Employment Law

'This book presents the issues in employment law in innovative ways and successfully puts the law in its political, social and economic context. The range of different materials stimulate discussion and debate [and it is] attractive to students as it presents the law in a clear and accessible fashion, is topical, and provides many activities to help students to cement their learning.'

Lisa Rogers, Senior Lecturer, Birmingham City University

'The real life context provided in this book is extremely rich and appropriate. It will prove very useful in engaging students in a fuller appreciation of the legal issues raised.'

Carol Kilgannon, Lecturer/Programme leader LLB, Winchester University

Employment Law

Roger Welch and Caroline Strevens
University of Portsmouth

PEARSON

Harlow, England • London • New York • Boston • San Francisco • Toronto • Sydney
Auckland • Singapore • Hong Kong • Tokyo • Seoul • Taipei • New Delhi
Cape Town • São Paulo • Mexico City • Madrid • Amsterdam • Munich • Paris • Milan

LIVINGLAW

Pearson education limited

Edinburgh Gate
Harlow CM20 2JE
Tel: +44 (0)1279 623623
Website: www.pearson.com/uk

First published 2013 (print and electronic)

ISBN: 978-1-4082-7232-9 (print)
978-1-4082-7233-6 (PDF)

British Library Cataloguing-in-Publication Data
A catalogue record for the print edition is available from the British Library

Library of Congress Cataloging-in-Publication Data
Welch, Roger.
  Employment law / Roger Welch and Caroline Strevens.
    p. cm.
  Includes index.
  ISBN 978-1-4082-7232-9
  1. Labor laws and legislation — Great Britain.   I. Strevens, Caroline.   II. Title.
  KD3009.W45 2013
  344.4101—dc23

                                                                2012041610

10 9 8 7 6 5 4 3 2 1
16 15 14 13 12

Print edition typeset in 10.5/13pt Minion Pro by 35
Printed by Ashford Colour Press Ltd, Gosport

NOTE THAT ANY PAGE CROSS REFERENCES REFER TO THE PRINT EDITION

Brief contents

Contents

premium
mylawchamber
unrivalled support for legal education

Join over 5,000 law students succeeding with MyLawChamber

Visit **www.mylawchamber.co.uk/welch** to access a wealth of tools to help you develop and test your knowledge of employment law, strengthening your understanding so you can excel.

✦ Interactive 'You be the judge' multiple choice questions to test your understanding of each topic

✦ Practice exam questions with guidance to hone your exam technique

✦ Annotated weblinks to help you read more widely around the subject and really impress your lecturers

✦ Case summary and key case flashcards to test yourself on legal terms, principles and definitions

✦ Legal newsfeed to help you read more widely, stay right up to date with the law and impress examiners

✦ Answer to Lawyers' brief simulation

✦ Legal updates to help you stay up to date with the law and impress examiners

For information about teaching support materials, please contact your local Pearson sales consultant or visit **www.mylawchamber.co.uk**.

The regularly maintained mylawchamber site provides the following features:

✦ Search tool to help locate specific items of content.

✦ Online help and support to assist with website usage and troubleshooting.

Guided tour

Key points
Identify the essential elements of each chapter, aiding your core understanding of the chapter.

Key points In this chapter we will be looking at:

- ✦ The significance of the distinction between employees, workers and the self-employed
- ✦ How to determine whether a worker is employed under a contract of employment and thus has employee status
- ✦ The formation of a contract of employment

- ✦ The statutory requirement on employers to provide a written statement of terms
- ✦ Distinguishing between express and implied terms as sources of a contract of employment
- ✦ Contract terms derived from collective agreements between employers and trade unions
- ✦ Statutory standards and contract terms

People in the law
Read the interviews from people working in employment law and gain insight from their first-hand work experience.

People in the law

Interview with **Piers Bateman**, a solicitor for more than 30 years. Piers became a Partner with Stokes Solicitors LLP in Portsmouth in 1986 and where, presently as a consultant to the firm, he has practiced in business and employment law for more than 20 years, representing small and medium-sized enterprises and individual clients across the counties of SE England and in London.

Where clients have been dismissed, how often, if at all, do you have to tell them that they are not eligible to claim unfair dismissal? About 30% of clients are advised that they will not succeed in claiming unfair dismissal.

without notice. One is where the employer is a small business and either the employer or employee feels 'stressed' and the dismissal is made in the

Law in action
Learn how the system works in practice through examples and problem scenarios found in the news.

Law in action

The reasons for the dispute between public sector workers and their employers over their occupational pensions were documented earlier (see the 'Law in action' feature in Chapter 8). This dispute led to what was effectively a one-day general strike by public sector workers on 30 November 2011. This strike was co-ordinated by the TUC and saw members of unions representing a wide range of public sector workers taking part. They ranged from podiatrists and radiographers to cleaners and construction workers.

The relevant unions were: the Association of Educational Psychologists, Aspect, Association of Teachers and Lecturers, Chartered Society of Physiotherapy, Educational Institute of Scotland, First Division Association, GMB, National Association of Head Teachers, Napo (family court and probation staff), the teachers' union NASUWT, Northern Ireland Public Service Association, National Union of Teachers,

Source: Debbie Rowe, Pearson Education Ltd

graphers, UCAC (one of the Welsh teachers' unions), Union of Construction, Allied Trades and Technicians, University and College Union, Unison and Unite.

Case summary

Learn the essential facts, details of the case and the decision, all in these concise summaries, integrated into the text yet pulled out in the margins for easy reference.

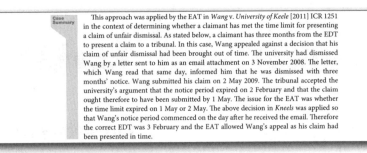

Case Summary

This approach was applied by the EAT in *Wang* v. *University of Keele* [2011] ICR 1251 in the context of determining whether a claimant has met the time limit for presenting a claim of unfair dismissal. As stated below, a claimant has three months from the EDT to present a claim to a tribunal. In this case, Wang appealed against a decision that his claim of unfair dismissal had been brought out of time. The university had dismissed Wang by a letter sent to him as an email attachment on 3 November 2008. The letter, which Wang read that same day, informed him that he was dismissed with three months' notice. Wang submitted his claim on 2 May 2009. The tribunal accepted the university's argument that the notice period expired on 2 February and that the claim ought therefore to have been submitted by 1 May. The issue for the EAT was whether the time limit expired on 1 May or 2 May. The above decision in *Kneels* was applied so that Wang's notice period commenced on the day after he received the email. Therefore the correct EDT was 3 February and the EAT allowed Wang's appeal as his claim had been presented in time.

Documenting the law

See real-life employment law documents reproduced within the text to give you a sense of how the law looks and feels in practice.

Documenting the law

It is clear from the above that an employer will incur legal liability if it does not have policies and rules in place to protect its employees from unlawful harassment. Similarly (as discussed in Chapter 3), an employer may be in breach of the duty to maintain trust and confidence if it fails to protect employees from bullying, even though such conduct may not amount to unlawful harassment. Therefore, all employers should adopt rules and procedures designed to protect employees from bullying or unlawful harassment. The following policy provides an example of how appropriate rules and procedures can be drafted.

L CO. LTD
COMPANY POLICY ON BULLYING AND HARASSMENT

As an equal opportunities employer the company believes that all it employees should be treated, and should treat each other, in ways that recognise the right of the individual to be treated with respect and the dignity at the workplace.

The purpose of this policy is to explain to employees the types of behaviour that constitute bullying and/or harassment and this includes acts which are rendered unlawful by the Equality Act 2010. The company will not tolerate such behaviour and any employee guilty of it will be committing a disciplinary offence which, in certain circumstances, will constitute gross misconduct warranting instant dismissal.

This policy sets out the procedures that an employee should follow if he or she believes that she is the victim of bullying or harassment.

Key stats

Information about what is actually happening in the real world helps you to relate to the practical side of the law.

Key stats

For the first 25 years after the Second World War trade unions grew significantly in terms of their membership levels and influence in British society. In 1979 there were around 13 million trade union members and trade union density was around half the workforce as a whole. Trade union density means the proportion of the workforce which is in a position to join trade unions and choose to do so. Figure 8.1 demonstrates the rise and fall in trade union membership over the past 100 years or so.

Diagrams and flowcharts

These visual aids will make complex legal processes easier to follow and understand.

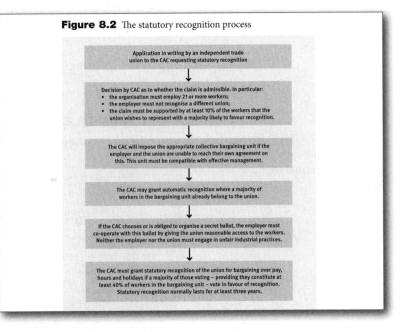

Figure 8.2 The statutory recognition process

You be the judge

Use your knowledge and apply it as you go to real-life scenarios to fully test your understanding.

You be the judge

Q: Do you think that John is entitled to a statutory redundancy payment in the following situation?

The managing director of X Co. Ltd. decides that the company is not sufficiently competitive and should move to introducing night working. Currently, employees work nine-hour shifts between 8.00 a.m. and 6.00 p.m. The company informs its employees that it is proposing to change their contractual hours of working so that in alternate weeks they will be required to work from 6.00 p.m. until 4.00 a.m. The employees are informed that any employees who refuse this change to their contracts of employment will be dismissed with salary in lieu of notice. All the employees other than John accept these new working conditions. John has been dismissed with pay in lieu of notice but believes he is entitled to a redundancy payment.

Source: Steve Cole, Photodisc

A: John does not have the right to a redundancy payment as the employer had no intention of reducing the size of the workforce.

The above situation is very similar to the facts of the cases of *Johnson* v. *Nottinghamshire Police Authority* [1974] ICR 170 and *Lesney Products Ltd* v. *Nolan* [1977] ICR 235. In both these cases it was clarified that any dismissals could not constitute redundancy dismissals if the employers required the

Writing and drafting

Put your knowledge of employment law into practice by completing the writing and drafting exercises contained throughout to enhance your practical legal skills and employability

Writing and drafting

The above cases establish that the key factor to recognition of a trade union is that the employer has expressly or impliedly agreed to *negotiate* with the union. In order to avoid doubt and uncertainty, best practice demonstrates that the proper prerequisite for routine collective bargaining is a written recognition agreement between an employer and a trade union. In real life an employer and/or a trade union may seek the advice of a person with legal expertise, although this will not necessarily be a legal practitioner, in drafting collective agreements.

Therefore imagine that you have been approached by the HR manager of an engineering company which employs 100 staff. It is contemplating recognising the General Workers Union (GWU) for its 80 engineers.

Source: Steve Cole, Photodisc

However, it does not want its administrative and managerial staff to be within the scope of collective bargaining. The HR manager has asked you to provide her with a written memorandum containing the 'Heads of agreement' for recognising the GWU. By this she

Out and about

Venture out and visit the suggested places or stay in and visit the websites to enhance your understanding of the areas covered.

Out and about

In understanding how the law works, it is valuable to appreciate the different forms that bullying at work can take, and to consider the steps that an employee may take to secure protection from the employer to prevent further acts of bullying from taking place.

The following website is useful for these purposes: http://www.direct.gov.uk/en/Employment/ResolvingWorkplaceDisputes/DiscriminationAtWork/DG_10026670

When visiting this website consider the following questions:

1. What examples of bullying at work did you identify?
2. What informal action would you take if you were a victim of bullying by colleagues at work?
3. In what circumstances would you consider taking formal action internally, that is, within your employing organisation?
4. What do you think formal action would consist of?

Reflective practice

How well did you really do? Use these sections to critically analyse your answers to exercises, deepening your understanding and raising your marks in assessments.

Reflective practice

What do the above cases tell you about the nature of the implied term of trust and confidence as defined in *Woods* by Browne-Wilkinson J? The term is a dynamic one which is capable of further development in terms of the type of employer behaviour that it can cover. The articles by Brodie in the *Industrial Law Journal*, which are cited in the 'Further reading' section of this chapter, shed further light on the nature of the term. In the next section of this chapter we consider the case of *United Bank* v. *Akhtar*. This case demonstrates that contrary to the normal position in contract law the implied duty of trust and confidence can override an express term in an employment contract.

Your reading of the EAT and Court of Appeal decisions in *Woods* should have enabled you to appreciate that what could be considered bad behaviour by an employer will not always amount to a breach of trust and confidence – in which case a resignation by an employee cannot constitute a constructive dismissal. As you may have ascertained, in this case the company had taken over the business in which Woods had been employed and, contrary to a promise initially given to her, persistently sought to persuade her to accept changes to her working conditions with respect to pay and hours. The tribunal decided that the company had not committed a repudiatory breach of contract. The EAT disagreed with this conclusion, but decided that it had no jurisdiction to overturn the

Summaries
Identify and recall the important cases and legal principles you need to aid revision and guarantee you go into assessments with confidence.

Summary

- An employee will have been dismissed by reason of redundancy where the employer closes or sells the business (unless the TUPE Regulations apply).

- Alternatively, there will be a redundancy dismissal where for any reason the employer reduces the size of the workplace because fewer employees are required to undertake a particular job.

- Where, in either of the above situations, an employee is required to move to a new workplace there will still be a redundancy dismissal, even where there is an appropriate mobility clause in an employee's contract, if the employee is being required to move from his or her established place of work.

- Employees with at least two years' continuous employment are entitled to a statutory payment which is calculated on the basis of

- be unfair where the employer has failed to carry out the reorganisation in a reasonable way.

- Where the transfer of a business is a relevant transfer within the meaning of the TUPE Regulations, employees should be transferred to the new employer on their existing contractual terms and conditions of employment.

- Where an employee is dismissed before or after a relevant transfer, this dismissal is automatically unfair unless the employer can show that the dismissal was for an economic, technical or organisational reason, and the employer had acted reasonably in deciding to dismiss.

- Where an employer is making 20 or more employees redundant at a single establishment, there is a duty to inform and

Question and answer
Test and apply your knowledge of employment law by answering the questions provided using the guidance to help and structure your answers.

Question and answer*

Problem: Peggy is the owner of a public house called 'The Prince Albert'. Peggy discovers that money is missing from the cash till. In addition to herself, the only people who have access to the till are the two members of the bar staff, Alfred and Katherine, and her son, Philip. Alfred, Katherine and Philip are all employed by Peggy under contracts of employment. Peggy interviews Alfred and Katherine and they both deny taking the money. Peggy asks Philip whether he has borrowed any money from the till and he tells her that he has not done so. Peggy is unable to identify the thief and decides to dismiss both Alfred and Katherine with net salary in lieu of notice. A police investigation subsequently discovers that the thief was in fact Philip.

Advise Alfred and Katherine to their legal rights and remedies (if any).

You should spend approximately 40 minutes on answering this question.

Essay: 'Unfair dismissal law places a disproportionate emphasis on procedural issues as, providing an employer follows a proper procedure prior to dismissing an employee, the subsequent dismissal will normally be found by an employment tribunal to be fair. The substantive fairness of the dismissal will often not be given an appropriate weight.'

Critically examine this statement with reference to the range of reasonable responses test.

If you treat this question as an exam question, you should spend approximately 40 minutes on answering it. However, this is the type of question that may be set for an in-course essay – in which case, having undertaken your research, you might well take approximately three hours in writing it.

✳ Answer guidance is provided at the end of the chapter.

Further reading
Annotated references to journals and websites point you to that extra reading necessary to ensure you hit the higher marks.

Further reading

IDS Handbook (2009) Contracts of Employment (Income Data Services: London).
Chapters 7 and 8 provide in-depth coverage of wrongful dismissal, constructive dismissal and damages as a remedy for wrongful dismissal. Chapter 10 provides a clear and comprehensive discussion of how an employment contract can be frustrated.

Deakin, S. and Morris, G. (2012) Labour Law (Hart: Oxford).
Pages 426–89 of Chapter 5 provide comprehensive and contextual explanation and analysis of the law concerning wrongful dismissal.

Freedland, M. (2005) The Personal

Brodie, D. (2004) 'Protecting Dignity in the Workplace: the Vitality of Mutual Trust and Confidence', Industrial Law Journal, vol. 33, pp. 349–54.
This article examines damages for breach of mutual trust and confidence, after the decision of the House of Lords in Unisys v. Johnson, with emphasis on the decision in Eastwood where damages were granted to cover lost earnings resulting from psychiatric injury.

Ewing, K. D. (1993) 'Remedies for breach of the contract of employment', Cambridge Law Journal, vol. 52, pp. 405–36.

premium
mylawchamber
unrivalled support for legal education

Visit **www.mylawchamber.co.uk/welch** to access a wealth of tools to help you develop and test your knowledge of employment law, strengthening your understanding so you can excel.

✦ Interactive 'You be the judge' multiple choice questions to test your understanding of each topic

✦ Practice exam questions with guidance to hone your exam technique

✦ Annotated weblinks to help you read more widely around the subject and really impress your lecturers

✦ Case summary and key case flashcards to test yourself on legal terms, principles and definitions

✦ Legal newsfeed to help you read more widely, stay right up to date with the law and impress examiners

✦ Answer to Lawyers' brief simulation

✦ Legal updates to help you stay up to date with the law and impress examiners

Preface

As part of the Living Law Series this text is intended to provide a comprehensive explanation of employment law and to bring the law alive by demonstrating the practical role that the law plays in the world of work. We have sought to achieve the latter objective by combining elements of traditional academic contextual and critical analysis with the use of key statistical data and news reports of cases and/or events where employment law issues have attracted significant media interest. To make our discussion of the law less abstract we have included realistic documents which are of importance to the key players – employees/workers, employers, human resource managers and trade unions – as well as to employment lawyers. Similarly, the *People in the law* feature in each chapter contains interviews with lawyers and others who engage with employment law in their working lives.

These features are supplemented by *Writing and drafting* activities which are designed to enable you to develop and reflect on your skills in using your knowledge of employment law in practical situations. The final chapter of this book replicates real life by putting you in the position of a lawyer instructed to represent a client who has been dismissed by his employer. Each chapter also includes *You be the judge* short problem questions which are designed to enable you to self-test and confirm your understanding of some of the key issues and cases covered in the chapter. At the end of each chapter we have included essay and problem questions, along with outline answers, of the sort LLB students are typically required to undertake on their courses.

The text is aimed at students studying employment law as part of an LLB programme, but it is hoped the book will prove of interest and value to students on other degree or professional programmes and indeed trade union courses which include employment law on their syllabi. This text is intended to provide a practical approach to employment law, but the subject is inherently practical in its own right given its impact on the many millions of people who are part of, or wish to become part, of the labour market. Therefore, it is hoped that anyone who reads this text will find that, as a result, they can use the law to advance their own interests at the workplace, and perhaps even provide some advice and assistance to family members or friends who are faced with problems of an employment law nature.

We have stated the law as we believed it to be at 1 June 2012. Any errors or important omissions are, of course, entirely our responsibility. We will be updating the law twice a year on our website **www.mylawchamber.co.uk/welch** – where you will also find other materials to support your studies. Employment law is a dynamic and fascinating subject so we hope you enjoy reading and using this book as part of your study of it.

Authors' acknowledgments

We would like to express our profound gratitude to all of our interviewees who took the time and trouble to answer our questions in ways that readers should find interesting and stimulating. We would particularly like to thank Zoe Botterill who first commissioned us to write this book, Gabriella Playford for all her help as assistant editor and Cheryl Cheasley who, as our editor, provided countless invaluable comments and suggestions which have improved the book in its final form.

I would also like to thank my wife Chris for being Chris, and my Mum and Dad, Joyce and Richard Welch, for encouraging a working-class boy from Pompey to take getting educated seriously.

Roger Welch and Caroline Strevens

Publisher's acknowledgements

We are grateful to the following for permission to reproduce copyright material:

Figures

Figure 7.1 from number of claims brought to employment tribunals, http://www.personneltoday.com/articles/2011/07/01/57739/age-discrimination-claims-up-by-one-third.html, Personnel Today/Reed Business Information; Figure 8.1 from James Acher, Trade Union Membership 2010, National Statistics Publication, Department for Business, Innovation & Skills, http://www.bis.gov.uk/policies/employment-matters/research/trade-union-stats, Crown copyright.

Text

Key stats box on p. 173 after Ministry of Justice Employment Tribunal and EAT statistics 2010–2011, published by the Ministry of Justice in September 2011, http://www.justice.gov.uk/downloads/statistics/mojstats/employment-trib-stats-april-march-2010-11.pdf, Crown copyright; quote on page 221 from *the Guardian*, 14/12/2011, http://www.guardian.co.uk/business/intractive/2009/jun/22/unemployment-and-employment-statistics-recession (Allen, P. & Mead, N.); Key stats box on p. 265 adapted from 'Tribunal awards: which discrimination cases attract the biggest payouts?', Laura Chamberlain, *Personnel Today*, 12 September 2011, http://www.personneltoday.com/articles/2011/09/12/57940/tribunal-awards-which-discrimination-cases-attract-the-biggest.html, Personnel Today/Reed Business Information.

Interviews

Interview and photo on pp. 65–6 from Vicki Brown; interview and photo on pp. 123–4 from Charlotte Rayner; interview and photo on pp. 147, 206–7 from Piers Bateman; interview and photo on pp. 246–7, 329, 406–7 from Mick Tosh; interview and photo on pp. 247–8, 330, 407 from Peter Brook; interview and photo on pp. 303–4 from Wendy Comerford.

In some instances we have been unable to trace the owners of copyright material, and we would appreciate any information that would enable us to do so.

Table of cases

Table of statutes

Table of statutory instruments

Table of European legislation

Abbreviations

The following sets out the full names of the main abbreviations used throughout this book.

ACAS – Advisory, Conciliation and Arbitration Service
AML – Additional Maternity Leave
ASLEF – Associated Society of Locomotive Engineers and Firemen
AWR – Agency Workers Regulations
BA – British Airways
BBC – British Broadcasting Association
BT – British Telecom
CA – Court of Appeal
CAB – Citizens Advice Bureau
CAC – Central Arbitration Committee
CBI – Confederation of British Industry
CCO – Continuation of Contract Order
CEAEB – Conduct of Employment Agencies and Employment Businesses Regulations
CIPD – Chartered Institute of Personnel and Development
CO – Certification Officer
DDA – Disability Discrimination Act 1995
DRA – Default Retirement Age
EAT – Employment Appeals Tribunal
ECHR – European Convention on Human Rights
ECJ – European Court of Justice
EctHR – European Court of Human Rights
EDT – Effective Date of Termination
EEC – European Economic Community
EHRC – Equality and Human Rights Commission
EqA – Equality Act 2010
ERA 1996 – Employment Rights Act 1996
ERA 1999 – Employment Relations Act 1999
ET – Employment Tribunal
ETD – Equal Treatment Directive
ETO – Economic, Technical or Organisational
EWC – Expected Week of Childbirth (Chapter 7)
EWC – European Works Council (Chapter 8)
EU – European Union
GOR – Genuine Occupational Requirement
HL – House of Lords
HR – human resources
HRA – Human Rights Act 2000
HSE – Health and Safety Executive
HSWA – Health and Safety at Work etc. Act 1974

IAWBH – International Association of Workplace Bullying and Harassment
ICE – Information and Consultation of Employees Regulations
ICR – Industrial Cases Reports
ILO – International Labour Organisation
IRLR – Industrial Relations Law Reports
J – Judge
JES – Job Evaluation Study
JNB – Joint Negotiating Board
LIFO – Last in first out
LJ – Lord Justice
MPL – Maternity and Parental Leave Regulations
NASUWT – National Association of Schoolmasters Union of Women Teachers
NEC – National Executive Committee
NHS – National Health Service
NMWA – National Minimum Wage Act
NUJ – National Union of Journalists
NUM – National Union of Railwaymen
NUT – National Union of Teachers
NZEI – New Zealand Education Institute
OML – Ordinary Maternity Leave
PCE – Principal Executive Committee
PCP – Provision, Criterion or Practice
PCS – Public and Communication Services Union
PHA – Protection from Harassment Act 2011
ROB – Religion or Belief Regulations
RRA – Race Relations Act 1976
RMT – National Union of Rail Maritime and Transport Workers
SC – Supreme Court
SDA – Sex Discrimination Act 1975
SI – Statutory Instrument
SMP – Statutory Maternity Pay
SOGAT – Society of Graphical and Allied Trades
TFEU – Treaty on the Functioning of the European Union
TGWU – Transport and General Workers Union
TICE – Transnational Information and Consultation of Employees Regulations
TU – trade union
TUC – Trades Union Congress
TULRA – Trade Union and Labour Relations Act 1974
TULRCA – Trade Union and Labour Relations (Consolidation) Act 1992
TUPE – Transfer of Undertakings Protection of Employment Regulations
UCAC – Undeb Cenedlaethol Athrawon Cymru
UCU – University and College Union
UCW – Union of Communication Workers
USDAW – Union of Shop, Distributive and Allied Workers
WTD – Working Time Directive
WTR – Working Time Regulations

Chapter 1
Introduction to employment law:
the institutions and people involved

Key points In this chapter we will be looking at:

✦ The composition and jurisdiction of employment tribunals and the Employment Appeals Tribunal (EAT)

✦ People involved in employment law: employers, employees, workers and trade union members

✦ The role of the Advisory Conciliation and Arbitration Service (ACAS) and other institutions such as the Central

Arbitration Committee (CAC) and the Equality and Human Rights Commission (ECHR)

✦ European Union law as a source of employment law

✦ The impact of the Human Rights Act and the European Convention on Human Rights on employment law

Introduction

Imagine you have a problem at your place of work. It may be that you are unhappy with the way you are being treated by your managers or colleagues, or that you fear that your employer is going to dismiss you or, indeed, your employment has already been terminated against your will. Other possibilities include a belief that your employer is not complying with your legal rights regarding limits on working hours, to paid holidays or to a minimum wage. On the other hand, it may be that you application for a job was unsuccessful and you suspect that this was because of your race, gender or sexual orientation.

This text explains the rights that you may have in any of these situations.

Conversely, it is also important to consider the duties that you owe to your employer whilst you are at work. Such duties will be primarily stipulated by your contract of employment. This contact is, of course, a legally binding agreement between you and your employer. As well as detailing your contractual rights, such as your how your wage or salary is calculated and what your holiday entitlement is, it will lay down the duties that you owe to your employer, such as what you are required to do by way of performing your job and when you are required to attend the workplace. As you will see, employees are also under contractual duties that have been put into all contracts of employment by previous decisions of the courts. The most important of these duties is the duty to obey any reasonable instruction given to you by your employer and a duty to act in good faith (see Chapter 2).

However, before we look at the law in depth it is important to have some idea about how the law works. The ordinary civil courts have a role to play – particularly in deciding whether either an employer or an employee has acted in breach of contract. However, it is employment tribunals which are at the heart of our system of employment law, as it is these tribunals rather than the ordinary courts which will hear most claims based on employment rights that are granted to employees by legislation. Other institutions are also of importance: first and foremost of these is ACAS, the Advisory, Conciliation and Arbitration Service. ACAS may assist you in reaching a settlement with your employer when you have been dismissed. It also has a rule-making role through drafting and issuing codes of practice. Here we will examine the roles played by both employment tribunals and ACAS in processing and resolving employment law claims.

The sorts of rights and duties identified above are part of what we call individual employment law, that is, the law governing the relationship between an individual employee and an individual employer. However, it may well be that having obtained a job you decide to join a trade union. Trade unions are common throughout public sector employment and in larger private sector companies. Important trade unions include the National Union of Teachers (NUT), UNISON which represents workers in local government and the National Health Service and UNITE which represents workers in both the public and private sectors.

Trade unions exist to represent their members in their relations with their employer. A trade union will represent you individually if you have a problem at work. It may also represent you and your colleagues collectively through negotiating some or all of your terms and conditions of employment. This is known as **collective bargaining**. If there is a breakdown in this collective bargaining process then a formal dispute between the union and the employer may arise. ACAS also has an important role in assisting in the resolution of such disputes. Alternatively, it may be that a dispute results in a trade union deciding to organise industrial action. Today, such action is heavily regulated by statute law. The legal framework within which collective bargaining and the regulation of industrial action operate is known as **collective labour law** (considered in depth in Chapters 8 and 9).

From your studies of the English legal system you will know that most English law is either judge-made in the form of the common law or is contained in statutes and statutory instruments. Both the common law and statute are important sources of the law regulating the employment relationship. However, European law is also an important source of employment law. This is particularly the case with European Union (EU) law in the whole area of discrimination law. There can also be an overlap between rights at work and human rights law. In such cases we need to examine the impact of the European Convention on Human Rights as implemented in the UK through the Human Rights Act 1998.

Given the central role that employment tribunals play in deciding the outcome of legal claims that are brought against employers the initial focus of this chapter will be on tribunal practice and procedure.

The system of employment tribunals

If you have a dispute with your current employer over the operation of your contract of employment, then, should you take legal action, this will be in the form of an ordinary action for breach of contract and it will be heard by the ordinary civil courts. For example, you may believe that your employer has failed to pay you money that you are owed under your contract of employment. Normally, your claim will go to the County Court unless the legal issues involved are very complex, and/or the amount of compensation you are seeking is large, in which circumstances the claim is more likely to be heard by the High Court. Similarly, actions in tort, for example in the context of **employers' negligence**, are heard in the ordinary civil courts.

However, in practice, it is much more likely that the rights at work that you wish to enforce are derived from statute law, and under the relevant statute your claim will need to be presented to an employment tribunal rather than a court of law. There are two main Acts of Parliament containing such rights. One is the Employment Rights Act (ERA) 1996, which provides the large majority of employment protection rights enjoyed by employees, including rights covered in detail in this text such as the right not to be **unfairly dismissed** and the right to a **statutory redundancy payment**. The other is the Equality Act 2010, which contains nearly all the law concerned with discrimination and equal pay. Employment tribunals have exclusive jurisdiction to hear all legal claims arising from these Acts where the dispute occurs in the context of an employment relationship.

Table 1.1 on page 8 summarises the different jurisdictions of the civil courts and employment tribunals.

Although any type of legal proceedings will seem complicated to anyone who is not familiar with them, employment tribunals are less formal in their nature and procedure than is the case with courts of law. The venue for a tribunal hearing will more resemble a normal room than a courtroom. The tribunal panel will be dressed in ordinary clothes rather than wigs and gowns. Where a party represents himself or herself, the tribunal chair, known as an employment judge, is empowered to give some assistance to that party. Obviously, this will not amount to providing a party with the legal arguments which that party can use, but the chair may intervene to ensure that witnesses are asked appropriate questions to seek to ensure all the relevant evidence is revealed.

Contrary to the normal position in a court of law, both employees and employers can be represented by non-lawyers. Typically, employees who belong to a trade union are represented by officials of their union, and employers are represented by members of their human resources or personnel departments. It is normal for each party to bear their own costs in obtaining legal advice and legal representation. If a claimant belongs to a trade union then it may be one of the benefits of such membership that the union will pay all or some of the costs involved if the union decides to support the member in bringing a tribunal claim. It should be noted that costs may awarded against a party if, as is explained further below, that party has been warned by an employment judge that it is not reasonable to proceed with, or to resist, a claim; in short that proceeding with the claim constitutes wasting the time of the tribunal and the other party.

As is typically the case with claims heard by any sort of tribunal, and as a matter of long-standing government policy, legal aid is not available for claims to be presented to employment tribunals. The legal aid system is administered by the Legal Services Commission, and its purpose is to provide state funding to people on lower incomes to contribute towards the costs of obtaining legal advice and legal representation. However, generally, the availability of legal aid is restricted to civil court proceedings. Unfortunately, it must be the case that some people are deterred from bringing employment tribunal claims because they cannot afford to pay for legal advice and do not have the skills to represent themselves. The only source of advice and representation for individuals in this position will be seeking free advice from, for example, a Citizens Advice Bureau (CAB) or a free legal representation unit run voluntarily by legal practitioners or some university law schools. Going to a CAB will not always be enough, in practice, to enable a person to enforce his or her legal rights, and free legal representation units may not exist in the area of the country that the claimant lives. Although legal aid is not available to claimants for tribunal proceedings, as is explained further below, it is available for any appeal proceedings that an unsuccessful claimant decides to initiate.

Key statistics

The work done by employment tribunals and their importance to employees and workers seeking to enforce their employment rights is demonstrated by the following figures. Between 2007 and 2008 they disposed of 81,600 claims; between 2008 and 2009 this figure was 92,000 and between 2009 and 2010 the number of claims disposed of had risen to 112,400. Between 2010 and 2011, 122,800 claims were disposed of. This is 9% more than in 2009/10 and 33% more than in 2008/09.

One reason for the increase in claims in 2009/10 and 2011/11 was the state of the economy in contrast with the preceding years. The global banking and financial crisis that occurred in the autumn of 2008 has resulted in cuts in public sector expenditure and in private sector employers making employees redundant or restructuring their operations in ways that impact on the employment contracts of their employees. Inevitably, in times of economic uncertainty and increased job insecurity, workers will look to their legal rights as one way of protecting their interests at work.

Source: Ministry of Justice Employment Tribunal and EAT Statistics 2010–11, published by the Ministry of Justice in September 2011. The full report can be downloaded at **http://www.justice.gov.uk/downloads/statistics/mojstats/employment-trib-stats-april-march-2010-11.pdf**

Before looking at the composition of employment tribunals, their jurisdiction and the procedure governing the presentation of tribunal claims, it is useful to understand the structure of the tribunal system and the relationship between this system and the ordinary courts.

In the world of employment law, employment tribunals perform a similar role to that performed by the County Courts or the High Court in our ordinary system of civil law. Employment tribunals are akin to these courts of first instance in that it will be an employment tribunal which will first hear, for example, claims of unfair dismissal or claims of sex or race discrimination. The employee or person bringing the claim is known as the claimant and the employer will be the respondent. The tribunal will hear all of the evidence, which will be given by the parties and any witnesses that they call, and will decide what the true facts underlying the claim actually are. In exactly the same way that a court does, the tribunal will apply the relevant law to the facts of a case to decide whether a claim should succeed or fail.

If the losing party believes that the tribunal has misunderstood the law, or has misinterpreted the evidence, then that party may appeal. This appeal initially goes to another special tribunal, the Employment Appeals Tribunal, which is normally just referred to by its initials, that is, the EAT. The composition and jurisdiction of the EAT is considered below. Any further appeals operate in accordance with our normal civil law system, so that an appeal from the EAT will be made to the Court of Appeal (Civil Division) with a final right of appeal to the Supreme Court. The tribunal and court structure is summarised in Figure 1.1.

Figure 1.1 Employment tribunals and appeals structure

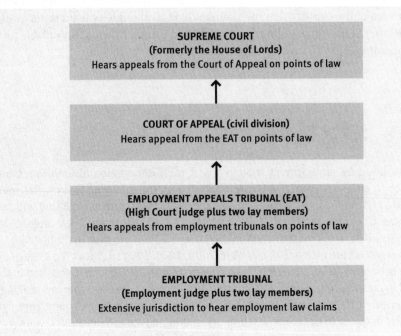

Composition of employment tribunals

As can be seen from Figure 1.1, an employment tribunal is chaired by an employment judge, who may be a solicitor or barrister with an expertise in employment law, or who may be a specialist in employment law who has been but is not currently a legal practitioner, such as a professor of employment law. Therefore, although an employment judge is appointed by the Judicial Appointments Commission, he or she is not a judge in the sense that this title is popularly understood – that is, individuals who once will have been solicitors or barristers but whose job function has become solely one of deciding legal cases.

As detailed below, employment judges may sit alone to hear a claim but they are normally assisted by two lay members. One of these lay members will be from a list consisting of employee representatives, such as officials of trade unions which are affiliated to the Trades Union Congress (TUC), a confederation of most British trade unions. The other lay member will be from a list of individuals with an employer background, and who may belong to an employers' organisation such as the Confederation of British Industry (CBI). Individuals can apply to become lay members, and the lists are approved by a government minister, the appropriate Secretary of State. The employment judge contributes legal expertise, whilst the lay members contribute their business expertise from their involvement in industry and commerce. An employment tribunal can therefore be regarded as acting, in part, as an industrial jury as its view of the facts of a case will be influenced by the practical experiences of the lay members. The lay members do, of course, act impartially when hearing a claim; it is not their role to advance the

> an employment tribunal can therefore be regarded as acting, in part, as an industrial jury

interests of either the employee claimant or the employer respondent. Lay members have an equal status to the employment judge and it is possible, although this is uncommon, for a decision of a tribunal to be a majority decision where the two lay members have voted against the decision of the employment judge.

Currently, employment judges may sit alone to hear a number of claims. These include claims that an employer has failed properly to provide an employee with a written statement setting out the terms of employment under which that employee is employed (see further in Chapter 2). Employers also have duties to consult with trade unions where the employer is proposing to make more than 20 employees redundant, or is proposing to sell all or part of the business to another employer. A trade union may seek compensation, on behalf of its members, from a tribunal where an employer has failed to comply with these duties (see Chapter 6). This is another type of claim that can be heard by an employment judge sitting alone.

The government has recently decided that employment judges should be able to sit alone to hear unfair dismissal claims. This change was made by the Employment Tribunals Act 1996 (Tribunal Composition) Order 2012, SI 2012/988. This change is controversial as it can be argued that it is precisely when tribunals are considering issues such as discipline and dismissal that the role of the tribunal as an industrial jury is most effective by virtue of the lay members drawing on their practical experiences of the world of work. Dismissals will be unfair where an employer has failed to act as a reasonable employer would act (see Chapter 5). Where employment judges sit alone they will no longer be able to take advantage of the expert views of lay members with respect to how reasonable employers can be expected to behave.

Jurisdiction of employment tribunals

Employment tribunals were first established in1964 by the Industrial Training Act, and were previously called industrial tribunals. Their original purpose was a relatively modest one: to hear appeals by employers against government levies imposed on them by way of contribution to industrial training. In 1965, tribunals were given jurisdiction to hear claims concerning an employee's entitlement to a statutory redundancy payment. In 1971, they were given jurisdiction to hear claims based on the then newly created right to claim unfair dismissal. Both of these claims remain an important part of an employment tribunal's workload but today tribunals have extensive jurisdiction over employment law matters and hear a large number of different types of claims.

Most of the chapters of this text are concerned to greater or lesser extents with statutory employment rights granted to employees and also, in some cases, to **workers** who do not possess **employee status** (see Chapter 2). These rights cover a very wide range of very different issues that arise at the workplace. Examples discussed in this text include: the minimum wage; entitlement to paid holiday; maternity and paternity leave; duties imposed on employers to consult with trade unions over proposed redundancies; and equal pay claims. Along with virtually all areas of discrimination law the right to claim equal pay is now contained in the Equality Act (EqA) 2010, and tribunals have exclusive jurisdiction to hear claims brought under this Act in the field of employment.

Therefore, it can be seen that the jurisdiction of employment tribunals is largely rooted in statute law. It will be an Act of Parliament or statutory instrument which will stipulate that claims brought under its provisions will first go to an employment tribunal. However, tribunals also have some jurisdiction to hear common law claims

Table 1.1 Jurisdiction of the courts and tribunals

Civil courts	Employment tribunals
Any action where employer or employee is claiming for a breach of the employment contract	Any claim to enforce statutory rights contained in ERA 1996 or EqA 2010
Any action by employer or employee based on tort law	Contractual jurisdiction where employment contract has been terminated and the amount of damages sought is no more than £25,000

where an employee is arguing that the employer has acted in breach of the contract of employment. Such claims can only be heard by tribunals after the employment contract has been terminated. Tribunals cannot award **damages** in excess of £25,000. It should be clarified that any contractual claim can still be brought to a County Court or the High Court in accordance with ordinary civil law procedure. Obviously, a claim should be taken to a civil court where the claimant is seeking damages over £25,000. The most important example of a tribunal's contractual jurisdiction is where it is hearing a claim that an employee has been dismissed in breach of contract. Such a dismissal is known as a **wrongful dismissal** (see Chapter 4). Where such an employee is also eligible to present a claim of unfair dismissal, the claimant can simultaneously present claims of wrongful and unfair dismissal to the same employment tribunal (see Chapter 5).

Table 1.1 distinguishes between the jurisdiction of the civil courts and that of employment tribunals.

Out and about

Visit http://www.justice.gov.uk/downloads/statistics/mojstats/employment-trib-stats-april-march-2010-11.pdf

From this site you can download the report from the Ministry of Justice's Tribunals Services for 2010–11. This report gives you an insight into the work done by employment tribunals and all the types of legal claims they have the jurisdiction to hear in addition to the types of claim that are specified above.

Tribunal hearings are held in public. If, in terms of geography this is possible, it would be a good idea for you, individually or with other members of your course, to visit a local employment tribunal. This will give you a good feel for how tribunals work and how all the parties involved conduct themselves. Should you visit a tribunal then, depending on what stage(s) of the proceedings you are able to observe, you should pay particular attention to how legal representatives and/or the employment judge question or cross-examine witnesses, and how legal representatives present their final legal submissions to the tribunal. If you are able to stay to the end of a hearing, you will be able to see how the tribunal gives its decision on whether the claim should succeed.

You can find your local tribunal via http://local.direct.gov.uk/LDGRedirect/MapAction.do?ref=employmenttribunal

Presenting claims to an employment tribunal

Presenting a claim to an employment tribunal is undertaken by completing an ET1 claim form and returning the completed form to the nearest tribunal office. As is detailed below, there are time limits for presenting tribunal claims. Normally, the ET1 must be received by the tribunal office no later than three months from the date that the claim arose. In completing the ET1 the claimant will give his or her name, address and other relevant personal details and the name of the organisation, company or person against whom the claim is being brought. The claimant will set out the reasons for the claim and the facts on which the claim is based. It is not necessary to have technical legal expertise to complete the claim, but it is in the claimant's interests for a tribunal to be able to ascertain from the form that the claimant has a genuine and sound basis for presenting a claim. Therefore, where claimants have professional advisers they should provide the adviser with the relevant information so that the adviser can complete the ET1 on the claimant's behalf. Once the ET1 is received by the appropriate tribunal office, the claim is regarded as formally presented.

If an employer wishes to respond to a claim, the employer or the employer's representative must complete a form ET3. Employers have 28 days to return the form from the date the employer received the ET1. The employer must give his, her or its personal details, the employer's version of the facts and the reason why the claim is being resisted. If an employer fails to complete and return an ET3 in time then the employer cannot participate in any proceedings to determine whether the claim should succeed.

Documenting the law

Forms ET1 and ET3 can be downloaded directly from **http://www.justice.gov.uk/global/forms/hmcts/tribunals/ employment/index.htm**. Download both forms in pdf format and save them to your PC or laptop, etc.

Read through both forms to ascertain the type of information that a claimant or respondent is required to provide. Essentially there are three component elements to the forms: the provision of personal details; setting out the salient facts and identifying the type of claim(s) to be brought, or providing arguments as to why a claim is being resisted; providing comment on the type(s) of remedy that the claimant is seeking to secure. The forms are easier to complete than is typically the case with legal forms, but completing a form in a thorough and clear way is still an important part of the tribunal process. Therefore, completing an ET1 or ET3 is best done by a person with the necessary legal or other professional expertise.

Presenting a claim in time

If you are considering presenting a tribunal claim, for example, a claim of unfair dismissal, or you are advising a friend or client to do so, it is very important that you understand that there are strict time limits for presenting a claim which should be adhered to. Failure to do so will generally mean that the tribunal will declare that it has no jurisdiction to hear the claim as it has been presented out of time, and this will be so irrespective of the claim's merits. A claim is deemed to be properly presented once it is received online or through the post by the relevant tribunal office.

Claims of unfair dismissal and most other complaints concerning violations of statutory rights must be presented to a tribunal no later than three months from the date the claim arises. In the context of a dismissal this will be the **effective date of termination (EDT)** of the employment contract. The EDT is determined by ss. 97 and 145 ERA 1996, and will normally be the date the dismissal takes effect (see Chapter 5). One exception to the three-month time limit is where an employee is presenting a claim for a statutory redundancy payment. The time limit for this claim is six months from the date of the redundancy dismissal (see Chapter 6). If you are presenting a claim based on discrimination law, the claim should be presented no later than three months from the date of the discriminatory act which constitutes the subject-matter of your complaint. Most such claims will be brought under the Equality Act 2010 (see Chapter 7).

Under s. 111(2) ERA 1996, a tribunal may hear a claim, which is received by it outside of the relevant time limit, if it considers that it was not reasonably practicable for the complaint to be presented within the proper time. As above, this will normally be three months from the date that the claimant's contract was terminated or from the date of the act complained of. The phrase 'not reasonably practicable' has been interpreted quite strictly, and case law suggests it is best understood as meaning that it was not feasible for a claimant to have presented a claim in time. Establishing a lack of feasibility requires more than what is normally understood as constituting reasonable practicability. For example, a claimant may only discover after it is too late to present a claim that he or she had a good basis for going to an employment tribunal. However, it has been long established that the claimant cannot argue that a claim was presented out of time because the claimant did not know his or her rights.

Nor can a claimant successfully argue that a claim was presented out of time because he or she was badly advised by, for example, a solicitor, a trade union officer or a volunteer worker at a Citizens' Advice Bureau. The reasoning here is that, although it might be reasonable for a claimant to rely on a specific adviser, it is always feasible for a claimant to seek advice from several sources to check that a particular piece of advice was accurate. As stated by the Court of Appeal, in *Dedman* v. *British Building and Engineering Appliances Ltd* [1974] ICR 53, where a claimant has been badly advised the appropriate course of action is to sue the adviser for breach of contract and/or under the tort of negligence. In *Dedman*, the claimant was dismissed and immediately consulted solicitors. He was not informed that there was a time limit for claiming unfair dismissal. By the time his claim was received, it was out of time. The claimant was not able to rely on the solicitor's failure to advise him properly to succeed in arguing that it was not reasonably practicable for him to have presented the claim in time.

Case Summary

One twist to this position is, however, provided by the case of *Jean Sorelle Ltd* v. *Rybak* [1991] IRLR 153. In this case, it was a member of the tribunal staff who had given incorrect advice by informing the claimant that weekends did not count in calculating the three-month time limit. It was held that it is reasonable for a claimant to assume that the advice provided by a member of the tribunal's own staff is accurate. Therefore *Rybak* was covered by the escape clause provided by s. 111(2) when his claim, which should have been received by the tribunal on a Saturday, was not received until the following Monday.

Case Summary

It might be considered natural that an employee who is challenging a dismissal internally through the employer's appeal procedures will wait until the outcome of the internal appeal before deciding to present a tribunal claim. However, a delay in presenting a tribunal claim may be fatal where the internal appeal is heard after a dismissal has taken place, as it is from this date of dismissal that the three-month period for presenting a tribunal claim will run.

In *Palmer* v. *Southend-on-Sea Borough Council* [1984] ICR 372, the employee was dismissed for theft but protested his innocence throughout the Council's disciplinary procedures. He was told by the Council's appeals committee that if he was subsequently found innocent by a criminal court the Council would reconsider the decision to dismiss. Approximately a year later his conviction for theft was quashed by the Court of Appeal (Criminal Division), but the Council refused to reinstate him. It was held that he could not proceed with the claim of unfair dismissal as it was out of time. It had been perfectly practicable for him to have presented a tribunal claim within the normal three-month time limit. There was no reason for him to have waited either for the decision of the Council's appeal committee or the outcome of the criminal proceedings against him.

In any situation where an internal appeal takes place after a dismissal has been made then, in light of the decision in *Palmer*, the best advice to be given to the dismissed employee is to present a tribunal claim whilst he or she is waiting for the internal appeal to be heard. If the internal appeal does succeed then the employee can simply withdraw the tribunal claim. If the internal appeal fails, the employee will have presented the tribunal claim in time and will be able to proceed with it. It should be clarified that with regard to an employer's appeal procedures it could be the case that the employee's contract continues until and if a dismissal is confirmed by an appeal hearing. In this situation the effective date of termination will be the date of the appeal hearing's decision confirming the dismissal, and therefore the three months for presenting a tribunal claim will run from that date.

However, there may be special circumstances that permit a tribunal to adopt a more flexible approach to that adopted in *Palmer*. In *John Lewis* v. *Charman* (2011) EAT Case 0079/11, the claimant, who was aged 20, waited for the outcome of an internal appeal before claiming unfair dismissal. Charman did not seek professional advice, and was out of the country on holiday when a letter arrived from John Lewis informing him that his appeal against his dismissal was unsuccessful. As soon as Charman read this letter he sought the advice of his father who found out about unfair dismissal rights on the internet and completed a form ET1 on his son's behalf. This claim was presented some six weeks out of time. The tribunal decided that the claim should be heard as it took into account Charman's age and lack of experience of employment rights. The tribunal decided that Charman had not acted unreasonably, either in waiting for the results of the internal appeal before seeking to ascertain the law, or in failing to arrange for his mail to be opened while he was away. The tribunal emphasised that this was not a case where a claimant had received bad professional advice, and concluded that it had not been reasonably practicable for Charman to have presented his claim in time. The EAT found that the tribunal had not made an error of law and therefore its decision should stand. It can be commented that this decision seems rather more generous to the claimant that has been so in earlier cases and perhaps should be regarded as very much decided on the basis of the case's special facts.

More typically, the circumstances in which the escape clause in s. 111(2) will apply to allow a claim to be presented out of time are very limited. Mental or physical illness which is so severe as to make it physically impossible for a tribunal claim to be presented is one situation in which s. 111(2) may apply. In *Schultz* v. *Esso Petroleum Co Ltd* [1999] IRLR 488, the Court of Appeal accepted that in the last six weeks of the three-month time limit Schultz had been too depressed to instruct solicitors to present a tribunal

Case Summary

Case Summary

Case Summary

claim on his behalf. The court rejected the argument that Schultz could have arranged for his claim to be presented before he started to suffer from depression and agreed that his depression meant that it had not been reasonably practicable for Schultz to have presented his claim in time. This decision seems fair, as the logic of the argument that Schultz's claim could have been presented earlier is that claimants who are vulnerable to serious illness should not have the full three months to present a claim in a way that is available to claimants who enjoy good health.

In discrimination law, under s. 123 EqA 2010, tribunals can hear claims presented out of time where the tribunal considers it *just and equitable* to do so. Tribunals have a wide discretion to decide whether or not a claim should be permitted to proceed, and they use this discretion more flexibly than is the case where the 'reasonable practicability' test is applied in respect of claims brought on the basis of ERA 1996.

Case Summary

For example, in *Chohan* v. *Derby Law Centre* [2004] IRLR 685, Chohan, a trainee solicitor, was dismissed and decided to claim sex discrimination under the Sex Discrimination Act 1975. This claim was presented 18 days out of time. The EAT accepted that the delay was the result of bad advice given to Chohan by her solicitors but ruled that it was just and equitable to allow her claim to proceed. In reaching this decision, the EAT also disagreed with the tribunal's view that, as a trainee solicitor, Chohan should have been able to find out for herself the time limit for presenting a discrimination claim. This approach is in stark contrast to that adopted by the Court of Appeal in the *Dedman* case, considered above, where it was held that bad professional advice is not a reason for allowing an unfair dismissal claim to be heard where it was presented out of time. The rationale behind the EAT's decision was that the respondent would have been presented with a windfall if Chohan was barred from presenting her claim. This approach seems sound, but, arguably, should not the same approach be taken with all types of tribunal claims? Presumably, the greater flexibility to tribunals granted by the EqA (and the previous legislation such as the Sex Discrimination Act 1975) is to ensure that British law is not in breach of EU law by imposing unjustifiable barriers to claimants pursuing discrimination claims.

You be the judge

Q: Advise Emily as to whether in either of the following two situations her claim of unfair dismissal could be heard by an employment tribunal:

(a) On 1 April, after five years of continuous employment, Emily was dismissed from her job as a journalist after an argument with the editor of her newspaper. Three weeks after her dismissal, Emily was about to seek legal advice when her daughter was knocked down by a drunken driver. Consequently, the daughter was in a coma for a period of three months. Emily presented a claim of unfair dismissal the day after her daughter awoke from this coma.

(b) On 1 April, after five years of continuous employment, Emily was dismissed from her job as a journalist after an argument with the editor of her newspaper. Three weeks after her dismissal, Emily was about to seek legal advice when she was knocked down by a drunken driver. Consequently, Emily was in a coma for a period of three months. Emily instructed her solicitors to present a claim of unfair dismissal one week after awaking from this coma.

A: In (a) it may well be that Emily's claim cannot be heard whereas in (b) a tribunal is likely to decide that her claim can be heard.

In both (a) and (b) Emily's claim is out of time as it has not been presented within the three-month period for claiming unfair dismissal. There is no direct precedent to Emily's situation in (a), but, given the strict way in which the escape clause in s. 111(2) has been interpreted, it could well be held that her daughter's coma did not render it unfeasible and therefore not reasonably practicable for Emily to present her claim in time; in which case the tribunal will decide it does not have the jurisdiction to hear her claim. Such a conclusion is clearly harsh, so it all depends on whether it is permissible for tribunals to be sympathetic to a claimant in Emily's position. The recent decision in *Charman* does suggest that where special circumstances exist tribunals can be more generous to claimants in the way in which they apply s. 111(2).

In (b) as it is Emily who was in a coma as a result of the accident, then s. 111(2) should apply to enable a claim to be presented out of time. The *Schultz* case could be regarded as a precedent in this second situation.

Note that if in (a) Emily was presenting a discrimination claim under the Equality Act then, given the decision in *Chohan*, it might well be held that it is just and equitable to hear her claim out of time.

Conciliated settlements and compromise agreements

Assuming forms ET1 and ET3 are returned in time to the tribunal office a case management process will then come into operation pending the convening of a tribunal hearing. As part of this process, copies of these forms will be sent to ACAS. The composition and functions of ACAS are considered further below, but ACAS conciliation officers play a very important role in seeking to resolve a legal dispute in a way that avoids the continuation of tribunal proceedings.

A conciliation officer can only become involved with the agreement of the parties. However, where this occurs then one possible outcome will be that the claim is voluntarily settled under the auspices of that conciliation officer. Where the parties do voluntarily agree to an **ACAS conciliated settlement** then the claim is withdrawn from the tribunal and the settlement is legally binding. This has the advantage to both parties of saving the time and money involved in going ahead with a tribunal hearing, and is advantageous to employment tribunals as it reduces their workloads. From an employer's perspective a settlement can avoid what has happened to the claimant becoming public knowledge. The employer can make it a condition of the settlement that the details of the claim and the settlement remain confidential.

Compromise agreements constitute an alternative method to an ACAS conciliated settlement to resolve a claim without tribunal proceedings needing to take place. Such an agreement must be in writing, and the claimant must have acted on independent advice from a lawyer or other qualified person such as a trade union official in approving the agreement.

Both conciliated settlements and compromise agreements can be subject to a confidentiality agreement. In either case it may be that, in return for confidentiality, the employer will agree to compensate the claimant with a larger sum of money than would have been awarded by an employment tribunal. Conversely, the claimant may settle for less than would have been awarded by a tribunal, but the circumstances are such that the claimant was not confident that the tribunal claim would succeed. These are the sorts of factors that the parties' representatives will take into account in seeking to negotiate a settlement or agreement on their client's behalf.

Later in this text (see Chapter 10) there is an activity that involves you acting on behalf of a client who wishes to claim unfair dismissal. One of the suggested tasks involves formulating a negotiating strategy on behalf of your client with a view to securing an ACAS conciliated settlement.

Key stats

The significance of the role played by ACAS with respect to individual employment law is demonstrated by the percentage of claims to employment tribunals which are resolved by an ACAS conciliated settlement.

For example, out of the 49,600 unfair dismissal claims disposed of in 2010–11, 41% were resolved by ACAS conciliated settlements. The percentages for breach of contract, national minimum wage and working time claims were 32%, 33% and 29% respectively.

The percentages for discrimination claims resolved by ACAS settlements were:

sex – 28%,
race – 36%,
disability – 46%,
religious belief – 34%,
sexual orientation – 41%,
age – 35%.

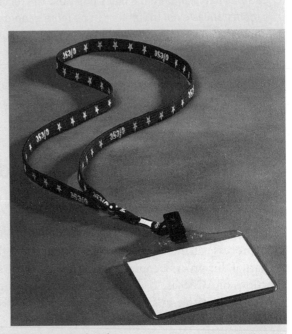

Source: Imagemore Co. Ltd

Source: Ministry of Justice Employment Tribunal and EAT statistics 2010–11, published by the Ministry of Justice in September 2011. The full report can be downloaded at http://www.justice.gov.uk/downloads/statistics/mojstats/employment-trib-stats-april-march-2010-11.pdf

Case management and pre-hearing reviews

Historically, it would often be the case that the parties to a tribunal claim and their representatives would have no personal contact with the tribunal prior to the day of the hearing. Today, in line with general civil law procedure, there will be a case management process which is largely conducted through the employment judge deciding that the effective processing of a claim will best be achieved through certain decisions being made prior to any full hearing taking place. At the discretion of the employment judge, or at the request of one or both of the parties, the judge can organise a case management meeting. This does not have to be a face-to-face meeting as, in consultation with the parties and their representatives, the judge can decide that the meeting is conducted over the phone or via a video link.

The purposes of such a meeting include clarifying the legal issues involved, identifying the witnesses to be called and their availability, and agreeing on the timing of the full hearing. The case management process is particularly important in complex claims such as equal pay claims. Such claims often involve tribunals having to decide whether there is a basis for deciding whether the job done by the claimant constitutes work of **equal value** to the employer to a different job undertaken by another colleague who is the claimant's chosen comparator of the opposite gender (see Chapter 7). Identifying the information that will be required – in particular, from the employer – to enable job analysis to be properly conducted is the sort of issue that can be dealt with through case management so that a hearing can be timed to take place after this information has been made available to and digested by the parties, their representatives and the tribunal members.

A pre-hearing review can be a very important part of the case management process. Although parties to a tribunal claim normally pay their own costs, tribunals are empowered to make costs orders against the losing party where the tribunal decides that a claim is misconceived. The maximum amount of costs that could be awarded was £10,000, but this figure was raised to £20,000 by the Employment Tribunals (Constitution and Rules of Procedure) (Amendment) Regulations 2012, SI 2012/468. At a pre-hearing review, which again can be convened by a decision of the employment judge, it can be determined whether a claim or the employer's response to it has *little* reasonable prospects of success. For example, if a female claimant is bringing an equal pay claim then the tribunal judge can inform her that it is highly unlikely that her job will be regarded as being of equal value to that undertaken by the chosen male comparator. In such circumstances the claimant is being warned that the claim is misconceived, and is effectively being advised not to continue with it.

If, contrary to a determination at a pre-hearing review, a party is determined that the claim should go to or be contested at a full hearing, the employment judge can require that party pay a deposit of up to £1,000. If the party does lose at full hearing and costs are awarded to the other party then the deposit will go towards paying the costs. If the party actually succeeds, or a costs order is not made, then the deposit will be refunded.

In extreme circumstances, the employment judge may decide to strike out a claim so that it does not proceed after a pre-hearing review. The judge is empowered to do this where it is decided that a claim has *no* reasonable prospects of success or is otherwise vexatious or scandalous. A claim may be considered vexatious or scandalous where allegations are made to cause, for example, distress and embarrassment to the other party. In *Jones* v. *Wallop Industries Ltd* ET Case No. 17182/81, the clamant argued he had been unfairly selected for redundancy and asserted that the company had done this as part of a criminal conspiracy against him. No evidence was presented to support this allegation and the whole claim was struck out on the basis that it was scandalous and vexatious.

Case Summary

A claim can also be considered vexatious, albeit not scandalous, where it is brought for an improper motive and amounts to an abuse of process. Where such a claim is permitted to proceed to full hearing this is also the basis on which a costs order can be made. In the case of *Keane* v. *Investigo* (2009) EAT/0389/09, Keane brought a number of claims for age discrimination with respect to jobs she had no intention of applying for. The EAT upheld the tribunal's decision to award costs against her as the sole aim of her presentation of the claims was to make money in circumstances in which she had no legal basis for seeking compensation.

Figure 1.2 illustrates the stages involved in pursuing a claim before an employment tribunal.

Figure 1.2 Employment tribunal claims

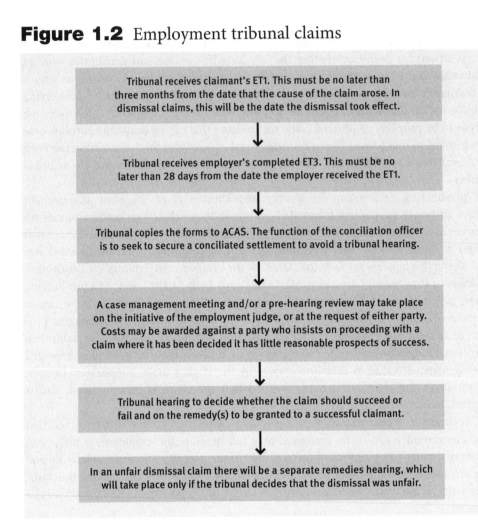

Tribunal receives claimant's ET1. This must be no later than three months from the date that the cause of the claim arose. In dismissal claims, this will be the date the dismissal took effect.

Tribunal receives employer's completed ET3. This must be no later than 28 days from the date the employer received the ET1.

Tribunal copies the forms to ACAS. The function of the conciliation officer is to seek to secure a conciliated settlement to avoid a tribunal hearing.

A case management meeting and/or a pre-hearing review may take place on the initiative of the employment judge, or at the request of either party. Costs may be awarded against a party who insists on proceeding with a claim where it has been decided it has little reasonable prospects of success.

Tribunal hearing to decide whether the claim should succeed or fail and on the remedy(s) to be granted to a successful claimant.

In an unfair dismissal claim there will be a separate remedies hearing, which will take place only if the tribunal decides that the dismissal was unfair.

Writing and drafting

It is clear from the above that good case management is facilitated if forms ET1 and ET3 are properly completed. This assists the tribunal judge in deciding whether to hold a case management discussion and, if so, what issues should be addressed. It also enables the judge to determine whether the claimant's or respondent's case has little reasonable prospects of success – in which case a pre-hearing review should be held in an attempt to save everyone's time and to avoid a party incurring expense in proceeding with a claim that is destined to fail.

As someone who has studied employment law, it might be the case that a member of your family or a friend comes to you with a legal problem that has arisen at work. Indeed, it is always possible that you may personally encounter such a problem and consequently consider making a tribunal claim. It is therefore very useful for you to familiarise yourself with forms ET1 and ET3 and how to complete them.

Forms ET1 and ET3 can be downloaded directly from **http://www.justice.gov.uk/ global/forms/hmcts/tribunals/employment/index.htm**. You can download both forms in pdf format from the tribunal website and save them to your PC or laptop, etc. You will then be able to edit the forms as often as you like in considering how different types of tribunal claims could be presented or responded to. Guidance on completing forms ET1 and ET3 can also be downloaded from this site.

Imagine you have recently applied for a job and were shortlisted for an interview. At the interview you were asked whether it was really feasible for a person of your gender to do the job effectively. You have been informed that your application for the job was unsuccessful. However, you have discovered that the successful applicant was of the opposite gender to you and was less well qualified for the post. You have now succeeded in obtaining another job, but you estimate that over the coming 12 months you will earn £3,000 less, after deductions for income tax and national insurance, than you would have earned had the initial job application been successful. What type of claim do you think you could present to a tribunal? If your claim succeeds, what type of remedy would you want from a tribunal in light of the above facts?

On the basis of the above scenario, complete the relevant sections of form ET1 setting out your personal details and the main details concerning the prospective employer and the job, which you can make up. In the appropriate part of the form, you should state the relevant facts and set out your arguments as to why you believe you have a good claim in law. You should specify what you think will be the appropriate remedy(s) for you to receive were your claim to succeed.

Handy tips: If you are completing an ET1 in real life then it can always be completed off-line and, if you are acting for a client, it can be emailed to the client for consideration before it is submitted to the tribunal. This is done by clicking on the red button towards the top of the form. In carrying out the above activity, you should not click on this button as otherwise your fictional claim could end up in a tribunal office!

It is not necessary to include cases in the ET1. However, if there is a previously decided case that is in your favour, particularly if it was one decided by the Court of Appeal or the Supreme Court, then it can do no harm to bring this case to the attention of the tribunal. It is also useful to identify briefly the statutory provisions on which your claim is based.

Reflective practice

Visit **http://etclaims.co.uk/tag/et1/** – to obtain advice on drafting an ET1. Have a look at the ET1 you completed earlier. Do you think these tips are useful in assisting claimants in drafting a tribunal claim? In drafting your ET1 you should have identified that the claim is one of sex discrimination. The fact that you were better qualified than the successful applicant could well constitute sufficient evidence that you were the victim of unlawful sex discrimination. The remedies for a successful claim of sex discrimination are fully explained later (see Chapter 7). However, in the above scenario, you should anticipate being awarded £3,000 compensation for loss of income as a result of your job application being unlawfully rejected. You would probably receive an additional sum of around £500 for injury to feelings as the prospective employer's discrimination was an intentional act.

The Employment Appeals Tribunal

The losing party before an employment tribunal may appeal to the Employment Appeals Tribunal, which is known universally as the EAT, and is chaired by a High Court or circuit judge. In the same way as is the case in employment tribunals, this judge is assisted by two lay members, and it is still permissible for either or both the parties to be represented by non-lawyers. As stated above, legal aid is not available for claims to tribunal hearings but it is available for proceedings before the EAT. This is very important as it is common for the parties to be represented by solicitors or barristers at EAT hearings, and claimants on low incomes would obviously be disadvantaged if there was no chance of them being able to afford representation by a legal practitioner.

An appeal can only be made to the EAT on a point or points of law. In other words, the appeal must be on the basis that the tribunal reached its decision on the basis of an error of law. For example, a tribunal misunderstood the law as contained in a precedent case or failed to take a relevant precedent into account. Appeals cannot succeed where the losing party believes the tribunal adopted a mistaken view of the evidence presented to it, unless the tribunal's view of the facts is so unreasonable as to amount to an error of law. Technically, in such a situation the tribunal's decision is said to be perverse. Where the tribunal has applied the law to the facts to reach a decision that any reasonable tribunal could reach then the tribunal's decision must stand. This is the case even if the EAT or an appellate court would have given a different decision.

Case Summary

An example of the EAT deciding it has *no* jurisdiction to overturn a tribunal's decision is provided by the case of *Woods* v. *WM Car Services Ltd* [1982] ICR 693. This case concerned a situation where the company had taken over a business but continued to employ Woods. At the time of the takeover the company assured Woods that it would not seek to change the terms of her contract of employment. The company repeatedly broke this promise and put pressure on Woods to agree to a new contract of employment and, ultimately, Woods decided to resign. The legal issue before the tribunal was whether in breaking its initial assurance to Woods the company had behaved in such a way as to mean that it had committed a breach of contract. The tribunal found that this was not the case as it is reasonable for employers to seek to persuade employees to accept new contracts of employment where the employer regards this as in the interests of business efficiency. On appeal, the EAT stated that it did regard the employer's behaviour to be so bad as to amount to a breach of contract. However, the tribunal had properly taken all the relevant evidence into account and the tribunal's view of this evidence was one that the tribunal was entitled to take. Therefore the appeal by Woods had to be dismissed, even though the EAT would have reached a different decision had it been in the tribunal's shoes. The Court of Appeal agreed that the EAT had no jurisdiction to overturn the tribunal's decision as this was a decision that any reasonable tribunal could reach. The Court of Appeal also stated that, in its view, the tribunal's view of the facts had been correct.

The above case vividly illustrates how different courts and tribunals can take different views of the same facts, and consequently reach different decisions in circumstances where any such decision is correct in law. An appeal will only succeed where the view of the facts which had been taken is one which no reasonable tribunal or court could take. You will find an 'Out and about' activity based on the *Woods* case later (see Chapter 3).

Distinguishing between issues of fact and issues of law can, in itself, be a very complex matter, and can be the basis of an appeal to the Court of Appeal by a party seeking to establish that the EAT had no right to overturn a tribunal's decision. The argument here will be that the EAT had disagreed with a tribunal's assessment of the facts, rather than regarding the tribunal as having been wrong in law, and therefore, as in *Woods*, should have upheld the tribunal's decision even though the EAT disagreed with it. Whether or not a worker has an employee status is regarded by the courts as an issue of fact rather than law, and the problems this position generates will be considered later (see Chapter 2).

If the EAT upholds an appeal, it can substitute its own decision for that of the employment tribunal. However, where the EAT believes that the facts need to be reconsidered in light of the law as expressed by the EAT, then it may remit the claim to the same or a different employment tribunal so it will still be a tribunal that decides the case.

Further appeals, which again can only be on a point or points of law, can be made to the Court of Appeal (Civil Division), and ultimately, albeit relatively rarely, to the Supreme Court. The Supreme Court has replaced the House of Lords, but for many years to come the leading authorities in employment law will be cases which were decided by the Law Lords as the senior judges sitting in the House of Lords. At the time of writing, as most such cases were heard by the House of Lords, the Supreme Court will be referred to only when it was actually that court that decided a case. However, outside the context of discrimination law, presumably for reasons of time and/or cost, relatively few appeals have been made to the House of Lords or the Supreme Court in cases which started their life in employment tribunals. It should be noted that, with respect to the doctrine of precedent, a decision of the EAT is not binding on a different EAT, but the EAT and employment tribunals are, of course, obliged to follow decisions of the Court of Appeal and the House of Lords/Supreme Court. Tribunals are also bound by decisions of the EAT.

Law in action

In January 2011, the government announced it wanted to reduce tribunal workload and find quicker and cheaper alternative methods to resolve workplace disputes. Set out below is an executive summary of the government's initial thinking, which it set out in a consultation paper, as to how it could achieve these objectives. As you read through this text you may wish to reflect on the below proposals and form your own opinions as to which, if any, you agree with.

The government sought views on how to:

Source: Ingram Publishing, Alamy

+ achieve more early resolution of workplace disputes so that parties can resolve their own problems, in a way that is fair and equitable for both sides, without having to go to an employment tribunal;

+ ensure that, where parties do need to attend an employment tribunal, the process is as swift, user friendly and effective as possible;

+ help businesses feel more confident about hiring people.

The consultation aims to identify measures to encourage parties to use early dispute resolution, including increased awareness of mediation and realistic expectations of what employment tribunals can award; it puts forward legislative proposals to simplify the employment tribunal process, encouraging earlier settlement of claims where possible and more efficient handling of claims; and it considers the qualifying period for employees before they can bring a case to an employment tribunal (ET) for unfair dismissal.

The proposals set out in this consultation cover:

✦ **Mediation** – the government is considering how we might enable greater use of alternative dispute resolution tools such as judicial mediation where an employment judge can propose ways to the parties as to how a dispute could be resolved. The consultation seeks to obtain more information about current use, costs and benefits, and barriers.

✦ **Early conciliation** – to require all claims to be submitted to ACAS in the first instance, rather than the Tribunals Service. This would allow ACAS a specified period (up to one month) to offer pre-claim conciliation in all cases.

✦ **Tackling weaker cases** – by making the power to strike out more flexible; allowing a judge to be able to issue a deposit order at any stage of the proceedings, to make the deposit order test more flexible and for the EAT to be able to make deposit orders; and increasing the deposit and cost limits for weak and vexatious claims from £500 and £10,000 to £1,000 and £20,000 respectively.

Encouraging settlements

✦ **Provision of information** – to provide for additional information about the nature of the claim being made and to include a statement of loss as required information for claims involving monetary compensation.

✦ **Formalising offers to settle** – where a party has made an offer to settle to avoid the need for a tribunal hearing but this offer has been rejected, then such an offer should be lodged with the ET. In the event that the ET finds for the party rejecting the offer but makes a less favourable award to what was offered, then there should be a mechanism for recognising the additional costs incurred by the other party as a result of the claim proceeding to a tribunal hearing.

Shortening tribunal hearings

✦ **Witness statements to be taken as read** in all hearings. This would mean that witness statements are provided in advance to the tribunal in writing and do not have to be read out by the witness as part of a hearing. This reduces the time that witnesses have to spend at the tribunal as their presence will be solely for the purposes of answering questions in examinations and cross-examinations. Consequently, tribunal hearings should be shorter and this results in saved costs for the system and business.

✦ **Withdraw the payment of expenses** in tribunal hearings – at present the parties and their witnesses are entitled to claim for expenses such as travel expenses and loss of earnings. Withdrawing this right will encourage parties to settle earlier and to think more carefully about the number of witnesses they call, so potentially reducing the length of hearings.

✦ **Extend the jurisdictions where judges can sit alone** in ETs to include unfair dismissal, and to remove the general requirement for lay members to be part of the EAT, allowing more efficient use of the lay member resource.

✦ **Introduce the use of legal officers** to deal with certain case management functions thus freeing up (more costly) judicial time to concentrate on matters requiring judicial expertise.

✦ **Introduce fee-charging** mechanisms in employment tribunals, for example where claimants lodge claims (and respondents choose to counter-claim), and/or for parties in claims that proceed to full hearing.

✦ **Introduce financial penalties for employers** found to have breached rights, to encourage greater compliance.

Source: Department for Business, Information and Skills, 'Resolving Workplace Disputes: A consultation', January 2011. The full consultation paper can be accessed from **http://www.bis.gov.uk/assets/biscore/employment-matters/docs/r/11-511-resolving-workplace-disputes-consultation.pdf**

One proposal, which was originally in the consultation paper, should be highlighted as it is particularly controversial and is now the legal position. This was the proposal to extend the qualifying period for claiming unfair dismissal from one year to two years' continuous employment with the same employer. This proposal was implemented by the Unfair Dismissal and Statement of Reasons for Dismissal (Variation of Qualifying Period) Order 2012, SI 2012/989 with effect from 6 April 2012.

A two-year qualifying period for unfair dismissal rights was originally introduced by Margaret Thatcher's Conservative government in the 1980s, and made many workers feel very vulnerable in the initial years of their employment. It also created additional difficulties for many women re-entering the labour market after taking a break in their careers to look after their young children, as it increased the time they had to work to re-acquire statutory employment rights. The qualifying period was reduced to one year by the Labour government in 1999, but is now once again two years for any employee who commenced employment on or after 6 April 2012.

The present government's rationale for making this change was summed up by the Business Secretary, Vince Cable, as follows:

'The priority of this government is to increase growth in our economy. We have one of the most flexible labour markets in the world but there is more we can do to give British business the confidence it needs to create more jobs and support the wider economy to grow.

Businesses tell us that unfair dismissal rules are a major barrier to taking on more people. So today we have announced that only after working for the same employer for two years can an employee bring an unfair dismissal claim.'

Source: http://nds.coi.gov.uk/content/detail.aspx?NewsAreaId=2&ReleaseID=421449&SubjectId=2

As well as extending the qualifying period for claiming unfair dismissal to two years, several other proposals contained in the consultation paper were implemented in 2012. These were:

✦ As commented on above, under the Employment Tribunals Act 1996 (Tribunal Composition) Order 2012, SI 2012/988, the government has implemented the proposal to enable employment judges to sit alone to hear unfair dismissal cases.

✦ Under the Employment Tribunals (Constitution and Rules of Procedure) (Amendment) Regulations 2012, SI 2012/468, witness statements can be taken as read, although an employment judge or tribunal can still rule that a witness should orally present his or her evidence.

✦ Also under SI 2012/468, employment judges and tribunals are now empowered to order a party to pay a witness's expenses in attending a tribunal.

✦ Under the Employment Tribunals (Constitution and Rules of Procedure) (Amendment) Regulations 2012, SI 2012/468, the maximum amount of costs that can be awarded by a tribunal has been increased from £10,000 to £20,000 and the deposit a tribunal can require a party to lodge had been increased from £500 to £1,000.

People **in the law**

The following interview is with **Max Craft**, who is an employment law judge in the Hampshire area. This interview provides valuable insights into how employment tribunals work, manage their very heavy workload and how voluntary settlements operate as an alternative to claims proceeding to full hearing. Max also comments on the likely impact of the recent changes to tribunal procedure which are summarised above.

Has it been of any practical importance that chairmen of employment tribunals can now use the title of employment judge? The employment tribunals are unique amongst other tribunals in that they operate within an adversarial arena involving party-to-party litigation rather than applications involving the state and challenging those decisions, for example, immigration, benefits, etc. My understanding is that it was thought that the title of employment judge was more consistent with the nature of the work and its responsibilities for that reason.

Do you have any views on the workload of employment tribunals and whether this needs to be reduced? If so, what do you consider to be the best ways for this to be achieved? Employment tribunals have seen a substantial increase in workload and it is a workload of increasing complexity. This reflects new legislation, particularly in the discrimination field and other areas such as family friendly policies and also the impact of European Directives and the interpretation of employment law before the European Court.

This has coincided with a reduction in available administrative resources which has been exacerbated more recently by the need to reduce costs across all areas of the public sector.

The employers' lobbying groups consistently advocate the perception that the employment tribunals do not deal robustly with weak, speculative claims. However, any judicial process that involves making findings of fact from amongst competing versions of events will make dismissing cases in the absence of receiving evidence difficult in most cases, particularly those involving discrimination.

There has also been an increase in group actions, for example, equal pay claims in the public sector and multi-day cases. This places substantial strain on judicial resources and uses up substantial amounts of judicial time to the detriment of a speedier process to hearing less complicated and onerous claims.

Employment tribunals are committed to rigorous case management and, in training, employment judges are consistently directed to those areas. This is to ensure that relevant issues can be identified and that the time and costs of preparation and attendance at hearing is proportionate to the issues involved to meet the published overriding objectives. The Employment Tribunals Service has also introduced its own mediation procedure to offer another avenue, free of charge, in more difficult and lengthy cases.

From 6 April 2012, the government has increased deposits required from parties to continue with cases viewed as weak to £1,000 and has also increased the costs that can be awarded by an employment tribunal from £10,000 to £20,000. It also intends to introduce compulsory pre-claim mediation, wants to reduce potential liabilities on smaller employers and will be introducing fees for issuing proceedings. Since 6 April 2012 it has also introduced employment judges sitting alone on unfair dismissal cases to save the time and cost involved in a tribunal sitting with three members in such cases.

There is also increasing encouragement of workplace mediation and, as in all litigation, this encouragement towards resolving issues before embarking upon the substantial expense of contested proceedings will continue.

It appears to me that this is achieving about the right balance to try and reduce the caseload and to assist employment tribunals in efficient case management. Ultimately, however, it is the parties themselves that have to take responsibility by having realistic expectations of the proceedings and working together with the employment tribunal to achieve proportionate and efficient conduct of the cases.

Please could you briefly describe how tribunals work with ACAS conciliation officers to enable a dispute to be resolved without the need for a tribunal hearing. The ACAS conciliation service works entirely separately from the employment tribunals. It is a principle of conciliation that any discussions with ACAS should not (and cannot) be referred to an employment tribunal hearing a case and these can play no part in determining the outcome of those proceedings. The effective screen between conciliation and judicial process is vital in ensuring that conciliation has the greatest prospect of success. Successful outcomes of ACAS conciliation will account for a substantial percentage of those claims that do not proceed to a full hearing.

A reasonably large number of claims to employment tribunals are rejected or withdrawn. In your experience what are the most common reasons for this? The statistics consistently show that around 65–70% of claims submitted to employment tribunals do not proceed to a hearing. Claims can be defeated by

procedural issues (for example, claims have not been submitted in time), be withdrawn and be settled between the parties. It is settlement that leads to the resolution of a substantial number of the claims that do not proceed to a full hearing. Very often the terms of settlement will involve a payment of financial compensation which will usually be paid without any admission of liability on behalf of the employer, but terms of settlement can encompass a variety of terms and do not always include paying compensation to the claimant.

In what circumstances would you consider imposing costs on a losing party? Broadly, a costs award can only be made within the terms allowed by the Employment Tribunals Rules of Procedure where a party to the proceedings or his or her representative has conducted the proceedings vexatiously, abusively, destructively or otherwise unreasonably, or the bringing or conducting of the proceedings by the paying party has been misconceived. The costs that can be awarded by an employment tribunal have recently been increased to a sum of up to £20,000. Alternatively, it can order that costs should be determined by way of assessment within the usual County Court procedures. This involves no cap on costs and is dealt with by the County Court.

People involved in employment law

Having examined the system of employment tribunals, we need to consider the characteristics of the main parties involved in an employment law claim which may be presented to a tribunal.

Employers

An employer will be any person running his or her own business who enters into a contract with another person to carry out work for the benefit of that business. Employers may be individuals or business people in partnership with one another. In the past, law firms were partnerships, but today they are generally limited partnerships and similar formalities apply to setting up a limited partnership as they do with setting up a private company. However, a partnership is still a form of business organisation which can be chosen by people who want fewer formalities, and consequently greater flexibility, than those involved in setting up a business in the form of a company. Nevertheless, most employers in the private sector will be companies with limited liability. A company is a legal person in its own right and is run by its directors. The advantage of limited liability is that if the company incurs legal liability the shareholders are not personally liable in terms of their personal income and savings being available for contribution to any compensation that a tribunal or court awards. Nor are shareholders personally liable to creditors seeking repayment of the company's debts. The shareholders' liabilities are limited to the value of their shareholdings. For example, if a company becomes insolvent and its employees are made redundant the shareholders cannot recover their investments, but they are not legally liable to pay employees any redundancy payments to which they are entitled. The other major type of employer will be public sector employers such as central government, local councils and the National Health Service (NHS).

Employees and workers

At first sight it may seem strange to refer to employees and workers as the latter will also be the former and the two words are often used synonymously. However, in employment law the difference can be crucial as workers with employee status enjoy many statutory employment rights, particularly those contained in ERA 1996, which are not granted to workers who do not have employee status. The original main statutory rights were the right to a statutory redundancy payment, which was granted in 1965, and the right not to be unfairly dismissed, which was granted in 1971. As a matter of government policy these rights were restricted to employees, but at the time it was typically the case that a worker would also have been an employee. However, patterns of untypical employment relationships have grown since those times so that, today, a significant number of workers are employed on a casual basis or via employment agencies. Often such workers are not employees and, consequently, do not enjoy the employment protection rights which are to be found in ERA 1996.

As a matter of social policy, governments can choose to confer rights on workers and this is the case with the right to a minimum wage granted by the National Minimum Wage Act 1998. This right is enjoyed by all workers irrespective of employee status. Discrimination law is derived from EU law and this requires all individuals who do work for another to be protected from discrimination in securing or carrying out work. Consequently, both workers and employees are protected from unlawful discrimination contrary to the Equality Act 2010. Indeed, generally, employment rights which are required by EU law, such as those contained in the Working Time Regulations 1998, which regulate working hours, apply to both employees and workers. It can be difficult to determine whether a worker has employee status and this is an issue that is fully dealt with later (see Chapter 2). It will be clarified at appropriate points in this text whether a particular right is restricted to employees or whether it is also granted to workers.

Trade union members

Whether an individual is a worker or an employee he or she can choose to join a trade union, although, unfortunately perhaps given their vulnerable position in terms of job security, many workers without employee status do not think about joining trade unions as they are not in permanent employment. It is also the case that many such workers will be employed in the private sector where trade unions are no longer as prevalent as they once were. As will be examined in greater depth (see Chapter 8), trade union membership has significantly declined in the years since 1979. In that year there were 13 million trade union members – today that figure has been halved and most of the decline is in the private sector. However, larger employer organisations in the private sector are often unionised, and UNITE is the best known example of a trade union that operates primarily in the private sector.

The main statute dealing with trade unions and the world of industrial relations is the Trade Union and Labour Relations (Consolidation) Act (TULRCA) 1992. Section 1 TULRCA defines a trade union as an organisation of workers whose principal purposes include regulating relations with employers or employer's associations. The latter will be a group of separate employers in the same trade, industry or profession who meet with one or more trade union representing workers in that job sector. For example, university employers have their own association, the Universities and Colleges Employers' Association, which negotiates with the University and College Union (UCU) and UNISON on the pay and conditions of their teaching and other administrative and technical staff.

The TULRCA is a very large and complex piece of legislation. Its provisions include: the rights that trade union members have with respect to their own trade unions; rights to time off at work for trade union activities; protection against discrimination or dismissal by employers on grounds of trade union membership; and the regulation of industrial action. This area of employment law is often known as collective labour law and aspects of it will be examined later (see Chapters 8 and 9).

One very important function of a trade union arises when it is recognised by an employer for the purposes of collective bargaining. This means that the employer has agreed with the trade union that the latter can negotiate with the employer on the terms and conditions of employment of all or some of its employees. Typically, such negotiations will cover matters such as rates of pay, hours of working, holiday and sick pay entitlement. An agreement reached through collective bargaining is known as a **collective agreement**. Normally, under s. 178(2) TULRCA, a collective agreement is not legally binding between the employer and the trade union who are the parties to the agreement.

However, a collective agreement may specify that its contents are to be incorporated into the individual contracts of employment of those employees on whose behalf the union made the agreement. Providing such a collective agreement is actually incorporated into an individual's contract of employment by an express term in that contract then the content of the collective agreement is legally enforceable between the employer and the employee. As above, a major example of such an agreement is where an employee's rate of pay has been determined by collective bargaining. Indeed, most workers who are collectively represented by a trade union will find that their wages or salaries are regularly negotiated on their behalf by a trade union. If a collective agreement is reached but the employee does not receive the increase in pay, then he or she can sue the employer for breach of contract to recover the money that is owed. This will be the case irrespective of whether the employee is a member of the trade union which negotiated the agreement. This process of collective bargaining and its legal consequences will be fully explored later (see Chapter 8).

The certification officer

Trade unions which have been recognised by an employer for the purposes of collective bargaining enjoy certain statutory advantages. Generally, this is only the case where the trade union is not just recognised by the employer but can also be regarded as independent of it; that is, not under the employer's control or influence. The certification officer is a civil servant whose functions include establishing whether a new trade union should be granted a certificate of independence (see Chapter 8).

Institutions involved in employment law

As well as the individuals discussed above, there are various institutions which play an important part in our system of employment law. First and foremost of these is ACAS, the government's conciliation and arbitration service.

The Advisory, Conciliation and Arbitration Service (ACAS)

ACAS was established by Harold Wilson's Labour government in 1975. ACAS consists of a chairman and up to 15 people who will have an employer or trade union background or who will be independents, such as academics with an expertise in industrial relations. Industrial conflict between employers and trade unions was a distinctive feature of the 1970s. Therefore, at the time ACAS was established its main role was to offer its services to employers and trade unions, which were in dispute with one another, in an attempt to resolve a dispute so that industrial action did not take place or was brought to an end. This remains one of the important functions of ACAS, and readers may recall the industrial action taken by cabin crew employed by British Airways in 2010. This was a high-profile industrial dispute and ACAS was involved in the talks between British Airways and the relevant trade union, UNITE, which ultimately led to the dispute being resolved. This dispute, some important case law it generated and this aspect of the work of ACAS will be fully considered later (see Chapter 9).

As explained above, another major role played by ACAS is to help individual employers and employees reach a conciliated settlement as an alternative to presenting a tribunal claim, or as an alternative to proceeding with a claim that has already been presented.

A third role is to provide guidance to employers, employees and trade unions on how important areas of employment law are to be understood and to be followed in practice. To this end ACAS is empowered to issue codes of practice. These codes do not consist of legal rules but they are authoritative guides on how the law is to be understood. The ACAS Code of Practice on Disciplinary and Grievance Procedures is a very important document in the area of unfair dismissal law (see Chapter 5). This code includes the disciplinary procedures that employers should follow before dismissing an employee. A failure to follow these procedures may result in a dismissal by an employer being found by an employment tribunal to be procedurally unfair. ACAS has also issued codes in the area of employee relations such as a code of practice concerned with time off rights for trade union representatives and members (see Chapter 8).

Out and about

Visit the ACAS website at **http://www.acas.org.uk/index.aspx?articleid=1461**. This will enable you to discover all the types of work that ACAS undertakes, as well as being able to download its annual report, its research reports and the codes of practice it has issued.

In particular, it is suggested that you click on the link entitled Disputes and Mediation. This will enable you to understand the role that ACAS plays in seeking to resolve both individual and collective disputes and conflict in the workplace.

From the website identify the differences between:

✦ mediation;

✦ conciliation; and

✦ arbitration.

Also what advice does ACAS provide on the issues of discipline and dismissal?

Handy tip: The ACAS Code of Practice on Disciplinary and Grievance Procedures 2009 is a particularly important document in employment law. You can download your own copy in PDF format from **http://www.acas.org.uk/index.aspx?articleid=2174**

The Central Arbitration Committee (CAC)

Like ACAS, the CAC was established by the Labour government in 1975, and it can arbitrate individual disputes between employers and employees. However, its main functions are in the world of industrial relations. It can, for example, determine whether an employer should be legally obliged to recognise a trade union. It also has functions concerning the disclosure of information by employers to trade unions for collective bargaining purposes, and enforcing legal rules requiring employers to consult collectively with their employees. All of these issues are considered later (see Chapter 8).

The Equality and Human Rights Commission (EHRC)

Prior to the Equality Act 2006, there were three separate commissions concerned with three separate areas of discrimination law: the Equal Opportunities Commission which focused on sex discrimination; the Commission for Race Equality; and the Disability Rights Commission. The 2006 Act established a single Commission, the EHRC, which is concerned not only with the above three areas of discrimination law but also other types of unlawful discrimination such as age discrimination and discrimination which relates to a person's sexual orientation.

The EHRC has a duty to encourage and support developments in society to promote anti-discriminatory attitudes and practices and human rights. It can issue codes of practice that, amongst others, employers should follow in complying with the law and in developing their own equal opportunities policies. It can investigate whether a person or organisation has committed an unlawful act, in violation of discrimination or human rights law, and can issue Unlawful Act Notices. These can require remedial action to be taken so that the unlawful acts are brought to an end, and can recommend what such remedial action should be. If necessary, it can apply to the County Court for a court order requiring an Unlawful Act Notice to be complied with.

The best way to find out about the work of the EHRC is to visit its website at **http:// www.equalityhumanrights.com/**. You will find particularly useful documents in the Advice and Guidance section on this website which expand on the law discussed later (see Chapter 7). It is recommended that you look at the Code of Practice on the Equality Act, guides for both employers and employees on what the law involves, and advice to workers as to how to go about presenting tribunal claims.

As well as combating discrimination, the Commission is charged with the duty of monitoring the compatibility of British law with the European Convention on Human Rights. This has been particularly important since the Human Rights Act (HRA) 1998 incorporated the European Convention into British law. The impact of the HRA is considered further below.

One function of the EHRC is to provide submissions to the **European Court of Human Rights (EctHR)** by way of independent legal expert opinion on cases in which the applicant is appealing against the decision of a British Court. The *Eweida* case (see Chapter 7), involved a Christian employee who was suspended without pay because she refused her employer's instructions not to display her crucifix whilst at work. Eweida lost her discrimination claim, but has taken her case to the EctHR on the basis of Article 9 of the Convention which provides individuals with the right to manifest a religious belief. In the view of the EHRC the wearing of religious symbols should be regarded as a manifestation of a religious belief, and the Equality Act should be interpreted to reflect this.

Further information on this can be obtained from **http://www.equalityhumanrights.com/ news/2011/september/commission-submits-intervention-on-religious-discrimination-in-the-wo/**

Finally, if you visit **http://www.equalityhumanrights.com/uploaded_files/who_we_ are.pdf** you will be able to download the Commission's own publication, *Who we are and what we do*, which explains its role and its powers.

Health and Safety Executive (HSE)

This is a body which is independent of government and was originally established by the Health and Safety at Work Act 1974. It provides advice to employers and workers on all areas of health and safety and is empowered to issue codes of practice. The HSE employs health and safety inspectors who visit workplaces to ensure that employers are complying with their legal duties under health and safety law (see Chapter 3). Health and safety inspectors can take enforcement action, including prosecuting employers in the criminal courts where they are in breach of their health and safety duties.

Further information about the work of the HSE can be obtained from its website at http://www.hse.gov.uk/index.htm

Sources of employment law

Having considered the people whose relationships are regulated by employment law, and the institutions that have been established to assist in the regulatory process, it is useful to identify precisely where employment law comes from.

British law

In accordance with the norms of our legal system, there are two main sources of employment law. The first source is judge-made law in the form of the common law. As stated above, the primary legal mechanism for regulating the relationship between individual employers and their employees is the contract of employment. As will be explained in depth later, the employment contract is made in exactly the same way as any other type of contract and most of the ordinary principles of contract law apply to it.

The common law in the form of the law of tort is also of some relevance to the employment relationship – particularly in the areas of health and safety and the organisation of industrial action. All employers owe their employees a duty to take reasonable care with respect to their health, safety and welfare at the workplace. It is the ordinary principles of the tort of negligence which determine whether an employer is in breach of this duty, and whether an injured employee is entitled to compensation from the employer as a result. It is a tort for any person to induce a party to a contract to act in breach of that contract. Effectively, this means that the organisation of strike action and most other forms of industrial action is inherently tortious (see Chapters 3 and 9 respectively).

Secondly, much of modern employment law is statute-based, either in the form of Acts of Parliament or in the form of statutory instruments. These statutory rights are considered throughout this text. The major Acts include the Employment Rights Act (ERA) 1996, the Equality Act (EqA) 2010 and the Trade Union and Labour Relations (Consolidation) Act (TULRCA) 1992. One important statutory instrument is the Working Time Regulations 1998 (see Chapter 2). As explained below, statutes and statutory instruments are also the mechanisms through which European law is implemented in the UK.

European Union (EU) law

EU law is of the utmost importance to employment law. Nearly all of our discrimination law is based on EU law as exemplified by the Equality Act 2010 and the Part-time Workers Regulations 2000, SI 2000/1551. As has been already explained, virtually all our discrimination law is now contained in the 2010 Act. However, the Part-time Workers Regulations are an exception this and the effect of these regulations is to prohibit discrimination against any part-time worker of either gender. The other main areas where EU law has an impact are:

✦ health and safety regulations, such as the Working Time Directive 1993 as implemented by the Working Time Regulations 1998;

✦ the transfer of a business by one employer to another employer as regulated by the Acquired Rights Directive 2001 (see Chapter 6);

✦ duties on employers to inform and consult with trade union or other employee representatives (see Chapters 6 and 8).

Articles 151 to 161 of the Treaty on the Functioning of the European Union (TFEU), which replaces the EC and EU Treaties, contain the legal bases for the EU legislating on social policy. Articles 154 and 155 are of particular importance as these provide the methods by which social, that is, employment legislation is introduced. In particular, the Commission must consult with the social partners, which consist of European employers' associations and the European Trades Union Confederation, before proposing legislation and permitting the social partners to negotiate Community-level agreements. Such agreements can be given the force of law by a decision of the European Council. The Parental Leave Directive 1996, Directive 96/34/EC, and the Directive on Part-time Work, Directive 98/23/EC, were made and implemented in this way. As a result of the Parental Leave Directive, new provisions were inserted into ERA 1996 to give parents the right to 13 weeks' unpaid leave to care for a child under the age of five. The Directive on Part-time Work was implemented by the Part-time Workers Regulations, as referred to above.

Article 157 TFEU, which provides the right for employees to receive equal pay for work of equal value irrespective of gender, is particularly noteworthy as this Article is **directly applicable**. This means that the Article is automatically law within member states and takes precedence over national legal rules. Therefore, should there be a conflict between the provisions on equal pay in the Equality Act and Article 157 an employee can rely directly on the latter as the basis of an equal pay claim in an employment tribunal.

EU Directives

EU legislation in the area of employment law is in the form of EU **Directives**. Normally, these are not directly enforceable by employers against their employees. It is first necessary for the Directive to be transposed into UK law, that is, given legal effect in the UK by an Act of Parliament or a statutory instrument. The Equality Act 2010 implementing the Equal Treatment Directive 2006/54 and the Framework Directive 2000/78/EC on Discrimination, and the Working Time Regulations 1998 implementing the Working Time Directive illustrate this process.

The latter Directive provides limits on working hours and rights to paid holidays and, in the UK, was of particular practical importance to workers in the private sector – in particular many lower-paid private sector workers traditionally did not receive any pay if they took holidays. The Directive should have been implemented in the UK in 1996, but actually was not implemented until 1998. It was only after this date of implementation that workers in the UK were able to benefit from and enforce the rights contained in the Directive.

However, some Directives take **vertical direct effect**. This means that, even though the Directive has yet to be implemented in the UK, state employees can enforce legal rights contained in the Directive once it comes into effect. The Directive will specify what this date will be. Moreover, if there is a conflict between a Directive and an Act of Parliament, state employees can rely on the Directive as the basis for a legal claim. The Equal Treatment Directive, which prohibits sex discrimination and originally came into effect in 1976, is a major example of a Directive which directly confers legally enforceable rights on state employees. The practical consequences of this are illustrated below by the *Marshall* cases.

> state employees can enforce legal rights contained in the Directive once it comes into effect

It is important to appreciate that even state employees can only directly rely on a Directive where its content is sufficiently clear, certain and precise to constitute a legally enforceable right. A Directive will not satisfy these criteria where it lays down general principles and leaves it to the governments of member states to decide on the detail of how the Directive will be implemented in their countries. For example, the abovementioned Working Time Directive provided for a maximum working week of 48 hours, but empowered governments of member states to decide whether domestic legislation should allow workers to opt out of this protection and choose to work more than 48 hours. This opt-out was included in the UK's Working Time Regulations. The impact of EU Directives on British employment law is summarised in Table 1.2.

On the other hand, the **European Court of Justice (ECJ)** has recently ruled, in *Dominguez* v. *Centre Informatique du Centre Ouest Atlantique* (C-282/10) [2012] IRLR 321, that a worker employed in the public sector in France could directly enforce the right contained in the Working Time Directive to four weeks' paid leave. Her rights under the Directive took priority over the relevant provisions in the French Labour Code. The right to four weeks' leave is clear and unambiguous and is consequently a right that can be directly enforced against state employers.

Case Summary

It should be appreciated that the meaning of 'state employer' in EU law is wider than this term would normally be understood. For example, in *Griffin* v. *South West Water Services Ltd* [1995] IRLR 15, the High Court held that, in accordance with legal principles formulated by the European Court of Justice, the water company could be regarded as a state employer despite the fact that it was a private company with shareholders. This was because the company still provided a service to the public, and was still controlled by the state to the extent that it could only operate on the basis of a licence granted by it. Therefore, redundancy rights given to workers under an EU Directive could be directly enforced by the water company's employees.

Case Summary

Essentially, any public sector employer will be a state employer for the purposes of EU law. Therefore, people employed in the armed forces, the police, the fire service, the civil service, local government, the NHS and the British Broadcasting Corporation (BBC), are all able to take legal action to enforce rights conferred by appropriate EU Directives. Employers such as universities, which are in part publicly funded and are subject to state regulation, will also be state employers. This is probably also the case with, for example, Network Rail and the Royal Bank of Scotland given their partially nationalised status. As the *Griffin* case illustrates, employees of private companies which are regulated by the state are also likely to be able to rely directly on EU law. However, some organisations, which were once fully nationalised, such as British Telecom (BT), now function completely as companies in the private sector and can no longer be regarded as state employers. BT operates in exactly the same way as other companies in the telecommunications and media industries such as Sky and Virgin Media.

Preliminary rulings by the European Court of Justice

The European Court of Justice (ECJ), which is the main court of the EU, plays an important role in interpreting EU law and in deciding whether a Directive can take direct effect. Under Article 267 TFEU, a national court can request a **preliminary ruling** from the ECJ where the national court is hearing a case which is based on EU law. If that court is the highest court in a member state, such as the Supreme Court in the UK, then a preliminary ruling should be requested before the national court decides the case. The preliminary ruling that the ECJ gives is not the decision in the case, but constitutes an authoritative interpretation of the point or points of EU law that the case involves. The ruling will be applied by the national court but it is still the latter that decides the case. Preliminary rulings are of general importance as they lay down legal principles that national courts throughout the EU must follow in the future, although the ECJ is not bound by its own previous rulings.

Case Summary

The interrelationship between state employees enforcing a Directive and the ECJ giving a preliminary ruling is illustrated by the cases of *Marshall* v. *Southampton Area Health Authority No. 1* [1986] IRLR 140 and *Marshall No. 2* [1993] IRLR 445. The original piece of EU legislation concerned with sex discrimination was the Equal Treatment Directive (ETD) 1976, Directive 76/207/EC. In Britain it was believed that the Sex Discrimination Act (SDA) 1975 properly implemented this Directive into British law. The SDA did not apply to employer policies on retirement and therefore it was not contrary to the SDA for employers to have different compulsory retirement ages for men and women. Marshall was employed in the National Health Service and was therefore a state employee. Contrary to her wishes she was required to retire at the age of 60, whilst her male colleagues were permitted to continue working to the age of 65. The Health Authority's retirement ages were based on the fact that the state retirement age for women and men was 60 and 65 respectively. Marshall claimed that this policy was unlawful sex discrimination as it was contrary to the ETD. The Court of Appeal decided to seek a preliminary ruling from the ECJ to ascertain whether the ETD covered retirement policies and whether Marshall, as a state employee, could directly rely on it. The ECJ replied in the affirmative to both these questions and the Court of Appeal decided that, in forcing Marshall to retire, the Health Authority was in breach of the ETD. In the second case, Marshall argued that she had not been given an effective remedy as, at that time, compensation for unlawful sex discrimination was subject to a statutory cap. Again a preliminary ruling was requested from the ECJ and again a ruling was given in her favour. The ECJ ruled that a member state is failing to provide an effective remedy for violations of rights provided by EU law if it imposes an arbitrary limit on the compensation that can be obtained. The Sex Discrimination Act 1975 was amended to comply with this ruling, and, today, there is no statutory cap for any claim that is brought on the basis of the discrimination law now contained in the Equality Act 2010. Therefore, compensation in discrimination cases can be for larger amounts of money than is possible, for example, in claims of unfair dismissal (see Chapter 7).

The litigation brought by Marshall has had important long-term consequences in this country. At the time of writing, there are still different state retirement ages for men and women, though these are in the process of being phased out. It is also the case (as will be explained in Chapter 7), that the law prohibiting age discrimination means that employers are no longer permitted to have a compulsory retirement age unless this can be justified. However, where a compulsory retirement age is permitted then in accordance with *Marshall* it must be the same for men and women.

Interpreting EU Directives

As a result of what is known as the Marleasing principle, as the law derives from the ruling of the ECJ in *Marleasing SA* v. *La Commercial Internacional de Alimentacion SA*

[1992] 1 CMLR 305, national law should be interpreted so that it is consistent with a Directive. This is because in applying national law, irrespective of the fact that national legislation may have been passed before a Directive came into effect, national courts must interpret national law, so far as it is possible to do so, in order to fulfil the objectives of the Directive. The only limit on interpreting statutes in this way is where to do so would be a clear distortion of the language used in the Act. In such a case it is necessary for the government to pass amending legislation so that UK law conforms to EU law.

> national law should be interpreted so that it is consistent with a Directive

For example (as explained in Chapter 7), it was held by both the British courts and the ECJ that neither the Sex Discrimination Act nor the Equal Treatment Directive (ETD) could be interpreted so that the word 'sex' could cover sexual orientation as well as gender. Therefore important changes to British and EU law were required to give effect to the decision of the European Court of Human Rights in the *Lustig-Prean* case which, as explained below, established that the European Convention on Human Rights prohibits discrimination against gay and lesbian people. These changes were implemented in British law in December 2003 and are now fully incorporated in to the Equality Act 2010.

Where the *Marleasing* ruling does apply this means the relevant Directive takes **indirect effect**. This is of practical importance for employees in the private sector, as such employees are unable to rely directly on Directives such as the ETD in the way that Marshall did in the case discussed above concerning different compulsory retirement ages for men and women. The significance of the ETD having indirect as well as direct effect is illustrated by rulings of the ECJ, which were given in the early 1990s, to the effect that the ETD made it unlawful for an employer to refuse employment to or to dismiss a woman because she was pregnant. Unless they had unfair dismissal rights, the only legislation that women in the UK could rely on at that time was the Sex Discrimination Act 1975. However, this Act had been interpreted in a way that prevented pregnant women from claiming sex discrimination unless it could be shown that a man in similar circumstances, such as prolonged absence from work through illness, would have been treated differently. In *Webb* v. *EMO Cargo Ltd* [1993] ICR 175, the House of Lords applied the *Marleasing* ruling to decide that it was unlawful to dismiss a woman on grounds of pregnancy. This was inherently sex discrimination, and it was no longer necessary for a pregnant woman to identify a male comparator who had been treated differently. Today, maternity rights are much more comprehensive (see Chapter 7).

Case Summary

Table 1.2 Impact of Directives on British law

Transposed into British law	Vertical direct effect	Indirect effect
Once a Directive is transposed into British law by a statute or statutory instrument, it is legally enforceable between employers and employees	Providing a Directive is sufficiently certain and clear, it is legally binding on all *state* employers and is legally enforceable by their employees	On the basis of the *Marleasing* principle, British courts must, where possible, interpret British legislation in a way that is compatible with a Directive and with interpretations of it contained in preliminary rulings by the ECJ

The impact of the Human Rights Act on employment law

As explained above, European law has been an important source of employment law ever since the UK joined what was the EEC in 1973. The European Convention on Human Rights (ECHR) 1953 is also of significance to employment law. There are provisions in the Convention which impact on employers and employees such as:

✦ Article 8 which guarantees the right to privacy and to a private life;

✦ Article 9 which guarantees the right to hold and manifest religious and other personal beliefs;

✦ Article 10 which guarantees the right to freedom of expression;

✦ Article 11 which guarantees rights of association, including the right to join a trade union, and rights of assembly.

It should be noted that all these rights can be restricted by national law on grounds of, for example, the maintenance of public order and public safety and to protect the rights and freedoms of others.

The decision of the European Court of Human Rights (EctHR) in *Lustig-Prean & Beckett* v. *the United Kingdom* [1999] IRLR 734, decided on the basis of Article 8, is a major example of how the Convention can impact on employment law. In this case the EctHR decided that it was unlawful to discharge individuals from the Royal Navy because they were gay men. This groundbreaking decision has resulted in major changes to EU and British employment law so that, today, it is unlawful for employers to discriminate in any way against gay, lesbian and bisexual employees. (This issue is fully examined in Chapter 7.)

Article 11 of the European Convention has also generated some EctHR decisions which are important for employment law. We explain above that employees may have some of their terms and conditions of employment determined by collective agreements entered into between their employer and their trade union. In connection with this collective bargaining process the EctHR decided, in *Wilson & NUJ* v. *UK* [2002] IRLR 568, that it was contrary to Article 11 for employers to discriminate against trade union members by, for example, withholding pay increases from employees who refuse to give up employment contracts which are derived from collective agreements. (This issue is fully examined in Chapter 8.)

British governments have also been subject to the European Convention and decisions of the EctHR since the 1950s, when Britain ratified the Convention. However, until recent times, the impact of the ECHR on British society in general, and the world of employment in particular, was of less significance than that of EU law as the British courts were not empowered to give effect to Convention rights where this conflicted with British law.

The importance of the ECHR has increased significantly as a result of the Human Rights Act (HRA) 1998. The HRA incorporated the European Convention on Human Rights (ECHR) 1950 into UK law with effect from 1 October 2000. The HRA overrules any case law which is incompatible with the ECHR, and requires the common law, Acts of Parliament and statutory instruments to be interpreted in ways consistent with the protection of the rights contained in the ECHR. Statutory instruments can be declared invalid on the basis that they conflict with the ECHR. However, judges cannot declare Acts of Parliament to be invalid but they are empowered to issue declarations of incompatibility. Government ministers are empowered to amend such legislation by statutory instrument. If the government decides not to do so then the individual's only recourse is to present a claim to the European Court of Human Rights (EctHR). Thus, ultimately and in contrast with EU law, the HRA does not contradict parliamentary sovereignty in that judges cannot declare Acts of Parliament to be invalid. Nevertheless, individual litigants, including employees, can now base legal actions and claims on the ECHR in a way that was not possible before the HRA came into effect.

For example, under s. 6, courts and tribunals must develop and apply the common law in a manner which is compatible with the Convention. Therefore, if a rule contained in the law of contract or the law of tort is in conflict with a right guaranteed by the Convention the relevant case must be overruled or restricted in its application. This has implications for legal rules regulating picketing activities by workers on strike. Common law cases deciding when demonstrations and picketing on the highway can be considered unlawful, on the grounds that they are **public nuisances**, must be understood as now being subject to Article 11 ECHR. As held by the House of Lords in *DPP* v. *Jones* [1999] 2 All ER 257, a case involving protestors who in previous years had been denied access to Stonehenge to celebrate the summer solstice, it is lawful to use the public highway providing the protest is entirely peaceful in nature and does not obstruct other users. It should be noted that this case was decided before the HRA came into effect but, in reaching its decision, the House of Lords considered the significance of Article 11 ECHR to public protest on the highway. It can be argued (as discussed in Chapter 9), on the basis of Article 11 and the decision in *Jones*, that case law which suggests that the number of pickets situated outside a workplace must be limited to six can no longer be regarded as correct.

Case Summary

Directly enforcing Convention rights

Despite what is explained above, it is important to understand that the ECHR still does not have the same overall impact on employment law as is the case with EU law. This is because, under s. 6(5) HRA, private acts are excluded from the provisions of the HRA in the sense that the Convention cannot be directly relied on to challenge such acts. The employment relationship is considered in English law to be a private relationship beyond the scope of public law, and this may be so even where the employer is regarded as being part of the public sector. We explained above that organisations such as universities, Network Rail and the BBC should be considered to be state employers for the purposes of EU law. However, under the HRA they should be considered as hybrid bodies. They exercise public functions in their relationship with the public, that is, with respect to their students, passengers and viewers or listeners. However, they are in the same position as private companies in their relationships with their employees. Therefore, for example, a university student is directly protected by the ECHR, but it is not possible for a university lecturer directly to enforce Convention rights against the university in its capacity as an employer.

Only employers which can be considered to be core **public authorities** such as the government in its relationship with civil servants, or local councils with respect to their employees, are fully subject to the ECHR. It is not possible to identify precisely which public sector employers are core public authorities and which are not. For example, the status of hospital trusts within the NHS is not certain. Hospital trusts have a degree of commercial autonomy in how they raise and spend money, and through, what is known as the Private Finance Initiative, can act in partnership with private businesses in, for example, securing capital for building projects. However, the NHS is controlled by government, and in the case of *Grampian University Hospital NHS Trust* v. *Napier* [2004] HRLR 18, the Hospital Trust was held by the Scottish High Court to be a governmental organisation. As such, although the Trust was subject to the Convention it was not protected by it. Therefore, it could not plead that it would have been a violation of its Convention rights to have permitted particular evidence to be used against it in court proceedings. On the basis of this decision it is possible that a NHS hospital trust is a core public authority. If this is the case then employees of hospital trusts can directly enforce Convention rights against their employers.

Case Summary

> employees who are not employed by a core pubic authority cannot directly plead Convention rights

Where employers are fully bound by these Articles, as is the case with government departments, the armed forces, the police force, the prison service, the fire service, local councils and possibly the NHS, then cases can be brought before the courts by employees seeking directly to enforce Convention rights against their employer. For example, if a police officer is dismissed on the grounds that he or she is gay or transgendered that officer can argue that the dismissal is a direct violation of his or her human rights under Article 8 of the Convention. Employees who are not employed by a core pubic authority cannot directly plead Convention rights and will need to argue that national law should be interpreted, developed and applied in a way that is consistent with the Convention.

As explained above, before December 2003 this argument was not available to, for example, a university employee, although such an employee is today able to claim unlawful discrimination under the Equality Act 2010. Therefore, as British law stands, it is the case today that all employees are protected from discrimination by their employers on the grounds of their sexual orientation. However, highly unlikely though this is, were the relevant provisions of the Equality Act to be repealed, employees of core public authorities would still able to enforce their rights under Article 8 of the Convention in the British courts. Employees of core public authorities would only cease to be protected by the Convention if a government enacted legislation which turned back the clock by expressly requiring or permitting employers to discriminate against gay and lesbian employees.

By way of summary, the type of employer which can be considered a core public authority is much more restricted than the type of employer which can be considered to be a state employer under EU law. As established above, with respect to the latter, all public sector employers will be state employers and this can even be the case with a privatised utility. This is one reason why EU law is of much more immediate relevance to employment law; the other reason is that one of the objectives of the EU is to provide for common legal standards in the social, that is, employment, field throughout the EU. The ECHR impacts on the employment relationship, but this is not one of the specific objectives of the Convention. Situations where Convention rights are relevant to employment law will be considered in the appropriate parts of this text.

There is one other important practical difference to identify between EU law and the ECHR as far as individual employees are concerned. As illustrated by Table 1.3, an employee, who bases a claim on the ECHR before national courts and tribunals but fails to do so successfully, can then take the claim to the EctHR as the final court of appeal.

Table 1.3 Distinguishing between the two European courts

European Court of Justice	European Court of Human Rights
Individual litigants have no rights of access to the ECJ	Individuals who have failed in their national courts can take their cases to the EctHR
Will give Preliminary Rulings but the national court applies the Ruling to decide the case	As the final court of appeal the EctHR's decision in a case is final
The ECJ's Ruling is binding on all member states and their courts	The EctHR's decision is binding on all signatory states and their courts

Individual employees do not have direct access to the ECJ. All they can do is to ask the national court to seek a preliminary ruling, under Article 267 TFEU, before deciding the case.

As will be explained further later (see Chapter 7), it is not clear that the Equality Act 2010 protects an individual employee who is intersexual rather than transsexual. The latter is a person who chooses to live as a member of the opposite gender to that person's birth gender. A person who is intersexual does not have a birth gender in that it cannot be said that that person was born either as a man or as a woman.

Although the EctHR has yet to make such a decision, it is reasonable to predict that the court will decide in the future that Article 8 of the Convention protects intersexuals from discrimination.

You be the judge

Q: Advise Jane as to whether she can claim in a British court or tribunal that her dismissal in the following situation is unlawful.

In answering this question, you should imagine that the EctHR has recently reached a decision that Article 8 applies to intersexuals in a similar way that it applies to transsexuals, and that the EU has adopted a Directive which implements this decision as part of EU law. This Directive has not yet been implemented by the British government.

Jane was employed as a lecturer by Barchester University for three years. As a result of a recent medical examination, Jane discovered that she should be classified as intersexual. Jane has been dismissed by the university on the grounds that her newly discovered sexual identity will cause too many practical complications and problems for it.

A: Jane cannot directly enforce her rights under Article 8 ECHR but she can enforce her rights under the EU Directive. As Jane is not employed by a core public authority, she will not able to argue in the High Court that her dismissal is contrary to Article 8 of the Convention. Her university employer is a hybrid body and, under the Human Rights Act, Convention rights can only be enforced against it when it is carrying out its public functions. In a situation such as this, a student who was intersexual and was excluded from the university could argue that this was a breach of the ECHR but, as the employment relationship is a private function, this argument is not available to Jane.

However, Barchester University will be considered as a state employer for the purposes of EU law. Consequently, using a case such as *Marshall* as a precedent, it is open to Jane to argue in an employment tribunal that the Directive should be regarded as taking direct effect on a vertical basis. Therefore, as a state employee, Jane is able to enforce her rights under this Directive, and she can argue that her dismissal is unfair as it is contrary to the Directive.

 Handy tip: If Jane was employed by a private company, she could not base a claim directly on the Directive. However, she could argue that unfair dismissal law and/or the Equality Act should be interpreted in ways that are consistent with both the EctHR decision and the EU Directive. Such arguments are sound but there can be no guarantee that they would succeed.

Summary

 Although the ordinary civil courts can be involved in deciding employment law cases based on the law of contract, the system of employment tribunals is of paramount importance to the enforcement of statutory employment rights.

Employment tribunals are chaired by an employment judge who is normally assisted by two lay members, who will have either an employee or employer background.

Tribunals hear all claims based on ERA 1996, such as a claim of unfair dismissal or a claim for a statutory redundancy payment.

Tribunals will also hear all discrimination claims based on the Equality Act 2010, where such claims arise in the context of the employment field.

The Employment Appeals Tribunal (EAT) hears appeals from employment tribunals. The EAT is chaired by a High Court or circuit judge and, in the same way as is the case with an employment judge, is assisted by two lay members. The EAT can hear appeals on points of law only.

 The Advisory Conciliation & Arbitration Service (ACAS) has an important role to play in disputes between employers and individual employees as it will seek to promote conciliated settlements as an alternative to a tribunal resolving the dispute.

 ACAS also has an important role to play in settling collective disputes between employers and trade unions.

One function of a trade union is to engage in collective bargaining with an employer to negotiate the terms and conditions of employment of the workers the union represents.

Collective agreements resulting from collective bargaining are not normally enforceable between the trade union and the employer. However, collective agreements which are incorporated into individual contracts of employment are enforceable by individual employees against the employer.

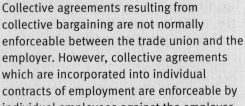 EU law is a major source of employment law in areas such as discrimination law, business reorganisations and employer duties to consult with employee representatives.

◆ As illustrated by the *Marshall* case, EU Directives can often be enforced directly by employees of state employers. Employees of private employers cannot directly rely on Directives, but national courts must and will generally interpret national legislation in order to give effect to rights contained in a Directive.

◆ As a result of the Human Rights Act, individuals employed by core public authorities, such as central government or local councils, can enforce rights contained in the European Convention on Human Rights against their employers in national courts.

◆ Other employees cannot do this, but can argue that the court interprets national law in a way that is compatible with the Convention.

◆ Individual employees of any type of employer can take a claim, based on the European Convention on Human Rights, to the European Court of Human Rights as a final court of appeal.

◆ Employees cannot take a claim, based on EU law, to the European Court of Justice. However, they can ask the national court to seek a preliminary ruling from the ECJ before reaching a decision. Such rulings are binding on national courts throughout the EU.

Question and answer*

Problem: Greyfriars Hospital Trust is a hospital operating within the National Health Service (NHS). As it is part of the NHS, the hospital is subject to government regulation as far as patient care and its general operations are concerned. However, it has its own budget and a large degree of autonomy in how that budget is spent. The hospital recently appointed Joan Sykes as its matron. She has a track record of being a strict disciplinarian. Joan is responsible for all patient care on the wards and is the line manager for all hospital staff other than doctors and surgeons.

Alice has been employed as a porter in the hospital's Orthopaedic Department, which cares for patients with broken bones, for the past 10 months. Alice is a latter day Cathar. Her religious beliefs are based on those of the Cathars in the Languedoc region of medieval France. These beliefs include: reincarnation until a state of purity is attained; the notion that Earth is Hell; and the belief that Jesus Christ was not the son of God but a man who was married to Mary Magdalene. (In *The Bible* Mary Magdalene is one of Jesus' followers but is not one of the disciples.)

Alice wears symbols associated with Catharism over her hospital uniform, and in conversations with medical staff and other patients seeks to convert them to her beliefs. This offends some people, who are practising Christians and find her beliefs both blasphemous and heretical. Joan instructed Alice to remove the symbols and to cease talking about her beliefs to other patients and staff. Joan made it clear to Alice that if she did not comply with these instructions she would be dismissed from the hospital for disobedience and breach of the hospital's dress code for its employees. Alice refused to comply with Joan's instructions, and, in accordance with the hospital's disciplinary procedures, Alice has been dismissed without notice.

Assuming Greyfriars Hospital may have breached Alice's rights under Article 9 and/or Article 10 of the ECHR, advise Alice as to whether she could seek redress from the High Court under the HRA. Alternatively, should she present an employment law claim to an employment tribunal? You are not required to discuss whether such a claim could succeed.

You should spend 40 minutes on answering this question.

Essay: 'To ease the burden on employment tribunals and to reduce the "red tape" on employers it is necessary to reduce the number of claims that are heard by employment tribunals. Good ways of doing this include requiring claimants to bear the costs of an unsuccessful claim, and to work longer before acquiring employment rights such as unfair dismissal.'

Critically evaluate this statement.

You should spend 40 minutes on answering this question.

✱ Answer guidance is provided at the end of the chapter.

Further reading

IDS (2006) *Handbook on Tribunal Practice and Procedure* (Income Data Services: London).

This handbook contains all that you will need if you are contemplating tribunal proceedings and wish to understand, in detail, what these proceedings will involve. In particular: Chapter 2 covers starting tribunal proceedings; Chapter 9 details the rules relating to conciliated settlements and compromise agreements; and Chapters 10 and 11 provide very useful guidance on preparing for tribunal hearings and the procedure that is followed at a hearing.

Allen, R., Crasnow, R. and Beale, A. (2007) *Employment Law and Human Rights* (OUP: Oxford).

This book provides a comprehensive and in-depth analysis of the application of the European Convention on Human Rights, as implemented by the Human Rights Act, and how it impacts on employment law. Chapters 1 to 4 provide detailed discussion of the issues contained in this chapter.

Barnard, C. (2012) *EC Labour Law* (OUP: Oxford).

This text provides a comprehensive and in-depth analysis of employment law in the EU. Chapter 1 is of particular relevance to this chapter as it explains in full detail how EU employment law is made.

Ewing, K. D. (ed.) (2000) *Human Rights at Work* (Institute of Employment Rights: London).

This book contains a collection of essays analysing the overall impact of the Human Rights Act on the employment relationship and the impact of specific articles of the European Convention. All of these essays discuss issues covered throughout this text, but Chapter 1, by Conor A. Gearty, provides a useful overview of the impact of the HRA on British law.

Boon, A., Urwin, P. and Karuk, V. (2011) 'What Difference Does It Make? Facilitative Judicial Mediation of Discrimination Cases in Employment Tribunals', *Industrial Law Journal*, vol. 40, pp. 45–81.

This article discusses research conducted into the use of judicial mediation to resolve disputes based on discrimination as an alternative to employment tribunal proceedings. It also compares judicial mediation with ACAS conciliated settlements.

Hand, J. (2010) 'The Compensation Culture: Cliché or Cause for Concern?', *Journal of Law and Society*, vol. 37, pp. 569–91.

This article considers and contrasts statistics for claims brought in the Queen's Bench, the County Courts and employment tribunals. It shows that only in employment tribunals has there been an increase in the number of claims presented, and analyses why this is the case.

Latreille, P., Latreille, J. and Knight, K. (2005) 'Making a Difference? Legal Representation in Employment Tribunals Cases: Evidence from a Survey of Representatives', *Industrial Law Journal,* **vol. 30, pp. 308–30.**
As you will have gathered from this chapter, it is common for parties to tribunal proceedings to choose to be represented by, for example, trade union officers or human resource managers, as alternatives to legal representation. This article discusses research on the impact the type of representative a party chooses to use on their success in pursuing or responding to a claim.

Question and answer guidance

Problem:
As you are not being asked whether any legal claim by Alice should succeed, your answer should focus on the type of claim that Alice can bring.

The main discussion in your answer should be concerned with whether Greyfriars Hospital is a core public authority or a hybrid body. The latter is any public sector employer which cannot be regarded as a direct organ of central or local government. However, the *Grampian Hospital Trust* case suggests that NHS hospitals are part of the state and, if this is confirmed to be so, then Greyfriars Hospital will be a core public authority. If the hospital is a core public authority then it is fully bound by the European Convention and Alice can challenge her dismissal in the High Court on the basis of Article 9 and/or Article 10 of the Convention. Her argument would be that rules of employment, which are in violation of the Convention, are invalid and unenforceable. Therefore, a dismissal on the basis of such rules is also contrary to the Convention.

If the hospital is found to be a hybrid body then, as the employment relationship is a private relationship, she can only present a claim, based on domestic law, to an employment tribunal. Your answer could explain that, although an employment tribunal cannot decide a claim directly on the basis of the Convention, it is required by s. 3 HRA to interpret domestic legislation as far as is possible in a way that is consistent with Convention rights. Similarly, under s. 6, a tribunal (or court) must ensure that the common law is applied so that Convention rights are properly respected.

In your conclusion you could clarify that, even if the hospital is not a core public authority, Alice can present the same type of arguments to an employment tribunal as she would have used in the High Court to seek to persuade the tribunal that UK law should be interpreted and applied in a way that leads to a decision that her dismissal was unlawful.

Handy tip: Although this will not be in your answer, if Alice does need to bring a tribunal claim, she will be able to combine a claim of wrongful dismissal – that is, that she was dismissed in breach of her employment contract – with a claim under the Equality Act 2010 to the effect that she has been subjected to unlawful discrimination on grounds of her religious beliefs. These areas of the law will be covered later (see Chapters 4 and 7 respectively).

Essay:
This question requires you to discuss whether the way in which employment law operates creates an undue and expensive workload for employment tribunals, and is also unduly onerous on employers. A good answer to this question would first set out an explanation of the composition and jurisdiction of employment tribunals.

Following this introduction, your answer should consider why the workload of tribunals is so big and discuss whether the ways of reducing it, which are suggested in the question, are appropriate. Your answer should clarify that in April 2012, the qualifying period for claiming unfair dismissal was increased from one year to two years. Your essay should discuss whether this change and other suggested changes, such as imposing costs on the losing party, will or could have an adverse impact on providing effective employment protection rights. Alternatively, will such changes strike a reasonable balance between maintaining effective employment rights and reducing undue burdens on employment tribunals and employers?

Your answer should also discuss other ways of reducing tribunal workload. In doing this you could draw on the extracts from the government's consultative paper and the interview with the employment judge, which are contained in this chapter, and on the abovementioned article by Boon, Urwin and Kurak, which discusses the possible advantages of judicial mediation over tribunal proceedings and ACAS settlements. A good answer would summarise what the government and the authors of the article propose, and then with reasons state whether and to what extent you agree or disagree with these proposals.

Your answer should finish with your own reasoned conclusion agreeing or disagreeing with the statement.

Visit **www.mylawchamber.co.uk/welch** to access tools to help you develop and test your knowledge of employment law, including interactive 'You be the judge' multiple choice questions, practice exam questions with guidance, annotated weblinks, case summary and key case flashcards, legal newsfeed, legal updates and answer to Lawyers' brief simulation.

Chapter 2
Nature, formation and sources of the contract of employment

Key points In this chapter we will be looking at:

✦ The significance of the distinction between employees, workers and the self-employed

✦ How to determine whether a worker is employed under a contract of employment and thus has employee status

✦ The formation of a contract of employment

✦ The statutory requirement on employers to provide a written statement of terms

✦ Distinguishing between express and implied terms as sources of a contract of employment

✦ Contract terms derived from collective agreements between employers and trade unions

✦ Statutory standards and contract terms

Introduction

In any type of employment it is important for you to know what types of rights and duties you will enjoy and owe, the information that the employer is legally obliged to supply you with and where the terms and conditions of your employment are to be found. These are the issues that this chapter is concerned with. The main source of your terms and conditions will be your contract of employment. In accordance with the ordinary principles of employment law this may, but need not be, in the form of a written document. Where an employment contract is entered into orally, employers are under a statutory duty to provide their employees with what is called is a **written statement of terms**. This document constitutes written evidence of what the main terms of your contract of employment are. The specific information that the employer must provide through the written statement will be detailed in this chapter. You will also be able to compare a written statement with a full written contract of employment.

Where employees are employed by an employer which has agreed to negotiate terms and conditions of employment with a trade union, they may find that this impacts on their own contracts of employment, as provisions contained in a **collective agreement** between the employer and the union may be incorporated into employees' employment contracts. This chapter will enable you to appreciate how **collective bargaining** between an employer and a trade union may impact on the individual employee.

As indicated in the previous chapter, it is very important to determine whether a person who enters into a contract to provide work for another is an employee or a worker. The majority of statutory employment protection rights, particularly those provided by the Employment Rights Act 1996, are given to employees only.

However **workers** who are not employees, such as casual workers and many agency workers, do enjoy some statutory rights. Important examples of such rights, which will be covered in this chapter, are rights under the Working Time Regulations 1998 and the National Minimum Wage Act 1998. Any person who enters into a contract to provide personal services by undertaking work for another is protected by discrimination law (see Chapter 7). This is so not just for employees and workers but also for individuals who are self-employed.

The first major issue to be examined in this chapter is how the tribunals and courts determine whether a person working for another has **employee status** and, therefore, possesses the statutory rights such status confers.

Determining employee status

Whether a person who is employed to work for another should be regarded as an employee is important for the following reasons:

✦ An employer owes an employee a common law duty of reasonable care with respect to health, safety and welfare at the workplace and there are corresponding statutory duties under legislation such as the Health and Safety at Work Act 1974.

✦ An employer is legally liable for any wrongful acts committed by an employee – this is known as **vicarious liability**.

✦ Many statutory employment protection rights, such as the right not to be dismissed unfairly and the right to a **statutory redundancy payment**, are only granted to employees. **Unfair dismissal** is a particularly important employment right as it enables a dismissed employee to seek remedies from an employment tribunal even where a dismissal is not a breach of contract. A dismissal is unfair where the employer has acted unreasonably in deciding to dismiss an employee.

Table 2.1 (overleaf) summarises the different legal protections accorded to employees, workers and the self-employed.

Identifying an employee

The legal basis of the employment relationship is the contract of employment. An employee is defined by s. 230 ERA 1996 as an individual who has entered into or works under a contract of employment. This somewhat circular definition is not very useful in establishing whether a person who does work for another is an employee, as no indication is given as to how we decide whether a contract to work personally for another is also a contract of employment. Workers also contract to provide work to an employer.

Table 2.1 Employment rights and employment status

Employment status	Employment rights
Employees who are employed under a contract of employment with a specific employer	Employment rights, such as unfair dismissal, contained in the ERA 1996 Working time regulations National minimum wage Discrimination law
Workers who enter into a contract to work for another where that contract is not a contract of employment. (The main examples of such workers are agency and casual workers.)	Working time regulations National minimum wage Discrimination law
Self-employed people who enter into contracts to provide services to others	Discrimination law

Self-employed people, such as plumbers or electricians, also enter into a contract to provide work when, for example, the occupier of a house employs their personal services to carry out repairs.

The tests for determining whether a person enjoys **employee status** have been developed by judges, and therefore are to be found in case law rather than any relevant legislation. You should be aware that in older case law, contracts of employment were called contracts of service and contracts to provide personal services were described as contracts for services.

The courts have developed various tests to determine whether a person providing work to another is an employee, and we will now examine these tests and assess their important in the world of work as it exists today.

The control test

This test was important historically, and is still of some relevance today. Under the traditional **control test** a person was controlled by an employer if he or she was told both *what* to do and *how* to do it. The difference between a chauffeur and a taxi driver provides us with a classic illustration of the control test. The employer of a chauffeur can tell him where to drive to and (within the legal speed limit) can instruct him at what speed to drive. A person who hires a taxi will give the driver the destination, but how the latter drives will be completely up to her.

The control test remains adequate for relatively unskilled workers as employers will typically give full instructions to such workers as to how their work is to be carried out. However, as explained further below, even fully controlling a worker will not always mean that worker has employee status. Casual workers may be fully controlled by an employer but, typically, are not regarded in law as employees.

Moreover, it has been clear since the middle of the last century that the test is not appropriate in many modern employment relationships, as often it is the employee, and not the employer, who has the professional expertise to determine how a job should be performed. For example, the owner of a company may employ accountants, human resource managers and, indeed, lawyers but may have no idea herself as to how such professionals carry out their work. Nevertheless, such professionals will often have employee status.

It is interesting to note that the control test can still be applied to some highly skilled employees such as professional footballers – even those that play in elite premier leagues.

As Lord Cozens-Hardy MR stated in *Walker* v. *Crystal Palace Football Club* [1910] 1 KB 87:

> 'It has been argued before us . . . that there is a certain difference between an ordinary workman and a man who contracts to exhibit and employ his skill where the employer would have no right to dictate to him in the exercise of that skill; e.g. the club in this case would have no right to dictate to him how he should play football. I am unable to follow that. He is bound according to the express terms of his contract to obey all general directions of the club, and I think in any particular game in which he was engaged he would also be bound to obey the particular instructions of the captain or whoever it might be who was the delegate of the authority of the club for the purpose of giving those instructions' (at page 92).

Today, it is the manager, rather than the team captain, who should be regarded as the person empowered by the owners of the club to instruct players what to do and how to play. A professional footballer must obey the instructions of his manager in all training sessions and even on the field of play in competitive matches. Obviously, the footballer uses his discretion as to, for example, whether to pass the ball or to make a shot at goal. However, if he strays completely from the team tactics decided on by the manager he is liable to be substituted and may find himself dropped from the team for future matches. Therefore, the above argument put forward by Lord Cozens-Hardy remains correct over 100 years after it was made.

However, it was and is the case that a rigid application of the control test will result in individuals not being regarded as employees when common sense points to the contrary, and this can have rather startling results. For example, in the 1940s in cases that have been long overruled, the courts decided that, as skilled persons, doctors and nurses could not be regarded as employees of the hospitals in which they worked. Therefore, if they negligently conducted an operation a hospital could not incur vicarious liability as it was not their employer.

The integration test

One attempt to overcome such problems which were created by the rigidity of the control test was provided by Lord Denning in formulating the integration test. In *Stevenson, Jordan and Harrison Ltd* v. *Macdonald and Evans* [1952] 1 TLR 101, the Court of Appeal had to decide whether the company had ownership of work produced by the defendant in his own time on the basis that work derived from knowledge developed in undertaking his job belonged to the company as his employer. On the facts, the court held that the defendant was an employee, but in the circumstances had generally not acted in breach of his contract of employment as he had used his general skill and knowledge rather than information that was available to him only in his capacity of an employee of the company. The law with which this case is concerned is considered later (see Chapter 3).

Lord Denning used his judgment in the case to state:

'It is often easy to recognise a contract of service when you see it, but difficult to say where the difference lies . . . One feature which seems to run through the instances is that, under a contract of service, a man is employed as part of the business, and his work is done as an integral part of the business; whereas, under a contract for services, his work, although done for the business, is not integrated into it but is only accessory to it.'

In other words, rather than placing the emphasis on the extent to which a person is controlled by an organisation, the whole picture needs to be looked at to determine whether a person belongs to an organisation as an employee as against being external to the organisation but doing work for its benefit.

In his judgment Lord Denning gave the following examples: 'A ship's master, a chauffeur, and a reporter on the staff of a newspaper are all employed under a contract of service; but a ship's pilot, a taxi-man, and a newspaper contributor are employed under a contract for services.'

If this integration test is applied, for example, to doctors employed by a particular hospital trust in the National Health Service (NHS), it can be seen they are sufficiently integrated into the organisation to be employees of it. By way of contrast, a visiting consultant would not be so integrated and therefore would not be an employee.

Whilst the integration test clarifies that the issue of employee status is complex and cannot be determined solely be focusing on the extent to which a person is controlled, it does not provide us with an analytical method to determine whether a particular individual is an employee. Greater insight in this respect is provided by the multiple test.

The multiple test

An approach based on this test recognises that there is no single test for determining employee status. Rather, a number of factors will be considered in analysing the relationship between the parties.

Case Summary

The multiple test was first used in the case of *Ready Mixed Concrete Ltd* v. *Minister of Pensions* [1968] 2 QB 497. This case concerned an appeal against a Ministerial decision that the Ready Mixed company was liable to pay the national insurance contributions of its drivers as required by the National Insurance Act 1965. This was only the case if it was correct to regard the drivers as the employees of the company. The company argued that the drivers were not employees. Drivers were employed in accordance with a scheme described as one of owner-driver delivery. Under the contract between the company and a driver the latter agreed to buy a lorry on credit from another of the group's companies and became the lorry's owner. However, the company paid for the insurance of the lorry and had the right to acquire the vehicle at the end of the contract. The driver had to pay all the running costs involving in driving and maintaining the lorry. The lorry bore the company colours and signs. Drivers were required to wear the company uniform, comply with the company's rules and obey the orders of its managers. Drivers were obliged to drive the vehicles themselves unless they could excuse themselves as they would validly be able to do if they were employees. For example, if a driver was unable to work as a result of illness or injury. Drivers' services were reserved to Ready Mixed, and the company could consent to the appointment of a substitute driver if a driver was unable to drive himself. In such a situation, the driver was to pay the wages of the substitute driver and was deemed to employ him. Clause 30 of the contract declared the drivers to be **independent contractors**.

It was held that an employment contract exists if: (1) a worker provides his own work or skill for payment in performing some service for the employer; (2) he agrees to be sufficiently subject to the other party's control to make the other party an employer; (3) the other provisions of the contract are consistent with its being a contract of employment.

On this basis, the court decided that, despite the degree of control the company exercised over its drivers, a driver should be regarded as being in business 'on his own account' and therefore should not be considered an employee. The court argued that the underlying economic reality of the case was that a driver owned his lorry and was therefore using his own business assets and thereby incurring a business risk. This meant that a driver was a self-employed businessman rather than an employee of the company.

Whilst the economic reality underpinning a relationship between the contracting parties is clearly important in deciding whether a person providing work is an employee or is self-employed, it is still possible to take different views of the facts of a case on this issue. In *Ready Mixed Concrete*, the court reached the decision that the drivers were self-employed because a driver was deemed to own his vehicle and was able to sub-contract by appointing a substitute driver. However, whether a driver was the real owner of the lorry can be questioned, given that the company had the option to buy back the lorry at the end of the contract, and normally drivers were expected to drive the lorries themselves. Therefore, whilst the judgment in this case provides a valuable analytical method for determining whether an individual is an employee, somewhat ironically perhaps the actual decision of the court can be subject to criticism.

The economic reality factor, emphasised in *Ready Mixed Concrete*, was applied in *Market Investigations Ltd* v. *Minister for Social Services* [1969] 2 QB 173. In this case a person was engaged by a market research company to act as an interviewer. She agreed, for a fixed remuneration, to provide her own work and skill, but detailed instructions on interview technique were issued to her by the company, as were details of the questions to be asked. She was required to do a certain number of days' work within a given time, although she could choose her own hours of work. No provision was made in the contract for sick pay or for holidays. It was held that on the basis of the extent and degree of control exercised by the company she was an employee. In reaching this decision, particular attention was paid to the fact that the interviewer invested no capital or equipment of her own, and therefore could not have incurred the risk of any business loss if the project did not fulfil its objectives.

Case Summary

The irreducible minimum for employee status

The cases discussed above demonstrate how the courts analyse a specific relationship to determine whether a person providing work to another is or is not an employee. Modern case law also emphasises the necessity of establishing whether the irreducible minimum for possessing employee status is present in any given case. As approved by the House of Lords in the case of *Carmichael & Leese* v. *National Power plc* [2000] IRLR 43, which is explained below, there are three aspects of this irreducible minimum.

(i) A requisite degree of control

As clarified by the *Stevenson, Jordan and Harrison* case, which is discussed above, it is not necessary for control to be in the form of instructing an employee as to how a job should be carried out. Control can be exercised in other ways, such as instructing an employee when and where to work, stipulating the procedures that must be followed for an employee to exercise his or her holiday entitlement, imposing dress codes and subjecting employees to **disciplinary procedures**.

(ii) Mutuality of obligations must be present

For a contract to be one of employment each party must owe duties to the other. This is what is meant by the phrase **mutuality of obligations**. In a contract of employment an employer is obliged to pay for work that he or she requires to be done and the employee is obliged to accept and carry out work as instructed. Where the relationship is more casual the employer is not obliged to offer work and the worker is not obliged to accept any work that is offered. A contract to complete a particular job only comes into existence where work is offered and the worker chooses to accept it. At that point the employer is then obliged to pay the agreed rate for any work that is completed.

This situation is illustrated by the cases of *O'Kelly* v. *Trusthouse Forte Ltd* [1983] ICR 728 and *Carmichael & Leese* v. *National Power plc* [2000] IRLR 43.

Case Summary

In *O'Kelly* a bar worker regularly contacted the company to ascertain if he was wanted for work as a wine butler. However, he was not obliged to ask for work or to accept it if offered. Similarly, the company was not obliged to offer work, although it regularly did so. The Court of Appeal held that in the absence of the requisite mutuality of obligations O'Kelly was a worker but not an employee.

In *Carmichael* individuals agreed to work as tour guides for National Power 'if and when required'. This clause meant that the parties were never under any legal obligation to offer or accept work and again this meant that the tour guides were workers but not employees.

(iii) Personal service

A worker must be contractually obliged to perform a job personally. If a worker has the discretion to appoint another person to undertake the work then he or she cannot be an employee.

Case Summary

In *Express & Echo Publications Ltd* v. *Tanton* [1999] IRLR 367, a driver was obliged to arrange at his own expense for another trained driver to do his work if he was unable or unwilling to do the work himself. It was held that, as he had a genuine choice between carrying out the work himself or choosing to pay someone else to do so, he was not an employee.

Case Summary

By way of contrast, in *Macfarlane* v. *Glasgow CC* [2001] IRLR 7, a gymnastics instructor was obliged to arrange for another person on a list drawn up by the Council to do her work if she was unable to do so. Although she had to make the arrangements for a replacement, the latter was paid directly by the Council. It was held that the obligation on her to arrange for a substitute was an additional contractual duty which did not negate the requirement of personal service. Macfarlane was not in the same position as Tanton who had the discretion to arrange for and pay another to do the contracted work.

If you look back at the facts of the *Ready Mixed Concrete* case, you will see that a driver was able to use a substitute driver, with the company's consent, if he was unable personally to drive the lorry. The driver was deemed to employ the substitute driver. This could be perceived as a power to sub-contract and therefore the driver was not subject to a duty to provide personal performance. However, arguably, given that a driver was obliged to have a good reason for not driving the lorry himself, and required the company's consent to use a substitute driver, the situation was more akin to that in

Macfarlane than to that in *Tanton*. If this view is correct, this reinforces the argument that the drivers should have been found to be employees of the Ready Mixed company.

Umbrella contracts and mutuality of obligations

It is possible for the courts to identify an **umbrella contract** giving rise to a mutuality of obligations. This occurs where a relationship between an employer and a worker is of a significant duration and over that period of time the worker has regularly been offered work which he or she has accepted to undertake. This is demonstrated by two cases involving homeworkers, that is, individuals who work in their own homes to carry out the work required by their employers. Typically, homeworkers will be women, and the work will involve making items, such as articles of clothing, out of materials supplied by the employer. The finished articles are then collected from the homeworkers at their homes.

In *Airfix Footwear Ltd* v. *Cope* [1978] ICR 1210, a homeworker made shoes for the company over a period of seven years. Normally, she worked for five days a week. She was held to be an employee. Similarly, in *Nethermere (St Neots) Ltd* v. *Taverna and Gardner* [1984] ICR 612, two workers made trousers for the company in their own homes. They had done this respectively for periods of four or five years. Materials for making the trousers was delivered to them and the finished trousers were collected from them on a daily basis, though they could choose how much work to accept, and could take time off providing advance notice was given of an intention to do so. In both cases, it was held that the long-standing relationships between the parties gave rise to an expectation that work would be provided and normally undertaken. This gave rise to a sufficient mutuality of obligations for the workers to be employees.

Case Summary

Table 2.2 summarises the meaning of mutuality of obligations and the rules for establishing whether the irreducible minimum exists for regarding a contract as a contract of employment.

Table 2.2 Establishing the irreducible minimum

Elements of the irreducible minimum	Application of the law	Relevant case law
Requisite degree of control	Not necessary to tell a person how to do a job providing there are other forms of control, and the individual incurs no personal business risk.	The law is illustrated by the contrasting cases of *Market Investigations Ltd* and *Ready Mixed*.
Mutuality of obligations	Employer must be obliged to offer work and the employee must be obliged to accept. May be present as a result of long-established practice giving rise to an umbrella contract.	The law is illustrated by contrasting the *O'Kelly* and *Carmichael* cases with *Nethermere (St Neots)*.
Personal performance	No discretion to choose to employ another person to do the job.	The law is illustrated by contrasting the *Tanton* and *Macfarlane* cases.

You be the judge

Q: In the following situations should Jack and/or Tiffany be considered to be employees?
Jack has for several months worked as a waiter at banquets held at the Queen Victoria Hotel. Every day he phones in to ask if his services are needed. Normally, he is offered work, which he accepts.

As has regularly been the case for the past five years, Tiffany works at home making trousers for Sanjay Co Ltd. Every week, except when she is on holiday, a driver employed by the company delivers materials to Tiffany's home and collects the finished trousers from her. When she works is up to her provided the trousers are completed by the stipulated deadline.

A: Jack is a worker but not an employee, whereas Tiffany has employee status.
Applying the *O'Kelly* case (see above) the casual nature between Jack and the Queen Victoria Hotel suggests there is no mutuality of obligations between the parties and this means that Jack is a worker, but not an employee. Jack is not required to ask for work, the company is not obliged to offer work and if work is offered Jack is not obliged to accept it.

Applying the *Nethermere* case (see above) an umbrella contract of employment can be identified which gives rise to a mutuality of obligations between Tiffany and Sanjay. This is because of the length of the relationship between the contracting parties combined with the regular pattern of working.

Labelling a contract and tax status

It is possible for the irreducible minimum for an employment contract to be present but the actual contract describes a contracting party as a self-employed independent contractor. The case law considered below demonstrates that how two parties label or describe their relationship is a factor to be taken into account by the courts, but it will not normally be a decisive factor. Moreover, an individual may pay income tax as though he or she is self-employed but this will not, in itself, prevent that individual from having employee status as far as employment law issues are concerned.

In particular, the label contracting parties attach to their relationship will not be given any significance by a court where the economic reality of that relationship largely contradicts this label. This is illustrated by two health and safety cases, *Ferguson* v. *Dawson Ltd* [1976] IRLR 346 and *Lane* v. *Shire Roofing Co Ltd* [1995] IRLR 493, in which builders were injured through the negligence of the employing companies. The builders were described as self-employed persons and paid tax and national insurance on this basis. Otherwise, they were subject to the complete control of the companies, as the building site foremen instructed them when to work and how they were to undertake their work. Moreover, the builders supplied no building materials of their own. It was held that the builders were employees and were owed a duty of care by the companies.

Even where workers request to become self-employed because of the tax advantages this will bring, courts and tribunals will still regard them as employees if that remains the reality of the contractual relationship. In *Young and Woods Ltd* v. *West* [1980] IRLR 201, West, a sheet metal worker, asked the company to treat him as self-employed. Consequently, he was paid without deductions for income tax and national insurance contributions. He was not given holiday entitlement or sick pay or the benefit of disciplinary procedure. Otherwise, there was no difference between his working conditions

Case Summary

Case Summary

and those of other sheet metal workers who remained employees. Subsequently, he was dismissed by the company and it was held that, despite the tax position, he was in all other respects an employee and therefore he was entitled to bring a statutory claim of unfair dismissal.

The *West* case can be contrasted with *Massey* v. *Crown Life Assurance* [1978] ICR 590; IRLR 31. From 1971 to 1973, Massey worked as manager of a branch office as an employee of Crown Life which paid him wages and deducted income tax on a pay as you earn basis. In 1973, at his own request, Massey entered into an agreement with the company whereby he continued to do the same job but became self-employed. In entering into this new agreement he used a company name registered for business purposes rather than his own name. In 1975, Crown Life terminated the contract and Massey brought a complaint of unfair dismissal. The Court of Appeal agreed with the industrial tribunal and the EAT that, in 1973, Massey had ceased to be an employee and therefore had ceased to possess statutory rights that are only possessed by employees. Therefore he was no longer eligible to bring a claim of unfair dismissal.

Case Summary

The distinction between *West* and *Massey* is that in the latter case the employee was a senior manager and in a position to negotiate freely the terms of his contract and to change his employment status. Given that he had chosen to become self-employed he could not have his cake and eat it. Once he decided to enjoy the financial advantages of being self-employed he could not seek to renege on this agreement by asserting he continued to possess the right to claim unfair dismissal. However, as the *West* case demonstrates, the courts are generally reluctant to permit employees to contract out of their statutory rights, and it is for HM Revenue & Customs to take action to recover the tax that should have been paid. *Massey* can be considered to be an exceptional case which reflected the senior position within the company that Massey enjoyed, and the fact that he had a registered company name he was able to use for business purposes.

The Supreme Court has recently emphasised the importance of the relative bargaining position of contracting parties, and held that it is appropriate for courts to look behind what is stated in a contract to determine the reality of the relationship between contracting parties and whether one party is actually an employee.

In *Autoclenz Ltd* v. *Belcher* [2011] ICR 1157, the Supreme Court found that individuals who had been engaged as car valeters were employees for the purposes of the National Minimum Wage Act and the Working Time Regulations. This was despite the fact that in their contracts they were described as sub-contractors and they were responsible for paying their own tax and national insurance. The contract provided that they were entitled to provide a substitute to carry out the work. Moreover, the contracts also stated that the valeters were not obliged to work and Autoclenz was not obliged to provide them with work. In practice, the company told them how to carry out the work, provided the cleaning materials, determined the rate of pay, prepared their invoices and required them to give prior notification if they were unable to work. The employer's practices therefore conflicted with the position as stated in the valeters' contracts. In practice, a mutuality of obligations did exist and the valeters were expected to provide personal performance. As stated by Lord Clarke, in cases such as this the essential question was: 'What was the true agreement between the parties?' The relative bargaining power of the parties had to be taken into account when deciding whether the terms of any written agreement represented what was agreed. The true agreement would often have to be gleaned from all the circumstances of the case, of which the written agreement was only a part. Courts should therefore adopt a purposive approach to the exercise of determining the true employment status of an individual as the Court of

Case Summary

Appeal had done in this case. The court had been right to conclude that, in fact, the valeters were employed under contracts of employment and were employees.

The following case demonstrates an application of the approach that tribunals are now required to take as a result of the above Supreme Court (SC) decision. In this case the EAT focused on the reality of the relationship between a lap dancer and the club where she worked.

Law in action

The appearance of lap dancing clubs in many British cities and towns is a relatively recent phenomenon but, issues of morality and sexploitation aside, they provide a source of income for a fair number of young women – some of whom are students or unemployed graduates. One of the first lap dancing clubs was the Stringfellows club in central London, and it is the Stringfellows company which is at the heart of an important recent EAT decision on the employment status of women dancers.

The case arose from an unfair dismissal claim brought by Nadine Quashie, a former students' union women's officer. Quashie worked as a lap dancer for more than a year at one of the Stringfellows clubs. She was not given any form of contract or written statement and was treated as self-employed by the club. She was responsible for making her own arrangements to pay income tax and national insurance contributions. During her time at the club she made a number of complaints about working conditions and was described by the club manager at the tribunal hearing as a troublemaker. Her contract with the club was terminated for her alleged involvement in dealing drugs. The tribunal ruled that she was not eligible to present a claim of unfair dismissal as she was not an employee. In the tribunal's view, Stringfellows did not pay Quashie for anything. Rather, she paid Stringfellows to be able to dance at the club, and it was the club's customers who paid her the money that she earned. On 26 April 2012, four years after Quashie's dismissal, the EAT upheld her appeal and found that the tribunal had erred in law in concluding that she did not possess employee status.

Quashie was not paid in cash by customers but they gave her what was known as 'Heavenly Money', which were in fact vouchers which she exchanged with the club for real money. Various deductions were made from the money she earned by way of the club's commission and to cover a variety of club expenses. The EAT found that the tribunal had placed too much emphasis on the traditional wage–work bargain and the club's treatment of her as self-employed. The EAT held that, although her earnings came entirely from customers rather than the club, she was paid for work done. Employment status is not decided by reference to the source, or the route, of the payment. Moreover, in the contemporary labour marker there are a number of forms of bargains within employment relationships. As examples, employees may be paid with free accommodation or with free meals, or by fees being paid directly to a university.

Quashie was able to establish that a significant degree of control was exercised over her by the club management. She had to attend the club on the nights designated in a rota and could be fined if she failed to arrive or was late. Fines could be imposed for other reasons such as missing a floor-show, talking to a customer before he bought a drink or chewing gum. She was also required to attend a meeting on a weekly basis for which she was not paid. Again any failure to attend was punishable by a fine.

Overall, the EAT found that the irreducible minimum for employee status was met. The degree of control over her was significant and she was clearly required to provide personal performance. Quashie was employed under an umbrella contract. The imposition of fines or deductions by agreement implied the existence of an ongoing relationship: it was a form of discipline built into the contractual relationship which was consistent with a contract of employment. A mutuality of obligations was present as Quashie was subject to an obligation to dance on the nights specified in the rota and the club was obliged to provide her with the opportunity to earn money.

Quashie's success in establishing that she was an employee is only the first phase of her legal battle. Her case has now been remitted to a tribunal to hear evidence and arguments as to whether she was unfairly dismissed. However, as reported in the *Guardian*, Quashie is motivated by a desire to improve the lot of all dancers. If the EAT's finding that she was an employee is extended across the industry this means that the exploitation and arbitrary treatment of women employed in clubs will be mitigated by them having not just unfair dismissal rights but also other employment rights such as paid holidays and paid maternity leave.

Source: Quashie v. *Stringfellows Restaurants Ltd* UKEAT/0289/11/RN, 26.04.2012. For a newspaper report see 'I want to make a difference', an interview with Julie Bindel, the *Guardian*, 19 June 2012.

The SC's decision in *Autoclenz* clarifies that a contract term seeking to exclude the presence of a mutuality of obligations should be disregarded when in practice employees are expected to attend work and are provided with work. If the decision in *Quashie* is extended across the industry then this should mean that clubs will be unable to construct non-employment relationships by using agreements which on the surface appear to give dancers a choice as to whether they work on particular nights. It can also be commented that the decision in *Autoclenz* casts further doubt on whether the decision that the High Court reached in the *Ready Mixed* case, discussed above, was correct on the facts.

You be the judge

Q: In the following situation would you consider Michelle to be an employee?
Michelle is engaged under a contract with B Co. Ltd to provide what the contract describes as the service of a sales representative. Michelle receives a basic remuneration of £300 a week and earns a 10% commission on everything that she sells. She is treated as self-employed for tax purposes. Michelle is required to: work a 35-hour week, Mondays to Fridays; report to the office daily to receive her instructions from Dennis, the head of the sales department; and arrange with Dennis when she can exercise her six-week holiday entitlement. She is also required to use her own car but is entitled to claim travelling expenses when using it whilst engaged on business for the company.

A: Michele is probably an employee.
It is not possible to conclude with complete certainty that Michelle is or is not an employee. However, on the facts as stated, it is probable that Michelle is an employee rather than self-employed. As established in cases such as *Ferguson*, the fact that the contract is described as one under which she provides a service rather than a contract of employment will not be a major consideration; nor will her tax status be a decisive factor. Applying the multiple test, as established in the *Ready Mixed* case, the focus should on control, personal performance and the underlying economic reality. Michelle is required to use her own car but this is not that unusual in the modern world of employment. It is more typical to pay travel expenses to employees than to self-employed contractors. She is paid, in part, on a commission basis but this can be regarded as a form of performance-related pay rather than constituting the assumption of a business risk. Clearly, she is required to work personally on the company's behalf. The overall extent of the company's control over her is more consistent with her being an employee rather than a self-employed person.

Employee status: issue of law or fact?

The Employment Appeals Tribunal (EAT) only has the power to overturn the decision of an employment tribunal where the tribunal is mistaken in its understanding of the law (see Chapter 1). It is for a tribunal to decide what the relevant facts of a case are, and the EAT cannot overturn a tribunal decision on the basis that it has a different view of the evidence. Given the technicality of the above discussion of employee status it might be thought that whether or not an individual should be viewed as an employee is a matter of law, as the issue involves applying the judicial tests to the facts of a case. However, it was held by the House of Lords in the *Carmichael* v. *National Power* case that the issue is one of fact, and therefore the EAT cannot uphold an appeal on the basis that it disagrees with the tribunal's decision.

However, a tribunal's view of the facts of a case may be so erroneous that this amounts to an error of law. In this situation the EAT can uphold an appeal and substitute its decision for that of the tribunal. An example of this could be where a tribunal identifies the existence of an umbrella contract giving rise to a sufficient mutuality of obligations to permit the tribunal to decide that a contract of employment exists. However, the actual evidence of how the parties have behaved in practice contradicts any notion of the employer being obliged to provide work or of the worker being obliged to accept it. This could be regarded as an error of law enabling the EAT to decide that the tribunal was wrong in finding that the individual worker had employee status. Conversely, as in *Quashie*, the EAT could decide that a tribunal has erred in failing to identify an umbrella contract where the reality of the relationship is that it is an ongoing one generating a mutuality of obligations.

There are occasions where even senior judges will disagree on the question of whether an issue is one of fact or law and whether the latter has been applied correctly. For example, in the *Nethermere* case involving homeworkers, the majority of the Court of Appeal agreed with the tribunal and the EAT that a mutuality of obligations arose through the length of the relationship between the company and the homeworkers. However, Kerr LJ dissented from this decision. In his view, a lengthy course of dealing could not convert itself into a contractually binding obligation to continue to enter into individual contracts or to be subject to some 'umbrella' contract.

As is discussed fully below, agency workers will often not possess employee status. In the case of *James* v. *Greenwich BC*, it was held that tribunals cannot infer the existence of a contract of employment from facts which merely establish a long-standing relationship between an agency worker and an employing organisation to which the worker is assigned by an agency. To do so is to make an error of law and if, on that basis, the tribunal decides that an agency worker is an employee then that decision will be wrong.

Overall, it is perhaps best to regard the issue of employee status as a mixed issue of law and fact. It is for the tribunal, and the tribunal only, to establish and interpret the evidence and to decide whether, overall, the facts point to the existence of a contract of employment or, for example, to a contract where the individual cannot be an employee because he or she is in business on his or her own account. However, where its view of the facts reveals a misunderstanding of the law then, as in *James*, an appeal against the tribunal's decision will succeed.

If an individual who carries out work for another is not an employee then that person will either be self-employed or a worker. The latter does not enjoy the same level of employment protection as an employee, but workers do possess some statutory rights which we will now consider.

Workers and statutory rights

A worker is a person who enters into a contract to provide work to another without acquiring employee status because, for example, a mutuality of obligations is not present. Whilst workers do not generally enjoy the employment protections rights provided by ERA 1996, they are protected by some statutory provisions – in particular the Working Time Regulations 1998 and the National Minimum Wage Act (NMWA) 1998. They are also protected by the Part-Time Workers Regulations 2000. On the other hand, self-employed persons are neither workers nor employees so they do not enjoy any of these rights. However, the self-employed may be protected by the provisions of the Equality Act 2010.

In distinguishing between workers and those who are self-employed it is again important to ascertain whether a person is in business on his or her own account. This is demonstrated by the case of *Commissioners of Inland Revenue* v. *Post Office Ltd* [2003] IRLR 199. Sub-postmasters were required to provide and maintain at their own expense sufficient office accommodation and pay such assistants as were needed to carry out post office business. They had to operate during specified hours unless permission was given to vary those hours. They also had to meet certain quality standards and assume full responsibility for the running of their post office, although they did not need to be present. It was held that the sub-postmasters were neither employees nor workers of the Post Office because in providing their own accommodation, equipment and staff they were running their own separate businesses.

Case Summary

As stated above, the right to a minimum wage and rights relating to working hours and paid holidays are rights enjoyed by both employees and workers.

The national minimum wage

Both employees and workers are entitled to receive a minimum wage. The National Minimum Wage Act (NMWA) 1998 lays down the minimum rate that employers must pay to their employees and workers. Typically, this hourly rate is increased annually to take into account cost of living increases created by rates of inflation. In October 2012, the highest rate for workers over the age of 21 was £6.19. The rate for those aged 18–20 was £4.98 and for school leavers aged 16 and 17 it was £3.68. Apprentices under 19, or over 19 but in the first year of their apprenticeship, were entitled to at least £2.65. It is common for those employed in the hotel, catering and retail industries to receive only this minimum wage. However, based on experiences before the NMWA was introduced, rates of pay would be even lower if the right to a minimum wage did not exist.

If an employer fails to pay the national minimum wage then an employee or a worker can take action in the civil courts or in an employment tribunal to recover the amount of money the claimant is owed.

The Working Time Regulations

The Working Time Regulations 1998 provide for:

✦ a maximum working week of 48 hours;

✦ this may be averaged out over the period of weeks – the norm for this is 17 weeks;

+ a minimum rest period of 11 hours between working days;

+ a rest break of 20 minutes in any working day of more than six hours;

+ a minimum of one day off a week;

+ night workers, that is workers who work at least three hours between 11.00 p.m. and 6.00 a.m., should not work for more than an average of eight hours in any 24-hour period;

+ paid holiday entitlement – in 2011 this was 28 days, though part-time workers have their holiday rights reduced on a pro rata basis.

As stated above, in determining an individual's working week it is permissible for an employer to impose a working pattern which means that a person has averaged 48 hours a week over a 17-week period. For example, if a worker works 50 hours for eight weeks and 46 hours for nine weeks this will meet the 48 hour average for that 17-week period. This figure is arrived at by totalling the number of hours a person has worked over 17 weeks and then dividing this total figure by 17. In this example, the total number of hours worked is 814 and if divided by 17 this produces an average of 48 hours a week. In calculating a person's working hours it should be appreciated that lunch breaks and any other rest breaks are not to be taken into account.

The most controversial aspect of the regulations is that employees and workers are able to opt out of their rights with respect to the maximum working week of 48 hours. Despite the adverse effect of long working hours on personal health and family life, many employees and workers do choose to opt out of their rights and accept contractual obligations to work for more than 48 hours in any one week. This is either in order to earn more money or because they fear the consequences for longer-term job security or prospects if they refuse to do so. Arguably, the impact of the opt out is that workers only enjoy a working week of 48 hours or less where this is the preferred policy of the employer.

Regulation 4 requires an opt-out agreement to be in writing and to be entered into by a worker on an individual basis. Under regulation 5 a worker may give seven days' written notice of his or her wish to end the agreement. However, the agreement can expressly specify that up to a maximum of three months' notice must be given to being the agreement to an end.

It is also possible for an employer to secure a longer working week through entering into a written workforce agreement which provides for this. Where the employer recognises a trade union, this will be in form of a collective agreement which is made in the same way as any other type of collective agreement. In the absence of a recognised union, the employer can seek to negotiate a workforce agreement with employee representatives elected by the workforce. Alternatively, where the employer employs 20 or fewer workers, a workforce agreement can be secured by the employer obtaining the signatures of at least 51% of the workforce approving the agreement. A workforce agreement can extend the working week to an average of 52 hours a week. A single workforce agreement can be for no more than five years.

Under regulation 30, workers may present a claim to an employment tribunal if an employer is in breach of its statutory duty with respect to rest periods or holiday pay. If the claim is well-founded, the tribunal may make a declaration to that effect and award compensation on the basis of what it considers to be just and equitable. The tribunal will order an employer to pay any holiday pay which the worker should have received.

Case Summary

In *Barber* v. *RJB Mining Ltd* [1999] ICR 679, it was held that the right to an average of 48 hours a week is a contractual right implied into the contracts of employees and workers by the regulations. Barber and other pit deputies were required to work in excess of the statutory maximum as they were required to work at weekends in order to keep coalmines open. The High Court granted a declaration to the effect that it was open to the pit deputies to refuse to work until such time as their average working time fell within the statutory limit.

Another consequence of the right to an average of 48 hours a week being part of the contract is that an employee is entitled to resign and claim **constructive dismissal** if the employer seeks to require the employee to work in excess of the statutory maximum. Constructive dismissal is fully discussed later (see Chapters 3–5), but where termination of an employment contract by an employee is a constructive dismissal then the employee is able to claim compensation for wrongful and/or unfair dismissal.

Under s. 45A ERA 1996, a person may complain to a tribunal that he or she has been subject to a **detriment** by the employer if he or she has suffered any form of disadvantage as a result of asserting a right under the regulations. Section 23 NWMA provides for similar rights where a person is subjected to a detriment for asserting his or her rights under the Act. For example, an individual may be discriminated against by being barred from receiving non-contractual benefits such as use of the company's car park because that person has presented a tribunal claim to enforce his or her rights under the Working Time Regulations or the NWMA. If a claim under s. 45A ERA 1996 or s. 23 NMWA is upheld, then an award of compensation will be made.

It may even be that a person has been dismissed for seeking to enforce these statutory rights. Workers are not able to present claims of unfair dismissal but, under s. 45A or s. 23, they can still obtain some compensation because the dismissal will be unlawful. If an employee, but not a worker, has been dismissed for asserting statutory rights under the Working Time Regulations or the NWMA then, under s. 101A and s. 104A ERA 1996 respectively, such a dismissal will be **automatically unfair**. As will be fully explained later (see Chapter 5), this means that a tribunal is obliged to decide that a dismissal for these reasons is unfair. The appropriate remedies will be the normal remedies for unfair dismissal, which are detailed later (see Chapter 5).

Out and about

Many students are employed in jobs where employers only pay the national minimum wage. Some unscrupulous employers also fail to pay their workers when they are on holiday as such employers operate on the basis that their workers do not know their statutory rights. Therefore anyone at work or seeking to secure work must be fully aware of their statutory rights. Up-to-date information can be obtained from the government's website that provides advice to employees on employment rights: **http://www.direct.gov.uk/en/Employment/index.htm**. If you visit this website, you will be able to ascertain the current minimum wage rates and entitlement to paid holiday.

Source: Ben Nicholson, Pearson Eduction Ltd

In accessing this website you will find more detail on the following very important issues:

+ Workers employed in hotel and catering often receive tips from customers but, contrary to what employers may say to their staff, these tips do *not* count towards the minimum wage. For example, if a waiter is paid a tip, he is entitled to keep this tip and receive (at least) the minimum wage.

+ Workers have no rights to take public holidays such as the August bank holiday. If you do take a public holidays, such days are *included* in the statutory minimum entitlement to paid holidays. Therefore, public holidays are not in addition to the statutory entitlement.

+ Workers are not entitled to any additional pay for working on public holidays. Therefore, if an employer chooses, it is still entitled to pay only the national minimum wage.

Are you, or to your knowledge, any of your family or friends, being employed by organisations which are not observing the minimum statutory standards? If so, you might want to consider bringing a claim to an employment tribunal, or advising others to do so.

Agency workers

Many students will undertake paid work on a temporary basis, and may secure such work through employment agencies. It is not uncommon for agency workers to regard the agency as the employer, but in law, as is explained fully below, often this will not be the case. This will be so even though it is the agency that pays the worker and is responsible for deducting income tax and national insurance contributions. Agency workers who are not employees have no job security as they are not protected by unfair dismissal and redundancy rights.

Agencies are regulated by the Employment Agencies Act 1973 and the Conduct of Employment Agencies and Employment Businesses (CEAEB) Regulations 2003, and there are two forms of agencies. Employment agencies, which are properly so called, provide a service to the worker of finding them permanent employment. Once the agency has done this, its relationship with the worker normally comes to an end. Clearly, in this context there is no employment relationship between the agency and the worker. The latter is more accurately to be regarded as being a client of the agency and using its services to secure employment. Where the agency successfully finds work for the client with an organisation, it is that organisation which will become the employer.

there are two forms of agencies

Agencies which find work for temporary workers with other organisations are strictly speaking employment businesses in accordance with s. 13(3) of the 1973 Act. Such agencies are required by the CEAEB Regulations to provide agency workers with written statements setting out the main terms of their engagement as well as paying wages, income tax and national insurance contributions. Typically, they will also be responsible for ensuring that the worker's rights under the National Minimum Wage Act and Working Time Regulations, as explained above, are respected. However, these regulations do not assist in determining the employment status of an agency worker.

Key stats

Statistics show that temporary workers finding work through agencies are a significant part of the UK labour force. There are around 1.3 million agency workers and, at just over 5%, the proportion of agency workers in the UK is higher than in any other EU member state.

Around a quarter of agency workers work in production, around a third in the private services sector and the rest in the public sector – particularly education and health. The statistics reveal that large firms are more likely to use agency workers than is the case with smaller firms. Presumably, this is because they are better placed financially to pay the fees that agencies charge. It is also common for schools and NHS hospitals to use temporary workers to cover for absent full-time staff or where there is a temporary staff shortage.

Some 50% of agency workers would like to have their temporary jobs put onto a permanent basis.

The Labour Force Survey reveals that agency workers earn less than comparable, inexperienced, permanent workers, that is, those with less than two years' service. Their hourly earnings were 94% of the level of permanent employees. As explained below, this position could be remedied, at least in part, by the Agency Workers Regulations 2010. These regulations provide for circumstances where agency workers must enjoy the same basic pay and conditions as comparable permanent employees.

Source: 'Agency Working in the UK: A Review of the Evidence', *BERR Employment Relations Research Series no. 93*, October 2008.

Agency workers and employee status

It is possible, in theory, for an agency worker to be the employee of an employment business. However, for this to be the case the worker must be sufficiently controlled by the business, and the business must be obliged to offer work, or at least training, which the worker is obliged to accept. As a hypothetical example, an agency permanently employs individuals who are obliged to report to it on a daily basis and are required to undertake work at any organisation to which they are assigned. In return the agency is obliged to assign work to these individuals or to pay them despite the fact that no work is available on a particular day. In this situation the irreducible minimum for employee status, as explained above, will be present and the persons employed by the agency will be its employees.

However, the more typical relationship is a tripartite one under which the employment business or agency has a contract with the worker to find work for the latter, and there is a separate contract between the agency and the organisation to which the worker is assigned (the end-user) under which the end-user pays a fee to the agency for the worker's services. The agency pays the worker's wages and national insurance contributions. There is no contractual relationship whatsoever between the worker and the client organisation as the end user. This tripartite relationship is illustrated by Figure 2.1 (overleaf).

Even where the acceptance by the worker of a specific assignment gives rise to a mutuality of obligations in that the worker must then undertake the work for an agreed period in return for payment by the agency, the worker will be controlled by the end-user on a day-to-day basis. The irreducible minimum for the existence of a contract of employment requires the worker both to be controlled by the employer and a mutuality of obligations between them to be present. In the typical triangular relationship the elements of mutuality of obligations and control are split between the agency and the end-user, and there is no contract at all between the worker and the latter.

Figure 2.1 The agency relationship

Can it be argued that an agency worker becomes an employee when the worker works for a particular end-user for a long period of time? This was the issue in *Dacas* v. *Brook Street Bureau (UK) Ltd* [2004] IRLR 358, where Dacas worked exclusively as a cleaner for Wandsworth Council for four years. After a dispute, the Council asked the agency to terminate her assignment, which the agency did and also removed her from its books. It was held by the Court of Appeal that she could not claim unfair dismissal against the agency as control over her work resided in the Council. However, in the court's view a contract of employment could have been inferred between Dacas and the Council because of the length of the relationship between them. Had this been argued on behalf of Dacas, then it may have been possible to conclude that Dacas was an employee of the Council and had been unfairly dismissed by it.

This approach could have led to the situation where an agency worker who has a long-standing relationship with a particular employer organisation secures statutory employment protection rights with respect to that organisation. Unfortunately, both the EAT and the Court of Appeal rejected the approach suggested in *Dacas* in the case of *James* v. *Greenwich Borough Council* [2008] ICR 545, where James worked for the Council again for a four-year period. She was informed by the Council that she was no longer required after she was absent through sickness, as the agency had supplied a replacement. Her claim of unfair dismissal against the Council failed as it was held that she was not its employee. The key judgment is that of Elias J in the EAT in which he explained that the fact that there is a long-standing and continuous relationship between an agency worker and the end-user is not in itself sufficient to enable a tribunal to infer a contract of employment between the parties. The key feature in agency arrangements is that the end-user cannot insist that the agency supplies a particular worker, even though in practice this is what has occurred. An employment contract can only be inferred where it is necessary to do this to give effect to the business reality of a particular relationship.

An example of such a business reality is provided by the case of *Cable & Wireless plc* v. *Muscat* [2006] ICR 975, in which Muscat operated his own company and, in accordance with the requirements of Cable & Wireless, provided his services to the company as a contractor through an employment business. The latter was responsible for ensuring his wages were paid, but in all other respects Muscat was treated as an employee of Cable & Wireless. The latter subsequently informed Muscat that it no longer wanted his services, and the tribunal found that he was an employee of Cable and Wireless and therefore entitled to bring a claim of unfair dismissal against it. The Court of Appeal agreed that

Case Summary

Case Summary

Case Summary

the business reality was that agency arrangements had been superimposed on a contractual relationship between Muscat and Cable & Wireless and the tribunal had been right to conclude that it was necessary to find that an implied contract of employment existed.

It can be argued that though the position in *James* is consistent with established legal principles, the position adopted by the majority in *Dacas*, which focuses on the length of the relationship between an agency worker and the end-user, is to be preferred. As the law stands, an agency worker who in practice has operated as an employee of a specific organisation for a long period of time exists in a form of legal limbo. The worker is not the employee of the agency, but nor can he or she become the employee of the end-user unless the latter chooses to offer the worker a contract of employment. As the *James* case illustrates, if the worker ultimately loses the work he or she has no rights whatsoever, even where the circumstances are such that had the worker been an employee there may well have been an unfair dismissal.

It is worth noting that the government has provided for a solution to the vulnerable position of both agency workers and casual workers via s. 23 of the Employment Relations Act 1999. Under this provision the Secretary of State is empowered to extend statutory rights to workers who are not employees, but, to date, no government has sought to exercise these powers. In practice, governments have maintained a deregulatory policy which allows employers to construct employment relationships where those working for such an employer only enjoy those statutory rights which are conferred on workers as well as employees.

> the Secretary of State is empowered to extend statutory rights to workers who are not employees

Law in action

The EC Directive on Temporary Agency Work (No. 2008/104) provides for equal treatment between temporary workers and permanent employees with regard to pay, working hours and holidays. However, it is important to appreciate that the Directive makes no difference to the employment status of agency workers. The Directive is implemented in a diluted form by the Agency Workers Regulations (AWR) 2010. One practical problem with the regulations is that a survey has shown that many British employers are not geared up to ensure that they are properly implemented. This survey, entitled 'Shifting Sands', conducted by recruitment company Randstad UK, revealed that only 7% of employers have conducted an impact assessment in preparation for implementing the AWR whilst 37% are completely unfamiliar with the regulations.

The research, which surveyed a total of 862 candidates and clients, claims that the impact of the AWR will vary across industries, according to their use of temporary workers, with sectors such as construction, education and healthcare likely to face some of the greatest challenges. Around half of organisations using agency workers will be affected by the AWR.

Brian Wilkinson, head of Randstad, stated: 'It is a concern that such a high proportion of organisations are so unprepared. We urge all users of agency workers to conduct a thorough assessment of their human capital resources and the impact of the Regulations. Doing this properly will enable organisations to optimise the structure and efficiency of their workforces.'

Wilkinson adds: 'The equalisation of basic working and employment conditions for agency workers will encourage more people that don't want permanent work to enter the labour market. That is good for them and it's good for UK employers.'

Source: Beth Holmes in *Personnel Today*, 7 March 2011, see http://www.personneltoday.com/articles/2011/03/07/57448/employers-in-the-dark-over-agency-workers-regulations.html

The Agency Workers Regulations

The Agency Workers Regulations (AWR) 2010, SI 2010/93, which are the subject-matter of the above 'Law in Action' feature, came into force on 1 October 2011. The regulations do not impact on the employment status of agency workers as discussed above. The regulations are specifically designed to cover agencies that assign workers to employers on a temporary basis. As we have seen, typically such agency workers will not possess employment status and do not enjoy the employment protection rights contained in the ERA 1996. As workers they are, however, entitled to the national minimum wage and are protected by the Working Time Regulations 1998 and the Part-time Workers Regulations 2000.

The general purpose of the AWR is to give agency workers some degree of equality with comparable permanent employees who are employed by the hirer organisation to which the agency worker is assigned. A permanent employee is a comparable employee if that person is employed on the same work as, or on work that is broadly similar to, the work which is undertaken by the agency worker. There are two categories of equal treatment. The first applies from day one of the agency worker's assignment, and the second applies after the worker has been deployed in the same role by the hirer organisation for 12 weeks.

> there are two categories of equal treatment

Regulation 12 provides that, from day one, the agency worker is entitled on the same basis as comparable permanent employees to collective benefits that permanent employees enjoy such as access to the staff canteen, transport facilities, car parking and child-care facilities. Less favourable treatment with respect to access to these facilities is permitted if the hirer can justify this by reference to the objective needs of the organisation. A possible example of such justification might be where the creation of additional car parking spaces could be considered by an employer to be logistically difficult or unduly costly. The other day one right is provided by regulation 13, which requires the hirer to provide the same information on job vacancies as is provided to comparable permanent employees. Regulation 13 does not permit a hirer to justify a failure to provide this information.

The most important aspect of equality of treatment, which only arises if the agency worker is deployed in the same role for at least 12 weeks, is the right to equality of treatment with respect to *basic* pay and conditions as provided by regulation 5. Pay covers basic pay, which is calculated by reference to the annual salary or hourly or daily rate received by comparable permanent employees. It also extends to overtime payments, contractual bonuses and shift payments for working unsocial hours such as working at night. Occupational sick pay and occupational pensions are excluded from the scope of the regulation. Agency workers must also be treated equally with respect to rest breaks and contractual rights to paid annual leave where these are more generous than the statutory minimum required by the Working Time Regulations.

The right of an agency worker, who is protected by the AWR, to receive the same rate of pay as comparable permanent workers partly overcomes the problems for agency workers arising from the ECJ ruling in *Allonby* v. *Accrington and Rossendale College* (C-256/01) [2004] ICR 1328. In this case Allonby, who was a part-time lecturer, was supplied by an agency to teach at the college. The ECJ ruled that she could not compare her pay with that received by a male full-time teacher who was employed directly by the college. Equal pay law does not apply to a situation in which the differences in the pay of workers performing equal work cannot be attributed to a single source. As Allonby and her chosen male comparator were paid by different organisations, their pay could not be compared for the purposes of an equal pay claim. Under the AWR, an agency

Case Summary

worker can now claim for equal pay once the worker has worked in a specific role for the same organisation for 12 weeks. Equal pay law is examined in depth later (see Chapter 7).

It may be that an agency worker is intermittently hired by the same organisation, but a new qualifying period of 12 weeks will not be required where there is a break of less than six weeks between different assignments and the agency worker is being deployed in the same role. However, hirers could avoid treating agency workers equally with respect to basic pay and conditions by changing their roles within the organisation on a rotating basis, or by ensuring there is a gap of more than six weeks between separate assignments. To pre-empt such attempts to circumvent the AWR, regulation 9 provides that if a worker is employed on a series of assignments a tribunal is empowered to form the view that the structure of these assignments has been devised with the specific purpose of avoiding the equal treatment provisions of the AWR and decide that the worker is protected by regulation 5. An example of such a structure could be where each assignment is for a period of 11 weeks and at the end of any given period of 11 weeks the agency worker is assigned to a new role. If a tribunal decides that a hirer is seeking to avoid compliance with regulation 5 it can award compensation of up to £5,000 in addition to any other compensation that the claimant receives.

Under regulation 18, the worker has three months from the date of the breach of the regulations to present a complaint. Both the agency and the hirer can be liable for breach of regulation 5, although the agency will have a defence to liability if it can show that it took reasonable steps to secure relevant information from the hirer and, on the basis of that information, acted reasonably to determine the pay and conditions that the worker should receive on the basis of equality of treatment. The hirer is solely liable for any breach of regulations 12 and 13 regarding access to collective benefits and the provision of information on job vacancies. A successful clamant will receive a declaration of his or her rights along with either compensation or a recommendation to the agency and/or hirer on actions that should be taken to comply with the regulations. A claimant will be entitled to a minimum of two weeks' pay where there has been a breach of regulation 5.

People in the law

The following interview is with **Vicki Brown,** who is an adviser at a Citizens Advice Bureau (CAB) in Portsmouth. Citizens Advice Bureaus are an important source of legal advice for individuals who cannot afford to obtain legal advice from solicitors and who do not have access to other sources of advice, such as a trade union. It is interesting that Vicki makes reference to people being afraid to enforce their employment rights. Arguably, this demonstrates the vulnerable position many individuals, whose only course of action is to seek advice at a CAB, perceive themselves to be in.

From your own experience, or that of your colleagues, is it a common problem that casual workers and agency workers have to be informed that they cannot, for example, claim unfair dismissal because in law they are not regarded as employees? It is my experience that this is not a common issue. My belief is that the reason for this is that most casual workers in this area are migrant workers and they do not seek advice because they do not know what their rights might be.

From your experience, or that of your colleagues, how common is it that some employers fail to comply with the National Minimum Wage Act and/or the Working Time Regulations on matters such as the length of the working week, the provision of rest breaks or allowing workers their full entitlement to paid holidays? We have very few claims in respect of the minimum wage. We have only had one of these in the last six months as far as I recall. I think the reason for this is that people fear losing their jobs if they try to raise this issue and this is a particular concern for casual and low paid employees.

However, we do have quite a few queries about the right to holidays, particularly the right to have a holiday on a bank holiday, and also the right to take breaks. In my experience, members of the public are surprised by the limited rights to take breaks and often think their entitlement is higher than the minimum specified by the regulations.

Where it appears that an employer is in breach of the National Minimum Wage Act and/or the Working Time Regulations, what courses of action do you typically advise individuals to take in order to enforce their statutory rights? We advise individuals to look at their own contracts of employment and advise them on the statutory minimum. We then suggest that they attempt to negotiate informally before considering a more formal challenge by raising a grievance. However, our overriding concern is to avoid being directive and to ensure individuals are informed so that they can make their own decision about what action to take.

The government has the power to extend statutory employment protection rights to workers who do not have employee status. What are your views on whether or not the government should do this? I think it would be a good move to give people more options. However, I am unsure if this move would make much of a difference at the moment when many fear claiming employment rights for fear of losing their jobs.

Formation of a contract of employment

Having identified the approach to be taken by the tribunals and courts in determining whether a person is working under a contract of employment, and is therefore an employee, it is necessary to consider how a contract of employment is made and to examine what its contents will be.

In theory, the ordinary rules of offer and acceptance apply to contracts of employment in the same way that they do to any other type of contract. Typically, it will be the employer who acts as the offeror by offering a job to the prospective employee on the basis of specified terms and conditions of employment. Indeed, the normal rules of offer and acceptance will be adhered to where, prior to the contract coming into existence, a written contract is sent to the prospective employee, which he or she is asked to sign and return, this constituting acceptance of the employer's offer.

However, as readers may have experienced for themselves, in practice it is not that uncommon for an employment contract to be discussed informally at an interview, and the interview is followed by the employer sending out a letter of appointment offering the job to the interviewee. The full contract is only later put into written form. Therefore, contrary to the normal way in which contracts should be made, the terms of the contract may not be certain on the date the contract comes into effect. The following two cases illustrate the problems that can result from the informal ways in which employment contracts may be made.

In *Stransky* v. *Bristol Rugby Ltd* (11/12/2002 QBD unreported), the club's director of rugby was authorised to approach Joel Stransky, a former international player, to discuss his possible employment as a club coach. Following these negotiations Stransky met the club's chief executive in a restaurant in Bath in April. The terms of the contract were discussed and agreed to over the meal. Stransky returned to his home in Leicester and informed his wife that he had a new job and thus they would be looking for a new home in the Bath/Bristol area. In the months after this meal, to the knowledge of the chief executive, preliminary steps were taken to secure a work permit for Stransky and he was introduced to the players. The chief executive was also asked to draw up the written contract for Stransky and his response indicated that he was intending to do so. In June, Stransky discovered that the club had decided not to employ him, and the club argued that no contract between it and Stransky had ever been made. In court, the chief executive stated that he did not recall meeting Stransky for a meal let alone offering him employment. Fortunately for Stranski all the evidence contradicted the club's arguments, and the court concluded that a contract had been entered into orally during the meal in April. Thus the club was in breach of this contact in refusing to employ Stranski for the agreed period.

Case Summary

In *White* v. *Bristol Rugby Club* [2002] IRLR 204, White, a professional rugby player, signed a three-year written contract to move from his previous club to Bristol. The contract expressly stipulated that it was subject to an 'entire agreement' clause, so that no oral representations made in the course of negotiations applied in respect of its express terms and conditions. White subsequently decided not to join the Bristol club and asserted that he had been told during pre-contract negotiations that he could opt out of the contract on repayment of the advance of his salary that had been paid to him. The High Court held that the 'entire agreement' clause prevented White from relying on the existence of any opt-out term, which had only been agreed orally. Only the terms contained in the written contract were binding on the parties. Therefore, White was in breach of this contract in refusing to take up his appointment by the club.

Case Summary

The latter case demonstrates that whilst employers are not required to use written contracts of employment, where they choose to do so the courts will normally work on the basis that all express terms of the contract, that is the terms actually agreed on by the employer and the employee, are to be found in the written contractual document. Where, as in *White*, the contract is specified as an entire agreement, the courts will not entertain evidence that there are other terms that have been agreed to orally. It is in the interests of employees in such circumstances to carefully scrutinise a written contract before formally accepting it to confirm that, from the employee's perspective, all of the terms that he or she expects to be in the contract are in the written document.

The written statements of terms

As stated above, like most other contracts a contract of employment may be made orally. Employees do not have a right to a written contract of employment. This can cause practical problems at a future date if the employee argues that a particular term was orally agreed to by the employer and the employer is now denying that such an agreement was made. The employee will be unable to establish a breach of contract unless evidence can be produced to prove the term was agreed to. Obviously, in practice, this will be very difficult, as there will often be no witnesses to what was agreed between the employer and employee.

However, in many important contexts this problem is avoided as, in the absence of a written contract of employment, the employer is under a statutory duty to provide a **written statement of terms**. This duty is provided by ss. 1–4 ERA 1996, and also requires written notification of any changes to the particulars contained in the original statement. The written statement must be given to the employee no later than two months after commencement of the employment. As is fully detailed below, this written statement must contain the details of the terms of the contract that employees would typically regard as being of importance to them, such as how their pay is calculated and what their contractual hours of working are. It should be understood that the written statement is *not* a contract of employment but provides evidence of the terms agreed by the employer with the employee.

> written statement is *not* a contract of employment but provides evidence of the terms agreed

Employers do not always comply with this statutory duty, and therefore it is important to appreciate that if an individual has not been given either a written statement or written contract, this does not prevent that person from being considered an employee in law. This was held to be the case in *Singh* v. *FA & the Football League* (2001 unreported) in which it was decided that, despite the fact that Singh had not been given any written information as to the terms on which he was employed, referees in Football League games are employees of the League and therefore have unfair dismissal rights. The same position will apply to referees in the Premier League.

As we have stated, the details that an employer is required to include in a written statement provide much of the information that is important to employees in establishing their contractual rights and in carrying out their jobs. The detail of the terms and conditions of employment that must be contained in a written statement are as follows.

Contents of the written statement

Under s. 1(2) ERA 1996 the written statement can be given to the employee in instalments during the first two months of employment providing the full information has been provided to the employee by the end of that period. However, under s. 2(4) the following information must be contained in a single document which can be regarded as the principal statement.

+ the names of the employer and employee;
+ the date when employment began;
+ the date when continuous employment began – this is of significance where any periods of employment with previous employers count towards the employee's continuous employment with the current employer;
+ the rate of remuneration or the method of calculating remuneration;
+ the intervals at which remuneration will be paid;
+ terms relating to hours of work;

+ terms relating to holidays, including public holidays and holiday pay;

+ the job title or a brief job description – the latter is necessary if the job title is not self-explanatory or does not accurately reflect the duties the employee is to perform;

+ details of the place or places of work.

Under s. 1(4) other information that must be contained in the written statement includes:

+ Any terms relating to incapacity for work due to sickness or injury – including any provision for receiving some or all of the employee's normal pay during an absence through sickness or injury. Note that there is no legal right to receive any proportion of the contractual wage during such an absence.

+ Any terms relating to occupational pension schemes.

+ The length of notice the employee is obliged to give and entitled to receive to terminate the contract. Note that minimum rights to notice are contained in s. 86 (see Chapter 4). Essentially, employees are entitled to one week's notice during the first two years of employment and an additional week for each completed year thereafter subject to a maximum of 12 weeks.

+ Whether the employment is intended to be permanent or, if it is for a fixed term, the date on which it is to end.

+ Details of any collective agreements between the employer and a trade union directly affecting the terms and conditions of employment.

+ Details regarding any work to be undertaken outside of the UK.

Under s. 3, the written statement may include a note specifying where documents containing **disciplinary procedures** and **grievance procedures** can be found. Such documents must be reasonably accessible to the employee. Typically, they will be included in a staff handbook which the employee will be given in addition to the written statement.

Under s. 2(2), the written statement can also refer the employee to other such documents to ascertain terms relating to absence through sickness or injury and the details of an occupational scheme.

Under s. 2(3), with respect to terms relating to notice the employee is entitled to receive, the statement may refer the employee to the law contained in s. 86 which sets out the minimum statutory periods of notice, or to the provisions of a reasonably accessible collective agreement.

Employers are required to keep the written statement up to date. Under s. 4 employees must be informed of any changes to the written statement no later than one month after the change has come into effect. This notification can be provided collectively, for example, by email or through a circular which sets out the proposed changes.

Writing and drafting

In your future professional employment, for example, as a legal adviser in a company or as a human resource manager, your job duties may include drafting written statements on behalf of your employer. Try drafting your own statement on behalf of L Ltd in accordance with its instructions as set out below.

L Ltd has recently opened a leisure and sports centre and is proposing to employ 25 employees. All these employees will have the same terms and conditions of employment, and will be required to undertake the same duties which include acting as fitness instructors, working on the reception desk, serving behind the bar at the centre and keeping the centre clean and tidy.

All employees are aged 18 or over. The majority of the employees are aged between 20 and 30. It is proposed to pay all employees £5.00 an hour. All employees will work nine-hour shifts; either between 6.30 a.m. to 3.30 p.m. or 3.30 p.m. to 12.30 a.m. for a six-day period in any week. They will be permitted a meal break of half an hour during a shift. They will be allowed to take four weeks' unpaid leave, but will be required to work on public holidays if so instructed. Employees working on public holidays will not receive any additional payments. Employees will have no contractual rights to be paid whilst absent through injury or illness.

Employees will be employed on permanent contracts, which can be terminated by the employer or employee by giving one month's notice.

The company does not have an occupational pension scheme, and does not recognise a trade union for the purposes of collective bargaining. It has drafted disciplinary and grievance procedures, which are included in a handbook which is to be provided to all staff on the first day of their employment.

You should spend about an hour on this activity in terms of both accessing the websites, suggested below, and then drafting a written statement in accordance with L Ltd's instructions to you. However, you should ensure that, irrespective of these instructions, your statement will enable the company to meet its statutory obligations on matters such as rates of pay and working hours.

◆ **Handy tips:** The government has created a website providing guidance to employers concerning their employment rights and duties (**http://www.businesslink.gov.uk/bdotg/action/home**). If you click on employment and skills, and then click on *staff documents and employment policies*, you will be able to read the advice on creating a written statement.

The following link will take you directly to a model blank statement, which can be downloaded in PDF format, demonstrating how a statement can be set out and specifying the categories of information it must contain: **http://online.businesslink.gov.uk/bdotg/action/stmtEmpLanding?r.l1=1073858787&r.l2=1073858914&r.l3=1084822756&r.s=tl&topicId=1075225309**

Also remember that you can remind yourself of the legal position relating to working time and the national minimum wage by revisiting the relevant sections of this chapter and accessing governmental advice at **http://www.direct.gov.uk/en/Employment/index.htm**

Remedies for failure to provide a written statement

Breach of the statutory duty to provide a written statement does not give an employee any rights to compensation, but does permit the employee to present a complaint to an employment tribunal. Where appropriate, under s. 11 ERA 1996, the tribunal can amend or complete a written statement to reflect what the parties agreed. In doing this the tribunal will seek to establish whether there is evidence as to what the parties agreed, or whether such evidence can be obtained by looking at the policies of the employer regarding other employees of the same or similar category to the claimant. A statement may also be completed by implying terms in order to give business efficacy to the contract (see below). The weight of opinion, however, is that tribunals cannot complete a statement by inventing terms on the basis that they are reasonable, although this is contrary to an *obiter dictum* of Stephenson LJ in *Mears* v. *Safecar Security*. This case is discussed below in the context of considering an employer's obligation to pay an employee who is absent through illness.

As held in *Construction Industry Training Board* v. *Leighton* [1978] IRLR 60, a case concerning a dispute over whether Leighton's salary included additional special payments, if the issue relates to the interpretation of a contractual term as opposed to its accuracy then the matter can be dealt with only by a civil court and not by employment tribunals. The latter do not possess the jurisdiction to interpret the meaning of an employment contract whilst it is still in operation.

This position was applied by the Court of Appeal in *Southern Cross Healthcare Co. Ltd.* v. *Perkins* [2011] ICR 285. In this case the court decided that, although tribunals may amend written statements to reflect what the parties had actually agreed, a tribunal had no jurisdiction to interpret a term where the parties had different views on what the contact provided. In this case the employee and the employer were in dispute over whether the employee had a permanent right to five days' leave over and above the minimum requirements for leave provided by the Working Time Regulations. This was an issue of interpretation of the employment contract which was outside the jurisdiction of a tribunal to undertake.

Case Summary

Where the statutory duty is not complied with, there is no general right to compensation, although there is one important exception to this. Under s. 38 of the Employment Act 2002, compensation can be granted for breach of the statutory duty if another statutory claim, for example of unfair dismissal, succeeds. Such compensation will normally be two weeks' statutory pay, although tribunals have the discretion to increase this to four weeks' pay if it deems this just and equitable in the circumstances. The concept of a **statutory week's pay** is explained later (see Chapter 5) but it is subject to a statutory limit, which in 2012 was £430.

The lack of an effective monetary remedy means that some employers do not take the statutory duty seriously, and do get away with violating the law without incurring any consequences. Nevertheless, employers should be cautious in adopting a flippant attitude. It can be the case that in failing to provide a written statement an employer does end up with a term in the contract which is put there by the tribunal, but it is not one which the employer would have chosen to have included in the employment contract.

Reflective practice

In drafting a written statement of terms it is important for an employer to ensure that the written statement is fully in accordance with other duties that statutes impose on the employer. If an employer fails to do this, a tribunal will amend a written statement so that it properly reflects the statutory duty concerned.

Revisit the information you discovered in undertaking the 'Out and about' activity earlier in this chapter on the National Minimum Wage Act (NMWA) 1998 and the Working Time Regulations 1998. As you may have realised, there are changes required to L Ltd's proposed policies in order for the company to be in compliance with its statutory duties (see the 'Writing and drafting' activity above).

The company is seeking to pay a lower rate of pay than will be required by the NMWA at the time you carry out this activity. The company is also failing to comply with its obligations under the Working Time Regulations to permit its employees to take paid holidays. The company is proposing a standard 51-hour working week. This exceeds the maximum of 48 weeks which is stipulated by the Working Time Regulations. The company must either reduce its proposed working week or ask each individual employee to sign a written agreement that the employee waives the right to a 48-hour working week. All of the other proposed policies of the company are in accordance with the law.

If necessary you should amend your written statement so that the company is complying with its legal obligations.

School leavers and contractual capacity

With respect to the formation of a contract of employment, one further issue to consider is whether there are age restrictions on who can enter into a contract of employment. As minors, individuals under the age of 18 do not normally possess contractual capacity and consequently will not be legally bound by any contracts they enter into. Many school leavers are of course under the age of 18, but there is not normally a problem concerning contractual capacity in employment law. A contract of employment, or an analogous contract for training or apprenticeship, is deemed to be for a minor's benefit and, consequently, is legally binding on both the employer and the minor employee. This position has long been accepted in contract law. For example, in *Roberts* v. *Gray* [1913] 1 KB 520, damages were awarded against a minor who broke a contract to accompany a professional snooker player on a world tour in order to receive training and develop experience.

It matters not that the contract contains particular terms which the minor regards as detrimental, providing that the contract taken as a whole is to the minor's benefit. This is illustrated by *Doyle* v. *White City Stadium Ltd* [1935] 1 KB 520, in which a minor boxer was bound by rules permitting suspension and a fine for hitting his opponent below the belt. Indeed the court held that the rules were just as much for his protection as for the protection of his opponents. This can be contrasted with *De Francesco* v. *Barnum* [1890] 45 Ch 430, in which a minor was released from her contract as a professional dancer where she was contracted to work only for the defendant, whilst he was under no duty to find her engagements, and her remuneration was deemed inadequate. Overall, the contract operated in a way that was to her disadvantage.

Contracts of apprenticeship are important in current economic conditions as they provide school leavers with the opportunity to obtain a job and receive vocational training as an alternative to seeking to enter the increasingly costly worlds of further and higher education. Contracts of apprenticeship put apprentices in a special position. The contract must be in writing, and the contract cannot be terminated during its currency other than by reason of **gross misconduct** on the part of the apprentice. For example, if an apprentice was caught stealing the employer's property, or physically assaulting another apprentice or an employee, this would clearly be gross misconduct on the apprentice's part and would permit the employer to terminate the apprenticeship.

Case
Summary

Case
Summary

If an apprentice is not guilty of gross misconduct and is dismissed during the contract of apprenticeship, the apprentice may sue the employer for breach of contract. As held in *Dunk* v. *George Waller & Son Ltd* [1970] 2 All ER 630, and contrary to the normal principles of contract law (which are explained in Chapter 4), apprentices who are dismissed in breach of contract can receive damages for loss of future prospects as well as immediate financial loss. Therefore, employers are ill-advised prematurely to terminate an apprentice's contract.

However, as held in *North East Coast Ship Repairers Ltd* v. *Secretary of State for Employment* [1978] IRLR 149, there is no dismissal where an apprentice is not offered a job after his contract of apprenticeship has expired. In this case, an apprentice fitter was not offered a contract of employment because the employer did not have any work for him to do. However, he was not entitled to a statutory redundancy payment as he had not been dismissed. The EAT stated a contract of apprenticeship is a special one-off contract under which the employee receives training. The purpose of the contract is completed when the specified period of training has come to an end. It is not akin to a fixed-term contract of employment so that non-renewal of a contract of apprenticeship does not constitute a dismissal. This decision means that, contrary to the normal statutory position (which will be examined in Chapter 5), non-renewal of a contract of apprenticeship does not constitute a dismissal. Therefore, an apprentice is unable to claim either a statutory redundancy payment or unfair dismissal if, on expiry of the contract of apprenticeship, the apprentice is not offered a contract of employment.

Case Summary

Sources of the contract of employment

Having considered how a contract of employment is made, it is now necessary to identify where the terms of an employment contract can be found. These terms may come from a variety of places which can be regarded as the sources of the employment contract. As explained below, all contracts of employment will contain a mix of express and implied terms. The collective bargaining process between an employer and a trade union (briefly explained in the previous chapter), may also be a source of the terms and conditions of employment for some employees.

Express terms

The main source of any person's employment contract will be the express terms of that contract. These are the contract terms actually agreed to, orally or in writing, by the employer and the employee. The types of terms that must be contained in a statutory written statement of terms, as detailed above, are examples of major express terms which will be in any contract of employment. Some employment contracts also contain more complex express terms. For example, employees may be bound by terms prohibiting disclosure of the employer's **confidential information**, and/or by terms prohibiting the employee taking up employment with the employer's competitors if the employee leaves his or her job (see Chapter 3).

Where a full written contract is provided, then normally the courts will not look outside the contractual document to ascertain the existence of any other terms. Disputes over the meaning of contractual terms are outside the jurisdiction of employment tribunals and will be dealt with in the ordinary civil courts. It is a court of law, and not an employment tribunal, which has the jurisdiction to hear claims for breach of contract which occur during the currency of the employment contract (see Chapter 1).

Judicially implied terms

As will be explained later (see Chapter 3), judges will more readily imply terms into contracts of employment than is the case with contracts in general, as they view certain rights and duties as a necessary feature of all employment contracts. On the basis of such **judicially implied terms** employees are bound to obey all lawful and reasonable instructions of the employer. An employer will be in breach of a judicially implied term if the employer treats an employee so badly, for example, through bullying, that the employer has destroyed the mutual trust and confidence on which modern employment relations are viewed by the courts as being based.

In other circumstances a court will only imply a term into an employment contract on the basis of the principles of the ordinary law of contract. The **business efficacy** test provides the main basis for a court deciding that a particular term needs to be implied into a contract to ensure the contract works in a proper businesslike manner and in accordance with what the parties themselves must have intended.

Case Summary

An example of the operation of the 'business efficacy' test is provided by the case of *Courtaulds Northern Spinning Ltd* v. *Sibson* [1988] IRLR 305. Sibson was employed as a lorry driver and had worked from a particular depot. There was no provision in his contract which empowered the company to move him to a different depot, and Sibson objected to moving when he was instructed to do so. In fact, the new depot was a similar distance to his home as was the case with the original depot. The Court of Appeal found that as Sibson spent most of his working day 'on the road' it was of no real significance to him which depot he worked from. At least this was so providing that requiring him to change depots made no difference to the travelling distance from his home to his workplace. Therefore, a term to the effect that he could be required to work from any depot within reasonable daily travel from his home could be implied into his contract. In order to ensure the contract operated in an efficient manner, both parties would have intended such a term to be included when they made the contract had they anticipated the need to do this.

Case Summary

However, a term cannot be judicially implied into a contract where this appears to be reasonable but where there is no evidence that *both* parties would have intended such a term to be included in the contract. In *Mears* v. *Safecar Security Ltd* [1982] IRLR 183, a problem arose when Mears was ill and he argued that the employer must have intended to pay him during the period of absence caused by the illness, as otherwise, there would have been an express term in his contract stipulating that there was no contractual right to sick pay. The tribunal accepted this argument, but the EAT held that it was wrong to do so as there was no evidence that the company had ever intended to be obliged to make such payments. This was not a situation where it could be argued that it was obvious that the parties must have intended such a term to be included in the contract. Nor was it necessary to imply such a term in order to give business efficacy to the contract. It is perfectly possible for a contract of employment to operate on the basis that an employee will not receive any remuneration during periods of absence caused by illness.

In fact, some employers do pay employees their normal wages during periods of illness, and others choose not to do so. This is therefore a matter which should be covered by the express terms of an employment contract, but if the contract is silent on the issue then the courts cannot normally imply a term to the effect that sick pay must be paid. In line with what is explained below, such a term could only be implied by reference to the **custom and practice** of a particular employer. Another possibility is that the issue of sick pay is covered by a collective agreement between the employer and the employee's trade union.

A contractual right to receive normal pay, in whole or on part, whilst absent through sickness or injury is different to statutory sick pay. This is a statutory benefit available to all employees who do not receive any pay whilst they are ill. The entitlement arises on the fourth consecutive day of an employee's illness and payment is available for a maximum of 28 weeks. To be eligible for statutory sick pay the employee must earn the minimum to be making national insurance contributions. In 2012 this was £107 a week, and statutory sick pay was £85.85 for each week of illness or injury.

Further information on claiming statutory sick pay can be accessed from **http://www.direct.gov.uk/en/moneytaxandbenefits/benefitstaxcreditsandothersupport/illorinjured/dg_10018786**

Collective agreements

Trade unions are most significant in the workplace when they have an agreement with an employer under which the employer agrees to negotiate with the union with regard to some or all of the contractual terms and conditions of its employees that the union represents. Where such an agreement exists, the union is said to be a **recognised trade union** by that employer for the purposes of collective bargaining. The objective of collective bargaining is for trade unions to reach collective agreements with employers. In Britain such agreements are *presumed*, both at common law and under statute law, not to be legally binding on the respective parties, and thus normally do not have the status of contracts. This is the case as a result of the decision in *Ford* v. *AUEW* [1969] 2 QB 303, and under s. 179 of the Trade Union and Labour Relations (Consolidation) Act (TULRCA) 1992.

However, the content of a collective agreement can be incorporated into the individual contracts of employment of the employees on whose behalf the union was negotiating. This will be the case where a term in an employment contract specifies that the contents of a collective agreement, in whole or in part, are incorporated into individual employment contracts. Alternatively, the collective agreement may be listed as part of an employee's contract in that employee's written statement of terms. It is important to understand that incorporation of a collective agreement will apply to all categories of employees on whose behalf the union was negotiating, not just those who happen to belong to the union. A collective agreement so incorporated is legally enforceable between the individual employee and the employer. Future collective agreements can vary or add to the terms of the contract.

Collective bargaining may be centralised in that it takes place between a number of employers and trade unions representing workers in a particular industry or who share the same occupation, for example teachers or workers in the NHS. Typically, such collective bargaining will be termed **national collective bargaining**. In such bargaining teachers are represented by a number of different unions including the National Union of Teachers (NUT) and the National Association of Schoolmasters Union of Women

Teachers (NASUWT). It is up to an individual teacher to decide which union, if any, he or she wishes to join. Most workers in the NHS who decided to join a trade union will belong to UNISON.

Where trade unions are recognised in the private sector it is more typical these days for bargaining to be between a union and a particular employer. This is known as **local collective bargaining**. UNITE and the GMB are the largest trade unions operating in the private sector. USDAW (Union of Shop, Distributive and Allied Workers), which represents shop workers in the retail industry, is another important private sector union.

It is possible for an employer to have entered into both national and local collective agreements on the same issue and for particular provisions in such agreements to conflict with one another. This was the issue in *Gascol Conversions Ltd* v. *Mercer* [1974] IRLR 155, in which a national agreement specified that Mercer was to work a 40-hour week, but a local agreement between the company and the union provided for a 54-hour working week. It was held that normally a national agreement will prevail over local agreements unless there is an express agreement to the contrary between the parties to the national agreement. Therefore, in this case it was the hours specified in the national collective agreement that were incorporated into Mercer's employment contract.

Case Summary

The process of collective bargaining and the different types of collective agreements that can be made will be considered fully later (see Chapter 8).

Custom and practice

A term can be implied into a contract of employment by reference to the custom and practice of the employer. This was done by the Court of Appeal in *Sagar* v. *Ridehalgh* [1931] 1 Ch 310 in reaching a decision that deductions from a weaver's wages that had been made for 30 years were permitted by his contract. It was held in this case that for a term to be implied by custom it must be certain, general and reasonable. However, it was not necessary for the employee to know of the term.

Case Summary

By way of contrast in *Meek* v. *Port of London Authority* [1918] 1 Ch 415, it was held that pay deductions could not be implied into a dock worker's contract where he was unaware of the practice. It can be argued that the latter approach is to be preferred as the basis for implying a term is that an employee has accepted it, and this is not possible if the employee has actual no knowledge of the custom involved.

Case Summary

Today, custom and practice is most relevant in the world of industrial relations as it is one way in which the contents of a collective agreement, as explained above, can be incorporated into the employment contracts of the workers that a trade union represents. It can also be the way in which duties which are initially voluntary can become legally binding. In *Solihull Metropolitan Borough Council* v. *NUT* [1985] IRLR 211, teachers who took industrial action in the form of a ban on voluntary duties such as attending parents' evenings were held to be in breach of contract. Such duties had been consistently performed by teachers over a long period of time and accordingly had become part of their employment contracts.

Case Summary

Disciplinary rules and procedures

Many employers will choose to adopt disciplinary rules that their employees are required to comply with. In practice, employers should also have written disciplinary and grievance procedures. Usually, these are rules and procedures that reflect an employer's policy rather than constitute terms of the contract. The advantage to the employer in rules and procedures accompanying contracts, but not being part of them, is that they can be added to or varied unilaterally, that is, by a decision of the employer. The agreement of the employees to such changes is not required.

An employer may decide to agree that rules and procedures should have contractual force. However, if they are so incorporated into the employment contract, the employer cannot **unilaterally vary** them. Moreover, a failure to observe contract-based rules or procedures constitutes a breach of contract. Although it is rare that this will happen in practice (as will be explained in Chapter 4), an employee who has been dismissed in breach of contractual procedures might be able to secure a court order in the form of an injunction to prevent the employer from implementing the dismissal.

Statutory standards

Some statutes provide for minimum standards that cannot be altered by the parties to an employment contract. Examples, as discussed in this chapter, include the national minimum wage, the minimum notice periods that employers must give to employees and provisions on rights to paid holiday as laid down in the Working Time Regulations. The latter rights also illustrate the impact EU law may have on employment contracts as the Working Time Regulations are required by the Working Time Directive 1993 as consolidated into the Working Time Directive, 2003/88.

Table 2.3 summarises the sources of the terms which may be found in employment contracts.

Table 2.3 Sources of the contract of employment

Sources of terms	Examples of terms
Express terms	Terms contained in written contracts of employment Terms required to be in a written statement of terms under s. 1 ERA 1996
Judicially implied terms	Terms implied through the 'business efficacy' test Judicially implied terms such as the duty of obedience
Collective agreements between an employer and a trade union	Negotiated terms on pay rates incorporated into individual contracts of employment between the employer and its employees
Statute law	National Minimum Wage Act Working Time Regulations
Custom and practice	A term may be so implied providing it is certain, general and reasonable in accordance with the decision in *Sagar* v. *Ridehalgh*
Disciplinary rules and procedures	Employers can choose to incorporate these into employment contracts

Documenting the law

As explained above, when a person starts work it is the employer's choice whether to provide the employee with a full written contract of employment or a written statement of terms. It is useful to appreciate the differences between these documents, and the following contract of employment is an example of a full written contract. It is also an example of a contract that is derived from collective bargaining. It is based on a collective agreement between post-1992 universities and unions representing academic staff. Whilst the collective agreement is not legally enforceable, the resulting employment contract between an individual lecturer and the university employer is legally binding on both parties.

The first four provisions concern the names of the parties, the date of commencement of the contract and identifying when there will be continuous service with previous public sector employers.

5 CONTRACTUAL DUTIES

You are employed as a lecturer in law. This is a full time post and its nature is such that you are expected to work such hours as are reasonably necessary in order to fulfil your duties and responsibilities. Those duties include teaching and tutorial guidance, research and other forms of scholarly activity, examining, curriculum development, administration and related activities. You are expected to work flexibly and efficiently, and to maintain the highest professional standards in discharging your responsibilities, and in promoting and implementing the corporate policies of the University.

The make-up of your duties will be determined from time to time by your Head of Department in consultation with yourself, and will be reviewed regularly through the staff appraisal system. Guidelines for the determination of the duties of lecturing staff are set out in the Staff Handbook; in particular, when deciding upon your specific duties, your Head of Department shall have regard to the matters set out under Head 1.4 of those guidelines ('Factors to be taken into account'). Any dispute over duties or hours may, if not resolved in the first instance between you and your Head of Department, be referred to the Grievance Procedure.

Your formal scheduled teaching responsibilities should not exceed 18 hours in any week or a total of 550 hours in the teaching year.

6 WORKING YEAR

Your teaching year will not normally exceed 38 weeks, of which 2 weeks will be spent on teaching-related administration. While some flexibility may be required in organising the teaching year, you will not (except with prior agreement) be required to undertake more than 14 consecutive weeks of teaching at any one time, and any significant variations to the normal pattern of the teaching year at the University will only be made after consultation with the staff and the recognised lecturer unions.

7 HOLIDAYS

7.1 The University's holiday year runs from 1 August to 31 July. In addition to statutory Bank Holidays, local discretionary holidays and days when the institution is closed in the interests of efficiency, you are entitled to 35 working days paid holiday during the course of the holiday year. Leave not taken at 31 July may be carried over, to be taken in August or September of the following year. Leave may not be carried forward beyond 30th September. In the holiday year in which your employment commences or terminates, your holiday entitlement will accrue on a pro-rata basis for each complete month of service; on the termination of your employment, holiday pay will be worked out on a similar basis.

7.2 The timing of your holidays is subject to the agreement of your Head of Department. Subject to the organisational requirements of the University, you may request that up to 6 weeks of your normal holiday entitlement be taken in one continuous period, and such a request will not be unreasonably refused.

7.3 Wherever possible, detailed holiday schedules for individual lecturers will be made as soon as is reasonably practicable after the beginning of each academic year; in determining holiday schemes, special regard will be given to lecturers with family responsibilities and those who wish to attend conferences or courses that are held in normal holiday periods.

8 RESEARCH AND SCHOLARLY ACTIVITY

8.1 As part of your duties, you will normally be expected to engage in research and scholarly activity. The nature and extent of this will vary with the nature of the subject(s) you teach and the full range and balance of your duties and other commitments. In this context, 'scholarly activities' includes the production of books, contributions to books, articles and conference papers, and is to be construed in the light of the common understanding of the phrase in higher education.

8.2 While it is in the nature of research and scholarly activity that it may take place throughout the year and be integrated into the overall pattern of your activities, it is envisaged that normally the period (s) of the year outside normal teaching weeks (clause – 'Working Year') and your holiday entitlement (clause – 'Holidays') will primarily be devoted to research and scholarly activity.

8.3 Your research and scholarly activity will be principally self-managed. In addition, these activities (and their relationship with your other duties) will be considered as part of the staff appraisal and development system, under which objectives for the coming year (or other appropriate period) can be set and achievements over the past year (or other appropriate period) can be assessed. The University undertakes to give you such support as is reasonable in the circumstances in order to help you to realise the objectives so set.

9 RENUMERATION

Your initial salary in this post is £*. It is payable monthly in arrears by direct credit transfer. In determining your salary review the Board of Governors will refer to national recommendations arising from negotiations between PCEF and the recognised unions. Full details of salary scales and their operation are set out in the Staff Handbook.

10 SICKNESS

Subject to the provisions of the Sick Pay and Sick Leave Scheme, you are contractually entitled to time off with pay if you are absent from work due to illness or injury. Full details of your entitlements are included in the Staff Handbook.

11 MATERNITY LEAVE

Your contractual entitlement to maternity leave is in accordance with the procedures contained in the Staff Handbook.

12 STAFF APPRAISAL

In relation to the performance of your duties you will be required to participate in an appraisal scheme approved by the Board of Governors and included in the Staff Handbook.

Paragraphs 13, 14, 15 and 16 of the contract concern exclusivity of service, patents, confidentiality, and copyright. These sections of the contract are set out in the following chapter.

17 PENSION

17.1 You are entitled to participate in the Teachers' Superannuation Scheme subject to its terms and conditions from time to time in force. The scheme is contracted out of the State Earnings Related Pension Scheme. Should you choose not to join the Teachers Superannuation Scheme you must join the State pension scheme or take out a personal pension.

18 PROBATIONARY PERIOD

18.1 The first 12 months of your employment will be a probationary period, during which your suitability for the position to which you have been appointed will be assessed. The University reserves the right to extend your probationary period, if, in its opinion, circumstances so require.

18.2 During your probationary period your employment may be terminated by the University on giving one month's written notice.

19 GRIEVANCE, DISCIPLINARY AND OCCUPATIONAL PERFORMANCE PROCEDURES

The University has agreed procedures for dealing with disciplinary, grievance and occupational performance matters. Details of these procedures are set out in the Staff Handbook.

20 TERMINATION OF EMPLOYMENT

Your appointment shall be terminable, except in the case of probation or dismissal for gross misconduct by your giving the institution two months' notice in writing or by the institution giving you three months' notice in writing.

21 VARIATION

Agreements reached as a result of national or local negotiations between the employer(s) and the recognised unions shall, after adoption by the Board of Governors, be automatically incorporated into your contract.

This contract may be varied with the agreement of both parties.

Source: The national academic contract can be accessed from the UCU website at **http://www.ucu.org.uk/index.cfm?articleid=1972**

Reflective practice

Have another look at the written statement of terms you drafted. What additional terms are included in the above full written contract of employment, which are not required to be included in a statutory written statement?

Consider whether there is any information in the above contract which is of a type which should have been, but was not, included in your written statement.

Summary

- It is necessary to distinguish between workers who have employee status and those who do not. Only employees have the employment protection rights provided by ERA 1996. For example, only employees can claim unfair dismissal and have a right to a statutory redundancy payment.

- However, both employees and workers have rights under the National Minimum Wage Act and the Working Time Regulations.

- There is no single test for establishing whether a worker has employee status. On the basis of the multiple test derived from the *Ready Mixed* case, a court must analyse all the terms in a contract to determine whether, on balance, a person is an employee or is in business on his or her own account.

- As confirmed by the Law Lords in *Carmichael*, there is an irreducible minimum for a contract of employment. This requires a sufficient degree of control by the employer, mutuality of obligations and personal performance by the employee.

- As in cases involving homeworkers, such as *Nethermere* v. *Taverna*, mutuality of obligations requiring an employer to provide work and the employee to accept it can be derived from umbrella contracts that operate over a long period of time.

- An absence of mutuality of obligations prevents casual workers and many agency workers from securing employee status.

- Employers are not obliged to use written contracts of employment. However, under s. 1 ERA 1996 employees are entitled to a written statement of terms detailing matters such as job title, rate of remuneration, hours of work, holiday entitlement and place(s) of work.

- Terms can be implied to a contract of employment by judges on the basis of orthodox contractual principles in the form of the business efficacy test.

- Terms may also be implied into an employment contract by reference to custom and practice.

- For many workers, particularly in the public sector, some terms in their employment contracts will be derived from collective agreements. These are agreements between employers and trade unions.

- A collective agreement is presumed not to be legally enforceable between the parties to it, but a collective agreement incorporated into a contract of employment is enforceable between the employer and the individual employee.

Question and answer*

Problem: Cordelia entered the employment of Supastores plc as a trainee. The company owns a chain of supermarkets located throughout Britain. Cordelia was employed at the company's store in Southsea. Lear, the manager of the store, was responsible for supervising her work and issuing her with the conditions of her employment. The written contract of employment, which Cordelia received from Lear, stated that her terms and conditions of employment were governed by the national agreements in force between Supastores plc and the Union of Shop Workers (USW). However, the relevant agreements were not listed in Cordelia's contract. This contract stipulates that her annual salary is £13,400.

A current national agreement provides that all employees will receive full pay for the first four weeks of any absence caused by illness or injury. Cordelia has received an application form to join the USW but, to date, has forgotten to complete it.

Five months after she commenced employment, Cordelia was absent from work for three weeks as a result of a virus. She was told by Lear that she would not be paid for this period as it was the company's policy not to pay salary to employees who were in their first year of employment, whilst they were absent due to sickness. Lear emphasised to Cordelia that this policy was clearly stated in the staff handbook which she had received along with her contract of employment. Lear also informed her that it had been agreed with the USW officials at the store that the national collective agreement on sick pay would not apply to trainees.

Cordelia was unhappy with the way she was treated and tendered her notice of resignation. Cordelia has now worked out her notice and left the employ of Supastores. She still believes she is contractually entitled to payment of salary for the three weeks that she was ill.

Advise Cordelia as to her legal rights and remedies (if any).

You should spend 40 minutes on answering this question.

Essay: 'The judicial concept of an irreducible minimum for the existence of a contract of employment means that, in reality, many vulnerable workers are deprived of important statutory employment protection rights.'

Discuss this statement.

You should spend 40 minutes on answering this question.

✱ Answer guidance is provided at the end of the chapter.

Further reading

IDS Employment Law Handbook (2009)
***Contracts of Employment* (Income Data Services: London).**
Chapter 1 provides a detailed technical analysis of the case law concerned with employee status; and Chapter 3 contains a comprehensive explanation of an employer's statutory duty to provide a written statement of terms.

Deakin, S. and Morris, G. (2012) *Labour Law* (Hart: Oxford).
This is the seminal text on both individual and collective labour law. Chapter 3 provides comprehensive and contextual analysis of the issues surrounding employee status, and Chapter 4 focuses on terms in the employment contract and working conditions.

Freedland, M. (2003) *The Personal Contract of Employment* (OUP: Oxford).
This is regarded by many as the leading academic work on employment contracts. Chapter 1 focuses on the nature of the contract of employment and the issue of employee status. Chapter 2 analyses the ways in which employment contracts are made. This is a demanding book but invaluable for anyone researching into these issues and/or is looking for an academic analysis of the application of contract law to the employment relationship.

Busby, N. and Christie, D. (2005) 'The Regulation of Temporary Agency Work in the European Union', *The Cambrian Law Review*, vol. 36, pp. 15–28.
This article provides comparative analysis of the regulation of agency work in different EU member states and considers the basis for an EU Directive on temporary agency work.

Davidov, G. (2005) 'Who is a Worker?', *Industrial Law Journal*, vol. 34, pp. 57–71.
This article critically analyses the way in which the law distinguishes between employees and workers, and argues for the extension of employment rights to workers who are dependent on a single employer.

Honeyball, S. (2005) 'The Conceptual Integrity of Employment', *The Cambrian Law Review*, vol. 36, pp. 1–14.
This article discusses different meanings of the term 'employment' and critically analyses the judicial tests for determining employee status.

Leighton, P. and Wynn, M. (2006) 'Will the Real Employer Please Stand Up? Agencies, Client Companies and the Employment Status of the Temporary Agency Worker', *Industrial Law Journal*, vol. 35, pp. 301–20; (2011) 'Classifying Employment Relationships – More Sliding Doors or a Better Regulatory Framework', *Industrial Law Journal*, vol. 40, pp. 5–44.
These two articles provide an analysis and critique of the way in which the law classifies employment relationships and demonstrates the particular problems faced by agency workers.

Wynn, M. (2011) 'The Agency Worker Regulations: a very British version of flexicurity', *Contemporary Issues in Law*, vol. 11(1), pp. 54–68.
This article critically analyses the Agency Workers Regulations 2011 and argues that the regulations offer a weaker protection to agency workers in Britain than that envisaged by the Directive.

Question and answer guidance

Problem:

This problem is asking you to explain and apply the rules for determining whether a collective agreement between an employer and a trade union has been incorporated into the employment contract of an individual employee.

Your answer should start by explaining what a collective agreement is, that such agreements are presumed not to be legally enforceable between the employer and trade union parties to them, but that the content of collective agreements will be legally enforceable to the extent that they are incorporated into individual contracts of employment. You should then explain how this process of incorporation works, and that a trade union will be negotiating on behalf of all relevant employees, not just employees who are members of it.

The main part of your answer will focus on whether the national collective agreement between Supastores and the USW has been incorporated into Cordelia's contract.

Your answer should state that it is irrelevant that Cordelia is not in the union and it is therefore of no legal significance that she has forgotten to complete her membership form. What matters is that her contract of employment stipulates that appropriate terms in her contract of employment are derived from national collective agreements. It is a potential problem that the relevant collective agreements are not specified in her contract. However, if the national agreement concerning sick pay is implemented by the company then it is incorporated into the employment contracts of its employees.

Your answer should identify that the major problem for Cordelia is that the local collective agreement states that trainees are not entitled to sick pay. The issue is therefore one of conflicting collective agreements. It was held by the Court of Appeal in *Gascol Conversion* v. *Mercer* that, where collective agreements conflict, it is the national agreement that will apply unless the national agreement specifies that it can be varied by subsequent local agreement.

On the basis of this decision, Cordelia is able to present a claim to an employment tribunal for the three weeks' net pay owed to her as the company is in breach of contract by withholding her salary from her. However, the company will be able to rely on the local agreement as the legal basis for the policy contained in the staff handbook if this is in accordance with the national agreement. Your answer could also make the point that in this day and age local collective bargaining is more common that national bargaining, and therefore the *Gascol* case could be regarded as out of date. If this argument is accepted by a court then Supastores can rely on the local agreement to withhold sick pay from Cordelia.

Essay:

The question is asking you to assess whether the ways in which the courts determine whether a person is an employee has resulted in the situation where many individuals in the labour market are deprived of important statutory employment protection rights.

After providing an introduction to your essay, your answer should explain the judicial tests for determining employee status and should explain the three elements of the irreducible minimum: that is, control, mutuality of obligations and personal performance. Cases such as *Ready Mixed* should be explained. The important decision of the Supreme Court in *Autoclenz* v. *Belcher*, that tribunals and courts should focus on the reality of the relationship between contracting parties, should also be discussed.

In discussing mutuality of obligations your answer could distinguish between homeworkers as in the *Nethermere St Neots* case and casual workers as in *O'Kelly* v. *Trust House Forte*. Your answer should also deal with the position of agency workers. *James* v. *Greenwich Council* is a very important case to include in your answer. This case confirms that even where an agency worker has worked for a particular organisation for a long period of time, this does not permit a tribunal or court to infer that a contract of employment has come into existence.

Your answer should explain that casual and agency workers are protected by the National Minimum Wage Act and the Working Time Regulations. However, they do not enjoy the very important employment protection rights provided ERA 1996. In particular, such workers are very vulnerable with regard to job security. They cannot claim unfair dismissal or redundancy payments, and employing organisations and agencies can simply decide there is no available work for them to do. You could include some brief discussion concerning the Agency Workers Regulations 2011 and the extent to which they require equality of treatment with an employing organisation's permanent employees.

In your conclusion you could state, with reasons, whether or not the government should exercise its powers under s. 23 Employment Relations Act 1999 to extend such rights to workers irrespective of employee status.

Visit **www.mylawchamber.co.uk/welch** to access tools to help you develop and test your knowledge of employment law, including interactive 'You be the judge' multiple choice questions, practice exam questions with guidance, annotated weblinks, case summary and key case flashcards, legal newsfeed, legal updates and answer to Lawyers' brief simulation.

premium
my**law**chamber
unrivalled support for legal education

Chapter 3
Performance of the contract of employment

Key points In this chapter we will be looking at:

✦ Judicially implied terms imposing contractual duties on employers

✦ Judicially implied terms imposing contractual duties on employees

✦ An employer's rights to protect secret and confidential information

✦ Enforcing contractual restraints on an employee's right to work for another employer after the employment contract has ended

✦ The employer's duties regarding the health, safety and welfare of the employee

✦ The employer's duties to prevent workplace stress and bullying

Introduction

As was fully explained, when you are in employment the relationship between you and your employer is primarily regulated by your contract of employment (see Chapter 2). To a substantial extent this will be through the express terms of your contract. These will either be found in a full written contract of employment, or in the **written statement of terms** that s. 1 Employment Rights Act (ERA) 1996 requires an employer to give you if a written contract had not been used. However, even when you have been provided with a full written contract, it is unlikely to cover everything you must do at work in order properly to perform all the duties required of you under your employment contract. Conversely, you are likely to have certain rights, such as a right to be provided with work so that you can develop your professional skills, which the express terms in the contract do not identify. This is because over a period of time, which stretches back to the beginning of the last century and continues until this day, judges, in deciding specific cases, have implied terms which apply generally to all employment contracts.

We saw that a judge can imply a term into a contract of employment, in accordance with the established principles of contract law, where this is necessary to give proper effect to what the parties must have intended when the contract was first made (see Chapter 2). However, the **judicially implied terms**, with which this chapter is concerned, are regarded by judges as specifying certain rights and duties that arise naturally from the relationship between employers and their employees. These implied terms are also known as the common law rights and duties in contracts of employment. In understanding all that may be required of employers and employees in performing the contract of employment, it is important to understand the content of these judicially implied terms and to consider their impact on the employment relationship.

This chapter will focus on a relatively modern requirement imposed on employers not to act in a way which destroys the employee's trust and confidence in the employment relationship, as well as terms requiring the employee to obey reasonable instructions of the employer and to cooperate with the business needs of the employer. We shall look at an employer's legal responsibilities regarding the health, safety and welfare of the employee at the workplace; this includes actions the employer should take to protect employees from bullying or suffering from workplace stress. The chapter will also examine who owns information, which an employee possesses as a result of doing his or her job, and the extent to which an employer can prevent an employee who leaves the organisation from taking up work with a competing employer.

Judicially implied duties of the employer

Where an employer either uses a full written contract of employment or complies properly with the statutory duty to provide a written statement of terms, as required by s. 1 ERA 1996, employees will be informed of most of their important rights under the contract. However, there have been cases in which the courts have had to decide whether a contractual right should be implied, where this right is not be found in an employment contract, and whether such a right should be deemed to be implied into all contracts of employment. As a result of this process the following contractual duties are imposed on all employers.

✦ the duty to pay wages;
✦ the duty to provide work;
✦ the duty to take reasonable care;
✦ the duty to maintain mutual trust and confidence.

These duties will now be examined in turn.

The duty to pay wages

The wage or salary an employee is entitled to receive, as well as how it is calculated, will be detailed in the express terms of the contract (see Chapter 2). In the absence of a written employment contract, the information must be contained in the written statement of terms and detailed weekly or monthly in an itemised pay statement. The latter is required by s. 8 ERA 1996 and must detail deductions such as income tax, national insurance and occupational pension contributions. The net amount of wages or salary to be paid must be stated.

It is therefore going to be unusual for an employee to carry out work without there being an express agreement as to what the payment for this work will be. An exception could occur, however, if overtime working is unusual but an employee agrees to undertake overtime working on a one-off basis without the payment for this work being agreed in advance. In such a situation it will be implied into the contract that the employer must pay a reasonable remuneration for this work. What constitutes reasonable remuneration will depend on the circumstances. For example, it may be based on the employee's normal hourly rate, or it might be a higher rate if this is the norm in the organisation if overtime work is undertaken.

It is possible that in carrying out an employer's instructions the employee will incur legal liability with respect to a third party. This could occur, for example, where an employee has been authorised to borrow money on his employer's behalf, but the employer has failed to repay the loan. However, as far as the creditor was concerned it was the employee who was the actual debtor, as the creditor believed the employee was borrowing the money for his or her own purposes. If the employee repays the loan, the employer is under a duty to *indemnify* the employee by reimbursing the employee for the financial loss incurred on the employer's behalf.

It should be noted that travelling expenses and the like would not be included under this heading. However, there might be express agreement as to when such expenses could be recovered by the employee, or the right to recover such expenses might be implied into the contract by **custom and practice**. Custom and practice (as we saw in Chapter 2) can only be relied upon as a source of a term in the employment contract where the employer has consistently operated a particular practice over a long period of time.

Employers have no implied contractual right to deduct money from an employee's wages. Moreover, under s. 13(1) ERA 1996, an employer may not make deductions from an employer's wages unless such deductions have either been authorised by statute, as is the case with deductions by way of income tax and national insurance contributions, or have been agreed to in writing by an employee under, or as a result of, a term in the contract of employment.

Case Summary

Employees may present a claim to an employment tribunal to recover any sum of money which has been wrongly deducted from their pay. It was held, in *Delaney* v. *Staples* [1991] ICR 331, that withholding accrued wages is to be considered an unauthorised deduction from wages. Therefore, if, as in this case, the employer refuses to pay outstanding wages, including accrued holiday pay, to the employee on termination of the contract, then the employee can present a claim to an employment tribunal to recover the money owed.

It is, of course, permissible for the employee to sue for the outstanding debt in an ordinary civil court. However, there are cost advantages to employees in enforcing their rights through presenting claims to employment tribunals (see Chapter 1). Therefore, given the choice, employees are likely to prefer going to an employment tribunal over going to a court of law.

The duty to provide work

Employers are required to pay their employees whilst they are required to be at work, but are they obliged to give their employees work to do during such periods? Traditionally, this was only the case for those employees who were paid on a commission or piecework basis, rather than a pre-specified fixed wage or salary. In other words, employees who had to be given work to carry out in order to have an opportunity to earn their remuneration. The only other exception related to employees who needed to work in order to establish and enhance a professional reputation, for example, an actor or a singer.

For other employees, irrespective of their status, the following *dictum by* Asquith J in *Collier* v. *Sunday Referee Publishing Co Ltd* [1940] 2 KB 647 applied:

> 'It is true that a contract of employment does not necessarily, or perhaps normally, oblige the master to provide the servant with work. Provided I pay my cook her wages regularly, she cannot complain if I choose to take any or all of my meals out' (at page 160).

Interestingly, given the old fashioned language in this case reflecting the view that the relationship between employer and employee was one of master and servant, the case actually concerned a senior employee, who was the editor of a newspaper. In *Collier*, it was held that the employer was in breach of contract when it was unable to provide him with work to do as it had sold the newspaper he edited to another company. Therefore, the employer had wrongfully dismissed him, but while the contract had continued there had been no implied duty to provide him with work.

Case Summary

In *Langston* v. *AUEW* [1974] ICR 180, an alternative, and more modern, proposition was put forward by Lord Denning:

> 'In these days an employer, when employing a skilled man, is bound to provide him with work. By which I mean that the man should be given the opportunity of doing his work when it is available and he is ready and willing to do it. A skilled man takes a pride in his work. He does not do it merely to earn money. He does it so as to make his contribution to the well-being of all. He does it so as to keep himself busy, and not idle. To use his skill, and to improve it' (at page 190).

The case would not arise today as it concerned a **closed shop agreement** between a company and a trade union under which the company agreed not to employ workers who were not members of the union. Such agreements can no longer be enforced and have fallen into disuse. In this case, Langston left the union and the employer suspended but continued to pay him. Nevertheless, even though the case is not relevant to the contemporary law, the idea that all employees who need to develop their professional skills and expertise must be given appropriate work to carry out is one that accords with modern thinking, and is generally regarded as the correct legal position today.

Indeed, it was applied by the Court of Appeal in *Provident Financial Group plc* v. *Hayward* [1989] ICR 160 in the context of whether there is a duty to provide work which restricts the ability of an employer to impose **garden leave** on an employee. Essentially, this is where employees are required to work out long notice periods before they are able to resign, but are instructed not to come to work. Typically this will be to prevent employees from continuing to access **confidential information** and/or have dealings with the organisation's customers. In *Hayward*, it was held that in the absence of an express term permitting 'garden leave' the imposition of it constitutes a breach of the duty to provide work. Such express terms will not be enforceable if they are deemed to be in **restraint of trade** (see below).

However, an express term permitting an employer to put an employee on 'garden leave' will be enforced where the employer has legitimate commercial interests to protect, such as preventing competitors from obtaining confidential information, providing the term is reasonable. In particular, the term's duration must be no longer than is commercially necessary to protect the employer's interests. For example, in *Crystal Palace FC Ltd* v. *Bruce*, which is considered in further detail below, a period of 'garden leave' of

Case Summary

two months was considered reasonable when Steve Bruce wanted to break his contract of employment with Crystal Palace in order to manage Birmingham City in a situation where both clubs were in the same football league and had not completed their fixtures against each other.

The case of *William Hill Organisation Ltd* v. *Tucker* [1998] IRLR 313 provides an example of an employer who sought to put an employee on garden leave without there being an express term in the contract permitting this. The company did this when Tucker tendered his notice of resignation so that he could leave and work for a rival firm of bookmakers. The Court of Appeal upheld a decision of the High Court that Tucker was a skilled employee who was entitled to be provided with work whilst serving his notice period. The irony of William Hill's actions was that, as it had broken Tucker's contract, he was entitled to leave the company immediately to take up employment with the competing firm.

The duty to take reasonable care

All employers are subject to the common law duty to take reasonable care with respect to the health, safety and welfare of their employees, as well as complying with various statutory duties imposed by legislation and the requirements of EU law. This duty will be considered in greater detail later on in this chapter in the context of **employers' negligence**.

The duty to maintain mutual trust and confidence

The common law rights and duties are not cast in stone, and can be varied and added to as time progresses. The most important judicially implied term to be developed in modern times is the duty on the employer to maintain **mutual trust and confidence**. The duty was identified during the 1970s – particularly in order to expand the circumstances where a resignation by an employee could constitute a **constructive dismissal**. Such a dismissal occurs where an employee resigns in response to a repudiatory, that is, very serious, breach of contract by an employer, which entitles the employee to regard the employment contract as having come to an end. The nature of a **repudiatory breach** of contract will be explained and discussed fully later (see the following two chapters). Case law has established that the implied duty of trust and confidence is a fundamental term of an employment contract.

> the implied duty of trust and confidence is a fundamental term of an employment contract

The classic statement of the duty was provided by Browne-Wilkinson J. in *Woods* v. *W/M Car Services* [1981] ICR 666 EAT. He stated:

'it is clearly established that there is implied in a contract of employment a term that the employers will not, without reasonable and proper cause, conduct themselves in a manner calculated or likely to destroy or seriously damage the relationship of confidence and trust between employer and employee . . . To constitute a breach of this implied term it is not necessary to show the employer intended any repudiation of the contract: the tribunal's function is to look at the employer's conduct as a whole and determine whether it is such that its effect, judged reasonably and sensibly, is such that the employee cannot be expected to put up with it . . .' (at pages 670–71).

Out and about

The case of *Woods* is interesting because the EAT and the industrial tribunal took a different view, on the facts, as to whether the employer had committed a repudiatory breach of contract. However, the EAT can only overturn a tribunal's decision where the tribunal can be regarded as having made an error of law (see Chapter 1). The EAT must accept the tribunal's view of the facts.

Read the EAT and the Court of Appeal decisions in *Woods* v. *W/M Car Services* [1981] ICR 666 and [1982] ICR 693 respectively either from the Industrial Cases Reports or a database such as WESTLAW, and carry out the following activities:

1. Summarise the facts of the case.

2. Identify how the EAT viewed the employer's behaviour and therefore the decision it would have reached had it constituted the original tribunal.

3. What view of the employer's behaviour did the Court of Appeal take?

Many of the decided cases in which employers have been found to be in breach of this duty have revolved around the issues of verbal and physical abuse and harassment. Essentially, the employer's breach of contract in such circumstances constitutes a failure to treat the employee with respect, and this connects with the general issue of bullying which will be considered later in this chapter. An analogous situation is where an employer or senior manager seeks to humiliate an employee. For example, in *Courtaulds Northern Textiles* v. *Andrew* [1979] IRLR 84, a manager insulted Andrew by accusing him of not being able 'to do the bloody job anyway'. In fact, the manager did not even genuinely believe that Andrew was incompetent. It was held that this behaviour by a senior employee meant that the company, as the employer, was in breach of the duty to maintain mutual trust and confidence that it owed to Andrew.

Case Summary

Another example of a way in which the duty to maintain mutual trust and confidence may be broken is provided by the case of *Malik* v. *Bank of Credit & Commerce International* [1997] ICR 606. The bank went into liquidation after its directors had been found guilty of fraudulent trading. Malik was one of the bank's employees and was entirely innocent of any dishonest behaviour, but his reputation was adversely affected as a result of the bank's activities. It was held by the House of Lords that an employer is in breach of the implied duty of trust and confidence if it wilfully conducts its business in a dishonest and corrupt manner.

Case Summary

As will be explained further later (in Chapters 4 and 5), breach of this duty can give rise to an action for **damages** as well as enabling an employee to claim wrongful and/or unfair dismissal. In *Malik*, it was held by the Law Lords that in the exceptional circumstances of the case he was entitled to 'stigma' damages to compensate him for loss of his professional reputation.

Generally, an employer is not under a duty to provide a reference for an employee who wishes to take up employment with another employer. If the employer does supply a reference then the employer is subject to a duty owed to the recipient of the reference to take reasonable care in ensuring the reference is accurate. This is part of the operation of the normal principles of the tort of negligence. The employer will be in breach of the implied term of mutual trust and confidence, with respect to the employee, if the reference creates a misleading picture of the employee in a way that the employer knows

**Case
Summary**

or ought to know will damage the employee's chances of securing new employment. In *TSB Bank plc* v. *Harris* [2000] IRLR 157, the employer's reference suggested that Harris had dishonestly forged a customer's signature when, in fact, she had initialled a form to show that the signature had been changed. It was held that the employer had acted in breach of trust and confidence.

**Case
Summary**

In *Goold Ltd* v. *McConnell* [1995] IRLR 516 the EAT held that failure by the employer to provide a **grievance procedure** also constituted a repudiatory breach through breach of the implied duty of trust and confidence. McConnell suffered a substantial reduction in his take-home pay as a result of the company being in financial difficulties. McConnell sought to pursue a grievance with the company chairman but was prevented from doing this by his immediate manager. His terms of employment contained no reference to any grievance procedure. McConnell resigned and claimed constructive unfair dismissal. It was held that the right to obtain redress against a grievance was fundamental since the working environment might well lead to employees experiencing difficulties for a variety of reasons, including the fact that authority and control was sometimes exercised by persons insufficiently experienced to exercise it wisely. Therefore, as McConnell had been unable to present a formal grievance he had been constructively and unfairly dismissed.

Reflective practice

What do the above cases tell you about the nature of the implied term of trust and confidence as defined in *Woods* by Browne-Wilkinson J? The term is a dynamic one which is capable of further development in terms of the type of employer behaviour that it can cover. The articles by Brodie in the *Industrial Law Journal*, which are cited in the 'Further reading' section of this chapter, shed further light on the nature of the term. In the next section of this chapter we consider the case of *United Bank* v. *Akhtar*. This case demonstrates that contrary to the normal position in contract law the implied duty of trust and confidence can override an express term in an employment contract.

Your reading of the EAT and Court of Appeal decisions in *Woods* should have enabled you to appreciate that what could be considered bad behaviour by an employer will not always amount to a breach of trust and confidence – in which case a resignation by an employee cannot constitute a constructive dismissal. As you may have ascertained, in this case the company had taken over the business in which Woods had been employed and, contrary to a promise initially given to her, persistently sought to persuade her to accept changes to her working conditions with respect to pay and hours. The tribunal decided that the company had not committed a repudiatory breach of contract. The EAT disagreed with this conclusion, but decided that it had no jurisdiction to overturn the decision of the tribunal as the latter had neither misdirected itself in law nor taken an unreasonable view of the facts. The Court of Appeal confirmed that the EAT was right to conclude it had no jurisdiction to overturn that decision. However, the judgments in the Court of Appeal also suggest the court agreed with the decision of the tribunal. This is seen most clearly from the judgment of Watkins LJ in which he states: 'employers should not be put in a position where, through the wrongful refusal of their employees to accept change, they are prevented from introducing improved business methods' (at page 702).

The case demonstrates that although it is clear that the implied duty of trust and confidence is a fundamental term in any employment contract, judges may disagree on the facts as to whether or not it has been breached.

Judicially implied duties of the employee

A statutory written statement of terms is not required to specify the contractual duties that an employee is required to perform in undertaking his or her job (as explained in Chapter 2). All that is required is that the statement contains a job title or at most a brief job description. Similarly, many full written contracts of employment will not list all the duties an employee may be required to undertake. Employers are not required to draft disciplinary rules, though many chose to do so. Where employers do have such rules they should document these rules, along with **disciplinary procedures**, and inform employees where these rules and procedures can be located. However, as is the case with an employee's duties, there may still be rules which are not specified in any written document but which are still binding on employees. This is because the overall effect of the judicially implied duties on employees is to flesh out written statements and written contracts in respect of what an employer may require an employee to do.

The following contractual duties are imposed on all employees:

✦ the duty of obedience;

✦ the duty of co-operation;

✦ the duty to take reasonable care;

✦ the duty of fidelity.

These contractual duties will now be examined in turn.

The duty of obedience

The implied **duty of obedience** is the main term which has the effect of fleshing out in practice what the employer can require the employee to do in fulfilling his or her contractual obligations. The employee must obey all instructions of the employer provided they are reasonable. An instruction will be reasonable if it is consistent with the express terms of an employee's contract and relates to the work that the employee is contracted to carry out. For example, an employee is instructed to prioritise a particular job over others that form part of the employee's scheduled workload on a particular day or over a particular week. Providing an instruction is reasonable, it does not matter that the instruction is not to be found in any written document. However, as shown by *Morrish* v. *Henleys (Folkestone) Ltd* [1973] 2 All ER 137, an instruction is not reasonable if it is unlawful. In this case the employee refused to connive with his employer in falsifying records for the latter's personal gain. It was held that he was not guilty of disobedience.

> the employee must obey all instructions of the employer provided they are reasonable

Case Summary

Typically, breach of the duty of obedience will result in the employee being disciplined and this may result in an employee being given a disciplinary warning or, if permitted by the contract, suspended without pay for a period of time. Very serious disobedience by an employee, either as a one-off incident or through a series of events, may constitute repudiation, that is, a rejection, by an employee of his obligations under the employment contract. A repudiatory breach of the employment contract goes to the root, or very essence, of the contract, and therefore destroys its purpose. This permits the employer to dismiss the employee summarily, that is, instantly without notice. Issues of discipline and dismissal will be considered fully later (see the following two chapters).

Dress codes

The right of an employer to impose a dress code on employees is an interesting example of where an employee's duty of obedience may arise. Employers may, orally or in writing, stipulate dress codes for their employees, but a requirement to dress, or not to dress, in a particular way does not need to be contained as an express term in a contract of employment for it to be enforceable. Such rules of employment can be drawn up by employers outside of the framework of the employment contract. An advantage to an employer of drafting rules, which are not part of the contract of employment, is that such rules can be changed or added to as and when the employer decides that this is appropriate. As the rule is non-contractual it can be varied unilaterally by the employer. Acceptance of an amended or new rule by the employee is not required in order for that rule to be enforceable. Providing the rule is reasonable, the employee is contractually obliged to comply with it.

Case Summary

The following cases demonstrate the types of dress codes that employers may decide to impose. In *Schmidt* v. *Austicks Bookshop Ltd* [1978] ICR 85, it was held by the EAT that an employer could impose a requirement on a woman who worked in its bookshop to wear a skirt and to prohibit her from wearing trousers. This decision was approved in *Smith* v. *Safeway plc* [1996] IRLR 456 where the Court of Appeal held that it was not unfair to dismiss an employee who refused to have his hair cut to collar length. In *Department for Work & Pensions* v. *Thompson* [2004] IRLR 348, it was held that the employer could enforce an instruction that male employees should wear collars and ties. In all of these cases arguments to the effect that the dress codes discriminated on grounds of sex were rejected. It was accepted that the dress requirements were gender specific but it was held that an employer may impose such dress codes providing employees of the opposite gender are subject to equivalent requirements.

Essentially, the tribunals and courts accept that employers can impose dress requirements on employees of both genders requiring them to be smart and to dress in accordance with different conventional standards for men and women. In *Smith*, for example, it was accepted that he was prepared to wear his hair in a pony tail in the same way that his female colleagues did whilst at work, but the Court of Appeal rejected the argument that the rule should not have been imposed as it prevented him from having long hair in his private life. The court argued there were equivalent restrictions for the women employees in that they could not have shaven or partly shaven hair styles.

Case Summary

A variant of these decisions is provided by *Boychuk* v. *Symons Holdings Ltd* [1977] IRLR 395. Boychuk was a lesbian and proud of her sexuality. She was employed as an audit clerk and her duties brought her into contact with the public. She was dismissed for persistently insisting on wearing a badge bearing the words 'Lesbians Ignite'. It was held that the tribunal had not erred in law in finding her dismissal to be fair. It was within the employer's discretion to instruct Boychuk not to wear a badge which could be expected to be offensive to fellow employees and customers.

It would be interesting to discover if there would be a similar outcome to the *Boychuk* case today. Attitudes have changes since the 1970s and, arguably, being offended by a badge such as the one that Boychuk wore can be regarded as the product of homophobic attitudes. As explained later (in Chapter 7), employees have the right not be subjected to discrimination on the grounds of their sexual orientation, and a dismissal of an openly gay employee to avoid giving offence to others could constitute unlawful discrimination and therefore unfair dismissal.

More generally, there will be different opinions as to whether employers should have powers to impose dress requirements which are not needed, for example, to satisfy health and safety standards. However, it is clear that the law does not require employers to demonstrate that dress requirements are commercially necessary, for example, in order to attract or keep customers or clients. It is sufficient that the dress requirements are in accordance with the perceived norms of society. However, it can be commented that ever since the cultural revolution of the 1960s, many people will, at some point in their lives, have adopted unconventional styles of dress and overall appearance. Are most people today, in their capacities as customers and clients of a business, really shocked by the unconventional appearance of a particular employee that they happen to be dealing with? Similarly, should a gay employee be prevented from making explicit his or her sexual orientation? These issues have also arisen in the context of religious dress and the display of religious symbols and will be considered further later (see Chapter 7).

It is the case that, on occasion, an employer's dress code can attract unfavourable media coverage.

Law in action

A number of newspapers, including the *Guardian* and the *Daily Mail*, reported on the plight of Melanie Stark, who was a sales assistant in the HMV department of Harrods. Stark felt obliged to leave her job after she was put under pressure for refusing to comply with the store's dress code which stated: 'Full makeup at all times: base, blusher, full eyes (not too heavy), lipstick, lip liner and gloss are worn at all times and maintained discreetly (please take into account the store display lighting which has a "washing out" effect).'

Despite being described by one manager as among the best of their employees, and had worked without makeup for four years, she was on two occasions sent home and, on another, sent to work in the stockroom for refusing to wear makeup.

Melanie Stark resigned from the job as she said the store's attitude to her had left her 'exhausted, stressed and upset'. She was quoted as saying: 'Makeup can change your features completely, especially if I was to wear all of what they were asking. I would look like a different person to me. And I never chose to look like that.'

At the time of writing, this had not resulted in legal action, but the *Guardian's* legal expert was of the view that she could have had a claim under the Equality Act 2010, even though Harrods also had a dress code for men. Such a claim could also have been accompanied by claims for constructive **wrongful** and **unfair dismissal**.

Source: Caroline Davies (2011) 'Harrods "Ladies" code drives out Sales Assistant', the *Guardian*, 1 July.

It is the case that a dress code, which may not be considered to be sex discrimination, may constitute race discrimination and will be unlawful on that basis. In *G* v. *St Gregory's Catholic Science College Governors* [2011] EWHC 1452, G, who was African-Caribbean, wore his hair in cornrows. G was turned away from the school, on his first day, as he was told that his hairstyle was contrary to the school's dress code for boys. Black girls at the school were permitted to wear their hair in cornrows. It was held that, on the basis of the

Case Summary

above case law, there was no sex discrimination as cornrows worn by boys could be considered by the school to be unconventional. However, the wearing of cornrows was part of G's family tradition and was of cultural and ethnic importance to him. In these circumstances, refusing to admit him to the school constituted unlawful race discrimination. This is not, of course, a case decided in the context of employment, but there seems no reason in principle why it should not apply to an individual refused employment, or dismissed from employment, in similar circumstances.

Mobility clauses

It is possible for a court on the basis of **business efficacy** to imply a **mobility clause**, requiring an employee to move to a new place of work, into an employment contract (see Chapter 2). This was so, for example, in *Courtaulds Northern Spinning Ltd* v. *Sibson* [1988] ICR 451, where a lorry driver could be required to operate from any depot within a reasonable travelling distance from his home. In this case the additional travel involved in moving to a new depot was about one mile.

However, normally a mobility clause will be an express term of the contract; in which case an employee who refuses to move to a new place of work in accordance with it will be breach of the duty of obedience. The mere fact that a mobility clause is in a contract will normally be sufficient to enable an employer to invoke it. As held in *White* v. *Reflecting Roadstuds Ltd* [1991] ICR 733, an employer does not have to show it is reasonable to require an employee to move to a new workplace. In this case, it did not matter that the employee would have suffered a pay cut had he moved to a new place of work. Refusal to have moved would have constituted disobedience on the employee's part, and therefore his resignation could not be regarded as constructive dismissal.

As held in *Ottoman Bank* v. *Chakarian* [1930] AC 277, an employee can refuse to move to a country in which his life is in danger, as was the case for Chakarian who refused to transfer to a branch of his bank in Turkey where he was under the threat of a death sentence for his dissident political activities. However, as clarified in the very similar case of *Bouzourou* v. *Ottoman Bank* [1930] AC 271, an employee can only argue this where it can be proved that the threat to life or liberty is a real one. For example, in *Walmesly* v. *Udec Refrigeration Ltd* [1972] IRLR 80, it was held that an employee was in breach of contract in refusing to move from England to Belfast at the height of the Provisional IRA's bombing campaign in the early 1970s. Belfast was a dangerous place, but Walmesly had no connection with state or paramilitary forces, and therefore was in no greater danger than any other civilian living and working in the north of Ireland at that time.

A mobility clause cannot be enforced in a manner that constitutes breach of the employer's duty to maintain mutual trust and confidence. In *United Bank Ltd* v. *Akhtar* [1989] IRLR 507, Akhtar was instructed with very little notice to transfer from his bank's headquarters in Leeds to a branch in Birmingham. Such a transfer required Akhtar to relocate himself and his family, and the bank both refused him time to do this or, contrary to his contract, consider assisting him in the move by contributing to his relocation expenses. It was held that the manner in which the express mobility clause was invoked destroyed mutual trust and confidence and therefore Akhtar's resignation amounted to a constructive dismissal. It was the bank, not Akhtar, who had repudiated the contract of employment. As stated above, this case demonstrates that the implied term of trust and confidence is a fundamental term in an employment contract and has an overriding effect on express terms.

Case Summary

Case Summary

Case Summary

Case Summary

The duty of cooperation

As well as being under a duty of obedience, employees are subject to a wider **duty to cooperate** with the employer. This may require them to work more flexibly than is required by a strict interpretation of the terms of their contracts or, as illustrated by the *Creswell* case explained below, to perform their jobs in a different way to how they have done so in the past. A general example of the duty to cooperate with the employer by working flexibly would be an obligation to accept an instruction to cover for an absent colleague by doing some or all of that person's work as well as or instead of the work that the employee is normally required to do.

A duty to cooperate in such circumstances is not without limits. The work the employee is instructed to do must be consistent with an employee's skills set and with the employee's general role and status in the organisation. For example, a professional employee could not normally be expected to undertake menial work such as cleaning the office because the normal cleaner had not reported for work. It is not clear whether a duty to cooperate would extend to an employee being obliged to work overtime in circumstances where there was no express contractual obligation to this effect. Arguably, such a requirement could only be imposed on an employee in a genuine emergency, such as the need for work to be covered for health and safety reasons.

The origin of the implied duty to cooperate lies in case law from the world of industrial conflict, which established that the wilful impeding or obstruction of an employer's business is a breach of an employment contract. For example, in *Secretary of State of Employment* v. *ASLEF* [1972] 2 All ER 949, train drivers were instructed by their trade union, ASLEF, to 'work to rule'. This included following a number of safety checks contained in the rulebook before a train could be moved from any rail station. The rulebook was very out of date and adhering to it strictly resulted in a severe disruption of the railway network. The Court of Appeal held that the train drivers were acting in breach of contract as in following the rulebook they were in breach of their implied duty to cooperate with their employer. Further similar cases in the context of industrial action will be discussed later Chapter (see 9).

Case Summary

A very important consequence of the duty of cooperation is that employees must adapt to new methods and techniques in the way that they do their jobs even though such changes may mean developing and using new skills. In *Cresswell* v. *Board of Inland Revenue* [1984] IRLR 190, workers employed by the Inland Revenue, who had always worked with paper filing systems, were held to be in breach of contract in refusing to operate new computerised systems. It is important to appreciate that, where an employer introduces new ways of doing a job, it is implied into the contract that the employee's duty to cooperate with change is conditional on the employer having first provided reasonable training. Computerisation is, of course, not an issue in today's world of work, but the *Cresswell* case is good law in any future situation where new technologies and methods of working are created and enable particular work to be undertaken more efficiently.

Case Summary

The duty of care

This is discussed below in the context of an employer's **vicarious liability** for a tort committed by an employee whilst at work.

The duty of fidelity

All employees owe a **duty of fidelity** or loyalty to their employers during the currency of their contracts of employment. This is particularly important in circumstances in which the employee has access to the trade secrets or other **confidential information** which belongs to the employer, or has personal contact with and therefore influence over the employer's customers or clients. It is quite likely that readers who gain professional employment will be in this position and therefore this duty of fidelity will be of direct relevance to you. It is important to understand that there are limits to the scope of this implied duty and that, generally, the duty ceases to exist once the contract of employment has come to an end. Therefore, an employer may secure greater protection of its commercial interests through the inclusion of appropriate express terms in the contract. However, as explained below, such express terms will be invalid and unenforceable if they are unreasonable because they are wider than necessary to protect the employer's legitimate interests. Again, if you enter the professions or the commercial world you may well find such express terms in your employment contract.

Moonlighting

Generally, unless there are express terms in the employment contract to the contrary, an employee is free to 'moonlight', that is, work for other employers or himself outside of working hours. The duty of fidelity will only apply to prevent the employee from doing this where the employee has access to trade secrets. This is illustrated by *Hivac Ltd* v. *Park Royal Scientific Instruments Ltd* [1946] 1 Ch 169. In this case, Hivak Ltd secured an injunction against Park Royal Ltd, its main competitor, to prevent it from employing its employees in their spare time. The employees concerned had access to trade secrets. There was no evidence that they had disclosed these secrets but their employment by Park Royal Ltd meant there was a potential danger that secret information would be disclosed. Therefore, the employees were in breach of their duty of fidelity to Hivak Ltd by working for Park Royal Ltd.

An employee can be restrained, that is prevented, by an injunction from acting in breach of the duty of fidelity. As demonstrated by the *Hivak* case, an alternative course of action by the employer is to sue the competing employer. This is possible because it is a tort for anyone to induce an employee to act in breach of the contract of employment. Park Royal Ltd had committed this tort by recruiting the employees of Hivak Ltd and therefore inducing them to act in breach of their duty of fidelity.

Employers can prohibit 'moonlighting' through an express term in the contract of employment requiring exclusivity of service. However, an absolute prohibition on working for other employers will constitute a **restraint of trade**. Therefore, employers are advised to restrict such prohibitions to working for specified competitors, or by requiring employers to obtain the employer's permission prior to taking up additional forms of employment. An example of a reasonable term regarding exclusivity of service is to be found in clause 13 of the employment contract between some universities and its academic staff. This clause is set out below in 'Documenting the law' later in this chapter.

Fidelity and misuse of confidential information

Information which may be protected during the employment will cover trade secrets and other commercial and confidential information that the employee has acquired directly or indirectly within that employment. An employer has a wide discretion in identifying the type of information which is to be regarded as confidential and is not to be revealed to other persons without the employer's consent. Examples of such information include the personal details of the employer's staff, the details of any disciplinary issues that may have arisen within the organisation, the employer's business plans and the employer's pricing and marketing strategies.

The employer is in a strong position to enforce confidentiality whilst the employment lasts, as disclosure of confidential information can be regarded as gross misconduct which entitles the employer to dismiss an employee without notice. However, post-employment, the duty of fidelity is only enforceable with regard to trade secrets and analogous information. Such information must be secret in that it does not constitute knowledge that is also available outside of the employer's organisation and must give the employer a distinct competitive advantage in the relevant market. Examples include inventions, chemical formulae, new processes and new technological advances. A major example of such trade secrets in today's world will be the creation of new unique software and operating systems for laptop and tablet computers, smart phones, MP3 players, gaming consoles and the like.

> post-employment, the duty of fidelity is only enforceable with regard to trade secrets

Lists of the names and contact details of an employer's customers and clients are analogous to trade secrets. Therefore, the duty of fidelity also continues to apply to this type of information even after the employment has ended. In *Roger Bullivant Ltd* v. *Ellis* [1987] ICR 464, Ellis copied and removed a list of the company's customers with the express purpose of using the information to set up a competing business. It was held that he could be restrained from using this information for his own business purposes, as information consisting of customer details continued to belong to the company after Ellis had left its employ.

Case Summary

What is known as the 'equitable springboard doctrine' provides the basis for granting an injunction against an employee even though the employment contract has ended. The theory is that the employee can only have retained information, such as a trade secret or a list of customers, by taking away the information, without the employer's consent, whilst still in the latter's employ. This breach of the duty of fidelity by the employee provides the springboard for a court being able to enforce the contract against the employee even after it has come to an end. A court is able to use its equitable jurisdiction to prevent an employee from profiting from such a breach of contract to the detriment of the former employer.

In older case law the practical ways in which the duty would be broken was through copying or deliberately memorising the information. Newer ways of breaking the duty can be demonstrated by an employee retaining a memory stick on which the information is stored. Alternatively, an employee may, legitimately, have been able to access an employer's password protected database from home, but will have broken this duty by copying information contained in the database to a personal hard disk, smart tablet and the like without the employer's consent.

Distinguishing between trade secrets and confidential information

It is important to distinguish between trade secrets and information which is confidential but which falls short of a trade secret or information that is analogous to a trade secret such as lists of customers or clients. A term cannot be implied into an employee's contract to prevent the employee from using confidential information for his or her own purposes once the employment has come to an end. As is explained further below, an employee can only be prevented from using or disclosing confidential information, once the employment has ended, if there is an express confidentiality clause in the employee's contract.

Case Summary

In *Faccenda Chicken Ltd* v. *Fowler* [1986] ICR 297; IRLR 69, Fowler, in his capacity as the company's sales manager, had access to the detailed sales information of the company such as names and addresses of customers, their requirements and the prices they paid. Fowler did not copy this information or deliberately commit it to memory with the intention of using the information to his employer's detriment. He left the company, and formed his own company in competition with his former employer. Several of Faccenda Chicken's employees also left the company in order to work for Fowler. There were no terms in Fowler's contract, or those of the other employees who joined his business, concerning the use of confidential information or trade secrets. The only possibility therefore was that Fowler had acted in breach of his duty of fidelity. The Court of Appeal held that the information possessed by Fowler constituted confidential information but not trade secrets. As Fowler had not acted in breach of fidelity during his employment with Faccenda Chicken, he could not be prevented from using this confidential information once his employment with the company had come to an end.

It can be difficult in practice to distinguish between confidential information and trade secrets, and in Faccenda Chicken, Neill LJ suggested the following factors should be taken into account:

✦ The nature of the employment – does the work that the employee regularly undertakes require the employee to use information which he or she knows or can be expected to realise is of a sensitive nature in the form of a trade secret?

✦ The nature of the information – is the information of a sort which would normally be understood as constituting a trade secret, or is it material which, whilst not strictly speaking a trade secret, is of such a highly confidential nature as to require the same protection as a trade secret?

✦ Has the employer made it clear to the employee the information is a trade secret or is confidential in nature?

✦ Can the relevant information can be easily isolated from other information which the employee is free to use or disclose? If so, then it is easier to regard such information as a trade secret.

Table 3.1 summarises the differences between different types of information and an employer's rights to prevent misuse or disclosure.

One practical way in which an employer can seek to define confidential information and an employee's duties with respect to such information is by express terms in the contract. Such terms may be called confidentiality or non-disclosure clauses or covenants. Again, as set out below, clauses in the national contract between universities and their academic staff provide a good illustration of the use of such terms. In *SBJ Stephenson Ltd* v. *Mandy* [2000] IRLR 233 an insurance broker was subject to a term in his contract that after the termination of the contract he was prohibited from disclosing information about the affairs or identity of the employer's clients. It was held that this term was enforceable and could be applied even to those clients whom Mandy had simply remembered through doing business with them. It made no difference that he had not deliberately committed client details to his memory.

Case Summary

Table 3.1 Types of information and an employer's rights: *Faccenda Chicken* v. *Fowler*

Types of information	Example	Employer's rights
Trade secret	Secret formula or process unique to that employer	Employee can be prevented from disclosing/misusing this information during and after employment through the duty of fidelity.
Information analogous to a trade secret	Names and contact details of the employer's customers and clients	Employee can be prevented from disclosing/misusing this information during and after employment through the duty of fidelity.
Confidential information	Pricing and marketing strategies, identity of employer's customers or clients	Duty of fidelity applies to prevent employee from disclosing/misusing this information during the contract but not after it has ended. Duty of fidelity continues to apply where 'garden leave' can be imposed by an express term in the contract. Non-disclosure clauses can be enforced after the contract has ended.
General knowledge and skill	Professional or technical expertise developed through doing a particular type of work	Employer can include a term in the employment contract requiring exclusivity of service which prohibits the employee working for competitors. Employee cannot be prevented from using such knowledge once the employment has ended.

It should be noted that there are limits on the type of information which can be subject to non-disclosure clauses once the employment has come to an end. An employee cannot be prevented from using any general knowledge, skills or expertise, for his or her own benefit or for that of a new employer, which he or she acquires or develops simply through doing a particular job. For example, a trainee solicitor may well have learned of the expertise of particular barristers as a result of having contact with them whilst working for a particular firm. The trainee could not be prevented from drawing on this knowledge for the benefit of any other firm in which he is subsequently employed. There must be some way in which the information involved is special to that employer and is not available elsewhere in the same profession or industry.

Garden leave

An alternative contractual mechanism to the use of a confidentiality clause, and one which keeps the duty of fidelity alive, is placing the employee on 'garden leave'. As detailed above, an employer is likely to be in breach of the duty to provide work if the employee is placed on 'garden leave' without there being an express terms in the employment contract permitting the employer to do this. This is particularly important as it is the same type of employee that an employer might want to work out a relatively long period of notice as will be covered by the duty to provide work.

However, such terms are also *prima facie*, that is, initially to be regarded as a restraint of trade (see below). Therefore, such a term will be enforced only if it is reasonable. An employer must be able to show that it will be detrimental to its interests to allow an employee to leave and work for a competing employer without first serving a long period of notice. Moreover, there must be a reason to justify preventing the employee from being at work whist working out his or her notice period. Such reasons will include removing the employee's access to confidential information and his or her personal contact with the employer's customers and clients. If the employer does not have a legitimate commercial interest to protect, or the period of 'garden leave' is longer than necessary, the term will not be enforceable.

There is one important difference between a term imposing 'garden leave' and a restraint that continues to apply after the contract has ended. As explained below, the latter will normally only be applied strictly in accordance with the words used in the contract, and if these words mean the restraint is wider than necessary then it will be declared void and unenforceable. However, a court may interpret a 'garden leave' clause so that it applies to the extent that the court considers reasonable.

Case Summary

In *Symbian Ltd* v. *Christensen* [2001] IRLR 77, Christensen, a computer software sales executive, was placed on 'garden leave' and prevented from working for anyone during the notice period of six months. Christensen wished to work for Microsoft, the only real competitor. The court held that although the scope of the clause was too wide in that it applied to any other company it could be interpreted as applying only to Microsoft and thus enforced on that basis.

Case Summary

One context in which it appears to be increasingly common to find 'garden leave' clauses is in the contracts of managers of professional football teams. The case of *Crystal Palace FC Ltd* v. *Bruce* [2001] All ER (D) 331 NOV (unreported), illustrates why such terms are being used and the judicial view of them. At the time the case occurred, Steve Bruce was the manager of Crystal Palace. Bruce wished to leave the club to become the manager of Birmingham FC. Crystal Palace sought an injunction to enforce a 'garden leave' clause to prevent him from doing this. Burton J decided that Crystal Palace might well have legitimate interests to protect as it and Birmingham were both in the First Division and indeed were both rivals for a play-off position at the end of the 2001/02 season. Therefore, Steve Bruce's departure to manage Birmingham could have been detrimental to Crystal Palace's prospects for the rest of the season. Bruce could have used inside knowledge of the club, its coaching methods and the team's strengths and weaknesses to the benefit of Birmingham and the disadvantage of Crystal Palace. The court granted an injunction for a short period of around two months to restrain Bruce from leaving Crystal Palace in breach of contract.

Whistleblowing and protected disclosures

On the basis of the above it can be seen that employers are generally able to prevent 'whistleblowing' by an employee who discloses to the outside world incidents which have occurred within the employer's organisation. An employee who reveals such information, contrary to the employer's instructions, will be guilty of disobedience and this may well amount to gross misconduct. However, s. 43 ERA 1996 protects employees from dismissal, or being subjected to any other form of detriment, where they have made protected disclosures.

A disclosure may be so protected if, for example, an employee reports criminal acts to the police. For the statutory protection to apply, the employee must have acted in good faith and not for personal gain. There must also have been a good reason for the employee disclosing information outside of the employing organisation. For example, the employee has gone to the police because the employee reasonably believes evidence of a crime will be concealed or destroyed if the employee makes the disclosure to the employer.

> the employee must have acted in good faith and not for personal gain

There is also an overriding requirement that in all the circumstances of the case it was reasonable for the employee to have made the disclosure. Relevant circumstances include the identity of the person to whom the disclosure is made. It might not be reasonable, for example, for an employee to disclose criminal behaviour, which the employer has sought to conceal, to the press unless the employee has first gone to the police, and the police have failed to take any action. Alternatively, it may be generally reasonable for an employee to report such matters to his or her trade union in order to seek advice as to what further action the employee should take,

As is explained later (see Chapter 5) there are circumstances where the dismissal of an employee will be automatically unfair. Where an employee is dismissed for an automatically unfair reason then a claim of unfair dismissal must succeed and the employee will be entitled to receive the remedies for unfair dismissal (as explained in Chapter 5). Under s. 103A ERA 1996, a dismissal for making a protected disclosure is an example of an **automatically unfair dismissal**. Where an employee has been subjected to any form of detriment short of dismissal, such as demotion, a claim can be brought under s. 47B. This section also protects workers who are not employees. Where a worker is dismissed, although he or she cannot claim unfair dismissal, the worker can bring a claim under s. 47B.

Documenting the law

The below provisions concerning exclusivity, patents, confidential information and copyrights are from the contract of employment of academics in higher education (which is otherwise set out in Chapter 2). The provisions are instructive as they can be regarded as reasonable and therefore fully enforceable in a court of law. Overall, the terms can be seen as striking a balance between the interests of the employer and the professional interests of the employee.

13 EXCLUSIVITY OF SERVICE

13.1 External work which is supportive of your professional responsibilities is encouraged by the University.

13.2 Before you enter into an obligation to undertake any external work, including consultancy, you must inform (the institution); however, by way of exception, this requirement does not apply to the following:

external examining;

acting as an assessor or moderator;

the production of scholarly works such as books, articles and papers;

any other activity specified in the Staff Handbook as not coming within this requirement.

13.3 (The institution) will then decide (within 5 working days or whatever other period may be agreed as being reasonable in all the circumstances) if that work will interfere with the performance of your professional responsibilities, or compete or conflict with the interests of (the institution), in which case (the institution) may at its sole discretion require you not to undertake the work; such a requirement will not be made unreasonably, will be subject to full consultation with yourself and, if made, will be accompanied by full written reasons for it.

13.4 Where it is intended to use the facilities of (the institution) in connection with external work, then prior approval is required in accordance with procedures set out in the Staff Handbook.

14 PATENTS AND INVENTIONS

14.1 The provisions of sections 39, 40, 41, 42 and 43 of the Patents Act 1977 relating to the ownership of employees' inventions and the compensation of employees for certain inventions are acknowledged by (the institution) and by you.

14.2 You agree that by virtue of the nature of your duties and the responsibilities arising from them you have a special obligation to further the interests of (the institution).

14.3 Any matter or thing capable of being patented under the Patents Act 1977, made, developed or discovered by you either alone or in concert, whilst in the performance of your normal duties, duties specifically assigned to you or arising out of anything done by you to which paragraph 14.2 applies, shall forthwith be disclosed to (the institution) and subject to the provision of the Patents Act shall belong to and be the absolute property of (the institution).

14.4 You shall (and notwithstanding the termination of your employment) sign and execute all such documents and do all such acts as (the institution) may reasonably require: –

    14.4.1 to apply for and obtain in the sole name of (the institution), (unless it otherwise directs) patent registered design or other protection of any nature whatsoever in respect of the inventions in any country throughout the world and, when so obtained or vested, to renew and maintain the same;

    14.4.2 to resist any objection or opposition to obtaining, and any petitions or applications for revocation of, any such patent, registered design or other protection;

    14.4.3 to bring any proceedings for infringement of any such patent, registered design or other protection;

    14.4.4 (the institution) hereby undertakes to indemnify you in respect of all costs, claims and damages, howsoever and wheresoever incurred, in connection with the discharge by you of any and all such requests under 4.1, 4.2 and 4.3.

    14.4.5 (the institution) acknowledges section 7 and 42 of the Patents Act. In respect of any invention which belongs to (the institution) by virtue of section 39 of the Patents Act, it shall be for (the institution) in the first instance to decide whether to apply for patent or other protection.

    14.4.6 In the event that (the institution) decides not to apply for patent or other legal protection you have the right to be notified of that decision as soon as is reasonably practicable thereafter.

    14.4.7 If, following such a decision by (the institution) you wish to apply for Patent either yourself or with another you must first inform (the institution) of your intention to do so. Within a reasonable period of time following such notification (the institution) must tell you whether it would object to your proposed application. The sole ground for such objection is that the patenting of the invention will involve or result in the disclosure to third parties of trade secrets or other confidential information belonging to (the institution) and that such disclosure may damage the interests of (the institution).

    14.4.8 Where (the institution) objects under 14.5.3 you hereby undertake in consideration of the payment of compensation to be determined under 5.5 below, not to proceed to apply for patent of the invention concerned nor to assist any other person to do so.

    14.4.9 The calculation of compensation referred to above shall have regard to those factors set out in section 41 of the Patents Act. In the event that (the institution) cannot agree the amount of compensation, it shall be competent for either you or (the institution) to apply to the President of the Law Society to appoint an arbitrator under the terms of the Arbitration Act, whose decision shall be binding.

15 CONFIDENTIAL INFORMATION

15.1 You shall not, except as authorised by (the institution) or required by your duties hereunder, use for your own benefit or gain or divulge to any persons firm company or other organisations whatsoever any confidential information belonging to (the institution) or relating to its affairs or dealings which may come to your knowledge during your employment. This restriction shall cease to apply to any information or knowledge which may subsequently come into the public domain other than by way of unauthorised disclosure.

15.2 All confidential records, documents and other papers (together with any copies or extracts thereof) made or acquired by you in the course of your employment shall be the property of (the institution) and must be returned to it on the termination of your employment.

15.3 Confidential information must be determined in relation to individual employees according to their status, responsibilities and the nature of their duties. However it shall include all information which has been specifically designated as confidential by (the institution) and any information which relates to the commercial and financial activities of (the institution), the unauthorised disclosure of which would embarrass harm or prejudice (the institution). It does not extend to the information already in the public domain, unless such information arrived by unauthorised means.

15.4 Notwithstanding the above (the institution) affirms that academic staff have freedom within the law to question and test received wisdom, and to put forward new ideas and controversial or unpopular opinions, without placing themselves in jeopardy of losing their jobs and privileges they have at (the institution).

16 COPYRIGHT

16.1 Subject to the following provisions, (the institution) and you acknowledge sections 11 and 15 of the Copyright, Designs and Patents Act 1988.

16.2 All records, documents and other papers (including copies and summaries thereof) which pertain to the finance and administration of (the institution) and which are made or acquired by you in the course of your employment shall be the property of (the institution). The copyright in all such original records, documents and papers shall at all times belong to (the institution).

16.3 The copyright in any work or design compiled, edited or otherwise brought into existence by you as a scholarly work produced in furtherance of your professional career shall belong to you; 'scholarly work' includes items such as books, contributions to books, articles and conference papers, and shall be construed in the light of the common understanding of the phrase in higher education.

16.4 The copyright in any material produced by you for your personal use and reference, including as an aid to teaching, shall belong to you.

16.5 However, the copyright in course materials produced by you in the course of your employment for the purposes of the curriculum of a course run by (the institution) and produced, used or disseminated by (the institution) shall belong to (the institution), as well as the outcomes from research specifically funded and supported by (the institution).

16.6 The above sub-clauses (16.3–16.5) shall apply except where agreement to the contrary is reached by you and (the institution). Where a case arises, or it is thought that a case may arise, where such agreement to the contrary may be necessary, or where it may be expedient to reach a specific agreement as to the application of the above sub-clauses to the particular facts of the case, the matter should be taken up between you and (your Head of Department). By way of example, this sub-clause would apply where any question of assignment of copyright or of joint copyright may arise; other examples and guidance may be contained from time to time in the Staff Handbook.

Source: The national academic contract can be accessed from the UCU website at http://www.ucu.org.uk/index.cfm?articleid=1972

Post-employment restraints

Any term in an employment contract which seeks to prevent an employee from setting up his or her own business or working for any other company after the employee has ceased to work for the employer is regarded as being in restraint of trade. Consequently, any such term, or covenant as such a term is sometimes called, is *prima facie* void. This means that the term is of no legal effect and it is unenforceable in a court of law. Consequently, irrespective of the employee's knowledge and acceptance of the term, the former employee can act in violation of it.

However, a **post-employment restraint** will be enforced by a court if the term is considered to be reasonable. For this to be so the employer must have a legitimate interest to protect. This may be in the form of a trade secret. Alternatively, it may be legitimate for the employer to include terms in the contract which prevent its customers or employees being solicited by the former employee with a view to seeking to induce them to transfer their allegiances to, or to work for, a competing business. Such restraints must be for no longer than is commercially necessary to protect the employer's legitimate interests, and must be reasonable with regard to their area of geographical operation.

The following cases provide a useful comparison.

Case Summary

In *Forster and Sons Ltd* v. *Suggett* [1918] 35 TLR 87, the works manager of the company was instructed in certain confidential methods concerning the correct mixture of gas and air in the furnaces for the manufacture of glass and glass bottles. He entered into a contract which contained a term that he would not, during the five years following the termination of his employment, carry on in the UK, or be interested in, glass manufacture or any other business connected with glass making. It was held that the restraint was reasonable and therefore valid and enforceable. This was the case even though the term was to last for five years and applied throughout the UK. In the circumstances the trade secrets involved gave the company a competitive edge for a five-year period and the company was a UK-wide commercial undertaking.

Case Summary

In *Commercial Plastics Ltd* v. *Vincent* [1965] 1 QB 623, Vincent had access to trade secrets. A term in his contract prevented him from working for any other business in the industry for one year after his employment with the company. It was held that this term was unenforceable as it was potentially global in scope but the company only operated within the UK market. It was also suggested in this case that in more innovative industries the duration of a restraint should be for a relatively short time if it is to be considered reasonable. This is because where the market is rapidly changing, today's trade secret is tomorrow's general knowledge. Therefore, only short restraints are necessary to retain a competitive edge. This approach is clearly of contemporary relevance to businesses operating in the information technology industry.

Case Summary

The case of *FSS Travel & Leisure Systems* v. *Johnson* [1998] IRLR 382, illustrates just how difficult it can be to determine whether an employer does have legitimate interests to protect. Even in examining the evidence in the same case judges may disagree on the nature of the information that a former employee is seeking to use or disclose. During his employment Johnson had access to and a working knowledge of the company's computerised bookings systems. There was an express term in his contract preventing him for working for competitors for a period of one year after he left the employ of FSS Travel. Both the High Court and the Court of Appeal found this post-employment restraint to be void and unenforceable as a period of one year was longer than was commercially necessary for the company to protect its interests. However, the Court of Appeal disagreed with the High Court that the information constituted a trade secret. The appeal court took the view that Johnson's knowledge of the booking systems could not be separated from his normal working duties and the information he needed to carry these out. Therefore, FSS Travel had no right to seek to restrain Johnson from using this information after he had ceased to be one of its employees.

If a restraint is too wide, it will normally be unenforceable even though the business has legitimate interests to protect. However, in exceptional circumstances a court may interpret a term in such a way that it is reasonable but only where such an interpretation was clearly intended by the parties. In *Littlewoods Organisation* v. *Harris* [1978] 1 All ER 1026, General Universal Stores (GUS) was the chief rival to the plaintiff mail order company. The defendant was a senior employee with access to confidential information. He agreed that he would not work for GUS for one year after leaving Littlewoods. He resigned and was employed by GUS. Littlewoods sought an injunction to restrain him from doing this. Harris argued that the term in his contract was too wide since it stopped him working for GUS even in their companies which were not involved in mail order. The Court of Appeal held that where a contract is drafted in general terms which, without alteration, can be interpreted in a sense which was not unreasonable to protect the relevant confidential information or trade secrets, which the employer was seeking to protect, the court could interpret it in that sense thereby rendering it valid and enforceable. In this case the relevant terms were interpreted as only applying to GUS's mail order business and would be enforced on that basis.

Case Summary

Severance and the blue pencil test

Other than in an exceptional case such as *Littlewoods*, a restraint which is unreasonable because it is worded too widely is invalid and unenforceable unless a judge is prepared and able to sever the offending words from the main part of the contract term. However, severance is only possible if it is in accordance with the 'blue pencil test'. This requires the court to delete words from the restraint, that is run a blue pencil through them, without having to add new words for the remaining term to make sense. If the remaining term does make sense and is now reasonable then it can be enforced.

The following hypothetical example illustrates when severance is possible and impossible. Suppose that you are employed in a law firm which has offices throughout the county of Hampshire. The following term is in your contract of employment:

'If you leave the employment of the firm you may not, for a period of five years, work for any other law firm in the County of Hampshire or in any other part of the United Kingdom in which the firm may establish operations in the future.'

The objective of this term will be regarded as legitimate by a court in so far as it is designed to prevent you taking any of the firm's clients to a new firm in which you have accepted employment. However, the term is only enforceable to the extent that it is reasonable. If on leaving the firm you accepted employment with another law firm in Hampshire a court might decline to enforce it on the basis that five years is a longer period than is necessary for the firm to protect its clientele. Severance would not be possible as, if you strike out the period of five years, the term becomes more unreasonable as there would be no specified time limit and the term would operate for the rest of your life. The court is not empowered to replace the five-year time period with a shorter period which the court regards as reasonable.

By way of contrast, if the court agreed that five years was a reasonable period of time for the term to be enforceable, given the personal relationship between you and some of the firm's clients, the court is very likely to regard the geographical scope of the term as unreasonable as it also covers areas of the country in which the firm, to date, has never operated and therefore any clients will be future clients whom you have never met. In this situation severance is possible providing it is reasonable to enforce the term throughout Hampshire. Using the 'blue pencil test' the words 'or in any other part of the United Kingdom in which the firm may establish operations in the future' would be struck out. This would mean that the term would then read: 'If you leave the employment of the firm you may not, for a period of five years, work for any other law firm in the County of Hampshire.' If this amended term is reasonable it would then be enforced by the court.

You be the judge

Q: Can Basil be prevented from acting as he does in any of the following three situations?

(a) Basil is employed as the head chef at the Fratton Towers Steakhouse in the town of Portsea. Basil works out his notice and opens his own restaurant in the next street from the Fratton Towers Steakhouse. He advertises this in the local newspaper. The advertisement stresses that Basil is the former chef of the Fratton Towers Steakhouse.

(b) The situation is the same as above, but Basil writes personally to the regular customers of the Fratton Towers Steakhouse informing them of his new restaurant.

(c) The situation is the same as in (a) but there was a term in Basil's contract of employment prohibiting him from working as a chef in any other steak restaurant in Portsea, or within a 50-mile radius of the town, for a period of three months.

A: Fratton Towers can take no action in (a), is likely to be able to secure an injunction in (b) and, through the process of severance, may be able to enforce the term against Basil in (c).

There is nothing that the Fratton Towers Steakhouse can do in (a) if there are no terms in Basil's contract prohibiting him from seeking, through an advertisement, to solicit customers of the Steakhouse. The latter has no general right to prevent him from setting up a competing business.

However, in (b) the practical likelihood is that Basil only has the contact details of the customers through having copied them in some way whilst an employee of Fratton Steakhouse. Therefore, as shown in *Roger Bullivant* v. *Ellis* (see above), Basil will have been in breach of the implied duty of fidelity and can be restrained by a court injunction from profiting from this.

In (c), although it is legitimate for Fratton Steakhouse to seek to protect its clientele by an express term in Basil's contract, it is likely that the term is too wide in its geographical scope, even though the period of three months may well be reasonable. However, severance will be possible if it is reasonable to enforce the term throughout Portsea as the clause relating to the 50-mile radius can be severed from the term in accordance with the 'blue pencil test'.

Restraints and wrongful termination of the employment contract

It is possible that an employee who has a post-employment restraint in his or her employment contract is dismissed in a way that is a breach of contract by the employer. This is known as a **wrongful dismissal** and such dismissals will be considered fully later (see Chapter 4). In *General Bill Posting* v. *Atkinson* [1909] AC 118, the House of Lords confirmed that an employer cannot rely on a restraint clause where the employee has been wrongfully dismissed. In this case Atkinson was entitled to 12 months' notice and was subject to a post-employment restraint with a duration of two years. Atkinson was dismissed without notice, and he subsequently set up his own rival business in breach of the contractual restraint clause. It was held that his dismissal was wrongful, and in so repudiating the contract the employer had brought the contract and the post-employment restraint to an end. Therefore, irrespective of whether the restraint was reasonable it had ceased to exist, and could no longer be enforced against Atkinson.

Case Summary

As in this case, a wrongful dismissal may be an actual dismissal in that the contract is terminated by the decision of the employer. Wrongful dismissals may also be constructive in that it is the employee who terminates the contract through resigning or leaving, but this is in response to a repudiatory breach by the employer. Again, **constructive dismissal** will be explained fully later (see Chapter 4), but the following ruling concerning Kevin Keegan was given as a result of him being constructively dismissed by Newcastle Football Club.

Law in action

Kevin Keegan resigned as the manager of Newcastle FC in September 2008, and successfully brought a claim for constructive wrongful dismissal against the club before the Premier League Manager's Arbitration Tribunal. The reasons why his claim succeeded will be explored later (see Chapter 4). However, one of the issues that the Arbitration Tribunal had to consider was whether Newcastle could enforce a term in Keegan's contract, which prohibited him from working in any capacity for any other Premier League Club for a period of six months if his contract was terminated by the club. Keegan argued that the restraint was unreasonable and therefore unenforceable.

However, the tribunal found that the term was reasonable. It was only for six months, and did not prevent Keegan from working for clubs outside the Premier League, or for any other club in another country or at international level. The tribunal

Source: Sozaijiten

agreed with Newcastle's argument that it was reasonable to prevent Keegan from working in any capacity for another Premiership club, as putting his detailed knowledge of Newcastle's players and their contracts at the disposal of a rival Premiership club would have given the latter an unfair advantage. The tribunal also noted that during the operation of the restraint it was permissible for Keegan to negotiate a contract with another Premiership club; the restraint merely prevented the contract from commencing until the six-month period had expired.

On this basis the tribunal found for Newcastle FC and decided that it could enforce the restraint despite its repudiatory breach. As commented by Kevin Groome and Mike Townley, of Bates Wells & Braithwaite LLP's Sports Unit, it was surprising that Keegan did not argue that, on the basis of normal contractual principles, the wrongful termination of his contract brought the restraint to an end and therefore it could no longer be enforced against him.

Had Keegan taken his claim to the civil courts, rather than the Arbitration Tribunal, it seems likely that this would have been argued on his behalf and it would have been held that the restraint was no longer legally binding on him.

Source: Groome, K. and Townley, M. (2009) 'Managers Contracts: Constructive Dismissal: Kevin *Keegan* v. *Newcastle* FC', *World Sports Law Reports*, vol. 7(12). For a link to the actual ruling of the Premier League Manager's Arbitration Tribunal see **http://videos.icnetwork.co.uk/nejournal/kevinkeegan.pdf**

The employer's duties with respect to the employee's health, safety and welfare at work

Having examined the terms that are judicially implied into all contracts of employment it is necessary to consider in greater depth an employer's duty of reasonable care with the respect to the health and safety its employees. This contractual duty substantially overlaps with **employer's negligence** in tort law and, generally, the cases discussed in this part of the chapter were decided on the basis of tortious rather than contractual principles. Where an employee can sue both for breach of contract and in negligence, the employee is likely to base a claim on the latter in the ordinary civil courts of law, as damages in the law of tort can reflect losses such as loss of a limb and/or pain and suffering, whereas in contract law damages are restricted to the actual financial loss arising from the employee's injury. However, as will be explained below, the contractual duty is not without significance as there can be circumstances in which an employee has not suffered an injury. This means that the employer will not have committed a tort but there may still be a breach of the contract of employment on the employer's part.

The employer's duty of care

Case Summary

In *Wilsons and Clyde Coal Company* v. *English* [1938] AC 57, the House of Lords held that, at common law, under the law of tort, an employer owes a duty of care to take all such steps as are reasonably necessary to ensure the safety of its employees. In this case, a surface colliery worker was injured by haulage equipment used to raise miners from the pit. It was held that the company was in breach of this duty to take reasonable care as it should have stopped its employees from working near to the haulage equipment whilst it was in use.

In *Wilsons and Clyde Coal Company*, Lord Wright stated that an employer's obligation to his employee is of a three-fold nature, as set out below. However, it should be understood that, whilst it is often convenient to consider an employer's liability under these three headings, as clarified by Neill LJ in *McDermid* v. *Nash Dredging Limited* [1986] ICR 525 (see below), these are different practical aspects of a single duty that an employer personally owes to his employees. By personal duty we mean that an employer is responsible in law for ensuring the safety of his employees and therefore will be legally liable if the duty is broken. A company will incur personal liability where its directors and/or senior managers are at fault.

The three aspects of the duty of care as identified by Lord Wright, plus a fourth, are as follows.

The provision of competent staff

If an employer was aware that an employee had acted in ways that were dangerous to his or her colleagues on previous occasions, and failed to seek to prevent further misconduct either by dismissing or disciplining the employee, the employer will be liable to any employee who is injured as a result of a repetition of the dangerous behaviour involved. This is because the employer will have failed to take reasonable care to select and maintain competent staff.

Today, workplace bullying is a very important example of this aspect of the employer's duty of care, and is considered below.

The provision of adequate equipment and protective devices and clothing

An employer will not be liable unless it knew or ought to have known of a danger or defect against which the employee should have been protected. Although an employer is obliged to keep itself informed of contemporary knowledge in the field of accident prevention, it is not obliged to adopt all the latest improvements. Therefore, the fact that its equipment is less safe than that in use by other employers is not, in itself, proof of negligence. In *Parkes* v. *Smethwick Corporation* (1957) 55 LGR 438 it was held that an employer was not negligent in failing to fit an ambulance with retractable gear for a stretcher, even though other employers did use such stretchers. On the evidence, the court found that the ambulance was reasonably safe for use by the ambulance workers.

Case
Summary

The provision of a safe system of working and effective supervision

It is for the employer to devise a system for undertaking work in a way that is reasonably safe and to provide proper instructions – including warnings of identifiable dangers – to its employees accordingly. The case of *Wilsons and Clyde Coal Company* provides an example of how this aspect of an employer's duty may be broken. The duty continues to apply even though the employees are experienced in their work, but less practical instruction will be needed the more experienced an employee is. Similarly, although employees should be adequately supervised to ensure they are complying with an employer's instructions, less supervision will be required where employees are experienced and have a record of being reliable and efficient.

The patterns of working required by an employer are a very important feature of providing a safe system. For example, in *Pickford* v. *ICI* [1996] IRLR 622 the employee developed repetitive strain injury as a result of being required to type for long periods without breaks. The employer was found to be negligent through failing to provide for adequate rest breaks or in varying the work the employee was required to do.

As documented below, it is well established that stress is very much a problem in the contemporary workplace, particularly in office environments. Part of the employer's duty to provide a safe system involves taking reasonable care to protect an employee

from psychiatric injury resulting from stress at work. In *Walker* v. *Northumberland County Council* [1995] IRLR 35, the Council was held liable for the employee's second nervous breakdown, in circumstances where it knew that his first nervous breakdown had been caused by the stress and anxiety occasioned by his heavy workload as a social services officer. The Council should have taken adequate steps to lessen that workload when he returned to work after his first nervous breakdown.

As confirmed by the Law Lords in their decision in *McDermid* [1987] ICR 917, the duty to provide a safe system is non-delegable in the sense that it cannot be delegated to a senior manager who then becomes personally liable in the place of the employer if the manager fails to ensure the safe system is properly implemented. In this case the captain of a tug was responsible for ensuring the rope tying the tug to the jetty had been properly removed before instructing the tug to be moved off. Here the captain failed to wait for McDermid's knock to confirm the rope was clear and McDermid was injured as a result. The Law Lords held that the company was directly liable for its duty to ensure that not only had a reasonably safe system been devised but also that it was properly followed in practice.

It is important to emphasise that the employer was personally or directly liable in all the above cases. This can be contrasted with the situation where the employer's liability is vicarious in that the employer is legally responsible not for its own actions but for those of an employee. Vicarious liability will be discussed below.

The provision of a safe place of work

Although this is not included as a separate heading in *Wilsons & Clyde Coal Limited* v. *English*, it is clear from decided cases that an employer is under an obligation to provide a safe place of work. This includes access to and from the workplace. The case of *Latimer* v. *AEC Ltd*, which is discussed below, provides an illustration of the operation of the duty of care in the context of ensuring a workplace is reasonably safe.

Breach of the duty of care

In many cases the key issue is whether the employer is in *breach* of duty as this is only the case if the employer has failed to take *reasonable* care.

The factors in assessing breach of duty are:

(a) the magnitude of the risk of injury which consists of the likelihood of injury combined with its potential seriousness;

(b) the practicability of precautions the employer could have taken to avoid any injury;

(c) the importance of the employer's objectives in requiring the work to be undertaken in the circumstances that applied in a given situation.

The following cases illustrate how the courts apply these factors in determining whether an employer has failed to take reasonable care.

In *Paris* v. *Stepney* BC [1951] AC 367, Paris, a mechanic was working under a vehicle and lost his eye when it was hit by a flying chip of rusty metal. Paris was blind in his other eye and therefore as a result of the injury was now totally blind. It was held by the Law Lords that irrespective of whether goggles should have been provided to workers with two good eyes the magnitude of risk of injury in this case was very high – given the risk of total blindness – and this risk could have been easily eliminated by providing Paris with goggles. Therefore, the Council was in breach of its duty to take reasonable care.

Case Summary

By way of contrast, in *Latimer* v. *AEC* [1953] 2 All ER 449, it was held that the company was not in breach of duty to shut its factory after it had been flooded by an exceptionally heavy rainstorm. The company used all the sawdust at its disposal to make part of the factory floor safe, and it was not liable to the plaintiff after she slipped on an uncovered and still wet part of the floor. Whilst, the magnitude of risk of injury was relatively high, the employer had taken reasonable steps to reduce the risk of injury. The only way in which that risk could have been eliminated was by shutting the factory until the floor had dried naturally. Given the loss of production such a step would have caused, closure of the factory was more than could have been reasonably demanded of the employer.

Case Summary

The case of *Watt* v. *Hertfordshire* CC [1954] 2 All ER 368 demonstrates how emergency workers may have to accept a higher risk of injury than workers in general. Watt was a fireman and was called to an accident at which a heavy jack was required to free people trapped in a car crash. The engine carrying Watt and the jack was not equipped to secure the latter in an effective manner. Watt was seriously injured when the jack slipped on top of him. The Court of Appeal held that, although the magnitude of risk of injury was obviously very high in this situation, the employer was merited in taking the risk as it was essential that the jack was transported to the scene of the accident.

Case Summary

Contributory negligence

Even where an employer is in breach of duty he will have a partial defence where an employee has failed to take reasonable care with respect to his or her own safety and is therefore guilty of contributory negligence. It will be for the court to determine the extent to which the employee was responsible for his or her own injuries, and the compensation that the employer is obliged to pay to the employee will be reduced accordingly. A typical example of contributory negligence is where, contrary to the employer's instructions, the employee decides not to use safety equipment or wear protective clothing that the employer has provided.

Vicarious liability

This chapter has focused on the employer's personal liability where an employee is injured as work. However, it is not uncommon for an injury to occur at work because one employee through negligence has injured a colleague. In such a situation even if the employer is not personally liable he or she will be vicariously liable. Such liability is imposed on an employer with respect to any tort that an employee commits whilst acting within the scope of his employment. The meaning of scope of employment has been drawn very widely. An employer will be vicariously liable if the wrongful behaviour of an employee is related to his or her work, even where the employee acts wholly for his or her own benefit and in contradiction to the purposes for which the employee is employed. This was held to be so by the House of Lords in *Lister* v. *Hesley Hall Ltd* [2001] ICR 665. In this case the employer was liable for acts of child abuse carried out by employees at a residential home. The employees responsible for the abuse were obviously acting for their own perverse gratification in a way that was of no benefit to the employer and was in direct contradiction of their contractual duties to care for the children in the home. Nevertheless, they were deemed to be acting within the scope of their employment and the employer was vicariously liable.

As held in *Lister* v. *Romford Ice & Cold Storage Co Ltd* [1957] I All ER 125, where an employer is vicariously liable the employee is in breach of the duty to take reasonable care that is owed to the employer. Breach of this duty gives the employer a right to recover any compensation it has had to pay from the negligent employee by way of an indemnity. However, in practice it is rarely worth the employer's while to exercise this right as employees will not have the resources to indemnify the employer. It is much more likely that the employer will take disciplinary action, up to and including dismissal, against the employee.

Contractual liability

The employer's common law liability in the law of tort is reinforced by the law of contract as it is judicially implied into a contract of employment that an employer owes a duty to take reasonable care.

The essential practical difference between contractual and tortious liability is that an employer will only incur the latter if an employee has actually suffered an injury. This is because damage is an essential element of the tort of negligence. However, the contractual duty can be broken irrespective of whether the employee has been injured. This is important if an employee is dismissed by the employer without notice for refusing to work in a dangerous environment, or with dangerous equipment. The employee would not be guilty of disobedience but, as explained later (in Chapters 4 and 5), would be entitled to compensation from the employer for wrongful and/or unfair dismissal as it is the employer who is in breach of the contractual duty to take reasonable care. An employee who resigns in response to a breach of this duty will also be able to establish that he or she has been constructively dismissed. Table 3.2, below, summarises the comparison between an employer's contractual and tortious duties of care.

> the contractual duty can be broken irrespective of whether the employee has been injured

Health and safety dismissals

As referred to above, some dismissals will be automatically unfair and, in the context of health and safety, such protection is given to employees by s. 100 of ERA. This renders it automatically unfair to dismiss an employee for 'leaving a place of work because of a reasonable belief in serious and imminent danger'. Providing an employee can show that the belief that a danger was serious or imminent was reasonable and therefore an

Table 3.2 Comparing the contractual and tortious duties of care

Duty of care under the law of contract	Duty of care under the tort of negligence
Duty is broken if the employer fails to take *reasonable* care.	Duty is broken if the employer fails to take *reasonable* care.
Damages reflect loss of earnings resulting from the breach of duty, for example, as a result of a dismissal in breach of contract.	Damages reflect both loss of earnings and the pain and suffering the employee incurs as a result of the breach of duty.
The employer incurs liability even if the employee does not suffer an injury.	The employer will not incur liability if the employee does not suffer an injury.

objective one, any dismissal must be found by a tribunal to be unfair without further argument being necessary.

The following two cases illustrate the operation of s. 100 ERA 1996. Normally, a serious and imminent danger will arise from the state of the workplace or the equipment an employee is required to use. However, in *Harvest Press Ltd* v. *McCaffrey* [1999] IRLR 778, the danger was in the form of the claimant's colleague. McCaffrey was abused by this colleague after McCaffrey had complained about his behaviour and, fearing a physical assault, McCaffrey left his night-time shift. He subsequently phoned his manager stating that he was not prepared to return to work unless the abusive colleague was removed or dismissed. The employer decided that McCaffrey had broken his contract by refusing to work and dismissed him. The EAT upheld the tribunal's decision that McCaffrey had been automatically unfairly dismissed under s. 100 ERA 1996.

In *Balfour Kilpatrick Ltd* v. *Acheson* [2003] IRLR 683, a group of workers collectively left their workplace after it had become dangerous as a result of being flooded through a heavy rainfall. However, four days after the flood the workers were still refusing to return to work even though the weather had improved and the workplace had largely dried. The EAT confirmed that there was no reason why s. 100 could not cover a collective walkout. However, in the circumstances of the case, the men had lost the protection of s. 100 in refusing to return to work once it was no longer reasonable for them to continue to believe that the state of the workplace posed a serious danger.

Case Summary

Case Summary

Breach of statutory duties and strict liability

Legislation and statutory instruments, as well as the common law, have always had a large part to play in promoting health and safety at work by providing detailed regulation of particular types of work and workplaces. Typically, such regulation is part of the criminal law and employers can be prosecuted for being in breach of statutory duty. Moreover, in contrast with the common law, some statutory provisions impose strict liability. This means that employers can be legally liable even where they can show that have taken reasonable care. An example of this is provided by s. 14 of the old legislation covering factories.

Case Summary

Section 14 of the Factories Act 1937 imposed a duty on employers to fence machinery securely so as to prevent employees from coming into contact with dangerous parts of it. In *John Summers & Sons Limited* v. *Frost* [1955] AC 740, Frost was seriously injured whilst operating an unfenced machine. It was held that s. 14 imposed strict liability so that the employer was in breach of that duty even though the machinery in question could not have operated if it had been fenced. An employer would not normally be regarded as negligent with respect to a failure to provide safety devices where doing this would render equipment commercially useless. However, where a statutory duty imposes strict liability a failure to comply with it will render an employer legally liable irrespective of the consequences that proper compliance would generate.

This case also illustrates that some statutory duties impose civil as well as criminal liability on an employer. Where this is so, an employee who is injured as a result of an employer's failure to comply with a specific statutory duty may bring an action in tort to recover damages for the injuries that the employee has sustained. Typically, where breach of statutory duty does generate civil liability then the defence of contributory negligence, as explained above, will be available to an employer. For example, if an employee, who removed a safety guard supplied by an employer, was consequently injured, any damages awarded to that employee would be reduced on grounds of contributory negligence.

The relevant provisions in a statute or a statutory instrument will specify whether it is intended that employees should be able to sue for breach of statutory duty. For example, the Factories Act 1937 has been replaced by a number of regulations, which regulate all types of workplaces, including the Provision and Use of Work Equipment Regulations 1992, SI 1992/2932 and the Management of Health and Safety at Work Regulations 1999, SI 1999/3242. The former expressly imposes both criminal and civil liability whereas the latter is solely part of the criminal law.

One major change to the law, implemented by the Management of Health and Safety at Work Regulations, was the imposition of a duty on employers to carry out risk assessments of the ways in which work is being carried out. Where appropriate, employers should decide on and implement action to reduce any risk of injury to the lowest acceptable level. If an employer knows that an employee is pregnant then the employer must carry out a risk assessment to ascertain if there is anything about the workplace or the job the employee is employed to do which constitutes a risk to the health and safety of the employee or her child. If this is the case then the employee should be provided with alternative work to do. If it is not possible to provide alternative work then the employee should be suspended on full pay for as long as is necessary to protect her and her child.

It should be noted that regulation 11 of the Provision of Use of Equipment Regulations replaces s. 14 of the Factories Act 1937. However, regulation 11 requires suitable safety devices to be provided 'to the extent that it is practicable to do so'. Therefore, it may be that regulation 11 imposes a less strict duty than that which was contained in s. 14. Even if this is the case, the regulation is still requiring an employer to do more than is required where the legal duty is only to do what is *reasonably* practicable.

Criminal liability

Possibly the most well-known piece of health and safety legislation is the Health and Safety at Work Act (HSWA) 1974. This Act is part of the criminal rather than the civil law. Section 2 of the HSWA lays down duties requiring employers to do what is reasonably practicable to ensure the health, safety and welfare at work of all employees. These duties therefore reflect the common law duty to take reasonable care, which is explained above. Essentially, as a result of s. 2 HSWA, negligence by an employer is a criminal offence as well as a tortious act. However, unlike the tort of negligence, enforcement action can be taken against an employer even though, as yet, no employee has suffered injury.

negligence by an employer is a criminal offence as well as a tortious act

Employers can be prosecuted for a breach of a statutory duty by a health and safety inspector, who is employed by the Health and Safety Executive (HSE). This body was established by the HSWA to oversee and monitor the working of health and safety law (see Chapter 1). Although, enforcement action by a health and safety inspector can result in an employer being fined or even sent to prison, it is much more common for health and safety inspectors to serve an improvement or a prohibition notice. A prosecution will only take place if the notice is not complied with.

A prohibition notice will have the effect of prohibiting a workplace or equipment from being used until the safety requirements specified in the notice have been implemented. Prohibition notices may only be issued where an inspector considers there is a risk of serious personal injury. Prohibition notices may take immediate effect where the risk is imminent. An improvement notice may be issued in any situation where an inspector considers that the employer is in breach of a statutory duty. The employer must be given at least 21 days to carry out the improvements specified in the notice.

Employers may appeal to employment tribunals against the serving of a notice, but a failure to comply with it is a criminal offence punishable by fine or imprisonment. If the duty is strict, it is no defence for the employer to argue that there have been no previous accidents. For example, in *Murray* v. *Gadbury* (1979), in breach of the Agriculture Machinery Regulations 1962, a farmer had used an unguarded cutter for 26 years without incident. His appeal against the serving of an improvement notice failed as the duty to provide a guard was mandatory. However, in such circumstances, it will not be appropriate to serve a prohibition notice. In *Brewer & Sons* v. *Dunston* (1978), an unguarded hand guillotine had been used for 18 years without incident. An appeal against the serving of a prohibition notice succeeded as it could not be established that there was a risk of serious personal injury.

Case Summary

If a breach of statutory duty cannot be established then an appeal by an employer against the serving of a notice must be upheld. For example, in *Associated Dairies* v. *Hartley* [1979] IRLR 171, an improvement notice was served under s. 2 HSWA which required the company to provide free special footwear to 1,000 employees. It was held that the cost involved in doing this outweighed the risk to employees and, therefore, the company was not in breach of s. 2 as this only requires employers to do what is reasonably practicable.

Case Summary

Companies will be directly responsible for any breach of duty if the actual individual at fault was a director or manager. The individual(s) concerned can also be prosecuted. Companies may incur vicarious liability for breach of statutory duty on the basis of the law as explained above. Moreover, under s. 7 HSWA, employees owe a duty of reasonable care with respect to the health and safety of themselves and any other person in the workplace.

There are two issues arising from the employer's personal duties under both contract and tort that are worth highlighting as particularly important in the contemporary workplace: these are the issues of workplace stress and bullying.

Workplace stress

As you can see from the statistics provided below, research has established that workplace stress is a major contemporary issue in the world of work.

Key stats

Research on workplace stress was conducted in 2000 in Bristol and was based on a sample of 17,000 respondents. Some 20% of this sample reported high or very high levels of stress resulting from their jobs. Stress levels were highest in the 35–55 age groups and increased with levels of education and occupations linked to educational qualifications. For example, 41.5% of the sample who were teachers, and 31.8% of those who were in nursing, reported high stress levels, as did 26.7% of professional managers. Stress levels were low, for example, in catering where only 6.8% reported high stress. None of the respondents in hair and beauty reported high stress levels.

Source: The scale of occupational stress: A further analysis of the impact of demographic factors and type of job, by Andrew Smith, Carolyn Brice, Alison Collins, Victoria Matthews and Rachel McNamara, Centre for Occupational and Health Psychology, School of Psychology, Cardiff University. Research report prepared for the Health and Safety Executive.

Case Summary

Barber v. *Somerset County Council* [2004] ICR 457 is the leading authority for setting out an employer's responsibilities to take reasonable action to ensure employees do not suffer psychiatric injury as a result of workplace stress. In this case, the Law Lords held that the Council was in breach of its duty to Barber where it had become aware that his difficulties at work were having an adverse effect on his mental health, but had taken no steps to help him. Barber was a teacher who regularly worked 61–70 hours week and had complained of work overload to the deputy head teacher. He was subsequently absent from work for a three-week period and his absence was certified by his doctor as being due to stress and depression. On his return to work no steps were taken to reduce his workload. Finally, Barber left the school after losing control and shaking a pupil. Subsequently, Barber was unable to work as a teacher, or to do any work other than undemanding part-time work.

In upholding Barber's appeal, the Law Lords generally approved the guidance provided by the Court of Appeal in the case for determining whether stress-based claims should succeed. The key issue is whether psychiatric injury to a particular employee is reasonably foreseeable irrespective of whether such injury was foreseeable in a person of 'ordinary fortitude'. In other words, employers should take into account whether an employee is particularly susceptible to suffering from stress, even though other employees doing the same job under the same conditions would not be. Relevant factors include:

✦ the nature and extent of the work being undertaken – an employer is required to be more alert to the danger of stress if an employee is being overworked in a job which is intellectually or emotionally demanding;

✦ any signs of stress exhibited by the employee such as unusual irritability, tiredness which could be caused by lack of sleep and/or an inability to concentrate.

Employers should also realise that harm to health can become foreseeable where an employee uncharacteristically takes regular or prolonged absences from work even if he or she does not complain of stress. However, even though employers may have responsibility for taking the initiative, it is clear that if an employee is suffering from stress it is in the employee's own interests to inform the employer accordingly.

Bullying

The following statistics demonstrate the extent to which bullying in the workplace is an important problem. Interestingly it is older rather than younger workers who appear more likely to be the victims of bullying, and bullying appears to be more prevalent in the professions.

Key stats

Three and a half million people (14% or one in seven of the workforce) say they have been bullied in their current job according to a YouGov poll for the TUC. Just over 20% (one in five) say that bullying is an issue where they work.

Bullying is more likely in the public sector where 19% say they have been bullied compared to 12% in the private sector and 8% in the voluntary sector.

Bullying appears to be most common in professional jobs as 16% of people in such jobs reported that they had been bullied. According to the TUC, this may reflect the large number of professional and associate professional jobs in the public sector such as teaching, and across the NHS.

Men are more likely to be bullied (16%) than women (12%), and 45–54 year olds (19%), followed by 35–44 year olds (17%) are the age groups most likely to be bullied. The 25–34 year olds are the least bullied (8%).

It is not the low paid who are most likely to say they are bullied. Those earning less than £20,000 report much less bullying than those earning between £20,000 and £60,000 (17%). But among those earning above £60,000 only 7% cent say they are bullied.

Source: YouGov poll for the TUC published 5 September 2008, **http://www.emplaw.co.uk/lawguide?startpage=data/12maroo.htm**

Bullying can overlap with discrimination law in that it may take the form of sexual or racial harassment, for example. This type of bullying is covered by the Equality Act 2010 and will be examined later (see Chapter 7). Given that age appears to be a factor, bullying could also be a product of age discrimination. On the other hand, it may be that older employers, through their greater experience of work, are better at recognising that they are the victims of the more subtle forms of bullying behaviour such as unreasonable pressure to complete a job by a particular deadline. However, as the *Green* case shows (see below), bullying need not be based in discriminatory attitudes for an employer to incur liability, as the ordinary common law principles of tort and contract also apply.

Out and about

In understanding how the law works, it is valuable to appreciate the different forms that bullying at work can take, and to consider the steps that an employee may take to secure protection from the employer to prevent further acts of bullying from taking place.

The following website is useful for these purposes: **http://www.direct.gov.uk/en/ Employment/ResolvingWorkplaceDisputes/DiscriminationAtWork/DG_10026670**

When visiting this website consider the following questions:

1. What examples of bullying at work did you identify?

2. What informal action would you take if you were a victim of bullying by colleagues at work?

3. In what circumstances would you consider taking formal action internally, that is, within your employing organisation?

4. What do you think formal action would consist of?

Based on the law as explained so far, what types of legal claims do you think you could bring if a complaint to your employer of being bullied did not result in the bullying coming to an end?

Case Summary

In *Green* v. *DB Services Ltd* [2006] IRLR 764, Green had been subjected by a group of women to a relentless campaign of mean and spiteful behaviour designed to cause her distress. In presenting her evidence Green provided the following examples of the types of bullying behaviour to which she had been subjected:

✦ ignoring me or staring silently at me, often with their arms crossed; this was done in a way that was plainly intended to intimidate and unnerve me;

✦ greeting and acknowledging other members of the secretariat department in a very overt manner, in order to highlight the fact that they were not speaking to me;

✦ excluding me from conversations with other member of the secretariat department by either talking over me or pretending they could not hear anything I said;

✦ excluding me from group activities to which every other member of the secretariat department would be invited, typically when booking restaurants for departmental lunches;

✦ waiting for me to walk past the area of the office in which they sat before bursting out laughing;

✦ making crude and lewd comments that made me feel uncomfortable;

✦ interfering with office administration by removing my name from circulation lists, hiding my post from me and removing papers from my desk.

It was held that the company was in breach of its duty of care to Green in failing to take any adequate steps to protect her from such behaviour. Green's line managers had known or ought to have known what had been going on, and the bullying had given rise to a foreseeable risk of psychiatric injury. Green was granted general damages of £35,000, and £25,000 to cover the period in which she would not be able to work in the future as a result of the psychiatric injury she had suffered.

Owen J identified the following key factors in determining whether an employee could recover damages as a result of being bullied at the workplace:

+ Did the claimant's managers and/or members of the HR department know or ought reasonably to have known of the bullying?

+ Did they know or ought reasonably to have known that the bullying might cause psychiatric injury?

+ Could they, through the exercise of reasonable care, have taken steps which would have avoided such injury?

The decision confirms that employers are personally liable for managers who fail to protect employees from bullying. In this case, the company was directly liable as the claimant's managers knew or should have known of the bullying as it was conducted over a period of time, and Green and other employees had complained to HR managers that there was a bullying culture in the department in which she was employed. The departmental managers could have taken obvious steps to stop the bullying. They should have made it clear that such behaviour was unacceptable, and warned those involved that if they persisted in the bullying they would be subjected to disciplinary action. The managers could have taken immediate action to protect Green from further bullying by moving those responsible to a different location or to a different department. The judge was of the view that it was plainly foreseeable that the types of bullying to which Green had been subjected could cause any employee to suffer some degree of psychiatric injury. However, this was particularly so in this case as the company was aware that Green had suffered depression in the relatively recent past and had been prescribed anti-depressant medication. The company should have realised that she was more vulnerable than employees in general to becoming clinically depressed if subjected to the types of treatment that she had experienced whilst working for it.

Writing and drafting

Visit **http://www.businesslink.gov.uk/bdotg/action/detail?itemId=1073792621&type =RESOURCES**

On the basis of what you discovered in undertaking the above 'Out and about' activity and what you can ascertain from the advice on this website, attempt the following exercise.

You are the legal adviser to a company which supplies various types of information technology and employs 500 employees. The company is divided into 10 sections and each of these sections is run by a senior manager, although overall authority is vested in Alan, the managing director. Alan is concerned that the company does not have a written anti-bullying policy. Alan asks you to draft him a memorandum, which lists the key matters that the company should include in a written policy seeking to avoid bullying within the organisation, and which advises employees on the actions they should take internally if they believe they are the victims of bullying at work.

You should spend no more than one hour on this activity.

Handy tip: From the above website you can obtain further ideas by accessing the links to ACAS and the Chartered Institute of Personnel and Development (CIPD). In drafting your memorandum you should remember that Alan will have two key objectives. First, he will be concerned to prevent bullying from taking place within his company. Secondly, should bullying occur, he will want to be confident that the contents of the company's anti-bullying policy should ensure that it could not be subject to successful legal action by an employee who is the victim of that bullying.

Contractual liability for bullying

As well as liability in tort, an employer who bullies an employee, or is personally responsible for the injuries suffered by an employee as a result of bullying, will be in breach of both the implied duty to take reasonable care and the duty to maintain **mutual trust and confidence**. This is important where the employee resigns and seeks **damages** for wrongful dismissal. In addition to claiming wrongful dismissal, an employee who is eligible to do so may also claim unfair dismissal. Where this is advantageous to an employee, the claim of wrongful dismissal, as well as the claim of unfair dismissal, can be presented to an employment tribunal rather than a court of law.

Case Summary

Although it is not a case that directly involves bullying, *Gogay* v. *Herts CC* [2000] IRLR 703 illustrates that an action for damages for psychiatric injury can be based in contract law rather than the tort of negligence. Gogay suffered clinical stress as a result of being suspended pending an investigation into alleged child abuse. This was a breach of the contractual duty to take reasonable care on the employer's part as the evidence did not warrant suspension and there were other less draconian options available to the employer. It was held that the employer should have reasonably foreseen that Gogay could suffer stress and was liable to pay damages of around £40,000 for the period of time after the contract that she was unable to work as well as the costs of psychotherapy treatment.

An employee who is seeking damages for loss of future earnings may need to sue for breach of contract in a court of law rather than present a claim to an employment tribunal. This is because (as explained in Chapter 1) tribunals cannot award damages in excess of £25,000. If an employee is unable to work for a significant period of time it may well be the case, as illustrated by *Gogay*, that the resulting loss of earnings will be more than £25,000.

Table 3.3 summarises the contractual and tortious liabilities that an employer may incur where an employee has been bullied at the workplace.

Table 3.3 An employer's liability for bullying

Contractual liability for bullying	Tortious liability for bullying
Breach of the duties to maintain mutual trust and confidence and to take reasonable care	Breach of the duty to take reasonable care
Employee can resign and claim constructive dismissal	Whether or not the employee resigns he or she can sue for breach of the duty of care
Employee can claim damages for wrongful dismissal and compensation for unfair dismissal in an employment tribunal	Employee can recover damages from the civil courts through an action in negligence
Damages include loss of future earnings if bullying has caused psychiatric injury which prevents the employee from working	Damages include compensation for the pain and suffering caused by the bullying as well as any loss of actual or future earnings

Statutory vicarious liability for bullying

Outside the context of discrimination law, legal action resulting from an employee being bullied will generally be based on the common law through actions in contract and/or tort. However, an employee may also be able to bring a claim based on statute law. Under s. 1 of the Protection from Harassment Act 1997 (PHA), bullying can constitute 'a course of conduct' constituting harassment. This is defined as an act which has occurred on at least two previous occasions. The perpetrators of such harassment can be sued for damages and made subject to a court injunction to prevent the bullying from being repeated.

In *Majrowski* v. *Guy's and St Thomas's NHS Trust* [2006] ICR 1199, the claimant established that he had been regularly bullied and intimidated by his line manager, Sandra Freeman. She was rude and abusive to him in front of other staff. She was excessively critical of his time-keeping and work. She imposed unrealistic performance targets for him and threatened him with disciplinary action if he failed to meet them. She isolated him by refusing to talk to him. Majrowski, who was gay, believed this treatment was fuelled by homophobia. The House of Lords held that the PHA applied to the work-place and that, under s. 3, Majrowski could bring a claim for damages as the employer was vicariously liable for the acts of harassment to which he had been subjected.

Case Summary

In the *Green* case, discussed above, the company was also found to be vicariously liable under the PHA. It is worth noting that, in contrast to the common law, this statutory liability is imposed even when the employer and the appropriate senior managers have no knowledge that the bullying has taken place. Therefore, an employee who, for whatever reason, has failed to report to the employer or a line manager that he or she is a victim of bullying can still bring a claim on the basis of the PHA. Where acts of harassment are the product of homophobic attitudes then (as is explained in Chapter 7) an employee today can also present a claim under the Equality Act 2010 to an employment tribunal.

People in the law

Interview with **Charlotte Rayner,** who is Professor of Human Resource Management at the University of Portsmouth. Charlotte has been involved in the study of workplace bullying since 1996 when she undertook the first systematic study in the UK. She is especially interested in organisation-level prevention strategies. She is President of the International Association on Workplace Bullying and Harassment (IAWBH) which includes scholars and practitioners from around the world.

Other than in contexts such as racial and sexual harassment (which is dealt with elsewhere in this text), what type of behaviour would you regard as constituting bullying in the workplace?
This is not an easy question to answer. Academics have been trying to define a set of behaviour that amounts to bullying and have approached it by

asking victims. The response from victims groups behaviour into four types – personal attack, task attack, isolation and undermining behaviour – and all types may happen over a period of time. As a result, HR professionals define bullying from the perspective of the victim and thus are forced to draft policies that can potentially cover a wide range of behaviour. 'Bullying is in the eye of the beholder' so to speak. This does not help the manager and so most policies will give lots of examples.

From your research would you say that bullying by managers as well as by an employee's colleagues is a problem? Yes, it varies between countries, but in the UK around 80% of bullying is manager to subordinate, and that is the case in the USA, Australia and Canada. In the Nordic countries it is often somewhat less at around 50%.

Again, based on your own research, is bullying more prevalent in more highly paid professional occupations than in lower-paid jobs? No significant differences have been found in hierarchy. If 15% of front line workers say they are bullied, 15% of managers do too.

Based on your professional experience please could you identify, in brief, the key elements that a written anti-bullying and harassment policy should contain. I would suggest the following:

- a statement that the organisation is against bullying and harassment and that it will act on all complaints;
- a broad definition of bullying and harassment and lots of examples;
- a statement that one incident can be treated as bullying and harassment.
- procedures for dealing with complaints of bullying should include: an informal process where misunderstanding can be ironed out; and a formal process where a formal complaint is made to an appropriate manager who should act on the complaint by undertaking an investigation;
- if bullying and harassment is found the disciplinary procedure is instigated;
- serious cases should be designated gross misconduct and warrant dismissal.

It is interesting to note that, contrary to the above statistics compiled by the TUC, Professor Rayner's research does not suggest that lower-paid workers are less likely to encounter bullying than is the case with more highly paid professionals. It is inevitable that, in some cases of empirical research, findings will differ where different samples are used.

Reflective practice

Have another look at the memorandum you drafted listing what an anti-bullying policy should contain. Taking into account the answers provided in the above interview is there anything you would change or add to in your memorandum?

Summary

Historically, employers were generally not under a judicially implied duty to provide work to their employees providing wages were paid. Today, it is generally accepted that skilled employees must be given work to do in order to maintain and develop their professional skills.

As held in *Provident Financial Insurance* v. *Hayward*, where there is a duty to provide work an employer cannot put an employee on 'garden leave' during a period of notice unless there is an express term in the employment contract permitting the employee to do this. Such a term will be void on the basis that it is a restraint of trade unless the duration of the 'garden leave' is reasonable, and the employer has legitimate interests to protect by putting the employee on 'garden leave'.

The most important judicially implied duty that is imposed on employers is the duty not to act in any way that is calculated or likely to destroy the mutual trust and confidence on which all employment relationships are based (*WM Car Services* v. *Wood*).

On the basis of this duty employers must treat employees with respect and not bully, harass or humiliate an employee or allow others in the workplace to ill-treat an employee.

As held by the House of Lords in *Malik* v. *BCCI* adversely affecting an employee's professional reputation by operating a business in a corrupt or dishonest manner will also be a breach of this duty.

Employees are under an implied duty to obey all lawful and reasonable instructions of the employer. Breach of this duty may be so serious as to permit an employer to dismiss an employee summarily, that is, without notice. Complying with an employer's dress code is one important practical example of the duty of obedience.

Employees must also cooperate with the employer in the running of the business. As demonstrated by *Cresswell* v. *Inland Revenue*, providing an employer provides reasonable training, an employee must adapt to change by learning new methods or using new equipment to do a particular job.

During employment an employee must not act in breach of the duty of fidelity by disclosing or misusing confidential information. This duty continues to be enforceable against an employee, even though the employment contract has terminated, with respect to trade secrets or contact details of the employer's customers and clients.

An employer can also protect trade secrets and customer information by including express terms or covenants in the employment contract which prevent an employee from setting up his own business or working for a competitor for a period of time after the employment has ended.

Such post-employment restraints are *prima facie* void and unenforceable as being in restraint of trade. They can be enforced providing an employer has legitimate interests to protect and is not just seeking to prevent competition. A restraint must be reasonable in terms of its duration and area of geographical operation.

Under the law of tort, and as a result of a term judicially implied into contracts of employment, an employer owes an employee a duty of reasonable care with respect to the health, safety and welfare of the employee whilst at work.

One important aspect of this duty is to provide a reasonably safe system of working. This duty may be broken by unreasonably exposing an employee to workplace stress or, as in *Green* v. *DB Services*, by failing to prevent an employee from being bullied.

Such failures by the employer will also constitute breach of the duty to maintain mutual trust and confidence.

As illustrated by the *Gogay* case, breach of these duties will enable employees to resign and claim damages for loss of earnings arising from any psychiatric injury.

Question and answer*

Problem:

For the past 10 months, Paul Whittingham has been employed as assistant manager of a leisure centre in Pompey by L plc. The company operates leisure centres throughout the UK. Paul is given 48 hours' notice of an instruction to transfer to the company's leisure centre in Alfchester, which is 30 miles from Pompey, where Paul lives. He is told that he must act as the manager of this centre for the next six months. He will be paid on a manager's full salary during this period. Paul states that he will be unable to transfer at such short notice due to him having to take his two children to, and to collect them from, primary school. Paul undertakes these responsibilities on a regular basis, as his wife works in London and leaves home early and arrives home late. L plc has never objected to Paul organising his working day to accommodate these responsibilities.

There is a term in Paul's contract of employment which states: 'The employee may be required to engage in reasonable travel to work at any of the company's leisure centres in the Southern Region.'

Advise Paul as to whether he will be in breach of contract if he refuses to work in Alfchester until he has had the opportunity to arrange alternative child-care arrangements.

How, if at all, would your answer be different if there is no mobility clause in Paul's employment contract?

You should spend 40 minutes on answering this question.

Essay:

Evaluate the extent to which the judicially implied terms in contracts of employment effectively balance the interests of an employer to run an efficient business operation with the interests of employees to justice and dignity in the workplace. Illustrate your answer with examples from decided cases.

You should answer this question in 40 minutes.

✱ Answer guidance is provided at the end of the chapter.

Further reading

IDS Employment Law Handbook (2009) *Contracts of Employment* (Income Data Services: London).
Chapter 2 provides a detailed technical analysis of the case law concerned with judicially implied terms; and Chapter 5 contains a comprehensive explanation of an employer's rights to protect trade secrets and confidential information.

Deakin, S. and Morris, G. (2012) *Labour Law* (Hart: Oxford).
Pages 349–89 of Chapter 4 of this seminal text provide in-depth coverage and critical analysis of the issues dealt with in this chapter.

Freedland, M. (2003) *The Personal Contract of Employment* (Oxford: OUP).
Chapter 3 of this leading work analyses the terms to be found in employment contracts and provides 'guiding principles' for how they should be interpreted and applied by the courts.

Barrett, B. (2011) 'Should Employers Be Held More Responsible for Stress at the Work Place?', *Contemporary Issues in Law*, vol. 11(1), pp. 37–53.
This article explains and provides critical comment on the case law on workplace stress. It explores the ways in which an employee can frame a claim for compensation for stress at work.

Brodie, D. (1998) 'Beyond Exchange: The New Contract of Employment', *Industrial Law Journal,* **vol. 27, pp. 79–102; (2008) 'Mutual Trust and Confidence: Catalysts, Constraints and Commonality',** *Industrial Law Journal,* **vol. 37, pp. 329–46.**

These important articles trace and analyse the evolution of the judicially duty on employers to maintain mutual trust and confidence. The more recent article considers whether human resources standards and ethics will influence the future development of the implied term.

Brodie, D. (2007) 'Deterring Harassment at Common Law', *Industrial Law Journal,* **vol. 36, pp. 213–16.**

This case comment focuses on the case of *Green* v. *DB Group Services,* which is discussed in this chapter, and demonstrates its importance to protecting employees from bullying at work.

Palferman, D. (2011) 'Managing conflict and stress in the workplace: theory and practice' *Legal Information Management,* **vol. 11, pp. 122–5.**

This short article examines action taken by the HSE to tackle to workplace bullying and stress.

Question and answer guidance

Problem:

Your answer should start with an explanation that an employee owes a duty to obey all reasonable instructions of the employer. Therefore, where an employer invokes an express mobility clause in a contract the employee should normally transfer to a new workplace in accordance with the employer's instructions. On this basis, the company could argue that Paul is guilty of disobedience and liable to dismissal if he refuses to move to Alfchester.

However, your answer should also explain that, as held in *White* v. *Reflecting Roadstuds Ltd*, whilst an employer is not under a duty to act reasonably, the employer must not seek to enforce a mobility clause in a way that constitutes breach of the duty to maintain mutual trust and confidence. This is illustrated by the decision in *United Bank* v. *Akhtar*, and this case can be used by Paul that he should be given more than 48 hours' notice to arrange alternative child-care. You can argue that the company appears to know of his family arrangements as, to date, it has allowed him to work hours that enable him to take his children to and from school. Your answer should clarify that this would not permit him to refuse to transfer on a permanent basis, but he should be given additional time to make alternative arrangements for his children.

Your answer will be different if there is no mobility clause in Paul's contract, as he can argue that the employer has no power to instruct him to move to Alfchester. Occasionally, as in *Courtaulds Northern Spinning Ltd* v. *Sibson*, the courts have implied mobility clauses into employment contracts. However, in that case the employee's job required him to drive on a daily basis, and the term was restricted to travelling a reasonable travelling distance from his home. The actual additional travelling involved was about one mile. One possibility that you could argue with respect to Paul, albeit one that is not that likely to be accepted by a tribunal, is that a mobility clause could be implied, and then enforced as above, if it was the norm within the company for employees of Paul's status to commute to different centres if the company required them to do so. On this basis, it could also be argued that Paul is in breach of the duty of cooperation if he refuses to work in Alfchester. However, the more likely conclusion is that he will not be guilty of disobedience in the absence of an express mobility clause in his employment contract.

Essay:

This question requires you to demonstrate that you know and understand the terms which are judicially implied into contracts of employment, and to provide critical analysis of the impact of judicially implied terms on the employment relationship.

Therefore, your answer should explain, with case examples, the employer's duty to provide work, to take reasonable care and to maintain mutual trust and confidence. Similarly, you should explain the employee's duties of obedience, cooperation and fidelity. Cases you could cite as examples include: *Provident Financial* v. *Hayward*; *Wilson & Clyde Coal* v. *English*; *Woods* v. *WM Car Services*; *Cresswell* v. *Inland Revenue*; *Faccenda Chicken Ltd* v. *Fowler*.

In evaluating the impact of implied terms your answer should pay particular attention to mutual trust and confidence as this is a term of relatively modern origin, and prevents employers from acting badly with respect to their employees in ways that would not have amounted to a breach of contract in the past. However, your answer should clarify that an employer is not under a duty to act reasonably. The facts of *Woods* v. *WM Car Services* could be drawn on to provide an example of what could be regarded as bad behaviour by an employer without the employer being in breach of mutual trust and confidence. You could draw on the articles by Brodie in the *Industrial Law Journal* as a source of critical analysis of the nature and impact of the implied term of trust and confidence.

Your answer could use bullying as a practical example of the duties to maintain mutual trust and confidence and to take reasonable care in action. You should explain how breach of these duties will enable an employee to resign and claim damages for constructive wrongful dismissal, and/or compensation for unfair dismissal.

Your answer could include cases, such as *Schmidt* v. *Austick Bookshops* and *Smith* v. *Safeways*, to demonstrate an employer's wide powers to impose dress codes which employees are under a contractual duty to comply with.

You should provide a conclusion which gives your reasoned opinion as to whether the implied terms strike a balance of power between employers and employees. As an example, one conclusion could be that, whilst the duty to maintain mutual trust and confidence does protect employees in ways that were not so in the past, the balance of power remains with the employer. Employers are not under a duty to act reasonably, whereas employees must obey all reasonable instructions and are subject to the wider duty of cooperation. Your answer could, of course, reach the opposite conclusion if you provide arguments to this effect.

Visit **www.mylawchamber.co.uk/welch** to access tools to help you develop and test your knowledge of employment law, including interactive 'You be the judge' multiple choice questions, practice exam questions with guidance, annotated weblinks, case summary and key case flashcards, legal newsfeed, legal updates and answer to Lawyers' brief simulation.

Chapter 4
Common law termination of the contract of employment

Key points In this chapter we will be looking at:

✦ The relevance of the doctrine of frustration to contracts of employment

✦ Lawful termination of the contract of employment in accordance with its terms

✦ When a summary dismissal by the employer will be wrongful

✦ Constructive dismissal and grievance procedures

✦ Remedies for wrongful dismissal

Introduction

It is commonplace in any employment relationship for an employee to wish to leave a job, or for an employer to decide that it no longer wants the services of a particular employee. In such circumstances, as far as the ordinary common law principles of contract law are concerned, the employment contract can normally be easily terminated by either the employee or the employer. This is done either by the employee submitting a notice of resignation in accordance with the express terms of the contract, or by the employer dismissing the employee by providing the employee with the period of notice that the employee is entitled to receive under the contract.

However, there will be circumstances in which the employer will want to terminate the contract

instantly without giving the employee any notice whatsoever. Such a dismissal is technically known as a **summary dismissal**. This chapter will explore when such a summary dismissal is a breach of contract by the employer. This will constitutes a wrongful dismissal which will enable the dismissed employee to bring a claim for compensation in the form of **damages** in the ordinary courts or in an employment tribunal. However, a summary dismissal is lawful, that is, permitted by contract law, where the employer is justified in regarding the employee as being guilty of **gross misconduct**. As will be clarified during this chapter, there is an important overlap here between a dismissal and a breach of contract by the employee in the form of breach of the **duty of obedience,** or a breach of the **duty of cooperation** (see Chapter 3).

Similarly, an employee may be the victim of a serious breach of contract by the employer, for example, through breach of the duty to maintain mutual trust and confidence, which may entitle the employee to resign and claim damages for constructive wrongful dismissal. This chapter will examine when a resignation constitutes a **constructive dismissal** and the **grievance procedures** an employee is advised to follow before deciding to terminate the contract. Table 4.2 on page 142 summarises the different types of dismissal which can take place.

The first issue considered in this chapter concerns termination of the employment contract through the operation of the law in the form of the contractual doctrine of frustration, rather than termination of the contract by either the employer or the employee.

Frustration of contracts of employment

A contract is frustrated where an unexpected event destroys the purpose of a contract by making its performance fundamentally different to what was envisaged by the contracting parties when the contract was first entered into. Under the Law Reform (Frustrated Contracts) Act 1943 where a contract is frustrated the normal consequence is that neither party continues to be bound by their obligations under the contract, but money owed prior to the frustrating event remains payable. In the context of the contract of employment this means that the employee is entitled to be paid up to the date that the contract is terminated through frustration, but there is no dismissal by the employer even if the employee wishes to continue with the contract. In short, where an employment contract is frustrated, an employee is unable to claim wrongful or unfair dismissal. The latter type of dismissal is the subject-matter of the next chapter, but the essence of an unfair dismissal is that an employer has acted unreasonably in deciding to dismiss an employee even though the dismissal has not involved any breach of contract on the employer's part.

The imprisonment of an employee provides one important example of how an employment contract can be frustrated. The leading case on this is *F. C. Shepherd & Co Ltd* v. *Jerrom* [1986] ICR 802; IRLR 358 where an apprentice was sent to a young offenders institution for nine months. At the time of the sentence the apprenticeship had just over two years to run. It was held that the sentence frustrated the contract as it meant Jerrom would be absent for a significant proportion of the remainder of the apprenticeship. On the other hand, a short sentence, such as one for 20 days imposed on the employee for maintenance arrears in *Mecca Ltd* v. *Shepherd* EAT 7379/78, will not frustrate the contract.

Case Summary

An employee's absence through illness or injury provides the major example of how a contract of employment may be frustrated. If an absence is temporary then, regardless of its length, be the absence due to imprisonment or illness an employer will not be able to plead frustration where it is practical to replace the employee on a temporary basis.

For example, in *Marshall* v. *Harland & Wolff* [1972] ICR 101, Marshall had been employed by the company since 1946. The company did not pay employees whilst they were absent through illness, but it was not its practice to terminate employees' contracts on grounds of illness. Marshall was absent for 18 weeks through a heart condition, but

Case Summary

when he was fit to return to work he was told that his job no longer existed. It was held that Marshall had been dismissed by reason of redundancy and he was entitled to a redundancy payment. His absence was temporary in nature and it was the company's practice to arrange for the work of employees to be covered when they were absent through illness. Therefore, the company could not regard the contract as frustrated.

Frustration is more likely to occur in a **fixed-term contract** in circumstances where absence through illness or injury accounts for a large proportion of the duration of the contract. However, it is also possible for frustration to apply to contracts which can be terminated through notice. The main principles are set out in the case of *Egg Stores Ltd* v. *Leibovici* [1977] ICR 260. The employee was injured in an accident and was paid for the first five weeks of his absence. He was unable to work for a total period of five and a half months, and when he sought to return to work he was told that another person had been permanently employed to replace him. The tribunal decided that the contract was not frustrated as the employer had taken no steps to terminate the employee's employment. The EAT decided that the tribunal had made an error of law as frustration automatically terminates an employment contract without any action being required on the employer's part.

In remitting the case to a different tribunal to determine whether the contract had been frustrated, the EAT identified the following factors to be taken into account in considering when illness may frustrate an employment contract:

✦ The length of previous employment – the longer an employee has been employed the greater the onus on the employer to keep the job open unless temporary cover or replacement is not a practical option.

✦ How long the employment had been expected to continue in the future – this is particularly important where the contract is for a fixed-term and the employee will be absent for much of the remainer of the contract.

✦ The nature, length and effect of the illness or injury – where the employee's incapacity is permanent or long-term it is more likely that the contract is frustrated.

✦ The nature of the job, the need for the work to be done and for a replacement to do it – frustration is more likely where the employee has a key role in the organisation so that the work must be covered but it is not practical to appoint a temporary replacement.

✦ The risk to the employer of acquiring obligations in respect of redundancy payments or unfair dismissal compensation to the replacement employee if the latter is to be dismissed when the absent employee returns to work.

✦ Whether all or any part of an employee's salary or wages have continued to be paid during the period of the absence.

✦ The acts and statements of the employer – has the employer behaved in way that suggests that the contract is still continuing despite the employee's absence?

✦ Whether a reasonable employer could have been expected to wait longer before permanently replacing the employee.

A contract is unlikely to be frustrated if an employee is still receiving sick pay as this demonstrates that the contract is still in existence. A contract will be frustrated where the incapacity caused by illness or injury is permanent. For example, in *Notcutt* v. *Universal Equipment Co. Ltd.* [1986] ICR 414, the employee's doctor stated that he did not think Notcutt would work again after suffering a heart attack. It was held that the contract was frustrated. It is interesting to note in this case that the employer had given

Notcutt notice of dismissal. However, as in law the contract was already frustrated by the time this notice was given, there was no dismissal.

Employers need to be cautious in seeking to rely on the doctrine of frustration to argue that an employment contract has come to an end as a result of an employee's illness or injury. If an employer's calculations are wrong and the contract is not frustrated, the employee will be able to claim damages for wrongful dismissal if the contract has been terminated without notice. If the employee is eligible to claim unfair dismissal, such a claim may succeed even though the employee has received due notice. To avoid being liable for unfair dismissal it is normally very important that the employer consults with the employee and obtains full medical reports prior to reaching a decision to dismiss (as will be examined in Chapter 5). Finally, employers also need to be wary of acting in violation of the disability discrimination provisions in the Equality Act 2010. Employers should not normally dismiss employees on grounds of an illness or injury, which also constitutes a disability, without first considering whether reasonable adjustments to the employee's work, patterns of working or the equipment the employee uses can be taken to enable the employee to remain in employment (see Chapter 7).

Lawful termination of the contract of employment

Other than in circumstances in which a contract of employment is brought to an end by the doctrine of frustration, employment contracts will be terminated through the actions of one or both of the contracting parties. A dismissal may constitute a breach of contract by the employer but, before considering the circumstances in which this will be the case, we will examine the different ways in which an employment contract can be lawfully brought to an end. If an employment contract is terminated lawfully this means that neither the employer nor the employee has acted in breach of contract. The ways in which in employment contract can be lawfully terminated are summarised in Table 4.1.

Table 4.1 Lawful termination of employment contracts

Lawful termination	Method of termination
Resignation	Employee terminates employment contract by submitting a resignation with due notice
Dismissal	Employer terminates employment contract by dismissing employee with due notice
Expiry of a fixed-term contract	The period of time that the parties agreed the contract should last has come to end, and the contract is not renewed
Mutual agreement	Employer and employee agree that the employment contract should be terminated

Resignation by an employee

Normally where it is the employee who has terminated the contract by resigning, he or she will have no legal rights against the employer. The major exception to this is where the employee can establish that there has been a constructive dismissal, and this will be considered below.

Under s. 86(2) of the Employment Rights Act (ERA) 1996, an employee who has been continuously employed for one month or more is obliged to give at least one week's notice. This is the minimum that an employee must give. If the contract specifies a longer period of notice then the employee must give this period of notice or the resignation will be a breach of contract. If the contract does not specify a notice period then the employee must give reasonable notice of a decision to resign. What constitutes reasonable notice depends on all the circumstances of the case. These include any normal practice in the employing organisation or the area of business in which the employee is employed.

Where an employee resigns in breach of contract, an employer may sue to recover damages for any financial loss that the employer incurs. In practice, an employer is only likely to sue where the employee is a senior employee or a valuable asset to the employer, so that the latter suffers a real financial loss as a result of the employee failing to work out his or her notice. Employees in the worlds of entertainment and professional sport are examples of the sorts of employees who may be sued for resigning in breach of contract. However, in most forms of employment, employers will not exercise their rights to sue. This is because either an employer will not incur any financial loss, or it will not be practical to recover this sum of money from the employee. The more likely penalty that an employer will use is to refuse to give a reference to an employee, or to state in a reference that the employee left the organisation in breach of the employment contract.

Despite what employers sometimes threaten, they cannot withhold accrued wages or holiday pay from an employee who resigns in breach of contract. Such conduct, unless permitted by a term in the contract or through prior written consent by the employee, will normally constitute an unlawful deduction from pay contrary to s. 13 ERA 1996 (as explained in Chapter 3). Consequently, the employee will be entitled to present a claim to a tribunal to recover the money that is owed.

Key stats

It is interesting to note that, although unlawful deductions from an employee's pay have not generated a lot of case law in terms of decided cases laying down important precedents for the future, disputes over deductions from pay are a major part of the annual workload of employment tribunals. After claims of unfair dismissal this is the second most popular type of claim that tribunals have to deal with.

In 2007–08, 34,600 claims were accepted by tribunals. In 2008–9, 33,800 such claims were accepted and in 2009–10 the number of accepted claims leapt to 75,500. It is not possible to discern from the figures why there were so many claims in 2009–10 but, possibly, the significant increase in the number of claims is linked to the economic recession in the wake of the global banking and financial crisis which exploded in 2008. There was a fall in the number of accepted claims accepted in 2010–11, but at a figure of 71,300 the number of claims was still high.

In the period between April 2010 and March 2011, 38,200 claims were dealt with: 14% of these claims were successful, 33% were withdrawn and 27% were resolved through ACAS conciliated settlements. Of the remaining claims 9% were struck out without a hearing taking place, and 8% were unsuccessful after a preliminary or full hearing.

The statistics also demonstrate that, generally, claims for breach of contract constitute an important part of the workload of employment tribunals. It is not possible to identify how many of these claims were for wrongful dismissal, or how many were for constructive rather than actual dismissal, but breach of contract claims heard by employment tribunals are the third most popular type of claim that tribunals deal with.

In 2007–08, 2008–09 and 2009–10, 25,100, 32,800 and 42,500 contractual claims were accepted by tribunals in these respective years. In 2010–11, 34,600 claims were accepted.

Between April 2010 and March 2011, 31,800 of these claims were dealt with: 17% of which succeeded at full tribunal, 23% were withdrawn and 32% were resolved through ACAS conciliated settlements. Of the remaining claims, 8% were struck out without a hearing and 9% failed after a preliminary or full hearing.

Source: Ministry of Justice Employment Tribunal and EAT statistics 2010–11 published by the Ministry of Justice in September 2011. The full report can be downloaded at **http://www.justice.gov.uk/downloads/statistics/mojstats/employment-trib-stats-april-march-2010-11.pdf**

Termination by mutual agreement

It is possible for an employer and an employee to agree that the employment contract should come to an end. In such a case there is neither a dismissal nor a resignation and there can be no question of either party being in breach of contract. A good example of such a termination is where employees are invited to apply for **voluntary severance** or early retirement in return for a lump sum payment over and above their normal salaries. If severance is subsequently offered by the employer and accepted by an employee, the contract is terminated by mutual agreement.

As in *Birch* v. *University of Liverpool* [1985] ICR 470, such schemes may operate in a context where the employer is seeking to reduce the size of the workforce, and voluntary severance and/or early retirement is seen as an alternative to the employer needing to make employees redundant. This should be contrasted with **voluntary redundancy**. This is a selection method for dismissal by reason of redundancy in a context where employees are being invited to volunteer for dismissal. The employees' rights in such a situation are to an agreed redundancy payment (see further in Chapter 6).

The courts will not permit an employer to disguise a dismissal as a termination by mutual agreement. In *Igbo* v. *Johnson Matthey Chemicals Ltd* [1986] ICR 505, an employee was granted leave of absence to visit her family in Nigeria. The employer required her to sign a document stating that if she did not return to work by a stipulated date her employment would terminate. Igbo failed to return by the due date. The Court of Appeal ruled that she had been dismissed. Despite the agreement she had made, it was clear that the decision to terminate her contract was made unilaterally by the employer and Igbo had not genuinely agreed to her employment coming to an end.

Case Summary

It is very important that the courts have adopted the position taken in *Igbo*, as otherwise such 'agreements' could be used by an employer as a device to exclude an employee's rights to bring a claim for unfair and/or wrongful dismissal.

Expiry of fixed-term contracts

A contract is for a fixed term if its date of expiry is stipulated as a term of the contract. Such a contract will be still for a fixed term even if can be terminated by notice during its period of operation. For example, a contract is to last for one year but during that year can be terminated by either party giving one month's notice to the other. This contract is still a fixed-term contract despite the fact that it can be terminated by notice. A contract which is to terminate on completion of a specified task is also a fixed-term contract. Non-renewal by an employer of a fixed-term contract is perfectly permissible at common law as an employer is under no obligation to offer an employee a new contract once the previous contract has come to an end. However, such a non-renewal is a dismissal for statutory purposes (as will be seen in the next chapter). Therefore an employee, who has been employed under a two-years fixed-term contract, or a series of fixed-term contracts which have lasted for at least two years, is able to present a claim of unfair dismissal.

Since 1 October 2002, the use of fixed-term contracts for employees, but not workers, has been regulated by the Fixed-Term Employees (Prevention of Less Favourable Treatment) Regulations 2002, SI 2002/2034. These regulations implement the EC Fixed-Term Work Directive No. 99/70. The main purpose of these regulations is to ensure that fixed-term employees are treated equally with permanent employees unless differential treatment can be objectively justified by the employer by reference to its commercial or organisational needs.

Additionally, regulation 8 limits the use of fixed-term contracts. Once an employee has been continuously employed under successive fixed-term contracts for a period of four years, then renewal of the most recent contract will transform the contract into a permanent one which can only be terminated by notice. At the very least the notice period will be the statutory minimum period detailed below. If a single fixed-term contract is for longer than four years, as may be the case in professional sport and the entertainment industry, regulation 8 does not apply unless this contract is renewed. Regulation 8(2) permits an employer objectively to justify the continued use of fixed-term contracts beyond the four-year period. Professional football provides a good example of such justification, as clubs typically employ both playing and coaching staff under a succession of fixed-term contracts and this is the agreed norm within the sport.

Case Summary

In *Duncombe* v. *Secretary of State for Children, Schools and Families* [2011] ICR 1313, the SC held that it was objectively justifiable to employ teachers in schools in other EU member states on fixed-term contracts for a period of up to nine years when, as a result of regulations governing those schools, it was unable to continue to employ them on the expiry of the nine-year period. It was always the intention that the employment would last for no longer than nine years and this was not an abuse of the use of successive fixed-term contracts as permanent contracts would not have been appropriate.

Dismissal by notice

The employer has a contractual right to dismiss for any reason, or indeed no good reason whatsoever, providing the employee receives due notice. The period of notice will normally be expressly stated as a term of the contract, otherwise it must satisfy the requirement of reasonableness. As explained above, in the context of a resignation by an employee, what is reasonable in any given situation will depend on all the relevant circumstances such as any norm in the employer's field of business or industry.

Statutory minimum periods of notice are provided by s. 86 ERA 1996. Once an employee has been employed for one month then during the first two years of employment the employee is entitled to receive one week's notice. The employee is entitled to receive an additional week's notice for each subsequent year that the employee is employed. For example, an employee who has completed six years' employment is entitled to six weeks' notice. These statutory notice periods are subject to a maximum period of 12 weeks. Therefore, for example, an employee who has been employed for 20 years is still only entitled, under s. 86, to 12 weeks' notice. Where the contractual notice period is more generous than the statutory period, it is the contractual period that applies. It is not uncommon in professional jobs for employees to be entitled to notice periods of several months, and for such notice periods to operate from the start of the employment.

Technically, an employer will be in breach of contract if an employee is dismissed instantly but is given contractual pay in lieu of notice; that is, the employee is not permitted to work out the notice period. However, as the only contractual claim that the employee can bring is one of damages for wrongful dismissal then, providing the employer has paid all contractual payments that the employee would have earned during the notice period, there is no point to an employee claiming wrongful dismissal. Payment of salary in lieu of notice does not prevent an employee from claiming **unfair dismissal** if that employee has at least two years' **continuous employment** (see Chapter 5).

Termination of an employment contract by summary dismissal

The methods of terminating an employment contract, which are explained above, will normally result in the contract being terminated in a way that involves neither the employer nor the employee acting in breach of contract. By way of contrast, a summary dismissal, where no notice or inadequate notice is given or a fixed-term contract is terminated prior to its date of expiry, is *prima facie* a breach of contract. Such a dismissal is termed a wrongful dismissal, and will enable the employer to sue the employer for breach of contract.

However, not all **summary dismissals** will result in an employer being in breach of contract. A summary dismissal is permissible where the employee is guilty of **gross misconduct**. For this to be the case, the employee must be in breach of a term – express or implied – which is at the heart or root of the contract, or have refused to perform the contract in its entirety. Such a breach of contract by an employee is technically known as a **repudiatory breach**. Disobedience of a lawful and reasonable instruction by the employer *may* constitute gross misconduct. However, if, in the circumstances of a given case, the employee's disobedience does not constitute a repudiatory breach then a summary dismissal will be wrongful. Table 4.2, on page 142, distinguishes between lawful and wrongful summary dismissals.

Essentially, a summary dismissal is always a wrongful dismissal unless it is the employee who has committed a repudiatory breach of contract by behaving in a way that constitutes gross misconduct. Where the employee is guilty of gross misconduct then the dismissal is justified and is lawful. It is for the courts to decide whether the employee has been guilty of misconduct and, if so, whether the misconduct is so serious as to constitute a repudiatory breach of contract on the employee's part. The following cases provide examples of how the courts approach the issue of gross misconduct.

Case Summary

In *Laws* v. *London Chronicle Ltd* [1959] 2 All ER 285 CA, Laws, who was employed as a personal assistant, accompanied her immediate superior to a meeting called by the managing director. A quarrel broke out between her superior and the managing director. The former left the meeting and instructed Laws to leave with him. The managing director instructed her to stay. She left the meeting and was summarily dismissed by the managing director for wilful disobedience. The Court of Appeal upheld her complaint of wrongful dismissal on the basis that she had been posed with a dilemma resulting from conflicting loyalties. The managing director of a company is really the employer in human form, and therefore there could not be any doubt that Laws had been guilty of disobedience as his orders took precedence over any instructions issued by any other manager in the company. However, in the circumstances, although Laws had committed a breach of contract, it was not a repudiatory breach amounting to gross misconduct.

The judgment of Lord Evershed, the Master of the Rolls at the time of the case, clarifies that it is the ordinary principles of contract law that apply to summary dismissals, and there are no special principles that apply to contracts of employment. His judgment also clarifies what is meant by a repudiatory breach. He stated:

> 'To my mind, the proper conclusion to be drawn . . . is that, since a contract of service is but an example of contracts in general, so that the general law of contract will be applicable, it follows the question must be – if summary dismissal is claimed to be justifiable – whether the conduct complained of is such to show the servant to have disregarded the essential conditions of the contract of service. It is, no doubt, generally true that wilful disobedience of an order will justify summary dismissal, since wilful disobedience of an order shows a disregard – a complete disregard – of a condition essential to the contract of service, namely, the condition that the servant must obey the proper orders of the master, and that unless he does so the relationship is, so to speak, struck at fundamentally . . . one act of disobedience or misconduct can justify dismissal only if it is of a nature which goes to show (in effect) that the servant is repudiating the contract, or one of its essential conditions . . .' (page 287).

> **there is no standard test for ascertaining whether misconduct is gross**

There is no standard test for ascertaining whether misconduct is gross. The circumstances of the case must be taken into account in determining whether or not the employee has committed a repudiatory breach of contract. Only if this is so is the employer justified in deciding immediately to terminate the contract. From a contractual perspective the dismissal is simply the employer communicating to the employee that the latter's breach has discharged the employer from its obligations under the contract, and the employer has consequently elected to treat the contract as at an end.

The case of *Pepper* v. *Webb* [1969] 2 All ER 216 both illustrates when misconduct will amount to a repudiatory breach and that gross misconduct may take the form of a series of incidents which culminate in a single event which can be regarded by the employer as the 'final straw'. In this case Pepper was employed as a gardener and the employer's wife was in charge of him on a day-to-day basis. For the first three months of his employment Pepper was regarded as a good employee, but a personality clash developed between Pepper and his employer's wife. The latter formed the view that Pepper had generally become insolent and uncooperative. Matters came to a head one Saturday, just before Pepper was due to finish work for the week. Pepper was instructed to put some plants into the greenhouse and he refused to do so. He said to the employer 'I couldn't care less about your bloody greenhouse and your sodding garden'; and then walked off.

It was held that Pepper's insolence and disobedience on the Saturday, combined with his history of unsatisfactory behaviour, amounted to a repudiatory breach of contract, and therefore he could be summarily dismissed for gross misconduct. Interestingly, the court took no note at all of the fact that had the gardener complied with the instruction he would have extended his working week by at least half an hour by way of what, almost certainly, would have been unpaid overtime.

The case of *Wilson* v. *Racher* [1974] IRLR 114 CA also involved a gardener who swore at his employee and therefore provides an interesting comparison with *Pepper*. In this case, Wilson was unjustly and without foundation accused by his employer of shirking his work. In fact he had stopped work, which involved trimming a hedge with an electric cutter, as there had been a heavy rainstorm and continuing with the job would have put him at the risk of being electrocuted. In the course of an argument with his employer over why the work had not been completed, Wilson stated: 'If you remember it was pissing with rain on Friday. Do you expect me to get fucking wet?' Subsequently, Wilson ended the argument with the words 'Get stuffed', and 'Go and shit yourself'.

In contrast to Pepper, until this incident, Wilson had been regarded as an impeccable employee. The court decided that, given his work record combined with the fact that he had been unjustly provoked by the employer, his insolence did not amount to gross misconduct and his dismissal was wrongful.

It is interesting to note that this case perhaps marks the moment when the courts moved away from viewing the employment relationship as one of master and servant. Indeed, the court introduced a new perspective on the employment relationship, which in the years since has been of fundamental significance.

In the words of Edmund Davies LJ:

'Many of the decisions which are customarily cited in these cases date from the last century and may be wholly out of accord with current social conditions. What would today be regarded as almost an attitude of Czar-serf, which is to be found in some of the older cases where a dismissed employee failed to recover damages, would, I venture to think, be decided differently today. We have by now come to realise that a contract of service imposes upon the parties a duty of mutual respect . . .' (page 115).

As explained in the previous chapter, in the years since these words were spoken the notion of a duty of mutual respect has been at the core of the development of the implied duty to maintain **mutual trust and confidence**.

The case of *Macari* v. *Celtic Football & Athletic Assoc* [1999] IRLR 787 illustrates the interrelationship between the duty of obedience, the duty to maintain mutual trust and confidence and summary dismissal.

You be the judge

Q: Read the facts of the *Macari* case as set out below. Which of the following do you think is the ratio of the case?

(a) Breach of mutual trust and confidence by an employer does not excuse an employee from the duty of obedience whilst the contract continues.

(b) Breach of mutual trust and confidence by an employer releases an employee from the duty of obedience. Thus the employee can choose to refuse to obey any future instructions by the employer that the employee regards as onerous.

Lou Macari was appointed manager of Celtic in October 1993. In March 1994 the club was taken over by a consortium headed by Fergus McCann. The latter made it clear from the outset that he did not want Macari as manager and excluded him from meetings of the board which, under the previous regime, Macari had attended. In June 1994 Macari was summarily dismissed for wilful acts of disobedience: in particular, a failure to comply with a residence requirement to live in or near to Glasgow. Macari had previously been the manager of Stoke FC and his family home remained in Stoke. This resulted in him being frequently absent from Celtic Park as he was with his family in Stoke. The Scottish Court of Session accepted that the club's treatment of Macari amounted to destruction of mutual trust and confidence. The issue was whether, despite its breach of the duty to maintain mutual trust and confidence, the club was entitled to dismiss Macari summarily for disobedience.

A: (a) is correct. Where the employer is breach of the duty to maintain mutual trust and confidence the employee can resign and claim constructive dismissal. However, if the employee chooses to continue with the contract he remains fully bound by all his duties under the contract including the duty of obedience. In this case Macari's disobedience amounted to a repudiatory breach of contract and therefore his summary dismissal was lawful.

Constructive dismissal

As explained above, if an employee resigns without giving due notice to the employer, the resignation will be a breach of contract by the employee. However, this will not be the case where, in law, a resignation by an employee constitutes a constructive dismissal and breach of contract by the employer. *Western Excavating Ltd* v. *Sharp* [1978] ICR 221 is the leading case on what constitutes constructive dismissal. It is this case that made it clear that for a constructive dismissal to occur it is not enough that the employer has treated the employee unreasonably. The employer's conduct must amount to a repudiatory breach of an express or implied term of the employment contract.

Case Summary

In *Western Excavating*, Sharp was suspended for five days without pay after he was absent from work without leave in order to play a game of cards. Sharp was short of money and asked the company if he could be given either a loan or accrued holiday pay during his period of suspension to cover his living expenses. These requests were refused as being contrary to company policy. Sharp's suspension was in accordance with the terms of his contract, and he had no contractual entitlement to accrued holiday pay unless he left the company. Consequently, Sharp resigned from his job so that he could collect his holiday pay. The Court of Appeal held that there was no constructive dismissal and Sharp had resigned voluntarily. Irrespective of whether the employer's behaviour in this case was reasonable it had not committed any breach of contract, let alone one that was repudiatory in nature.

The decision in *Western Excavating* confirms that the test for establishing constructive dismissal is entirely contractual in nature. The employer must either have committed a repudiatory breach or have announced an intention to so. In the latter situation the employer will have committed an anticipatory breach and, as is the case in ordinary contract law, the employee as the injured party is entitled to accept the proposed breach immediately and to treat the contract as at an end.

A repudiatory breach may be a breach of implied duties, discussed in the previous chapter, such as the duty to maintain mutual trust and confidence or the duty to take reasonable care. For example, as in cases such as *Courtaulds* v. *Andrew* or *Green* v. *DB Services*, an employer may be in breach of either or both of these duties by bullying an employee or allowing an employee to be bullied by his or her colleagues. Alternatively, there may be a breach of an express term in an employment contract, which will constitute a repudiatory breach by the employer, such as **unilaterally varying** the terms of the contract by, as examples, reducing an employee's pay or changing the hours that the employee has contracted to work. Such changes to an employee's contract should only be made with the employee's consent. In *United Bank* v. *Akhtar* (see Chapter 3), the employer committed a repudiatory breach by seeking to enforce a mobility clause in the employee's contract in circumstances where this required the employee to relocate his family home and the employer failed to give him reasonable time to do this. In short, just as gross misconduct in the form of a repudiatory breach by the employee enables the employer to treat the contract as at an end, so an equivalent breach by the employer enables the employee to do likewise.

Therefore, any constructive dismissal will inherently be a wrongful dismissal as the employer has committed a breach of contract. An employee will always be able to bring an action for constructive wrongful dismissal in the ordinary civil courts, or present a claim of constructive wrongful dismissal to an employment tribunal. Where an employee is also eligible to claim unfair dismissal then the employee may also present a claim of constructive unfair dismissal to an employment tribunal (see Chapter 5).

Table 4.2 (overleaf) summarises the different types of dismissal which may occur and the common law consequences of the dismissal.

Law in action

The nature of constructive dismissal was at the heart of Kevin Keegan's successful claim against Newcastle FC after he resigned as manager of the club in September 2008. The case also illustrates how an arbitration scheme, which operates in a particular industry, can provide an alternative mechanism to the courts for resolving employment law disputes. The background to the case is the introduction into the English game over the past decade of a continental-style management structure where the team manager operates alongside a director of football. Obviously this can create tensions where the lines of responsibility are not clear and/or not kept to.

At Newcastle, Kevin Keegan was the manager and Dennis Wise was the director of football. The tribunal found that it had been expressly agreed with Keegan that he was to have the final say regarding the recruitment of players, and that his contract should be interpreted accordingly. Subsequently, Newcastle entered into a loan agreement for the Uruguayan International, Ignacio Gonzalez, on the recommendation of Dennis Wise, but contrary to the wishes of Kevin Keegan. The latter made several attempts to resolve the ensuing conflict with the Newcastle board before deciding he had no option other to resign. The Premier League's Manager Arbitration Tribunal found that there had been a fundamental breach of Keegan's contract and therefore he had been constructively and wrongfully dismissed.

As illustrated by the *Macari* case discussed above, delay in resigning can constitute affirmation of the employer's breach and the right to claim constructive dismissal is consequently brought to an end. As explained below, a series of events culminating in one event which can be regarded as constituting the final straw can justify a decision to resign. The tribunal found that Keegan's attempts to ascertain whether the dispute could be amicably resolved did not constitute affirmation, and that the final straw was provided by a letter to Keegan stating that the board did not accept that he had a right to the final say over the recruitment of Gonzalez.

Similar facts led to a claim for constructive wrongful dismissal by Alan Curbishley against West Ham in 2009. Contrary to a term in Curbishley's contract, West Ham sold Anton Ferdinand and George McCartney to Sunderland against his wishes. In finding that Curbishley had been constructively and wrongfully dismissed, the Manager's Arbitration Tribunal viewed the Keegan case as a direct precedent.

Source: For a summary of the ruling see **http://www.premierleague.com/page/Headlines/0,,12306~1845645,00.html**; also see Guardian Sport, 4 November 2009.

Table 4.2 Dismissal terminology

Type of dismissal	Definition	Legal consequences
Dismissal by notice	Employer provides the employee with the notice required by the contract	Dismissal is lawful as no breach of contract is involved
Wrongful summary dismissal	Employer dismisses employee without notice, or during the operation of a fixed-term contract, where the employee has done nothing wrong, or any misconduct does not amount to gross misconduct	Employer is liable for breach of contract and must compensate employee for the actual financial loss incurred (e.g. the net pay that would have been earned during the notice period)
Lawful summary dismissal	Employee has committed gross misconduct going to the root of the contract	Employer is entitled to treat the employee's repudiatory breach as having brought the contract to an end
Constructive dismissal	Employee resigns in response to a repudiatory breach of contract by the employer	Dismissal will be wrongful, and the employer must compensate the employee for the actual financial loss incurred

Constructive dismissal and affirmation

The necessity of applying the principles of contract law to determine whether there has been a constructive dismissal means that an employee must not delay unreasonably in deciding to rely on an employer's repudiatory breach as the basis for regarding the employment contract as having come to an end. Such a delay in resigning is likely to constitute acceptance of the employer's breach and **affirmation** of the contract. If the employee leaves the job having already affirmed the employment contract then the employee will have

> a delay in resigning is likely to constitute acceptance of the employer's breach

resigned and will no longer be able to claim there has been a constructive dismissal. Moreover, as demonstrated by the *Macari* case discussed above, once an employee affirms the employer's breach the employee must continue to perform his or her contractual duties properly.

However, a delay by the employee in resigning is not always fatal to establishing a constructive dismissal. The employee may be able to rely on the 'last straw' principle as in *Lewis* v. *Motorworld Garages* [1986] ICR 157. The employer demoted Lewis without due cause and refused to grant him a pay increase that had been given to other employees. Such behaviour by the employer clearly amounted to destruction of mutual trust and confidence, but Lewis decided to remain in his job. In itself this would have constituted affirmation by Lewis. However, the employer continued to unjustly criticise Lewis, who ultimately decided that he had had enough and resigned. It was held that where there is continuing pattern of behaviour by an employer, which constitutes a repudiatory breach, the employee continues to be able to argue that, in law, a resignation is a constructive dismissal. Moreover, it is not necessary that the employer's act that constitutes the 'last straw' for the employee is in itself a repudiatory breach. It is sufficient that that act contributes to the employer's destruction of mutual trust and confidence.

Case Summary

The 'last straw' principle was further clarified by the decision of the Court of Appeal in *London Borough of Waltham Forest* v. *Omilaju* [2005] IRLR 35. Omilaju had made several complaints to an employment tribunal alleging race discrimination and victimisation. As permitted by the contract, the Council refused to pay Omilaju's wages for the time that he was absent through attending the tribunal. Omilaju resigned, claiming that the non-payment was the last in a series of acts which had destroyed the relationship of mutual trust and confidence between him and his employer. The Court of Appeal confirmed that the final act in a series of actions which cumulatively entitled an employee to repudiate his contract and claim constructive dismissal need not be a breach of contract and need not be unreasonable or blameworthy. However, the act complained of had to be more than very trivial and had to be capable of contributing, however slightly, to a breach of the implied term of mutual trust and confidence. It would be rare that reasonable and justifiable conduct would be capable of contributing to that breach. The test of whether an act was capable of breaching the implied term of trust and confidence was objective. The Council's conduct, viewed objectively, was not capable of contributing to a breach of the implied term of trust and confidence, and therefore Omilaju had affirmed any breach of contract by the employer and it was he who had terminated the contract. Therefore, he could not argue that there had been a constructive dismissal.

Case Summary

Writing and drafting

You are employed as a solicitor by a firm which provides advice on employment law matters to C Co. Ltd, a company which specialises in marketing computer software. The managing director is seeking your advice after being informed by Helen, one of the secretaries in the company, that she is being bullied by two of her female colleagues, and is considering resigning. The managing director asks you to draft a letter to be sent to Helen which seeks to assure her that the company regards bullying, if proven, as a serious disciplinary matter. The letter should set out the steps that you think Helen should take internally, that is, within the company, to seek to resolve the issue without the need for her to leave her job. The ultimate objective of the letter is to ensure that should Helen leave she has no basis for taking legal action against the company.

You should spend no more than 40 minutes on this activity.

Handy tip: In drafting this letter on behalf of the company, you need to think about the style an employer should adopt in seeking to demonstrate sensitivity to an employee who has complained of bullying, combined with persuasive argument based on the law as to why she should not resign.

Grievance procedures and constructive dismissal

In *Goold Ltd* v. *McConnell* [1995] IRLR 516 the EAT held that failure by the employer to provide a grievance procedure constituted a breach of the implied term of trust and confidence (see Chapter 4). As a result of the Employment Act 2002 (Dispute Resolution) Regulations 2004, SI 2004/752 employers were effectively required to have written grievance (and disciplinary) procedures. However, this is no longer the case as these statutory procedures were abolished with effect from April 2009 by the Employment Act 2008. The reason for this was that the statutory procedures were introduced to reduce tribunal workload and to simplify the law but, in practice, the procedures generated case law involving some complex technicalities. Given that these procedures are no longer in operation, the decision in *Goold* is once again of practical importance.

The primary purpose of grievance procedures is to encourage employers and employees to resolve problems internally rather than regarding tribunal claims as a first course of action. Thus, in general terms, employees who have a grievance should not resign in order to claim constructive dismissal until the employer has been given an opportunity to provide appropriate redress through internal procedures. Under s. 207A Trade Union & Labour Relations (Consolidation) Act (TULRCA) 1992, failure to do this may result in any damages for constructive wrongful dismissal or, the **compensatory award** for unfair dismissal being reduced by up to 25% (see Chapter 5). An example of where a claimant could find his or her compensation reduced would be where, having received an employee's written complaint, the employee invites the employee to a grievance hearing. However, the employee decides to resign rather than attend this hearing. Assuming the claimant succeeds in claiming constructive wrongful dismissal, the refusal to attend the hearing would be a basis for making a statutory deduction to any compensation the tribunal awards.

Similarly, if an employer does not have an adequate grievance procedure, or refuses to allow an employee to invoke it properly, any damages or compensatory award may be increased by up to 25%. One of the main function of ACAS is to draft codes of practice that employers and employees should adhere to if the employer wishes to discipline an employee, or the employee wishes to make a formal complaint concerning how he or she is being treated within the organisation (see Chapter 1). As documented below, the current ACAS Code of Practice sets out the basis for grievance procedures which employing organisations can use as a model for drafting their own procedures.

Documenting the law

ACAS grievance procedures

LET THE EMPLOYER KNOW THE NATURE OF THE GRIEVANCE

31. If it is not possible to resolve a grievance informally employees should raise the matter formally and without unreasonable delay with a manager who is not the subject of the grievance. This should be done in writing and should set out the nature of the grievance.

HOLD A MEETING WITH THE EMPLOYEE TO DISCUSS THE GRIEVANCE

32. Employers should arrange for a formal meeting to be held without unreasonable delay after a grievance is received.

33. Employers, employees and their companions should make every effort to attend the meeting. Employees should be allowed to explain their grievance and how they think it should be resolved. Consideration should be given to adjourning the meeting for any investigation that may be necessary.

ALLOW THE EMPLOYEE TO BE ACCOMPANIED AT THE MEETING

34. Workers have a statutory right to be accompanied by a companion at a grievance meeting which deals with a complaint about a duty owed by the employer to the worker. So this would apply where the complaint is, for example, that the employer is not honouring the worker's contract, or is in breach of legislation.

35. The chosen companion may be a fellow worker, a trade union representative or an official employed by a trade union. A trade union representative who is not an employed official must have been certified by their union as being competent to accompany a worker.

36. To exercise the right to be accompanied a worker must first make a reasonable request. What is reasonable will depend on the circumstances of each individual case. However it would not normally be reasonable for workers to insist on being accompanied by a companion whose presence would prejudice the hearing nor would it be reasonable for a worker to ask to be accompanied by a companion from a remote geographical location if someone suitable and willing was available on site.

37. The companion should be allowed to address the hearing to put and sum up the worker's case, respond on behalf of the worker to any views expressed at the meeting and confer with the worker during the hearing. The companion does not however, have the right to answer questions on the worker's behalf, address the hearing if the worker does not wish it or prevent the employer from explaining their case.

DECIDE ON APPROPRIATE ACTION

38. Following the meeting decide on what action, if any, to take. Decisions should be communicated to the employee, in writing, without unreasonable delay and, where appropriate, should set out what

action the employer intends to take to resolve the grievance. The employee should be informed that they can appeal if they are not content with the action taken.

ALLOW THE EMPLOYEE TO TAKE THE GRIEVANCE FURTHER IF NOT RESOLVED

39. Where an employee feels that their grievance has not been satisfactorily resolved they should appeal. They should let their employer know the grounds for their appeal without unreasonable delay and in writing.

40. Appeals should be heard without unreasonable delay and at a time and place which should be notified to the employee in advance.

41. The appeal should be dealt with impartially and wherever possible by a manager who has not previously been involved in the case.

42. Workers have a statutory right to be accompanied at any such appeal hearing.

43. The outcome of the appeal should be communicated to the employee in writing without unreasonable delay.

Handy tip: You can download the full ACAS Code of Practice in PDF format from **http://www.acas. org.uk/media/pdf/h/m/Acas_Code_of_Practice_1_on_disciplinary_and_grievance_procedures.pdf**

Source: ACAS Code of Practice 1 on Disciplinary and Grievance Procedures, April 2009.

In summary the main aspects of a grievance procedure are that:

+ an employee should present a formal complaint in writing;
+ the employer should arrange a formal hearing to enable the employee to present the complaint;
+ the employee has the right to be accompanied at the hearing by a trade union representative or a colleague;
+ if the employee is not satisfied with the outcome of the hearing, the employer should arrange for a second hearing by way of an appeal.

Reflective practice

Look back at the letter you drafted to Helen on behalf of her employer. In the light of the content of the ACAS Code, are there any changes or additions that you would like to make to the advice you gave Helen as to steps she should take internally to enable the company to protect her from any further bullying?

The following interview is with a solicitor who has many years' experience in advising employers and employees on employment law matters. It is interesting to note that, in his experience, lack of **continuous employment** or **employee status**, is not a common reason for individuals being unable to claim unfair dismissal, and therefore having no option other to claim wrongful dismissal. His responses also demonstrate that handling claims for wrongful dismissal – be the dismissal actual or constructive – is an important part of his case work.

People **in the law**

Interview with **Piers Bateman**, a solicitor for more than 30 years. Piers became a Partner with Stokes Solicitors LLP in Portsmouth in 1986 and where, presently as a consultant to the firm, he has practiced in business and employment law for more than 20 years, representing small and medium-sized enterprises and individual clients across the counties of SE England and in London.

Where clients have been dismissed, how often, if at all, do you have to tell them that they are not eligible to claim unfair dismissal? About 30% of clients are advised that they will not succeed in claiming unfair dismissal.

If clients have not been eligible to claim unfair dismissal, to what extent is this because they have not worked long enough, or they do not have employee status? Is it common for them to be ineligible on both these grounds? About one-fifth of the above proportion of clients will not be eligible on grounds that they have not worked long enough or do not have employee status. The split between these reasons is about 50/50: therefore it is not common for ineligibility to be on both of these grounds.

Where employees, not eligible to claim unfair dismissal, have been summarily dismissed without notice have you ever been able to advise them that they have a good case to claim wrongful dismissal? Yes about 25% of clients who are not eligible to claim unfair dismissal are advised that they could succeed in claiming wrongful dismissal.

In your experience are there any common reasons for employers deciding to dismiss without giving proper notice in accordance with the contract? There are two common reasons for employers dismissing

without notice. One is where the employer is a small business and either the employer or employee feels 'stressed' and the dismissal is made in the 'heat of the moment'. The other context is where it is alleged that the employee has been dishonest.

Have you had experience of being able to tell clients that, despite the fact that it was the client who terminated the employment contract, the client has a good case for establishing constructive dismissal? If so, are there any common reasons, in terms of employer behaviour, why constructive dismissals have taken place? Yes constructive dismissals do arise, and the underlying reason, in almost all cases, has been because of poor (or entire lack of) management ability at the applicable level of line management.

Specifically, in descending order of 'commonality', the reasons are:

✦ inadequate redundancy procedures, with resulting 'unfairness';

✦ verbal bullying and/or harassment;

✦ 'office politics' combined with lack of management 'grip', thereby enabling self-interested mid-level managers (or an ambitious HR department) to try manipulating procedures to remove target employees from post, and recruit/parachute in target replacements.

Remedies for wrongful dismissal

As established above, an employee who is dismissed in breach of contract, or who is constructively dismissed, has been wrongfully dismissed. The primary remedy for wrongful dismissal is damages. The purpose of damages is to compensate the employee for the actual loss suffered as a result of the wrongful dismissal. Typically, this will be the wage or salary that the employee would have earned between the date of the wrongful dismissal and the date that the contract could have been terminated lawfully by the employer.

It should be clarified, as was held in *British Transport Commission* v. *Gourley* [1956] AC 185, a case concerning damages awarded to an employee who was injured in a railway accident through his employer's fault, that damages are assessed on **net pay** rather than **gross pay** as damages are not taxed. It is the loss of net pay therefore that constitutes the employee's actual financial loss. Similarly, the national insurance contributions an employee would have made are deducted from the damages the court awards. As a result of ss. 401 and 403 Income Tax (Earnings and Pensions) Act 2003 damages in excess of £30,000 are taxable. Therefore, any sum of damages over and above £30,000 will be awarded on the basis of the dismissed employee's gross pay.

Before considering in greater depth how damages are calculated, we shall look at other remedies, in the form of court orders, which may be available to some employees who have been wrongfully dismissed.

Injunctions

It is a fundamental principle of contract law that a court will not compel an employee to continue to work for a particular employer or vice versa. Therefore, the courts will not grant decrees of **specific performance** in the contexts of employment contracts. However, the courts may, in appropriate circumstances grant **injunctions** to prevent an employer or employee from acting in breach of contract. The courts are able to do this where the effect of an injunction is to encourage but not compel performance of the contract. In *Warner Bros* v. *Nelson* [1936] 3 All ER 160, the actress Bette Davis agreed as part of a contract with Warner Bros that she would not act in films for any other movie studio for the period of that contract. The court granted Warner Bros an injunction to prevent her from acting in violation of this negative undertaking in her contract.

Case Summary

By way of contrast, in *Page One Records Ltd.* v. *Britton* [1967] 3 All ER 822, the court refused to grant an injunction to the record company to prevent the Troggs, a successful pop group in the 1960s, from breaking an undertaking in their contract that they would not employ any other record company as their manager for the duration of the contract, as this would have had the effect of compelling the group to continue with the contract with Page One Records.

Case Summary

The reason for the different decisions is based on the courts' perceptions of the different capabilities of the artistes in the two cases. Bette Davis was regarded by Branson J, the judge in her case, as a person of intelligence, capacity and means, who could have earned a reasonable remuneration by engaging in occupations other than acting in films for the duration of her contract with Warner Bros. The Troggs, on the other hand, were regarded as simple persons with no business experience. Therefore, they could not have secured a similar income to what they were earning as a pop group in any other type of occupation. Nor, for example in contrast to a band composed of intelligent and talented people, such as the members of the Beatles or the Stones, could they have continued to succeed as professional musicians without a manager. Therefore, if the court had granted an injunction to Page One this would have presented the Troggs with no option other than to continue their contract with the company.

The most important employment context in which injunctions may be granted is to restrain an employer from dismissing an employee in breach of procedures incorporated into contracts of employment. Such a dismissal is procedurally wrongful. The impact of the injunction is not to force the employer to continue to employ the employee, but does prevent the employer from implementing a dismissal until the contract-based procedures have been observed.

The case of *Irani* v. *Southampton and South West Hampshire Health Authority* [1985] IRLR 203 provides an example of an injunction being granted in such circumstances. Irani, a specialist doctor, was dismissed in breach of the procedures contained in his contract. The reason given for his dismissal was that he had a bad working relationship with the consultant supervising him, and that as he was the junior of the two it was his contract which should be terminated. The court found that, despite the dismissal, the employer continued to have trust and confidence in him. Moreover, an award damages would have been an inadequate remedy as his dismissal rendered him virtually unemployable within the National Health Service. Therefore, the court decided that it was appropriate to grant an injunction to prevent Irani from being dismissed until the procedures in his contract had been properly followed. The ultimate fate of Irani was not subject to a subsequent legal action so it is unknown. However, the rationale behind granting an injunction in such a case is that if procedures are adhered to then the employer might not reach a decision to dismiss.

It is important to understand that injunctions are not frequently granted even where disciplinary procedures are contract-based. They can be refused on the grounds that an award of damages is an adequate remedy, or on the grounds that mutual trust and confidence between the parties has been destroyed or because the employee has accepted the employer's repudiatory breach of contract.

The case of *Dietman* v. *Brent LBC* [1987] ICR 737 illustrates the latter possibility. Dietman was dismissed by the Council in the wake of a public outcry over the killing of a child by her step-father. Dietman was one of the social workers responsible for the welfare of the child. There was evidence that her dismissal was the result of public pressure rather than a genuine belief by the employer that she had been guilty of gross misconduct. Certainly, her dismissal was wrongful in the sense that procedures in her contract were not followed prior to her dismissal. However, Dietman subsequently accepted an offer of employment by a different council. It was held that her acceptance of a new job constituted acceptance by her of Brent Council's breach of contract and therefore an injunction was no longer a remedy available to her. The fact that she could secure another job in the same field also showed that damages were adequate as a remedy in this case. However, in calculating damages, it was necessary for the court to grant a sum of compensation which covered the net pay she would have received during the period of time that would have elapsed if the disciplinary procedures had been properly followed, as well as covering the period of notice which her contract entitled her to receive.

Case Summary

Case Summary

Contract law theory and injunctions

The granting of an injunction or, as in *Dietman*, the granting of damages to cover the period in which the employee would have remained in employment had such procedures been properly followed, are based on orthodox contractual principles. Essentially, what was termed the 'acceptance view' by Hodgson J in *Dietman*, gives the injured party a choice where that party is a victim of a repudiatory breach of contract by the other contracting party. The injured party can choose to treat the contract at an end, or can choose to accept the breach of contract and to continue with the contract. Earlier in this chapter we saw that an employee has such a choice in deciding whether to resign and claim constructive dismissal or to stay in a job where an employer's conduct constitutes a repudiatory breach.

Case Summary

The 'acceptance view' was first applied to employment contracts by the majority of the Court of Appeal in *Gunton* v. *Richmond upon Thames LBC* [1980] ICR 755. In this case, Gunton was appointed as a college registrar under a contract of employment which could be terminated with one month's notice. However, termination on disciplinary grounds could only be made after disciplinary procedures contained in Gunton's contract had been followed. Gunton was dismissed without these procedures being properly followed, but with one month's salary in lieu of notice, on the basis of bad work performance. The court held that he was entitled to damages for the period for which he would have remained employed if the procedures had been correctly carried out. In the circumstances of the case, it was estimated that this would have been for one further month and he was awarded one month's net salary by way of damages.

Case Summary

An alternative theory known as the 'automatic termination view' had been put forward in *Sanders* v. *Ernest A Neale Ltd* [1974] ICR 565. In this case employees who were taking industrial action were given an ultimatum to the effect that they would be dismissed if they did not agree to work normally by a specified date. The day after this ultimatum expired, the employees reported for work. It was held that they had already been dismissed and that, even if the dismissals were wrongful, they had no choice other than to accept that their contracts had come to an end. The contract of employment was viewed as a special case in which an employee cannot ignore the effect of a dismissal even where it is a repudiatory breach by the employer. In reaching its decision in *Gunton*, the Court of Appeal disapproved of the 'automatic termination view'.

Case Summary

Doubt was cast on the validity of the 'acceptance view' by the Court of Appeal in *Boyo* v. *Lambeth LBC* [1994] ICR 727. In this case Boyo was summarily dismissed after it was alleged he had been guilty of fraud. The Council dismissed Boyo without following disciplinary procedures which were in his employment contract. After his dismissal the police dropped the criminal charges against him. Throughout this period Boyo had protested his innocence and asserted his desire to return to his job. The court found that Boyo had not accepted his dismissal and decided it was obliged to follow the decision in *Gunton*. Consequently, the court awarded Boyo damages amounting to five months' net salary, as this was the period of time that it was estimated that the procedures would have taken to be completed. However, the court also stated that had it not found itself obliged to follow *Gunton*, it would have restricted damages to any loss of the period of notice to which the employee was entitled. Therefore, the court was making it clear that it would have preferred to have decided the case on the basis of the 'automatic termination view'.

Case Summary

Most recently, the decision in *Gunton* has been applied by the Court of Appeal in *Edwards* v. *Chesterfield Royal Hospital NHS Foundation Trust* [2010] ICR 1181. In this case, following allegations that he had conducted an improper examination of a female patient, a surgeon was dismissed without disciplinary procedures being properly followed by the hospital trust. The Court of Appeal held that, if it was established that these procedures were incorporated into his contract, he could receive damages covering not just the notice period but also the period he would have stayed in employment had the procedures been fully adhered to.

An appeal by the Supreme Court was heard in *Edwards* and the decision by the Court of Appeal in *Gunton* appears to have been impliedly approved by it. However, the Supreme Court also had to deal with other issues arising from the case relating to how damages are calculated, and these issues are fully considered below.

In the authors' opinion, the 'acceptance view' should be applied to contracts of employment in the same way that it is applied to any other type of contract. As was established in the previous chapter, an employer has a choice between adopting disciplinary rules and/or procedures as policies which operate alongside an employment contract, and incorporating them into the contract as part of its express terms. Where an employer chooses the latter option it seems appropriate that it should accept the normal consequences for acting in breach of a contract's terms. Injunctions will be granted relatively rarely, as often damages will be an adequate remedy for an employee who is dismissed in breach of contractual procedures. However, it is the case that an employee will continue to be paid, or at least suspended on full pay, if such procedures are properly followed by the employer. Therefore, it is right that damages are awarded to cover loss of pay where the employer prematurely terminates the contract in a way that is procedurally wrongful.

Judicial review

Historically, Crown servants were not considered to be employees but 'office holders' appointed by the Crown and therefore subject to public law. This branch of the law regulates both relationships between the different institutions of the state and relationships between the state and individuals. In the latter context, individuals who are adversely affected by a decision of a state body can challenge the validity of that decision by applying for it to be judicially reviewed and declared by a court to be null and void. This public law remedy is available to individuals who should be regarded as office holders rather than employees. For example, in *Ridge* v. *Baldwin* [1964] AC 40, the Chief Constable of Brighton was able to have his dismissal declared null and void where he was not given a chance to state his case and was therefore dismissed in breach of the principles of natural justice.

Today, most Crown servants, or as they are more normally called civil servants, are treated the same way as employees in general and enjoy the same statutory employment protection rights. Moreover, most public sector workers are employed under ordinary contracts of employment and their rights and duties are regulated by private rather than public law. Therefore, as made clear in *R* v. *East Berkshire Health Authority ex p Walsh* [1984] ICR 743, a senior nursing officer could not challenge a dismissal through an application for judicial review. His appropriate course of action was to present a claim of unfair dismissal to an employment tribunal.

However, public law remedies may still be available to senior civil servants or senior managers in the public sector. There is no established category of which such public servants will be entitled to apply for **judicial review** and the issue must be established on a case-by-case basis. The essential criteria are that the individual's terms and conditions of employment are set out in a statute, or are decided on by a government minister, rather than contained in an ordinary contract of employment.

This was the case with Sharon Shoesmith, whose case is the subject-matter of the following 'Out and about' feature. Shoesmith was dismissed from the post of Director of Children's Services by Haringey Council. She was able to challenge her dismissal through an application for judicial review as her post was established and regulated by legislation – the Children's Act 2004.

Out and about A puzzle: fitting the pieces together

In May 2011, Sharon Shoesmith succeeded in an application for judicial review. Her dismissal by Haringey Borough Council from the post of Director of Children's Services was declared null and void by the Court of Appeal. Her dismissal came about after the death of Baby P in August 2007. Using sources such as newspaper articles see if you can discover the answers to the following questions. A good starting point is to search for the case in WESTLAW.

1. How did Baby P die?
2. Why was Sharon Shoesmith deemed to be responsible for Baby P's death?
3. Which government minister intervened to secure her dismissal?
4. Why did Sharon Shoesmith's application for judicial review succeed?
5. According to newspaper reports how much compensation may Sharon Shoesmith receive?

You should be able to secure all the information you need from internet sources, and you should spend no more than one hour on this activity.

Handy tip: In the Party Names box of the Cases section of WESTLAW use the search words 'Shoesmith Haringey Council'.

Damages

As stated above, an award of damages is the only remedy that will be available to most employees who have been wrongfully dismissed. As is normally the case with contractual claims, damages may be claimed from the County Court or the High Court. However, under the Employment Tribunals Extension of Jurisdiction (England and Wales) Order 1994, SI 1994/1623, employment tribunals also have jurisdiction to hear claims arising out of, or which are outstanding on, the termination of on employee's employment. Such claims include actions in damages for wrongful dismissal and the recovery of money due to the employee under the employment contract. It is important to understand that breach of contract claims can only be presented to employment tribunals if the employment contract has been terminated. Contractual claims which are brought while the contract still exists can only be heard in the ordinary civil courts. However, it should be remembered that, as a result of s. 13 ERA 1996 a tribunal claim can be brought to recover money an employee is owed where an employer has made unlawful deductions from wages, and this includes a situation where accrued wages have been withheld altogether (see Chapter 3).

Tribunals can only grant damages up to a sum of £25,000. If an employee chooses to go to a tribunal to bring an action for wrongful dismissal, but the loss suffered is greater than £25,000, it is not possible to bring a second action to a civil court to recover the outstanding loss. Therefore, if the employee wishes to recover damages in excess of £25,000 the action for wrongful dismissal should be taken to the County Court or the High Court. Where an employee has been summarily dismissed and has successfully claimed unfair dismissal, the compensatory award for unfair dismissal is subject to a statutory cap – in 2012 this was £72,300. Where the employee's contractual losses are greater than this figure, then subject to the normal limitation period of six years from the date of the dismissal, the employee can still bring an action for wrongful dismissal in a court to recover damages for the outstanding losses.

Calculating damages

In calculating damages for wrongful dismissal the normal contractual rules, as formulated *in Addis* v. *Gramaphone Co Ltd* [1909] AC 488 and re-affirmed by the House of Lords in *Johnson* v. *Unisys Ltd* [2001] IRLR 279, apply. In both these cases it was held that the purpose of damages is to compensate wrongfully dismissed employees for the actual financial loss incurred as a result of the wrongful dismissal. Therefore, damages cannot be recovered for the damage to an employee's reputation caused by the manner of the dismissal.

> purpose of damages is to compensate wrongfully dismissed employees for the actual financial loss incurred

In the latter case, the Law Lords made it clear that to award damages on this ground would be to usurp the statutory position concerning unfair dismissal. As we shall see in the next chapter, it is Parliament's intention that the compensatory award, which may be given to an unfairly dismissed employee, can cover loss of future earnings, but this remedy is only available to an employee with at least two years' continuous employment. Damages are restricted to recovering the money the employee would have received had the contract been terminated lawfully, and this does not normally include money the employee would have earned in the future.

Where the employment contract can be terminated by notice the employee's actual financial loss will normally be the net pay the employee would have received during the notice period plus any accrued holiday pay. If the contract is for a fixed-term then, subject to the duty to mitigate as discussed below, the employee will receive damages to cover the remainder of the period that the contract still has to run from the date of the dismissal. Other benefits, such as bonuses and pension entitlements, will be included in a sum of damages where these are part of the contractual benefits an employee is entitled to receive.

In *Horkulak* v. *Cantor Fitzgerald International* [2005] ICR 402, Horkulak had been employed by the company in a senior management position, on a three-year fixed term contract at a basic annual salary with bonus clauses. He resigned after nine months in the job and claimed that he had been constructively and wrongfully dismissed by reason of constant bullying, and abusive and intolerable behaviour directed at him by his superior. It was held that his damages should include discretionary bonus payments where the withholding of such payments was arbitrary and a breach of good faith by the employer. Horkulak was entitled to believe that in the normal course of his employment his contract entitled him to some bonus payments over and above his basic salary. However, bonuses will not be included in an award of damages where their payment is at the absolute discretion of an employer and they are not a normal feature of the remuneration that an employee receives.

Case Summary

Earlier in this chapter we considered the legal consequences of an employer agreeing that its disciplinary procedures are part of its contracts with its employees. *Edwards* v. *Chesterfield Royal Hospital NHS Foundation Trust* [2012] ICR 201 is a recent important case on this issue. Edwards was a consultant surgeon with the Royal Hospital Trust. He was summarily dismissed for gross professional and personal misconduct following a disciplinary hearing. The disciplinary process was conducted in breach of procedures which Edwards argued were incorporated into his contract of employment. These breaches consisted of: a failure to include a clinician of the same discipline as Edwards on the disciplinary panel; the panel should also have been chaired by a legally qualified person; and Edwards should have been permitted legal representation. Edwards argued that, had these procedural requirements been observed, the panel would not have found him guilty of personal and professional misconduct. As a result of the dismissal, Edwards was unable to obtain permanent employment in the NHS. Edwards claimed damages for loss of earnings and pension entitlements and other losses totalling over £4 million.

As stated above, the Court of Appeal confirmed that Edwards was entitled to damages covering loss of earnings in respect of the period that he would have remained employed while contractual disciplinary procedures ran their course.

The Court of Appeal also held that he could recover loss of future earnings if the evidence established that breach of contract-based procedures prevented him from continuing in his career. The Supreme Court reversed this part of the Court of Appeal's decision. It held that the Court of Appeal had been wrong in concluding that a breach of contract of this type was an exception to the decision in *Unisys Ltd* v. *Johnson*. Although statutes such as ERA 1996, the Employment Act 2002 and the Employment Act 2008 had introduced various models for dealing with dispute resolution, Parliament had throughout linked a failure to comply with disciplinary procedures with the outcome of unfair dismissal proceedings. The unfair dismissal legislation precluded a claim for damages for breach of contract in relation to the manner of a dismissal, and this included the situation where the breach arose through a failure to follow contractual disciplinary procedures.

As explained below, one situation where the decision in *Unisys* will not operate to limit damages will be where an employer's breach of contract *prior* to a dismissal causes an employee to suffer from psychiatric injury.

Law in action

Earlier in this chapter it was suggested that you discover what happened to Sharon Shoesmith's application for judicial review challenging her dismissal by Haringey Borough Council. You may have ascertained that her application was upheld by the Court of Appeal. Subsequently, the Council sought leave to appeal to the Supreme Court and this was refused. Contrary to the above case of *Edwards*, where the Supreme Court decided that damages for breach of contract cannot reflect the manner in which an employee was dismissed, as a result of succeeding in her application for judicial review

Source: Imagemore Co. Ltd

Shoesmith will be able to recover damages for loss of future earnings. It has been estimated by employment law expert Philip Henson, of City firm Bargate Murray, that Sharon Shoesmith is in line for compensation of up to £1 million for the loss of her career. Her salary had been worth £133,000 a year to her.

◆ **Handy tip:** if you have not yet had a look at the Court of Appeal decision in the *Shoesmith* case, you can do so from the Industrial Cases Reports or on WESTLAW using the citation *Regina (Shoesmith)* v. *Ofsted and others* [2011] ICR 1195.

Source: Marsden, S. and Woodcock, A. (2011) 'Sharon Shoesmith in line for compensation', the *Independent*, 2 August. http://www.independent.co.uk/news/uk/home-news/sharon-shoesmith-in-line-for-compensation-2330560.html

It was once thought that damages for wrongful dismissal could include compensation for the loss of eligibility to acquire statutory rights. However, it was held, in *Harper* v. *Virgin Net Ltd* [2004] IRLR 390 and The *Wise Group* v. *Mitchell* [2005] ICR 896, that damages for wrongful dismissal cannot reflect loss of opportunity to claim unfair dismissal. This is so even if, as in these cases, providing the employee with proper notice and/or following contract-based disciplinary procedures would have meant that the employees would have acquired the requisite continuity of employment, and therefore would have been eligible to claim unfair dismissal by the date their dismissals would then have occurred.

It may be thought that these decisions are unfair. Effectively, like the decision in *Unisys* and, most recently, the Supreme Court's decision in *Edwards*, they are policy decisions designed to restrict the compensation that employees can obtain from claiming wrongful dismissal in circumstances where the courts believe it is Parliament's intention that such compensation should only be available to employees who, at the date of their dismissals, possess the statutory right not to be unfairly dismissed.

'Stigma' damages

As established above, an employee cannot normally recover any damages for the adverse effect on his or her professional reputation resulting from a wrongful dismissal. However, in exceptional cases 'stigma' damages may be awarded for a breach of mutual trust and confidence by the employer which occurs during the period that the contract was still in operation. Such damages were awarded by the Law Lords in *Malik* v. *BCCI* [1997] ICR 606, where honest employees suffered damage to their reputations as a result of the employing bank operating a corrupt and dishonest business.

Law in action

Readers will recall the massive scandal that broke in July 2011 over allegations that the *News of the World* had hacked into the phones, not just of politicians and celebrities, but also into the victims of crimes such as the murdered schoolgirl, Millie Dowler, and people killed or maimed by the London 7/7 bombings in 2005. This scandal resulted in Rupert Murdoch and his son James appearing before a House of Commons Select Committee, and in the arrests of Andy Coulson and Rebekah Brooks, former editors of the *News of the World*. One consequence of the scandal was the decision to close the *News of the World*, with its final edition appearing on Sunday 10 July 2011.

It was generally accepted that the journalists who lost their jobs as a result of the closure of the paper were wholly innocent of any wrongdoing. As reported in the *Guardian*, this raised the issue of the journalists being able to claim 'stigma' damages by invoking the decision of the House of Lords in *Malik*. Certainly, should it prove to be right in law to regard their employer, News International, as legally responsible for the phone hacking then the journalists should be able to argue breach of the implied term of trust and confidence.

Source: SuperStock, Ingram Publishing, Alamy

It can be questioned, however, whether their reputations really were tainted as a result of the scandal. The view of the authors of this text is that the accepted view that the journalists who lost their jobs were honest professionals might, somewhat ironically, prevent them from successfully claiming compensation for loss of earnings by way of 'stigma' damages.

Source: Bowcott, O., Jones, S. and Quinn, B. (2011) 'Dismissed staff may have grounds to sue', the *Guardian*, 11 July.

Psychiatric injury

Damages may also be covered for psychiatric injury which is a reasonably foreseeable consequence of the breach of an employer's duty to take care and/or to maintain mutual trust and confidence. This was discussed (in Chapter 3) with regard to the decisions in: *Walker* v. *Northumberland CC* [1995] ICR 702, which concerned causing an employee to suffer from stress by requiring that employee to work excessively long hours; and *Gogay* v. *Herts CC* [2000] IRLR 703 and *Green* v. *DB Services Ltd* [2006] IRLR 764, where employees suffered from clinical depression as a result of behaviour akin to bullying by the employer, or as a result of the employer failing to protect an employee from bullying by colleagues.

Case law also establishes that where there has been a breach of mutual trust and confidence it is necessary to distinguish between loss that occurs prior to the dismissal and loss arising from that dismissal. As confirmed by the Supreme Court in *Edwards*, the decision of the House of Lords in *Unisys* prevents a wrongfully dismissed employee from claiming damages for any loss, other than actual financial loss, that results from the employer's decision to dismiss. This includes a situation where the dismissal causes the employee to suffer from psychiatric injury which prevents him or her from seeking and taking up new employment.

However, in *Eastwood* v. *Magnox Electric plc; McCabe* v. *Cornwall County Council* [2004] ICR 1064 the House of Lords distinguished *Unisys* from a situation where the employer is in breach of the duty to maintain mutual trust and confidence before the dismissal occurs, and the psychiatric injury suffered by the employee is caused not by the dismissal but by the breach of this implied term. In these cases the employers were guilty of deliberate misconduct in the way that disciplinary procedures were operated. In *Eastwood*, disciplinary procedures were invoked in order to intimidate two employees and other employees were encouraged to give false evidence. In *McCabe*, the employer refused to mount a proper investigation in circumstances where such an investigation was clearly warranted: McCabe was a teacher who had been accused of inappropriate behaviour towards female school students. All the employees concerned subsequently suffered from psychiatric illnesses. The medical evidence established that these illnesses dated from the period of the disciplinary proceedings rather than the period immediately after the dismissals. Damages were awarded to cover the loss of earnings suffered by the employees as a result of their being unable to work.

Table 4.3 summarises the principles on which an award of damages will be made.

Case Summary

Table 4.3 Calculation of damages

Type of loss	Damages
Loss of net salary during notice period or remainder of fixed-term contract	Subject to employee's duty to mitigate damages will be awarded to cover this loss in full
Loss of reputation as a result of the dismissal	As a result of the decision of the House of Lords in *Unisys*, damages will not be awarded for this loss. The only exception is where 'stigma' damages are awarded where an employer has been corrupt or dishonest
Loss of earnings resulting from breach of contract-based disciplinary procedures	Damages for period employment would have lasted if procedures had been observed
Loss of future earnings resulting from psychiatric injury	As a result of the decision of the House of Lords in *Unisys*, damages will not be awarded where the injury arises as a result of the dismissal. As in *Eastwood*, damages will be awarded where the injury arises from an employer's failure to maintain mutual trust and confidence where this occurs *prior* to the dismissal

Reduction of damages

There are two grounds on which damages for wrongful dismissal may be reduced. One is where the employee has failed take reasonable action to reduce his or her loss. The other, which applies only to tribunal claims, is where the employee was responsible for grievance or disciplinary procedures in the ACAS Code not being properly followed prior to the dismissal. It should be noted that, in contrast to compensation awarded for unfair dismissal, damages cannot be reduced on the grounds that through misconduct the employee contributed to the dismissal.

Duty to mitigate damage

Any victim of a breach of contract is under a duty to take reasonable steps to **mitigate**, that is, reduce or if possible eliminate, the damage, that is, the financial loss, incurred as a result of the breach of contract. Consequently, wrongfully dismissed employees should seek new employment and accept a suitable job if one is offered. However, there will not be a breach of this duty to mitigate if the available employment is not commensurate with the employee's qualifications and/or the job that the employee was dismissed from.

Case Summary

A complete failure to mitigate may result in a wrongfully dismissed employee only receiving nominal damages of, for example, one pound. This is illustrated by the case of *Wilding* v. *British Telecommunications plc* [2002] ICR 1079. This case concerned disability discrimination and unfair dismissal, but the duty to mitigate in these areas of the law operates in the same way as it applies to damages for wrongful dismissal. Wilding was dismissed as he was no longer able to do his job because of a back injury. After he had been dismissed the employer offered him new employment which took his disability into account. Had Wilding accepted this job offer he would not have suffered any financial loss. However, Wilding refused what the tribunal considered to be reasonable offer of re-employment and it was held that he had completely failed to mitigate his loss.

Case Summary

By way of contrast, in *Yetton* v. *Eastwoods Froy Ltd* [1967] 1 WLR 104 a dismissed managing director refused re-employment as an assistant managing director on the same salary that he had previously received. It was held that his refusal of this position was not a breach of his duty to mitigate even though he would have suffered no financial loss had he accepted the alternative job. The significant reduction in his status justified his refusal to accept the offer of re-employment.

The ACAS Code and damages

Although failure to follow the ACAS Code of Practice has no impact on whether or not a dismissal is wrongful it is relevant to the damages that an employee receives if the claim for wrongful dismissal is dealt with by an employment tribunal. As referred to above, under s. 207A TULRCA1992, where there has been an unreasonable failure to follow grievance procedures, or disciplinary procedures, damages will be increased or reduced by up to 25% depending on whether it was the fault of the employer or the employee that the procedures were not adhered to.

In the context of constructive wrongful dismissal, an employee may be excused from invoking internal grievance procedures in circumstances where the employee has been the victim of bullying, harassment or failure by the employer to take reasonable care. However, this is only in the situation where it is reasonable for the employee to fear that there could be ongoing bullying, or a continuing danger to his or her personal safety, during the period that the employee remains at work whilst the internal procedures are being completed.

It should be understood that the ACAS Code is of no consequence where an action for wrongful dismissal is heard at first instance by an ordinary civil court. Therefore, no increases in or deductions from damages will be made by a court where procedures in the code have not been followed.

Summary

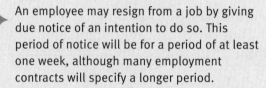

- An employee will not have been dismissed in circumstances in which the employment contract has been terminated through frustration as a result of an employee being imprisoned or being absent from work through illness or injury.

- An employee may resign from a job by giving due notice of an intention to do so. This period of notice will be for a period of at least one week, although many employment contracts will specify a longer period.

- An employer may terminate a contract by giving due notice or by deciding not to renew a fixed-term contract which has expired. Employers must comply with the minimum statutory notice periods, or with the notice period stipulated in the contract if this is longer.

- A summary dismissal by an employer is *prima facie* wrongful and thus a breach of contract. However, a summary dismissal will be lawful if it is in response to gross misconduct by the employee in the form a repudiatory breach of contract.

- Where the employer commits a repudiatory breach of contract the employee may resign and claim there has been a constructive dismissal.

- A repudiatory breach may occur through a series of events culminating in a final incident which constitutes the last straw entitling the

employee to regard him or herself as constructively dismissed.

- Unreasonable delay by an employee in deciding to resign will amount to acceptance of the employer's breach of contract. Once an employee has so affirmed the contract, it is no longer possible to rely on the employer's breach to argue there has been a constructive dismissal.

- In special circumstances an employee may be able to restrain a procedurally wrongful dismissal by securing an injunction or successfully applying for judicial review.

- An action for damages is the normal remedy available to a wrongfully dismissed employee. Normally, damages are restricted to the actual financial loss that an employee suffers as a result of the wrongful dismissal. Typically, this will be accrued holiday pay and the net pay the employee would have earned during the period of notice that should have been given by the employer.

- Damages may be recovered for loss of future earnings in the form of 'stigma' damages, or where an employee suffers psychiatric injury, as a result of the employer destroying mutual trust and confidence before the dismissal occurred.

- Damages cannot be recovered for loss of reputation or psychiatric injury resulting from the manner of the dismissal.

Question and answer*

Problem: L Co. Ltd operates a leisure centre in the town of Barchester. Six months ago L Co. Ltd entered into a contract to employ Susan as the head of its marketing department. Susan soon discovers that Pauline, the managing director, is not impressed with her work. For the past four months Pauline has regularly criticised her performance in front of junior colleagues. One day, Pauline publicly informs Susan that she has decided to demote her, without any deduction in her salary, to deputy head of the marketing department, as she does not have the appropriate attitude for a senior management position. Susan responds by submitting her notice of resignation, which is to take immediate effect.

At the date of her resignation, Susan's net pay was £3,000 a month, and under her contract she was entitled to three months' notice. Since her resignation Susan has been diagnosed by her doctor as suffering from a stress related illness, and has informed her that she will not be fit to work in any capacity for any employer for another 12 months.

Advise Susan as to her contractual rights and remedies (if any) against L Co. Ltd.

You should take no longer than 40 minutes in answering this question.

Essay: 'What would today be regarded as almost an attitude of Czar-serf, which is to be found in some of the older cases where a dismissed employee failed to recover damages, would, I venture to think, be decided differently today. We have by now come to realise that a contract of service imposes upon the parties a duty of mutual respect . . .' (*per* Edmund Davies LJ in *Wilson* v. *Racher*).

Discuss this dictum in the context of considering the circumstances in which an employee may succeed in claiming that there has been a wrongful dismissal.

You should take no longer than 40 minutes in answering this question.

✱ Answer guidance is provided at the end of the chapter.

Further reading

IDS Handbook (2009) Contracts of Employment (Income Data Services: London).

Chapters 7 and 8 provide in-depth coverage of wrongful dismissal, constructive dismissal and damages as a remedy for wrongful dismissal. Chapter 10 provides a clear and comprehensive discussion of how an employment contract can be frustrated.

Deakin, S. and Morris, G. (2012) Labour Law (Hart: Oxford).

Pages 426–89 of Chapter 5 provide comprehensive and contextual explanation and analysis of the law concerning wrongful dismissal.

Freedland, M. (2005) The Personal Employment Contract (OUP: Oxford).

This is the leading specialist text on employment contracts and Chapters 6, 7 and 8 focus on termination of employment contracts. Chapter 7 is of particular interest as this covers wrongful dismissal and actions for damages.

Brodie, D. (2004) 'Protecting Dignity in the Workplace: the Vitality of Mutual Trust and Confidence', Industrial Law Journal, vol. 33, pp. 349–54.

This article examines damages for breach of mutual trust and confidence, after the decision of the House of Lords in *Unisys* v. *Johnson*, with emphasis on the decision in *Eastwood* where damages were granted to cover lost earnings resulting from psychiatric injury.

Ewing, K. D. (1993) 'Remedies for breach of the contract of employment', Cambridge Law Journal, vol. 52, pp. 405–36.

This article provides useful explanation and analysis of when injunctions can be granted to restrain a breach of an employment contract, and of the principles involved in calculating the damages a successful claimant should receive.

Question and answer guidance

Problem: In answering this problem you need to do two things. First you need to discuss whether Susan has been constructively dismissed. In all probability Pauline's behaviour means the company has committed a repudiatory breach through destruction of mutual trust and confidence. You need to discuss the possibility of Susan having affirmed the contract but, as in the *Lewis* v. *Motorworld* case, the 'last straw' principle should be applied in her favour.

Your answer should conclude that it is very likely that Susan can present a claim of constructive wrongful dismissal. The answer should explain that she cannot claim constructive unfair dismissal as she has only been employed for six months, that is, she does not have the requisite two years' continuity of employment.

The second thing you should do in your answer is to discuss how her damages will be calculated assuming her claim succeeds. She will receive £9,000 to cover her net pay during the three-month notice period. There can be no question of any failure to mitigate on her part given her depression. Whether she can recover damages for loss of earnings after the notice period depends on the medical evidence. She can recover such damages if her illness pre-dates the dismissal and is caused by the employer's breach of mutual trust and confidence. However, she cannot recover such damages if her depression is the result of the dismissal.

Essay: This question is asking you to consider and discuss whether, in the modern law of employment, misconduct by an employee has to be examined in light of the behaviour of the employer. Is it the case that misconduct which may once have been considered to constitute gross misconduct will not necessarily be seen in that way today?

Your answer should explain how an employer may lawfully terminate a contract of employment by giving due notice or choosing not to renew a fixed-term contract which has expired. Consequently, a summary dismissal will be a *prima facie* breach of contract and thus wrongful.

Your answer should then discuss cases illustrating the nature of gross misconduct justifying a summary dismissal through considering whether or not an employee has committed a repudiatory breach of contract. Cases you could use include *Laws* v. *London Chronicle*, *Pepper* v. *Webb* and *Macari* v. *Celtic*. The last case is a particularly useful example as it demonstrates the interrelationship between an employer's implied duty to maintain mutual trust and confidence and an employee's implied duty of obedience. An employer's breach of duty does not justify disobedience by the employee, and a dismissal will be lawful where the employee's disobedience constitutes a repudiatory breach of contract. As the question is based on the dictum of Edmund Davies LJ in *Wilson* v. *Racher*, your answer should include discussion of the decision in this case.

Your conclusion could agree with the dictum and explain how mutual trust and confidence is now at the heart of the modern employment relationship. This can transform what once would have been disobedience by an employee into a breach of contract by the employer. The case of *United Bank* v. *Akhtar* concerning the invoking of a mobility clause (see Chapter 4) is a good example of this. Therefore, although gross misconduct by an employee still justifies summary dismissal, the nature of gross misconduct is different to how it was perceived by judges in the past. Consequently, claims of wrongful dismissal which once would have failed may today succeed.

Chapter 5
Unfair dismissal

Key points In this chapter we will be looking at:

✦ Eligibility to claim unfair dismissal
✦ Automatically unfair dismissals
✦ Potentially fair reasons for dismissal with the emphasis on incapability and misconduct dismissals

✦ Substantive fairness and the range of reasonable responses test
✦ Procedural fairness and the ACAS Code
✦ Remedies for unfair dismissal

Introduction

Imagine that you have been dismissed by your employer. You know that your employer, in dismissing you, could not have been in breach of your employment contract if you were given the right amount of notice as specified in the contract. Where the dismissal is not a breach of contract, it will not be possible for you to claim **wrongful dismissal** (see Chapter 4). Indeed, before 1971 there would have been nothing in law that you could have done about such a dismissal, even though you did not understand why your employer had decided to dismiss you, and you believed that you had been treated completely unjustly.

However, the picture has been very different since 1971 when the statutory right not to be unfairly dismissed was first introduced by the Industrial Relations Act. Since that time, despite the employer not being in breach of contract, employees have been able to present claims of **unfair dismissal** to an employment tribunal. For you to have this statutory right you must have **employee status** (as discussed in depth in Chapter 2), and you must have been continuously employed by your current employer for at least two years.

The essence of unfair dismissal law is that it restricts the ability of an employer to terminate a

contract of employment by giving due notice to an employee or by refusing to renew a fixed-term contract of employment on its expiry. Both of these forms of termination of an employment contract are lawful at common law (see Chapter 4). The employer must be able to show that the dismissal is for a permissible reason as set out in s. 98(2) of the Employment Rights Act (ERA) 1996, which is explained fully below. Moreover, even where this is the case, the employer must be able to satisfy an employment tribunal that it has acted as a reasonable employer would act in deciding to dismiss the claimant. A dismissal may be unfair on a procedural basis by virtue of the employer failing to follow the formal procedures set out in the **ACAS Code on Disciplinary and Grievance Procedures**.

This chapter will also fully explain the remedies a claimant might receive from an employment tribunal where the claim of unfair dismissal has succeeded. It may be that a successful claimant will get back his or her job. This would happen where the tribunal has granted a remedy known as **reinstatement**, and the employer has agreed to the claimant returning to the former job and to receiving arrears of pay, etc. It is more likely that a successful claimant will receive compensation.

However, this compensation will often be more generous than what claimants receive by way of damages where they have successfully claimed wrongful dismissal. The primary monetary remedy for unfair dismissal is called a **compensatory award** and, in contrast to damages for wrongful dismissal, may cover loss of net earnings for the whole period during which a claimant remains unemployed after the dismissal. This compensatory award is subject to a statutory cap which, in 2012, was £72,300.

On a technical note, in reading cases on unfair dismissal you should be aware that the right not to be unfairly dismissed was included in the Employment Protection (Consolidation) Act 1978 (EPCA). The right is now contained in ERA 1996 which came into force in August 1996. However, a number of important cases are based on provisions of the EPCA, as ERA 1996 merely further consolidated the law. Therefore, many cases decided under the EPCA remain authoritative interpretations of the law.

Contrasting wrongful and unfair dismissal

Before examining the law of unfair dismissal in depth it is useful to clarify the differences between wrongful dismissal (which we discussed in the previous chapter) and unfair dismissal. It is very important to understand that they are quite separate claims in law based on quite separate legal principles, and the two claims must not be confused by using the legal language appropriate for one claim in connection with the other claim. This is of practical importance because employment tribunals have the jurisdiction to hear claims of wrongful dismissal where an employee has been summarily dismissed without due notice by the employer (see Chapter 4). Where such an employee also has at least two years' **continuous employment**, the employee can simultaneously present claims for wrongful dismissal and unfair dismissal to the same employment tribunal. It is possible for the employee to succeed in both claims, but it is also possible for the employee to succeed in one claim but to fail in the other. Therefore, in presenting legal arguments in support of these claims it is vital that the distinction between the different natures of the two claims is carefully drawn and maintained. Similarly, where either or both of the claims succeed the employee will receive different types of remedies from the tribunal. The ways in which an unfair dismissal differs from a wrongful dismissal will become fully clear as this chapter develops, but it is useful to have a general idea of the differences before examining the law of unfair dismissal in depth.

Handy tip: The key to distinguishing between the two claims is to remember that wrongful dismissal is a common law claim based on the ordinary principles of contract law, whereas unfair dismissal is a statutory claim based on its own special principles as provided by ERA 1996. Table 5.1 sets out the main points of distinction between the two claims.

A pre-condition for a claimant who has been dismissed being able to present a claim of unfair dismissal to an employment tribunal is that the claimant possesses the statutory right and is therefore eligible to present the claim. This issue of eligibility is the first aspect of unfair dismissal law which this chapter will discuss in depth.

Table 5.1 Contrasting wrongful and unfair dismissal

Wrongful dismissal	Unfair dismissal
A claim based on a dismissal constituting a breach of contract by the employer	A claim to enforce a statutory right, which is independent of contract law, and is acquired through having two years' continuous employment
Dismissal must be without notice or prior to the expiry of fixed-term contract	A claim can be made even though due notice has been given or a fixed-term contract has expired
Dismissal may be constructive where the employee resigns in response to a **repudiatory breach** of contract by the employer	Dismissal may be constructive where the employee resigns in response to a repudiatory breach of contract by the employer
Summary dismissal permitted where the employee commits gross misconduct through a repudiatory breach of contract	In reaching any decision to dismiss the employer must have acted as any reasonable employer might act
Breach of disciplinary procedures is only relevant if the procedures are part of the employment contract	Usually a breach of the ACAS Code will render a dismissal procedurally unfair
Dismissal can be justified on the basis of evidence of gross misconduct, constituting a repudiatory breach of contract, which comes to light after the dismissal	Dismissal must be based on facts known by the employer at the date of the dismissal
The primary remedy will be an award of damages based on actual financial loss arising from the breach of contract – typically this will be the net pay the employee would have earned during the contractual period of notice	The primary monetary remedy is called a compensatory award and this includes loss of future earnings, up to a statutory maximum, where the employee is unemployed as a result of the dismissal: other remedies include a **basic award** and reinstatement

Eligibility to claim unfair dismissal

In order to be eligible to claim unfair dismissal the claimant must satisfy a number of criteria. These are:

✦ The claimant possesses employee status.

✦ The claimant has been continuously employed by the employer for at least two years.

✦ A dismissal has taken place.

✦ The claim is presented in time.

These criteria will be examined in turn.

Employee status

Only an employee can present a claim of unfair dismissal (as explained in Chapter 1). Workers who are not employees, such as casual workers and many agency workers, are not able to claim unfair dismissal if they are told that their services are no longer required. Government employees may be considered Crown servants rather than individuals employed under contracts of employment (as was established in Chapter 4). However, this is not a problem as far as unfair dismissal rights are concerned as, under s. 191(1) ERA 1996, the rights are expressly applied to 'persons in Crown employment' in the same way as to other employees. Section 191(1) does not cover members of the armed forces and consequently they do not enjoy unfair dismissal rights, Individuals in certain other categories of employment are also excluded from the protection of unfair dismissal rights. For example, as a result of s. 200(1), police officers are generally not able to claim unfair dismissal.

Continuity of employment

Normally, under s. 108(1) ERA 1996, an employee must have at least two years' continuous employment to be eligible to present a claim of unfair dismissal. A year means a calendar year. Therefore, if an employee commenced employment on 1 May 2012 that employee will acquire two years' continuous employment and unfair dismissal rights on 30 April 2014. It should be noted that governments are empowered by s. 200 to vary the qualifying period for claiming unfair dismissal rights by statutory instrument. The government did this in 2012 through the Unfair Dismissal and Statement of Reasons for Dismissal (Variation of Qualifying Period) Order 2012, SI 2012/989, which increased the qualifying period for unfair dismissal from one year to two years. This qualifying period of two years' continuous employment relates to employees who commenced their employment on 6 April 2012. Employees who were already in employment before this date are covered by the previous qualifying period of one year's continuous employment. Therefore, for example, an employee who commenced employment on 1 January 2012 will have acquired unfair dismissal rights on 31 December 2012.

For most employees, establishing they have the necessary continuity of employment by the date of their dismissals is all that they have to do to ascertain that they can present claims of unfair dismissal. This issue, however, is a crucial one. Therefore, if you are ever asked for advice, however informally, by a person who has been dismissed the first thing you should ascertain is for how long that person was employed prior to the dismissal. Moreover, it will also be necessary to determine whether that person commenced employment before, on or after 6 April 2012. If the employee commenced employment before this date then, as above, that employee will be eligible to claim unfair dismissal as he or she will have been in continuous employment for more than one year.

The effective date of termination

In determining whether an employee has acquired the statutory right it is necessary to identify the precise date on which a dismissal took effect as well as the date on which the contract commenced. This date is known is the **effective date of termination (EDT)** of the employment contract. The rules for identifying the EDT are set out in s. 97(1)

ERA 1996. This section provides that where the contract is terminated by notice of dismissal the EDT is the date on which the notice expires. The period of notice to which an employee is entitled will be set out in the employee's employment contract or written statement of terms. This must be accordance with the minimum statutory periods of notice set out in s. 86 (see Chapter 4). In the first two years of their employment employees are entitled to a statutory minimum of one week's notice. This notice period is for a full seven days even though the working week will normally be for five or six days.

The case of *West* v. *Kneels Ltd* [1987] ICR 146 illustrates the interrelationship between s. 86 and s. 97(1) ERA 1996. West began working for the company on 23 July 1984. After she had started work on 15 July 1985, her employers dismissed her and gave her a 'week's notice from now'. The EAT held that the computation of the period of notice of termination of employment excluded the day on which the employee had actually commenced work where notice is received on that day. It was in accordance with good industrial practice that seven days' notice meant seven clear days. Therefore 22 July 1985 was the effective date of the termination of the contract, and West had the necessary qualifying period of one year's continuous employment to pursue her claim for unfair dismissal.

This approach was applied by the EAT in *Wang* v. *University of Keele* [2011] ICR 1251 in the context of determining whether a claimant has met the time limit for presenting a claim of unfair dismissal. As stated below, a claimant has three months from the EDT to present a claim to a tribunal. In this case, Wang appealed against a decision that his claim of unfair dismissal had been brought out of time. The university had dismissed Wang by a letter sent to him as an email attachment on 3 November 2008. The letter, which Wang read that same day, informed him that he was dismissed with three months' notice. Wang submitted his claim on 2 May 2009. The tribunal accepted the university's argument that the notice period expired on 2 February and that the claim ought therefore to have been submitted by 1 May. The issue for the EAT was whether the time limit expired on 1 May or 2 May. The above decision in *Kneels* was applied so that Wang's notice period commenced on the day after he received the email. Therefore the correct EDT was 3 February and the EAT allowed Wang's appeal as his claim had been presented in time.

The recent decision of the Supreme Court in *Gisda Cyf* v. *Barratt* [2010] ICR 1475 clarifies how the EDT is to be determined where an employee is dismissed by letter. The company sent Barratt a letter of dismissal. She was not at home when the letter arrived on 30 November 2006 as she was visiting her sister. She opened the letter when she returned home on 4 December. She presented a claim for unfair dismissal on 2 March 2007. Her claim was out of time if the EDT was 30 November. It was confirmed by the Supreme Court that her claim was presented in time as the EDT was 4 December. The EDT is the date on which an employee actually reads the letter of dismissal, or has a reasonable opportunity to do so, rather than the date on which the letter is posted or delivered. Barratt had not acted unreasonably in failing to arrange for her mail to be opened in her absence and therefore she had no reasonable opportunity to read the letter until 4 December. The Supreme Court commented that if an employer wishes to ensure that the dismissal is communicated to the employee on a particular day then the employer should communicate the dismissal directly to the employee.

Under s. 97(1) ERA 1996, if the contract is for a fixed-term the EDT will be the date the contract expires. Therefore, if an employee was employed under a fixed-term contract for two years on 1 May 2012, the effective date of termination will be 30 April 2014.

Where the employee has been dismissed summarily without notice, s. 97 specifies that the EDT is the date the dismissal took effect; that is, the date on which the employee is instructed to leave the employment or, as held in the *Gisda Cyf* case above, the date that the employee reads a letter of dismissal. This is the position even where the employee is paid salary in lieu of notice. In *Robert Cort & Son Ltd* v. *Charman* [1981] ICR 816, Cort started employment on 15 October 1979 and he was entitled to one month's notice. On 26 September 1980 he was summarily dismissed and given one month's salary in lieu of notice. The EAT held that 26 September constituted the effective date of termination of Cort's contract and therefore he did not possess the necessary one year's continuity of employment to enable him to claim unfair dismissal.

Case Summary

However, as held in *Chapman* v. *Letheby & Christopher Ltd* [1981] IRLR 440, where the employer intends to terminate the contract with due notice, and pays the employee for the notice period but does not require the employee to work, or be available for work, during it, then the EDT is the date on which the notice period expires. Such a dismissal should be understood as a dismissal with notice. An employer might act in this way where the employer wishes to ensure the employee has no further contact with clients and/or colleagues. It may be that the employee has been put on 'garden leave'. An employer can require an employee to work out notice without coming into work providing this does not break a duty on the employer to provide work and does not constitute a restraint of trade (see Chapter 3).

If the employee has resigned then normally the EDT will have no relevance for the purposes of claiming unfair dismissal as the claim cannot be brought in the absence of a dismissal. The exception to this is, of course, where in law the employee's resignation constitutes a **constructive dismissal**. As we discuss further later in this chapter, a constructive dismissal occurs where the employee resigns from the employment in response to behaviour by the employer which constitutes a repudiatory breach of an express or judicially implied term of the employment contract, such as the duty to maintain **mutual trust and confidence**, by the employer. Where an employee has been constructively dismissed the EDT will normally be the date on which the employee physically left the employment. However, should an employee, who has been constructively dismissed, give notice of an intention to resign then the EDT will again be the date the notice expires.

An employer can prevent the employee from acquiring statutory rights by summarily dismissing the employee before the right has been acquired (see Chapter 4). In such circumstances, although the dismissal will normally be wrongful, the employee cannot be awarded damages to cover the loss of statutory rights. However, a wrongfully dismissed employee may be able to rely on s. 97(2) ERA 1996 to acquire the necessary period of continuous employment. This section applies where an employee has been given no notice or a shorter period of notice than that to which the employee is entitled under s. 86, as referred to above.

For example, an employee commenced employment on 10 April 2012. That employee acquires the right not to be unfairly dismissed on 9 April 2014. If the employee was summarily dismissed without any misconduct on his part on 3 April 2014 then, under s. 97(2), the employee will be able to add on the statutory minimum one week's notice he or she should have received. This means that the EDT will be the date this notice expires, that is 9 April, rather than the date of the **summary dismissal**, and therefore the employee will be able to claim unfair dismissal. It is important to appreciate that it is only the statutory period of notice that can be used for this purpose. The employee cannot use any longer period of contractual notice to take advantage of s. 97(2). Moreover, this provision does not apply where the summary dismissal is justified by the employee's gross misconduct in the form of a repudiatory breach of contract, for example where an employee has stolen from or defrauded the employer.

The meaning of continuity of employment

In determining whether an employee has the necessary continuity of employment to be able to claim unfair dismissal we need to understand how continuity of employment may be broken so that previous periods of employment with an employer cannot be taken into account. For example, if every summer you work for two months with the same employer each period of employment is a separate period of employment. You cannot add the periods of employment together in order to begin to build up a period of continuous employment.

The definition of continuous employment is contained in s. 212 ERA 1996. Under s. 212(1), providing the contract continues to exist, weeks count even although no work is actually done at all. In other words, weeks of absence through, for example, holiday or sickness will still count providing the contract is not terminated. However, as in the above hypothetical example, continuity of employment will be broken if the contract of employment ceases to exist. If the employee is subsequently re-employed by the same employer the employee will have to start from scratch in terms of building up continuous employment.

Under s. 212(3) ERA 1996, there are three exceptions to this rule and these exceptions cover a number of typical situations where the employee does not have a contract of employment for a period of time. As a result of these exceptions, weeks may be counted and continuity is not broken even though the employee has not worked and the contract has ceased to exist.

These are as follows.

(a) Where the employee is absent from employment for up to 26 weeks through sickness or injury

It must be emphasised that this provision only comes into play where the employee's contract ceases to exist during the period of absence. Each period of illness must be treated separately. For example, an employee is ill for 20 weeks and during this period of time the contract of employment ceases to exist. The employee returns to work for one day. The following day the employee is again unfit for work and is absent for another 10 weeks. Each period of illness is for less than 26 weeks and therefore continuity of employment will be maintained in this situation. It is by no means unusual for an employee's contract to continue during periods of absence through illness or injury, and in these circumstances continuity is not broken and s. 212(3) is of no relevance.

(b) Where the contract ceases to exist as a result of a temporary cessation of work

Such temporary cessations may occur because there are routine breaks between successive employment contracts, or because an employee has been laid off by the employer because there is no work available for the employee to undertake.

The decision of the House of Lords in *Ford* v. *Warwickshire County Council* [1983] ICR 273 illustrates the approach that may be taken in the former situation. Ford was employed under a series of fixed-term contracts for a number of years by the council in one of its further education colleges. Effectively, every July her contract ended but she was re-employed under a new contract in September after the summer vacation period had ended. Ultimately, Ford was made redundant and she argued that she had been continuously employed for the whole period that she had been employed in the college and her redundancy payment should be calculated on this basis. The Law Lords adopted a mathematical test and on that basis agreed with her. Essentially, over a long period of time she had been employed for a period of 10 months and had ceased to be employed for a period of two months in any one year. Given the proportion of the period of employment to the proportion of the period of unemployment the latter constituted a temporary cessation in her employment, and continuity of employment was maintained.

As held in *Flack* v. *Kodak* [1986] ICR 775 the mathematical test should not be rigidly applied as it only really works where there is a pattern of successive employment contracts as was so in the *Ford* case. In *Flack*, a number of employees had each been employed according to seasonal needs on an intermittent basis over periods varying from 3–11 years until they were finally dismissed by their employer. In deciding whether they had sufficient continuity to acquire statutory rights – in this case the two years' continuity of employment required for eligibility for statutory redundancy payments – the tribunal analysed each of the breaks in employment as percentages of the preceding and ensuing periods of employment and concluded that the breaks in employment were too substantial to amount to temporary cessations of work. This meant that in each case continuity of employment had been broken and they were not entitled to redundancy payments. The Court of Appeal agreed with the EAT that the tribunal had applied the wrong test in determining continuity of employment. The court held that where an employee had worked intermittently over a period of years in an irregular pattern a tribunal ought to have regard to all the circumstances over the whole period of employment to ascertain whether the breaks in the employment were temporary so that continuity of employment was not broken. Tribunals should not confine themselves to looking only at each such breaks in relation to the adjoining periods of employment. Therefore, the tribunal had erred in law in adopting a purely mathematical approach and the case should be remitted to it so that the right test could be applied in deciding the case.

In short, where there is no consistent pattern to the seasonal periods that employees work a 'broad brush' rather than a mathematical approach should be taken. Tribunals should examine and consider the whole period of the employee's employment, looking at all the circumstances including the length of an employee's employment before and after breaks in the employment contract.

This 'broad brush' approach was first adopted by the House of Lords in *Fitzgerald* v. *Hall Russell Ltd* [1969] 3 All ER 1140. In this case, Fitzgerald was a welder employed in the shipbuilding industry. His employment had commenced in 1958. On 28 November 1962 he was dismissed because the respondents had a shortage of work and were therefore obliged to lay off a large number of workers. The foreman told the dismissed workers that they would soon be back. Fitzgerald was re-engaged by the company on 21 January 1963 and finally dismissed because of redundancy on 8 December 1967. It was held that given his history of employment before and after the period of lay-off, which was for less than two months, he had been continuously employed between 1958 and 1967, and his redundancy payment should be calculated on that basis. Another relevant factor in this case, as evidenced by the foreman's statement, was that it was envisaged by both the employer and Fitzgerald that the period of lay off would be temporary in nature.

Unfortunately, irrespective of whether a tribunal uses a mathematical approach or a 'broad brush' approach, employees such as students who work for a particular

Case Summary

Case Summary

employer during the summer holiday whilst at school, college or university will not acquire the continuity of employment required to claim either unfair dismissal or redundancy rights.

(c) An absence in circumstances where by arrangement or custom employment is regarded as continuing by the employer

Case Summary

The most common example of this exception applying is where an employee is permitted leave of absence for personal reasons and the contract ceases to exist during the period of such a career break. However, as demonstrated by *Curr* v. *Marks & Spencer plc* [2003] ICR 443, it is very important from the employee's perspective that the employer not only agrees to keep the job open for the employee to return to, but also agrees that continuity of employment will be maintained during the career break. In this case no such promise was given to the employee, and when she returned to work she had to start building up her period of continuity all over again.

You be the judge

Q: Consider whether Bert is eligible to claim unfair dismissal in the following situation.
On 1 September Bert was employed as an assistant school caretaker. He was absent from work through illness for the whole of the following March and returned to work on 1 April. For the remainder of this year Bert worked continuously except when he exercised his contractual entitlement to leave. On 5 January of the following year, Bert was informed by the head teacher that it had been decided to lay him off, as the school needed to save money and the head teacher wanted to see if the school could make do with just one caretaker. On 2 February of that year, Bert was re-employed as it was decided his services were needed. In April, Bert broke his arm playing football for his pub team and was unable to work for two months. On 25 August, the head teacher informed Bert that, although he had done nothing wrong during his time at the school, he was being dismissed with immediate effect.

A: Bert is almost certainly eligible to claim unfair dismissal. His periods of absence though illness or injury will not impact on his continuity of employment. Either Bert's contract will have continued during these periods, or he can take advantage of s. 212(3) ERA 1996 so that any weeks in which he was not employed under a contract count, and continuity of employment is not broken. This is so because each period of illness was well under the 26-week limit. Similarly, he may not have been employed under a contract during the period of lay-off, but given its relatively brief duration it is likely to constitute a temporary cessation and therefore again continuity of employment will not be broken. He is dismissed before he has worked for two years but, as his dismissal is wrongful, he can take advantage of s. 97(2). This enables Bert to add on his statutory notice period of one week which will give him the two years' continuity of employment required to render him eligible to claim unfair dismissal.

The meaning of dismissal

For an employee to be able to claim unfair dismissal it is of course necessary for him or her to show that a dismissal has actually taken place. This will not be so (as we saw in the previous chapter) if the employment contract has been frustrated or terminated by mutual agreement, or the employee has resigned.

Section 95(1) ERA 1996 provides that an employee is dismissed by his employer if:

(a) the contract under which he is employed is terminated by the employer (whether with or without notice);

(b) he is employed under a contract for a fixed term and that term expires without being renewed under the same contract; or

(c) the employee terminates the contract under which he is employed (with or without notice) in circumstances in which he is entitled to terminate it without notice by reason of the employer's conduct.

A dismissal with notice, and thus in accordance with the contract, may still be unfair, even though it will not be wrongful. Similarly non-renewal of a fixed-term contract, which is of no legal consequence at common law, may constitute an unfair dismissal. As explained above, an employee who has been summarily dismissed may bring simultaneous claims of wrongful and unfair dismissal to the same employment tribunal.

As held in *Western Excavating* v. *Sharp* [1978] ICR 221, a resignation may constitute a constructive dismissal only where it is the employee's response to a repudiatory breach by the employer (see Chapter 4). In this case, the employee was suspended without pay for misconduct and the employer refused to give the employee his accrued holiday pay. As the employer was contractually entitled to do this, it had not committed any breach of contract let alone one which was repudiatory in nature.

Although the concept of constructive dismissal is based on the common law, the overwhelming number of cases that are based on such dismissals will be concerned with claims of unfair dismissal. Many such claims will be based on the argument that the employer has acted in a way that destroys mutual trust and confidence. Any behaviour by an employer which amounts to bullying, harassing or seeking to humiliate an employee will be a breach of this duty and will entitle an employee to resign and claim constructive unfair dismissal (see Chapter 4). It is inherently going to be the case that if a breach of this duty is established then the claim of constructive unfair dismissal will succeed.

The case of *Watson* v. *University of Strathclyde* [2011] IRLR 458 provides a recent example of a constructive dismissal arising out of a breach of the employer's implied duty of trust and confidence. In this case Watson had presented an internal grievance to the university against her line manager. The university convened a grievance hearing but appointed on to the panel hearing the grievance a senior employee who had a close working relationship with Watson's line manager. The university rejected Watson's protest that this employee was not neutral and was likely to be biased against her, and she decided to resign. It was held that in the circumstances the university's refusal to appoint another employee on to the grievance panel was a breach of the duty of trust and confidence and Watson had been constructively and unfairly dismissed.

Case Summary

One of the other main instances of constructive dismissal is where the employer unilaterally imposes changes to the terms and conditions of employment, for example, by cutting pay or altering the agreed hours that the employee should work. Such a **unilateral variation** to an employee's contract, if it is not agreed to by the employee, is a repudiatory breach of contract by the employer. Therefore, the employee can resign and claim constructive dismissal rather than accept new terms and conditions of work. However (as we shall see in the next chapter), it is by no means the case that such dismissals will always be found to be unfair. A tribunal may well take the view that an employer has acted reasonably in imposing new working conditions on employees where the motive for doing this is to enhance the efficiency or competitiveness of the business. Whilst this may give rise to a constructive dismissal, a tribunal may also find it to be a fair dismissal.

However, it is also be possible that a unilateral variation to an employee's contract constitutes an actual rather than a constructive dismissal. This is illustrated by the case of *Hogg* v. *Dover College* [1990] ICR 39, where a head of department was informed that he was demoted with other very substantial changes to his terms and conditions of employment being made. It was held that in these circumstances the employer had actually dismissed Hogg from his original job, and therefore it was not necessary for him to have resigned in order to establish a constructive dismissal. Hogg was therefore able to continue in his new job under his new terms and conditions of employment, whilst claiming unfair dismissal from the job he had previously been employed by the college to undertake.

It can be difficult to determine whether an employee has been dismissed or has resigned. This is most likely to be a problem where a contract is terminated through the use of informal and ambiguous language – particularly where the employer and/or employee have lost their tempers. For example, in *Tanner* v. *Kean* [1978] IRLR 110, Tanner was told by his employer, Kean, not to use the company's van outside working hours and was lent £275 to buy a car. When Kean found that Tanner was still using the van outside working hours, Kean said: 'What's my fucking van doing outside; you're a tight bastard. I've just lent you £275 to buy a car and you are too tight to put juice in it. That's it, you're finished with me.' It was held that the tribunal was entitled to find Kean's words to have been spoken in annoyance and in the circumstances did not constitute words of dismissal.

Similarly, in *Futty* v. *Brekkes* [1974] IRLR 130, Futty, a fish filleter, was told by his foreman to fuck off if he did not like his job. Futty interpreted these words as a dismissal and left the company's employ. The evidence established that in Hull docks, where Futty had been employed, more formal language was used when dismissal was involved. The foreman's words had to be interpreted in their context, which in this case meant: 'if you are complaining about the fish . . . or you do not like what . . . you are doing . . . clock off and . . . come back when you are disposed to start work again the next day.' Therefore, Futty had resigned from his employment and, as there had not been a dismissal, he could not present a statutory claim.

It is important to remember that although contracts may be terminated by an agreement to this effect between the employer and the employee, case law has established that the courts will not permit a dismissal to be disguised as a termination of the contract through mutual agreement. This was illustrated by the Court of Appeal's decision in *Igbo* v. *Johnson Matthey* [1986] IRLR 215 (see Chapter 4). In this case the employee agreed that if she did not return to work from holiday by a particular date this meant that her contract had automatically terminated. It was held that the subsequent termination of her contract was in reality the product of a unilateral decision by her employer and she was able to proceed with a claim of unfair dismissal.

Presenting a claim in time

Before considering the circumstances in which a dismissal may be considered unfair it is important to take one procedural issue into account. If you are considering claiming unfair dismissal, or advising a friend or client to do so, it is very important to remember (as explained in Chapter 1) that there is a strict time limit of three months from the effective date of termination for presenting a claim. Failure to adhere to this time limit will generally mean that the tribunal will declare that it has no jurisdiction to hear the claim. Under s. 111(2) ERA 1996, a tribunal may hear a claim if it considers that it was not reasonably practicable for the complaint to be presented within three months but, as we have seen, the phrase 'not reasonably practicable' has been interpreted quite strictly. A claim to a tribunal is made by completing a form ET1 which is then sent online or by post to the relevant tribunal office (see Chapter 1). A claim is deemed to be properly presented once it is received by the latter.

Key stats

As the following statistics demonstrate, unfair dismissal is a major area of employment tribunal workload. This demonstrates the importance of the statutory right to employees. Even where the employer has not committed any breach of contract in dismissing the employee, the justice of the dismissal can still be challenged through a tribunal claim. However, given that employees who were employed on or after 6 April 2012 will have to work two years in order to secure unfair dismissal rights, it can be anticipated that in the future the number of unfair dismissal claims will fall. This will be, of course, in line with the intention of the coalition government and its desire to ease the burden of employment rights on employers. Alternatively, the increase in the qualifying period for unfair dismissal rights can be seen as weakening the ability of the law to ensure that employees are treated justly by their employers.

In 2009–10, 57,400 claims were accepted by employment tribunals. This is in comparison with 2008–09 when there were 52,700 claims, and 2007–8 when there were 40,900 claims. The increase in claims in 2009–10 is partly accounted for by the fact that the statutory disputes procedures, introduced by the Employment Act 2002 (Dispute Resolution) Regulations 2004 SI 2004/752, which had the effect of encouraging or requiring employers and employees to seek to resolve disciplinary and grievance issues internally, were abolished with effect from April 2009 by the Employment Act 2008. Therefore, as in the past before the statutory procedures were introduced, employees who were actually or constructively dismissed were able to proceed directly to the presentation of tribunal claims. In 2010–11, the number of accepted claims had fallen to 47,900.

Between April 2010 and March 2011, 49,600 claims were dealt with and 4,200 of these claims (8%) succeeded. Some 25% of these claims withdrawn, 41% were resolved through ACAS conciliated settlements and 13% were unsuccessful after a preliminary or full hearing.

Source: Ministry of Justice Employment Tribunal and EAT statistics 2010–11 published by the Ministry of Justice in September 2011. The full report can be downloaded at **http://www.justice.gov.uk/downloads/statistics/mojstats/employment-trib-stats-april-march-2010-11.pdf**

Automatically unfair dismissals

As explained above, if an employee does not have two years' continuity of employment that individual will not normally be able to claim unfair dismissal even if the employer has acted wholly unreasonably in reaching the decision to dismiss. However, there are important exceptions to this requirement of continuity of employment. Various sections of the ERA provide that a dismissal for a specified reason is automatically unfair. In such instances of **automatic unfair dismissal** it is not necessary for the employee to have acquired two years' continuous service. The right not to be dismissed for an automatically unfair reason applies from day one of the employment contract, that is, the date of the commencement of the contract. Moreover, all that the employee

> the right not to be dismissed for an automatically unfair reason applies from day one

has to establish is that the dismissal is for a reason that a statutory provision designates to be automatically unfair. Whether or not the employer has acted reasonably in deciding to dismiss ceases to be of any relevance. However, where the employee has been employed for less than two years, the **burden of proof** is on the employee to prove that the dismissal was for an automatically unfair reason. Otherwise, the burden of proof remains with the employer to show the real reason for the dismissal and, therefore, that it was not for an automatically unfair reason. The rules relating to the burden of proof will be further considered below.

Dismissal by reason of pregnancy provides a very good example of this process in action. Under s. 99 ERA 1996, it is automatically unfair to dismiss a woman on grounds of pregnancy, or because she has given birth to a child or has exercised her right to take maternity leave. This is so even though a woman was pregnant at the time she accepted the offer of a job and therefore ceases to work well under two years from the date that she was employed. Some employers complain that this is unfair on them as they have to incur the costs of the woman's pregnancy without receiving the benefit of receiving work from her. However, without the protection of s. 99 many women who become pregnant towards the start of their careers would find their careers jeopardised as a result of having conceived a child, whereas the would-be father faces no such consequences. From an equal opportunities perspective s. 99 is therefore vital. This issue will be considered further later (see Chapter 7), but it should be pointed out that a woman who is refused employment on grounds of her pregnancy also has legal rights. Such a refusal of employment is unlawful sex discrimination contrary to s. 18 of the Equality Act 2010.

The main circumstances when a dismissal will be considered automatically unfair are summarised as follows and, as specified, are dealt with in more detail at the relevant points throughout this text:

+ dismissal for a reason relating to pregnancy, maternity or family leave (see Chapter 7);

+ dismissal in connection with the right to request flexible working (see Chapter 7);

+ dismissal in connection with the right to time off for dependants (see Chapter 7);

+ dismissal for reasons relating to jury service – s. 98B ERA 1996;

+ dismissal for a health and safety reason – s. 100 (see Chapter 3);

+ dismissals of shop and betting workers who refuse to work on Sundays – s. 101 ERA 1996;

+ dismissal in connection with rights under the Working Time Regulations – s. 101A ERA 1996 (see Chapter 2);

+ dismissal for assertion of a statutory right – s. 104 ERA 1996. (It is automatically unfair to dismiss any employee for seeking to enforce the statutory employment rights discussed throughout this text.)

+ dismissal for making a protected disclosure – s. 103A ERA 1996 (see Chapter 3);

+ dismissal because of a 'spent' conviction as defined by the Rehabilitation of Offenders Act 1974 – under s. 4(3)(b) of that Act (note the normal qualifying period of two years' continuous employment applies to the exercising of this right);

+ dismissal of a trustee of an occupational pension scheme – s. 102 ERA 1996;

+ dismissal for trade union membership, participating in a trade union activity at any appropriate time or using trade union services – s. 152 TULRCA (see Chapter 8);

+ dismissal for a reason relating to a prohibited trade union blacklist – s. 104F ERA 1996 (see Chapter 8);

◆ dismissal for a variety of activities concerned with acting as a trade union or employee representative (see Chapter 8);

◆ dismissal for participating in protected industrial action – s. 238 A TULRCA (see Chapter 9).

The claim of unfair dismissal

There are normally two main aspects to a claim of unfair dismissal once it is being heard by an employment tribunal. The burden of proof is on the employer to establish the real reason for the dismissal of the employee, and that this reason is potentially fair as it is for a reason set out in s. 98 ERA 1996, as detailed below. If the tribunal does not accept that the dismissal is for a potentially fair reason then it must find the dismissal to be unfair, and the tribunal will go on to consider the remedies that are appropriate to grant to the successful claimant.

However, often the employer will be able to satisfy the burden of proof. Indeed, it is not unusual for this stage of the proceedings to be a formality as the claimant will accept that the dismissal was for a potentially fair reason and the employer's reasons for the dismissal will not be contested. Where this is the case the hearing will continue on to its second stage to enable the tribunal to decide whether the employer has acted reasonably or unreasonably. If the tribunal decides that the employer's decision was unreasonable, or was reached in an unreasonable way, then the dismissal will be found to be unfair. The tribunal will determine the reasonableness of the decision to dismiss on the basis of s. 98(4) ERA 1996, and this issue is discussed in depth below.

The employer's reasons for the dismissal

In establishing the real reason for the dismissal, the normal burden of proof in civil law cases applies. Therefore, the employer will have satisfied this burden of proof if the tribunal accepts that, on the balance of probabilities, the employer is telling the truth. This burden of proof can be contrasted with that in criminal cases, where an accused person can only be found guilty if it is established beyond reasonable doubt that he or she committed the crime.

Under s. 98(1) ERA 1996, the employer must show that the principal reason for the dismissal is either a reason falling within subsection (2) or some other substantial reason of a kind such as to justify the dismissal of an employee holding the position which the employee held.

A reason falls within subsection (2) if in the following circumstances:

(a) it relates to the capability or qualifications of the employee for performing work of the kind which he or she was employed by the employer to do;

(b) it relates to the conduct of the employee;

(c) the employee was redundant;

(d) the employee could not continue to work in the position which he or she held without contravention of a statutory duty or restriction.

Incapability dismissals include dismissals on grounds both of poor work performance and absences through ill-health or injury. Dismissals on the grounds of misconduct by the employee are the most common type of dismissal, and the sorts of issues that we have seen considered in the context of wrongful dismissals are also the sorts of issues that give rise to claims of unfair dismissal. In particular, an employee will have been dismissed on grounds of disobedience, insolence or failure to cooperate with the employer. Both incapability and misconduct dismissals are fully considered below. Redundancy dismissals are also very important but these are considered in depth in the next chapter.

An example of (d), where an employee has been dismissed by virtue of a statutory restriction, would be where an employee is employed to drive vehicles and loses his driving licence. If the employee cannot be redeployed for the period that he is unable to drive, then his dismissal will be on the basis that the law prevents the employer from employing the employee in his normal job. In this situation the employer will be able to show that the dismissal was for a potentially fair reason. Moreover, the employer's decision to dismiss will normally be regarded as reasonable by an employment tribunal and it will find that the dismissal is fair. An employer cannot reasonably be expected to continue to employ an employee where the law prohibits that employee from continuing to work.

Under s. 98(1)(b), a dismissal can be considered to be for some other substantial reason where the reason given is 'of a kind such as to justify the dismissal of an employee holding the position which the employee held'. This constitutes a miscellaneous category of dismissal whereby the employee cannot be regarded as having committed any form of misconduct, but the employer can view the circumstances as warranting the dismissal. The most important example of a dismissal in this category, as will be discussed in the following chapter, is where an employee is dismissed for refusing to accept variations to the employment contract arising from a business reorganisation.

Another important example of such a dismissal relates to an employee who is employed under a fixed-term contract, or series of fixed-term contacts, lasting for more than two years, and the contract is not renewed in circumstances where the non-renewal is not connected to the personal conduct of the employee. An employer may well have a good business reason not to renew the contract. For example, the employee was employed under a fixed-term contract to act as a temporary replacement for an employee on secondment, and the latter has now returned to work. However, if the employer has failed to act reasonably in refusing to renew the fixed-term contract, the dismissal will be unfair.

Written reasons for the dismissal

Employers and employees will often agree that the reason the employer advances for the dismissal is genuine and this will not be an issue of contention before the tribunal. However, the employee may wish to argue that the reason given by the employer is untrue. This is important because, as explained above, if the employer is unable to show that the genuine reason for the dismissal falls within s. 98(2) or s. 98(1)(b) the tribunal must find the dismissal to be unfair.

To help the employee decide whether or not to challenge the evidence of the employer, under s. 92 ERA 1996, an employee can request that the employer provides a written statement detailing the reasons(s) for the dismissal. Under s. 93, if the employer refuses to do this and the tribunal agrees such a refusal is unreasonable, it will award the employee two weeks' pay. The right to request written reasons for the dismissal is independent of any actual claim of unfair dismissal, and therefore the remedy of two weeks' pay can be sought even where the claim of unfair dismissal is withdrawn or is unsuccessful. A week's pay is calculated on the basis of gross pay, that is, the pay an employee earns before deductions for tax and national insurance contributions have been made. However, the amount of a week's pay is subject to a statutory limit which may be less than the actual week's pay that the employee earned. In 2012 the maximum statutory week's pay was £430. What is meant by a statutory week's pay will be considered further towards the end of this chapter with regard to the remedy of a basic award. It should be noted that the employer's duty to provide written reasons arises automatically where the employee is dismissed during pregnancy or while taking maternity leave or adoption leave, and is not dependent on the employee requesting that written reasons be provided.

Figure 5.1 illustrates how a claim of unfair dismissal may progress. The following parts of this chapter will explore the issues to be taken into account by employment

Figure 5.1 Claiming unfair dismissal

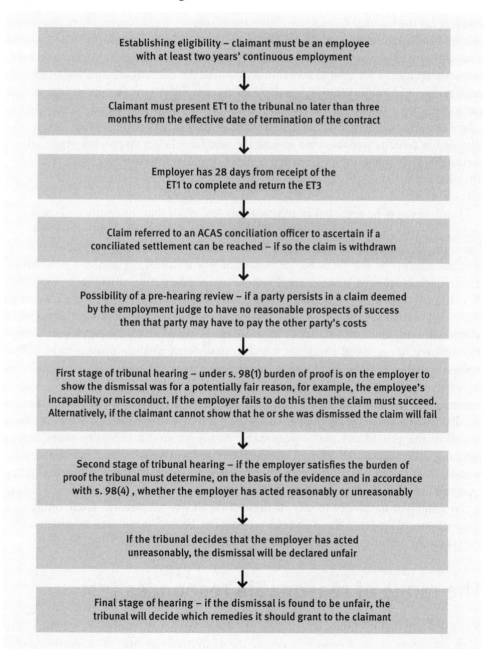

tribunals in determining whether or not the employer has acted reasonably in reaching a decision to dismiss an employee.

The reasonableness of the dismissal

Where the employer has fulfilled the requirements of s. 98(1) ERA 1996, by showing that there was a potentially fair reason for the dismissal, the determination of the question whether the dismissal is fair or unfair is made by a tribunal under s. 98(4). This provides that it is for the tribunal to decide whether the employer acted reasonably or unreasonably in dismissing the employee on the basis of whether the dismissal was 'in accordance with equity and the substantial merits of the case'. In reaching its decision s. 98(4) expressly requires a tribunal to take into account all the relevant circumstances, including the size and administrative resources of the employer's undertaking. In practice, particularly with respect to the formal procedures the employer could be expected to follow prior to reaching a decision to dismiss, it may be easier for a small business to show it has acted reasonably than will be the case for a larger employing organisation. Section 98(4) does not impose a burden of proof on either the employer or the employee. The decision as to the reasonableness and therefore the fairness of the dismissal is for the tribunal to make.

Dismissals may be regarded as substantively unfair, in that the tribunal decides that an employer did not have a sufficiently good reason for deciding to dismiss the employee. For example, the employer may be able to show that the employee's misconduct was the genuine reason for the dismissal. However, if the misconduct involved is relatively minor, such as lateness, and the employee has received no prior disciplinary warnings, then the tribunal might conclude that a reasonable employer would have chosen to impose a lesser penalty than dismissal. Indeed, lateness is the type of disciplinary offence which will normally lead to a series of warnings being given to the employee. Only if an employee has received a warning which is designated by the employer to be a final written warning and the employee is then late for work yet again will it normally be reasonable to dismiss that employee.

Even if the tribunal decides the dismissal was substantively fair, it can still decide that the dismissal is procedurally unfair. This will be the case where the employer has failed to follow the procedures that a reasonable employer would normally adopt before reaching a decision to dismiss. A reasonable employer will conduct an appropriate investigation into the facts and give the employee a formal disciplinary hearing with a final right of appeal before deciding that a dismissal is an appropriate penalty. A failure by an employer to adhere to any of these sorts of procedures will often result in a tribunal concluding that the dismissal was unfair. The circumstances in which a dismissal can be considered to be procedurally unfair will be fully discussed below.

The range of reasonable responses test

It is for a tribunal to decide whether an employer has acted reasonably and therefore fairly. However, it is of primary importance to understand that, as a matter of law, a tribunal must not substitute its views for that of the reasonable employer. A tribunal cannot find a dismissal unfair on the grounds that, if it had been in the employer's shoes, it would not have regarded the employee's behaviour as justifying the ultimate penalty of dismissal. Alternatively, it cannot argue that the dismissal was procedurally unfair because the tribunal members would have adopted a different procedure before reaching a decision to dismiss. Employers may operate within a band or range of reasonable responses. Only if a dismissal is outside of this range, and therefore

> ## a tribunal must not substitute its views for that of the reasonable employer

the employer has acted in a way that no reasonable employer would act, can a tribunal find a dismissal to be unfair. This **range of reasonable responses test** was formulated and explained in the following cases.

In *British Leyland (UK) Ltd* v. *Swift* [1981] IRLR 91, the tribunal had found that the employer had acted unreasonably in failing to consider a penalty short of dismissal with regard to a long-serving employee who had displayed a vehicle licence belonging to the company on his own car. The Court of Appeal found that, as the employee was guilty of dishonesty, the employer had acted as any reasonable employer might act and the dismissal was fair. In explaining that what is meant by a band or range of reasonable responses, Lord Denning stated:

'The correct test is: was it reasonable for the employer to dismiss him? If no reasonable employer would have dismissed him, then the dismissal was unfair. But if a reasonable employer might reasonably have dismissed him, then the dismissal was fair. It must be remembered that in all these cases there is a band of reasonableness within which one employer might reasonably take one view; another quite reasonably take a different view . . . if it was quite reasonable to dismiss him, then the dismissal must be upheld as fair: even though some other employers may not have dismissed him . . .' (page 93).

This test was applied by the EAT in *Iceland Frozen Foods Ltd* v. *Jones* [1982] IRLR 439 EAT, a case concerning an employee who attempted to make a false claim for an overtime payment. Browne-Wilkinson, J explained the law as follows:

'(1) the starting point must be the words [of the section] themselves; (2) in applying the section an Industrial Tribunal must consider the reasonableness of the employer's conduct, not simply whether they (the members of the Industrial Tribunal) consider the dismissal to be fair; (3) in judging the reasonableness of the employer's conduct an Industrial Tribunal must not substitute its decision as to what was the right course to adopt for that of the employer; (4) in many (though not all) cases there is a band of reasonable responses to the employee's conduct within which one employer might reasonably take one view another quite reasonably take another; (5) the function of the Industrial Tribunal, as an industrial jury, is to determine whether in the particular circumstances of each case the decision to dismiss the employee fell within the band of reasonable responses which a reasonable employer might have adopted. If the dismissal falls within the band the dismissal is fair, if the dismissal falls outside the band it is unfair . . .' (at page 442).

It is clear that a dismissal may be reasonable, even if a particular tribunal regards it as harsh, if it can be shown that other employers, particularly those in the same line of business, would regard dismissal as an appropriate penalty. The range of reasonable responses test has been subject to substantial academic and even judicial criticism by the EAT – these criticisms are discussed below. However, in the combined cases of *Post Office* v. *Foley* and *HSBC Bank plc* v. *Madden* [2000] IRLR 827 the Court of Appeal confirmed the range of reasonable responses test and ruled that it is binding on the EAT. In *Foley*, the employee was dismissed after he was allowed to leave work early to go home to look after his wife, who was ill, but was seen going into a pub prior to going home. The EAT decided that the dismissal was too harsh and therefore unfair. In *Madden*, a bank employee was dismissed for fraud, but the tribunal and the EAT decided that the bank had not carried out a proper investigation and had closed its mind to the fact that the employee might have been innocent. The Court of Appeal decided that both employers had acted within the range of reasonable responses, and therefore the EAT had no legal basis for concluding that the dismissals were unfair. The EAT had made an error of law in failing to apply the range of reasonable responses test.

Capability and reasonableness

Incapability dismissals on the grounds of an employee's lack of competence or ill-health provide a very important context for understanding the application of the range of reasonable responses test. Such dismissals fall within s. 98(3) ERA 1996 which defines 'capability' as referring to skill, aptitude, health or any other physical or mental quality, and 'qualifications', as relating to any degree, diploma or other academic, technical or professional qualification relevant to the position which the employee held. A reasonable employer might decide to dismiss an employee on grounds of poor work performance, but only after an employee has been warned that his or her work is not up to the standards required by the employer, and has been given a chance to improve. Where possible an employee should be given assistance to improve through additional training or mentoring by a colleague. Similarly, persistent absences as a result of illness might result in an employer concluding that it is reasonable to dismiss the employee because of the operational difficulties that the employee's absences create. However, as is demonstrated by the case law discussed below, a decision to dismiss on grounds of an employee's ill-health is not a decision that an employer should make lightly.

The case of *Cook* v. *Thomas Linnell & Sons Ltd* [1977] ICR 770 provides a good example of an employer acting within the range of reasonable responses in deciding to dismiss an employee for lack of competence. Cook was appointed as manager of one of the employer's wholesale food cash-and-carry depots. He had previous managerial experience with the company, but had never been employed on the food side of the employer's business. It became quickly apparent that he was not performing his job satisfactorily and there was a fall in the depot's profits due to his poor management. Despite warnings and advice Cook's performance did not improve. Cook was offered the managership of another non-food depot at the same salary but he refused this offer of re-deployment. In upholding Cook's dismissal as fair, the EAT stated that 'the operation of unfair dismissal legislation should not impede employers unreasonably in the efficient management of their business'.

Many employers operate systems of staff appraisal which will contain methods for assessing objectively whether an employee has efficiently met the performance targets which have been set by the employer. Indeed, it is important that the view that an employee lacks the necessary competence is based on an objective assessment of his or her performance, and is not simply the subjective view of a manager or supervisor.

This is illustrated by the decision in *Post Office* v. *Mughal* [1977] ICR 763. Mughal was engaged as a trainee clerical officer for a probationary period of one year. She was given several warnings by the sales manager that her work was unsatisfactory and that she would be dismissed if it did not improve. During the tenth month of the probationary period Mughal was told by her immediate superior that her clerical work was up to the required standard, and no further complaint concerning her work was made after that date. However, at the end of the probationary period the sales manager, who did not know that she had been told her clerical work was satisfactory, dismissed Mughal on the grounds her work was not up to the standard of the permanent staff. The EAT held, that although the employer had an appropriate appraisal procedure, it had not been operated properly in this situation as Mughal had been led to believe that her work had reached the proper standard. Therefore, her dismissal was unfair.

Many employers do impose probationary periods on employees. This case shows that it can be dangerous for employers to believe that they can treat probationers differently to other staff. Once they have acquired the right not to be unfairly dismissed probationers are entitled to have their work performance appraised in a way that is objective and fair. However, with effect from 6 April 2012 this point is of rather less practical significance. This is because probationary periods typically last for one year, but employees who start their employment on or after this date will have to work for two years before they are protected by unfair dismissal law. During the first two years of employment an employer is now able to dismiss an employee simply by giving that employee due notice. Providing a dismissal is not in breach of the employment contract, an employee who is perceived as not being of the right standard can be dismissed even though there has been no formal appraisal of that employee's performance and the employee has not been given any chance to improve.

Normally, an isolated act of incompetence would not merit dismissal and any dismissal would be beyond the range of reasonable responses. However, exceptionally, as in *Taylor* v. *Alidair* [1978] ICR 445, a single act of incompetence may constitute the basis for a fair dismissal. In this case a pilot, through negligence, crashed his plane. It was held that it was reasonable for the employer to conclude that the pilot should not be given a second chance, given the potentially calamitous consequences were the pilot to repeat his negligence.

Case Summary

Writing and drafting

Jill Smith was employed by X Co. Ltd for two years and one week prior to her dismissal. X Co. Ltd is owned by Pam Michaels, the managing director, and is a small company employing 50 employees. Jill seeks your advice. She informs you that she was dismissed because she was regarded as incompetent by John Stevens, her male supervisor. She has evidence that this supervisor had persistently invited her to go out to dinner with him and was upset that she always turned him down. Pam Michaels summoned Jill to a meeting with her at which she told Jill that she had decided to dismiss her, with full pay in lieu of notice, on grounds of incompetence. Pam told Jill that as she was receiving full pay there was no point in her taking any legal action against the company.

Jill has informed you that despite what has happened to her she would like to get her job back. Draft a letter seeking to persuade Pam Michaels that Jill should be reinstated.

In drafting this letter you should be aware, as will be explained later in this chapter, that employment tribunals can grant an order of reinstatement to an employee who has been unfairly dismissed, and if an employer refuses to reinstate then additional compensation can be granted.

You should spend approximately 30 minutes on this activity.

> ◆ **Handy tip:** Your letter should be written in a style which you regard as appropriate for a legal practitioner seeking to act on behalf of a client, though it is not necessary to make up and include the addresses of the company and your firm. Your letter should be formal and technical in its tone as you are seeking to persuade Pam that the law is on your client's side. Therefore, it is in Pam's and her company's interests to reinstate Jill.

Ill-health and reasonableness

Where, as a result of ill-health or injury, an employee is absent for a long period the essential question is whether in all the circumstances a reasonable employer can be expected to wait any longer. The employer should treat the employee with sympathetic consideration and hold the job open as long as possible, but, ultimately, the reasonable employer can regard the needs of the business as paramount.

It is normally essential that, prior to reaching a decision to dismiss an employee, the employer will take reasonable steps to ascertain the full medical position and adequately consult with the employee. In *East Lindsey DC* v. *Daubney* [1977] ICR 566, Daubney, a surveyor, was absent from work for long periods because of illness. The council's personnel director wrote to a doctor asking him to indicate whether the employee's health was such that he should be retired on grounds of permanent ill-health. The Council decided to dismiss Daubney on the basis of the doctor's response that this was the case. The EAT found the dismissal to be unfair as the reasonable employer will ensure the employee is able to state his case and obtain an independent medical opinion. Daubney had been denied these opportunities.

Case Summary

Where an employee is unfit to carry out his normal job, but could undertake alternative employment, the reasonable employer should offer redeployment to the employee if alternative work is available. The fact that such redeployment will involve demotion or the employee receiving a lower of rate of pay will not in itself render an offer of redeployment unreasonable. In *British Gas Services Ltd* v. *McCaull* [2001] IRLR 60 the employee was diagnosed as an epileptic and was informed that it was no longer safe for him to continue in his job as an engineer. The company offered him the only other available job that it was safe for him to do. The market rate of pay for this job was lower than that which McCaull had previously earned. McCaull refused this offer of redeployment and was dismissed. It was held that the employer had acted reasonably in the circumstances and the dismissal was fair.

Case Summary

Ill-health may cause a series of short-term absences. Providing the ill-health is genuine then any dismissal will be on grounds of capability, rather than absenteeism in the form of misconduct, and the above approach should generally apply. The employer should seek to establish the true medical position, unless, as in *International Sports Ltd* v. *Thompson* [1980] IRLR 340, the illnesses are unconnected and transient. This will be the case where an employee suffers from illnesses such as separate bouts of colds of flu but does so more frequently than is typically the case with the population at large. However, the employer must still give the employee the chance to be heard, and the employee must be warned that if the absences continue, so that there is an unacceptable level of absence, then dismissal will occur.

What constitutes an unacceptable level cannot be determined in advance, and will be decided on a case-by-case basis. In *Thompson*, the dismissal was found to be fair where the level of absence was 25% over an 18-month period. It cannot be assumed that a lower level of absence would never justify a dismissal. There will be some industries or professions in which any level of absence will cause particularly damaging operational consequences. For example, in *Patval* v. *London Borough of Camden* ET Case No. 2203464/07, the users of the employer's IT services required flexible and reliable IT support. Any absence caused severe disruption to the employer. In this sort of context any level of absence which is beyond what an employer should consider to be the norm may justify it in reaching a decision to dismiss. The determining factor in this type of situation is whether the employer has a sickness absence policy in place which specifies what constitutes an unacceptable level of absence. Providing this policy is not wholly unreasonable, given that any employee may occasionally be too ill work for a day or so, and the employer properly communicates its policy to the workforce and applies it in a consistent manner, any dismissal on the ground of sickness absence may well be accepted by a tribunal as reasonable and fair.

Case Summary

Lynock v. *Cereal Packaging Ltd* [1988] ICR 670 is another case where the employee was regularly absent as a result of unconnected illnesses. He was dismissed by the company after a series of meetings and warnings, which culminated in a final warning, to the effect that his attendance record needed to be improved so it was nearer to the average attendance record within the company. In finding his dismissal to have been fair, the EAT stressed that the provision of warnings should not be akin to a system of warnings for misconduct. The employer should approach the situation with 'sympathy, understanding and compassion'. The purpose of the warning of dismissal was to advise the employee that the stage was close to being reached where, 'with the best will in the world', continued employment would become impossible.

Misconduct and reasonableness

Employers may draw up their own disciplinary rules and an employee is subject to an implied duty to obey all reasonable instructions (see Chapters 2 and 3). Breach of a rule and/or disobedience on an employee's part will constitute misconduct, and tribunals must apply the range of reasonable responses test, as explained above, in deciding in any given case whether the misconduct involved justifies a dismissal. It is in misconduct cases that, in practice, there is most likely to be a range of responses that tribunals must take account of. Some employers will take a more lenient view than others, but those who take a harsher view and choose to dismiss must still be regarded as acting reasonably where other employers would also regard it as reasonable to dismiss.

It was established (in Chapter 4) that for the purposes of wrongful dismissal, misconduct can only be considered gross where it amounts to a repudiatory breach of contract by the employee. This is a very serious breach going to the root of the contract which entitles the employer to treat the contract as at an end. However, in an unfair dismissal claim the meaning of gross misconduct is more flexible. This is because employers have substantial discretion as to what types of behaviour they may specify as constituting gross misconduct in their own disciplinary rules. Providing these rules are clear as to what types of behaviour will constitute gross misconduct then, only if an employer has acted beyond the range of reasonable responses in specifying an offence as gross misconduct, will a consequent dismissal be considered unfair. The following cases illustrate the application of the range of reasonable responses test to misconduct dismissals.

Case Summary

In *Trust Houses Forte Hotels Ltd* v. *Murphy* 1977 [IRLR] 186, Murphy, a night porter, was summarily dismissed after his stock of alcohol for guests at night was checked and Murphy admitted taking some alcohol for his own use, though he had intended to replace it. It was held that, although some employers may have adopted a more lenient attitude, strictly speaking Murphy's behaviour amounted to theft. It is within the range of reasonable responses for any employer to regard theft as gross misconduct, and the company had acted fairly in deciding to dismiss Murphy for stealing property which had been entrusted to his care.

Case Summary

In *British Railways Board* v. *Jackson* (CA) 1994 [IRLR] 235, Jackson, a buffet car steward for British Rail, was dismissed after having been seen with a bag containing food with which to make bacon sandwiches. British Rail believed he intended to sell sandwiches to its passengers in competition with it and was in contravention of its disciplinary rules which specified that this was gross misconduct. The tribunal and the EAT upheld his complaint of unfair dismissal on the ground that British Rail's decision was unreasonable as there was no evidence that he had actually made any sandwiches. The Court of Appeal upheld British Rail's appeal on the basis that the tribunal had erred in concentrating on whether the employer had been reasonable in treating Jackson as being in actual infringement of the rule. The decisive factor should have been whether British Rail was acting reasonably in forming the belief that Jackson intended to sell the food in his possession. The tribunal's finding that British Rail's decision was not within a range of reasonable responses was declared to be perverse.

Case Summary

The case of *Bowater* v. *North West London Hospitals NHS Trust* [2011] IRLR 331 is a recent case, decided by the Court of Appeal, which illustrates when a tribunal may find a dismissal to be substantively unfair because the decision to dismiss falls outside of the range of reasonable responses. Bowater, a nurse, was dismissed for making a sexual comment while straddling the naked genitals of a patient who was suffering from a fit. The employment tribunal found that the comment could be described as lewd but that most people would consider it to be merely humorous. Consequently, it held that the decision to dismiss Bowater fell outside the band of reasonable responses a reasonable employer could have adopted. The EAT found that the tribunal had wrongly substituted its own opinion of what would have been reasonable, and that it had taken account of an irrelevant factor when finding that Bowater's remark would be considered to be merely humorous. The Court of Appeal restored the decision of the tribunal. The court found that the EAT had been over critical and wrong in its criticism of the tribunal's finding that a large proportion of people would find the lewd remark humorous, and it had no basis for concluding that the tribunal had substituted its own opinion for that of the employer. In the view of the Court of Appeal, Bowater had made a misguided and wholly inappropriate remark. However, this was intended to be humorous, and there was no evidence that the patient was conscious of it having been made. Nor was any other patient or member of the public present at the time. The court regarded it as significant that neither the doctor nor the nurse in charge had admonished her at the time of the incident or reported her conduct. The tribunal was clearly aware of the context in which the incident took place and it was entitled to find that summary dismissal was outside the range of reasonable responses to Bowater's conduct.

In reaching this decision the Court of Appeal stated that it was important in cases such as *Bowater* that the EAT and the appellate courts pay proper respect to decisions of the employment tribunal. The court emphasised that it is employment tribunals to whom Parliament has entrusted the responsibility of making what are sometimes difficult and borderline decisions in relation to the fairness of a dismissal. Presumably, therefore, had the tribunal decided in *Bowater* that the hospital trust had acted *within* the range of reasonable responses, and therefore the dismissal was fair, then this finding could not have been overturned on appeal either. It can be commented that the decision that the tribunal actually reached seems correct. It is fairly common knowledge that in operating theatres, where the patient is unconscious, doctors and nurses performing the operation may indulge in black humour. The facts of *Bowater* are akin to this situation as neither the actual patient nor any other patient or member of the public overheard the comment that the nurse made.

The following two cases illustrate how it may be reasonable for an employee to be dismissed for acts of misconduct committed by an employee as part of his or her private life; and that evidence from sources external to the employer organisation can be drawn upon. However, inconsistency of treatment is unreasonable and will render a dismissal unfair.

In *Post Office* v. *Liddiard* June 2001 (CA) (unreported), Liddiard was employed as a coder in the Post Office and worked nights. He commenced his employment in 1986 and had a good record of employment. In 1998, following riots involving English football hooligans attending the World Cup, the respondent was arrested and convicted in France of offences amounting to football hooliganism. He was sentenced to 40 days' imprisonment. Following the violence in France, there was widespread condemnation by the Prime Minister and the press of those involved in the violence. Liddiard was identified in a national newspaper as being a Post Office employee and being involved. The Post Office suspended Liddiard pending disciplinary proceedings, and he was subsequently dismissed for gross misconduct that brought the Post Office into disrepute.

The employment tribunal took into account the fact that Liddiard had had an excellent employment record, the incident for which he had been convicted in France had no relation to his employment, and that he was employed within the Post Office and not in contact with the public. The tribunal also took into account the facts that the legal proceedings in France had a number of anomalies, and although convicted, Liddiard continued to deny the offences. Moreover, the manager who had dismissed Liddiard had admitted that he had been influenced by the press reports. On those grounds, the tribunal had found that Liddiard had been unfairly dismissed.

The Court of Appeal upheld the appeal by the Post Office as the central issue that the tribunal should have addressed was whether it was reasonable for the Post Office to conclude that Liddiard had committed gross misconduct through behaving in a way which brought the Post Office into disrepute. The tribunal had failed to apply the range of reasonable responses test and thus had wrongly found the dismissal to be unfair.

A reasonable employer will normally take into account an employee's length of employment and previous record. Consistency of treatment is also an important factor in determining whether an employer has acted within the range of reasonable responses. These issues were considered in the cases of *T Doherty* v. *Consignia plc and M Doherty* v. *Consignia plc* EAT 2001) Case Number 2204805/00; (2001) Case Number 2205635/00, which were not dissimilar to that of *Liddiard*. These cases are discussed together though there were some factual differences and the cases were heard at different times by differently constituted tribunals. Thomas Doherty (TD) and Michael Doherty (MD) were full-time employees with the Post Office (Consignia), and both were Arsenal fans. Both also worked, in their spare time, as stewards for Flight Options, a travel company, assisting fans travelling to and from football matches in countries outside the UK. Neither of the brothers had any record of football hooliganism, and both were highly regarded by Flight Options. The cases arose out of violence that preceded the 2000 UEFA cup final between Arsenal and Galatasary played in Copenhagen. It was established at the time that it was the Galatasary fans who initiated the violence as they attacked a square set aside for use by Arsenal supporters. Subsequent video footage did show TD kicking a Turkish fan but the footage was less clear with respect to MD. The footage did not identify either of the brothers as employees of the Post Office. However, subsequent coverage in the tabloid press did and the Post Office decided to initiate separate disciplinary proceedings against both of them.

In deciding to dismiss MD and TD the Post Office failed to consider the previous impeccable employment records of both of the brothers. It was found that this was particularly the case with MD who had 13 years' exemplary service and had put himself at risk defending the Post Office against armed robbery. Moreover, in the case of TD, the employer failed to take into account its treatment of other Post Office employees accused of acts of hooliganism in Copenhagen. In one of these cases disciplinary action was dropped for want of evidence, even though the individual concerned was shown in the same newspaper article as that concerning TD to be throwing a bicycle. The employer also failed to take into account that it had earlier reinstated an employee who was a Millwall fan and had been sentenced to nine months' imprisonment for football hooliganism. Thus the dismissals of both Doherty brothers were deemed unfair in that no reasonable employer would have reached a decision to dismiss in the circumstances of either case.

Case Summary

The case of *Saunders* v. *Scottish National Camps Assoc. Ltd.* [1980] IRLR 174 was a particularly controversial example of the range of reasonable responses test. In this case, Saunders was employed as a maintenance man by the company. He was dismissed on grounds of some other substantial reason after he was seen going into a gay club in Glasgow and subsequently admitted to the employer that he was gay. Unsurprisingly, since his sexuality had nothing to do with paedophilia, it was accepted that he did not pose any danger to the children using the camp. Nevertheless, the employer believed that parents of children, as the customers, could be concerned by his employment and thus his presence as an employee was potentially harmful to the employer's commercial interests. The EAT held that his dismissal was within the range of reasonable responses and thus fair.

Case Summary

It must be emphasised that this decision could not be reached today as the dismissal would be in breach of s. 12 of the Equality Act 2010 (which will be examined in Chapter 7). In fact such a dismissal has been unlawful since December 2003 when the Sexual Orientation Regulations came into effect. Moreover, as confirmed in *X* v. *Y* [2004] IRLR 625, such a dismissal is contrary to Article 8 of the European Convention on Human Rights. Section 3 of the Human Rights Act 1998 requires statutory provisions to be interpreted in a way that is consistent with the Convention, and this applies to the range of reasonable of responses test (see Chapter 1). Therefore, normally a dismissal on grounds of the employee's sexual orientation must be unfair. However, in *X* v. *Y*, X was employed by a company linked to the probation service, and was dismissed after being found guilty of 'cottaging', the criminal offence of gross indecency through engaging in consensual sexual activity with another man in a public place. This dismissal was held to be fair, as it was for being found guilty of a criminal offence and was thus beyond the scope of the right to a private life as guaranteed by Article 8. In short, the dismissal was on grounds of X's criminality not his sexuality.

Critiquing the range of reasonable responses test

Some employers regard statutory unfair dismissal rights as an undue constraint on managerial prerogative – the right to manage – and responsible for increasing the amount of 'red tape' employers must follow in order to dismiss employees whose work performance is regarded as being below the employer's required standards. They argue that unfair dismissal law impedes business efficiency and generates unemployment as employers are discouraged from employing more employees. For such employers the range of reasonable responses test provides at least some safeguard as their decisions to dismiss and dismissal procedures are being judged on the basis of what a reasonable employer might do rather than on what an employment tribunal thinks an employer should have done.

On the other hand, there has been academic and judicial criticism of the effects of the range of reasonable responses test. Unfair dismissal law is an important mechanism for enabling employees to achieve something approaching workplace justice – this is particularly the case for employees who are not collectively represented by a trade union. Without effective statutory employment protection rights non-unionised employees have no protection other than their employment contracts. However, for many employees the contract of employment is an inadequate instrument for securing their interests as they do not negotiate their terms and conditions of employment. The contents of most employment contracts are exclusively determined by the employer. Where this is the case the employment contract may primarily operate as a source of control of an employee rather than a mechanism for providing employment protection. If an employee is dismissed then, providing the dismissal is not in breach of contract, the employee will have no legal basis for challenging the dismissal.

Unfair dismissal law provides an employee who has been treated unjustly with some access to legal redress in circumstances where a dismissal is wholly in accordance with the employment contract. Unfair dismissal rights do not prevent employers from dismissing unsatisfactory employees, or employees who have been guilty of serious acts of misconduct. Their effect is to impose standards on employers which many employers would wish to adhere to voluntarily in the name of establishing good employee relations. It can be argued that the consequence of the range of reasonable responses test is, in requiring tribunals to base their decisions on what some employers regard as reasonable, to weaken significantly the protection that unfair dismissal law provides for employees.

Towards the end of this chapter you will find references to articles written by Hugh Collins in the 1982 volume of the *Industrial Law Journal*. These articles encapsulate the criticisms of many academic employment lawyers of the notion that there is a range of reasonable responses and, providing an employer acts within this range, the reason for the dismissal should not be challengeable as unfair. The essence of the criticisms is that there is an overemphasis on the procedure that an employer followed prior to the dismissal. Providing an employer has followed procedures, which are consistent with the provisions contained in the ACAS Code of Practice, a dismissal is likely to be found to be fair. A tribunal must accept the employer's substantive reason for dismissing an employee as fair if any other employer, deemed to be a reasonable employer, could also have chosen to dismiss. It matters not that a tribunal panel regards the employer as having acted too harshly or otherwise unjustly. If the employer has acted within the range of reasonable responses, the tribunal has no option other than to find that the dismissal was substantively fair. On the other hand, by way of a counter argument, it is contended in the *Industrial Law Journal* article by Elias, which is cited at the end of this chapter, that the use of a properly fair procedure will normally result in a fair decision being reached.

In our view, the inability of a tribunal to review the fairness of the employer's decision from its own perspectives restricts the tribunal's power to function fully as an industrial jury in deciding whether a dismissal was justified. As an example, long before the law was changed to render it unlawful to discriminate against employees on grounds of their sexual orientation the above decision of *Saunders* received much criticism. The decision suggests that a reasonable employer may act to protect its business interests by dismissing an employee in order to accommodate homophobic attitudes held by some of its customers.

Out and about Reflecting on judicial criticism of the range of reasonable responses test

Judicial criticism of the range of reasonable responses test can be found in the following judgment of Morison J. in *Haddon* v. *Van Den Bergh Foods* [1999] ICR 1150 EAT. The facts of this case were that Haddon, a technical operator with the company, was invited to attend a ceremony to mark his 15 years' service with it. On the day of the ceremony, Haddon was required to work a shift commencing at 2.00 p.m. and finishing at 10.00 p.m. The ceremony was to begin at 5.15 p.m. and to finish at 7.30 p.m. Haddon had been told by his line manager that he would be required to complete his shift after the ceremony because of staffing problems. Another manager had told Haddon most people did not return to work because they had usually had something to drink, and Haddon should sort this out with his line manager. Haddon did not do this, but did have a drink at the ceremony and consequently decided not to return to work. He was then summarily dismissed for gross misconduct. The tribunal recognised that the dismissal was harsh and that few reasonable employers would have taken such action. It, nevertheless, regarded itself as bound to hold that the dismissal was fair on the basis of the range of reasonable responses test and in light of the employer's disciplinary rules. The dismissal was found to be unreasonable and therefore unfair by the EAT.

You can read this case from the *Industrial Cases Reports* or by accessing the case on WESTLAW. Have a look at and reflect on paragraphs 20 to 31 of Morison J's judgment.

Do you agree with Morison J that the range of reasonable responses test has become a 'mantra' which makes it unduly difficult for employees to succeed in establishing substantive unfairness? Is the test too 'loaded' in favour of employers? Or is it more the case that, providing a proper procedure is followed, the resulting decision by the employer is likely to be inherently fair?

Handy tip: At the end of the case analysis on WESTLAW there is a list of journal articles discussing the case and the range of reasonable responses test in general. If you are doing research into this area, for example, for an extended essay or a dissertation, you will find it useful to look at the synopses of these articles to ascertain whether any of the articles will be useful to your research.

Also, do remember that even if you agree with the approach adopted by Morison J, it is clear, as a result of the Court of Appeal decisions in *Foley* and *Madden*, which are cited above, that this approach is wrong in law.

Investigations and establishing the facts

As stated above, even it is decided that an employer had a good reason for dismissing an employee, bad procedure on an employer's part can result in the dismissal being found to be procedurally unfair. An important part of any procedure that the reasonable employer will normally adopt will be the conducting of a reasonable investigation to ascertain whether the employee has committed any misconduct and, if so, what the surrounding circumstances were. Such an investigation should be a prerequisite both to the convening of a formal hearing and the reaching of a decision by the employer. As a general rule, failure to conduct an investigation, or one that in the circumstances will be considered adequate by a reasonable employer, will render a dismissal unfair. The cases involving the Doherty Brothers, discussed above, are a good illustration of this, as the employer attached much too much importance to allegations in the tabloid press, and insufficient weight to the testimonies of the Doherty Brothers and other witnesses.

British Home Stores v. *Burchell* [1980] ICR 303 is the leading case on the importance of an employer conducting a reasonable investigation before deciding to take disciplinary action against an employee. The EAT was satisfied that the employer in this case had acted reasonably to secure evidence that the dismissed employee was guilty of abusing the system of staff purchases to pay less than the proper staff price for purchasing clothing from the store in which she worked. The employer had interviewed all the relevant witnesses, including a store detective who had been monitoring the activities of Burchell, and had taken a reasonable view of documentary evidence which pointed to guilt on the employee's part.

Case Summary

Arnold J's judgment sets out a three-staged approach that tribunals should follow in determining whether the employer has acted reasonably to determine the facts and in deciding to dismiss on the basis of them:

✦ First, the employer must genuinely believe that the employee committed the act or acts for which he was dismissed.

✦ Secondly, the employer must have reasonable grounds for believing the employee to be guilty.

✦ Thirdly, the employer will have acquired reasonable grounds for believing the employee to be guilty by carrying out as much investigation into the matter as was reasonable in all the circumstances of the case.

This approach has subsequently been confirmed as correct by the Court of Appeal in *HSBC Bank plc* v. *Madden* [2000] IRLR 827, and as explained above, the extent and nature of the employer's investigation is to be examined within the context of the range of reasonable responses test. In this case the bank had employed one of its security personnel to investigate whether Madden was involved in the misappropriation of customers' debit cards or their fraudulent use. The tribunal was not convinced that Madden was the culprit and stated that the investigation had failed to look into the financial affairs of other employees. Therefore, it decided that the investigation was unreasonable and the dismissal was unfair. The Court of Appeal reversed this decision as the tribunal had in effect decided that, had it been the employer, it would not have been satisfied by the evidence that Madden was the culprit and would not have dismissed

Case Summary

him. The tribunal had made an error of law by focusing on the fact that the investigation had not proved to *its* satisfaction that Madden was guilty of misconduct. Rather, it should have determined whether the bank's investigation into Madden's alleged misconduct was one that a reasonable employer might make and, on the basis of it, conclude that the employee was guilty.

Case Summary

The decision in *Madden* confirms that a tribunal cannot decide the employer's investigation was inadequate if the investigation was one that a reasonable employer would have considered to be appropriate in the circumstances. A tribunal cannot substitute its view of the facts for the view that a reasonable employer could adopt. Another case example of this principle is provided by *Sainsbury's Supermarkets Ltd* v. *Hitt* [2003] ICR 111. The employer found stolen goods in Hitt's locker, and refused to believe Hitt's claims that the property could have been planted in his locker by another employee. The tribunal concluded that it was unreasonable for the employer to have concluded that Hitt was the thief. The Court of Appeal held that the wrong test had been applied. The question was not whether Hitt was actually guilty, but whether it was reasonable for the employer to have concluded that he was guilty after it had conducted a reasonable investigation. As this was the position in this case, the dismissal was fair.

It is important to understand that it does not follow that an employer who fails to conduct an investigation must have acted unreasonably. There are circumstances where a dismissal, which is not preceded by an investigation, can nevertheless still be considered to be fair. For example, an employee is caught removing the employer's property from the workplace and is dismissed summarily 'on the spot'. As the employee is guilty, the failure to conduct a formal investigation will not in itself render the dismissal unfair, even though the employer has not sought to establish the facts.

Case Summary

Where a reasonable investigation should have been, but was not, carried out, then, as demonstrated by the decision in *A* v. *B* [2003] IRLR 405, the dismissal will be unfair. In this case A appealed against an employment tribunal's decision that he had not been unfairly dismissed from his employment as a residential social worker. A was suspended in June 1997 following allegations that he had been involved in an inappropriate relationship with a 14-year-old female resident of the home where he worked. Those allegations were the subject of an investigation by his employer, B, and the police. Although insufficient evidence was found to sustain a prosecution, A was dismissed following an internal hearing in December 1999. In upholding A's appeal, the EAT accepted his contentions that the decision to dismiss was unfair as the investigation had been subject to lengthy delays and that he had been denied access to evidence relied on by B at the internal hearing. The two and a half year period between suspension and dismissal was unacceptable. The failure to disclose witness statements to A, and the admitted failure by B to take statements from other potential witnesses, had also materially prejudiced A's case.

Case Summary

If an appropriate investigation does establish that it is reasonable to view an employee as guilty of misconduct, a dismissal will stand as fair, providing other appropriate disciplinary procedures in the ACAS Code were followed, even if, by the time of the tribunal hearing, the employee's innocence has been established. Moreover, as held in *Monie* v. *Coral Racing Ltd* [1981] ICR 109, if an employee has narrowed down employees suspected of misconduct to several employees, but cannot through further investigation identify the actual culprit, it is reasonable to dismiss all the suspects, even though one or more of the employees so dismissed may be innocent. In this case the employer's investigation had established that it could only have been Monie or another employee who could have stolen money from the employer's safe. It was not possible to determine which one of the employees was the actual culprit and both were dismissed. It was held that, even though Monie may have been innocent, his dismissal was on the basis of a reasonable investigation and therefore it was fair.

This decision may be considered as creating an injustice in that it permits employers fairly to dismiss employees when they are wholly innocent of any dishonest conduct. However, the decision has to be understood within the framework of the range of reasonable responses. The decision is based on an acceptance by the courts that a reasonable employer may take whatever disciplinary steps are necessary to protect its property. In a case such as *Monie*, if the employer dismisses an employee who turns out to be innocent, and a reasonable investigation would have established that fact, then the dismissal will be unfair. The problem for the employer in *Monie* was that it was not possible to ascertain which employee was actually guilty.

An unusual twist on this legal position is provided by the case of *Frames Snooker Centre* v. *Boyce* [1992] IRLR 472. In this case, Boyce was dismissed from his job as manager of a snooker centre, together with another manager, following a series of thefts which the police believed to have been an 'inside job'. The police were unable to eliminate any of the suspects. A third manager, the daughter of the proprietor, was not dismissed. It was held that the dismissal could not be regarded as unfair simply on the basis that not all the potential suspects had been dismissed. The employer was acting reasonably in deciding not to dismiss his own daughter, as an employer is entitled not to dismiss all potential suspects provided that he can show solid and sensible grounds for differentiating between members of the suspected group.

Case Summary

Law in action Unfair dismissal of Carol Hill

Some readers may regard 'whistle blowing' by an employee as an honourable thing to do where this involves giving people information which it can be argued they have a moral right to hear, but which an employer wants to keep secret. However, in law, although some disclosures are deemed protected and the employee 'whistle blower' has special rights to claim unfair dismissal, 'whistle blowing' is more likely to constitute a disciplinary offence (see Chapter 3). This was the situation Carol Hill, who was employed as a school dinner lady by a primary school in Essex, found herself in.

Source: Photodisc

She was suspended after telling a couple that their seven-year-old daughter had been tied to a fence and hit with a skipping rope by a group of boys. She was subsequently dismissed by the school's governors after telling a local newspaper what had happened to her.

The school argued at the tribunal that Hill had been dismissed for gross misconduct as, by talking to a journalist, she had brought the school into disrepute.

Hill was represented by her trade union, UNISON, and it was successfully argued on her behalf that her dismissal was procedurally unfair because the school did not carry out a reasonable investigation into the allegations, and that the disciplinary and appeal hearings were not fair hearings.

The case also illustrates how winning an unfair dismissal claim may be a moral victory for the dismissed employee, but the remedy the employee receives is somewhat underwhelming. Carol Hill withdrew her attempt to secure reinstatement once the tribunal had ruled in her favour because of the effect on her health in pursuing the claim. Ultimately, she received £350 by way of compensation.

Source: For a full newspaper report see http://www.guardian.co.uk/law/2011/jan/06/school-dinner-lady-unfairly-sacked?INTCMP=SRCH; and BBC News 2 February 2011 at http://www.bbc.co.uk/news/uk-england-essex-12345393

Procedural fairness and the ACAS Code

In practice employers are required, or at least well advised, to draft disciplinary rules and procedures and ensure these are effectively communicated to and understood by their employees. Moreover, the reasonable employer will develop and comply with disciplinary procedures, which are consistent with the model procedures provided by the Advisory Conciliation and Arbitration Service (ACAS). The current version of the ACAS Code of Practice on Disciplinary and Grievance Procedures came into force on 6 April 2009.

The ACAS Code does not generally have a legal status in that it lays down guidelines that it is prudent for employer to follow, rather than setting out duties that employers are legally obliged to comply with. However (as was established in the last chapter), a failure by an employer to comply with the ACAS Code may result in the compensation that a tribunal awards to a dismissed employee being increased by up to 25%. This is so both with respect to compensatory awards for unfair dismissal claims and to successful claims in damages for wrongful dismissal.

Documenting the law

The ACAS Code sets out the following as the salient features of a disciplinary procedure that a reasonable employer will adopt. Employers are well advised to draft their own disciplinary procedures on the basis of these provisions of the code.

+ Employers and employees should raise and deal with issues promptly and should not unreasonably delay meetings, decisions or confirmations of those decisions.
+ Employers and employees should act consistently.
+ Employers should carry out any necessary investigations, to establish the facts of the case.
+ Employers should inform employees of the basis of the problem and give them an opportunity to put their case in response before any decisions are made.
+ Employers should allow employees to be accompanied at any formal disciplinary or grievance meeting.
+ Employers should allow an employee to appeal against any formal decision made.

With respect to investigations:

+ It is important to carry out necessary investigations of potential disciplinary matters without unreasonable delay to establish the facts of the case. In some cases this will require the holding of an investigatory meeting with the employee before proceeding to any disciplinary hearing. In others, the investigatory stage will be the collation of evidence by the employer for use at any disciplinary hearing.

+ In misconduct cases, where practicable, different people should carry out the investigation and disciplinary hearing.

+ If there is an investigatory meeting this should not by itself result in any disciplinary action. Although there is no statutory right for an employee to be accompanied at a formal investigatory meeting, such a right may be allowed under an employer's own procedure.

+ In cases where a period of suspension with pay is considered necessary, this period should be as brief as possible, should be kept under review and it should be made clear that this suspension is not considered a disciplinary action.

Disciplinary Meetings and Appeals should be in accordance with the following requirements.

+ The meeting should be held without unreasonable delay whilst allowing the employee reasonable time to prepare their case.

+ Employers and employees (and their companions) should make every effort to attend the meeting. At the meeting the employer should explain the complaint against the employee and go through the evidence that has been gathered. The employee should be allowed to set out their case and answer any allegations that have been made. The employee should also be given a reasonable opportunity to ask questions, present evidence and call relevant witnesses. They should also be given an opportunity to raise points about any information provided by witnesses. Where an employer or employee intends to call relevant witnesses they should give advance notice that they intend to do this.

+ Where an employee feels that disciplinary action taken against them is wrong or unjust they should appeal against the decision. Appeals should be heard without unreasonable delay and ideally at an agreed time and place. Employees should let employers know the grounds for their appeal in writing.

+ The appeal should be dealt with impartially and wherever possible, by a manager who has not previously been involved in the case.

+ Workers have a statutory right to be accompanied at appeal hearings.

+ Employees should be informed in writing of the results of the appeal hearing as soon as possible.

◆ **Handy tip:** You can download a full PDF version of the ACAS Code from **www.acas.org.uk/drr**

Source: ACAS Code of Practice 1 on Disciplinary and Grievance Procedures, April 2009.

A good disciplinary procedure

The key features of a good disciplinary procedure can be summarised as follows:

+ Where misconduct by employee is alleged, as thorough an investigation as is reasonably practical should be conducted before formal disciplinary procedures are invoked.

+ If the investigation produces evidence that an employee is, or may be, guilty of misconduct, a formal hearing should be convened.

+ This hearing should be conducted fairly and chaired by an impartial manager.

+ The employee should be permitted to be accompanied by a trade union representative or a colleague.

+ If a penalty is imposed on the employee as a result of the initial hearing, the employee should be invited to exercise a right of appeal.

✦ If possible, the appeal hearing should be chaired by a different and more senior manager to the one who conducted the first hearing. Again the employee should be permitted to be accompanied by a trade union representative or a colleague.

The key aspects of these points are discussed in turn below.

Conducting a thorough investigation

As established in the *Burchell* case above, a failure to carry out a reasonable investigation will often result in the dismissal being found to be unfair. However, a dismissal may be fair, despite the fact that no investigation has taken place, if the employee is caught red-handed in an act of misconduct.

Carrying out a formal hearing

If the investigation produces evidence that an employee is, or may be, guilty of misconduct a formal hearing should be convened. The main purpose of a formal hearing is to enable the employee to give his view of the facts, and to put forward arguments as to why he should not be disciplined or dismissed. Generally, if a hearing does not take place a dismissal will be procedurally unfair. In *Chrystie* v. *Rolls Royce Ltd* [1976] IRLR 336, Chrystie was summoned to a formal disciplinary hearing for assaulting a co-employee when provoked. Chrystie failed to attend this hearing but sent a letter explaining that he had been acting in self-defence and that he had been ill on the day of the hearing. The company decided to dismiss him on the basis that he failed to exercise his opportunity to be heard and that fighting clearly constitutes gross misconduct. The EAT upheld the tribunal's decision that the company had failed to act reasonably in refusing to postpone the hearing until Chrystie was well enough to attend.

Case Summary

Ensuring that a disciplinary hearing is properly conducted

A formal hearing should be chaired by an impartial manager who has had no previous involvement in the investigation of the employee or the decision to instigate formal disciplinary proceedings. Where a disciplinary hearing is not conducted properly this may be enough to render a dismissal unfair even if the employee has subsequently exercised a right of appeal. This is demonstrated by the case of *Wise* v. *Filbert Realisations Respondent* (Formerly Leicester City Football Club) EAT/0660/03 9 February 2004. This case involved the dismissal of the footballer Dennis Wise for punching a team-mate, Callum Davidson, in the face. As a result of the blow, Davidson suffered a fractured cheekbone. Wise was dismissed after a disciplinary hearing, which was chaired by the club's owner. The employment tribunal found that this hearing was flawed in a number of ways. Wise exercised a right of appeal but this appeal was restricted to hearing arguments from both sides. No witnesses were heard and the evidence was not examined. It was held that the dismissal was procedurally unfair. In order to cure initial substantial procedural failings, the appeal process should normally be by way of a full rehearing, involving witnesses once again presenting their evidence, and allowing the employee, or his representative, to cross-examine those witnesses.

Case Summary

However, as is always the case in applying the provisions of the ACAS Code, there is no rule of law to the effect that defects in a disciplinary hearing can only rectified if the appeal was in the form of a full rehearing. In *Taylor* v. *OCS Group Ltd* [2006] ICR 1602, the employer appealed against a decision that Taylor had been unfairly dismissed because

Case Summary

an appeal had not constituted a full rehearing. Taylor had been employed as a database programmer/analyst. He was profoundly deaf and his deafness amounted to a recognised disability under the Disability Discrimination Act 1995. In the course of his work, in breach of company policy, he gained remote access to the terminal of another employee and acquired confidential information about staff salary levels. Taylor was dismissed following a disciplinary hearing. At this hearing Taylor was not represented and, because of his disability, he did not fully understand what was happening. The decision to dismiss was confirmed at a subsequent appeal hearing. At this appeal hearing the employer had provided Taylor with an interpreter but for part of the time only. The employment tribunal found that the dismissal had been unfair because Taylor had been unable to participate effectively in the disciplinary process leading to his dismissal, particularly at the first hearing, and that the appeal hearing had not rectified the defects of the first hearing. The Employment Appeal Tribunal upheld the employment tribunal's decision that the appeal hearing fell short of what was required to correct the earlier defect. The Court of Appeal held, allowing the employer's appeal, that there was no rule of law that only an appeal by way of rehearing was capable of curing earlier defects in disciplinary proceedings and that a mere review never was. Under s. 98(4) ERA 1996, a tribunal should not consider procedural fairness separately from the other issues arising such as the reasons for dismissal. Both the tribunal and the EAT had erred in deciding that the dismissal had to be unfair because the appeal had not been in the form of a full rehearing. The case was remitted to a differently constituted tribunal to consider whether on the facts the appeal process should be regarded as curing the defects in the disciplinary hearing.

Respecting the right of accompaniment

As well as being a recommendation in the ACAS Code, s. 10 of the Employment Relations Act (ERA) 1999 gives the employee the statutory right to be accompanied at a formal disciplinary hearing and any further appeal hearing by a trade union representative or friend. Where this right is denied then, irrespective of the fairness of any dismissal, the employee may present a complaint to a tribunal under s. 11 ERA 1999. The normal remedy will be two weeks' statutory pay. A **statutory week's pay** is based on the claimant's gross pay, that is, pay before income tax and national insurance contributions have been deducted, and is subject to a statutory limit. In 2012, the statutory maximum for a week's pay was £430. The concept of a statutory week's pay is explained fully below in explaining the basic award which will normally be granted to claimants who successfully claim unfair dismissal. A claim can be brought under s. 11 irrespective of whether the employee is also claiming unfair dismissal, and the claim can succeed even if a claim of unfair dismissal fails.

Although employees have the right to be accompanied by a trade union representative or a friend, a recent decision by the Supreme Court in *R (on the application of G)* v. *Governors of X School* [2011] UKSC 30, confirms that employees have no right to legal representation at a disciplinary hearing unless this is part of an employer's contract-based procedures. In this case, a teaching assistant was accused of sexual misconduct with a minor. At a disciplinary hearing to consider his guilt, G was permitted representation by a trade union official or a colleague but not his solicitor. Given the criminal nature of the allegations against him, both the High Court and the Court of Appeal held that the denial of legal representation was in breach of G's rights to a fair trial as guaranteed by Article 6 of the European Convention on Human Rights. A majority of the Supreme Court disagreed and held that Article 6 does not apply to an employer's internal disciplinary proceedings.

Case Summary

Appeal hearings

If a penalty is imposed on the employee as a result of the disciplinary hearing, the employee should be invited to exercise a right to appeal. The case of *Stoker* v. *Lancashire County Council* [1992] IRLR 75 demonstrates the importance of the appeal process. If the appeal hearing is procedurally flawed the dismissal will be unfair. Stoker was employed by the council at a higher education institution (HEI). His contract of employment incorporated the HEI's disciplinary procedure, which was then subject to the council's disciplinary procedure. Stoker was dismissed after the HEI had properly followed its disciplinary procedure, but he exercised his contractual right of appeal to the council. The council's procedures stipulated that this right of appeal involved a full re-hearing of a case. However, the council decided that it was only required to review the dismissal and then either confirm it or remit the case to the HEI for reconsideration. In the event, the council confirmed the HEI's decision to dismiss. The Court of Appeal upheld Stoker's appeal to it on the basis that a reasonable employer will comply fully with its own contractual disciplinary procedure and Stoker should therefore have been afforded a full rehearing by the council.

It is important to appreciate that full procedure, in accordance with the ACAS Code, should be adhered to each and every time that an employer is considering disciplining an employee. It should be the case that, except in instances of gross misconduct, a series of formal written warnings should be given to an employee each time an offence is committed or repeated. A final written warning should make it clear to the employee that repetition of the offence will result in the employee being summarily dismissed. A written warning should be removed from an employee's work record after a period of time if the employee does not repeat the offence. The norm is that it should be removed if the employee 'keeps a clean sheet' for one year. Generally speaking, an employee cannot challenge a disciplinary warning in an employment tribunal. However, if the procedure followed prior to a warning being issued was defective, and the employee is ultimately dismissed, then it will be unsafe for the employer to rely on this warning in seeking to argue that the dismissal was fair.

Reflective practice

Look back at the letter you may have written earlier on behalf of Jill Smith. Are there any matters of a procedural nature that you think should be added to your letter in the light of the provisions of the ACAS Code? The more it can be persuasively argued that bad procedure on the part of the employer makes it more likely that the employee will win a claim of unfair dismissal, the greater the incentive for the employer to agree to a voluntary settlement.

The legal status of the ACAS Code

It is very important to understand that the ACAS Code sets out guidelines not binding legal rules. Therefore, it is possible for a dismissal in a given case to be fair even though there were aspects of the ACAS Code that were not followed by the employer. Nevertheless, the importance of the code must not be underestimated. As confirmed by the House of Lords in *Polkey* v. *AE Dayton Services Ltd* [1988] ICR 142, a failure to follow the code will normally render a dismissal procedurally unfair. However, the Law Lords also clarified that a failure to follow the code will not definitely mean that the dismissal was unfair. There will be circumstances where a reasonable employer could decide that following the code in its entirety, or particular parts of it, would be futile or useless.

> **a failure to follow the code will normally render a dismissal procedurally unfair**

One example of where it is not necessary to follow the ACAS Code will be where an employee is caught red-handed in the act of theft. As we saw earlier in this chapter, in discussing the EAT's decision in *Burchell*, it is not necessary to carry out a full investigation in such circumstances. All that needs to be established is that the employee was actually stealing, that is, had not been given any permission to remove property belonging to the employer from the workplace. The reasonable employer might also conclude in such a situation that there is no point to giving the employee a hearing as there can be no justification for an act of theft.

Another possibility might be that the employee has fully confessed to gross misconduct and, in the light of this confession, no further procedure is necessary. This is illustrated by the case of *Mathewson* v. *R.B. Wilson Dental Laboratory* [1988] IRLR 512. In this case Mathewson, who worked in a dental laboratory, was late back from his lunch. Mathewson was interviewed by his employer and confessed that he had been arrested by the police for being in possession of cannabis. He was summarily dismissed without any formal disciplinary procedure being followed. It was held that the dismissal was fair as, given the nature of Mathewson's offence and the work he was employed to do, it was reasonable for the employer to rely on his confession to conclude that he had committed gross misconduct. Therefore, Mathewson's dismissal was fair.

Case Summary

The following case provides what could be regarded as a controversial example of where a dismissal can be regarded as fair despite a failure to follow the ACAS Code. In *Sartor* v. *P&O European Ferries (Felixstowe) Ltd* [1992] IRLR 271, Sartor was employed as a stewardess on a ferry and was dismissed after a customs officer had found company teabags in her car. After two managers conducted an investigation, Sartor was instructed to attend a disciplinary hearing. Contrary to the ACAS Code, she was not informed of the allegations against her. She exercised her right of appeal against the decision of dismissal and this appeal was heard by the same managers who had carried out the investigations. This was a second breach of the code as these managers had already been involved in the disciplinary proceedings against her. The Court of Appeal held it could not reverse the tribunal's decision that the dismissal was fair. Although the employer had failed to follow the code, the defects were relatively minor in nature and therefore the tribunal was entitled to conclude that the employer had acted reasonably in the way the decision to dismiss was reached. It can be argued that a decision of this sort unduly downplays the importance of the ACAS Code. Should it really be perceived as a minor procedural defect where managers investigating an employee's alleged misconduct are empowered to make the ultimate decision on whether that employee should be dismissed?

Case Summary

The *Polkey* case itself involved making the employee redundant without first having a consultation meeting with him to discuss the proposed redundancy. As will be explained further (in Chapter 6), consulting with individual employees over proposals to make them redundant is generally considered to be a very important procedural step. For example, it is possible that as a result of such a consultation the employer agrees with an employee that redeployment of the employee through giving the employee a different job in the organisation is a feasible alternative to redundancy. Therefore, as a general rule, an employer who makes an employee redundant without first having a consultation will have acted unreasonably and the redundancy dismissal will be unfair.

However, in *Polkey*, the employment tribunal decided that the dismissal was fair despite the fact that no consultation had taken place. The tribunal accepted the employer's argument that the failure to hold a consultation had made no difference to the employer's decision, as even if a consultation had taken place the employer would still have decided to make Polkey redundant. In reaching this decision the tribunal followed a number of cases which had established that failing to follow the ACAS Code could not make a dismissal procedurally unfair where the procedural defects involved had made no practical difference to the employer's decision to dismiss.

When the House of Lords considered Polkey's appeal it decided that these cases were wrong in law and overruled them. This meant that the employment tribunal had made an error of law in applying the no difference approach. The Law Lords held that the correct law to be applied was whether a reasonable employer could have concluded that it was futile or useless to hold a consultation before reaching a decision to make an employee redundant. Only if this was the case could a dismissal be regarded as fair. Therefore, an employer cannot argue at the tribunal hearing that had it followed the ACAS Code a decision to dismiss would still have been reached, and therefore the failure to follow the code has made no difference to the outcome. The employer must be able to demonstrate that, at the time of the dismissal, the failure to follow the code was in the circumstances a course of action that a reasonable employer could adopt. The question to be addressed is: could a reasonable employer have concluded that following the code was futile or useless?

> **could a reasonable employer have concluded that following the code was futile or useless?**

Earlier in this chapter we established that whether an employer has good reason to dismiss the employee is to be understood within the framework of the range of reasonable responses test. A dismissal will be substantively fair, even if the tribunal considers it to be harsh, if a reasonable employer could have reached a decision that dismissal was an appropriate penalty. The Court of Appeal made it clear, in the case of *Duffy* v. *Yeomans* [1994] IRLR 642, that the range of reasonable responses test applies equally to determining whether the employer has adopted a reasonable procedure prior to reaching a decision to dismiss.

Case Summary

The significance of applying the range of reasonable test to procedural fairness is illustrated by the facts of *Duffy*. The facts of the case were very similar to those in *Polkey* in that an employee was made redundant without the employer first having a prior consultation with him. However, there was a subtle difference to *Polkey* in that the evidence revealed the employer had not even considered whether a consultation with Duffy should have taken place. It was held that the decision in *Polkey* did not require an employer personally to consider whether there is any point to holding a consultation. A tribunal should find a dismissal to be fair, despite the fact a consultation did not take place, if a reasonable employer could have considered a consultation to be futile or useless.

The decision in *Duffy* can be criticised, as it can be argued that it enables an employer, who has not even thought about the right procedure to be followed, to get away with bad practice where a decision not to follow particular procedures is within the range of responses open to a reasonable employer. In short, the issue is to be resolved objectively on the basis of what a reasonable employer might do; the subjective thought processes of the actual employer at the time of the dismissal are not relevant.

It can be seen from the above discussion of the cases that have been decided since *Polkey* that it is by no means easy to predict in advance when a failure to follow to the

ACAS Code will render a dismissal procedurally unfair, and where the dismissal should be considered fair despite procedural defects on the employer's part. It certainly seems that there can be what some might consider important breaches of procedure by an employer, but the dismissal will still be found to be fair.

However, there is one part of the Law Lord's decision in *Polkey* that has been clear since the case was decided. An employer will never be able retrospectively to rely on facts, which only come to light after the dismissal, to justify that dismissal as fair. The decision to dismiss must have been reasonable on the basis of the evidence the employer had established at the date the dismissal occurred. However, as will be explained below, facts that come to light after the dismissal may impact on the level of compensation a successful claimant receives, and indeed may permit a tribunal not to award any compensation whatsoever.

Polkey: a summary of the law

In the light of the House of Lord's decision in *Polkey*, and the cases decided in its wake, the legal status of the ACAS Code can be summarised as follows:

✦ The procedure an employer follows prior to a decision to dismiss will be reasonable if it is in accordance with the code.

✦ Normally, a failure by an employer to adhere to the provisions of the code will mean that the dismissal is procedurally unfair.

✦ An employer *cannot* justify a failure to follow the code by arguing this has made *no difference* to the decision to dismiss.

✦ A dismissal may be fair, despite a failure to follow the code, where it is within the range of reasonable responses for an employer to conclude that that it would be futile or useless to follow particular provisions of the code.

✦ An employer can only rely on evidence available to it at the date of the decision to dismiss. Information that the employer discovers after this date cannot be used to justify the dismissal.

Law in action

It was suggested (in Chapter 5) that you should track what happened to Sharon Shoesmith, after she was removed from her post as Haringey Council's Director of Children's Services by former Children's Secretary Ed Balls. This action was taken in light of a report by OFSTED into the causes of the death of the baby, Peter Connolly. Shoesmith applied for judicial review of her dismissal, and the Court of Appeal found in her favour because she was never given the chance to be heard, this being a breach of the rules of natural justice. Subsequently, the Supreme Court refused leave of appeal to the Department of Education and Haringey Council. At the time her court case succeeded there was speculation in the media that she could receive in the region of £1 million by way of compensation.

It is interesting to note that had Shoesmith claimed unfair dismissal her claim may well have succeeded given the complete lack of procedure prior to her dismissal. However, on the basis of the *Polkey* principle explained above, she may have received little or nothing by way of compensation as a tribunal may have regarded her dismissal as deserved. Her case is therefore an example of a situation where taking legal action, other than unfair dismissal, can work to a dismissed employee's advantage.

Source: Marsden, S. and Woodcock, A. (2011) 'Sharon Shoesmith in line for compensation', the *Independent*, 2 August, http://www.independent.co.uk/news/uk/home-news/sharon-shoesmith-in-line-for-compensation-2330560.html

Remedies for unfair dismissal

Imagine that you have successfully claimed unfair dismissal in an employment tribunal. The next stage of the hearing will be to decide what remedies will be granted to you, and you, as the successful claimant, will have an input into this. It may be that you would like your old job back or an alternative job with the same employer. If the tribunal agrees with you that this is appropriate, it will grant you either an order of reinstatement or of **re-engagement**.

If you do not want to return to your former employer – perhaps because you are apprehensive as to how you will be treated given that you have successfully claimed unfair dismissal – financial compensation in the form of what is called a **compensatory award** will be your remedy of choice. Such compensatory awards are also attractive to many claimants as the sums of money involved are typically higher than what an employee normally receives by way of damages for wrongful dismissal. As detailed below, this is because the dismissed employee's loss of earnings for the whole period in which he or she is likely to remain unemployed can be taken into account. Damages are restricted to the actual financial loss arising out of the employer's breach of contract. Typically, this will just be the pay that an employee would have earned during the contractual notice period. Moreover, of course, damages will not be available where the dismissal did not involve a breach of contract by the employer, as such a dismissal will not have been wrongful.

Like damages, the compensatory award is based on the **net pay** that an employee was receiving at the date of dismissal. Net pay is the actual money that an employee receives after deductions for income tax and national insurance contributions have been made to an employee's salary or wage. The colloquial term is 'take-home pay'. Whilst the compensatory award reflects an employee's actual losses which arise from the dismissal, s. 124(1) ERA 1996 places a statutory cap on the amount of compensation a claimant can receive. Consequently, some claimants may not receive full compensation for the loss that they suffer. The statutory cap is normally increased annually by statutory instrument to take account of inflation. In 2012, as a result of the Employment Rights (Increase of Limits) Order 2011, SI 2011/3066, the statutory maximum for the compensatory award was increased to £72,300.

The compensation that successful claimants may receive will also include a **basic award**. This is composed of a statutory week's pay and reflects the claimant's weekly wage, age and completed years of employment at the date of dismissal. A statutory week's pay is based on the **gross pay** that the claimant earned. Gross pay is the pay that a person earns before deductions for income tax and national insurance contributions are made by the employer. A statutory week's pay may be less than the actual gross pay that the claimant earned as, like the compensatory award, it is subject to a statutory maximum. The maximum for a week's pay is normally increased annually by statutory instrument along with the increase in the statutory maximum for the compensatory award. In 2012, under SI 2011/3066, the statutory maximum for a week's pay was increased to £430. The low level of this statutory limit is controversial, as it is well below the actual weekly gross pay of many employees who are earning what are generally regarded as moderate incomes.

There is one potential drawback with respect to compensation for unfair dismissal. Contrary to the position with damages, both a claimant's compensatory and basic awards for unfair dismissal can be reduced by the extent a tribunal regards the employee as having contributed to the dismissal through having been guilty of some misconduct. A claimant will only receive full compensation for unfair dismissal where, prior to the dismissal, he or she was innocent of any misconduct.

Key stats

In 2010–11, eight successful claimants were awarded reinstatement or reengagement, and 2,600 were awarded compensation by the tribunal. Some 12% of successful claimants received compensation below £1,000 and 21% received compensation of between £1,000 and £2,999; 5% received compensation in the average salary range of £20,000 to £29,999. Fifty one claimants, that is, 2% of claimants receiving compensation, were granted compensation in excess of £50,000.

These statistics demonstrate just how uncommon it is for tribunals to order reinstatement or re-engagement. The small numbers of claimants who receive largish sums of compensation demonstrate that, in practice, the statutory cap on compensation, this being £68,400 in 2011, is not an issue for most successful claimants.

On a speculative basis, the figures might also suggest that employees with middle range incomes, such as university lecturers and many solicitors, are less likely to be the victims of unfair dismissals than is the case with those in the lower income brackets. Alternatively, it may be that more highly paid professional employees are better placed to negotiate a settlement with an employer under which they receive compensation in return for withdrawing the unfair dismissal claim and keeping the terms of the settlement confidential.

Source: Ministry of Justice Employment Tribunal and EAT statistics 2010–11, published by the Ministry of Justice in September 2011. The full report can be downloaded at http://www.justice.gov.uk/downloads/statistics/mojstats/employment-trib-stats-april-march-2010-11.pdf

Orders of reinstatement and re-engagement

Sections 114 and 115 ERA 1996 provide for the tribunal orders of reinstatement and re-engagement. The difference between the two remedies is that a reinstated employee returns to the job he or she was doing prior to dismissal, whereas re-engagement requires the claimant to be engaged in different but comparable employment. This could be with the same employer but, for example, in a different department of the employer's business, or at a different workplace location. Alternatively, it could be with a different employer in the form of an associate company of the former employer. In deciding whether to grant either of these orders, a tribunal will take into account the wishes of the claimant, as an employee will not be reinstated or re-engaged contrary to his or her wishes.

A reinstated employee must receive arrears of pay and the full restoration of rights, including the continuity of employment and pension rights the employee would have accrued had the dismissal not taken place. The tribunal sets out the terms on which an employee must be re-engaged. Typically, this will be on the same terms which applied to the employee prior to the dismissal, but they may be different in order to reflect the fact the employee was guilty of some misconduct and this contributed to the employer's decision to dismiss.

Under s. 116, a tribunal may decline to grant either of these orders to the claimant on the basis that it is not just and equitable to require an employer to take back an employee who has contributed to the dismissal through misconduct or incapability. In practice, most unfairly dismissed employees were guilty of some misconduct and this is sufficient reason for a tribunal deciding that it is not appropriate to order either reinstatement or re-engagement.

Alternatively, a tribunal can refuse to grant either order because it is not reasonably practicable for the employer to comply with it. This includes the situation where, as a result of all the circumstances surrounding the dismissal, trust and confidence between the employer and the dismissed employee have been destroyed. This will often be the case in small businesses in which the employer and employee will be working alongside one another, as ill-feeling resulting from the fact that the dismissal occurred will mean that it will be impossible for a proper working relationship between them to be resumed.

Economic factors can also be taken into account. In *Port of London Authority* v. *Payne* [1994] IRLR 9, the Court of Appeal accepted the employer's argument that re-engagement was not reasonably practicable as the employer was in the middle of implementing a number of redundancies. This decision was particularly controversial as the unfairly dismissed dockers had been dismissed for their trade union activities (see Chapter 8).

In practice, as evidenced by the above statistics and for the reasons given above, it is relatively rare for either reinstatement or re-engagement to be granted. However, with respect to the cases, brought by the Doherty brothers, which are explained above, both tribunals took the view that they should be reinstated. Had the Post Office acted reasonably on the basis of the available evidence, and consistently with respect to how the brothers' colleagues were treated, neither would have been dismissed for the alleged offences involving football hooliganism. Moreover, the tribunals took into account that there was strong support amongst the workforce for the reinstatement of both brothers, and the relevant managers had either changed or could be expected to respond professionally by accepting that the decisions to dismiss had been mistaken. Therefore, the issue of trust and confidence was not a barrier to the practicality of reinstatement.

Section 116(5) expressly provides that the fact that the employer has permanently replaced the claimant shall not be taken into account by the tribunal in deciding whether orders of reinstatement or re-engagement are reasonably practicable. There are two statutory exceptions to this position.

The first of these is where it was not practicable for the dismissed employee's work to be done without engaging a permanent replacement, and therefore the dismissed employee's job no longer exists. The importance of the role that the dismissed employee played within the organisation is a key factor in determining whether it was necessary for the employer to appoint a permanent replacement. The approach that tribunals take is similar to that taken in the frustration cases that we examined earlier (see Chapter 4). Some employees, such as senior managers, or highly skilled professionals or technicians, are so important to an employing organisation that it cannot function effectively without that person's job being performed. It will be difficult or impossible to recruit a substitute employee on a temporary basis, and therefore the employer has little option other to appoint a permanent replacement for the dismissed employee.

Secondly, it may be that the employer waited for a reasonable period of time before employing a replacement, and at that time the employer had not heard from the dismissed employee that he or she wished to be reinstated or re-engaged. What constitutes a reasonable period will vary with the circumstances of the case. However, the more difficult it is for the employer to continue to arrange for temporary cover the more reasonable it will be for the it to decide to appoint a permanent replacement.

Employers are not obliged to comply with an order of reinstatement or re-engagement. Where an employer does refuse to comply with an order, the employee will return to the employment tribunal so that the claimant can be granted the monetary remedies for unfair dismissal. These remedies are in the form of a basic award and a compensatory award and, normally, the claimant will receive both of these awards. The ways in which these awards are calculated are fully explained below.

The employee will also receive an **additional award**. This award acts as compensation to the claimant for the fact that the employer refused to comply with the tribunal's order of reinstatement or re-engagement. The additional award will consist of between 26 and 52 statutory weeks' pay. In 2012, given that the statutory limit for a week's pay was £430, the maximum additional award that could be made was £22,360. Tribunals have a wide discretion in deciding how many weeks pay will be awarded, and it is permissible to take into account the conduct of the employer in refusing to comply with an order.

Where a tribunal declines to grant an order of reinstatement or re-engagement, or an order is made but the employer declines to comply with it, then the tribunal will calculate the basic award and the compensatory award that the claimant will receive.

The basic award

The purpose of the basic award is to compensate the employee for the loss of his or her job security. It therefore has the same purpose as the statutory redundancy payment to which an employee is entitled if he or she has been dismissed by reason of redundancy (see Chapter 6). Under s. 119 ERA 1996, a basic award is calculated on the same basis as a statutory redundancy payment. This reflects the employee's age, completed years of employment and gross weekly pay, subject to the statutory limit for a week's pay, at the date of the dismissal.

Three scales apply in calculating a basic award. The claimant will receive:

1. half a week's pay for every year of employment completed under the age of 22;

2. plus one week's pay for every year completed aged 22 to 40;

3. plus one and a half week's pay for every year completed aged 41 or more.

However, with respect both to a basic award and a redundancy payment the employee can only be credited with the last 20 years of employment that he or she completed. In 2012, given the maximum of £430 for a statutory week's pay, the maximum basic award that could be granted was £12,900. Claimants must have at least 20 completed years of employment in the highest band based on one and a half week's pay to receive this amount. Therefore, the statutory maximum can only be awarded to a claimant aged 61 or more at the date of dismissal. If such a claimant was dismissed in April 2012, had earned a gross salary of £600 a week and had been in the same employment for 40 years then he or she would receive a basic award based on a calculation of $20 \times 1.5 \times £430$, and so would receive the maximum possible amount of £12,900. Further examples of how basic awards/statutory redundancy payments are calculated will be given in the next chapter.

Under s. 122 ERA 1996 the basic award can be reduced on the following grounds.

✦ The employee has already received a statutory redundancy payment – if this is the case then the employee will not also receive a basic award for unfair dismissal.

✦ The employee was guilty of misconduct prior to the dismissal – under s. 122(2) ERA 1996, in contrast to deductions for contributory fault from the compensatory award, deductions can be made from the basic award for any misconduct prior to the dismissal, even though the misconduct has only come to light since the dismissal, and therefore did not contribute to it.

✦ The employee unreasonably refused a voluntary offer of full reinstatement by the employer. For example, the employer offers to reinstate the employee to the same job, at the same workplace and on the same terms and conditions of employment. The employee is to receive full arrears of pay and any other benefits such as pension benefits. The employee has no reason to believe that he or she will be subjected to any form of detrimental treatment if he she returns to work for the employer or that a proper working relationship is no longer feasible. An employee who refuses such an offer of reinstatement has acted unreasonably.

The compensatory award

the compensatory award may cover all of the claimant's financial loss arising from the dismissal

The most significant monetary award that a successful claimant will receive is the compensatory award. The compensatory award may cover all of the claimant's financial loss arising from the dismissal. This award is granted in addition to the basic award. Section 123(1) of ERA 1996 specifies: 'the amount of the compensatory award shall be such amount as the tribunal considers just and equitable in all the circumstances having regard to the loss sustained by the complainant in consequence of the dismissal in so far as that loss is attributable to action taken by the employer'. In determining what is just and equitable in any given case, tribunals will take the following losses into account.

Contractual losses

As is the case with damages for wrongful dismissal, the compensatory award will cover the net pay an employee would have earned during the period of contractual notice that he or she should have been given by the employee. Alternatively, if the contract was for a fixed-term, the award will include the net pay the employee would have earned over the period of time the contract still had to run at the date of dismissal.

Immediate losses

In providing for compensatory awards for unfair dismissal it was Parliament's intention that unfairly dismissed employees should receive compensation for losing their jobs as a result of the unfair dismissal. Therefore, in contrast to an award of damages for wrongful dismissal, the compensatory award will also include immediate and future loss of earnings beyond the date of expiry of the period of contractual notice or the fixed-term contract. The immediate loss is the financial loss suffered by the claimant between this date and the date of the tribunal's decision. The future loss is any financial loss the claimant will continue to incur as a result of still being unemployed after the tribunal's decision.

In calculating the immediate loss there are two main possibilities that will apply. First, in the period between the dismissal and the date of the tribunals' decision, the employee has obtained a new job on the same or at a higher salary to that he or she received prior to the dismissal. Here, the compensatory award will cover the overall financial loss the claimant suffered as a result of any unemployment during the period between the dismissal and the commencement of the new contract of employment. For example, the claimant was summarily dismissed and was entitled to one month's notice. The claimant's net pay was £2,000 a month. Three months after the dismissal the claimant obtained a new job at the same rate as the claimant received from the respondent employer. The compensatory award will be £6,000, that is, £2,000 for loss of notice and £4,000 for the other two months during which the claimant was unemployed.

Secondly, as above, but in a situation where the net pay the claimant now receives is £500 less a month than the claimant received from the respondent employer. Here the ongoing immediate loss will be £500 for each month up to the date of the tribunal hearing. For example, if the tribunal's decision is given nine months after the date of dismissal the claimant will receive a compensatory award of £9,000. This is £6,000 as above plus £500 a month for the additional six months leading up to the tribunal's decision.

Future losses

The compensatory award will also reflect any future loss the claimant is likely to suffer after the date of the tribunal's decision. In the above example, the tribunal would have to estimate for how much longer after the tribunal's decision the pay differential is likely to continue. For example, it is likely that in one year's time the claimant will be promoted and will then earn more than he or she was receiving in the previous job. The claimant's future loss will therefore be £6,000, giving him a total compensatory award of £15,000.

It is possible that a claimant will still be unemployed at the date of the tribunal's decision. Here the compensatory award will include all of the claimant's loss of net earnings up to the date of the tribunal hearing plus the loss of future earnings the employee is likely to incur. The actual amount of such future loss cannot be identified with any certainty. The tribunal will have to estimate for how much longer the claimant is likely to remain unemployed, and the compensatory award will reflect the net pay the employee would have earned during this period. The statutory cap is of particular practical importance where the claimant suffers a loss of future earnings, as it imposes a statutory limit on the compensatory award that the claimant can receive.

The Court of Appeal has recently confirmed that in rare cases the loss of future earnings reflected in the compensatory award can cover the whole of the remainder of the claimant's working life. In *Wardle* v. *Credit Agricole and Investment Bank* [2011] ICR 120, Wardle was dismissed after he had brought a claim of race discrimination against the company. In accepting that this dismissal was unfair, the court found that on the basis of the available evidence Wardle had a 70% chance of securing another post in the future and his loss of future earnings should be calculated on that basis. However, the court stated that where the evidence does show that a claimant has no prospect, or only limited prospects, of securing new employment in the future then the compensatory award can reflect the claimant's total loss of his or her career.

Case Summary

The compensatory award will also include other financial losses such as the loss of occupational pension rights, which would have accrued had the employee not been dismissed, and the loss of statutory rights. As detailed in this text, a number of statutory rights are only acquired by an employee by working for the same employer for a specified period of time. An unfairly dismissed employee has to build up employment rights, including unfair dismissal, all over again if he secures employment with a new employer. Typically, tribunals award a sum of between £200 and £300 for the loss of statutory rights. The basis for calculating lost pensions rights is very complex and beyond the scope of this text. However, it is reasonably well-paid employees, who also have occupational pension schemes, that are more likely to receive compensation at or near to the maximum award a tribunal can make.

We saw (in Chapter 4) that damages cannot include compensation for injury to feelings or loss of reputation as these are not financial losses. In *Dunnachie* v. *Kingston upon Hull City Council* [2004] ICR 1052 the House of Lords held that this principle also applies to the compensatory award for unfair dismissal. In this case, Dunnachie successfully claimed constructive unfair dismissal on the basis of a prolonged campaign of bullying against him. This did not cause him to suffer psychiatric injury, but in the view of the tribunal reduced him to a 'state of overt despair'. The tribunal awarded him £10,000 to reflect injury to feelings. The House of Lords held that his compensatory award could not include this sum of money as the compensatory award is restricted to losses of a financial nature.

The following interview with a solicitor experienced in employment law provides insights into why unfair dismissal claims succeed and how lawyers approach the issue of the remedies a successful claimant should receive – particularly where the claimant can bring overlapping claims of unfair and wrongful dismissal. It is interesting to note that, despite a common perception that most unfair dismissal claims succeed on grounds of procedural defects by employers, in this solicitor's experience it is more typical for dismissals to be found to be substantively unfair.

People **in the law**

Interview with **Piers Bateman**, a solicitor for more than 30 years. Piers became a Partner with Stokes Solicitors LLP in Portsmouth in 1986 and where, presently as a consultant to the firm, he has practised in business and employment law for more than 20 years, representing small and medium-sized enterprises and individual clients across the counties of SE England and London.

Do you think tribunals are less likely to believe the reasons advanced by an employer for dismissing an employee where the employer has failed to provide the employee with written reasons for the dismissal? Yes, I believe this is the case: the more so the larger the size of the employer organisation.

Which would you say is the most important factor in a claim of unfair dismissal succeeding: the employer's reason for the dismissal or defects in the procedure the employer adopted prior to the dismissal? The employer's reason for the dismissal.

From the presentation of a claim to a decision on remedies, how long does a claim of unfair dismissal typically take? This is very variable, depending on the day-to-day workloads of regional tribunal centres, and the complexity of issues that may impact on tribunal case management throughout. Broadly it takes 6–9 months.

In the successful claims were your clients reasonably satisfied with the remedies that they received? The great majority are satisfied – and interestingly, even where a claim fails, at least half, in my experience, feel they were given a good opportunity to 'state their case in public', even if they would not agree with the final decision.

How often do successful claimants secure reinstatement? I can only answer for the cases I've dealt with. The figure is 2 or 3% which represents roughly a 10% success rate in respect of those cases where the client has sought reinstatement. In most cases I've advised the client not to persist with request for re-instatement, or otherwise to persist – but only for tactical reasons. Often clients have thought an employer might have a change of mind, and the client wouldn't be persuaded otherwise – almost invariably, the client was wrong! In my experience, no order has ever been made where the respondent employer had not already been persuaded to agree to have the

employee back in accordance with the tribunal order. Overall, there have been just a few happy occasions where proceedings have ended with it being agreed that employees can return to their jobs.

How often, if at all, have you been able to advise clients that they can present simultaneous claims of wrongful and unfair dismissal? I have given clients this advice but only where the claim for damages for wrongful dismissal is not likely to exceed the statutory cap for damages of £25,000 – otherwise I advise the client to run the wrongful dismissal claim in the High Court.

Where such clients have succeeded in both claims has this ever advantaged them in terms of any sum of damages being separated out from the compensatory award the tribunal decides it can make? Yes, one reason will be to ring fence the compensatory award so that the maximum award can be granted. The other reason will be where deductions from compensation for unfair dismissal could be made on grounds of contributory fault or *Polkey*/'just and equitable' reasons. Damages will be safe from deductions on these grounds.

Deductions from and adjustments to the compensatory award

As referred to in the above interview a tribunal can make deductions from or adjustments to the compensatory award for a number of reasons. The ground for such deductions/ adjustments and the order in which they should be made are as follows.

(a) Failure to mitigate loss

As a result of s. 123(4) ERA 1996, in the same way that applies to damages, the compensatory award can be reduced as a result of the claimant's failure to act reasonably to **mitigate** the loss resulting from the dismissal. The dismissed employee should try to find another job (as we saw in Chapter 4). Failure to do so or an unreasonable rejection of a job offer will result in the compensatory award being reduced by the appropriate amount. For example, if an employee is unemployed at the date of the tribunal's decision, but was offered an appropriate job three months after the date of dismissal, then the compensatory award will be limited to the first three months of unemployment.

(b) Deductions which are just & equitable

Under s 123(1) ERA 1996, it is permissible to reduce the compensatory awards to nil where this can be considered by a tribunal to be just and equitable. One example of this will be where evidence of misconduct justifying the dismissal only came to light after the dismissal. Such a dismissal must be unfair, as the employer had no reasonable grounds to dismiss the employee at the date of the dismissal. In *W Devis & Sons Ltd* v. *Atkins* [1977] ICR 662, the employee was dismissed on grounds of his work performance and this dismissal was unfair. After the dismissal, the employer discovered Atkins had been guilty of dishonesty and could have been fairly dismissed on that basis. The Law Lords stated that unfair dismissal law should not be used to allow a rogue's charter under which employees can obtain compensation even though they deserved to be dismissed. Therefore, it was just and equitable not to make a compensatory award in this case.

A second example is where the tribunal can make what is known as a **Polkey reduction**. A tribunal can do this, in line with the decision of the Law Lords in *Polkey* which was considered above, where the tribunal decides that the dismissal would have been fair had a proper procedure been followed. As established above, the employer cannot argue that failure to follow the ACAS Code has made no difference to the decision to dismiss and therefore it is a fair dismissal. However, this 'no difference' approach can be applied by the tribunal to enable it to decide that, although the dismissal had to be declared unfair on procedural grounds, the employee would have been dismissed had a proper procedure been followed. Therefore, the claimant should receive nothing by way of a compensatory award. In the claim brought by the footballer Dennis Wise, which is explained above, the EAT commented that this was a case in which a 'Polkey reduction' might be appropriate as the evidence clearly established that Wise had struck his teammate, Callum Davidson. However, in remitting the case to a tribunal, the EAT stated that this was a matter for the tribunal to decide.

(c) Failure to follow the ACAS Code

Under s. 207 Trade Union and Labour Relations (Consolidation) Act 1992, as explained above, the compensatory award can be adjusted upwards or downwards by up to 25% where there has been a failure by the employer or employee to comply with the ACAS Code.

(d) The employee's misconduct contributed to the dismissal

Under s. 123(6) ERA 1996, as noted above, the compensatory award can be reduced by the amount the tribunal regards as appropriate because the employee was not entirely innocent but was guilty of some misconduct or some degree of incompetence. In this sense the employee has contributed to the dismissal because, were it not for the employee's behaviour, he or she would not have been dismissed. The more serious the employee's misconduct was, the greater the deduction from the compensatory award will be.

Making deductions from the compensatory award

Deductions from the compensatory award should be made from the actual loss the individual incurs. Only after such deductions should the reduction to the statutory maximum amount take place. For example, the full compensatory award the employee would be entitled to is £100,000, but the tribunal decides the compensatory award should be reduced by 10% on grounds of the employee's contributory fault. This reduces the compensatory award to £90,000. If this occurred in 2012, the tribunal would then reduce the compensatory award to £72,300. The important point to appreciate is that the 10% deduction is made to the full loss of £100,000 not to the statutory cap. If the latter were the case the award the employee would receive would be reduced to £65,070. As in this example, the correct compensatory award is the statutory maximum of £72,300.

The interrelationship between the compensatory award and damages

We examined when a summary dismissal by an employer will be a wrongful dismissal entitling the dismissed employee to bring an action for damages (see Chapter 4). As explained, where an employee has been continuously employed for at least two years and is summarily dismissed there is an overlap between being able to claim wrongful and unfair dismissal. Indeed, both claims can be presented simultaneously to the same employment tribunal. For the reasons explained above, typically, the compensatory award a successful claimant will receive will be for a larger sum of money than what the claimant may also have been able to recover by way of damages for wrongful dismissal, and the award of damages will not impact on the size of the compensatory award. In effect, damages which, for example, cover loss of notice will be subsumed into the compensatory award.

However, strictly speaking, any award of damages is separate to the compensatory award and is not to be included in the compensatory award in determining whether the statutory limit has been reached. Where the claimant succeeds in both claims then damages can be awarded to cover the net pay the claimant would have earned during the notice period or during the remainder of a fixed-term contract. The compensatory award can then cover loss of earnings that arise during the period after the contract could have been lawfully terminated. This can benefit more highly paid employees on longer periods of notice than is the norm.

For example, a claimant received £3,000 a month net pay and was entitled to three months' notice. If the claimant successfully claims wrongful and unfair dismissal the he or she will receive £9,000 by way of damages. The claimant could then receive the full compensatory award – currently £72,300 – if the actual losses entitle him or her to receive this sum.

It is also important to take into account that deductions cannot be made to any sum of damages that is awarded on grounds of the claimant's contributory misconduct. Therefore, in the above example, if the tribunal decided that the claimant was equally responsible for his or her dismissal this means the compensatory award will be halved. However, the claimant will still receive the full £9,000 damages for loss of notice. In reducing the compensatory award it should be remembered that this is done before the tribunal ascertains whether the award must be reduced to the statutory limit. It should also be remembered that damages, as well as the compensatory award, may be adjusted upwards or downwards where one party is responsible for any non-compliance with the ACAS Code.

Table 5.2 summarises the remedies that may be granted to a claimant who successfully claims unfair dismissal, and the basis on which compensation may be awarded.

Table 5.2 Remedies for unfair dismissal

Remedy	Purpose or effect	Calculation
Reinstatement or re-engagement	Employee returns to former job or different job with the employer. Arrears of pay, seniority, etc. restored	Additional award if employer does not comply with the order Statutory week's pay of between 26 and 52 weeks
Basic award	Equivalent of a statutory redundancy payment and compensates employee for loss of job security	Based on employee's age, gross pay and completed years of employment Week's pay subject to statutory limit
Deductions from basic award	Depending on employee's fault the award may be reduced by an appropriate percentage or reduced to nil	Deductions on grounds of: refusal of employer's voluntary offer to reinstate; and/or contributory fault through employee misconduct
Compensatory award	Subject to statutory cap, compensation reflects actual financial loss arising from the unfair dismissal Includes loss of net earnings and other losses such as lost pension rights	Immediate loss between dismissal and tribunal hearing Loss of future earnings and benefits after the tribunal hearing
Deductions from compensatory award	Reduces compensation employee receives but deductions must be made before statutory cap is imposed Nil compensatory awards are possible	Deductions on grounds of: • any failure to mitigate; • deductions which are just and equitable, including '*Polkey* reductions'; • deductions or increases of up to 25% if ACAS Code not followed; and/or • contributory fault through employee misconduct

Summary

- Only workers who have employee status may claim unfair dismissal.

- An employee with two years' continuous employment may claim a dismissal was unreasonable and therefore unfair even though the employer has not acted in breach of contract, as the employee has been dismissed with due notice, or the employer has decided not to renew a fixed-term contract of employment.

- Continuity of employment is broken if there are breaks between employment contracts, unless, under s. 212 ERA 1996, these are due to a period of sickness of up to 26 weeks or to a temporary cessation in employment.

- Exceptionally dismissals may be automatically unfair and the requirement of two years' continuous employment will not apply. Under s. 99, a dismissal by reason of pregnancy is an example of an automatically unfair dismissal.

- A dismissal will have occurred where it is the employer who has decided to terminate or not renew the employment contract.

- A dismissal may also be constructive where the employee has resigned in response to a repudiatory breach of contract by the employer. For example, the employer is in breach of the implied duty of trust and confidence.

- Under ss. 98(1) and 98(2), dismissals must be for potentially fair reasons such as incapability, misconduct or redundancy.

- Under s. 98(4), a dismissal will only be fair if the employer has acted reasonably. In determining whether an employer has acted reasonably the tribunal must not substitute its own view for that of a reasonable employer, but should decide whether the employer has acted within the range of reasonable responses.

- Dismissals should be procedurally fair in accordance with the ACAS Code of Practice. Normally, employers will conduct reasonable investigations to determine the facts and conduct a formal hearing and permit a formal right of appeal before deciding to dismiss an employee.

- As held by the Law Lords in *Polkey*, although employers should normally adhere to the ACAS Code, failure to do so does not necessarily render a dismissal unfair. A dismissal can be fair despite procedural defects where a reasonable employer could regard full adherence to the code to be futile or useless.

- A dismissal can never be fair where evidence which justifies the dismissal only comes to light after the dismissal has taken place.

- An employee who successfully claims unfair dismissal may be granted reinstatement or re-engagement. However, typically, such employees will receive a basic award and a compensatory award.

- There can be deductions from the basic and compensatory awards on a number of grounds including contributory misconduct by the employee. Nil awards can be granted where evidence discovered after the dismissal retrospectively justifies it.

Question and answer*

Problem: Peggy is the owner of a public house called 'The Prince Albert'. Peggy discovers that money is missing from the cash till. In addition to herself, the only people who have access to the till are the two members of the bar staff, Alfred and Katherine, and her son, Philip. Alfred, Katherine and Philip are all employed by Peggy under contracts of employment. Peggy interviews Alfred and Katherine and they both deny taking the money. Peggy asks Philip whether he has borrowed any money from the till and he tells her that he has not done so. Peggy is unable to identify the thief and decides to dismiss both Alfred and Katherine with net salary in lieu of notice. A police investigation subsequently discovers that the thief was in fact Philip.

Advise Alfred and Katherine to their legal rights and remedies (if any).

You should spend approximately 40 minutes on answering this question.

Essay: 'Unfair dismissal law places a disproportionate emphasis on procedural issues as, providing an employer follows a proper procedure prior to dismissing an employee, the subsequent dismissal will normally be found by an employment tribunal to be fair. The substantive fairness of the dismissal will often not be given an appropriate weight.'

Critically examine this statement with reference to the range of reasonable responses test.

If you treat this question as an exam question, you should spend approximately 40 minutes on answering it. However, this is the type of question that may be set for an in-course essay – in which case, having undertaken your research, you might well take approximately three hours in writing it.

✱ Answer guidance is provided at the end of the chapter.

Further reading

IDS (2010) *Unfair Dismissal Employment Law Handbook* (Income Data Services: London).
This handbook is an excellent reference source for unfair dismissal law in its entirety and contains a very detailed and readable explanation of the law. Chapters 3, 4, 5, 6, 14, 15, 16 and 18 are particularly relevant to the issues covered in this chapter.

Deakin, S. and Morris, G. (2012) *Labour Law* (Hart: Oxford).
Chapter 5 of this leading text on all areas of employment law provides comprehensive explanation of unfair dismissal law which is combined with critical and contextual analysis.

Collins, H. (1992) *Justice in dismissal: the law of termination of employment* (Oxford University Press: Oxford).

As this book was written more than 20 years ago its explanation of the law is obviously no longer fully up to date. However, it critically analyses the law in its social, political and philosophical contexts and this analysis remains pertinent to the law as it is today. The book is therefore valuable for anyone who wishes to research further into the law of unfair dismissal from a critical standpoint.

Pitt, G. (1993) 'Justice in Dismissal: a Reply to Hugh Collins', *Industrial Law Journal*, vol. 22, pp. 251–68.
This article provides a useful summary and critical discussion of the perspectives advanced in the above text by Collins.

Collins, H. (1982) 'Capitalist Discipline and Corporatist Law Part 1', *Industrial Law Journal*, vol. 11, pp. 78–93; 'Capitalist

**Discipline and Corporatist Law Part 2',
pp. 170–7;**

**Elias, P. (1981) 'Fairness in Unfair
Dismissal: Trends and Tensions', *Industrial
Law Journal*, vol. 10, pp. 201–17.**

These three articles by Collins and Elias should be
read altogether. Despite being written in the very
early 1980s, the debates the articles provide remain
highly relevant in providing a critique of the range
of reasonable responses test and whether or not
unfair dismissal law gives too much weight to
procedural fairness at the expense of substantive
fairness.

**Collins, H. (2004) *Nine Proposals for the
Reform of the Law on Unfair Dismissal*
(Institute of Employment Rights: London).**

As the title of this short book indicates, this work
proposes nine reforms to unfair dismissal law. One
proposal that Collins makes is to replace the range

of reasonable responses test with one that is akin
to the test for justifying indirect discrimination
(which is explained in Chapter 7 of this text). For
a dismissal to be fair an employer must be able
show that it was a proportionate means of securing
that employer's legitimate commercial and/or
organisational objectives. A dismissal will be unfair
if the employer's legitimate objectives could be met
by other means including lesser disciplinary action.

**Sanders, A. (2009) 'Part One of the
Employment Act 2008: "Better" Dispute
Resolution?', *Industrial Law Journal*,
vol. 38, pp. 30–49.**

This article provides a useful analysis of the rules
relating to procedural fairness as they were at the
time this text was published. Of particular interest
is the discussion of changes to the law in the light
of the abolition of the statutory disputes procedures
which were in operation between 2004 and 2009.

Question and answer guidance

Problem:
Your answer should start by establishing that Alfred and Katherine cannot claim
wrongful dismissal as they have received salary in lieu of the periods of notice to
which they were contractually entitled. They must each have two years' continuous employment to be able to
claim unfair dismissal.

The problem requires you to focus on the procedural aspects of the ACAS Code, in line with *Burchell* and
Polkey, and considering issues such as the carrying out of a reasonable investigation and holding a disciplinary hearing. The cases of *Monie* v. *Coral Racing* and *Frames Snooker* v. *Boyce* are of direct relevance to the
answer. The key issue is whether it was within the range of reasonable responses for Peggy to dismiss Alfred
and Katherine, but not Philip. On the basis of *Frames Snooker*, it may be reasonable for Peggy to believe that
Philip was innocent of the theft, even though it later transpires that he was the guilty party. Your answer
should emphasise that it can only be reasonable to dismiss employees who may be innocent of theft if proper
procedure is fully followed, the actual culprit cannot be identified and the employer believes that dismissal
of the employees is the only effective way to prevent further thefts.

The final part of your answer should discuss the remedies Alfred and Katherine should receive if their
claims of unfair dismissal succeed. Reinstatement is probably impractical despite their innocence. This is
because mutual trust and confidence between Alfred/Katherine and Peggy has been destroyed thereby rendering a proper working relationship impossible. However, both Alfred and Katherine should receive full basic
and compensatory awards. Your answer could explain that the latter can reflect loss of net earnings for any
period of unemployment arising from an unfair dismissal. This includes both immediate losses up to the date
of the tribunal's decision and any future losses arising from any period of unemployment that the tribunal will
predict will continue after the hearing.

Essay:

This question requires you to demonstrate your understanding of unfair dismissal law, and, in particular, to subject the range of reasonable responses test to critical analysis.

Your answer should display a comprehensive knowledge and understanding of how unfair dismissal law works with emphasis on s. 98(4) ERA 1996 and cases demonstrating substantive fairness and procedural fairness within the framework of the range of reasonable responses test. Cases you could cite on substantive fairness include cases such as *Iceland Frozen Foods* v. *Jones* which sets out the range of reasonable responses test, and cases such as *Jackson*, *Bowater*, *Liddiard* and *Doherty* which illustrate the use of the test. *Polkey* should be explained as the leading authority on procedural fairness along with cases such as *Duffy* and *Mathewson* which illustrate how a dismissal may be procedurally fair even though the ACAS Code was not followed by the employer. *Burchell* could be cited to demonstrate how an employer may act fairly in dismissing an employee after a reasonable investigation has been conducted even though it is subsequently established that the employee was innocent of any misconduct.

In addition to showing that you know and understand the law, your essay must contain critical analysis discussing the statement if your answer is to address the essay question properly. Despite the fact that they were written in the 1980s, the *Industrial Law Journal* articles by Elias and Collins, which are cited above in 'Further reading', remain invaluable as sources of arguments which your answer can draw upon. Your essay could also discuss Morison J's criticisms of the range of reasonable responses test in *Haddon*, which you may have considered in the 'You be the judge' feature earlier in this chapter.

Your answer should contain conclusions in which you state your own reasoned opinion as to whether the range of reasonable responses should be retained, or whether it should be overruled by the Supreme Court or subject to statutory repeal. You could also make reference to some of the proposals for reform that have been advanced. For example, as Collins proposes, the range of reasonable responses test should be replaced with one that requires an employer to act proportionately in dismissing an employee to protect its legitimate commercial or organisational objectives.

Chapter 6
Redundancy and other economic dismissals

Key points In this chapter we will be looking at:

✦ The legal definition of redundancy and how to determine whether an employee is eligible to receive a statutory redundancy payment

✦ How to calculate a statutory redundancy payment

✦ The legal position where an employee is offered redeployment in another job as an alternative to being made redundant

✦ When a redundancy dismissal will also be an unfair dismissal

✦ Dismissals for economic reasons where an employer has reorganised the business

in ways which change the existing employment contracts of its employees

✦ When a transfer of a business by one employer to another employer is regulated by the Transfer of Undertakings Protection of Employment (TUPE) Regulations

✦ When a dismissal arising out of a business transfer will be unfair

✦ Statutory duties on employers to consult with trade unions or other employee representatives as a result of an employer's proposals to make collective redundancies or a business transfer

Introduction

We have focused on how an employee, who has been dismissed on grounds of incapability, incompetence or misconduct, may succeed in claiming **unfair dismissal** (see Chapter 5). It is also common for employees to be dismissed not by reference to their individual circumstances or behaviour but for economic or commercial reasons beyond their control. This may be because the employer decides to reduce

the size of the workforce, decides to reorganise a business in a way which leads to new contractual terms and conditions being imposed on the workforce or decides to transfer the business to a new employer. Any of these decisions by an employer may lead to employees being dismissed, and this chapter focuses on the statutory rights that employees so dismissed may have against their employer.

Where an employee is dismissed as a result of a reduction in the size of the workforce, or because the business is closed down altogether, that employee has been dismissed by reason of redundancy. The employee's standard statutory right in this situation will be to receive a **statutory redundancy payment**. However, there is a potential overlap with unfair dismissal law in that the redundancy may have been carried out in an unfair way by the employer. In such a case the employee will be entitled to claim compensation for unfair dismissal in addition to being able to claim a statutory redundancy payment. This chapter will explain the statutory definition of redundancy, how a redundancy payment is calculated and the circumstances in which such a payment can be successfully claimed, and will discuss how a **redundancy dismissal** may also be an unfair dismissal.

As an alternative to, or in addition to, making redundancies, an employer may make changes to the ways in which the organisation functions and this may necessitate changing the terms and conditions of employment of existing employees. This situation can result in particular employees refusing to accept changes to their contracts of employment and the consequent dismissals of such employees.

This chapter will examine the factors that employment tribunals take into account in deciding when such dismissals should be considered fair and when they will be found to be unfair.

Where an employer sells the business this may constitute the transfer of an undertaking regulated by the TUPE Regulations. As this chapter will explain, the general effect of these regulations will be that existing employees of the current employer will be transferred to the new employer and will keep their existing contracts of employment. However, circumstances may arise where, as a result of the **business transfer**, some employees are dismissed either prior to or after the transfer has taken place. This chapter will explain when such dismissals will be fair and when they will be unfair.

Where an employer proposes to make redundancies, or to engage in a business transfer, the employer may be under a statutory duty to consult with a trade union or, if there is no relevant union, with elected representatives of the relevant employees. The final part of this chapter will consider when the statutory duty to consult arises, what statutory consultations must involve and the consequences for an employer if the duty to consult is not properly complied with.

The meaning of redundancy

As identified above, employees who lose their jobs as a result of a reduction in the size of the workforce or the business being closed down may be dismissed by reason of redundancy and may be entitled to a redundancy payment, However, redundancy has a technical meaning in law and there have been circumstances where employees have thought they have been made redundant but case law has established that this was not the case. It is therefore important to understand when, in law, a dismissal will be a redundancy dismissal. If there is no redundancy, the dismissed employee will not be entitled to a redundancy payment, although, as will be discussed below, the employee may be able to succeed in a claim of unfair dismissal. Conversely, where a dismissal is by reason of redundancy, and the redundancy has been carried out in a fair way, the dismissed employee's only right will be to a statutory redundancy payment.

The definition of redundancy is contained in s. 139(1) Employment Rights Act (ERA) 1996. For a dismissal to be a redundancy dismissal it must be attributable wholly or mainly to:

(a) cessation of the employer's business; or

(b) the employer's requirements for employees to carry out work of a particular kind having ceased or diminished.

Examples of (a) will be where the employer closes all or part of the business or sells off some of the business assets such as buildings and/or premises. Such closures or sales may be as a result of insolvency or an attempt to keep some of the business solvent. It is also possible that an employer may sell part or all of the business as a going concern so that the business is taken over by a new employer. Where the selling and buying employers are both companies, the sale is likely to be effected by the latter purchasing the shares in the company. Where this is the case, any employees who are dismissed by the selling or buying company will have been made redundant.

However, where a sale is not by share purchase and is deemed a 'relevant transfer' special protection may be given to employees under the Transfer of Undertakings Protection of Employment (TUPE) Regulations 2006, SI 2006/246 which are designed to implement EU law. In particular, the transfer will not operate as a dismissal and the contract of employment will automatically continue with the substitution of the buying company as the employer. What constitutes a 'relevant transfer' and its legal consequences are fully explained in a later section of this chapter.

The main example of (b) is where the employer simply reduces the size of the workforce at one or more of its business premises. This may be because, for example, the employer wishes to reduce costs by reducing the wages bill, or there has been a decline in the demand for employer's products or services. It is important to understand that there will be redundancy dismissals where the employer's requirements for the same number of employees have diminished. It does not matter that the volume of work remains constant or has even increased, but fewer employees are required as a result, for example, of the introduction of new technologies.

There will be a redundancy where the employee's job function continues to exist but the employer is able to reorganise work so that an employee's job is shared between other employees. In this situation, the employer has reduced the workforce by one employee, and therefore there will be a redundancy within the meaning of s. 139(1)(b) ERA 1996. There will also be a redundancy dismissal, even though, under the employee's contract of employment, there were different jobs that he or she could be required to undertake. It is sufficient for the definition of redundancy that the employer no longer wants the employee in that particular role. Older case law, which held to the contrary, was overruled by the House of Lords in *Murray* v. *Foyle Meats Ltd* [1999] IRLR 562 on the basis that that they were unnecessarily over-technical interpretations of the statutory provisions. The facts of this case illustrate how employees can be redundant despite the fact that their jobs have not completely disappeared.

Case Summary

In *Murray*, livestock slaughterers were informed they were to be dismissed by reason of redundancy even though, under their employment contracts, they could be required to undertake other jobs in the factory. They argued that the employer's failure to provide them with other work meant their dismissals were unfair. It was held by the Law Lords that they had been fairly dismissed by reason of redundancy. On a straightforward interpretation of the statutory definition the employer required fewer employees to act as slaughterers; it mattered not that the employer could have exercised a contractual option to provide them with alternative work.

> if an employer requires fewer employees to do a particular job, there is a redundancy dismissal

The effect of this decision is that the law has been simplified. If an employer requires fewer employees to do a particular job, there is a redundancy dismissal. This includes circumstances where the employee's job function still exists, or where the employee could have been given alternative work to carry out in accordance with his contract of employment. The only issue to be resolved is that the evidence demonstrates that it was the employer's requirement for fewer employees that was the *cause* of the employer's decision to dismiss the relevant employees. Providing this is the case, the employees will have been dismissed by reason of redundancy.

The impact of new technologies

Technological developments can result in employers requiring their employees to use new equipment or new processes to carry out their jobs. The obvious examples of such new technologies in recent decades was first the introduction of computerised systems into many workplaces and then the intensive use of the internet to undertake a variety of tasks and activities in a variety of locations, including employees' homes and whilst travelling on public transport. The introduction of new technologies does not always result in employees being made redundant. However, it is not untypical that the use of new technologies does enable the employer to obtain the same, or even an increased, volume of work with fewer employees. This situation provides the main example of redundancy dismissals taking place even though the employer is not in commercial or financial difficulties.

However, in determining that an employee has been dismissed by reason of redundancy it is important to establish that an employee has lost his or her job because the employer no longer requires the employee to do 'work of a particular kind', that is, a specific job. Another possibility, which will not constitute a redundancy dismissal, is that the job still exists and the employer continues to wish to employ the employee to undertake it. However, the employee is unable to get on with the new way of carrying out the job and is ultimately dismissed. Such a dismissal should be understood as being by reference to the employee's capability and should not be regarded as a redundancy dismissal.

The meaning of 'work of a particular kind' in s. 139(1)(b) ERA 1996 is illustrated by the case of *Hindle* v. *Percival Boats Ltd* (1969) 1 All ER 836. In this case Hindle was a highly experienced and skilled boat builder. Until the late 1960s he had been required to make boats out of wood but the company decided to replace wooden boats with ones made of fibre glass. This should be understood as constituting a new technological development at that particular time. Hindle was unable to get on with using fibre glass and was dismissed for being 'too good but too slow'. At the time of his dismissal, unfair dismissal law did not exist, but Hindle argued that he should be entitled to a redundancy payment as the company no longer needed skilled woodworkers. The Court of Appeal rejected this argument as his job, as a boat builder, still existed. The cause of his dismissal was not that the company required fewer employees to undertake work of a particular kind. Rather, as the company argued, the cause of his dismissal was his inability to cope with the new ways of doing his job.

It is important to understand that, today, as established in the case of *Cresswell* v. *Inland Revenue* [1984] ICR 508 where office systems were computerised, an employee should be provided with adequate training to become familiar with working with new technologies. Employees in such circumstances are subject to a **duty to cooperate** by adapting to change (see Chapter 3). However, if an employee is dismissed without such training being provided, the dismissal will be unreasonable and consequently unfair.

By way of contrast to *Hindle*, in *Murphy* v. *Epsom College* [1985] ICR 80 the college replaced its traditional central heating system with a computerised one. Murphy's skills were as a plumber but these skills were no longer required to maintain the new system. It was agreed by the Court of Appeal that the college no longer wanted a plumber and

Case Summary

Case Summary

219

that the new job required the employee to be a heating engineer. Therefore, as Murphy's job had disappeared he was entitled to a redundancy payment.

Mobility clauses and redundancy

It is possible that, where an employer decides to make employees redundant by closing a workplace or requiring fewer employees to work at that particular location, some or all of the employees concerned are redeployed, that is, provided with work, at a different location. However, it may be the case that at least some of those employees do not wish to move to the new workplace. For many years the legal position was that such an employee will not have been made redundant, if the employer was relying on a **mobility clause** in the employee's employment contract which entitled the employer to require the employee to move to a different place of work.

Case Summary

However, in *Bass Leisure Ltd* v. *Thomas* 1994 IRLR 104, the EAT took a factual approach based on where the employee actually worked as against where the employee could be required to work under the contract. Thomas was employed to collect money from fruit machines situated in a number of public houses in Coventry. The company decided to close its establishment in Coventry and invoked a mobility clause in Thomas's contract. She was informed that she was to be redeployed, in accordance with this contractual term, at a different workplace some 20 miles from Coventry. Thomas refused to move as travelling this distance would have disrupted her domestic arrangements and so she decided to resign. The EAT decided that the mobility clause in her contract did not permit the company to require her to make this particular move. Consequently, instructing her to move constituted a breach of contract by the employer which entitled to Thomas to resign and claim constructive dismissal by reason of redundancy. Therefore, she was entitled to a statutory redundancy payment. However, the EAT also stated that, as a matter of fact, her established workplace was in Coventry, and even if the mobility clause in her contract could have been invoked by the company it could not have been relied upon to prevent an actual dismissal from being a redundancy dismissal.

Case Summary

This approach was confirmed by the Court of Appeal in *High Table Ltd* v. *Horst* [1997] IRLR 513. In this case three waitresses, who had always been based at a business situated in the City of London, were told that their services were no longer required. It was held that despite the presence of mobility clauses in their contracts there was a redundancy situation as they were no longer required at their established place of work. The Court of Appeal did clarify that the presence of a mobility clause in a contract is not wholly irrelevant. It might be the case, for example, that an employee is regularly required to work in different places but is informed that he or she will be longer be employed at a specific location. In these circumstances there will not be a redundancy as it cannot be argued that the employee is no longer required at his or her established place of work. Rather, the employee has a number of different workplaces and the closure of one of them does not constitute a redundancy situation.

It is important to appreciate that where an employee is redundant as a result of being instructed to move to a new workplace then the transfer constitutes an offer of alternative employment. As will be discussed further below, where such an offer is suitable and is unreasonably refused then the employee will lose the right to a redundancy payment.

It is important to distinguish between situations where a mobility clause is invoked to instruct an employee to move to a different workplace as part of a process of implementing redundancies, and where such an instruction is given as part of a policy of redeploying employees in their same jobs, but at a different workplace, with the objective of avoiding the need for any redundancies.

In *Home Office* v. *Evans* [2008] IRLR 59, in the knowledge that the Eurostar operation on Waterloo Station was to close, the Home Office decided to invoke mobility clauses in the contracts of immigration officers as an alternative to dismissing any of them by reason of redundancy. There was no longer any point in having immigrations officers at Waterloo as passengers would no longer be using the station to leave or enter the country. However, the Home Office did not want to reduce the number of immigration officers it employed, and therefore, in accordance with the mobility clauses in their employment contracts, it opted to redeploy those officers stationed at Waterloo at new geographical locations. The Court of Appeal held that those employees who refused to move were not dismissed by reason of redundancy as their jobs still existed. The whole purpose of the exercise was to avoid the need for any employee to lose his or her job. In such situations (as explained in Chapter 3), employees who refuse to move are dismissed for refusing to comply with a reasonable instruction of the employer.

Case Summary

It was very important, as a matter of evidence in the above case, that the Home Office had not made any announcement of pending redundancies and nor had it initiated its redundancy procedures. The reasoning in this case will not be applicable where the decision to dismiss by reason of redundancy has been proposed or taken prior to employees being informed that they are to be redeployed at a new workplace. In this situation relocation is part of the redundancy process, and the employer's proposals should be in accordance with its normal redundancy procedures.

The circumstances in which a dismissal will be by reason of redundancy can be summarised as follows:

✦ closure of part or all of a business;

✦ employer decides to reduce the number of employees it employs;

✦ the introduction of new technology leads to the disappearance of an employee's job;

✦ in any of the above contexts, under a mobility clause the employee is instructed to move to a new workplace, which is not his or her established base, but declines to move.

Key stats

In 2007–08 there were 7,800 claims presented to employment tribunals relating to redundancy pay. Between 2008 and 2009 there were 10,800 claims and between 2009 and 2010 the number of claims had risen to 19,000. Between 2010 and 2011 the number of claims fell to 16,000 despite continuing recession, but it is likely that the number of claims will remain high, in comparison with earlier years, whilst mass unemployment continues to be a significant feature of the economy.

In an article by Paddy Allen and Nick Mead in the *Guardian* of 14 December 2011 it was reported that one in five young people are now out of work. Moreover, in the context of redundancies:

'UK unemployment has hit a fresh 17-year high after the public sector shed thousands more jobs and the private sector failed to pick up the slack. The total number of unemployed people rose to 2.64 million, while the number of unemployed young people remained above 1 million. People claiming unemployment benefit rose to nearly 1.6 million.'

Source: the source of the statistics for the number of employment tribunal claims was *Ministry of Justice Employment Tribunal and EATS Statistics 2010–11*, published by the Ministry of Justice in September 2011. The full report can be downloaded at http://www.justice.gov.uk/downloads/statistics/mojstats/employment-trib-stats-april-march-2010-11.pdf; and the *Guardian* quote is from http://www.guardian.co.uk/business/interactive/2009/jun/22/unemployment-and-employment-statistics-recession

Claiming a redundancy payment

Having established the circumstances in which an employee can rightly be regarded as dismissed by reason of redundancy, the next issue to explore is the circumstances in which a dismissed employee will be entitled to a statutory redundancy payment. Only **employees** are entitled to statutory redundancy payments; **workers** do not have this entitlement (see Chapter 2). In order for an employee to be eligible to present a claim for a redundancy payment, the employee must have been **continuously employed** for at least two years and must have been subjected to a dismissal. An employee will have been continuously employed for any period of time during which the contract has continued to exist (see Chapter 5). It matters not that the employee may not have actually worked for significant periods during the currency of the contract providing the contract itself is not terminated by the employer. Normally, a dismissal will be an actual dismissal in that the evidence shows that it was the decision of the employer that the contract should be terminated. Moreover (as explained in the last chapter), non-renewal of a **fixed-term contract** which has expired is a dismissal under s. 95 ERA 1996, and therefore employees are still dismissed and are entitled to redundancy payments where redundancies are implemented through this mechanism.

Alternatively, there will be a **constructive dismissal** where the employee has resigned in response to a **repudiatory breach of contract** by the employer. A repudiatory breach is any breach by a contracting party that goes to the root of the contract so that the basis of it is destroyed. In the context of redundancy a common repudiatory breach by the employer will be a requirement by the employer that the employee should do an entirely different type of job, as illustrated above by the case of *Murphy* v. *Epsom College*. Another major example will be an instruction to an employee to move to a different workplace where there is no relevant mobility clause in the employee's contract that the employer is able to invoke.

A twist on this latter possibility is provided by the decision in *Maher* v. *Fram Gerrard Ltd* [1974] ICR 31. It is an established principle of general contract law that an announcement by a contracting party that he or she will commit a repudiatory breach at a future date constitutes what is termed an *anticipatory breach* of contract. Such a breach entitles the injured contracting party to opt to terminate the contract with immediate effect. It is not necessary for the injured party to wait until the date that the breach of contract actually takes place. In this case, the employer informed Maher that he would be required at a future date to move to new place of work as he would no longer be required at his existing workplace. As there was no mobility clause in Maher's contract, this constituted a repudiatory breach of his contract. Therefore, it was held that Maher was entitled to resign immediately and secure a statutory redundancy payment on the basis that there had been a constructive dismissal.

Case Summary

It follows from what has been stated above that there is no entitlement to a redundancy payment where the employee has not been dismissed. This is illustrated by the case of *Morton Sundour Fabrics* v. *Shaw* [1967] 2 ITR 84. The company warned Shaw that he was likely to be made redundant in the immediate future. On the basis of this warning Shaw secured employment with a different company and handed in his notice. It was held that he was not entitled to a redundancy payment as he had voluntarily resigned from his job.

Whilst this decision is unsurprising in terms of how the law operates it is nevertheless controversial. This is because it enables an employer to warn of impending redundancies in the hope that some employees will leave to take up new employment and consequently the costs of implementing redundancies will be reduced. Essentially, employees are presented with a choice between taking up new jobs elsewhere or postponing doing this until the date of dismissal has occurred so that they can retain their entitlement to redundancy payments. Effectively, this involves employees in gambling on there being available jobs with other employers at the dates of their dismissals.

Voluntary redundancies

It is not uncommon for an employer to offer voluntary redundancies to the workforce. Typically, the sums of money that employees will be offered will be higher than the statutory redundancy payment to which an employee will be entitled. In such circumstances the redundancy will be implemented by contractual agreement with individual employees and the statutory scheme will not be applicable. If the terms of such an agreement are not complied with, this will be governed by ordinary contract law. It should be remembered that employment tribunals can hear claims for breach of contract, on termination of an employment contract, providing the amount being claimed is for no more than £25,000. Therefore, if a contractual redundancy payment, or any unpaid element of it, is for less than £25,000 and the employer fails to pay, the amount can be recovered through a contractual claim presented to an employment tribunal. If the unpaid amount is above £25,000, the action for breach of contract must be taken to an ordinary civil court.

However, it may still be necessary to determine whether an employee, whose contract has been terminated by **voluntary redundancy**, has been dismissed by the employer. This is possible despite the use of the term 'voluntary' as it may be the case that voluntary redundancy is the selection method that the employer is using to identify employees who are to be made redundant. In other words, such employees are volunteering for dismissal and the decision to dismiss still rests with the employer.

One example of how this can be important is where, as detailed below, employers are under a statutory duty to consult with **recognised trade unions** or **employee representatives** because collective redundancies, involving at least 20 employees, are being proposed. Dismissals through voluntary redundancy count in determining the number of employees as a whole that the employer is proposing to dismiss, and calculating the total number of such employees impacts on establishing whether the employer has properly complied with consultation duties.

By way of contrast, as an alternative to redundancy, an employer may offer **voluntary severance** and/or early retirement. Employees are invited to apply to benefit from such schemes, but there is no question of any employees being dismissed by reason of redundancy if the desired numbers of employees choose not to apply. Where an employee does apply and the application is accepted by the employer then again this is an agreement covered by contract law. In short, the termination of the employment contract is by mutual agreement.

Calculating redundancy payments

A claim to a tribunal for a statutory redundancy payment must be presented within *six* months from the effective date of termination. This is in contrast to a claim for unfair dismissal, and indeed most other tribunal claims, where employees have three months to present a tribunal claim.

The amount of statutory redundancy pay is based on the employee's age, completed length of service and week's pay at the date of dismissal. The maximum service which can be counted is 20 years. A week's pay is subject to the current statutory maximum, which in 2012 was £430. A week's pay is based on **gross pay** and not **net pay**, that is, the pay an employee receives before there have been any reductions for income tax, national insurance and the like.

The employee is entitled to:

✦ one and a half weeks' pay for each *complete* year of service after reaching the age of 41;

✦ one week's pay for each complete year between the ages of 22–40 inclusive;

✦ up to the age of 21 half a week's pay for each complete year of employment.

It should be noted that when the Labour government introduced age discrimination regulations in 2006 it did consider whether different age bands were appropriate in that they favour older and longer serving employees. The government concluded that age should continue to be a factor as it is right to recognise an employee's loyalty to a particular employer, and it is often the case that the older an employee is when made redundant the more difficult it is for that person to secure a job with another employer.

In 2012, the maximum payment that an employee could receive was £12,900. This is the product of a calculation of 30 weeks multiplied by £430. To receive this amount the employee would need to be aged at least 61 and to have at least 20 years' completed employment. The employee would also have needed to have earned gross pay of at least £430 a week.

Examples of calculating statutory redundancy payments

John is aged 27 and has completed 10 years' employment and his gross pay is £320 a week. His payment will be based on having completed five years' employment aged 22 and over for which he will receive one week's pay for each of these years. John will be credited with half a week's pay for each of the first five years of his employment.

Therefore the calculation will be a product of multiplying 7.5 weeks by £320 giving John a payment of £2,400.

Jane is aged 50 and has completed 30 years' employment and her gross pay is £500 a week. Her payment will be based on having completed nine years' employment aged 41 and over for which she will receive one and a half weeks' pay for each of these years. Jane will be credited with one week's pay for 11 years of her employment. It is important to remember that only the last 20 years of Jane's employment can be taken into account and to reduce her actual gross pay to the statutory maximum (as in 2012) of £430.

Therefore the calculation will be 24.5 weeks multiplied by £430 giving Jane a payment of £10,535.

Out and about

Visit the government's website at http://www. direct.gov.uk/en/Employment/Redundancy AndLeavingYourJob/Redundancy/ DG_174330. This website provides information about claiming a redundancy payment and provides a link to an online calculator which enables an individual to ascertain the redundancy payment he or she is currently entitled to receive.

The first thing you should do is to ascertain the statutory maximum week's pay which is currently in force. Once you have done this you can access the calculator and enter different

Source: Imagemore Co. Ltd

hypothetical data to see what the different results are. If you have family or close friends of different ages, who have been in their jobs for at least two years, then ask them for their relevant details so you can advise them on their entitlement to a redundancy payment. If you are employed and are eligible to receive a statutory redundancy payment then, of course, you should ascertain what your own current entitlement is.

Offers of alternative employment

It is possible that, even though an employee should be regarded as dismissed by reason of redundancy in accordance with s. 139 ERA 1996, that employee will not be entitled to a statutory redundancy payment. This is the consequence of s. 141 which applies where the employee has received notice that he or she is to be dismissed by reason of redundancy but, as an alternative to making that employee redundant, the employer makes that employee an **offer of suitable alternative employment**. Unreasonable rejection of suitable alternative employment will result in the employee losing a redundancy payment.

Cases demonstrating the working of s. 141 are to be found below. However, the following short example provides an illustration. An employee is made redundant from an office in his or her home town

> unreasonable rejection of suitable alternative employment will result in the employee losing a redundancy payment

but is offered redeployment in another office in the immediate area. The new job is exactly the same as the job the employee was previously doing, and he or she is to be employed on exactly the same terms and conditions of employment. In such a scenario, an employee who refuses redeployment will normally lose the right to a statutory redundancy payment as the offered alternative employment will be suitable and the refusal of it will be unreasonable.

Whether the offer of alternative employment is to be regarded as suitable alternative employment is ascertained largely through an objective comparison between the two jobs. Where the alternative employment should be regarded as objectively suitable but is rejected by the employee, the employee will lose the right to a redundancy payment unless the employee can show that he or she has acted reasonably. Whether this is so is determined by subjective factors personal to that specific employee.

The objective factors to be taken into account in determining whether the offered alternative is suitable include: whether the jobs are the same or similar with respect to pay and other terms and conditions of employment such as hours and holiday entitlement; the skills the employee is required to use; the physical working environment; and job status.

Case Summary

An example of the relevance of job status is provided by *Taylor* v. *Kent County Council* [1969] 2 QB 560. Taylor had been employed as a headmaster of a boys' secondary school. A girls' secondary school was situated on the other side of the road. Kent County Council decided to merge the two schools with the result that only one head teacher was required, and Taylor's application for this post was unsuccessful. Taylor was offered continued employment as a teacher without any changes to his salary or other conditions of employment. Taylor rejected this offer and claimed a statutory redundancy payment. It was held that the loss of status involved rendered the offer of alternative employment unsuitable and therefore Taylor was entitled to a redundancy payment.

Case Summary

It is important that there is a real loss of status and not merely a change in job title, but the employee's perception of whether or not there is a genuine demotion should be taken into account. In *Bird* v. *Stoke-on-Trent Primary Care Trust* (2011) Appeal No. UKEAT/0074/11/DM, Bird was made redundant from a job that involved some clinical work but primarily involved managerial duties. She was offered alternative employment in a role which involved some managerial responsibilities but was largely a clinical one. Moreover, she would no longer have been regarded as a manager within the organisation. It was held by the EAT that, providing her perception that this constituted a demotion was a reasonable one for her to hold, then the offered alternative employment was unsuitable and she would be entitled to a redundancy payment.

These cases demonstrate the very important point that where an offer of alternative employment is unsuitable it is not necessary for the employee to establish that the refusal of the alternative employment was reasonable. The subjective reasons for the employee's rejection of the offer are only of importance where the alternative employment is objectively suitable. However, it should be understood there are no rigid lines between factors which render an offer unsuitable and factors which can be considered in deciding whether an employee has acted reasonably or unreasonably in rejecting the offer of alternative work.

For example, the offer may involve the employee in having to relocate to a different part of the country or to engage in significant additional daily to travel to undertake work in a different geographical location. Even if relocation or additional travel is logistically possible for that employee, the offer could be considered unsuitable if any additional costs involved are to fall entirely or mainly on the employee without any financial contribution from the employer. Alternatively, tribunals might simply decide that the adverse impact on the employee's standard of living constitutes a good reason for the employee to reject the offer of work at a different workplace. It should be remembered, as explained above, that, as a result of the decision in *High Table* v. *Horst*, these arguments may apply even if there is an appropriate mobility clause in the employee's employment contract but the employee is no longer required at his or her *established* place of work.

Reasons for refusing offers of suitable alternative employment

Where the employee is offered the same job on the same terms and conditions and without any effective reduction in the rate of pay, but at a different place of work, the domestic circumstances of that employee provide one example of where the employee's personal needs may constitute sufficient reason to justify the refusal of suitable alternative employment. Examples of such domestic circumstances include child-care responsibilities, or caring for an elderly relative or the career needs of a spouse or partner. The latter would be an important issue if relocation would require the spouse or partner to resign from her or his job where that would disrupt that person's career or result in that person becoming unemployed.

The case of *MacCullum* v. *William Tawse Ltd* [1967] IRLR 199 provides a case example of domestic circumstances justifying a rejection of suitable alternative employment. In this case, moving to a new place of work would have meant the employee would only have been able to spend one weekend every six weeks at home with his family. It was held that he was acting reasonably in rejecting this offer when his wife was in poor health and she would have had to look after five children for considerable periods on her own.

In *Landry* v. *Wedlake Saint Solicitors* ET Case No. 3300098/10, the employee had no family commitments to take into account but moving to a new workplace would have resulted in her travelling an additional two and a quarter hours a day. It was held that, even if this did not involve her incurring the travelling costs, she was acting reasonably in rejecting this job as she was 57 and was therefore making a reasonable lifestyle choice not to increase the time spent travelling to and from work. Indeed, she was at an age when many people are looking to reduce the time they spend at work let alone travelling to it.

Case law in this area of redundancy law does not provide hard and fast precedents as each case will be decided on its own merits. However, the following two cases provide examples of other kinds of subjective factors which will be assessed by tribunals in deciding where an employee's refusal of suitable alternative employment should be considered reasonable or unreasonable.

In *Fuller* v. *Stephanie Bowman (Sales) Ltd* [1977] IRLR 87, the employee was made redundant at her office in Mayfair but offered identical work at an office in Soho. The problem for Fuller was that the Soho office was situated above a sex shop and she was apprehensive about being harassed by men in the vicinity of the office. The tribunal decided that she was unlikely to be mistaken for a sex worker as she was in her fifties and therefore she had nothing to fear. Consequently, the tribunal decided that her refusal to move to the new office was unreasonable and she had lost the right to a redundancy payment. Given its sexist, ageist and rather naive assumptions, this reasoning would probably not be followed today. However, the case does illustrate that if an employee refuses to relocate for reasons which can be regarded as based on a personal whim then the rejection of suitable alternative employment will be unreasonable.

By way of contrast, in *Wragg & Sons Ltd* v. *Wood* [1976] ICR 313, the employee was a man in his fifties who, having been given notice of redundancy, found a new job with a new company which was due to start the day after his notice period expired. The day before the expiry of Wood's notice the company decided to revoke his redundancy and offered him continued employment in the same job on the same rate of pay at the same premises. It was held that Wood was acting reasonably in rejecting this offer of suitable

Table 6.1 Offers of alternative employment

Suitability of alternative employment offered by the employer	Reasonableness of employee's decision to reject suitable alternative employment
Objective comparison between the two jobs	Acceptable reasons based on **subjective** factors relating to that claimant
Rates of pay	Family care responsibilities
Other contractual conditions	Career needs of spouse or partner
Skills involved in performing the job	Difficulty in finding a new job if made redundant in the future
Job status	
Work environment	Employee is to bear the costs involved in redeployment or relocation
Who bears the costs involved in redeployment or relocation?	*Personal whim* will *not* justify rejecting suitable alternative employment

alternative employment. The offer was made late in the day, and Wood was acting reasonably in deciding he was more secure in taking up employment with the new company than he would be if he accepted the offer of continued employment by his current employer. Having been made redundant once, it was reasonable for him to apprehend that he might be made redundant again at a future date, at which point it would have become even more difficult for a man of his age to secure employment elsewhere.

Table 6.1 summarises the factors to be taken into account in determining whether alternative employment is suitable and, if so, whether a rejection of it is reasonable.

Trial periods

Under s. 138 ERA 1996, the provisions relating to offers of alternative employment continue to apply over a statutory trial period of four weeks. Therefore, an employee may be able to experience what undertaking the alternative employment involves, but will still be able to claim a statutory redundancy payment if the employee decides not to continue with the employment during or at the end of a four-week period. The right to a statutory payment remains dependent, of course, on the alternative employment being objectively unsuitable or on the employee having acted reasonably in deciding not to continue with it. *Hindes* v. *Supersine Ltd* [1979] IRLR 343 provides an illustration of the operation of s. 138. Hindes was made redundant but was offered a different job in a different factory on a slightly lower rate of pay. Hindes left this job during the statutory trial period. It was held that he was still entitled to a redundancy payment as he was able to establish that the new working environment was physically less pleasant – indeed it caused him to feel nauseous – and this combined with the reduction in pay meant that the alternative employment was unsuitable.

It should be understood that this *statutory* trial period only applies where the employee is under notice of dismissal, or where he was employed under a fixed-term contract

Case Summary

which the employer has decided not to renew. It is possible that the redundancy is implemented in a way that constitutes a repudiatory breach of contract by the employer which entitles the employee to resign and claim constructive dismissal. This is illustrated by the case of *Maher* v. *Fram Gerrard Ltd*, which is discussed above.

In such circumstances, it was held in the case of *Turvey* v. *Cheney Ltd* [1979] ICR 341 that the employee is entitled to a common law trial period which, in accordance with the principles of contract law, enables the employee to work for a reasonable period of time before deciding whether to accept or reject the employer's breach of contract. In this case, as a result of redundancy, four employees were transferred on to new work without being offered new contracts. More than four weeks after starting on the new jobs they left the company, as they decided that the new work did not suit them. It was held by the EAT that s. 138 and its provisions relating to a four-week trial period did not override the common law. Therefore, it was necessary to remit the case to another tribunal to determine on the facts whether, at the time the employees left the company, they were still exercising their contractual rights to decide whether or not to accept the employer's breach of contract. Only when this common law trial period has ended will the four-week statutory trial period begin.

Case Summary

In summary, if the employee leaves the employment during the common law trial period this constitutes an acceptance by the employee that the employer's breach of contract has brought the contract to end, and there is still a constructive dismissal by reason of redundancy. Once this common law trial period has ended, the employee is then entitled to add on and work the four-week statutory trial period. If the employee leaves during or at the end of this latter period, the right to a redundancy payment is only lost where the employee can be regarded as unreasonably refusing a suitable offer of alternative employment.

Lay-offs and short-term working

Where there is no work for an employee to do, or there is a reduction in the work required from an employee, an employer may decide to **lay-off** that employee or impose short-term working as an alternative to making the employee redundant. If an employee is laid-off, he or she is not provided with any work whatsoever. Short-term working is defined by s. 147(2) ERA 1996 as where the employee will receive less than half a week's pay. As an example, the employee is normally contracted to work a five day week but the employer reduces this to two days a week.

Under s. 148(2), an employee who is laid-off or kept on short-term working without pay for four or more consecutive weeks may resign and claim a redundancy payment. Alternatively, where the consecutive period is no more than three weeks, an employee has this right where the lay-off or short-term working is for a total of six weeks in any period of 13 weeks. The employee is only entitled to receive a statutory redundancy payment once the employee has worked out his or her contractual period of notice.

In order to exercise this right the employee must provide the employer with written notice of an intention to claim a redundancy payment within four weeks of the last of the weeks of lay-off or short-term working on which the claim is based. An employer is entitled to respond by giving the employee a written counter-notice contesting the liability to make a redundancy payment. Under s. 152, this counter-notice will successfully defeat a claim for a redundancy payment if the employer can show that it is reasonably expected that no later than four weeks from the date of the counter-notice the employee will be employed for a period of at least 13 continuous weeks without being laid-off or put on short-term working. This defence will fail if an employee remains laid-off or on short-term working during each of the four weeks after the date that the counter-notice was served. Where the employee is entitled to a statutory redundancy payment, this can be claimed from an employment tribunal in the normal way if the employer fails to pay.

Guarantee payments

Where an employee is laid-off without pay, the employee may be able to claim a guarantee payment. This is an alternative or *additional* right to claiming a statutory redundancy payment on the basis of the above procedure. For an employee to be eligible to claim a guarantee payment that employee must have been continuously employed for at least one month prior to the day on which the guarantee payment is claimed. Payments can only be claimed for days on which employees are provided with no work whatsoever. Under s. 31 ERA 1996, a full-time employee is entitled to payment for a maximum of five days in any period of three months. If an employee only works, for example, for three days a week then the employee will only be entitled to guarantee payments for three days in a three-month period.

Under s. 34 Employment Relations Act 1999, the maximum daily amount for a guarantee payment is generally increased annually in line with the Retail Prices Index. In 2012, the daily maximum was £23.50 a day giving a total of £117.50 for five days in any three-month period. If an employer fails to make a guarantee payment, the employee has three months from the day in respect of which the payment is claimed to present a claim for the payment to an employment tribunal. If the claim is upheld by the tribunal, it will order the employer to pay the employee the money that is due.

Redundancy and unfair dismissal

So far in this chapter we have been concerned to explain when a dismissal by the employer constitutes a dismissal by reason of redundancy, and whether, where there is such a dismissal, the employee is entitled to a statutory redundancy payment. It is possible that in any given situation there is an overlap between redundancy law and unfair dismissal law. This section of the chapter discusses when this will be the case and the remedies to which the unfairly dismissed employee will be entitled as a result.

The employer is required by s. 98(1) ERA 1996 to establish the genuine reason for a dismissal and to show that the reason is a potentially fair one as defined by s. 98(2) (see Chapter 5). This section lists the types of dismissal that are potentially fair and, as well as dismissals for reasons such as incapability and misconduct, identifies redundancy as a potentially fair reason for dismissing an employee. Moreover, providing there is a genuine redundancy, an employer does not have to justify the reasons for making an employee redundant. This was held to be the case in *Moon* v. *Homeworthy Furniture Ltd* [1977] ICR 117 where it was held that the employees could not challenge the employer's view that continuing to operate a factory was not economically viable by producing a business plan seeking to demonstrate that the factory could be made profitable.

Case Summary

Conversely, a sham redundancy will always constitute an unfair dismissal as the employer will not be able to satisfy the requirements of ss. 98(1) and 98(2). A redundancy could be regarded as a sham where the employer is unable to produce any evidence that there are commercial and/or organisational reasons for closing a business or reducing the number of employees required to operate it. A case example of a sham redundancy is provided by *Catton* v. *Rye Street Coachworks Ltd* (2008) ET Case No. 3201204/08. The employer discovered that Catton was pregnant. Four days later she was told that because of a 'reshuffle' she was redundant. There had been no previous mention within the organisation of redundancies and there were no signs of any downturn in work. The tribunal held that the company had failed to prove that Catton's dismissal was by reason of redundancy. The real reason for her dismissal was her pregnancy. Therefore, the dismissal was both unfair and unlawful sex discrimination.

Case
Summary

In considering the overlap between redundancy dismissals and unfair dismissal law, it is important to remember that, although the qualifying period for claiming a statutory redundancy payment is two years, prior to 6 April 2012 the qualifying period for unfair dismissal was one year. It is only employees, who commenced employment on or after 6 April 2012, who will need to have two years' continuous employment to be eligible to claim that a redundancy dismissal was unfair. It is also important to remember that where a dismissal is **automatically unfair** then the normal qualifying period for claiming unfair dismissal is not applicable. The right not to be automatically unfairly dismissed arises on commencement of the contract of employment. Under s. 105 a selection for dismissal by reason of redundancy will be automatically unfair if it is for one of the listed inadmissible reasons. (These reasons, such as dismissal for reasons connected with trade union membership or activities, or because of pregnancy or the exercising of maternity rights, are listed and briefly explained in Chapter 5.)

Fair redundancy procedures

Even where a redundancy dismissal is genuine and is not automatically unfair, it may still be unfair by reference to s. 98(4) ERA 1996. As in any other unfair dismissal claim, a dismissal by reason of redundancy will be unfair if the employer has not acted reasonably, that is, within the **range of reasonable responses** open to the employer. (This test is explained and discussed in Chapter 5.) A reasonable employer should adhere to the following procedures and practices prior to dismissing an employee by reason of redundancy. Providing the employer does this then any redundancy dismissal should be fair and the only statutory right possessed by the dismissed employee will be the right to a statutory redundancy payment.

The provision of adequate warning and consultation

The decision of the Law Lords in *Polkey* v. *Dayton* [1988] ICR 142, which was discussed in the previous chapter with respect to the **ACAS Code on Disciplinary and Grievance Procedures**, arose out of an employer's failure to consult before making the employee redundant. Unlike its predecessors, the current ACAS Code does not apply to redundancy dismissals but the decision in *Polkey* does continue to apply. Therefore, normally, an employer should have redundancy procedures under which individual employees are to be warned that they are at risk of redundancy, and are to be invited to a consultation meeting with a member of management in the event that it is proposed to select any such employee for redundancy. In larger organisations, where the outcome of such a meeting is confirmation that the employee is to be made redundant, the employee should be granted a right of appeal to a more senior level of management, such as the directors of a company or the senior managers or governing bodies of a public sector organisation.

As explained by Lord Bridge in *Polkey*, the purpose of consultation is to discuss steps the employer could take to avoid making the employee redundant, and to ascertain the selection method for redundancy that the employer is using is a fair one. However, failure to consult will not render the dismissal unfair where the employer can show that consultation can reasonably be considered futile or useless. Therefore, if the employer can show that the commercial and/or financial circumstances are such that the employer has no option other than to make compulsory redundancies and no option other than to select the employee for redundancy, then a failure to consult might not render the dismissal unfair. Arguably, however, except in very drastic circumstances the employer should always be aware that redundancies are inevitable in time to warn the workforce of this. Remember, and perhaps rather ironically, employees who leave to take up new jobs in the wake of such a warning will not have been dismissed and will not be entitled to statutory redundancy payments.

The consideration of alternatives to redundancy

As illustrated by the staff reduction policy (see below), where an employer believes that it is necessary to reduce the size of the workforce there may be ways of doing this which will avoid the need for making employees redundant, or will reduce the number of redundancies which the employer will decide it is necessary to make. Such methods include: ending overtime working; implementing natural wastage so that employees who leave the organisation are not replaced; inviting employees to apply for voluntary severance and/or early retirement in return for receiving specified payments such as a year's salary and/or early access to accrued pension benefits. There is no actual duty on employers to consider these sorts of alternatives prior to implementing redundancies, but failure to do so in the context of consultation with an employee at risk of redundancy may mean that the employer has failed to act reasonably and consequently the dismissal of that employee will be unfair.

A reasonable employer will also normally consider whether voluntary redundancies are feasible, that is, to invite employees to volunteer for redundancy dismissals. This is only likely to be acceptable to employees if the employer can offer redundancy payments which are more generous than a payment an employee is entitled to under the statutory scheme. Where voluntary redundancy is not feasible from the employer's perspective, for example because of the additional costs involved, or where insufficient numbers of employees volunteer, the employer can be regarded as having acted reasonably in deciding that it is necessary to proceed with making redundancies on a compulsory basis.

Even where it is reasonable for an employer to conclude that compulsory redundancies will take place, consultations with an employee at risk of compulsory redundancy should still consider alternatives to making that specific employee redundant. Individual employees should still be given the opportunity to question their individual selection for redundancy, and to explore individual alternatives to redundancy such as redeployment elsewhere within the organisation. An example of an employer failing to follow the latter course of action is provided by the case of *Vokes Ltd* v. *Bear* [1974] ICR 1. The company employed Mr Bear in a managerial capacity and without prior warning or any discussion with him informed him that he was to be redundant. The company was part of a network

Case Summary

of companies and, at the time Bear was made redundant, other companies within the group were advertising managerial vacancies. Whilst there was no guarantee that Bear would have been considered suitable for filling one of these vacancies, the failure even to discuss this possibility with him meant that the employer had failed to act reasonably and therefore Bear's dismissal was unfair.

In the context of redeployment, it is important to remember that if an employee under notice of redundancy is offered suitable alternative employment that employee will lose the right to a statutory redundancy payment if such an offer is unreasonably rejected. Clearly, providing proper procedures have been followed by the employer, the employee's dismissal in such a situation will be reasonable and fair.

The adoption of fair selection methods for redundancy

Historically, if in a given sector of industry there were customary procedures to be followed by the employer in implementing redundancies a dismissal would have been automatically unfair if such procedures were not adhered to. Similarly, employers were required to abide by redundancy procedures contained in a **collective agreement** with a trade union if claims of **automatic unfair dismissal** were to be pre-empted. These provisions were repealed by the Deregulation and Contracting Out Act 1994 as part of the deregulatory policies of John Major's Conservative government. However, the existence of such procedures will be taken into account by tribunals in considering whether an employer has acted reasonably in accordance with s. 98(4) ERA 1996. Where an employer is unable to establish a good reason for such procedures not being followed, consequent dismissals are likely to be found to be unfair.

A selection method for redundancy based on last in first out (LIFO) is a major example of a customary procedure or one which may be found in a collective agreement. The logic behind this method is that it is the most recently recruited members of the workforce who will be selected first for compulsory redundancies. There is, however, a problem with the use of LIFO which connects with discrimination law (as discussed in Chapter 7). Self-evidently LIFO disproportionately impacts on the younger members of the workforce and thus constitutes age discrimination. Moreover, women are also often disproportionately affected by LIFO as many women have breaks during their careers to give birth to and look after children. LIFO can therefore amount to what is termed **indirect discrimination** (the nature of such discrimination will be fully explained in Chapter 7). As shown by the following 'Law in action' feature, discrimination law notwithstanding, LIFO can still constitute a fair selection method for redundancy.

Law in action

In May 2009, the use of a selection method for redundancy, contained in a collective agreement between Rolls-Royce plc and the UNITE trade union, which included the use of points for each year worked with Rolls-Royce was declared lawful by the Court of Appeal on the basis that the procedure was a proportionate method of securing the legitimate objectives of rewarding loyalty and creating a stable workforce.

This decision of the Court of Appeal supported the decision given in the High Court to the effect that: 'The criterion of length of service respects the loyalty and experience of the older workforce and protects the older employees from being put onto the labour market at a time when they are particularly likely to find employment hard to find.'

Rolls-Royce had argued that taking long service into account when selecting workers for redundancy amounted to indirect age discrimination and wanted to ignore provisions in their collective agreement with UNITE that rewarded length of service when making redundancies.

In giving his reaction to the court's decision, Unite's General Secretary, Derek Simpson, said:

'We are delighted with this decision. The ruling sets a precedent, where other factors are equal, for protecting older workers from the effects of redundancy. It has always been clear to Unite that loyalty seen in length of service should be recognised when an employer takes the drastic step of making redundancy dismissals ... We look forward to using this decision to help defend our members' rights in many other companies as well as Rolls-Royce.'

Source: The above is derived from an article by John Charlton in *Personnel Today*, 14 May 2009, entitled 'Rolls-Royce loses key age discrimination appeal'. This can be accessed at **http://www.personneltoday.com/articles/2009/05/14/50693/rolls-royce-loses-key-age-discrimination-appeal.html**; also see *Rolls-Royce plc* v. *Unite the Union* [2010] ICR 1 for the full law report of the Court of Appeal's decision.

Other justifications for LIFO include retaining more experienced employees and keeping down the costs of implementing redundancies. It is important to understand that the decision of the Court of Appeal in the *Rolls-Royce* case does not mean that LIFO has been declared to be objectively justifiable in all circumstances. In any redundancy situation where an employer decides to use this selection method, it will still have to be justified by reference to the specific circumstances in which redundancies are being made.

Case Summary

Age discrimination was also the issue in *Woodcock* v. *Cumbria Primary Care Trust* [2012] IRLR 491. In this case the Court of Appeal decided that it was lawful to make the chief executive of the trust redundant before he reached the age of 50 at which point he would be entitled to take advantage of a very beneficial early retirement scheme. The court held that cost is a permitted factor for justifying age discrimination providing there other factors present contributing to the justification. In this case the trust had given him a year's warning that he had was at risk of redundancy and had expected him to obtain alternative employment in the National Health Service. If his dismissal had been further delayed he would have secured a windfall in the form of being able to access an enhanced occupational pension. Therefore, the cost involved in not dismissing him, combined with preventing him from benefiting from a scheme that he would not have enjoyed if he had continued in employment with the trust to his expected age of retirement, justified the age discrimination present in this case. It can be noted that had Woodcock claimed unfair dismissal then, on the basis of the above arguments, it is likely the dismissal would have been regarded as within the range of reasonable responses and therefore fair.

Where any selection method for redundancy is based on unlawful discrimination, such as sex, race or age, any resulting dismissal will be unfair. Discrimination law, as you will see (in Chapter 7), is contained in the Equality Act 2010 rather than in ERA 1996. As summarised in Table 6.2, dismissed employees are more likely to rely on the Equality Act in preference to ERA 1996 for two reasons. First, there is no qualifying period of employment to satisfy in order to present a tribunal claim. Secondly, as was of practical relevance in the case of *Woodcock* above, there is no statutory cap on the compensation that a tribunal can award for unlawful discrimination. The maximum amount that a claimant can receive by way of a compensatory award for unfair dismissal was, at the time of writing, £72,300 (see Chapter 5). Furthermore, a worker who does not have employee status (as explained in Chapter 2), will not be entitled to a statutory redundancy payment or be eligible to claim unfair dismissal. Such a worker is, however, protected by the Equality Act.

Table 6.2 Comparing ERA 1996 and the Equality Act with respect to claims of unfair selection methods for redundancy

ERA 1996	Two years' continuity of employment required	Only employees may claim unfair dismissal	Statutory cap on the compensatory award
Equality Act 2010	No qualifying period required	Workers as well as employees can claim	No limit on compensation

A selection method for redundancies that employers may choose to adopt, which will normally be free from the constraints of discrimination law, is one based on employee performance. This may reflect an employee's attendance record, providing periods of absence caused by injury or illness are excluded as, failing to do this, could bring the disability discrimination provisions of the Equality Act into play. Disciplinary records can also be used, as can an employee's performance as reflected in any formal employee appraisal records. It is important that employee performance is assessed on an objective basis, such as merit points achieved through an employee's contribution to the organisation, and not on the subjective perceptions of particular managers.

If an employee is selected for redundancy because a manager regards his or her performance as deficient, but there has been no formal appraisal of the employee's performance, the selection for redundancy is likely to be unfair. For example, in *Williams* v. *Compair Maxam Ltd* [1982] employees, who in the manager's opinion 'would keep the company viable', were excluded from being selected for redundancy. It was held that the company's selection method was entirely subjective and unreasonable and therefore those who were selected for redundancy were unfairly dismissed.

Case
Summary

Writing and drafting

You are employed as a paralegal in a firm of solicitors specialising in employment law. You have been instructed by a senior partner to write a letter to C plc seeking compensation on behalf of Doris, who has been dismissed by reason of redundancy.

Doris was employed as the finance manager at the Manchester office of C plc. The company has a number of offices situated in various large towns and cities throughout Britain. Doris was informed by James, the senior manager at the office in Manchester, that, in order to reduce costs, he had decided to take over her functions and to dismiss her with notice by reason of redundancy. Doris has received her statutory redundancy payment. At the time of her dismissal Doris was aware that there was a vacancy in the finance department in the company's head office in London, which she was qualified to be considered for. Doris would have been prepared to move to London to stay in employment. After her dismissal, Doris discovered that the person employed to fill the vacancy at the London office was less experienced than her and had not been employed by the company before.

Handy tip: You should write this letter in a technical and persuasive style with a view to convincing C plc that Doris has been unfairly dismissed and therefore it should pay compensation to her.

The following summarises the factors employment tribunals will take into account in determining whether a redundancy dismissal is unfair.

Determining whether a redundancy dismissal is unfair

A redundancy dismissal will be unfair if an employer has failed to act reasonably in accordance with s. 98(4) ERA 1996. The following factors are taken into account in assessing reasonableness:

✦ Have individuals been warned they are at risk of redundancy?

✦ Have individuals been consulted over proposed redundancies to consider alternatives such as redeployment?

✦ Has the employer adopted a fair method for selecting employees for redundancy?

✦ Is the selection method in accordance with customary practice or collective agreements with trade unions?

✦ If the selection method is based on work performance does it reflect objective appraisal of individual employees?

A redundancy dismissal will be *automatically* unfair if it is for an inadmissible reason such as pregnancy or membership of a trade union.

Remedies for unfair redundancies

It will only be in rare circumstances, such as a sham redundancy, where a tribunal might be able to grant an order of **reinstatement** or **re-engagement** to an unfairly dismissed employee as, if the redundancy is genuine, the dismissed employee's job will no longer exist. Therefore, assuming an employee who is unfairly dismissed by reason of redundancy has received a statutory redundancy payment, the normal remedy will be a **compensatory award**. Normally, this will be based on the actual financial loss suffered by the employee and will be calculated in the same way as explained in the last chapter, and subject to the same statutory cap – at the time of writing this was £72,300. However, an employee with less than two years' service will not be entitled to a redundancy payment but will receive a **basic award** reflecting one year's completed employment. This will not be the case with employees who commenced employment on or after 6 April 2012 as such individuals will need two years' continuity of employment before becoming eligible to claim unfair dismissal.

Some categories of automatic unfair dismissal, such as selection for redundancy for a trade union reason, will entitle an employee to a minimum basic award, which at the time of writing was £5,300. An automatically unfair dismissal for a health and safety reason, contrary to s. 105(3) ERA 1996, will entitle the employee not only to this minimum basic award but also to an uncapped compensatory award. An example of a health and safety reason would be where an employee is dismissed, or in this context is selected for redundancy, because the employee left a place of work 'because of a reasonable belief [he was] in serious and imminent danger' (see Chapter 3).

In our examination of the decision of the Law Lords in *Polkey* (see Chapter 5), it was established that defective procedure can make a dismissal unfair even though an employer can show that the failure to follow proper procedure has made *no difference* to the employer's decision to dismiss. If a *reasonable* employer would have followed the procedure concerned, then a failure by an employer to do so will mean that the dismissal must be unfair. However, it is permissible for a tribunal to conclude, on the basis of the 'no difference' principle, that the employee should not receive a compensatory award for unfair dismissal. This is known as a **Polkey reduction**.

This is illustrated by the Court of Appeal's decision in *Arhin* v. *Enfield Primary Care Trust* [2010] EWCA Civ 1481, where the employee was denied the opportunity to put forward a case as to why she should not be selected for redundancy. It was held that, although this meant her dismissal was unfair as the employer had failed to act reasonably, she should not receive a compensatory award as the award should be subjected to a 100% reduction. The evidence revealed that her job had disappeared. Although there was one vacancy for redeployment, she was clearly not the most suitable candidate to be considered for this post. In short, though the reasonable employer would have consulted with her, the failure to do so in this case made no difference to the decision to select her for redundancy.

As explained above, the current ACAS Code does not apply to redundancy dismissals. Whilst this makes no difference to the procedures that employers are advised to follow in implementing redundancies this does have one practical consequence. The compensatory award granted to an unfairly dismissed employee cannot be increased or decreased as a result of the code not being properly followed.

The following staff reduction policy contains a comprehensive set of procedures which if properly followed should prevent any claim of unfair dismissal from succeeding.

Documenting the law

STAFF REDUCTION POLICY

1 GENERAL PRINCIPLES

1.1 In order to sustain the overall health, viability and success of the organisation, the employer may from time to time find itself in financial or other circumstances requiring reductions in the number of staff employed. In such circumstances the employer will seek to avoid compulsory redundancies by considering steps such as the use of natural wastage, reorganisation, redeployment and voluntary reductions, in order to prevent compulsory redundancy.

1.2 Should situations occur in which it is necessary to reduce the number of staff within the organisation, every effort will be made to avoid redundancy. In order to achieve responsible but effective management of such situations, the employer will proceed in the following manner.

2 NATURAL WASTAGE

2.1 In the first instance, should natural wastage occur in areas of the organisation where staff reduction might be needed, every effort will be made to manage those areas so that the wastage should remove the need for any other reduction.

2.2 Subject to ensuring the effective continuation of the organisation's work, the employer will seek across the organisation, through management, redeployment and retraining, to use natural wastage to minimise or remove any need for other severance.

3 VOLUNTARY SEVERANCE

3.1 Where staff reduction in the judgment of the employer is deemed necessary, the employer may either sequentially or at the same time implement a voluntary severance and premature retirement scheme. This may be confined to specific parts of the organisation and/or to certain categories of staff or may be operated generally.

3.2 The invitation to apply for voluntary severance and premature retirement should include a redundancy payment based upon actual salary and actual completed years of employment.

3.3 Responses to the employer's invitation to apply for voluntary severance and premature retirement will be considered by the employer in the light of its operational and strategic requirements. The decision to allow voluntary severance and premature retirement is at the discretion of the employer.

4 COMPULSORY REDUNDANCIES

4.1 The employer will initiate compulsory redundancy procedures only as a last resort after operating fully the voluntary severance and premature retirement procedures.

4.2 All employees are entitled to notice of the termination of their employment as provided for by their contract of employment.

4.3 The employer will provide to any employee whom it is proposed to make compulsorily redundant a statement of the reason for that redundancy.

4.4 Following the issuing of this statement a meeting shall be arranged between the employee and his or her line manager and the Head of Human Resources at which the reasons for the proposed redundancy will be discussed. The employee has the right to be accompanied by a trade union representative or friend.

4.5 If the outcome of the above meeting is not satisfactory to the employee he or she may request a final meeting with members of the organisation's executive board. At this meeting the employee may appeal

(i) against initial selection for compulsory redundancy

(ii) and/or the termination of employment.

The employee has the right to be accompanied by a trade union representative or friend at this final meeting.

Reflective practice

Look back at the letter you drafted on behalf of Doris. From the facts as stated it appeared that Doris was simply informed that she was redundant and no procedure was followed. This situation was very similar to the case of *Vokes Ltd* v. *Bear*. Had Doris been consulted, she could have put it formally to James that she should be considered for redeployment at the London office. The company's failure to consult with Doris and to consider alternatives meant that it has acted unreasonably and Doris's dismissal was unfair. Consequently, if C plc refuses voluntarily to compensate Doris for loss of earnings, she will be entitled to present a tribunal claim to seek a compensatory award for unfair dismissal.

Had the company adhered to procedures such as those which are detailed in the above staff reduction procedure, this problem should have been avoided. Doris' dismissal would have been fair providing C plc could show that it had discussed redeployment with her but had acted reasonably in concluding that Doris was not suitable for employment in the London office. Alternatively, the company would have acted reasonably if, after allowing Doris to participate in a competitive interview for the London post, it had an objective basis for deciding that the successful candidate was stronger than Doris.

Business reorganisations and unfair dismissal

A dismissal by reason of redundancy is the major example of an employee being dismissed for economic reasons which are not connected to the personal behaviour of the employee. However, not all **economic dismissals** will constitute redundancies. It is important to remember that the statutory definition of redundancy requires the dismissal to be the result of an employer deciding that fewer employees are required to undertake work of a particular kind. Therefore, if an employee is dismissed for economic reasons, such as the maintenance or enhancement of cost efficiency or productivity, but in circumstances in which the employer is not seeking to reduce the number of employees required to undertake a particular job, that dismissal cannot be a redundancy dismissal. Although, as we shall see, there may be circumstances in which it will be an unfair dismissal.

You be the judge

Q: Do you think that John is entitled to a statutory redundancy payment in the following situation?

The managing director of X Co. Ltd. decides that the company is not sufficiently competitive and should move to introducing night working. Currently, employees work nine-hour shifts between 8.00 a.m. and 6.00 p.m. The company informs its employees that it is proposing to change their contractual hours of working so that in alternate weeks they will be required to work from 6.00 p.m. until 4.00 a.m. The employees are informed that any employees who refuse this change to their contracts of employment will be dismissed with salary in lieu of notice. All the employees other than John accept these new working conditions. John has been dismissed with pay in lieu of notice but believes he is entitled to a redundancy payment.

Source: Steve Cole, Photodisc

A: John does not have the right to a redundancy payment as the employer had no intention of reducing the size of the workforce.

The above situation is very similar to the facts of the cases of *Johnson* v. *Nottinghamshire Police Authority* [1974] ICR 170 and *Lesney Products Ltd* v. *Nolan* [1977] ICR 235. In both these cases it was clarified that any dismissals could not constitute redundancy dismissals if the employers required the same number of employees to carry out the same jobs they had always been employed to undertake. Therefore, the dismissals fell outside the statutory definition of redundancy. The changes required by the companies in these cases and by X Co. Ltd were to employment contracts not to the number of employees required to work under these contracts.

Although in the above cases the dismissals were not by reason of redundancy, such dismissals *may* be unfair. The employer can argue on the basis of s. 98(1)(b) ERA 1996 that the dismissals are for 'some other substantial reason', and that the decision to dismiss is reasonable within the meaning of s. 98(4) on grounds of necessary business

Case
Summary

reorganisation. This was held to be the case by the Court of Appeal in *Hollister* v. *NFU* [1979] IRLR 238 in which the the National Farmers Union decided to reorganise its Cornwall business so that the pay of its secretaries were calculated on the same basis as applied in all other parts of the country. Hollister declined to accept a new contract of employment based upon the revised terms and was accordingly dismissed. His claim for unfair dismissal was rejected by an industrial tribunal on the grounds that the reorganisation amounted to 'some other substantial reason' justifying dismissal. The Court of Appeal upheld this decision on the basis that the dismissal may be justified as within the range of reasonable responses where employers need to reorganise their business and the employee declines to cooperate with such reorganisation.

In assessing reasonableness the key factors to be taken into account are:

✦ Was there a sound business reason for the reorganisation?

✦ Was it necessary to insist that a specific employee be required to accept the changes?

✦ Had the majority of employees accepted the changes?

✦ Had there been adequate consultation in line with the decision in *Polkey*?

Case
Summary

These principles are illustrated by *St John of God (Care Services) Ltd* v. *Brooks* [1992] IRLR 546. The employees were nurses at a hospital run by the company. In order to avoid closure following a reduction in funding, it was considered necessary to employ the staff on less beneficial terms. A letter was sent to all employees informing them that entitlement to holiday would be reduced, overtime rates abolished, the general sick pay scheme replaced by statutory sick pay and the imposition of a pay freeze. The employees were informed that the changes would be discussed with them, they would be given a reasonable period of time in which to decide whether to accept the new contracts, but if they did not they would be dismissed. Four of the nurses did not accept the new terms and were given notice of dismissal. The EAT held that the circumstances showed that there was a sound business reason for the reorganisation, and that the employer had acted reasonably. Therefore, the dismissals of the four nurses who refused to accept the changes to their employment contracts were fair. This case shows that dismissals may be fair even where the employer has unilaterally varied employment contracts if it is the dismissed employees who can be regarded as unreasonable because they have refused to accept changes to their terms and conditions of employment.

Therefore, although the general impact of unfair dismissal law is to protect employees in circumstances in which dismissals are in accordance with the employment contract, dismissals in the context of business reorganisations may be fair even though they arise out of a **unilateral variation of contractual terms** without the consent of employees who find themselves dismissed as a result. This is another consequence of dismissals being fair providing an employer has acted within the range of reasonable responses. Effectively, employers are able to justify acting in breach of contract in circumstances where they can establish that a reasonable employer would act in this way in furtherance of business efficiency.

This legal position perhaps demonstrates that (as discussed in Chapter 5), the range of reasonable responses test can operate to reinforce managerial authority at the expense of providing effective employment protection. Alternatively, it can be argued that varying employment contracts is a way in which employers can maintain the job security of their employees. However, it should be emphasised that, as illustrated by *Hollister* above, it is not a prerequisite for a finding of fair dismissal that the business reorganisation was necessary to avoid redundancies. It is sufficient that an employer can show that the aim of the reorganisation is to improve the efficiency, productivity and/or competitiveness of the business.

Business transfers and the TUPE Regulations

Another business context which may result in employees being dismissed for economic reasons is where an employer is proposing to transfer all or part of a business to another employer. Imagine that you are employed in a public house and the owner of the pub decides to sell it to another publican, who will continue to trade using the same name for the pub and intending to retain its regular clientele. The buying publican has informed your employer that he wishes to employ his own staff, on lower rates of pay, and therefore a condition of the sale is that your employer dismisses you by reason of redundancy. In this situation, although there are no questions relating to your competence, and the same numbers of employees are required, you have lost your job through no fault of your own.

However, in such circumstances the TUPE Regulations will apply to protect you. These regulations use the terminology of transferor and transferee rather than seller and buyer of the business. They require the buying publican, as the transferee, to accept that you and any other existing employees are transferred to him as your new employer on your existing pay and other contractual conditions. If you are dismissed as a result of the sale of the pub, you will be able to bring a claim of unfair dismissal against the *transferee*, and normally such a claim will automatically succeed.

Note: the original Transfer of Undertakings Regulations were made in 1981 to transpose the EU's Acquired Rights Directive 1977. This Directive was replaced in 2001 with the Acquired Rights Directive 2001/23. This Directive is transposed by the Transfer of Undertakings (Protection of Employment) Regulations 2006, SI 2006/246 (abbreviated to TUPE).

Relevant transfers

Not all business transfers will be covered by the TUPE Regulations. Under regulation 3 there must be a relevant transfer, which is defined as the transfer of an undertaking or business, or part of such an undertaking or business, where there has been the transfer of an economic entity which retains its identity.

Therefore, the regulations will only apply where a business has been sold as a going concern. For example, in a similar situation to the above, if the pub in which you work is sold to a property development company, which intends to knock it down and build residential flats on the land, the pub will cease to exist as an economic entity after the sale. Therefore, your only rights will be to a statutory redundancy payment, which you will be able to claim from your employer. This will always be the case where the sale is of land and/or business assets, such as furniture and equipment, and the buyer will not be taking over the previous business.

However, there will be a relevant transfer, and therefore TUPE will apply, where an organisation decides to transfer part of its operations to another business. For example, a university decides that it will no longer employ its own employees to provide catering services to its students and staff. It enters into a contract with an external catering company to provide these services. TUPE will apply so that the catering company will be obliged to continue to employ the catering staff previously employed by the university. If the contract between the university and the catering company is for a defined period of time then, on expiry of the contract, the catering staff will revert to being university employees. If the university then makes a contract with another catering company, TUPE will continue to apply to protect the catering staff.

A case example of this process is provided by *Dines and others* v. *(1) Initial Health Care Services Ltd (2) Pall Mall Services Group Ltd* [1995] ICR 11. The Court of Appeal held that TUPE continued to apply where a health authority changed the contractor responsible for cleaning its hospitals. The court decided that there had been a 'relevant transfer' between the contractors which took place in two phases: (i) the handing back of the cleaning services to the health authority and (ii) the handing over of these services by the authority to the new contractor.

From the perspective of protecting an employee's security of employment, a major gap in TUPE is that the regulations will not normally govern the situation where a business is transferred through share purchase, that is, where one company purchases the majority of shares in another company from the latter's shareholders. In Britain, this is normally the way in which one company will take over another company. However, as the purchase of the latter's shares means that it continues to exist there is not deemed to be a change in the employer's identity. It is not uncommon before such takeovers occur for the company buying up the shares to insist that all or any of the existing employees are dismissed. Alternatively, it may be that the buying company agrees to continue to employ the workforce but then makes redundancies. In either of these situations, providing proper redundancy procedures are followed, the employees who lose their jobs are only entitled to statutory redundancy payments from the employer which implemented the redundancies.

The effect of a relevant transfer on employees

> transferred employees keep their jobs on their existing terms and conditions of employment

Under regulation 4(1), a relevant transfer shall not operate so as to terminate the contract of employment of any person employed by the transferor in the undertaking, or the part transferred, where the contract would otherwise have been terminated by the transfer. The contract shall have effect after the transfer as if originally made between the persons so employed and the transferee. For example, Company A transfers part of its operations to Company B. As a result of regulation 4, this transfer does not result in the dismissal of Company A's employees. Moreover, not only are the employees transferred to Company B, but so are the contracts of employment under which those employees were employed by Company A. In short, the transferred employees keep their jobs on their existing terms and conditions of employment.

Under regulation 4(3), this protection is provided to any person who was employed immediately before the transfer, or would have been so employed had he not been dismissed prior to the transfer taking place. The fact that TUPE may apply to dismissals carried out prior to the transfer taking place is illustrated by the decision of the House of Lords in *Litster* v. *Forth Dry Dock and Engineering Co Ltd* [1989] ICR 341. In this case the Forth Dry Dock Company was insolvent and went into receivership, and all of its employees were dismissed. One hour after these dismissals, the business was acquired by another company which only employed a few of the former employees of Forth Dry Dock. These employees were employed on lower wages than they had previously received. The Law Lords held that the dismissal of the workforce was for a reason that was solely connected to the transfer and therefore TUPE applied so the dismissals were automatically unfair. In such circumstances, it is the *transferee* who incurs liability for the unfair dismissals.

It is not the case that all dismissals that occur before a transfer will be covered by TUPE. In the case of *Secretary of State for Employment* v. *Spence* [1986] ICR 651, a company went into receivership. The receiver was uncertain that he would be able to sell the company and all the employees were dismissed. As it turned out, the receiver had been unduly pessimistic and later on, during the day on which the dismissals took place, the business was sold. Moreover, the dismissed employees were hired by the new owners of the business. The Court of Appeal held that the dismissed employees had not been employed immediately before the transfer. Therefore, they were entitled to redundancy payments from their *previous* employers. The difference between *Spence* and *Litster* is that in the latter case there had been collusion between the transferor and the transferee to carry out the dismissals in order to evade the regulations. In *Spence*, at the time of the sale, the receiver genuinely believed that a transfer might not take place and had dismissed the employees to protect the interests of the creditors of the company.

Later (in Chapter 8) we discuss the situation where an employer agrees to negotiate with a trade union on the pay and other contractual conditions of employment of its employees. An employer which acts in this way is said to have recognised the relevant union and has entered into a **recognition agreement**. If negotiations between the employer and the trade union result in a collective agreement, the contents of this agreement may be incorporated into the employment contracts of the relevant employees. For example, a college agrees to raise the pay of its administrative staff by one pound an hour. This agreement becomes part of the individual contracts of employment of the administrative staff. Were the college to fail to increase their pay as agreed then it would be liable for breach of contract to each of the employees. As will be explained further (in Chapter 8), collective agreements between employers and trade unions may or may not be incorporated into individual contracts of employment, but they are presumed *not* to be legally enforceable between the employer and the union.

Under regulation 6, where employees who are transferred belong to a trade union which was recognised by the transferor then collective agreements, including a recognition agreement, are transferred to the transferee. It should be clarified that this is only the case where the transferred employees and/or their resources maintain an identity which is distinct from the rest of the transferee's undertaking. This would be the case in the above examples of a university or health authority contracting out its catering or cleaning services. However, as a recognition agreement is not legally enforceable, there is nothing to prevent the transferee from ending the agreement once the transfer has taken place. This is known as **derecognition** of the union. It is important to understand that derecognition of the union will not alter the position that, as in the above example, at least part of the contracts of employment of the transferred employees will be derived from collective agreements, and the transferee will continue to be bound by such contractual conditions.

TUPE and automatically unfair dismissals

Transfers may result in particular employees being actually or constructively dismissed by the transferor or transferee. Under regulation 7, 'where either before or after a relevant transfer, any employee of the transferor or transferee is dismissed, that employee shall be treated . . . as unfairly dismissed if the transfer or a reason connected with it is the reason or principal reason for his dismissal'. It should be noted that only employees who have sufficient continuity of employment to claim unfair dismissal against the transferor will be able to claim unfair dismissal against the transferee.

It may be the case that there is some significant lapse in time between the transfer and a dismissal, but this will not prevent a dismissal from being automatically unfair where there is still a causal connection between the transfer and the dismissal. In *Taylor* v. *Connex South Eastern Ltd* EAT 12432/99, Taylor was dismissed two years after the transfer for refusing to accept a variation to his contract which would have made his terms and conditions of employment consistent with other employees on his grade, who were employed by Connex prior to the transfer. Other employees who had been transferred along with Taylor had accepted new contracts. The EAT held that there was no break in the chain of causation between the transfer and the attempt to vary Taylor's employment contract. Therefore, TUPE continued to apply and Taylor's dismissal was automatically unfair.

Case Summary

As a result of regulation 7(2), a dismissal will not be unfair where the reason or principal reason for dismissing an employee is 'an **economic, technical or organisational (ETO) reason** entailing changes in the workforce of either the transferor or the transferee before or after a relevant transfer'. In such circumstances, the dismissal will be regarded as being for redundancy, or some other substantial reason under ERA 1996, and will be subject to s. 98(4). In other words, the dismissal will be for a potentially fair reason and will be fair if the employer can show that it has acted reasonably.

Examples of ETOs which will make dismissals potentially fair include genuine redundancy dismissals where redundancies are necessary either to keep the business viable or ensure it remains profitable. An example is provided by *Meikle* v. *McPhail (Chesterton Arms)* [1983] IRLR 351. In this case, the EAT held that the dismissal of Meikle, a barmaid, after McPhail had taken over a pub was fair as, after the transfer, the latter was informed by his accountant that he had over-committed himself to the number of staff he would employ and substantial salary savings were required.

Case Summary

The *Connex* case also demonstrates that a desire by an employer to standardise terms of employment after the transfer, so that transferred employees have the same contracts as the rest of the transferee's employees employed to undertake the same work, will not normally be considered to be an ETO reason, and a dismissal will be unfair. This applies equally to a constructive dismissal where an employee resigns in response to the transferee's imposition of a new contract on that employee. In *Delabole Slate Limited* v. *Berriman* [1985] IRLR 305, the employee resigned because the transferee sought to impose a lower rate of pay on him. This would have brought his contract in line with the rest of the transferor's workforce. He successfully claimed unfair constructive dismissal. The Court of Appeal found that the dismissal was automatically unfair. A variation to contracts can only be regarded as being for an ETO reason where it is part of changes in the overall numbers or functions of the workforce. For example, all employees doing a particular job, irrespective of whether they were employed by the transferee before or only as a result of the transfer, are redeployed in different jobs under new contracts. Here the change in contracts would be the result in the change in the jobs and would not be connected to the earlier transfer.

Case Summary

In the joined cases of *British Fuels* v. *Baxendale and Wilson* v. *St Helen's Borough Council* [1998] ICR 1141, the House of Lords had to decide whether variations to the contracts of transferred employees by the transferees, where the employees had consented to new contracts, meant that the employees were bound by their agreement to accept new contracts. The Law Lords held that the agreements were void and of no legal

Case Summary

effect. Therefore, employees who were dismissed for failing to work in accordance with new contractual conditions were unfairly dismissed. These should be understood as policy decisions based on the principle that employees cannot contract out of their statutory rights. Such an approach by the courts is important as, in reality, employees may feel pressurised into accepting changes to their contracts as they fear that they will lose their jobs, or be penalised in some other way, if they do not so agree.

It is important to remember that even where the employer's reason for a dismissal is accepted as an ETO this only means the dismissal ceases to be automatically unfair. For the dismissal to be fair, the employer must still show that it has acted reasonably in accordance with s. 98(4) ERA 1996. In particular, the decision of the Law Lords in the HL in *Polkey* v. *AE Dayton Services Ltd* [1987] IRLR 503, means that the employer must normally follow appropriate procedures prior to reaching a decision to dismiss.

Case Summary

You be the judge

Q: Do the TUPE Regulations apply in the following situation and, if so, who is legally responsible for the dismissals?

Company A decides to contract out maintenance and upgrading of its computerised information systems to Company B. Ownership and legal responsibility for all computerised equipment is to be transferred to Company B. Both companies employ staff with the relevant technical expertise for this work. Company B does not want to employ staff currently employed by Company A. It informs Company A that it will agree to the contract only if, prior to the transfer, Company A dismisses the relevant employees. Company A agrees to this. Twenty-four hours after the employees are made redundant Company A and Company B conclude the contract.

A: The TUPE Regulations do apply and therefore it is Company B which will be liable in unfair dismissal.

Applying the decision of the Law Lords in *Litster*, although the employees were dismissed prior to the transfer, it is the transfer that is the reason for their dismissals. As there is a 'relevant transfer' in this situation, regulation 7 applies to make all the dismissals automatically unfair. It will be Company B, as the transferee, which bears the legal liability for the dismissals.

Collective redundancies and business transfers: an employer's statutory duties to inform and consult

As explained above, where an employer is proposing to dismiss an employee by reason of redundancy or in relation to a business transfer it is very advisable for the employer to engage in consultations with that employee prior to the dismissal. Failure to consult will generally mean that the employer has failed to act reasonably and the dismissal will be unfair. In addition to consultations with individual employees there are circumstances where there is a statutory duty to consult with representatives of the relevant section of a workforce. Any breach of this statutory duty gives rise to a special remedy known as a protective award, which will be explained below, and this remedy is quite separate to any compensation that an individual may be granted for unfair dismissal.

The statutory duties to inform and consult are designed to transpose Directive 98/59 on Collective Redundancies and the Acquired Rights Directive 2001/23 into UK law. Consequently, the ECJ has provided important guidance, through the **preliminary ruling** process and decisions against member states, on how the duties are to be understood and applied. The statutory duty to inform and consult over collective redundancies is set out s. 188 of the Trade Union and Labour Relations (Consolidation) Act 1992 (TULR(C) A). The corresponding duties relating to proposed business transfers are contained in regulations 13–15 of TUPE.

People in the law

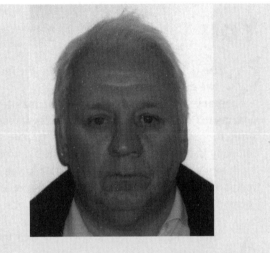

Before examining the detail of statutory duties to inform and consult is valuable to consider the perspectives and experiences of a trade union lay official and a HR practitioner who have participated in these consultation processes.

The first interview is with **Mick Tosh,** a port representative of the National Union of Rail, Maritime and Transport Workers (RMT).

What do you consider to be the main practical purposes of an employer consulting with recognised trade unions over proposed redundancies or business transfers in accordance with the legal requirements? The recognised union understands the requirements of business transfers including the appropriate consultation period and the rights of workers under TUPE legislation. Local union reps will be able to assist members in making choices about alternative work and or voluntary redundancy arrangements. A union can seek collective 'deal makers' such as early retirement, retraining, relocation and financial incentives for workers to volunteer for severance. In these circumstances the employer only deals with the collective rather than trying to resolve every individual need.

In your experience have consultations with a union ever made any difference to the employer's initial proposals? Yes, I have been involved in several redundancy exercises where the union has been able to negotiate improved terms.

If so, please could you give a few examples of the sorts of changes that consultations with your union have led to? A management proposal to replace a defined benefit pension scheme with an inferior money purchase arrangement was withdrawn following union counter proposals.

The company proposed to remove 100+ jobs and to severely reduce the conditions of the remaining workers by cutting leave, restricting sick pay qualification, increasing working hours and generally attempting to introduce flexibility of working arrangements. The latter was akin to having staff at the beck and call of the company like casual workers waiting for a call. The consultations lasted for five months and the union had to hold two ballots to get the members' views. The final agreement involved 69 redundancies, no reductions to leave, no increase in working hours, a 95% removal of flexible clauses and a welcomed improvement to sick pay arrangements.

Where consultations with a union over proposed redundancies are taking place do you consider it also to be important for the employer to consult with individual employees who are at risk of being made redundant? Yes, where possible but employees must be able to bring a TU rep as an advocate/adviser.

In your experience have consultations with such individuals ever produced changes to the employer's initial proposals? Again if the answer is yes please could you provide some actual examples? Yes, mainly small adjustments to benefits other than financial ones – in particular, a continuation of privilege travel after employees had left.

Many employers and recognised unions negotiate a redundancy procedure agreement. Please could you identify what the key elements of such a procedure should be? These are: (a) the freezing of job vacancies to maximise alternative employment; (b) advanced warning of redundancies at the earliest opportunity preferably 3–6 months before the consultation period starts; (c) provision of a reasonable period of retraining and assessment of job suitability by employer and employee; (d) options for relocation with resettlement; (e) transfer of employment to another employer; and (f) severance arrangements.

The following interview, asking essentially the same questions, is with **Peter Brook**, Head of the Human Resources Department at the University of Portsmouth. It is interesting to see that the views of both Mick Tosh and Peter Brook are reasonably similar on the issues of the purposes and consequences of statutory consultation despite the fact that they are, respectively, representing employees and an employer.

What do you consider to be the main practical purposes of consulting with recognised training unions over proposed redundancies or business

transfers in accordance with the legal requirements? It is unfortunate but in practice redundancies happen and it is the union's business to seek the best deal for their members. In my opinion, the main practical purposes of consulting are that we demonstrate to our staff that we have a transparent process as we are prepared to have our business case challenged by an independent body such as a trade union. In practice it is valuable to work with trade union officials who have experienced change elsewhere. In addition we are able, through this consultation process, to establish the real concerns that staff and unions have.

Have such consultations ever made any difference to the organisation's initial proposals? If so, please could you give a few examples of the sorts of changes that consultations with the union have led to? Yes, in my experience consultations have led to changes. An example of an impact that we had not thought of was with an organisation that had several sites and was asking staff to change the location of their place of employment. As a result of the consultations we changed the timescales for the implementation and the phasing of the changes in order to facilitate the implementation of the change and to mitigate the effects on individuals.

Where consultations with a union over proposed redundancies are taking place, do you consider it also to be important

to consult with individual employees who are at risk of being made redundant? Yes, I do think it is important to consult with individual employees after we have talked to the unions to ensure that we have listened to individual preferences and to maximise the options available. Individuals are given time to reflect and we ensure that they have full knowledge of their rights and their options.

In your experience have consultations with such individuals ever produced changes to the organisation's initial proposals? Again if the answer is yes, please could you provide some actual examples? In my experience consultations have resulted in redeployment opportunities arising for the individual because in consulting them we do an employee skills audit. This is about finding different, more acceptable ways to achieve the organisation's original objective.

The organisation has a redundancy procedure agreement. Please could you identify what the key elements of such a procedure should be? In my view, a good redundancy procedure agreement should ensure timely and meaningful consultation that leaves room for negotiation to mitigate the impact on individual employees. Procedures should be legally compliant, provide transparency as to the business case, have clear stages and ensure that staff affected can explore all options, including redeployment and retraining.

Collective redundancies

Under s. 188 TULR(C)A there is a duty to consult over proposed collective redundancies. A collective redundancy is where the employer is proposing to make 20 or more employees redundant. Section 188 specifies the information that the employer provides and stipulates that consultation must begin 'in good time'. In any case consultation must begin at least 90 days before the first dismissals take effect if 100 or more employees at one establishment are to be made redundant. This minimum period is reduced to 30 days if 20–99 employees are to be made redundant.

The employer is obliged to provide the following information in writing to the appropriate representatives:

✦ the reasons for the employer's proposals;

✦ the numbers and description of employees whom it is proposed to dismiss as redundant;

✦ the total number of employees of any such description employed by the employer at the establishment in question;

✦ the proposed method of selecting the employees who may be dismissed;

✦ the proposed method of carrying out the dismissals, with due regard to any agreed procedure, including the period over which the dismissals are to take effect.

Case Summary

As held by the EAT in *UK Mining Ltd* v. *NUM (Northumberland Area)* [2008] ICR 163, the Directive requires s. 188 to be interpreted as requiring the employer to consult over the business reasons behind the redundancies as well as their implementation. In this case the employer falsely stated that the closure of a pit was for health and safety reasons when the real reasons were of a commercial and financial nature. The EAT held that there was a breach of the duty to consult as the employer is obliged to provide the union with the reasons for proposed redundancies and clearly this requires the genuine reasons to be stated. The purpose of providing this information is to enable the union to challenge the need for redundancies, or at least the specific number required by the employer, by suggesting other ways in which an employer's commercial needs can be met.

The other information the employer is required to provide enables a union to establish the proportion of a workforce, or specific section of it, which it is proposed to make redundant as well as the types of work such employees are doing, and when it is proposed that redundancy notices will be issued to individual employees. The union is also able to comment on the employer's proposed selection method – in particular to ensure that it is not discriminatory or based on subjective criteria – and to ensure that if a redundancy procedure has been agreed with the union this procedure is being adhered to by the employer.

There is no duty to consult if fewer than 20 employees are to be made redundant. In calculating the number of employees who are to be dismissed there will still be a dismissal where a fixed-term contract which has expired is not renewed. As explained above, voluntary redundancies should also be counted where the employer's selection method for redundancy consists of the employer inviting employees to volunteer for dismissal.

For the *purposes of statutory consultation only*, the definition of redundancy, which we examined above, is widened to include any dismissals not related to the individual employee. This covers, in particular, the introduction of new contractual terms in the context of business re-organisations where employees are to be dismissed prior to new contracts being issued to them. As we saw above, this is not normally a redundancy situation as the employer is not requiring fewer employees to carry out particular jobs. However, such dismissals are redundancy dismissals for the purposes of triggering statutory consultations in accordance with s. 188 TULR(C)A.

Calculating the number of employees to be dismissed

A problem that may occur in calculating the number of employees to be made redundant arises where the employer has a number of workplaces and employees are being made redundant across these workplaces. If these workplaces constitute a single establishment then all the redundancies are to be added together to ascertain the number of employees the employer proposes to dismiss. Conversely, if each workplace constitutes an establishment in its own right then the duty to consult arises only at any of those establishments where the numbers of employees to be dismissed amount to 20 or more.

As stated above, the statutory duty to consult is derived from the EU's Collective Redundancies Directive and there have been important rulings from the ECJ on how the Directive is to be understood. One such ruling was given in *Rockfon A/s* v. *Nielson* [1996] IRLR 168, where the ECJ ruled that, in the context of a group of companies, associated companies may constitute separate establishments even if the decision to implement redundancies has been taken centrally by the parent company. Where an employee is assigned to a specific economic unit that unit constitutes a separate establishment for the purposes of calculating the number of redundancies to be made. The ECJ also stated in this case that courts should not permit employers to erect business structures which are designed to evade the EU's requirements for employers to engage in statutory consultations.

Case Summary

Case Summary

On this basis, the decision in *Barratt Developments Ltd* v. *UCATT* [1977] IRLR 403, would be the same today. The company had a large workforce engaged on building houses at 14 different sites. A site foreman was in charge of each site and there was a telephone to enable communication to be made with the company's headquarters. When the company was faced with a reduction in demand, it decided to reduce its labour force and some 24 employees on eight of the sites were dismissed on one week's notice. The company maintained that each of its sites was a separate establishment and hence was outside the statutory provisions requiring consultation with the union before redundancy dismissals could take place. The EAT upheld the tribunal's decision that it would be contrary to common and business sense to regard each of the company's sites as a separate establishment.

It is clear in a case such as this one that there is just one centralised layer of management capable of taking strategic commercial decisions. The site foremen were essentially employed in a supervisory capacity to ensure the building operations were being properly carried out by the workforce on each site. A similar decision would be reached where a company has a number of offices throughout the country, or particular parts of it, but the office managers have no authority to make policy decisions and their responsibilities are restricted to day-to-day operational decisions. On the other hand, where managers in different geographical workplaces do possess the power to decide on issues such as making redundancies, then each separate workplace is likely to constitute an establishment in its own right.

The period of consultation

Another problem, which has also required interpretation from the ECJ, is the date on which consultations should commence. It is the case that it is not necessary for consultations to commence as soon as an employer has decided that redundancies *may* be necessary. The requirement in the Directive, as reproduced in s. 188 TULR(C)A is that consultations begin 'in good time'. The key issue is that consultations begin in sufficient time for the consultations to be meaningful. As ruled by the ECJ in *Junk* v. *Kuhnel* [2005] IRLR 310, a case concerned with how German law should be interpreted so that it conformed with EU law, an employer is not required to consult where it is considering redundancies as part of its commercial and financial strategy. However, it must begin consultation before deciding that redundancy dismissals *will* take place.

Case Summary

For example, as held in *NUT* v. *Avon CC* [1978] ICR 626, there will be a clear breach of duty if redundancy notices have been served prior to consultations commencing. In this case redundancy notices were served the day before statutory consultation commenced, but did not take effect until after the minimum statutory consultation period had expired. In such circumstances the consultations will be a sham as the employer has already decided on the course of action it is going to take. A similar decision will be reached if redundancy notices are issued in the early stages of the consultation process.

The specified periods of 30 and 90 days are the minimum periods required and often consultations will be for longer periods if the purposes of statutory consultations are to be fulfilled. These purposes are defined as an obligation on the employer to consult with a view to *reaching agreement* with trade union or employee representatives about ways of:

✦ avoiding the need to make any redundancy dismissals;

✦ reducing the number of employees to be dismissed by reason of redundancy;

◆ mitigating the consequences of dismissals through, for example, making redundancy payments based on an employee's actual pay rather than the statutory payments required by the ERA.

The duty to reach agreement falls short of a duty to negotiate in that there may come a time where an employer can reasonably conclude that agreement with a union is not going to occur, and the employer may then proceed to implement redundancies. However, meaningful consultations must involve an employer giving a union the time to respond to its proposals, and this will be followed by some discussion of any counter proposals by the union and the employer's responses to them.

the duty to reach agreement falls short of a duty to negotiate

Whilst it may be prudent for an employer not to issue redundancy notices until after the appropriate minimum statutory consultation period has ended, it may be permissible to do this in the latter stage of such consultations providing the employer can demonstrate that at that point consultations have been meaningful. An example of this could be where the union has agreed to a voluntary redundancy process and the employer has received sufficient volunteers to cover the number of redundancies that the employer requires.

Trade union and employee representatives

An employer may recognise a trade union for the purposes of collective bargaining (see Chapter 7). This means that an employer has agreed to negotiate with that union on the terms and conditions of its employees that the union represents. It is sufficient that just one aspect of collective bargaining, for example over rates of pay, is subject to negotiation between the employer and the union. A union may be recognised for all employees, or just for those in a specific bargaining unit covering, for example, production but not clerical workers. The duty to consult requires the union to be independent of the employer as well as recognised by it. A staff association which is controlled or financed by an employer would not be independent though, as we shall see below, its officers could still be the appropriate **employee representatives** with whom statutory consultations could be entered into.

Where an **independent trade union** is recognised, and its members are directly or indirectly affected by the proposed redundancies, the employer *must* consult with that union in order to comply with statutory duties. It should be clarified that the employer can engage in consultations with other employee representatives providing its consultations with the recognised union fully comply with s. 188 TULR(C)A. A union's members could be indirectly affected by redundancies where they are not at risk of redundancy but will be affected, for example, by increased workloads once the redundancies have taken place.

Prior to March 1996, consultation was only required *if* the employer recognised an independent trade union. In *Commission of the EC* v. *UK* [1994] ICR 664 the ECJ ruled that UK legislation failed properly to implement EU law in the contexts of collective redundancies and business transfers, as there were no statutory provisions for consultation in the absence of a recognised trade union. The UK was and is unusual in this respect, as employers in other EU member states are generally obliged to recognise specified trade unions and/or consult with permanent bodies consisting of elected employee representatives sitting on what are generally known as works councils. As a result of this decision, where

Case Summary

the employer does not recognise a trade union, or there is no appropriate recognised union in that all the affected employees are outside the agreed collective bargaining unit, consultation must be with appropriate employee representatives. The current provisions for employee representatives are to be found in the Collective Redundancies and Transfer of Undertakings (Amendment) Regulations 1999 (SI 1999/1925).

An employer may consult with an existing body of employee representatives, such as the officers of a staff association or staff consultative committee, providing such persons are appointed or elected by the relevant employees rather than by the employer. The constitution of such bodies must also be such that they can be regarded as having the authority to engage in redundancy consultations even if this is not one of their stipulated or normal functions. For example, they do engage in consultations with the employer over its proposed business plans. By way of contrast, an association which simply has a social function would not be an appropriate body for the employer to consult with over proposed redundancies.

Where there are no appropriate existing employee representatives for the employer to consult with then it is the employer's responsibility to make such arrangements as are 'reasonably practicable' for the fair election of elected employee representatives. Candidates for election must be affected employees, and all affected employees must be given a vote. Where it is reasonably practicable, election should be by secret ballot.

Employee representatives have equivalent employment protection rights to those contained in ss. 146 and 152 TULRCA (which are examined in depth in Chapter 8). Therefore, they should not be subjected to any form of detriment or be dismissed for any reason which relates to the proper exercising of their functions as employee representatives. Under s. 61 ERA 1996, they also have statutory rights to reasonable time off with pay in order to perform their functions. Employers must allow representatives to have access to the workforce, and must provide them with appropriate accommodation and other office and communication facilities to enable them properly to carry out their role.

Where it is not possible for an election to take place, because the affected employees decide they do not wish to elect representatives, then the employer must provide each and every affected employee with the information set out in s. 188(4).

Remedies

Under ss. 189 and 190, a union can seek a protective award if the employer fails to comply with the duty to consult. This claim is brought on behalf of the employees who have been made redundant. Therefore, whilst it is the union that presents the claim, the money awarded goes to the affected individual employees. The amount of the award will be based on the statutory definition of a week's pay, although the normal statutory cap does not apply. The specific amount will be determined by the tribunal on basis of what it determines to be just and equitable. The maximum protective award is 90 days' pay. Where there is no relevant recognised trade union, the claim for the protective award can be presented by the employee representatives or, if there no such representatives, the employees themselves.

Case
Summary

In *Susie Radin Ltd* v. *GMB* [2004] IRLR 400, the Court of Appeal held that the award is based on punitive rather than compensatory factors and thus serious default by the employer may lead to the granting of the maximum award irrespective of whether the dismissed employees suffered any loss as a result of the breach of the statutory duty. In this case, the company closed its factory without engaging in any consultations with the GMB, a recognised trade union. The employer argued that the purpose of a protective award was compensatory and not punitive, and the award should reflect the fact that consultation would not have made any difference in that the factory would still have been closed if consultations had taken place. The Court of Appeal held that the purpose of a protective award was to ensure that consultation took place by providing a sanction against non-compliance by the employer. There was nothing in the statutory provisions to link the length of the protected period to any actual financial loss suffered by the employees. The focus was not on compensating employees, since these were not individual awards, but on the default of the employer and the seriousness of that default. It was that seriousness which governed what was just and equitable in the circumstances. A decision to make a protective award for the maximum period was permissible where, as this case, no meaningful consultation had taken place, and there were no circumstances mitigating the failure to consult.

An employer may invoke the defence of 'special circumstances which render it not reasonably practicable for the employer to comply' with the statutory requirements. In *Clark of Hove Ltd* v. *Bakers Union* [1978] IRLR 366, the employer, who was a confectioner, employed about 380 people. The company had been in financial difficulties for some time, but the company kept quiet about these as it hoped to find ways of continuing in business and so averting the need for redundancies. The company finally accepted that insolvency was inevitable and dismissed its entire workforce without any consultations with the Bakers Union, which it recognised. The EAT upheld the tribunal's decision that the defence was not available to the employer on the basis that 'special' in the context of 'special circumstances' meant circumstances which were uncommon or out of the ordinary. Therefore, an insolvency which had been foreseen by the employer could not constitute a special circumstance. The EAT commented that insolvency could amount to 'special circumstances' where it is unexpected and sudden. An example would be where was a sudden significant loss of demand for a company's product caused by a natural disaster or a trading boycott imposed by overseas countries.

Business transfers

Generally, the statutory duty to inform and consult over proposed business transfers operates in similar ways to the statutory consultation process for collective redundancies. In particular, the statutory duty is owed to a relevant recognised trade union. Only where there is no such union may the employer choose to inform and consult with employee representatives. The same rules apply to identifying or electing such representatives as are set out above. The granting of a protective award remains the appropriate remedy for breach of the statutory duty, and the special circumstances defence operates in the same way as explained above,

However, there are important differences between the statutory duties relating to collective redundancies and those relating to business transfers, First, whilst there is always a duty to inform, in the latter context a duty to consult does not always arise. Secondly, only *one* employer is involved where collective redundancies are proposed. With respect to proposed business transfers *both* the employer constituting the transferor and the employer constituting the transferee are subject to statutory duties. Moreover, as explained below, where the former has failed to comply properly with these duties it may be the latter that will actually incur legal liability.

The duty to inform

Regulation 13(2) of the TUPE Regulations requires the appropriate employer to inform the appropriate representatives of:

✦ the fact that the relevant transfer is to take place, the date when it is to take place and the reasons for the transfer;

✦ the legal, economic and social implications of the transfer for any affected employees;

✦ the measures which the employer envisages that it will take in connection with the transfer in relation to its own affected employees or, if it envisages that it will take no measures, it must inform them of that fact;

✦ if the employer is the transferor, the measures which the transferee envisages that he or she (the transferee) will take in connection with the transfer, in relation to such of those employees of the transferor who will become employees of the transferee after the transfer.

For the transferor to comply with this last obligation, regulation 13(4) provides that the transferee must give the transferor such information 'at such time' as will enable the transferor to comply with those obligations. Both the transferor and the transferee must provide the requisite information long enough before the transfer to enable meaningful consultations with the appropriate trade union or employee representatives to take place, should consultations prove necessary.

The duty to consult

Paragraphs 5 and 7 of regulation 13 of the TUPE Regulations impose a duty to consult with trade union or employee representatives where the employer envisages that it will, in connection with the transfer, be taking measures in relation to any employees affected by the transfer. The purpose of consultation is to seek agreement on any measures to be taken. The employer is under an express duty to consider any representations that are made to it, to reply to those representation, and, if it rejects them, to state its reasons for doing so.

Again, this is an obligation imposed on both the transferor and the transferee and owed by them to their own 'affected employees'. However, whilst there is always a duty to inform, there is no duty to consult if an employer does not envisage taking any measures in connection with the transfer. The word 'measures' has been given a very wide interpretation. It goes beyond changes to contracts of employment and includes any action, step or arrangement. For example, if the transferee is considering derecognising a trade union, which is recognised by the transferor, the transferee must inform the transferor of this so that the latter can inform and consult with trade union representatives accordingly.

Remedy

Under regulation 15 of the TUPE Regulations the remedy for failing to inform and consult is a protective award. As explained above in the context of redundancy, the union (or employee representatives) presents the claim on behalf of the relevant individual employees. The award will consist of a sum of money of up to 13 weeks' pay. This is gross pay, but there is no statutory cap, so it will be the actual gross pay that an employee earns during a week.

Under paragraph 5 of regulation 15, the transferor may, in its defence, argue that it was not reasonably practicable for it to comply with its statutory duties because the transferee did not give it sufficient information to enable it to do so. However, this defence can only be pleaded where the transferor gives the transferee notice of its intention to plead this defence and to make the transferee a party to the action under regulation 15. Although the transferor and transferee are jointly and separately liable for any breach of statutory duty, in this situation the tribunal may order the transferee to pay the appropriate compensation.

Under paragraph 2 of regulation 15, an employer may plead the 'special circumstances' defence in the same sorts of circumstances as where the defence can be pleaded to a failure to consult over collective redundancies. For example, where a transfer takes place in the context of an unexpected insolvency.

Table 6.3 summarises the differences and similarities between the duties to inform and consult over proposed collective redundancies and business transfers.

Table 6.3 Contrasting the duties to inform and consult

Proposed collective redundancies of 20 or more employees	Proposed business transfers
Duty to inform *and* consult – minimum consultation period of 30 days, or 90 days where 100 or more employees to be made redundant	Transferor and transferee under to duty to provide information about the transfer at such time to enable consultations to take place should they prove necessary
Purpose of consultation is to reach agreement on avoiding or reducing redundancies or mitigating their consequences	Duty to consult only where transferor and/or transferee envisage measures with a view to seeking agreement on measures to be taken
Duty owed to a recognised and independent trade union	Duty owed to a recognised and independent trade union
If no union duty is owed to elected employee representatives	If no union, duty is owed to elected employee representatives
Remedy for breach of duty is protected award of up to 90 days' pay for each affected employee	Remedy for breach of duty is protected award of up to 13 weeks' pay for each affected employee
Employer may plead the 'special circumstances' defence	Employer may plead the 'special circumstances' defence

Summary

◆ An employee will have been dismissed by reason of redundancy where the employer closes or sells the business (unless the TUPE Regulations apply).

◆ Alternatively, there will be a redundancy dismissal where for any reason the employer reduces the size of the workplace because fewer employees are required to undertake a particular job.

◆ Where, in either of the above situations, an employee is required to move to a new workplace there will still be a redundancy dismissal, even where there is an appropriate mobility clause in an employee's contract, if the employee is being required to move from his or her established place of work.

◆ Employees with at least two years' continuous employment are entitled to a statutory payment which is calculated on the basis of their age, completed years of employment, subject to a maximum of 20 weeks, and gross week's pay.

◆ An employee who has been dismissed by reason of redundancy will lose the right to a redundancy payment if he or she unreasonably rejects an offer of suitable alternative employment.

◆ A redundancy dismissal will be an unfair dismissal if the employer has acted unreasonably in selecting an employee for redundancy or by implementing a redundancy without adequate warning and consultation.

◆ If an employer dismisses an employee for refusing to accept unilateral changes to his or her contact of employment as a result of a business reorganisation, that dismissal will

be unfair where the employer has failed to carry out the reorganisation in a reasonable way.

◆ Where the transfer of a business is a relevant transfer within the meaning of the TUPE Regulations, employees should be transferred to the new employer on their existing contractual terms and conditions of employment.

◆ Where an employee is dismissed before or after a relevant transfer, this dismissal is automatically unfair unless the employer can show that the dismissal was for an economic, technical or organisational reason, and the employer had acted reasonably in deciding to dismiss.

◆ Where an employer is making 20 or more employees redundant at a single establishment, there is a duty to inform and consult with a recognised union or, in the absence of a recognised union, elected employee representatives.

 Where there is a proposed relevant transfer, the employers who are the transferor and the transferee are obliged to provide information to a recognised union or, in the absence of a recognised union, elected employee representatives.

◆ There is a similar statutory duty to consult where an employer envisages taking measures as a result of the transfer.

◆ Where an employer is in breach of a statutory duty to inform or consult, a trade union, or elected employee representatives, may claim a protective award on behalf of the affected employees.

Question and answer*

Problem:

June is employed as the senior clerical assistant at the Hampshire office of Marley Co. Ltd. June is a single mother, but June's mother also lives in June's house. The company has recently fully computerised its office with the most up-to-date equipment available on the market. After fully following the company's redundancy procedures, Luke, who is June's manager, informs her that she is no longer needed at the Hampshire office as the computerisation will enable Luke to exercise June's functions. Luke states that, in accordance with the mobility clause which is in her contract of employment, the company is offering June alternative work as a clerical assistant at its regional office which is 30 miles away. She is to receive the same rate of pay and will be employed under the same conditions of employment. In accordance with the mobility clause, the company will pay her travelling costs to and from the new place of work. June rejects this offer as her current job allows June to take and collect her seven-year-old child to and from school. Consequently, June is dismissed with notice.

Advise June as to whether she is entitled to receive a statutory redundancy payment.

You should spend 40 minutes on answering this question.

Essay:

Critically evaluate the effectiveness of the statutory duty of an employer to inform and consult over proposed redundancies or proposed business transfers as a mechanism for ensuring that employees' interests are properly protected.

You should spend 40 minutes on answering this question.

✱ Answer guidance is provided at the end of the chapter.

Further reading and references

IDS (2011) *Redundancy Employment Law Handbook* (Income Data Services Ltd: London).

This handbook provides a comprehensive and clear explanation of all of the law of redundancy. Chapter 2 on defining redundancy, Chapter 3 on alternative job offers, Chapter 8 on unfair redundancy and Chapter 10 on collective redundancies will be particularly useful to readers of this text.

IDS (2011) *Transfer of Undertakings Employment Law Handbook* (Income Data Services Ltd: London).

This provides a comprehensive and up-to-date account of how the TUPE Regulations work. Chapters 2 and 3 on the effects of a transfer, Chapter 4 on unfair dismissal and Chapter 8 on information and consultation will be particularly useful to readers of this text.

Deakin, S. and Morris, G. (2012) *Labour Law* (Hart: Oxford).

Chapter 5 of this work provides comprehensive and contextual analysis of the whole of the law concerning dismissal. Pages 561–93 of this chapter specifically deal with redundancies and other economic dismissals.

Freedland, M. (2009) *The Personal Contract of Employment* (OUP: Oxford).

Chapter 9 of this seminal text on employment contracts provides critical analysis of the effect on individual employment contracts where employees are transferred to a new employer.

McMullen, J. (2011) *Redundancy: The Law and Practice* (OUP: Oxford).

This book provides a comprehensive and practical guide to redundancy law. It contains chapters on redundancy payments, unfair dismissal and collective consultation which readers will find particularly useful.

McMullen, J. (2006) 'An analysis of the Transfer of Undertakings (Protection of Employment) Regulations 2006', *Industrial Law Journal*, vol. 35, pp. 113–39.
This article provides a critical review as to why the current regulations were brought in to replace the former regulations and assesses the extent to which these regulations meet their objectives.

Hall, M. and Edwards, P. (1999) 'Reforming the statutory redundancy consultation procedure', *Industrial Law Journal*, vol. 28, pp. 299–318.

This article draws on research on how redundancy consultation processes have operated to evaluate the changes to the statutory consultation procedure introduced by the Labour government in 1999.

Wynn-Evans, C. (2009) 'Redundancy and Age Discrimination', *Industrial Law Journal*, vol. 38, pp. 113–21.
This article discusses recent case law on when selection for redundancy can be considered to be unlawful discrimination and when it can be justified as in the *Rolls-Royce* v. *Unite* case. (The article is also relevant to the content of the next chapter of this text, which is on discrimination law.)

Question and answer guidance

Problem: Your answer should start by the stating the definition of redundancy in s. 139(1)(b) ERA 1996 and explaining this will potentially cover June's dismissal as the company has reduced the size of the workforce by one employee. You should apply the decision of the House of Lords in *Murray* v. *Foyle Meats* to clarify that she has been made redundant under the definition in s. 139(1)(b) despite the fact that her job function still exists.

Your answer should then discuss the significance of the mobility clause. It is clear that June has always worked at the Hampshire office and that is her base. Therefore, *High Table* v. *Horst* can be applied to conclude that she is dismissed by reason of redundancy despite the mobility clause in her contract. However, the company has offered alternative employment, and, under s. 141, she will lose the right to a redundancy payment if she has unreasonably rejected a suitable offer of alternative employment.

In discussing this issue, your answer should explain that in assessing whether the alternative employment is suitable the tribunal will make an objective comparison between her job and the offered alternative. Generally, the alternative is suitable as she is to be employed on the same pay and conditions and the company is covering the costs of her travelling to and from the regional office. However, applying *Taylor* v. *Kent CC*, the alternative employment is unsuitable if it involves a loss of status. At the Hampshire office she was a designated as a senior clerical assistant whereas at the regional office she would have been a clerical assistant. If this more than just a change in job title, and is a genuine reduction in her status, then she will be entitled to a redundancy payment despite rejecting the offer.

Even of the alternative is suitable she may still be viewed as having acted reasonably in rejecting it. The tribunal will examine the subjective reasons for her refusal. Relevant factors here will include whether she does need to take her child to and from school or, for example, could her mother do this for her? Alternatively, is June's mother also in need of her care?

As is typically the case, you will not be able to reach one solution so your conclusion should emphasise that June's entitlement to a statutory redundancy payment will depend on which of the above facts actually apply.

Essay:

The essay question is asking you to assess how effective the statutory duties to inform and consult are in protecting employees affected by collective redundancies or business transfers. Therefore, it is important that your answer contains critical analysis of how the duties work and their practical impact.

Your answer should start by outlining the duties to inform and consult as provided by the TULRCA in the context of collective redundancies and the TUPE Regulations in the context of business transfers. Your answer should explain that the duties are derived from EU Directives and are therefore subject to rulings and decisions of the European Court of Justice (ECJ). This provides some assurance that the duties must be applied in the same way in Britain as in other EU member states. For example, as a result of the ECJ's decision in 1994 in *EU Commission* v. *UK*, in the absence of an appropriate recognised trade union, the employer is under a duty to seek to make arrangements for the election of employee representatives with whom consultation can be undertaken.

Your answer should clarify that employers must always consult, as well as provide information, where collective redundancies involving more than 20 employees are proposed. However, in the context of a business transfer, there is only a duty to consult where the employer envisages taking measures as a result of the transfer.

In evaluating the effectiveness of the duties you should emphasise that the purpose of consultation is to reach agreement over redundancies and to seek agreement over the consequences of a business transfer. Despite the slight difference in wording, the employer is required to engage in meaningful consultation with trade union or employee representatives, although in both cases this falls short of a duty to negotiate. Therefore, ultimately, an employer is able to implement proposals even though the workforce might remain adamantly opposed to them.

Your answer could also state that consultation is likely to be more effective where there is a recognised trade union. This is because trade union representatives will be trained to handle statutory consultation, but this is less likely to be the case with elected employee representatives. You could question the adequacy of the remedy of the protective award. It could be argued that a failure to inform and/or consult makes it more expensive for an employer to implement its proposals, but does not prevent an employer from doing so. If an injunction was available as a remedy then an employer could only implement proposals once the statutory duties had been fully complied with. The article by Hall and Edwards in the 1999 *Industrial Law Journal*, which is cited in 'Further reading', can be drawn on to understand why changes were made to the statutory duties in 1999 and to help assess whether these changes have been of any practical significance.

Your conclusion could identify that the main consequence of the statutory duties is that an employer should not carry out collective redundancies or business transfers without warning representatives of the workforce and discussing their plans with them. However, providing this is done properly, an employer is free to proceed with its proposals irrespective of the impact on the workforce.

Chapter 7
The law of discrimination

Key points In this chapter we will be looking at:

- ✦ The characteristics of employees which are protected against discrimination by the Equality Act 2010 including race, religious belief, sex and sexual orientation
- ✦ The distinction between direct and indirect discrimination
- ✦ When indirect discrimination by a prospective or actual employer will be justifiable

- ✦ Associative and perceptive discrimination
- ✦ Pregnancy, maternity and parental rights
- ✦ The special rules that apply to age and disability discrimination
- ✦ Harassment and victimisation
- ✦ Proving discrimination
- ✦ Remedies for unlawful discrimination
- ✦ Equal pay laws

Introduction

Everyone has some idea about discrimination law in that they will be aware that it is generally unlawful for an employer to refuse to offer a job to a person because of that person's age, gender or racial group, or because a person is disabled. Many readers will also be aware that, unlike many of the employment rights that have been covered in previous chapters, issues such as length of employment are not relevant in establishing whether an individual is able to present a discrimination claim to an employment tribunal. Discrimination law applies from when an employer makes arrangements to advertise a job vacancy and covers the whole period, up to and including any dismissal, that a person is employed.

Moreover, in contrast to the requirements of the Employment Rights Act (ERA) 1996, protection is not restricted to 'employees'. Under s. 83(1) of the Equality Act (EqA) 2010 workers and self-employed persons, as well as employees, are protected by its provisions. The EqA covers any individual under a contract 'personally to execute any work or labour'. The other major practical difference between the EqA and ERA 1996 is that in discrimination claims there are no fixed caps on the amount of compensation that a successful claimant can be awarded.

The original three main pieces of discrimination legislation were the Equal Pay Act 1970, the Sex Discrimination Act 1975 and the Race Relations Act 1976. These Acts are now repealed, as are later Acts and regulations extending the scope of discrimination law to disability, sexual orientation, religious belief and age. Under EqA the whole area of discrimination law is contained in a single piece of legislation. The enactment of EqA was preceded by the Equalities Act 2006, which abolished the Equal

Opportunities and Disability Rights Commissions and the Commission for Racial Equality. There is now a single body, the Equality and Human Rights Commission (EHRC), which is responsible for overseeing the whole area of discrimination and human rights law. The role and powers of the EHRC was explained elsewhere in this text (see Chapter 1). One of the main functions of the EHRC is to issue codes of practice. If you visit **http://www.equality humanrights.com/legal-and-policy/equality-act/ equality-act-codes-of-practice/** you will be able to download your own copies of the EHRC's Codes of Practice on Employment and Equal Pay which provide official guidance on how EqA is to be understood.

This chapter will examine the nature of the different types of discrimination covered by the provisions of EqA and the different rules that apply to different forms of discrimination. The chapter will consider the issue of proving discrimination claims and explain the remedies available to a successful claimant. The chapter will also discuss the working of the equal pay laws.

Origins and objectives of discrimination law

Discrimination against oppressed groups is an historic feature of Western societies. This is in part because these societies are patriarchal in that it has historically been men in whom power has been vested – be this with respect to political leadership, owning and running businesses or domestically in the context of the family. Patriarchy can be perceived as providing the main cause of discrimination which is based on gender and sexual identity. Similarly, racism is in part derived from the legacy of colonialism in that persons of colour and/or members of specific national or ethnic groups were regarded as inferior by their colonial overlords. Moreover, divide and rule along ethnic and national lines has long been a tool of ruling groups at least from the time of the Roman Empire, if not earlier. Specific forms of racism such as anti-Semitism and Islamophobia have been and are combined with religious discrimination and date back to medieval Christianity and the crusades.

It is only in recent times, essentially since the 1960s, that discriminatory attitudes and practices have been challenged and increasingly subjected to legislative regulation. Indeed, in the past, the law often acted to reinforce bigotry and prejudice. For example, until 1967 all forms of sexual activity between gay men was illegal, and it was not until the New Labour government of the 1990s that the age of consent for heterosexual and gay sex was equalised at 16.

Arguably, there are three main contributory factors underlying the developments in the field of anti-discrimination legislation which have taken place from the 1970s onwards. In a societal context, anti-discrimination legislation was preceded by the seismic shift in cultural and social values that occurred in the late 1960s. In the wake of the anti-colonial liberation movements in the developing world and the civil rights movement in the USA, many people in the Western world, particularly the young, challenged the sexism (at least in theory as far as the men were concerned), racism and homophobia of previous generations. As this generation matured, and the women's and gay liberation movements it created gained strength, its members entered the labour market and the trade union movement and imported their values into the workplace. Discrimination law falls far short of what the more radical members of this generation demanded, which was liberation not legal reform, but there can be no doubt that the counter-cultural revolution of the 1960s was an important part of the creation of an environment in which legal change became inevitable.

The second contributory factor was from a more traditional source – the industrial working class. In 1968, sections of the working class symbolised by London dockers had shown their support for bigotry by marching in support of the politician, Enoch Powell, after he had made his infamous and racist anti-immigration 'rivers of blood' speech, or rather, rant. However, in the same year, any assumption that the traditional working class was imbued with discriminatory attitudes was exposed as ill-founded by the equal pay strike mounted by women sewing machinists employed by the Ford motor company, This strike, which has recently been immortalised by the film *Made in Dagenham*, was a pivotal moment in trade union history as it marks the time when slowly but surely the trade unions realised they could not ignore the concerns and interest of their women members. The next big equal pay strike was by women factory workers employed by the Trico company in 1976. The women were members of the Engineering Workers Union and the strike attracted widespread practical support from across the then still-male dominated trade union movement. Today, as has been the case for some time, trade unions are at the forefront of campaigns to strengthen equal pay laws and maternity and paternity rights.

The third and rather less dramatic contributor to progress in anti-discrimination legislation has been the European Union (EU). In Britain, the original pieces of legislation were the Race Relations Acts of 1965 and 1968. This legislation was part of the criminal law and was designed to criminalise acts of race hatred, and to outlaw practices such as refusing to provide accommodation, in the words of the highly shocking but not uncommon door notices of the period, to 'blacks, dogs or the Irish'. The Acts were the forerunners of the Race Relations Act 1976, which was the first piece of legislation designed to combat race discrimination through granting employment protection rights. In the context of gender, a similar approach was taken by the Equal Pay Act 1970 and the Sex Discrimination Act 1975. However, these two Acts were also required as part of the UK's membership of what is now the EU and was then called the EEC (European Economic Community).

One objective of the EEC was to prevent one member state from gaining an economic advantage over other member states by allowing businesses to treat their workers less fairly. In short, businesses in the EEC should operate on the basis of a level playing field. Therefore, Article 119 of the founding treaty of the EEC, the Treaty of Rome, required Member States to enact laws providing for equal pay for work of **equal value**. Article 119 was supplemented by the Equal Pay Directive 1975, and this **Directive** was complemented by the Equal Treatment Directive 1976, which was concerned with prohibiting sex discrimination more generally at the workplace. Today, the relevant Directive is the Equal Treatment Directive, 2006/54, which covers both sex discrimination and equal pay. Moreover, Article 13 of the Treaty of Amsterdam empowered the EU Council of Ministers by unanimous agreement to approve legislation drafted by the Commission to prohibit a variety of forms of discrimination. Such legislation was adopted in the form of Council Directive 2000/78/EC of 27 November 2000, the Framework Directive, establishing a general framework for equal treatment in employment and occupation. This Directive prohibits discrimination on grounds of religion or belief, sexual orientation, disability and age. As will be seen during this chapter, the European Court of Justice (ECJ) has delivered a number of major rulings in the areas of discrimination law and equal pay, which the courts in all member states are required to apply in interpreting national laws.

Human rights law derived from the European Convention on Human Rights (ECHR) has also impacted on discrimination law. This has been particularly the case with Article 8, which guarantees the right to a private life, and Article 9, which guarantees the right to manifest a religious belief. Human rights law has played a particularly significant role in creating an environment in which gay, lesbian, bisexual and transgendered persons, including employees, are protected by the law rather than being victimised by it. The EU's Framework Directive was designed in part to implement significant decisions of the European Court of Human Rights (EctHR) such as *Lustig-Prean*, which found discrimination on grounds of sexual orientation to be contrary to Article 8 ECHR and is explained below. On the basis of this Directive there were major developments in UK law from 2003 onwards. All of these newer developments were consolidated into the Equality Act 2010.

> human rights law has also impacted on discrimination law

The general purpose of discrimination law has been to create equality of opportunity by outlawing specific types of discrimination in specific contexts – including the workplace. Today, many people would agree that a worker should not be refused work or barred from promotion because of personal characteristics such as that person's race, gender, age or sexual orientation. Discrimination law is not without its critics, for example, those who regard it as both a cause and manifestation of 'political correctness'. Moreover, some employers regard the law, or at least aspects of it, as imposing undue burdens on them which adversely impact on cost-efficiency and organisational performance.

It is probably the case that most lawyers, at least in academic circles, concerned with employment rights and human rights have welcomed the ways in which discrimination law has evolved since the 1970s. Our major concern has been, in welcoming legal regulation, to examine critically the extent to which the law has and can eliminate discrimination and its economic and social consequences from our society. As demonstrated by some of the articles cited at the end of this chapter, employment lawyers have also sought to identify and propose ways in which the law could be amended to make it a more effective mechanism for combating discrimination at the workplace.

The Equality Act 2010 and protected characteristics

Under the old system of discrimination law each form of unlawful discrimination was regulated by legislation specific to it. The Equality Act (EqA) 2010 works through specifying the **protected characteristics** which are regulated by its provisions. Under s. 4 EqA these protected characteristics are:

✦ age;

✦ disability;

✦ gender reassignment;

✦ marriage and civil partnership;

✦ pregnancy and maternity;

✦ race;

✦ religion or belief;

✦ sex;

✦ sexual orientation.

Key stats

Figure 7.1 demonstrates the number and types of discrimination clams presented to employment tribunals between 2008 and 2011. It is interesting to note that claims based around religion or belief and sexual orientation are the smallest number of claims, but as will be elaborated later in the chapter, they have generated very significant case law, including the *Eweida* and *Ladele* cases which, at the time of writing, had been appealed to the European Court of Human Rights. Statistically, it is the number of age discrimination claims that have increased most significantly in recent years.

Source: Steve Cole, Photodisc

Statistics relating to each of the above types of discrimination claim will be provided at the start of the sections of this chapter in which each type of claim is discussed.

Figure 7.1 Number of claims brought to employment tribunals

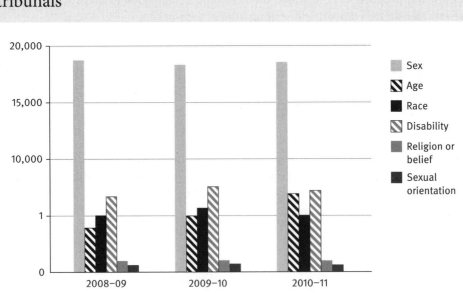

Source: Personnel Today, 1 July 2011, accessed at http://www.personneltoday.com/articles/2011/07/01/57739/age-discrimination-claims-up-by-one-third.html

The scope of unlawful discrimination in employment relates to all the above protected characteristics and covers: arrangements for recruiting employees – including short-listing and interviewing processes; refusal of employment; the terms on which employment is offered; opportunities for promotion or training; access to benefits, facilities or services; dismissal or subjection to any **detriment**.

The provisions in the EqA relating to age and disability will be considered later in the chapter. The next section of the chapter will focus on discrimination which is linked to race, religion or belief, gender and sexual orientation as the law operates on similar principles with respect to these types of discrimination.

Race discrimination

Key stats

Race discrimination saw falls in both the number of cases and the size of awards in 2010–11. The number of cases accepted by employment tribunals fell from 5,700 to 5,000, while the average award dropped from £18,584 to £12,108. The largest payout also fell significantly, from £374,922 to £62,580.

The majority of cases were settled through ACAS conciliation (36%) or withdrawn (28%), with 3% of all race discrimination claims being successful at tribunal.

Source: 'Tribunal awards: which discrimination cases attract the biggest payouts?', Laura Chamberlain, *Personnel Today*, 12 September 2011, **http://www.personneltoday.com/articles/2011/09/12/57940/tribunal-awards-which-discrimination-cases-attract-the-biggest.html**

Case Summary

Under s. 9 EqA, race includes colour, nationality and national or ethnic origins. The meaning of ethnic origins was determined by the House of Lords in the leading case of *Mandla* v. *Dowell Lee* [1983] ICR 385 HL. This case involved a student, who was a Sikh, who was excluded from his school because he refused to remove his turban. It was argued that this was not race discrimination as his desire to wear a turban was the result of his religious beliefs not his ethnic origins. The Law Lords held that Sikhs were a distinct ethnic group and therefore they were protected, as Sikhs, by the Race Relations Act. In the words of Lord Fraser:

'It is not suggested that Sikhs are a group defined by reference to colour, race, nationality or national origins. In none of these respects are they distinguishable from many other groups, especially those living, like most Sikhs, in the Punjab. The argument turns entirely upon whether they are a group defined by "ethnic origins" . . .

For a group to constitute an ethnic group . . . it must, in my opinion, regard itself, and be regarded by others, as a *distinct community by virtue of certain characteristics. Some of these characteristics are essential; others are not essential but one or more of them will commonly be found and will help to distinguish the group from the surrounding community'* (our emphasis) (pages 389–90).

The two conditions which appeared to Lord Fraser to be *essential* are:

1. a long shared history, of which the group is conscious as distinguishing it from other groups, and the memory of which it keeps alive; and

2. a cultural tradition of its own, including family and social customs and manners, often but not necessarily associated with religious observance.

The following characteristics are, in Lord Fraser's opinion, also *relevant*:

✦ either a common geographical origin, or descent from a small number of common ancestors;

✦ a common language, not necessarily peculiar to the group;

✦ a common literature peculiar to the group;

✦ a common religion different from that of neighbouring groups or from the general community surrounding it;

✦ being a minority or being an oppressed or a dominant group within a larger community, for example, the inhabitants of England shortly after the Norman conquest and their conquerors might both be ethnic groups.

If the two essential conditions are met, and all or, at least, most of the above relevant characteristics are present then a group of people will be considered to possess distinct ethnic origins and will constitute a racial group for the purposes of s. 9 EqA.

On this basis, Jews can be considered to have a racial as well as a religious identity. In the *Commission for Racial Equality* v. *Dutton* [1989] QB 783) a publican put a notice on the door of his public house to the effect that travellers were not permitted on his premises. It was held that gypsies are a racial group, by virtue of their distinct ethnic origins and, as they were included in the term 'travellers', the publican was potentially guilty of unlawful race discrimination.

In *Dawkins* v. *Department of the Environment* [1993] IRLR 284, it was held that Rastafarians do not have an ethnic status different to that of the wider African-Caribbean community. Therefore, Dawkins was not protected by the Race Relations Act (RRA) 1976 when he was refused employment because he refused to cut off his dreadlocks. However, as explained below, Rastafarians are now protected by s. 10 EqA which covers discrimination by reference to a person's religion or belief.

In the context of race, the *Dawkins* case can be contrasted with the recent decision in *G* v. *St Gregory's Catholic Science College Governors* [2011] EWHC 1452. G, who was African-Caribbean, wore his hair in cornrows. G was turned away from the school, on his first day, as he was told that his hairstyle was contrary to the school's dress code for boys. The wearing of cornrows was part of G's family tradition, and was of cultural and ethnical importance to him. The court accepted expert evidence that some people of African-Caribbean ethnicity, for reasons based on their culture and ethnicity, regarded the cutting of hair as wrong and required it to be kept in cornrows. There was sufficient evidence to establish that G was a member of an ethnic group which would be particularly disadvantaged by a refusal to permit them to wear cornrows. In these circumstances, refusing to admit him to the school constituted unlawful race discrimination. This decision was given in the context of the prohibition of discrimination in education, but there is no reason why the same decision would not be reached in an employment situation.

The English, Northern Irish, Scots and Welsh are different racial groups as, even though they all share UK nationality, they have different national origins because each country was historically a separate nation. This was confirmed to be the case in *BBC Scotland* v. *Souster* [2001] IRLR 150. Souster, an English journalist, was employed to present a sports programme covering Scottish rugby. His contract was not renewed and he was

Case Summary

Case Summary

Case Summary

Case Summary

replaced with a Scottish presenter. It was held that he could present a claim under the RRA as the English have separate national origins to the Scots and therefore he could argue that he had been subject to race discrimination on the basis of his English origins.

Religion or belief

Key stats

Payouts for religious discrimination claims were lower than in other discrimination cases, with 90% being less then £15,000. However, the average award of £8,515 was higher than in 2009/10 when the average came in at £4,886.

The largest payout also jumped, from £9,500 in 2009/10 to £20,221 in 2010/11. The number of cases fell from 1,000 to 880.

Most cases were withdrawn (29%) or settled through ACAS conciliation (34%), with 3% being successful at tribunal.

Source: 'Tribunal awards: which discrimination cases attract the biggest payouts?', Laura Chamberlain, *Personnel Today*, 12 September 2011, http://www.personneltoday.com/articles/2011/09/12/57940/tribunal-awards-which-discrimination-cases-attract-the-biggest.html

Section 10 EqA prohibits discrimination by reference to a person's religious or philosophical belief. The section expressly includes a lack of religious belief, so that atheists and agnostics are also protected by EqA. All mainstream religions are obviously covered by s. 10 as are sub-divisions of such religions such as Catholicism and Protestantism and the different branches of Islam. The EHRC's Code of Practice makes it clear that adherents to less mainstream religions, such as the Baha'i faith, Jainism, Rastafarianism and Zoroastrianism, are protected by EqA.

One reason why the extension of discrimination law to religious beliefs is important is because of the overlap between race and religion and the fact that a person's religion can be used to disguise discrimination which is in fact based on race. For example, discrimination against Muslims cannot constitute race discrimination in the way that is so with discrimination against Sikhs or Jews. Muslims do not share the same national or ethnic origins. However, Islamophobia is a contemporary problem in Western societies, and far right groups, which in Britain include the likes of the English Defence League and the British National Party, use religion as a code for race. To a typical supporter of these groups anyone with a brown face is a 'Paki' and therefore a Muslim. This is the case irrespective of that person's nationality or national or ethnic origins and the fact that that person may be a Buddhist, a Hindu, a Jain or of no religion whatsoever.

Section 10 is not restricted to religious beliefs as other philosophies, including political philosophies, are covered by it though an exhaustive list of such philosophical beliefs cannot be provided in advance, and decisions will be made on a case-by-case basis. It is clear that membership of political parties or campaigning groups is outside the protection of EqA. For example, in *Baggs* v. *Fudge* Employment Tribunal (Bristol), Case No. 1400114/05, Baggs, who was not interviewed for a job as a practice manager in a small medical practice because he was an active member of the British National Party, was not able to bring a discrimination claim under EqA.

Case Summary

The EAT decision in *Grainger plc and ors* v. *Nicholson* [2010] ICR 360 sets out factors to be taken into account in determining whether a given philosophy falls within s. 10. Nicholson was made redundant from his post as head of sustainability at the company. He successfully argued that a belief in climate change was a philosophical belief covered by EqA. The EAT proposed the following guidelines for determining what is a 'philosophical belief' for the purposes of EqA. The belief must be:

✦ genuinely held;

✦ not merely an opinion or viewpoint based on information publicly available;

✦ weighty and concerning a substantial aspect of human life and behaviour;

✦ able to attain a certain level of cogency, seriousness, cohesion and importance;

✦ worthy of respect in a democratic society, not incompatible with human dignity and not in conflict with the fundamental rights of others.

The latter factor rules out philosophies based on notions of racial superiority such as Fascism, but, as examples, Darwinism, Marxism or a belief in free market economics as the best basis for organising human society probably constitute protected secular philosophies on the basis of these guidelines.

An application of the guidelines was provided by the case of *Hashman* v. *Milton Park (Dorset) Ltd t/a Orchard Park*, Southampton Tribunal, 31.1.11, ET Case No. 3105555/09. The tribunal held that an employee's fervent opposition to fox-hunting and hare-coursing formed part of his belief in the sanctity of life, including the lives of animals, and amounted to a protected philosophical belief within the meaning of the legislation.

Sex and sexual orientation

Key stats

Sex discrimination had the highest amount of cases accepted by employment tribunals, compared with other types of discrimination claims. However, the figure remained at around the same level as 2009–10, rising slightly from 18,200 cases to 18,300. The average award of compensation was £13,911.

A sex discrimination claim topped the rankings for the highest payout given for a discrimination claim in 2010–11, with the highest award reaching £289,167. However, almost all (97%) awards were less than £50,000.

Nearly half of claims were withdrawn (49%) and 2% were successful at tribunal.

Despite ranking second in list of awards for 2009–10 the average sexual orientation discrimination award fell from £29,384 to £11,671 in 2010–11.

The highest payout also saw a large fall, from £163,725 to £47,633, although the largest award in 2009–10 was the only sexual orientation discrimination payout to exceed £30,000 that year. Similarly, in 2010–11, all but one of the awards were less than £30,000.

Most cases were settled through ACAS conciliation (41%) or were withdrawn (31%): 3% of claims were successful.

Source: 'Tribunal awards: which discrimination cases attract the biggest payouts?', Laura Chamberlain, *Personnel Today*, 12 September 2011, http://www.personneltoday.com/articles/2011/09/12/57940/tribunal-awards-which-discrimination-cases-attract-the-biggest.html

Under s. 13 EqA, an employer discriminates on grounds of sex if it treats a woman differently to a man or vice versa. Much of the case law, which this chapter includes, arises through sex discrimination claims and therefore the relevant law will be explained through these cases. Whilst the source of laws prohibiting gender discrimination can be found in EU law, it is the European Court of Human Rights (ECtHR) which played the pivotal role in outlawing discrimination on grounds of sexual orientation as a result of its interpretation of Article 8 of the European Convention which guarantees the right to a private life.

The trigger for this historic change in the law was the decision of the ECtHR in *Lustig-Prean and Beckett* v. *the United Kingdom* [1999] IRLR 734. In this case the ECtHR ruled that it was contrary to Article 8 to discharge individuals from the Royal Navy on the sole ground that they were homosexuals. The wide-sweeping consequences of this decision were immediately clear as the European Court rejected arguments from the Ministry of Defence that the presence of homosexuals in the armed forces 'can cause offence, polarise relationships, induce ill-discipline and, as a consequence, damage morale and unit effectiveness', and therefore any discrimination could be justified as being in the interests of national security.

Case Summary

However, the impact of the decision in *Lustig-Prean* was significantly reduced by the fact that the Human Rights Act 1998 only permits rights guaranteed by the European Convention to be enforced directly against public bodies. Moreover, it was decided that discrimination against an employee on the basis of his or her sexuality could not be considered unlawful either under the Sex Discrimination Act or under the EU Equal Treatment Directive 1976, as these pieces of legislation only covered gender-based discrimination.

As stated above, the Framework Directive included discrimination on grounds of sexual orientation and these provisions of the Directive were implemented by a statutory instrument, which originally came into force in December 2003. The EqA re-enacts the relevant provisions. Under s. 12(1) 'sexual orientation' means a sexual orientation towards:

✦ persons of the same sex;

✦ persons of the opposite sex; or

✦ persons of the same sex and of the opposite sex.

This definition obviously prohibits discrimination against gay and lesbian employees. The definition also protects bisexual employees and, although this is not common, discrimination against employees on the basis that they are heterosexual.

As explained above, the Framework Directive also covers religion or belief and a statutory instrument prohibiting discrimination on these grounds also came into force in December 2003. More recently, there have been several important cases, which will be considered below, concerning conflicts of rights between gay and religious employees.

Gender reassignment

Although the ECJ ruled that the Equal Treatment Directive did not cover sexuality, it did rule, in *P* v. *S and Cornwall County Council* [1996] ICR 795, that the dismissal of an employee was contrary to the Directive where the reason for the dismissal was that the employee proposed to undergo gender-reassignment surgery. The basis of this ruling was the ECJ's view that sex discrimination arose through comparing the treatment of a person of the sex to which he or she was deemed to belong with how that person would have been treated before undergoing, or proposing to undergo, gender reassignment.

The Sex Discrimination Act (SDA) 1975 was amended to cover discrimination against a transgendered, or in the language of the statute, transsexual person, and the law is now contained in s. 7 EqA. A transsexual is defined by s. 7(1) as a person who has started, is undergoing or has undergone a process (or part of a process) of gender reassignment by changing physiological or other attributes of sex. Under the SDA, gender reassignment was primarily seen as a medical process under which the individual would be under medical supervision culminating in gender reassignment surgery. On the basis of the above definition this is no longer the case. It is sufficient that a man decides to live as a woman or vice versa, although it should be noted that the legislation still excludes transvestism – this being where a man as a man, or a woman as a woman, regularly engages in cross-dressing.

However, medical considerations cannot be completely discarded as there are persons who are intersexual, rather than transsexual, who fall between the definitions of men and women and have not embarked on any process of gender reassignment. A famous example of a person who may be considered intersexual comes from the world of sport. Caster Semenya is a South African athlete who won the 800 metres gold medal in the World Championship for athletics in Berlin and competed in women's events in the 2012 London Olympics. There has been much media discussion as to whether she has the physiological constitution of a man and thus should be banned from competing in her sport as a woman. At the time of writing, the International Athletics Federation had sought to get round this problem by altering its regulations so that the focus is not on determining an athlete's gender but on the level of male hormones in the athlete's body.

As explained below, EqA also prohibits perceptive discrimination. This occurs where a person is subjected to discrimination because it is perceived that that person has a protected characteristic. It could be argued that an intersexual could be perceived to be transsexual and thus protected by s. 7.

An ongoing issue, arising from the legislation as it was previously worded, is illustrated by the Court of Appeal decision in *Croft* v. *Royal Mail Group Plc* (CA) [2003] IRLR 592. It appears that an employer will not be committing unlawful discrimination in providing for separate toilet facilities for pre-operative transsexuals, despite the offence to a person's dignity that might be caused. If anything this problem is likely to be exacerbated by the fact that a transgendered person no longer has to undergo gender reassignment surgery, and therefore may be permanently subject to such arrangements.

As a result of a decision of the European Court of Human Rights, in *Goodwin* v. *UK* [2002] IRLR 664, and as implemented by the Gender Recognition Act 2004, a post-operative transsexual is entitled to have his or her new sex fully recognised through a change in that person's birth certificate. It is clear, therefore, that a decision such as the one in *Croft* will cease to be applicable once a person has completed an operation to change his or her birth gender. Once gender reassignment surgery has taken place, an employee must be treated in all respects as though he or she had always been a member of that employee's acquired gender.

Marriage and civil partnership

Under s. 8 EqA, it is unlawful to discriminate against an employee because that person is married or has entered into a civil partnership with a partner of the same sex. A gap in the protection offered by s. 8 is that it does not protect single persons, including single parents. Nor does it cover couples, be they of the opposite sex or same sex, who cohabit with one another but have not undertaken a marriage or civil partnership ceremony.

Pregnancy and maternity

In the landmark rulings of *Dekker* v. *VJV Centrum* and *Hertz* v. *Aldi Marked* [1991] IRLR 27, 131, the ECJ ruled that refusal of employment to or dismissal of women on grounds of pregnancy was contrary to the Equal Treatment Directive. It was initially unclear whether it was unlawful to refuse employment to a pregnant woman under a temporary contract where she would be unable to fulfil all or most of that contract. The problem is best illustrated by a situation where a pregnant woman accepts a temporary contract to cover for another woman who is on maternity leave, and then, as a result of her own pregnancy, will also be on maternity leave for much of the same period of time. In the *Tele Danmark (Brandt-Nielsen)* Case [2001] IRLR 853, the ECJ ruled that refusal of employment to a woman because she is pregnant will be unlawful in all circumstances, irrespective of the economic consequences for the employer. Therefore, a pregnant woman who is refused employment on the basis that she will be unable to perform a substantial amount of the employment contract will be the victim of unlawful discrimination.

Section 18 EqA renders it unlawful discrimination to subject a woman to any form of unfavourable treatment, including refusal of employment, demotion or dismissal, during the protected period relating to her pregnancy. This protected period begins at the start of a woman's pregnancy and continues until the end of the period of her compulsory maternity leave. For women who are not employees this is two weeks after the end of her pregnancy. For women who are employees this will be for the ordinary maternity leave (OML) period of 26 weeks or the additional maternity leave (AML) period of 52 weeks.

A pregnant employee also possess the statutory right, under ss. 55–57 ERA 1996, to request paid time off from work to receive ante-natal care. If the employer unreasonably refuses such a request then the woman can recover compensation from a tribunal if she attended a medical appointment and has lost pay as a result. If a woman is dismissed for exercising this right then the dismissal will be **automatically unfair**. It should also be remembered that (as explained in Chapter 5), under s. 99 of ERA 1996 a woman who is an employee and is dismissed by reason of her pregnancy will automatically succeed in a claim of unfair dismissal.

Statutory maternity leave

The EqA does not provide for maternity leave but to understand its scope it is necessary to look at the relevant rules which are set out in Part VIII of ERA 1996 and the Maternity and Parental Leave (MPL) Regulations 1999, SI 1999/3312. In order to qualify for statutory maternity leave an employee must, no later than the fifteenth week before the expected week of childbirth (EWC), inform the employer that she is pregnant and the date on which intends to start her maternity leave. This date cannot be earlier than the beginning of the eleventh week before the EWC. In return the employer must notify the employee – preferably in writing – of the date her statutory maternity leave will end. If the employer fails to provide this notice, the employer may not be able to take any action if the employee returns after the date that her maternity leave actually expired. Should the employee wish to return earlier than this date, she must give the employer at least eight weeks' notice of the date she intends to return to work.

Where the employee takes OML for 26 weeks, she has the right to return to the same job, on the expiry of the maternity leave, on terms and conditions of employment which are no less favourable than those that she enjoyed prior to taking maternity leave. The significance of the phrase 'no less favourable' is that the employee is entitled to improvements to terms and conditions of employment which took place whilst she was on maternity leave, for example, any pay increases the employer has granted to other employees on the employee's grade.

Where the employee takes AML, and therefore the full period of leave totalling 52 weeks, the employer is permitted to establish that it is not reasonably practicable for the employee to return to her old job. Where this is genuinely the case, the employer *must* offer the employee an alternative job which is suitable and appropriate for her to do in the circumstances. The terms and conditions under which this job is done must again be no less favourable than the terms and conditions which applied to her previous job.

Providing an employee is earning a sufficient wage to be paying national insurance contributions, she is entitled to receive statutory maternity pay (SMP) if she has 26 weeks' continuous employment by the beginning of the fourteenth week before the EWC. In 2012, the mother had to be earning at least £107 a week, and the SMP for the first six weeks of maternity leave is 90% of the employee's average gross weekly earnings. For this initial period there is no upper limit. The employee is entitled to SMP for another 33 weeks at the standard rate of £135.45 (in 2012), or 90% of her average gross weekly earnings, whichever is the lower sum.

Parental and carers' rights

One of the ongoing consequences of the patriarchal nature of our society is that, as is discussed further later in this chapter, work traditionally undertaken by men is better paid than work traditionally done by women. Moreover, many women in work often bear the brunt of unpaid work in the form of caring for children and other family members. This is not always because of sexism on the part of fathers. Rather, it is the inevitable consequence of the family budget being primarily dependent on his income. However, over the past decade statutory rights have been introduced with the purpose of enabling both parents to be involved in child-care whilst continuing to work. These rights, which, like maternity leave, operate independently of EqA, are only available to employees.

The Paternity and Adoption Leave Regulations 2002, SI 2002/2788, provides for a period of two weeks' paid paternity leave. This right is only available to fathers with at least 26 weeks' continuous employment ending with the fifteenth week before the EWC. The leave must be taken in one block of either one week or two consecutive weeks and must be completed within 56 days of the actual birth of the child. This right to paternity leave was extended by the Additional Paternity Leave Regulations 2010, SI 2010/1055, which permit fathers, who have acquired the right to take paternity leave to take up to an additional 26 weeks' paid leave to care for a newborn child or support the mother. The right is conditional on the mother having returned to work. Statutory paternity pay is subject to the same statutory maximum as statutory maternity pay, which for 2012 was £135.45 or 90% of an employee's average gross weekly earnings, whichever was the lesser amount.

Effectively, these regulations permit the father to take over the right to paid leave if the mother decides to return to work after she has taken a minimum period of 20 weeks' maternity leave from the date the baby was born. This right is particularly valuable for parents where it is the mother who is on the higher salary or wage. It may also be useful for parents who earn more or less the same amount of money. Obviously, exercising this right is less attractive to parents in the fairly common position where it is the father who is the higher earner. It should be noted that adoptive parents have similar statutory rights. It is for the adoptive parents to choose which one of them is deemed the adoptive parent for the purposes of exercising the rights to paid adoption leave.

As a result of the EC Parental Leave Directive, Directive 96/34, the MPL regulations contain provisions which provide right to parents, that is, both mothers and fathers, with one year's service to 13 weeks' *unpaid* leave to care for a child under the age of five. This is extended to 18 weeks in the case of a disabled child until that child's eighteenth birthday.

Under s. 57A ERA 1996, employees are also entitled to take reasonable *unpaid* time off to care for children and other dependent family members, including spouses, partners and parents, in emergency situations of illness or injury where it is necessary to care for them or to arrange for care, for example, by taking the dependant to hospital or obtaining other appropriate professional care. In order to exercise this right, the employee must inform the employer of the reason for his or her absence as soon as is reasonably practicable and how long the employee expects to be absent for. Employers are not permitted to require employees to make up the lost time when they return to work. Nor can they require employees to treat the time taken off as part of their annual leave.

It is unlawful to subject an employee to any detriment, such as depriving the employee of any benefits granted to other employees or reducing seniority rights, for exercising any of the above family rights. Any dismissal on any of the above grounds will be automatically unfair (see Chapter 5).

The right to request flexible working

In recent times there has been considerable discussion on the value to employees and employers of employees being able to strike a good work–life balance, and the role that flexible working patterns can play in achieving this. However, the statutory right to request flexible working is restricted to employees who are parents of children under the age of 17, or 18 if the child is disabled, or who are carers of adults. Under Part 8A ERA 1996, such employees, providing they have at least 26 weeks' continuous employment, have the right to *request* that their employers allow them to adopt a flexible working pattern such as moving from full-time to part-time employment, job-sharing, changing the days on which the employee attends work or working from home. Providing employers adhere to a proper procedure, which is in accordance with the legislation, employers are able to reject a request.

Under s. 80F(2) ERA 1996 the employee's request must be:

✦ in writing and dated;

✦ state that the application is made under the statutory right to request a flexible working pattern;

✦ give details of the flexible working pattern the employee is applying for, including the date from which the employee wants it to start;

✦ explain what effect the employee believes the new working pattern would have on the employer, and how any effects might be dealt with.

The employer must consider the request and, under s. 80G(1)(b), it can only be rejected for one of the following business reasons:

✦ burden of additional costs;

✦ detrimental effect on ability to meet customer demand;

✦ inability to reorganise work among existing staff;

✦ inability to recruit additional staff;

✦ detrimental impact on quality;

✦ detrimental impact on performance;

✦ insufficiency of work during the periods the employee proposes to work;

✦ planned structural changes.

If the employer wishes to reject the request, he must invite the employee to a meeting to discuss this within 28 days from the date the employer received the request. If the employer then decides to reject the request, the employee must be permitted to exercise a right of appeal. The meeting to consider the appeal must take place within 14 days of the date on which the employer received notice of the employee's wish to appeal.

If an employee believes that the request for flexible working has been wrongfully refused, the employee may present a complaint to a tribunal within three months of the date of the employer's decision. The tribunal is not empowered to review the employer's reasons for rejecting the request if the reason is for one or more of the business reasons set out in s. 80G(1)(b). The tribunal can uphold the complaint if the employer has failed to follow the mandatory procedure, or the rejection was not for a permitted business reason, or the employer's decision was based on incorrect facts.

Under s. 80I, if the tribunal finds that the complaint is well founded it must issue a declaration to this effect. It can order the employer to reconsider the employee's request and make an award of compensation. The amount of compensation will be based on what the tribunal considers just and equitable and is subject to a maximum of eight **statutory weeks' pay**. Therefore, the statutory cap on a week's pay applies – in 2012 this was £430 a week. A tribunal may well decide to award the maximum amount in circumstances where the employer clearly did not have a permitted business reason to reject the request.

Handy tip: The statutory rights granted to parents and carers are very detailed but government websites provide clear and up to date advice. Readers can access this advice at: **http://www.direct.gov.uk/en/Parents/Moneyandworkentitlements/WorkAndFamilies/index.htm**

The forms of discrimination

Having identified the types of discrimination which are prohibited by EqA, it is important to understand that discrimination may be in a direct form or an indirect form, and both of these forms of discrimination are unlawful. However, there are important differences between these two forms of discrimination which are fully explored below.

Direct discrimination

Under s. 13(1) EqA, a person (A) discriminates against another (B) if, because of a protected characteristic, A treats B less favourably than A treats or would treat others. A straightforward example of **direct discrimination** is where a person is not shortlisted for a job, or not offered employment or overlooked for promotion because of a protected characteristic. For example, there is evidence that an individual was not considered suitable for a particular post because that person was a woman, and/or was black and/or was gay.

It is important to understand that direct discrimination may take place even though an employer was not motivated by discriminatory attitudes. This is the result of the leading judgment of the House of Lords in *James* v. *Eastleigh Borough Council* [1990] ICR 554 and its adoption of the 'but for' test. In this case, the Law Lords decided that Mr James was directly discriminated against when he was charged a higher price than his wife for admission to a swimming pool. The sole reason for the differential treatment was that the concessionary cheaper price was for pensioners only. Although Mr and Mrs James were both aged 61, she was a pensioner and he was not. Clearly, there was no discriminatory intent and motive on the part of the Council. Nevertheless, *but for* the fact that Mr James was a man, he would have been treated the same as his wife. As a result of the 'but for' test, direct discrimination is in theory easier to establish as it is not necessary to establish an intention to discriminate. However, there is a very real practical difficulty with regard to proof, and providing evidence of discrimination to an employment tribunal will be discussed below.

Case Summary

The decision of the Court of Appeal, in the controversial case of *Eweida* v. *British Airways* [2010] ICR 890, demonstrates that an employee will not succeed in claiming direct discrimination where all employees are treated alike by an employer even though an employer's policies or practices are specifically detrimental to a particular employee. The issue in *Eweida* was whether she had been subject to unlawful discrimination as a result of a blanket ban on employees displaying jewellery, including religious icons – in her case a crucifix. She lost her claim of direct discrimination as all employees, irrespective of any religious beliefs, were subject to this rule.

Case Summary

We considered (in Chapter 3) the issue of when employees are required to comply with an employer's dress code and established that employers have wide powers to require employees to dress in particular ways. There have been attempts to argue that dress codes, which can be regarded as derived from gender stereotypes, constitute unlawful discrimination. However, as held in cases such as *Schmidt* v. *Austicks Bookshop Ltd* [1978] ICR 85 and *Smith* v. *Safeway plc* [1996] IRLR 456, it is permissible for an employer to impose dress codes which are in accordance with conventional standards in society. Therefore, men can be required to wear suits and ties and to wear their hair short, whilst women can be prohibited from wearing trousers in the workplace. However, as shown by the *St Gregory College* case discussed above, it is possible for a dress code to constitute unlawful discrimination.

Direct discrimination and an employer's genuine occupational requirements

If direct discrimination is established then normally this will mean that an employer has acted unlawfully, and it will not be open to an employer to justify the discrimination by reference to the employer's commercial needs. This is one reason why, as we saw above, an employer cannot justify refusal of a temporary job to a pregnant woman even though she will not be able to carry out most of her contractual commitments.

However, whilst direct discrimination cannot be justified, it is lawful where the **genuine occupational requirement (GOR)** defence contained in Paragraph 1, Schedule 9 EqA can be pleaded successfully. This defence is available where an employer can show it is a genuine occupational requirement for an employee to have a particular protected characteristic. For the defence to be available, the employer must also be able to show that the requirement is a proportionate means of achieving a legitimate aim.

There were equivalent provisions in the earlier legislation and the SDA and the RRA both specified the circumstances where the defence would be available. Schedule 9 does not reproduce a similar list, but the previous provisions and case law can still be relied upon to establish the types of situations when the defence can be pleaded. It is permissible, for example, to require an employee to be of a particular gender or ethnic group where this is for reasons of authenticity, for example, in the acting or modelling professions.

It may also be permissible for an employer to refuse employment where the provision of personal services is concerned. For example, in *London Borough of Lambeth* v. *Commission for Racial Equality* [1990] IRLR 231, it was implicitly accepted that is permissible to require a counsellor to be of the same racial or ethnic group as the majority of the people he or she is employed to provide with advice. Similarly, it is probably the case that the defence is available to an organisation established to advise gay people on sexual matters, as only if an advisor is gay is she or he fully able to understand the complexities of a particular problem that another gay person may have.

The *requirement of proportionality* provides a limit on the extent to which an employer may engage in direct discrimination. For example, for reasons of decency and privacy it would be legitimate for the owner of a men's clothes shop to require at least one of the sales staff to be male for the purposes of entering a male changing room or measuring a man's trouser leg. However, this is not a reason to require all sales staff to be male, and the gender, for example, of a person specifically employed to work on the till to take customer's payments is of no relevance to being able to perform that particular job.

Religious celebrants, such as vicars, priests, imams and rabbis provide another example of where the genuine occupational defence can be pleaded, as a religious employer will be able to establish that it is a 'genuine occupational requirement' for its celebrants to hold the relevant religious beliefs. More controversially, Paragraph 2 of Schedule 9 provides organised religions with a special defence that, for example, permits a religious employer to require celebrants to be of a specific gender or heterosexual. This defence is available where the doctrines of an organised religion require a celebrant to possess or not possess a particular protected characteristic. The defence is also available where the requirement is imposed to avoid conflict with the strongly held convictions of a significant number of the religion's followers. This defence connects with debates in, for example, the Anglican Church as to whether women or non-celibate gay men should be permitted to become bishops.

It should be noted that GOR defences apply to the contexts of recruitment, promotion and dismissal. However, they do not apply to the terms and conditions under which persons are employed, or to access to benefits, facilities or services that an employer provides to its employees. Therefore, whilst there may be circumstances in which an employer can restrict employment to, for example, members of a particular gender, if members of the opposite gender are employed they must not be discriminated against with respect to the contractual and non-contractual benefits that they enjoy.

Positive action

Some argue that the most effective way of securing equality is to discriminate positively in favour of disadvantaged groups by treating them more favourably than those groups in society who, in effect, have benefited from discrimination. However, **positive discrimination** to overcome the legacy of past discrimination cannot constitute a GOR. For example, an employer cannot decide that a job vacancy will only be available to members of a particular racial group because employees from that group are under-represented in the workforce. Indeed, both the SDA and RRA inherently prohibited positive discrimination, and this remains the case under EqA.

However, positive action is permitted by s. 158 EqA, and has been increasingly encouraged by EU law. In *Badeck* v. *Hessischer Ministerprasident* [2000] IRLR 432, the ECJ ruled that positive action is not contrary to EU law unless it requires women to be afforded automatic and unconditional preference over men (or vice versa). The EU Directives concerned with prohibiting discrimination encourage Member States to take positive steps to compensate for disadvantages produced by past forms of discrimination.

Under s. 158, it is permissible for an employer deliberately to seek to increase the number of employees it employs from ethnic groups under-represented in the organisation. This could be done, for example, by targeting schools containing high numbers of members of the relevant ethnic groups or advertising in languages spoken by and/or in media popular with members of under-represented groups. The employer may emphasise that it welcomes applicants from the ethnic group(s) concerned. Employers may also put on special training courses to enable members from under-represented groups to be better placed to apply for a post or for promotion. Specific decisions to recruit one individual as against another must be made on objective criteria and not motivated by a desire to engage in positive discrimination. However, s. 159 EqA does permit employers to take ethnic, gender-based etc. under-representation into account in recruitment where candidates are as qualified as each other, although quota systems remain unlawful. As with the GOR defence, positive action under ss. 158 and 159 must constitute a proportionate means of obtaining the legitimate aim of overcoming under-representation which, for example, is the result of historic discrimination.

Indirect discrimination

The inherent difference between direct discrimination and **indirect discrimination** is that in the latter context an employer is treating all employees in an equal way, and therefore, on the face of it, is not behaving in a discriminatory manner. An example of discrimination which is indirect, but could not be direct, is where an employer imposes a rule on all employees, but members of a particular group of employees, sharing a protected characteristic, are disproportionately adversely affected by the rule in comparison to members of other groups of employees. In the *St Gregory's College* case, which is explained above, the school imposed a rule on hairstyles which was the same for all male pupils. As we saw, the rule constituted unlawful race discrimination. In fact, this was indirect discrimination, as the rule impacted detrimentally on the members of the ethnic group to which the claimant pupil belonged in a way that was not the case with respect to pupils of other ethnic groups. Once it is established that discrimination is indirect, rather than direct, than the key difference between the two forms of discrimination is that indirect discrimination is lawful if it can be justified by the employer.

The statutory definition of indirect discrimination is contained in s. 19 EqA. Under s. 19(1), a person (A) discriminates against another (B) if A applies to B a provision, criterion or practice (PCP) which is discriminatory in relation to a relevant protected characteristic of B's. Under s. 19(2), a PCP is discriminatory in relation to a relevant protected characteristic of B's if:

✦ A applies, or would apply, it to persons with whom B does not share the characteristic;

✦ it puts, or would put, persons with whom B shares the characteristic at a particular disadvantage when compared with persons with whom B does not share it;

✦ it puts, or would put, B at that disadvantage; and

✦ A cannot show it to be a proportionate means of achieving a legitimate aim.

Case Summary

The case of *Holmes* v. *Home Office* [1984] ICR 678 provides a good illustration of the concept of indirect discrimination in the context of employment. Holmes exercised her right to statutory maternity leave but, on its expiry, decided not to exercise her statutory right to return on basis of her existing employment contract. Rather, for child-care reasons, she requested that she be permitted to move from a full-time to a part-time contract but this request was denied. This constituted indirect sex discrimination as the way in which child-care typically operates in this society means that the number of working mothers who can satisfy a requirement to work full-time is substantially fewer than the number of working fathers who can do so. The Home Office was unable to provide any organisational reason for requiring its employees to work full-time, and therefore it was unable to justify its refusal to allow Holmes to move to a part-time contract. Consequently, she won her claim of unlawful indirect sex discrimination. This case established a general rule to the effect that discrimination against part-time workers will normally inherently be indirect discrimination against women.

It should be noted that part-time workers of *both* sexes are protected at work by virtue of the EU Part-time Work Directive (97/81), which was implemented in the UK by the Part-time Workers (Prevention of Less Favourable Treatment) Regulations 2000, SI 2000/1551. Regulation 5 states that a part-time worker has the right not to be treated by his or her employer less favourably than the employer treats a comparable full-time worker as regards the terms of the employment contract, or by being subjected to any other detriment. However, differential treatment will not be unlawful if it can be justified objectively by the employer. A part-time worker, who was previously employed as a full-timer by the employer, can compare his or her position with the way in which he or she was previously treated.

Examples of potentially unlawful discrimination include:

✦ imposing more onerous workloads;

✦ erecting barriers to part-time workers being eligible for promotion;

✦ providing for less favourable contractual benefits including different hourly pay rates;

✦ blocking access to pension schemes;

✦ selecting part-time workers first for redundancy.

Therefore, if a female part-time worker is subject to discrimination at work, she is able to bring a claim of indirect discrimination under EqA, and/or a claim of direct or indirect discrimination under the regulations. The test for objective justification is the same for each of these claims, and is fully discussed below.

An employee claiming indirect discrimination must establish that he or she belongs to a group that is disadvantaged by an employer's **provision, criterion or practice (PCP)**. As confirmed by the EHRC's Code of Practice, this may make it necessary to produce statistical evidence that establishes that a smaller proportion of the claimant's group can meet the PCP in comparison with another group or other groups in society. Alternatively, this may be self-evident. For example, as stated above, it is established knowledge that the majority of part-time workers are women.

If a claimant is unable to establish that he or she is a member of an identifiable protected group, which has been disproportionately discriminated against, then indirect discrimination will not have occurred. In *Eweida*, see above, the Court of Appeal upheld the decisions of both the ET and EAT that she was not the victim of indirect discrimination as the court took the view that, for Christians, the wearing or displaying of a crucifix was simply an issue of individual choice.

A different approach was taken in *Azmi* v. *Kirklees MBC* [2007] ICR 1154. In this case a Muslim woman, who was employed as a teaching assistant in languages classes for school children, was dismissed after she refused to remove her face veil in classes where male teachers were or might be present. It was accepted by the EAT that this was indirect religious discrimination as the ban on the veil only affects Muslims. However, for reasons that will be explained below, she lost her case as the council's actions could be justified.

Justifying indirect discrimination

The key difference between direct and indirect discrimination is that the former will always be unlawful unless the genuine occupational requirement defence can be successfully pleaded. However, indirect discrimination will be lawful if the employer is able to justify the PCP which constitutes the indirect discrimination. The test for justification is derived from EU law as propounded by the European Court of Justice in *Bilka-Kaufhaus Gmbh* v. *Weber von Hartz* [1987] ICR 110, an equal pay case which is discussed towards the end of this chapter. The employer must establish: (a) that there is an objective economic or operational need for the discriminatory practice; and (b) the discriminatory effects are no greater than necessary to secure the employer's objectives.

The requirement of **proportionality** operates to limit the circumstances where indirect discrimination can be justified as, even where an employer can establish genuine commercial objectives, the discrimination will not be justified if the employer's objectives can be secured by other non-discriminatory means, or if the discriminatory PCP produces merely marginal advantages to the employer.

The case of *London Underground* v. *Edwards* [1998] IRLR 364 provides a good example of justification failing on the basis of proportionality. Edwards was employed by London Underground as a train driver. The workforce was predominantly male and Edwards was the only single mother. As such, she was unable to work a new shift system introduced by London Underground. The court found that she had been indirectly discriminated against on the basis that the majority of single parents are mothers. The court accepted London Underground's argument that the new system did enhance efficiency. However, London Underground failed in its plea of justification as it disproportionately adversely impacted on Edwards as she had been forced to give up her job. The efficiency gains secured by the new shift system would not have been undermined if London

Case
Summary

Underground had exempted Edwards from it and allowed her to continue to work her established hours.

Case Summary

In *Manchester University* v. *Jones* [1993] IRLR 218, the claimant, who had obtained a degree as a mature student, answered an advert for the post of careers adviser at Manchester University which stated that the person appointed would be a graduate, preferably aged 27–35 years. Jones was aged 46 and was not selected for interview. The Court of Appeal held that, even if this age requirement was capable of amounting to indirect sex discrimination, it was justified as the evidence showed that the existing careers advisers were all middle-aged and a younger candidate, nearer to the age of the typical undergraduate, was required to balance the number of older people on the staff. It can be noted that, today, the university would clearly be regarded as having committed direct age discrimination. However, as this form of discrimination can also be justified, the result is likely to be the same as it was in the *Jones* case.

Case Summary

By way of contrast, in *Briggs* v. *North Eastern Education and Library Board* [1990] IRLR 181, Briggs, a science teacher, was promoted. The promotion was conditional upon her carrying out additional duties such as assisting with extra-curricular school games. Briggs subsequently adopted a baby, and stated that she would be unable to continue with extra-curricular activities until her daughter reached school age. Consequently, the school authorities decided to demote her to her former position. It was held that this constituted indirect sex discrimination as it is proportionately more difficult for women in comparison to men to undertake work outside of normal working hours. However, the employer's requirement that coaching is carried out after school was imposed in order to meet a reasonable educational need, and it was justifiable to make a promotion conditional on this work being undertaken. The educational needs of school children were also successfully invoked in *Azmi*, see above, to justify the refusal to permit Azmi to wear a face veil in the classroom, as it was necessary for the pupils to see her face if they were to learn linguistic skills effectively.

Table 7.1, below, summarises the differences between direct and indirect discrimination.

Table 7.1 Distinguishing between direct and indirect discrimination

Direct discrimination	Indirect discrimination
An employee is treated less favourably than other employees because of a protected characteristic	A PCP is imposed on all employees but the employee belongs to a group with a protected characteristic that is disproportionately disadvantaged by the PCP
Direct discrimination is normally unlawful and cannot be justified	Indirect discrimination is unlawful unless it can be justified by the employer
Direct discrimination will only be lawful if requiring an employee to have a particular protected characteristic is a GOR and is a proportionate means of achieving a legitimate aim	Indirect discrimination will be justified if the purpose of the PCP is to meet an objective commercial need or organisational interest of the employer, and it is a proportionate means of achieving that legitimate aim
Proportionality means that the employer's needs cannot be met by other means, and the advantage to the employer is not outweighed by the discrimination suffered by the claimant	Proportionality means that the employer's needs cannot be met by other means, and the advantage to the employer is not outweighed by the discrimination suffered by the claimant

You be the judge

Q: Assuming indirect discrimination has been established in both of the following two situations, could the PCP of requiring Olivia and Nancy to be full-time teachers be successfully justified by the school?

SPBS is a boarding school outside of the state sector. The school has both female and male pupils and a full-time teaching staff of 100, 35 of whom are women. The school has a policy of preferring to employ teachers on a full-time basis, as members of staff are expected not only to teach during the day but also to supervise homework sessions in the evenings, and to look after boarders prior to their bedtimes. Full-time teachers and their families live in accommodation provided by the school. However, to overcome a short-term lack of specialist expertise five part-time teachers are currently employed in the mathematics department. Four of these part-timers are women. There are six full-time members of the department, three men and three women.

Olivia Twist is one of four women out of a staff of eight in the English department. Olivia has just adopted a young child and asks Mark Tucker, the head teacher, if she can transfer to a part-time contract under which she will work for half the normal working week. Mark refuses this request on the basis that it will reduce the number of teachers available to care for the needs of female boarders.

Mark Tucker announces that there will be one promotion from current full-time staff in the mathematics department. Nancy Sykes, one of the part-time teachers in the department, wishes to work on a full-time basis and applies for the promotion. Although Nancy is extremely well qualified, she has only ever taught on a part-time basis. Nancy is not short-listed for the promotion interviews as only current full-time teachers are deemed to eligible to apply.

A: It is not possible to identify certain answers to these situations but justification is more likely to succeed with respect to Olivia than with Nancy.

If Olivia was employed in an ordinary secondary school then justification would be more difficult to plead as it would be more feasible for the school to arrange for a job share where Olivia and a new teacher each worked for half the working week. However, the school will probably be able to demonstrate that such an arrangement would be difficult to operate in a boarding school, and if Olivia was simply permitted to work for half the normal time this would increase the workloads of her colleagues. Note if Olivia exercised her right to request flexible working, these reasons would also constitute business reasons for refusing her request.

On the other hand, a PCP that only current full-time teachers are eligible to apply for promotion is harder to justify given that Nancy is happy to work full-time if appointed. Having experience of teaching full-time might be a relevant factor to be taken into account in comparing the candidates for promotion, but her lack of this experience is unlikely to justify not even giving Nancy an interview. Note that Nancy would also be able to bring a claim of direct discrimination under the Part-time Workers Regulations.

Justification and conflicts of rights

The extension of discrimination law to cover sexual identity and religious beliefs has generated a situation where employers may be forced to choose between the conflicting needs of gay and religious employees. This conflict is demonstrated by the cases of *Ladele* v. *Islington LBC* [2010] ICR 532 and *McFarlane* v. *Relate Avon Ltd* [2010] ICR 507. Ladele was a registrar who refused to conduct ceremonies for civil partnerships on the basis this conflicted with her beliefs as a Christian. Macfarlane was employed as a counsellor by Relate, and he contended that it was unlawful discrimination to

Case Summary

have dismissed him for refusing to counsel gay couples where again such relationships offended his Christianity. In both cases the Court of Appeal accepted there was indirect discrimination, but in both cases found the employers' actions were justified given that the employees' beliefs did not permit them to refuse the jobs they were employed to undertake. It is important to take into account that gay colleagues of Ladele and McFarlane were offended by the idea that they should be permitted to refuse to provide services to gay people, and the employers had equal opportunities policies which required gay employees to be treated with dignity.

The alternative approach that the employers could have taken in these cases would have been to reject the complaints of their gay employees and to insist that Ladele and McFarlane be permitted to refuse to undertake work which offended their religious beliefs. However, it is important to remember that, in the contexts of sexuality and religious beliefs, discrimination law is designed to reflect human rights law which is contained in the European Convention. Had the courts found in favour of Ladele and/or McFarlane, it could have been argued that the decisions would have been incompatible with the requirements of the Convention. It should be noted that, like the *Eweida* case, these decisions are being appealed before the EctHR, but in its submissions to the EctHR the Equality and Human Rights Commission has stated it believes the decisions are correct. At the time of writing it was expected that the EctHR will hear these cases in September 2012.

Case Summary

The significance of the ECHR is also illustrated by the case of *R (on the Application of Johns)* v. *Derby City Council* [2011] EWHC 375. In this case the High Court had to consider whether Derby City Council was right to refuse to permit Mr and Mrs Johns to foster young children because, as Pentecostal Christians, they regarded homosexuality as a sin. The court found for the council partly on the basis that it was necessary to subordinate the right to act on religious values to the recognition that being homosexual is an entirely natural form of sexuality, and gay people, including children who do not yet know they are gay, should not be exposed to individuals who are in a position to undermine their personal dignity. Whilst this is obviously not an employment case, there is no reason to think that a different approach could or should be taken in the context of the workplace.

Associative and perceptive discrimination

In general, EqA re-enacts the provisions contained in previous Acts and Statutory Instruments (SIs). It does however introduce some important innovations. In prohibiting direct discrimination, EqA no longer requires discrimination to be by reference to a protected characteristic possessed by the claimant. The current definition of direct discrimination, contained in s. 13 EqA, is drafted so as to include **associative discrimination**, that is, where the claimant is subjected to discrimination because of an association with a person who possesses a protected characteristic.

Case Summary

For example, in *Attridge* v. *Coleman* [2010] ICR 210, the EAT upheld a decision of an employment tribunal that it is unlawful to subject an employee to discriminatory treatment because that employee is a carer for a disabled child. In this case, Coleman complained that she had been treated in an offensive manner when she had asked for time off to look after her disabled child. The tribunal's decision was based on a preliminary ruling by the ECJ that in line with the Framework Directive the DDA had to be interpreted to cover associative discrimination even though the claimant was not herself a disabled person. Today, the same decision would be reached on the basis of s. 13 EqA.

Similarly, it will be unlawful age discrimination to discriminate against an employee because he or she had an older spouse or partner in need of care. In interpreting the Race Relations Act 1976, it was held, in *Showboat Entertainment Centre Ltd* v. *Owens* [1984] ICR 65, that it was unlawful to discriminate against a white employee who refused to comply with the employer's instructions not to deal with black customers. Again, today, such an employee would be protected by s. 13 EqA as the employee would be the victim of associative discrimination.

Case Summary

Section 13 is also drawn widely enough to cover **perceptive discrimination**, that is, discrimination because of an employee's perceived characteristic. For example, an employee, who is in fact heterosexual, is subjected to discrimination because he or she is perceived to be gay or lesbian. Another example of perceptive discrimination would be where a male employee, who was born a man, is discriminated against because he is perceived to be transgendered. Similarly, as mentioned above, a person who is intersexual may be protected by s. 7 EqA because that person is perceived to be transsexual.

Section 13 also covers the situation which occurred in a case that predates EqA, *English* v. *Thomas Sanderson* [2009] ICR 543, where the harassment of an employee was linked to his *imagined* sexual orientation. In this case, English was the victim of persistent homophobic 'banter' by colleagues because he had gone to boarding school and lived in Brighton. In fact, English was not gay and his colleagues did not actually believe that he was. The Court of Appeal nevertheless held that 'banter' which tormented a man because of his imaginary sexual orientation amounted to unlawful harassment on grounds of sexual orientation.

Case Summary

As argued by Sedley LJ, in paragraph 39 of the decision, there were policy reasons for not requiring an employee to be gay in order to claim unlawful harassment on grounds of sexual orientation. This is because sexual orientation is a fluid rather than a constant preference and a person's sexuality can change over the course of a lifetime. Employees also have the right to keep their sexual orientation private. In the words of Sedley LJ:

> 'Sexual orientation is not an either-or affair. Some people are bisexual, some, including heterosexuals, had unusual interests or proclivities. All might desire to keep their orientation to themselves but still be vulnerable to harassment by people who knew or sensed what their orientation was. It could not possibly have been the intention, when legislation was introduced to stop sexual harassment in the workplace, that such a claimant would have to declare his or her true sexual orientation in order to establish that the abuse was "on grounds of sexual orientation". What was required was that the claimant's (or someone else's) sexual orientation, whether real or supposed, should have been the basis of harassment directed at him or her.'

It should be noted that, oddly, the protection against associative and perceptive discrimination does not apply in the context of discrimination related to marriage or civil partnership. Section 13(4) makes it clear that an actual or prospective employee may only claim direct discrimination on these bases because he or she is married or in a civil partnership. However, discrimination which occurs because an employee is perceived to be in a civil partnership will normally also constitute discrimination based on the fact or perception that an employee is gay or lesbian.

Age discrimination

Key stats

Age discrimination cases saw a rise in both the size of the payouts and the amount of claims accepted by employment tribunals in 2010–11. While the average award grew from £10,931 in 2009–10 to £30,289 in 2011, the number of cases accepted by tribunals rose by nearly one-third to reach 6,800, overtaking race discrimination cases.

The highest payout given in an age discrimination cases in 2010–11 was £144,100, with 15% of winning claimants awarded £50,000 or more. This compares to a maximum award of £48,710 in 2009–10.

The majority of claims were withdrawn (40%), or settled without the need for a hearing through ACAS conciliation (35%). Some 2% of claims were successful at tribunal.

Source: 'Tribunal awards: which discrimination cases attract the biggest payouts?', Laura Chamberlain, *Personnel Today*, 12 September 2011, **http://www.personneltoday.com/articles/2011/09/12/57940/tribunal-awards-which-discrimination-cases-attract-the-biggest.html**

Age discrimination has been unlawful since 2006 when the Labour government implemented the Employment Equality (Age) Regulations 2006, SI 2006/1031. Age discrimination is unlike any other form of discrimination, in that it can happen to anyone including white, heterosexual, fully-abled males. However, ageism at the workplace is most likely to be experienced in the earlier or later periods of an individuals' career. There is a problem here in that there is an inherent tension in the way the law operates. In protecting older workers, who do not wish to retire or are unable to do so as occupational pension rights are lost and the state retirement age is incrementally raised, younger workers are prevented from obtaining paid employment or climbing the career ladder. This problem has been exacerbated by the abolition of the default compulsory retirement age of 65. However, as explained below, employers may be able to justify the imposition of a compulsory retirement age as a means of securing inter-generational fairness.

Age discrimination at work

Under s. 5 EqA, it is unlawful to discriminate against a person because of that person's age or membership of a particular age group. It will constitute direct discrimination if, for example, an employer decides to refuse employment to a person, or to select an employee for redundancy, because that person is aged 60. Similarly, job advertisements should not specify that applicants must be over 25 or less than 55 years old.

justification of direct age discrimination must be underpinned by public interest reasons

The key difference between age discrimination and the other forms of discrimination that we have examined is that direct age discrimination as well as indirect discrimination will be lawful if it can be justified by the employer. With respect to indirect age discrimination, the test for justification is the same as that for other forms of discrimination in that, in line with the *Bilka-Kaufhaus* **principles**, the employer must have an objective need for a provision, criterion or practice (PCP) which constitutes indirect age discrimination and must act proportionately in imposing the PCP. However, justification of direct age discrimination must be underpinned by public interest reasons. It cannot be solely by reference to the commercial interests of the employer.

Law in action

A very high-profile age discrimination case that was decided in early 2011 concerned the well-known TV presenter Miriam O'Reilly, who successfully claimed age discrimination when she was dropped as the presenter of the BBC programme, *Countryfile*. At the time she lost her job she was aged 53, and the tribunal heard allegations that O'Reilly had been asked by younger colleagues if it was 'time for Botox' and was warned to be 'careful with those wrinkles when high definition comes in'. O'Reilly told the tribunal she was not given a reason for her departure and was told only that *Countryfile* was being 'refreshed'.

At the tribunal, the BBC explained its decision in terms of the need to have presenters who could appeal to a younger audience when *Countryfile* was moved to a primetime slot on Sunday evenings. Although she lost part of her claim, which was based on sex discrimination, as a middle-aged male TV presenter would have been similarly treated, it was held that she was the victim of direct age discrimination. The tribunal held that seeking to widen the audience for the programme by appealing to younger viewers was a legitimate aim. However, age discrimination could not be justified as choosing younger presenters was not required to appeal to such an audience and, even if it was, it would not be proportionate to do away with older presenters simply to pander to the assumed prejudice of younger viewers.

After the tribunal decision was given, the BBC announced that it was going to introduce new guidance on fair selection procedures for presenters and give extra training for executives who make

Source: Photolink, Photodisc

these decisions. The BBC also stated that it would like to work with O'Reilly in the future and she stated that this desire was mutual.

With respect to the future, it has long been believed that the entertainment and media industries are infused with ageist attitudes, and both parties agreed the ruling will have an impact not just on the BBC but on the whole broadcasting industry.

Indeed, there have been other high-profile allegations of ageism by the BBC. Although this incident did not result in a legal claim, it was believed by many that Arlene Phillips was the victim of age discrimination when, at the age of 66, she was removed from the panel of judges on *Strictly Come Dancing*. There were similar suspicions when Moira Stewart was dropped at the age of 60 as a newsreader on *The Andrew Marr Show* (see **http://www.dailymail.co.uk/tvshowbiz/article-1193832/Strictly-ageist-How-Arlene-Phillips-66-giving-way-30-year-old-Alesha-Dixon.html**).

Source: **http://www.bbc.co.uk/news/entertainment-arts-12161045**. The O'Reilly case is discussed in *IDS Employment Law Brief* 918, February 2011.

Many jobs will require applicants to have academic and/or professional qualifications and this indirectly discriminates against persons who are not yet old enough to have secured such qualifications. Normally, this discrimination will be justifiable as employers will be able to show that it is essential that employees doing the relevant jobs are fully qualified to do so. Employers may also require employees to have previous experience. This requirement is also capable of justification providing employers can show why previous experience is essential or desirable if the successful applicant for a job is to be able to undertake that job effectively.

However, an unusual twist to the normal position regarding degree qualifications is provided by the case of *Homer* v. *Chief Constable of West Yorkshire Police* [2012] UKSC 15. Homer, a police officer aged 61, was prevented from being appointed to the top of his salary grade because of the employer's policy that a law degree was essential for this post. The Supreme Court held that this is was indirect age discrimination as police officers in the age band approaching compulsory retirement at 65 were disadvantaged in comparison with younger employees as they did not have the time left in the job which is needed for the completion of a degree. At the time of writing the Supreme Court had remitted the case to the tribunal to decide whether the requirement of being a law graduate could be justified and was therefore lawful. It can be commented that the decision in this type of case might be different in the future in any organisation where the employer does not have a compulsory retirement age.

At the other end of the scale, some jobs, such as being a fire fighter or a police officer, require a significant degree of physical fitness which employees over a particular age will generally not possess. In such contexts it may be permissible for the employer to have a compulsory retirement age, even though this constitutes direct age discrimination, as it is in the public interest that such workers are able to perform their jobs in a safe and effective manner. However, proportionality is also an important factor so that employers may need to consider whether desk jobs are available before forcing an employee to retire against that person's wishes.

The EAT decision in *HM Land Registry* v. *Benson*, UKEAT/2012/0197, is a recent case illustrating where *indirect* age discrimination can be justified. The employer was held to be justified in selecting employees for voluntary redundancy on the basis of whom it would cost least to dismiss, despite the fact that this gave rise to indirect age discrimination against employees aged 50–54. Using cost as the main criterion excluded employees in this age band from being able to volunteer for redundancy. The employer had allocated a budget of £12 million to the redundancy project, and the selection of employees in this age group would have cost almost £20 million more, since they would have been entitled to early retirement on an unreduced pension. Although the EAT declined to comment on the need for justification to be on a cost plus basis, this decision would appear to be in line with the Court of Appeal's decision in *Woodcock* v. *Cumbria Primary Care Trust* (which is discussed in Chapter 6). In *Woodcock*, the CA held that cost is only a permitted justification where there are other factors involved. In both *Woodcock* and this case the employers were seeking to avoid the situations where employees would receive 'windfalls' in the form of early retirement benefits.

Keane v. *Investigo and Others* (2009), EAT/0389/09, is an unusual discrimination case as it involved a claimant making multiple claims of age discrimination even though in reality she did not want to secure a job. Keane appealed unsuccessfully to the EAT against a tribunal decision dismissing her claim that the respondent employment agencies had discriminated against her on the ground of her age. Keane, an experienced accountant aged 50, had applied for a large number of jobs advertised online as suitable for newly qualified accountants. In the case of each of those applications, when it had become clear that she was not being offered an interview, Keane commenced tribunal proceedings claiming age discrimination. Some of the claims were settled before being heard, but the remainder were dismissed on the basis that Keane had no real interest in the vacancies and was making the applications only in order to claim compensation. Accordingly, she had suffered no actual detriment and therefore had no basis for bringing age discrimination claims. The EAT held that the tribunal had been correct to decide that on the basis of the evidence Keane had not been the victim of unlawful age discrimination. (There is an interview, later in this chapter, with a practitioner who was involved in representing some of the respondents in the *Keane* litigation.)

Writing and drafting

L Co. Ltd has a compulsory retirement age of 65 for its employees in senior management positions. There are 20 employees who are subject to this policy including John, who is the head of the company's human resource department and will be 65 in three months' time. As a solicitor who advises the company, you have been asked to draft a letter to John informing him that, in accordance with the company's compulsory retirement policy, he is to be dismissed after he has worked out his contractual period of notice of three months. The company informs you that the rationale for its retirement policy is the need to free up senior positions for younger colleagues and to avoid the need to subject elderly employees to the rigorous performance appraisal systems it uses for its senior managers. The company is aware that it is no longer legally permissible simply to have a default retirement age of 65 (see below).

◆ **Handy tip:** In drafting this letter, you should set out the reasons why L Co. Ltd is requiring John to retire in a way that should persuade him that the company's policy is lawful and he has no legal basis for making an age discrimination claim.

Compulsory retirement ages

The original regulations prohibiting age discrimination permitted employers to have a default retirement age (DRA) of 65 so that generally employees could be required to retire at that age. This default retirement age was considered and approved as lawful by the ECJ in *The Incorporated Trustees of the National Council for Ageing (Age Concern England)* v. *Secretary of State for Business, Enterprise and Regulatory Reform* (Case C388/07) [2009] ICR 1080, known generally as the Heyday case.

The provisions for the DRA were reproduced by Paragraph 8, Schedule 9 EqA, but have now been phased out as a result of the Employment Equality (Repeal of Retirement Age Provisions) Regulations 2011, SI 2011/1069. These regulations came into force on 6 April 2011, and the last possible date for compulsory retirement based on the old DRA was 5 October 2012. Employers must now justify a refusal to permit an employee to work even though that employee has passed the state pension age. Provisions which prevented employees over the age of 65 from claiming unfair dismissal or statutory redundancy payments have also been repealed. It remains permissible for employers to cease to provide financial benefits, such as health insurance and medical insurance, after an employee has reached the state pension age.

It is still permissible for an employer to have a contractual retirement age which may be under or over the age of 65, but such a uniform retirement age will only be lawful if it can be objectively justified. Given that the principle of proportionality must also be taken into account, it may be that many employers will decide that it is better to determine on a case-by-case basis whether an employee is failing to work effectively in circumstances where further training will be of no avail, and redeployment is not a feasible option. The dismissal would then be on grounds of individual capability, rather than age. Such a dismissal will be fair if it is within the **range of reasonable responses** in accordance with s. 98(4) ERA 1996 (see Chapter 5). Where a contractual retirement age can be justified then any dismissal should be fair on the basis of 'some other substantial reason' as provided by s. 98(1)(b) ERA 1996.

Out and about

In *Seldon* v. *Clarkson Wright & Jakes* [2012] UKSC 16, the Supreme Court had to consider whether a firm of solicitors was permitted to require a senior partner to retire at the age of 65. Clearly, this is direct age discrimination and is unlawful unless it can be justified. The employment tribunal had originally found in favour of the firm on the basis that the policy could be objectively justified by reference to the normal Bilka-Kaufhaus principles. You should access this case from WESTLAW and answer the following questions:

1. Why did the firm formulate its compulsory retirement policy?

2. Why did the Supreme Court decide that the employment tribunal had been wrong in law?

3. On what basis can direct age discrimination be justified?

4. Is it still possible that the firm was acting lawfully in requiring Seldon to retire?

Reflective practice

Revisit the letter you previously drafted on behalf of L Co. Ltd. In light of the SC's decision in *Seldon*, is there anything you would change or add to your letter? In carrying out the above 'Out and about' activity you should have understood that the Bilka-Kaufhaus principles do not apply to the justification of direct age discrimination. The employer's reasons must be underpinned by public interest aims and cannot be wholly based on the employer's own commercial or organisational interests. However, securing inter-generational fairness and preserving the personal dignity of older employees do constitute public interest reasons. With respect to the former it may be that it is necessary that older employees have previously benefited from employees in senior positions being made to retire at a particular age. Protecting an employee's dignity can cover not subjecting an older employee to the rigours of performance appraisal. Thus it is possible in the L Co. Ltd scenario that the company could justify its decision to compel John to retire. The *Seldon* case has been remitted to the tribunal for it to decide whether the firm's compulsory retirement age of 65 was a proportionate means of achieving the above aims.

Disability discrimination

Key stats

Although disability discrimination cases had the highest average award in 2009–10, in 2010–11 they fell behind age discrimination, with the average payout at £14,137, less than one-third of the figure for the previous year.

The highest award also fell significantly, from £729,347 in 2009–10 to £181,083 in 2010–11. The figure from 2009–10 was the largest ever disability discrimination award, given to Matt Driscoll, a sports writer at *News of the World*, who was subject to bullying and was sacked in 2007 while on long-term sick leave for stress-related depression.

Most claims were settled through ACAS conciliation (46%) and 3% of claims were successful.

Source: 'Tribunal awards: which discrimination cases attract the biggest payouts?', Laura Chamberlain, *Personnel Today*, 12 September 2011, http://www.personneltoday.com/articles/2011/09/12/57940/tribunal-awards-which-discrimination-cases-attract-the-biggest.html

In Britain, disability discrimination law dates from the Disability Discrimination Act (DDA) 1995. The DDA predates the requirements of EU law and was motivated by recognition that disabled persons are a disadvantaged group in society who should be protected from discrimination by the law. Discriminatory attitudes towards disabled people are not rooted in patriarchal power relations, as is the case with sexism, or in pathological bigotry, as is the case with racism and homophobia. The probable cause of discrimination is prejudice arising from an assumption that a person is not fit for employment because of a disability. Alternatively, it may be that an employer is unwilling to incur the cost and/or perceived inconvenience of employing a disabled person. The function of disability discrimination law is to enable a person to live as full a life as possible, including participation in the world of work, despite that person's disability.

The approach taken by the DDA was criticised because, despite its objective of protecting disabled persons from discrimination, it was based on a medical model which regarded disability as a personal problem for the individual. The objective of the DDA was to restrict the circumstances in which employers could use this problem as a reason to refuse employment or as a basis for dismissal. A social model of disability locates the problem as one which arises from the relationship between the disabled person and society, and the function of the law is to help challenge the ways in which society and work are organised to prevent disabled persons from participation in social and working life. However, in line with the Framework Directive, the way in which disability is defined by the EqA represents a limited movement towards a social model of disability.

Defining disability

Section 6 EqA defines disability as having a physical or mental impairment which has a substantial and long-term effect on a person's ability to carry out normal day-to-day activities. 'Substantial effect' is not defined, but it is clear that the effect must be more

Case
Summary

than trivial or minor. In *Anwar* v. *Tower Hamlets College* (2010) EAT 0091/10, Anwar suffered from recurrent headaches which caused moderate to severe pain. The EAT upheld the tribunal's decision that the headaches were more than trivial but had a minor rather than a substantial effect on her everyday life, and therefore Anwar was not suffering from a disability.

Normal day-to-day activities include mobility, manual dexterity and physical co-ordination. In determining whether the impairment affects a person's ability to carry out day-to-day activities, the focus should be on what a person cannot do, rather than what that person can do. For example, in *Leonard* v. *Southern Derbyshire Chamber of Commerce* [2001] IRLR 19, a tribunal decided that the employee who suffered from clinical depression was not protected by the DDA as, although she could not walk or drive for longer distances and suffered from memory loss, she could use a knife and fork and catch a ball. The EAT held that the tribunal had erred in law by focusing on what she could do rather than not do. She was disabled as her condition meant that she was unable to perform a number of day-to-day activities for any length of time.

On the other hand, as held in *Quinlan* v. *B&Q plc* (1998), an inability to engage in work involving heavy lifting is not a disability if the evidence shows the employee can lift everyday objects such as pieces of light furniture. Quinlan lost his job with B&Q after he underwent open heart surgery. His duties required him to carry out heavy lifting, but due to the risks it presented to his health, Quinlan was unable to do this work. The EAT upheld the tribunal's finding that as Quinlan was able to lift everyday objects he was not disabled within the meaning of the DDA.

The impairment must have a 'long-term' effect, and therefore short-term illnesses are not disabilities within the meaning of the Act. A disability is long-term if it has lasted, or is expected to last, for at least 12 months or for the rest of the person's life. This will include a terminal illness and recurring illnesses where a person will often have periods of well-being. Movement towards a social model means that certain progressive conditions, such as cancer, HIV infection or multiple sclerosis, are considered as disabilities from the point of diagnosis without the need to demonstrate a current effect on a person's ability to carry out an activity.

Section 6(4) also reflects a social approach as it provides that the legislation covers past disabilities. This recognises, for example, the prejudice that those with a history of mental illness may face. Other examples of past disabilities include a person who has an artificial limb, which enables that person to function normally on a day-to-day basis, and diabetes. A person with diabetes is 'disabled' even though the condition is controlled with medication.

A severe disfigurement such as a facial scar is regarded as a disability, but this does not include tattoos or facial or bodily piercings. Alcohol and drug addictions are not disabilities unless the addiction is the product of using drugs which were medically prescribed. Psychological conditions such as kleptomania or voyeurism are not covered. Surprisingly, perhaps, nor is hay fever, unless it aggravates the effect of another condition such as asthma in circumstances in which the asthma substantially affects a person's ability to work.

Forms of discrimination

The law concerning disability discrimination includes, but in practice does not primarily rest on, the distinctions between direct and indirect discrimination that apply to the other forms of discrimination discussed in this chapter. Section 13 renders it unlawful directly to discriminate against a person because of that person's disability. Therefore, it is unlawful to refuse to employ a person because that person is disabled in the same way that it is unlawful to refuse employment to a person because of that person's gender or racial group. On the other hand, s. 13(3) makes it clear that a person who is not disabled cannot claim direct discrimination because a disabled person has been treated more favourably. Disability discrimination law is the one context in which positive discrimination is legally permissible. The main thrust of the law is that an employer should take positive steps to enable an employee to work effectively despite that employee's disability.

> disability discrimination law is the one context in which positive discrimination is legally permissible

In *Archibald* v. *Fife Council* [2004] ICR 954, Archibald had been employed as a road sweeper and had been physically fit to do that job until she became disabled following minor surgery. The council dismissed her because her disability meant that she could no longer do her job. Archibald had argued before the tribunal that it would have been reasonable for the Council to have transferred her to a sedentary job without requiring her to undertake a competitive interview for the post. The tribunal found that that would have amounted to giving Archibald preferential treatment, and therefore the council had not failed to comply with its duty to make reasonable adjustments to her job. The Law Lords ruled that the tribunal had made an error of law as the duty to make reasonable adjustments might require the employer to treat a disabled person more favourably than other employees to remove the disadvantage which was attributable to the disability.

Case Summary

Although a disabled employee can be the victim of indirect discrimination, in practice s. 15 EqA is of much greater potential value to disabled persons as it prohibits discrimination against a disabled person if: (a) that person is treated unfavourably because of something arising in consequence of the disability; and (b) the different treatment cannot be justified as a proportionate means of achieving a legitimate aim. Although, as is the case with indirect discrimination, this form of discrimination can be justified it does not require the disabled person to show that he or she was treated less favourably than a comparator.

The wording of s. 15 EqA probably restores the law as it was understood after the decision in of *Clark* v. *TDG Ltd t/a Novacold* [1999] ICR 951. In this case Clark, who had allegedly suffered an injury at work, was dismissed from his employment with the company when a report from an orthopaedic consultant indicated that it was not possible to predict when Clark would be able to return to work. It was held by the Court of Appeal that it was only necessary for Clark to show that he had been treated less favourably than other employees because of his disability. It was not necessary for Clark to compare his treatment with how a person without his disability would have been treated in a comparable situation.

Case Summary

This decision was overruled by the House of Lords decision in *Mayor and Burgesses of the London Borough of Lewisham* v. *Malcolm* [2008] IRLR 700. As a result of this decision it was necessary for a disabled person to show that he or she had been treated less favourably than a comparator without his disability. Therefore, in a case like *Novacold*, it would be necessary for a disabled person who was unable to attend work to show that he or she was treated less favourably than a colleague without the disability would have been treated if absent from work for a similar period of time. Often this would not be the case and therefore claims would fail as claimants could not establish that they had been subjected to discriminatory treatment.

However, the wording of s. 15 would appear to restore the reasoning in *Novacold* and overrule the decision in *Malcolm*. This is because s. 15 prohibits treating a disabled person unfavourably because of something that arises in consequence of that person's disability. The fact that it is no longer required that a disabled person has been treated *less* favourably should rule out the need for a disabled claimant to compare his or her treatment with that of an employee without his or her disability. If unfavourable treatment is established, the onus will then be on the employer to justify this treatment if the claim is to be defeated.

The duty to make reasonable adjustments

Although indirect disability discrimination, or unfavourable treatment arising from a disability, is capable of justification this is not the case where the employer is under a duty to make **reasonable adjustments**, which would enable a disabled person to take up or continue in employment, and the employer has failed to do this. This duty only arises if the employer both knew of the employee's disability and knew that the employee was likely to be affected in the way complained of. However, the employer will have constructive knowledge where the employer could reasonably have been expected to know of the disability.

Case Summary

In *Wilcox* v. *Birmingham CAB Services Ltd* (2010) EAT 0293/10, the employee was unable to travel by car to city-centre work locations as she could not afford to pay for new car parking charges. She could not use public transport because of travel anxiety. The employer agreed that it would try to allocate her work which was close to her home but could not guarantee this would be a permanent arrangement. Wilcox resigned and argued that the employer had failed to make a reasonable adjustment. A subsequent medical report established that Wilcox was in fact agoraphobic and therefore afraid of being out in the open. It was only in light of this report that her phobia became known to the employer. It was held that employer did not have actual or constructive knowledge of her phobia. Therefore, it could not have known that a failure to make a permanent adjustment to her work location was putting her at a disadvantage because of her disability.

Section 20 consists of three requirements that apply in situations where a disabled person would otherwise be placed at a substantial disadvantage compared with people who are not disabled.

The first requirement involves modifying or disapplying a provision, criterion or practice which prevents a disabled employee from undertaking or continuing in a particular job. An example of this would be modifying the hours employees are normally required to work to enable a disabled employee to take up or stay in employment where the disability causes the employee to suffer from fatigue.

The second requirement involves employers making changes to overcome barriers created by the physical features of the workplace. An example of this would to provide a sufficient number of ramps and lifts to allow employees in wheelchairs to enter and exit buildings and reach their upper levels.

The third requirement involves providing an auxiliary aid by providing extra equipment, or providing an auxiliary service to assist the disabled person, to enable that person to perform the job involved. An example of this would be the provision of a telesensory device to enable a visually impaired employee to read important documents.

It is important to appreciate that the duty is only to make a reasonable adjustment. If there is no adjustment that could feasibly be made, or making an adjustment is more than what could be reasonably required of an employer, the employer will not be in breach of s. 20. The following factors can be taken into account in determining whether an adjustment is reasonable:

✦ how effective the change will be in avoiding the disadvantage the disabled person would otherwise experience;

✦ its practicality;

✦ the cost;

✦ the organisation's resources and size;

✦ the availability of financial support to implement the adjustment.

General examples of adjustments it might be reasonable for an employer to make include:

✦ making adjustments to premises;

✦ allocating some of the disabled person's duties to another person;

✦ transferring the person to fill an existing vacancy;

✦ altering the person's hours or pattern of working;

✦ assigning the person to a different place of work;

✦ acquiring or modifying equipment.

The decision in *Archibald* v. *Fife*, discussed above, provides an example of an employer failing to make a reasonable adjustment. As the case demonstrates, the employer cannot argue that an adjustment should not be made because it would lead to a disabled person being treated *more* favourably than other employees.

The case of *Chief Constable of South Yorkshire* v. *Jelic* [2010] IRLR 744 illustrates the failure to make a reasonable adjustment in the context of redeployment. Jelic was a police constable but when he started to suffer from chronic anxiety syndrome he was assigned work involving minimal face-to-face contact with the public. A few years later, the Chief Constable decided to retire him on medical grounds. The EAT confirmed that it was appropriate for a tribunal to find that it would have been a reasonable adjustment to have swapped Jelic's job with that of another officer, or to have offered him medical retirement and immediate re-employment as a civilian in a police staff post which was being advertised at the time.

Case Summary

The case of *Pervez* v. *Royal Bank of Scotland* ET Case No. 112677/08 illustrates how an employer can be regarded as acting reasonably in deciding not to make an adjustment. Pervez was partly blind and a job offer to act as a customer services adviser was withdrawn when the bank ascertained that it would cost at least £35,500 to provide equipment which would have enabled her to do this job. The tribunal found that a combination of the cost involved, uncertainty that the equipment would work and the disruption which would be caused to other employees meant that the bank had acted reasonably in deciding not to install the equipment.

Case Summary

An adjustment cannot be considered reasonable where it will make little or no impact on the disabled employee's ability to work or continue working. In *Lancaster* v. *TBWA Manchester* (2010) EAT 0460/10, the employee, who suffered from a panic and social anxiety disorder, was selected for redundancy. He argued that the employer had used selection criteria which disadvantaged him such as communication and inter-personal skills. The evidence established that even if other criteria had been used he would still have scored lower than anyone else and would have been made redundant. Therefore the employer had not failed to make a reasonable adjustment.

Case Summary

Unlawful harassment

The provisions in EqA prohibiting unlawful harassment cover all the types of discrimination we have examined in this chapter with the exception of marriage, civil partnership, pregnancy or maternity. This is curious, if not controversial, as pregnant employees and employees in civil partnerships, in particular, may well encounter harassment at work. However, harassment on these grounds should still be unlawful as it is likely to overlap with harassment on grounds of sexual orientation or gender, and/or constitute direct discrimination contrary to s. 13 EqA.

The relevant provisions are found in s. 26 EqA. Under this section, a person (A) harasses another (B) if he engages in unwanted conduct related to a relevant protected characteristic, and the conduct has the purpose or effect of:

✦ violating B's dignity; or

✦ creating an intimidating, hostile, degrading, humiliating or offensive environment for B.

In deciding whether the conduct has the above effect, each of the following must be taken into account:

✦ the perception of B;

✦ the other circumstances of the case;

✦ whether it was reasonable for the conduct to have that effect.

On the basis of the above definition, it is the case that, as examples, any homophobic, sexist or racist abuse perceived by the victim to be 'degrading' or 'offensive' will constitute unlawful harassment, even if this was not the actual purpose or intention of the perpetrator. However, an element of objectivity is included as it must be reasonable for the

Case Summary

employee to have such a perception. The case of *Thomas Sanderson Blinds Ltd* v. *English*, which is explained above, was remitted to a tribunal to decide whether, *on the facts*, English, who was heterosexual, had been the victim of discrimination through being subjected to harassment on the (imagined) basis that he was gay. The EAT decided (see EAT 0317/10) that the tribunal had been correct to conclude that he had not been the victim of harassment. He remained friends with the colleagues who had carried out the banter and had willingly participated in it himself.

Case Summary

Similarly in *Grant* v. *HM Land Registry* [2011] IRLR 748, a gay employee could not complain that he had been outed by a line manager in a new workplace, in breach of his personal dignity, when he had been openly gay in his previous workplace. It is true that in this case Grant's employer was the same, but it can be argued that it is for an employee to decide if and when he or she wishes to disclose his or her sexuality to a new set of colleagues. It is important in the *Grant* case that the evidence showed that the line manager had no bad motive for revealing Grant's sexual orientation.

The provisions in the former legislation contained a major gap in the law as a result of the decision of the House of Lords in *MacDonald* v. *AG for Scotland* [2003] ICR 937. This case specifically concerned sexual harassment, and the Law Lords stated that harassment was only unlawful sex discrimination where an employee was treated differently by reference to his or her own gender. However, as explained above, the EqA prohibits associative and perceptive discrimination, and this extends to harassment which is based on association and perception. Therefore, an employee who is harassed because he defends a woman who is subjected to sexual harassment by other colleagues, or because he has a disabled relative or friend or because he is perceived to be gay, will be protected by s. 26.

Section 26(2) EqA expressly covers sexual, as against sex-related, harassment. This is where an employee is the victim of unwanted conduct of a sexual nature. Examples of such harassment include: comments about the employee's personal appearance; 'jokes' of a sexual nature; the display of pornographic material; sending emails containing material of a sexual nature; and unwanted physical contact or a sexual assault.

Vicarious liability

It is clear that harassment of an employee is often conducted by a colleague or colleagues rather than the employer or by senior managers. In such circumstances, at least where the employer has no knowledge of the harassment, the employer cannot be directly liable. However, it is still possible for the employer to incur statutory **vicarious liability**.

Under s. 109 EqA, anything done by a person in the course of his or her employment must be treated as done by that person's employer as well as by him or her. This is the case whether or not any act was done with the employer's knowledge or approval. In *Jones* v. *Tower Boot Co* [1997] ICR 254, it was held by the Court of Appeal that the requirement that the perpetrator is acting in the course of employment does not mean that the acts of harassment must be connected to the work the perpetrator is employed to do. In this case the company was vicariously liable for acts of racist abuse and torture which were inflicted on the claimant by several of his co-workers. It is sufficient for the purposes of establishing vicarious liability that the acts of harassment occur whilst the employees are at work.

Moreover, it has also been held that the scope of an employer's vicarious liability includes behaviour where employees are 'socialising' with one another outside of working hours, away from the workplace, but as part of workplace culture. This was decided in *Chief Constable of the Lincolnshire Police* v. *Stubbs & Others* [1999] ICR 547. This case concerned the sexual harassment of a woman police officer during a police party in a pub. It was held that, as such social activities after police officers had finished their shift were perceived to be an integral part of police culture, the Chief Constable was vicariously liable. This case has obvious implications for the annual Christmas parties that many employers put on for their staff.

Under s. 109(4), an employer will have a defence to this vicarious liability if the employer has taken reasonable steps to prevent an employee from harassing or continuing to harass another employee. On this basis, an employer should be able to avoid vicarious liability if the employer drafts policies and rules prohibiting acts of discriminatory harassment, the rules are properly communicated to employees and complaints of harassment are investigated and properly acted upon, if necessary, through the dismissal of the perpetrator(s).

Third-party harassment

Another important gap in the law, which again resulted from the House of Lords' decision in *MacDonald*, was that employers could not be liable for third-party harassment.

Case Summary

Case Summary

Case
Summary

In reaching this decision the Law Lords overruled the decision in *Burton* v. *De Vere Hotels Ltd* [1997] ICR 1 (1996), in which it was held that an employer will be directly liable if its degree of control over a situation is such that it can take steps to protect employees from third-party racist abuse and fails to do so. In this case Burton and another person were African-Caribbean women who were employed by the hotel as waitresses. They claimed racial harassment after they had been serving at a dinner where the speaker, Bernard Manning, made racially offensive remarks to them and encouraged their abuse by other guests. It was held that the hotel was liable for the racially offensive comments as the event was sufficiently under its control, and the assistant manager should have been advised to withdraw the waitresses in the event of any harassment of them taking place. It was not necessary to show that the perpetrator of the abuse had any intention to discriminate and no specific degree of foresight was required.

Under ss. 40(2) and 40(3) EqA, it is once again possible to make the employer legally liable for third-party harassment. The employer will be liable where the employer fails to take such steps as would be reasonably practicable to protect the employee from harassment by a person who is not an employee. However, this will only be the case where the employer knows the employee has been subjected to third-party harassment on at least two other occasions, although it does not matter that the acts of harassment were carried out by different persons.

Case
Summary

It is not clear whether this 'three strikes' provision would cover the type of situation that occurred in the *De Vere* case. It depends on whether each comment by Manning was a separate act of harassment, or whether the whole of his after dinner speech constituted a single act. It is clear that the events which took place in *Pearce* v. *Mayfield School* [2003] ICR 937 would give rise to liability today. In this case, Pearce, who was a school teacher, was systematically subjected to homophobic abuse by her pupils for being a lesbian. The school authorities took no effective action to protect her from this abuse. However, in a combined decision with that given in *Macdonald*, it was held by the Law Lords that the school could not be liable as the pupils were not employees and the school was not directly or vicariously liable for their acts. Today, the school would be liable if it failed to have rules prohibiting pupils from engaging in homophobic abuse and/or failed to take effective disciplinary action against pupils who violated such rules.

Victimisation

As an alternative to harassment, an employee might be subjected to other forms of adverse treatment because he or she has brought a discrimination claim against the employer, or has been involved in such proceedings. Under s. 27 EqA, special rules apply to this situation as the employee will be the victim of unlawful victimisation. Section 27 provides that it is unlawful to subject a person to a detriment because he or she has done a protected act. Protected acts include bringing proceedings under the EqA, or giving evidence or information in connection with proceedings under the Act. A detriment excludes harassment as this is still covered by s. 26, even though the reason for it was that the employee has brought a tribunal claim. However, it would include, as examples, moving an employee to a new job or place of work, refusing access to training or other benefits, demotion or a refusal to consider that employee as a candidate for promotion.

Documenting the law

It is clear from the above that an employer will incur legal liability if it does not have policies and rules in place to protect its employees from unlawful harassment. Similarly (as discussed in Chapter 3), an employer may be in breach of the duty to maintain trust and confidence if it fails to protect employees from bullying, even though such conduct may not amount to unlawful harassment. Therefore, all employers should adopt rules and procedures designed to protect employees from bullying or unlawful harassment. The following policy provides an example of how appropriate rules and procedures can be drafted.

L CO. LTD
COMPANY POLICY ON BULLYING AND HARASSMENT

As an equal opportunities employer the company believes that all it employees should be treated, and should treat each other, in ways that recognise the right of the individual to be treated with respect and the dignity at the workplace.

The purpose of this policy is to explain to employees the types of behaviour that constitute bullying and/or harassment and this includes acts which are rendered unlawful by the Equality Act 2010. The company will not tolerate such behaviour and any employee guilty of it will be committing a disciplinary offence which, in certain circumstances, will constitute gross misconduct warranting instant dismissal.

This policy sets out the procedures that an employee should follow if he or she believes that she is the victim of bullying or harassment.

WHAT IS BULLYING OR HARASSMENT?

Bullying or harassment is unwelcome and unwanted behaviour that violates an individual's dignity or creates an intimidating, humiliating or offensive environment. It often involves an abuse of power or position and may be a single event, sporadic events or a continuing process. Bullying or harassment ranges from apparently insignificant acts or omissions through to verbal or physical violence. It impacts on an individual's work and/or social life. Individuals can feel uncomfortable, unsafe, frightened or embarrassed.

Examples of bullying or harassment include:

✦ shouting at or humiliating an individual in front of others;

✦ using sarcasm or aggression against an individual employee because of a perception that that employee has failed properly to perform his or her job function;

✦ spreading malicious rumours;

✦ blaming one person when there is a common problem or for something which others 'get away with';

✦ unfair allocation of work type or work load;

✦ adverse comments or 'jokes', for example, about a person's gender, race or religion, physical appearance, disability, family or other issues not connected to working tasks;

✦ excluding a colleague from activities or conversation unnecessarily;

✦ refusing, unreasonably, to communicate with others;

✦ undermining a competent individual by overloading and constant criticism;

✦ blocking promotion or training opportunities;

✦ putting pressure on a colleague to 'fit in' with others or to victimise another colleague;

✦ sending offensive emails or leaving offensive literature around;

✦ copying memos or emails that are critical about someone to others who do not need to know; or

✦ using gender stereotypes to demean or ridicule colleagues, for example 'women should stay at home and look after children' or 'men cannot multi-task'.

This is not an exhaustive list but it does provide major examples.

WHAT IS UNLAWFUL DISCRIMINATORY HARASSMENT?

The Equality Act 2010 protects individuals with specific characteristics from discrimination. Based on these protected characteristics the following types of harassment, which may involve one or more of the acts specified above, are unlawful.

Racial harassment

This is unwanted behaviour based on race, ethnic or national origin, nationality (including citizenship) or colour. This includes subjecting individuals of different racial groups to verbal abuse or physical violence, and making racist comments or 'jokes' about people's origins and backgrounds.

Religious harassment

This is unwanted behaviour based on religious beliefs or practices, including non-belief. This may take many forms including ridiculing items worn for religious reasons, denigrating cultural customs and dismissive treatment of requests for holidays for religious or cultural festivals, or derisory comments against an individual's beliefs or non-religious beliefs such as atheism or humanism.

Sexual harassment

This is unwanted behaviour of a sexual nature, or harassment on grounds of someone's gender. It includes unwanted attention of a sexual nature that denigrates or ridicules or is intimidating. This may be physical, ranging from unwanted touching, groping or the invasion of personal space to sexual assault, rape or indecent exposure. Sexual harassment can be verbal and may include unwanted personal comments or sexual slurs, belittling, suggestive, lewd or abusive remarks, explicit 'jokes' or innuendo, and compromising invitations, including demands for sexual favours. Examples of non-verbal sexual harassment include: suggestive looks, leering, explicit gestures, sending sexually explicit emails or the display of pornographic material on Company equipment or premises.

Acts of same sex sexual harassment, through any of the above forms of behaviour, are similarly unlawful.

Sexual orientation harassment

This is akin to sexual harassment and constitutes unwanted behaviour based on known or presumed sexual orientation whether gay, lesbian, bi-sexual or heterosexual. It is also unlawful to harass a person because he or she is in a civil partnership.

Harassment on the grounds of gender identity

This is unwanted behaviour directed at women or men who are known or assumed to have undergone gender reassignment treatment, or are living in a different gender than their birth gender, or are for some reason viewed as transgendered men or women. This could include breaching the confidentiality of someone who has undergone gender reassignment treatment, inappropriate exclusion of a transgendered man or woman from toilet facilities for their acquired gender, derogatory comments or intrusive questioning.

Disability harassment

This is unwanted behaviour based on disability, impairment or additional need. Such behaviour may include comments that are patronising or objectionable to the recipient or which creates an intimidating, hostile or offensive environment for disabled people.

Age harassment

This is unwanted behaviour based on known or presumed age. Such behaviour may include comments that are patronising or objectionable such as name-calling, stereotyping, derogatory comments, inappropriate reference to age, refusal to carry out management instructions because of a manager's age and exclusion of an individual from social events or meetings because of that person's age.

Associative and perceptive harassment

It is unlawful to engage in any of the abovementioned acts against an employee because that person associates with a colleague who possesses any of the above characteristics which are protected by the Equality Act. For example, a white male heterosexual employee is harassed because he befriends or defends another colleague who is black, or is a woman and/or is gay or lesbian. Similarly, it is unlawful to harass an employee because that employee is wrongly perceived to be, for example, gay or transgendered.

Third-party harassment

It may be that an employee is subjected to bullying or harassment not by a colleague but by a third party on the company's premises such as a customer or contractor. Should any employee be subjected to such bullying or harassment by a third party it is vital that the employee reports the matter as soon as is reasonably practicable to his or her line manager. This is so that the company can take appropriate steps to protect that employee from any further bullying or harassment from that third party.

PROCEDURE FOR DEALING WITH COMPLAINTS OF BULLYING OR HARASSMENT

(a) It may be possible for, or thought appropriate by, an employee who perceives himself or herself to be the victim of bullying or harassment to seek to resolve the matter in an informal manner. This can be achieved by arranging a meeting with the colleague or manager perceived to be acting in a bullying or harassing manner to discuss and seek to resolve the issues involved. At such a meeting both parties should be permitted to be accompanied by another colleague or a trade union representative.

(b) If an employee does not wish to pursue the matter informally because the employee believes that informal resolution will not work, or that an informal meeting could result in further acts of bullying or harassment, the employee should raise the matter with a relevant line manager through making a formal written complaint.

(c) Normally, this complaint will be presented to the employee's own line manager unless that person is the object of the employee's complaint or is believed to be complicit in the bullying or harassment that employee is complaining of. In such circumstances, the complaint should be presented to another or more senior line manager who is not believed to be involved in the behaviour which is the subject of the complaint.

(d) On receipt of a formal complaint, the relevant line manager should undertake an investigation to determine whether disciplinary proceedings should be taken against the employee(s) or manager(s) complained of. If it is decided to take disciplinary proceedings then the Company's normal disciplinary procedures will be invoked.

(e) If the employee presenting the complaint believes that the relevant line manger has wrongly refused to carry out an investigation or to instigate disciplinary proceedings then that employee should invoke the Company's normal grievance procedures.

(f) Where disciplinary proceedings do take place and an employee or manager is found guilty of bullying or harassment then the normal disciplinary penalties will apply. These range from the provision of a formal warning through to suspension or dismissal for gross misconduct. An employee or manager will be dismissed if, in breach of previous formal warnings, that person persists in acts of bullying or harassment. Alternatively, a very serious single act of harassment, such as a physical assault, may constitute gross misconduct warranting instant dismissal.

Presenting a discrimination claim

Often the most difficult part of presenting a discrimination claim will be providing the tribunal with evidence that discrimination has taken place. However, this will not always be the case. For example, sometimes an act will be overtly discriminatory, even though there was no discriminatory intent, as was the case in *James* v. *Eastleigh BC*, discussed above. Or it may be that a job advertisement contains discriminatory criteria, or an employer adopts a PCP which constitutes indirect discrimination. If the claimant was refused employment after an interview it may be that questions which suggest discriminatory attitudes were asked in the interview. However, perhaps ironically, it is in cases of the most serious form of discrimination, that is, where an actual or prospective employer intends to discriminate, that no concrete evidence of discrimination may exist. This will be because the employer was too clever to say or put anything in writing which could provide the claimant with evidence that she or he had been the victim of discrimination.

There are formal means available to claimants to assist them in providing evidence that discrimination has taken place. One of these means is the discrimination questionnaire. Under s. 138 EqA, statutory questionnaires are available for claimants to complete, and which employers can be asked to respond to. These questionnaires are designed to assist claimants in obtaining evidence that they have been subjected to discriminatory acts. It is not compulsory for a respondent to answer the questions which are posed, but if the respondent refuses to answer questions, or gives evasive or equivocal answers, then, under s. 138(4), tribunals are empowered to infer facts as a result.

Handy tip: These questionnaires can be accessed at: http://www.homeoffice.gov.uk/ publications/equalities/equality-act-publications/complaints-Equality-Act/

Section 136 EqA also has an important role to play in assisting the claimant to prove discrimination. Under this section, the **burden of proof** formally shifts to the employer where the evidence enables the tribunal to draw **inferences of discrimination**. Where this is the case, the tribunal must find discrimination to be proven if the employer is not able to provide an adequate explanation of its decisions or actions by reference to non-discriminatory factors. An example of a situation where the inference of discrimination can be drawn is where a successful applicant for a job or a promotion is less well-qualified and/or experienced than the claimant.

However, the employer might be able to show that the decision not to appoint the applicant was taken for grounds that are not discriminatory, such as the applicant's perceived personality and/or ability to fit in with an existing team of colleagues. Indeed, it is the fact that subjective value-judgements are so inherently connected to employers' decisions over matters such as recruitment and promotion that makes a direct discrimination claim so hard to win.

Case Summary

A case from the world of sport, *Singh* v. *The Football Association Ltd, The Football League Ltd & Others* (2001) ET Case Number 5203593/99, provides an example of how a discrimination claim may succeed as a result of a tribunal drawing inferences of discrimination. Mr Singh complained that he was the victim of direct race discrimination when he was withdrawn from the Football League's 'National List' of referees at the end of the 1998/99 season and thus ceased to be eligible to referee professional football matches. At this time he was the only person of Asian ethnic origin on the list. The reason given for the decision not to re-appoint him was that there had been a marked deterioration in his position on the merit list over the previous three years. However, there was no evidence to support the idea that there had been any such deterioration in Singh's performance.

The tribunal decided that there was evidence that individual respondents in this particular case were influenced by a stereotypical assumption that the applicant could never be a top-performing referee by virtue of his ethnic origin. The relevant evidence included a comment by one of the individual respondents, who was Secretary of the National Review Board established to ensure consistency of refereeing, that 'We don't want people like him [Mr Singh] in the PL [Premier League]'. This comment was viewed as a race-specific statement by the tribunal and, as such, formed part of the evidence that led to the tribunal deciding that there had been a sustained 'whispering campaign' against Singh from which the inference of racism could be drawn. Consequently, though Singh was unable to prove that his ethnic origin was the specific reason for his removal from the National List, the tribunal accepted his complaint of direct race discrimination on the basis that a hypothetical white referee, with the same performance record as Singh, would not have been removed from the 'National List'.

Remedies

As is typically the case with tribunal claims, under s. 123 EqA a claimant has three months from the date of the act complained of to present a claim to a tribunal. The only exception to this will be the limited circumstances in which a tribunal will decide that it is just and equitable to hear a claim presented outside of this period.

Section 124, which is largely based on the provisions in previous discrimination legislation, provides for three remedies that a tribunal may award to a successful claimant.

1. declarations stating that claimants have been the victims of unlawful discrimination, harassment or victimisation;

2. compensation;

3. recommendations.

Compensation

Unlawful discrimination is a statutory tort and therefore compensation is calculated in the same way that damages are calculated for the victim of a common law tort. Compensation can cover injury to feelings as well as financial loss, and there is no statutory cap on the sum of compensation that can be awarded. Moreover, in the case of intentional discrimination the sum of compensation can be increased to reflect the discriminatory motives on the respondent's part. On the other hand, damages may not reflect much more than the claimant's financial loss in cases of unintentional indirect discrimination. The statistics provided in this chapter identify the average awards of compensation for each type of discrimination claim.

In *Vento* v. *Chief Constable of West Yorkshire* [2003] ICR 318, the Court of Appeal considered the bases for determining the amount of compensation a successful claimant should receive. Vento joined the respondent's police force as a probationary officer at the age of 28, when she was married with three children. Two years later her marriage began to break down, and at the same time incidents occurred at work where fellow police

Case Summary

officers criticised her conduct, her personal life and her character in an unwarranted, aggressive and demoralising manner. She became clinically depressed but tried to continue. Further discrimination resulted in suicidal impulses, and she was subsequently dismissed from the force for alleged lack of honesty and performance.

Her complaint of sex discrimination against the Chief Constable was upheld by an employment tribunal and, in a remedies hearing, the tribunal concluded that the applicant would have completed her probation and qualified as a police officer and that she would have had a 75% chance of working in the force for the rest of her career. The applicant was awarded £165,829 for loss of future earnings, £65,000, including £15,000 aggravated damages, for non-pecuniary loss for injury to feelings, and £9,000 for psychiatric damage. The Court of Appeal upheld the compensation that the tribunal awarded to her for the loss of her career and for psychiatric injury. However, the court decided that the award for injury to feelings was excessively high and reduced it to £18,000 for injury to feelings and £5,000 for aggravated damages. The court ruled that three broad bands of compensation for injury to feelings could be identified:

1. between £15,000 and £25,000 for the most serious cases involving a lengthy campaign of discriminatory harassment;

2. between £5,000 and £15,000 for serious cases not meriting an award in the highest band;

3. between £500 and £5,000 for less serious cases, such as an isolated or one-off act of discrimination.

This judgment can be considered as providing guidelines for calculating compensation for non-pecuniary loss in the form of injury to feelings. It may be, however, that the specific monetary amounts are now out of date given that the case was decided in December 2002. It should also be noted that compensation for injury to feelings should not be understood as being capped at £25,000. The court explained that there should be considerable flexibility within each band allowing tribunals to fix what they determined to be fair, reasonable and just compensation in the particular circumstances of the case. There should be similar flexibility in exceptionally serious cases to allow compensation in excess of £25,000 to be awarded. It should also be understood that calculating a sum by way of aggravated damages should be done separately to calculating the sum of compensation for injury to feelings.

Recommendations

Tribunals also have the discretion to make a **recommendation** as to the action(s) that the respondent should take to remove or reduce the effects of the discrimination. The tribunal must set a time period during which such steps will be taken, and if the respondent fails to comply with the recommendation during this period then the compensation granted to the claimant may be increased. An example of such a recommendation would be for an employer to remove or amend a provision, criterion or practice (PCP) which the tribunal has found to constitute indirect discrimination. Where the claimant has been dismissed or has resigned from a job then, if this is consistent with the claimant's wishes, the tribunal can recommend that the claimant is reinstated. One difference between s. 124 EqA and the old legislation is that a recommendation can benefit the wider workforce as well as, or instead of, the claimant. For example, the removal of a PCP will not benefit a claimant who has left a job and has no desire to return to it. Nevertheless, a recommendation that the PCP be terminated can now still be made by the tribunal.

People in the law

This interview is with **Wendy Comerford**, who is a law graduate from the University of Portsmouth and qualified as a solicitor in May 2009. Wendy has since specialised in employment litigation including discrimination cases. Wendy worked and trained at a firm in Mayfair for six years, and now works for a large legal expenses company in Croydon.

Q1. The Equality Act 2010 sets out a common definition of unlawful discrimination that applies to nine protected characteristics. In which of these have you been involved with as a practitioner? Age, disability, pregnancy and maternity, race, religion or belief and sex.

Q2. From general observation as a practitioner, would you say that some types of discrimination are claimed more frequently than others? If so, could you please specify which the more common claims are? In my experience, the most common claims are concerned with age, disability and sex discrimination. Examples of my current files include indirect disability discrimination, a joint claim of direct age and direct sex discrimination and a joint claim of indirect sex, pregnancy and maternity discrimination.

Q3. Most claims you have handled are on behalf of the employer respondent. Why do employers normally contest claims? Is it a matter of lack of proof by the claimant or on the basis of legal argument as to how the legislation should be interpreted, or is it often a mixture of both? Most respondents deny discriminatory conduct outright. Many of the ET1 claim forms submitted by claimants do not particularise the discriminatory acts and, therefore, it is difficult for claimants to prove their claims. My submissions usually quote the relevant sections of the Equality Act 2010 and apply these to the facts of the case to show that the claimant was not discriminated against, or that the legislation does not protect the claimant from that particular conduct. For example, in one case the claimant attempted to argue unlawful discrimination when the dismissal was for being drunk.

Indeed, some claimants use the trick of adding on a discrimination claim to bolster their schedules of loss. That way they seek to justify throwing in a high-settlement proposal in the hope of being paid more than they would expect if they had just been claiming unfair dismissal.

Q4. Employers can justify indirect discrimination – have they sought to do so in any of the claims you have handled? If so, is it possible to give some brief details of arguments used by way of justification? I have not argued justification in indirect discrimination cases. However, I have a few clients who apply a requirement that a nurse/carer needs to be female to deal with sensitive caring requirements of female residents. I have not yet had a claim in relation to this, but I firmly believe that such a requirement for having a female carer will be considered to be a genuine occupational requirement and a proportionate means of meeting a legitimate aim. Therefore any claim for direct sex discrimination is likely to be unsuccessful.

In terms of disability discrimination, clients have dismissed employees who have been, or will be, absent for a long time due to ill-health as a result of their disability. To defeat both disability discrimination and unfair dismissal claims, we have needed to demonstrate that, prior to the dismissal, we acted reasonably and fairly, both in treating that reason as a sufficient reason to dismiss and in the dismissal procedure adopted. The first port of call was to seek consent for a medical report to gauge the prognosis of the employee's health and capabilities and then go through an incapacity procedure to dismiss. This usually includes several meetings to discuss the medical report and possible reasonable adjustments.

If a disabled employee is dismissed simply because of a poor attendance record and the employer did not go through a proper incapacity procedure to show the dismissal was a proportionate means of achieving a legitimate aim, that is, that it was objectively justified, then the prospects of successfully defending the claim will be very low. There is a defence that the employer did not know that the employee was disabled, and could not reasonably be expected to know that the employee had a disability. The onus is on what can be 'reasonably expected' of the employer, as it is not a defence simply to assert ignorance.

Q5. You were involved in age discrimination brought my Margaret Keane. In so far as it is permissible to do so, are you able to provide any insights into why employers contested her claims and the attitudes of the tribunals to the number of claims she brought? I was a trainee at the time and qualified and left the firm before this case got to appeal stage. We acted for some of the respondents. Obviously, for ethical reasons I am limited in what I can say. The EAT upheld the ET's finding that the claimant did not suffer age discrimination because her applications were not genuine.

The claimant was a 50-year-old experienced accountant. The claimant applied for numerous jobs that she was overqualified to do. When her applications were rejected she claimed age discrimination, that is, that she claimed she was refused employment because she was deemed too old for the job. If I remember rightly, her date of birth was not even included on her CV. The respondents argued that her claims were misconceived and a complete abuse of process. She was ordered to pay costs of several thousand pounds.

At the EAT stage, the EAT stated that discrimination required less favourable treatment and that indirect discrimination, the job advert being the provision, criterion or practice, required the person to suffer a disadvantage or detriment. The EAT held that the claimant made the applications in bad

faith and therefore was not genuinely interested in the jobs so she could not have suffered a detriment. Therefore, the EAT supported the respondents' arguments that her applications for the jobs were made with an ulterior motive.

Q6. Do you have any personal opinions on what she did? For example, do you think she was exploiting the law in a way that some might see this as an abuse of the process? She was most definitely exploiting the law. As a general rule, a claimant cannot claim unfair dismissal unless they have over 12 (now 24) months' service. It is therefore common to stick on a discrimination claim for good measure which will permit them to litigate. Even if claimants can claim unfair dismissal, a discrimination claim is complex and harder to defend and therefore more likely to raise the compensation bar and put them in good stead to negotiate a settlement. Eighty per cent of my claims end in a financial settlement without going to a hearing so what have claimants got to lose by having a go!

I had a case recently in which the claimant was claiming age discrimination for not being selected for a job. I put forward the argument that the claimant grossly overreacted to being rejected for the job in an attempt to substantiate his claim for age discrimination. I was successful in having this claim struck out and costs awarded. It turns out that he was a serial litigant and had made over 30 claims in the past – a complete abuse of the process.

In the *Keane* case I believe that she made a lot of money from previous settlements of similar claims against other companies because (i) they didn't want the publicity, and/or (ii) they did not have the financial resources to fund a discrimination claim, and/or (iii) they just wanted to get rid of the hassle. Either way she was quids in at the start. When Keane's claim got to the EAT stage, she was ordered to pay costs and lost all the money she made. The phrase 'quit whilst you are ahead' came to mind.

Equal pay

In the context of sex discrimination another form of discrimination that can occur is with regard to an individual's salary or wage and other contractual conditions relating to remuneration. Historically, such discrimination was prohibited not by the Sex Discrimination Act 1975 but by the Equal Pay Act 1970. Such discrimination has also always been contrary to European treaties. The current provision is to be found in Article 157 of the Treaty on the Functioning of the European Union (TFEU), which was formerly Article 141 of the EC Treaty, and provides for the right of equal pay for work of **equal value**. This Article is given detailed implementation by the Equal Treatment Directive, 2006/54. The Equal Pay Act 1970 has been replaced by ss. 64–70 of the EqA. As is generally the case with the provisions of the EqA, an applicant need not be an employee, but may be any individual who has entered into contract to perform work. As a **directly applicable** treaty provision, Article 157 can be relied upon as the basis of a claim in an employment tribunal. Claims can thus be brought under EU law, or under the EqA, or under both. In recent years, in particular, this area of law has been driven by rulings of the ECJ.

One major ruling of the ECJ in the field of equal pay which hugely impacted on member states and their nationals was *Barber* v. *Guardian Royal Exchange Assurance Group* [1990] ICR 616. In this case, the ECJ confirmed that EU equal pay law covered occupational pension schemes. As a result of this ruling, it became necessary for employers to equalise the age at which their male and female employees became eligible to take their occupational pensions. Prior to the ruling it was common for the occupational pension age to be linked to the state pension age. In Britain this meant that women were able to take their occupational pension at the age of 60 whereas men had to wait until they were 65. We have referred to the case of *Bilka-Kaufhaus Gmbh* v. *Weber von Hartz* [1987] ICR 110 in the context of the justification of indirect discrimination. The case itself was actually concerned with the entitlement of part-time workers to join occupational pension schemes. The ECJ ruled that part-timers should have such access unless their exclusion could be objectively justified. In making this ruling the ECJ paved the way for its subsequent ruling in *Barber*.

As well as occupational pension schemes, 'pay' covers all contractual forms of remuneration including sick pay, entitlement to paid holiday, contractual bonuses and redundancy pay.

Key stats

Although equal pay laws have been in existence for almost 40 years, a significant pay gap between the genders continues to exist. A major reason for this is that part-time pay rates are lower than full-time pay rates, but 42% of jobs done by women are part-time in comparison with 12% for men. The reason for this is that it is more likely that women will take on the role of carers, both for children and elderly relatives, and are only able to work on a part-time basis. Caring for children also often involves women in taking career breaks which adversely affect their opportunities for promotion. Certainly, there still appears to be a glass ceiling which operates as an obstacle to women obtaining positions such as senior executives of major corporations. Another major cause of the gender pay gap is that the job market remains segregated in that there are certain jobs that are predominantly undertaken by women where pay rates always have been and remain low. The way that the law operates also contributes to the gender pay gap, as employers may be able to justify pay differentials that operate to the benefit of men even though they arise through indirect discrimination against women.

The 2011 figures reveal that the average full-time man in work earned £16.44 an hour, whereas the female equivalent earned £14.00. This means that the average woman receives only around 85 pence for every £1 earned by the average man. Although more women than men work part-time, there is still a gender pay gap in favour of male part-timers. In 2011, the average part-time man earned £11.85 an hour whereas the female equivalent earned £10.77.

The overall comparison of both full-time and part-time men and women shows a pay gap of 18.6%. These figures for 2011 represent a small reduction in the size of the pay gap compared with the figures for 2010. However, given that the fall in the pay gap on a year-to-year basis remains very small, it would appear that it will take many more decades before the pay gap disappears.

Source: Office of National Statistics Annual Survey of Hours and Earnings 2011, http://data.gov.uk/dataset/annual_survey_of_hours_and_earnings

Identifying a comparator

In order to being an equal pay claim, s. 64(1) EqA requires the claimant to use a comparator who must be of the opposite sex, and is a real, rather than hypothetical, person. For reasons identified above, claimants will normally be women and this section of the chapter will proceed on that basis. As originally established by the ECJ in *Macarthys Ltd v. Smith* [1980] IRLR 210, the claimant can use a male predecessor as a comparator where the predecessor was earning a higher rate of pay. In *Macarthys*, a woman replaced a man but, despite the fact that she was doing the same job, she was paid £10 less a week than he had received. After a **preliminary ruling** by the ECJ it was decided by the Court of Appeal that she was entitled to same rate of pay.

Under s. 79 EqA, the comparator must be employed by the same employer, or an associated employer, at the same establishment, or at different establishments at which common terms and conditions of employment are observed. An associated employer is one controlled by, or which controls, the comparator's company or is controlled by the same company which controls the claimant's company. An example of employees, who are employed under common terms of employment, would be employees who have different jobs at different workplaces but whose terms and conditions are determined by the same collective agreement entered into between an employer and a trade union.

The decision of the EAT in *City of Edinburgh Council v. Wilkinson* [2010] IRLR 756 has broadened the meaning of same establishment for the purposes of equal pay law. The EAT decided all the employees employed by the council were employed at the same establishment irrespective of the different geographical locations at which they were employed. This meant that claimants working in schools, libraries and hostels could compare themselves with gardeners, grave-diggers and refuse workers. As council employees, they were all employed at the same establishment. This decision means that it is of much less practical importance to ascertain whether employees of the same employer who have different workplaces are employed under common terms of employment.

However, on the basis of Article 157 TFEU, employees of *different* employers may be able to use each other as comparators if they are employed under common terms of employment. This because of the ECJ's ruling in *Defrenne v. Sabena* [1976] ICR 672 that employees in the same service can make equal pay comparisons. In *Lawrence v. Regent Office Care Ltd* [2003] ICR 1092, the ECJ clarified that this means that a comparison can be made between employees of different employers where any pay differential can be attributable to a single source such as a national collective agreement covering all employees in a particular occupation.

An example of this is provided by the case of *South Ayrshire Council* v. *Morton* [2002] ICR 956, in which primary school head teachers in Scotland claimed equal pay with secondary school head teachers. The salary scales for both sets of teachers were determined by the same negotiating body, which, on the employers' side, consisted of different local education authorities. It was held that the education authorities constituted a single service and therefore the pay comparison could be made.

It should be appreciated that the decision in *Morton* is of less significance than once would have been the case. This is because it is common today, even where there is national collective bargaining covering different employers in the same sector, for employers to reserve the right to vary pay rates in their own companies or organisations. For example, in *Armstrong* v. *Newcastle upon Tyne Hospital Trust* [2006] IRLR 124, female domestic workers employed in one hospital trust sought to compare their pay with male porters in a different hospital trust. The porters received bonus payments which were not given to the domestic workers. It was held that, despite the fact they were all NHS employees, each trust was able to negotiate its own bonus schemes and therefore the workers were not employed by a single service within the meaning of EU law.

The routes to equal pay

A claimant can present an equal pay claim on the basis that she is employed on **like work** with the comparator, or her work has been rated as being of equal value to his. Most importantly in practice, the claimant will be employed on different work to that undertaken by the male comparator but she will be able to show that her work is of an **equal value** to the employer. Where the claim succeeds, a tribunal will insert a sex equality clause into the claimant's contract. Under s. 129 EqA, an equal pay claim can be presented to an employment tribunal during the employment or no later than six months from the date the claimant leaves that employment. However, *in Birmingham City Council* v *Abdullah* (24 October 2012) the SC held that, as an equal pay claim is also a claim for breach of contract, if a statutory claim cannot be heard by a tribunal because it is out of time, the claimant still has the normal six years to bring a contract claim in a civil court. This decision opens the door for a number of equal pay claims to be brought by women who left their jobs during the six years prior to the date of the decision. Where the claim succeeds a tribunal will insert a sex equality clause into the claimant's contract. Under s. 66 EqA, the claimant will have the right to have a term in her contract modified so that it is the same as the equivalent term in the contract of the male comparator. Alternatively, if there is a term in his contract, which is not in her contract, then the appropriate term will be incorporated into her contract.

Like work

Under s. 65(1) EqA like work is defined as work which is the same, or broadly similar in nature, to that undertaken by the comparator, and there are no differences of practical importance in relation to the terms and conditions of employment. In *Capper Pass Ltd* v. *Lawton* [1977] ICR 83, the EAT ruled that tribunals should not be required to undertake too minute an examination of the two jobs, or be constrained to find that work is not like work merely because of insubstantial differences. Lawton was employed by the company as the only cook in a kitchen where lunches were prepared daily for the directors and their guests. She worked a 40-hour week and was responsible to the catering manager. Two assistant male chefs worked under a head chef in the employees' canteen where 350 meals a day were prepared. They worked a 40-hour week, five and a half hours' overtime and one Saturday in three. They deputised for the head chef when required. The EAT upheld the tribunal's finding that her work was of a broadly similar nature to that undertaken by the male chefs.

Case Summary

As held in *Shields* v. *Coomes (Holdings) Ltd* [1978] ICR 1159, in ascertaining whether there are differences between the jobs it is necessary to examine what the jobs involve in practice rather than focusing on differences that may be contained in job descriptions or employment contracts. In this case, a female employee worked in a South London betting shop where she was paid less than male employees similarly so employed. The reason given by the employer for the pay differentials was that the men acted partly as security guards, as deterrents to trouble expected in that area and as carriers of cash. In fact there had never been any trouble at that particular shop. The Court of Appeal held that the differences in the contractual obligations of the two sexes were irrelevant unless these led to actual and not infrequent differences in practice, which they did not in this case. In reality, the pay differentials were based on sex, and Shields was entitled to equal pay.

Case Summary

The case of *Eaton and Nuttall* [1977] ICR 272 illustrates where there will be differences of practical importance between the work done by the claimant and that done by her chosen comparator. Nuttall was a production scheduler who was responsible for ordering supplies of 2,400 items up to a value of £2.50 each, and she earned £45.38 a week. A male production scheduler in the same department looked after 1,200 items worth between £5 and £1,000, and earned £51.88 a week. It was held that he had extra responsibilities, as if he made an error this had more serious financial consequences for the company than would be the case if Nuttall made an error. Therefore the claimant and her comparator were not engaged on like work.

Case Summary

The EAT's reasoning, in *Waddington* v. *Leicester Council for Voluntary Service* [1977] IRLR 32, shows how this approach can work to the detriment of a claimant. Waddington was a female play-leader and was senior to her comparator, a male play-leader, but was paid less than he was. It was held that if, in practice, she did undertake broader responsibilities then she would not be employed on like work with the male play-leader and could not argue that she was legally entitled to the same rate of pay.

Today, such a decision could not be reached as the claimant will be able to show that, even if she is not employed on like work with the male comparator, her work is, at the very least, of an equal value to his and therefore she is entitled to the same rate of pay. It was because the original Equal Pay Act of 1970 did not provide for work of equal value claims that the ECJ decided in, *Commission of the European Communities* v. *UK* [1982] ICR 578, that the 1970 Act did not conform to the requirements of the EU Treaty. The original Equal Pay Act was subsequently amended to permit equal value claims in the way that is detailed below.

You be the judge

Q: In the following two situations do you think A, a woman, is employed on like work with B, a man, and is therefore entitled to equal pay?

(a) A is employed as a fitness instructor by a gymnasium. Her hours of work are from 9.00 a.m. until 6.00 p.m. Her rate of pay is £8 an hour. B is also employed as a fitness instructor. His hours of work are from 1.00 p.m. until 11.00 p.m. and his rate of pay is £10 an hour. Both A and B work weekends on a rota basis.

(b) A is employed as a part-time fitness instructor at a gymnasium. Her hours of work are from 9.00 a.m. until 1.00 p.m. Her rate of pay is £7 an hour. B is also employed as a fitness instructor. His hours of work are from 9.00 a.m. until 6.00 p.m. and his rate of pay is £10 an hour. Both A and B are employed for five days a week from Monday until Friday.

A: In both situations A should be regarded as employed on like work with B and should be entitled to the same hourly rate of pay.

In *Electrolux* v. *Hutchinson* [1977] ICR 252, the EAT decided that working different hours does not constitute a difference of practical importance where employees do identical work. Workers may be entitled to a shift premium for working anti-social hours, such as evenings or nights, but this does not justify them being paid a higher basic rate of pay.

As explained below, it was decided in *Jenkins* v. *Kingsgate* that part-time workers are employed on like work with full-timers where the work is the same. Full-timers may be entitled to a higher hourly rate where they are genuinely more productive or efficient than part-timers, but it is difficult to see how this would be the case in situation (b).

Work rated as equivalent

Under the original Equal Pay Act it was provided that if an employer had carried out a job evaluation study (JES) then a woman was entitled to equal pay if the job evaluation had rated her job as being of equal value to the different job done by her male comparator. The problem with this provision is that equal value claims can only be brought if an employer has chosen to undertake job evaluation. The law did not and, indeed, does not require an employer to carry out job evaluation. The current provisions are to be found in s. 65(1)(b) EqA.

Equal value

Section 65(1)(c) EqA enables a woman to present an equal pay claim on the basis that, although the job that she does is different to that done by the male comparator, it is of an equal value to the employer. Under s. 65(6), work is of equal value if it is equal to the comparator's work in terms of the demands made on the claimant by reference to factors such as effort, skill and decision making.

There is no single method of job evaluation, but it does require an objective analysis of different jobs and a scoring system to ascertain if the different jobs are of an equal value to the employer. The case of *Hayward* v. *Cammell Laird Shipbuilders Ltd* [1985] 1CR 171 was the first case to be decided on the basis that different jobs were of equal value. The claimant was a female canteen assistant employed in a shipyard. She claimed she was doing work of equal value to male comparators who were shipyard workers and were paid at a higher rate as they were deemed to be skilled tradesmen, whereas she was deemed to be unskilled. An expert undertook a JES under the headings of physical demands, environmental demands, planning and decision making, skill and knowledge required, and responsibility. He assessed the demands of the jobs as low, moderate or

Case Summary

high. He concluded that, as the overall score awarded to the applicant's job was the same as that awarded to the shipyard workers, her job was of an equal value to theirs.

A potential bar to an equal value claim is where, for example, an employer employs its workers on two different types of jobs – Grade A and Grade B. Workers of both sexes are employed on both grades but the majority employed on Grade A are men whereas the majority employed on Grade B are women. Workers on Grade A enjoy a higher rate of pay than workers on Grade B. However, as women on Grade B are employed on like work with men on Grade B can they bring an equal value claim using men employed on Grade A as comparators? This was the issue that the House of Lords had to decide in *Pickstone* v. *Freemans Plc* [1988] IRLR 357. The Law Lords held that a woman may present an equal value claim even if she is employed on like work with a man. At the time this was a very important decision as, had the Law Lords ruled to the contrary, it would have been possible for employers to establish different job grades on different rates of pay and, in order to pre-empt the possibility of equal value claims, employ workers of both sexes on all job grades but in a context where the majority of workers on the higher paid grades were men.

The procedure for equal value claims

Under Schedule 6 to the Employment Tribunals (Constitution and Rules of Procedure) Regulations 2004, SI 2004/1861, the procedure for equal value claims normally consists of three stages.

Stage one will consist of an initial hearing to consider whether there is a sound basis to the equal value claim. A claim will fail at this stage if there are no reasonable grounds for regarding the two jobs as being of equal value, and therefore the claim has no real prospects of success. An employer may be able to defeat a claim by establishing that it has already carried out a valid JES, which has rated the claimant's job as being of a lower value to that undertaken by the comparator. Alternatively, the employer may successfully plead the **material factor** defence, which is discussed below.

It should be noted that the claimant cannot challenge the results of the JES undertaken by the employer unless it can be shown to be insufficiently objective and analytical, or it is tainted by discriminatory factors. For example, in *Inkersole* v. *Tungstone Batteries Ltd* ET Case No. 21349/90, female laundry workers claimed equal pay with male fork-lift truck drivers. Both jobs were compared in terms of the training required to the jobs but the women scored less under this heading. This was despite the fact that the drivers received a licence after two days training, whereas the women required considerably more training to learn how to use industrial sewing machines. Therefore, the JES was inherently discriminatory and invalid.

If the tribunal decides that the claim should proceed, it will need to decide whether it should commission a report by an ACAS appointed independent expert, who will conduct a JES and then report back to the tribunal. Tribunals can decide to dispense with a reference to an expert if they believe that the claim is well founded. An example of this would be where there have been previous cases where similar jobs have been found to be of equal value. Alternatively, both parties may have exercised their rights to commission their own job evaluation studies and the tribunal decides that a third report would be superfluous. In this situation the tribunal will hold a second hearing to determine which of the existing reports should be accepted.

If an ACAS expert is appointed there will be a stage two hearing to establish the facts on which the expert should base his report. These facts may be agreed by the parties or

Figure 7.2 Procedure for equal value claims

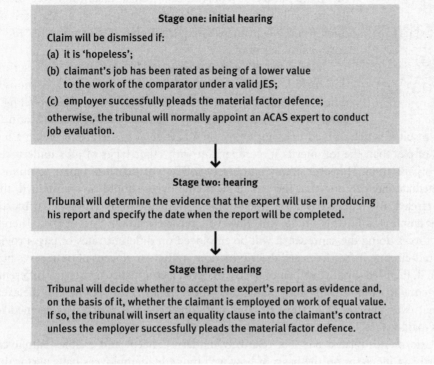

Stage one: initial hearing

Claim will be dismissed if:

(a) it is 'hopeless';

(b) claimant's job has been rated as being of a lower value to the work of the comparator under a valid JES;

(c) employer successfully pleads the material factor defence;

otherwise, the tribunal will normally appoint an ACAS expert to conduct job evaluation.

Stage two: hearing

Tribunal will determine the evidence that the expert will use in producing his report and specify the date when the report will be completed.

Stage three: hearing

Tribunal will decide whether to accept the expert's report as evidence and, on the basis of it, whether the claimant is employed on work of equal value. If so, the tribunal will insert an equality clause into the claimant's contract unless the employer successfully pleads the material factor defence.

determined by the tribunal. The tribunal will also specify the date by which the expert's report must be completed and fix the date for a stage three hearing.

Stage three consists of a final hearing. The tribunal will decide whether or not to accept the expert's report and whether the applicant's claim should succeed. It should be noted that both parties may commission experts to produce their own reports, in which case the tribunal must determine which of these reports it will accept. If the tribunal decides that the claimant's work is of an equal value to the work undertaken by the male comparator then the employer may plead the material factor defence to seek to defeat the claim. This defence can only be pleaded at this final stage if the point was not determined at the stage one hearing.

Figure 7.2, summarises the procedure that will be followed by a tribunal in deciding an equal value claim.

The material factor defence

Prior to the enactment of the Equality Act (EqA) 2010, case law had developed in quite complex ways primarily over the issue as to whether employers could use the material factor defence by justifying direct as well as indirect sex discrimination. Hopefully, the law has been clarified for the future by the new wording which is contained in s. 69. Under this section, a pay differential is permitted, where employees are employed on like work or work of equal value, if the employer can show that the differential is due to a material factor, examples of which are provided below, other than the gender of the

material factor defence will fail if the pay differential is the product of direct discrimination

employees. The material factor defence will fail if the pay differential is the product of direct discrimination. If the claimant can show that the material factor constitutes indirect discrimination then the defence will fail unless the employer can justify it on the basis of the *Bilka-Kaufhaus* principles requiring objective justification and proportionality, see above.

Material factors which are potentially free from sex discrimination include: qualifications; experience; geographical locations with different living costs; performance-related pay and red-circling. The latter arises where an employer has carried out job evaluation and as a result it is determined that employees on a particular grade are receiving a higher rate of pay than the job merits in comparison with other types of jobs undertaken in the organisation. However, many employers will accept that it is unfair to impose an immediate pay cut, and that the pay of such employees should be maintained, that is red-circled, and reduced over a period of time through the withholding of pay increases. New employees on this grade will, however, receive a lower rate of pay. Therefore, employees doing the same work will be employed on different rates of pay. Providing the red-circling is free from sex discrimination, in that employees of both sexes benefit from it, then red-circling will amount to a material factor justifying the pay differentials. Red-circling cannot justify a permanent pay differential, as the idea behind the exercise is that over the course of time all employees on the grade which was deemed to be over-paid will receive the same rate of pay.

Performance-related pay is a relatively modern concept and enables employers to award pay increases on the basis of how well individual employees have performed in their jobs. Performance must be assessed on an objective basis rather than the subjective perceptions of a manager, and the assessment must be free from factors which are inherently discriminatory. For example, the performance of part-time employees should not be assumed to be of a lower value than that of full-timers.

Case Summary

As held in *Leverton* v. *Clwyd County Council* [1989] IRLR 28, the overall value of a contractual package may also constitute a material factor justifying a difference between individual terms in the claimant's contract and that of the male comparator. For example, as in this case, the claimant may be on a lower annual salary but enjoy a better paid holiday entitlement. If this means that the overall contractual packages are of equal value the difference in the annual salary will be permissible.

Where the claimant shows that a pay differential is the product of indirect sex discrimination then the material factor defence will fail unless the material factor can be justified. The following are examples of the approach that tribunals will take. It is useful to note in passing that much of the law in this context is derived from rulings by the ECJ.

Part-time hours

Case Summary

Given the fact that the majority of part-time workers are women it is obvious that paying part-time workers a lower hourly rate of pay than that received by full-time workers will constitute indirect sex discrimination. As illustrated by *Jenkins* v. *Kingsgate Ltd* [1981] IRLR 388, the material factor defence can only be pleaded successfully if full-time working provides benefits to the employer that are not provided by part-timers. For example, in the context of a factory full-timers may be more productive if the machines of part-time workers are idle once part-timers leave work. However, it can be commented that in such a situation it should often be possible for an employer to prevent machines from being under-used by employing part-time workers at different times of the day or night.

As noted above, under the Part Time Workers (Prevention of Less Favourable Treatment) Regulations 2000, SI 2000/1551 discrimination against part-timers with respect to rates of pay is expressly unlawful unless it can be justified objectively. Thus part-time workers of both sexes, employed on like work with full-timers, can claim under these regulations as well as under EqA.

Market forces

Controversially, an employer may be able to justify a pay differential between a woman and a man because it can be argued that market forces justify him being paid at a higher rate. This is controversial because market forces can reflect an inherent gender pay gap where a man negotiates a higher rate of pay in agreeing to accept a new job with a new employer. This may be the case, for example, where the man is headhunted and he is only prepared to move employers if he is given a salary that is higher than the one he already enjoys. Consequently, his pay may be higher than that of female colleagues employed on like work or work of equal value.

Nevertheless, market forces have been capable of justifying pay differentials since the decision of the House of Lords in *Rainey* v. *Gtr Glasgow Health Board* [1985] IRLR 414. In this case there was a shortage of specialist medical practitioners. The health board decided to recruit specialists from the private sector into the Scottish National Health Service In order to do this it had to offer specialists coming from the private sector a higher salary than was enjoyed by practitioners, who were mainly women, already employed on NHS pay rates. It was held that the market forces operating in this situation constituted a material factor justifying the pay differentials.

Case Summary

In the case of *Enderby*, which is explained below, the ECJ agreed that market forces could constitute a material factor. However, the ECJ ruled that it is necessary for national courts to determine, on the basis of the principle of proportionality, whether and to what extent the shortage of candidates for a job constituted an objectively justified economic ground for the difference in pay between that job and another of equal value. There may be other ways, such as the introduction of overtime arrangements, whereby an employer can overcome a shortfall in staff without needing to recruit new employees on higher pay to that enjoyed by existing employees engaged in the relevant work.

Moreover, the national court should ensure that a pay differential attributed to permissible marker forces is no greater than what the relevant market forces demand. For example, to induce a man to move jobs the prospective employer may need to offer him a salary which is equal to or slightly higher than the one he is already receiving. Consequently, he earns a higher salary than female colleagues who were already employed in his new company. If, however, he is now receiving a much higher salary than he was previously earning, it may prove impossible to justify this pay differential by reference to market forces.

Collective bargaining and pay scales

Later we examine **collective bargaining** processes between employers and trade unions which result in **collective agreements** that constitute a source of terms in the employment contracts of individual employees (see Chapter 8). Negotiating rates of pay is a major purpose of collective bargaining, and pay differentials between workers employed on work of equal value may be the product of collective bargaining where unions have been unable to negotiate the same pay rates for workers employed on different jobs. Originally, case law operated on the basis that collective agreements resulting in different pay scales constituted material factors justifying pay differentials.

However, this approach is no longer permitted as a result of the ECJ ruling in *Enderby* v. *Frenchay Health Authority* [1994] ICR 112. In this case, as a result of collective bargaining agreements negotiated between National Health Service management and trade unions, speech therapists, pharmacists and clinical psychologists were given distinct pay structures with speech therapists, a predominantly female profession, being the lowest paid. The claimant, a woman speech therapist employed by a health authority, brought proceedings against the health authority claiming equal pay with two male comparators, a clinical psychologist and a pharmacist also employed by the health authority, on the ground that she was employed on work of equal value. The ECJ ruled that where significant statistics disclosed an appreciable difference in pay between two jobs of equal value, one of which was carried out almost exclusively by women and the other predominantly by men, EU law required the employer to show that that difference was based on objectively justified factors unrelated to any discrimination on grounds of sex. The fact that the different rates of pay were arrived at by collective bargaining processes did not preclude a finding of *prima facie* discrimination, and was not sufficient objective justification for the difference in pay between the jobs.

As a consequence of the ECJ's ruling in *Enderby*, employers can no longer simply assert that a pay differential is permitted because it is derived from collective bargaining arrangements with a trade union. Where collective bargaining structures reflect indirect sex discrimination, arising from the fact that particular work is undertaken predominantly by women, then the employer must objectively justify the pay differential on other grounds such as market forces.

Length of employment

Many pay scales award employees annual pay increments reflecting the number of years an employee has been employed. An employee with less service will consequently receive less pay than colleagues with longer service who are employed on like work or work of equal value. This issue was recently considered by the ECJ in *Cadman* v. *Health and Safety Executive* [2006] ICR 1623. In this case Cadman, a principal health and safety inspector was paid less than four male colleagues because she had been employed for a shorter period of time. The ECJ ruled that there is no general requirement on employers to justify length of service criterion because normally their intrinsic purpose is to reflect greater experience and/or to reward loyalty. However, an employer should be required to justify a specific salary scheme if the claimant can show that there are serious doubts that the scheme is required to meet the employer's needs.

This ruling was considered by the Court of Appeal in *Wilson* v. *Health and Safety Executive* [2010] ICR 302. Wilson claimed equal pay with three male comparators where a job evaluation study had rated her work as being of equal value to theirs. The salary structure required her to work for 10 years before she would enter the same higher band of pay as her comparators. The court held that as the original tribunal had regarded the requirement to work 10 years as excessive this did raise serious doubts about the validity of the salary structure. The serious doubts 'test' should be understood as a filter to ensure the claimant has some prospects for success. Once such doubts were established, the burden was on the HSE to justify its service criterion. As the HSE was unable to justify the requirement for 10 years' service, her equal pay claim succeeded.

Flexibility

The ability of an employee to work flexibly, both in terms of when and where an employee is prepared to work, may obviously work to the benefit of an employer. Naturally, employers may wish to award flexibility through giving the relevant workers a higher rate of pay than employees who are only prepared or able to work for specific hours and/or at a specific workplace. However, as the ECJ ruled in *Danfoss* [1991] ICR 74, rewarding flexibility can indirectly discriminate against women, as their role as carers may prevent them from working outside of their established hours or at different geographical locations. Therefore, it is necessary for employers to demonstrate that flexibility genuinely benefits the organisation in terms of enhancing efficiency. If this is not the case then flexibility is being used to disguise sex discrimination.

In conclusion, if a woman is employed on like work, or work of equal value, with a male comparator, and the material factor defence is not successfully pleaded by the employer, she is entitled to an equality clause in her contract of employment.

Summary

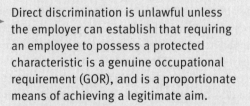

- The Equality Act operates through providing that characteristics possessed by employees, such as age, disability race, religious belief, sex and sexual orientation, are protected by its provisions.

- An employee will be the victim of direct discrimination if because of a protected characteristic the employee is treated less favourably than other employees.

- Direct discrimination is unlawful unless the employer can establish that requiring an employee to possess a protected characteristic is a genuine occupational requirement (GOR), and is a proportionate means of achieving a legitimate aim.

- An employee will be the victim of indirect discrimination if an employer applies a policy, criterion or practice (PCP) which, in comparison with other groups, disproportionally adversely impacts on members of a group to which the employee belongs where members of that group share a protected characteristic.

- Indirect discrimination is unlawful unless, in accordance with the *Bilka-Kaufhaus* principles, a PCP can be justified because it meets an objective commercial or organisational need of the employer and is a proportionate means of meeting that legitimate aim.

- It is unlawful to discriminate against an employee because that employee is perceived to have a protected characteristic, or he or she associates with another employee possessing a protected characteristic.

- A pregnant woman is protected from any unfavourable treatment, including refusal of employment and dismissal, from the commencement of her pregnancy to the expiry of her statutory maternity leave.

- As decided by the Supreme Court in *Seldon*, direct age discrimination, including a compulsory retirement age, can only be justified where the employer's policy reflects public interest issues.

◆ Under s. 15 EqA, where discrimination arises in consequence of a disability, it is not necessary for a disabled employee to compare how he or she has been treated with how an employee without that disability would have been treated in comparable circumstances.

◆ Under s. 20 EqA, discrimination which arises in consequence of a disability cannot be justified where an employer fails to make reasonable adjustments to premises, or to equipment or to how work is done to enable an employee to work despite the disability.

◆ An employee will be the victim of unlawful harassment where that person is the object of unwanted conduct related to a relevant protected characteristic, and the conduct has the purpose or effect of violating the employee's dignity, or it creates an intimidating, hostile, degrading, humiliating or offensive environment for the employee.

◆ Employers will be vicariously liable for acts of harassment carried out by employees at the workplace, or in work-related social activities, unless the employer has taken reasonable steps, for example, through the adoption and proper enforcement of a harassment policy, to protect an employee from harassment.

◆ Women who are employed on like work or work of an equal value with a male comparator are entitled to same pay as that enjoyed by the comparator.

◆ An employer will have a defence to an equal pay claim where the pay differential is due to a material factor other than sex, or the material factor is the product of justifiable indirect sex discrimination.

Question and answer*

Problem:

WT Ltd owns and runs a care home for elderly people. James is a white Englishman and a Rastafarian. Consequently, James wears his hair in the form of long dreadlocks. He has been employed as a gardener to maintain the grounds of the home for the past six months. WT Ltd has recently appointed Margaret as its senior manager. Margaret imposes a new dress code which applies to both sexes and, *inter alia*, requires all male employees to have hair which is no longer than collar length. On the basis of this code, Margaret informs James that he must cut off his dreadlocks. Margaret dismisses James when he refuses to comply with her instructions.

Peter has been employed as a carer in the home for the past three months. Rumours have circulated amongst other members of staff and the residents to the effect that Peter is homosexual. These rumours are erroneous. A person or persons send copies of *Gay News* to Peter, and put typed notices on notice boards, situated in various parts of the home to which everyone has access, which contain homophobic comments. Peter is very upset and complains to Margaret. Margaret informs Peter that she has no idea who is responsible, as it could be either staff or residents. Margaret reminds all members of staff that harassment on the grounds of a person's sexual orientation is specified as a disciplinary offence in the company's equal opportunities policy. Margaret also informs all of the residents that if they are guilty of homophobic behaviour then they can be excluded from the home. Margaret assures Peter that if the culprit or culprits are identified then appropriate action will be taken. However, until the culprits can be identified, Margaret states that she has no option other than to insist Peter continues to do his job as normal. Peter continues to receive offensive materials and decides he has no option other than to resign from his job.

Advise James and Peter as the legal rights and remedies, if any, that they have against WT Ltd.

You should spend 40 minutes on answering this question.

Further reading

IDS (2010) *Employment Law Guide to the Equality Act* (Income Data Services: London).
This invaluable as a starting point for detailed explanation of the EqA. Chapters 1 and 2, which explain the protected characteristics and forms of discrimination are particularly useful, as is Chapter 5 which deals with the enforcement of rights provided by the Act.

IDS *Handbooks on Disability Discrimination* (2010) and *Equal Pay* (2011) (Income Data Services: London).
These provide detailed explanation of these areas of the law based on the provisions of the EqA. Chapter 4 of the former provides an in-depth explanation of an employer's duty to make reasonable adjustments. Chapters 7 and 8 of the latter provide detailed explanation of equal value claims and the material factor defence.

Connolly, M. (2011) *Discrimination Law* (Sweet & Maxwell: London).
This is one of number of specialist texts on discrimination law which readers will find useful if they wish to go into any area of discrimination law in greater depth.

McColgan, A. (2005) *Discrimination Law: Text, Cases and Materials* (Hart: Oxford).
Another very useful text. The book obviously predates the Equality Act but contains valuable commentary on many cases which still constitute the law.

McColgan, A. (2011) *Equality Act 2010* (Institute of Employment Rights: Liverpool).
A short book containing critical commentary on the Equality Act 2010 which readers will find stimulating and easy to read.

Bowers, J. and Moran, E. (2002) 'Justification in Direct Sex Discrimination Law: Breaking the Taboo', *Industrial Law Journal*, vol. 31, pp. 307–20.

Gill, T. and Monaghan, K. (2003) 'Justification in Direct Sex Discrimination Law: Taboo Upheld', *Industrial Law Journal*, vol. 32, pp. 115–22.

Bowers, J., Moran, E. and Honeyball, S. (2003) 'Justification in Direct Sex Discrimination: a Reply', *Industrial Law Journal*, vol. 32, pp. 185–7.
As explained in this chapter, with the exception of age, direct discrimination cannot be justified by employers. An interesting debate on this issue is contained in the above articles in the *Industrial Law Journal*. These articles focus on sex discrimination but the arguments can also be related to the other forms of discrimination prohibited by the EqA.

Busby, N. (2011) 'Carers and the Equality Act 2010: Protected Characteristics and Identity', *Contemporary Issues in Law*, vol. 11, pp. 71–91.
This article argues that being a carer should be a protected characteristic under the Equality Act 2010 so carers would then be protected from employment-related discrimination.

Fredman, S. (2008) 'Reforming Equal Pay Laws', *Industrial Law Journal*, vol. 37, pp. 193–218.
This article explains the causes of the continuing pay gap between men and women and analyses why

equal pay laws have not adequately dealt with this problem. Fredman argues for legislation to impose positive duties on employers rather than relying on complaints being presented by individual claimants.

Volume 40 of the *Industrial Law Journal*, December 2011, is a special edition on Equality Law and the Act of 2010. Readers will find all the articles in this edition interesting and useful. In terms of the content of this chapter, critical analysis is provided by the following articles:

Solanke, I. 'Infusing the Silos in the Equality Act 2010 with Synergy', pp. 336–58.
This examines the way in which the EqA retains separate protected characteristics and proposes exploration of the scope for synergy, that is interconnecting the statutory provisions, across the different grounds of discrimination.

Lawson, A. 'Disability and Employment in the Equality Act 2010: Opportunities Seized, Lost and Generated', pp. 359–83.
This reviews the changes to the law made by the EqA and considers how far the way in which the law deals with disability discrimination could be extended to the other protected characteristics.

Pitt, G. 'Keeping the Faith: Trends and Tensions in Religion or Belief Discrimination', pp. 384–404.
This analyses case law on religion and belief including *Azmi* and *Eweida*, the conflict of rights demonstrated by the *Ladele* and *McFarlane* cases and explores the relationship between discrimiation law and human rights law.

As well as the above article by Pitt, the following articles provide interesting and different perspectives on these issues.

Carney, D. and Welch, R. (2011) 'Protecting Religious and Sexual Identities: Discrimination Law or Human Rights Law', *Contemporary Issues in Law*, vol. 11, pp. 92–116.

Hatzis, N. (2011) 'Personal beliefs in the workplace: how not to define indirect discrimination', *Modern Law Review*, vol. 74, pp. 287–305.

McColgan, A. (2009) 'Class Wars? Religion and (In)equality in the Workplace', *Industrial Law Journal*, vol. 38, pp. 1–29.

Vickers, L. (2010) 'Religious discrimination in the workplace: an emerging hierarchy?', *Ecclesiastical Law Journal*, vol. 12, pp. 280–303.

Vickers, L. (2008) *Religious Freedom, Religious Discrimination and the Workplace* **(Hart: Oxford).**
This book provides a comprehensive and seminal analysis as to why law should protect rights to religious beliefs.

Question and answer guidance

Problem: With respect to James, your answer should explain that as a result of cases such as *Schmidt* and *Smith* it has been established that employers can impose dress codes which are based on conventional notions of how men and women should look. Therefore, as Margaret's dress code applies to both male and female employees, James is unlikely to succeed in claiming direct sex discrimination. However, in the context of race, the case of *St Gregory's College* demonstrates how a dress code can constitute unlawful discrimination. James has not been subjected to race discrimination but he can argue he has been indirectly discriminated against on the basis of his religious beliefs. Applying *Azmi*, he can argue that Rastafarians are required to have dreadlocks and therefore the rule on hair length indirectly discriminates against him. On the basis of *Eweida*, he will have to demonstrate to a tribunal that dreadlocks are required by his religion rather than being an aspect of individual choice. He may also need to establish that his religious beliefs are genuinely held rather than his 'Rastafarianism' being, for example, the product of a sub-cultural liking for reggae music. Your answer should explain how indirect discrimination can be justified in accordance with the *Bilka-Kaufhaus* principles. Arguably, given that James is employed as a gardener, as against for example a carer, this may be difficult to do in this case.

With respect to Peter, your answer should explain that he has clearly been subject to harassment on grounds of his perceived sexual orientation contrary to s. 26 EqA. Assuming Margaret is not the culprit, it is necessary to discuss whether the employer is vicariously liable under s. 109 EqA, or liable for third party harassment under s. 40. On the face of it, the company should be able to demonstrate, given its rules on harassment and the action taken by Margaret, that it has taken reasonable steps to protect Peter and therefore will not incur liability. However, this will require evidence that Margaret has genuinely sought to discover the identity of the culprit(s) rather than just acting in a token way to appease Peter's concerns.

Your answer should give your conclusions as to whether and in what circumstances the claims by James and Peter will succeed. You should then explain the remedies to which they will be entitled. As well as declarations, they will be entitled to compensation covering both financial loss and injury to feelings. The tribunal might also recommend that James be reinstated. If the company refuses to comply with such a recommendation, the compensation awarded to James will be increased.

Essay:

This question is asking you both to discuss the accuracy of the statement and to engage in critical analysis of how the law operates.

The initial part of your essay should explain how to distinguish between direct and indirect discrimination, and confirm that the statement is correct with respect to discrimination relating to gender, race, sexual orientation and religion or belief. It is also correct, but not the main issue, with regard to disability discrimination. The statement is incorrect with respect to age discrimination.

You should explain the GOR defence which can be pleaded by employers in direct discrimination claims. You could explain that discrimination on grounds of pregnancy and maternity is never lawful. You should explain the *Bilka-Kaufhaus* ruling and some of the main case law on justification, for example, *Edwards* v. *London Underground*. You could briefly explain that s. 20 EqA is the key section in protecting disabled employees, and the duty on employers to make reasonable adjustments may require employers to treat disabled employees more favourably than other employees. With respect to age, you should emphasise that direct age discrimination is justifiable. However, in accordance with the decision of the Supreme Court in *Seldon*, justification is only permitted where the employer's practices and policies are underpinned by public interest considerations.

In discussing whether direct discrimination should be generally justifiable, you can draw on the arguments provided by Bowers, Moran and Honeyball and Gill and Monaghan in the articles cited above. The recent articles by Solanke and Lawson can also be used as sources of ideas and arguments. You could argue for the status quo, or support the position of Bowers *et al.*, and expand it to include all forms of discrimination other than perhaps pregnancy and disability, which you can argue should have their own special rules. You should clarify that if direct discrimination is to be generally justifiable then EU law will require the approach in *Seldon* to apply.

Your essay should have reasoned conclusions, which clearly state your own views, and are consistent with the arguments contained in your discussion.

Visit **www.mylawchamber.co.uk/welch** to access tools to help you develop and test your knowledge of employment law, including interactive 'You be the judge' multiple choice questions, practice exam questions with guidance, annotated weblinks, case summary and key case flashcards, legal newsfeed, legal updates and answer to Lawyers' brief simulation.

mylawchamber
unrivalled support for legal education

Chapter 8
Trade unions, collective bargaining and the law

Key points In this chapter we will be looking at:

✦ Introducing the British system of industrial or employee relations and the frames of reference for studying collective labour law

✦ The collective bargaining process and the legal status of collective agreements between employers and trade unions

✦ The incorporation of collective agreements into individual contracts of employment

✦ Determining whether a trade union is independent of an employer

✦ Voluntary recognition of a trade union by an employer for the purposes of collective bargaining

✦ How an independent trade union can secure statutory recognition

✦ Statutory rights to time off at work for trade union workplace representatives and trade union members

✦ Duties on employers to inform and consult with trade union or employee representatives

✦ Statutory rights to belong to a trade union and to participate in its activities

Introduction

If you secure employment in the public sector or larger employing organisations in the private sector, it may well be that your workplace will be unionised. The largest union in the public sector is UNISON which represents workers in local government and the National Health Service (NHS). UNITE and the

GMB, as well as representing workers in the public sector, are the largest unions representing workers across the private sector in a number of different occupations including car workers, tanker drivers, banking, publishing, retail and the public utilities. If your employer is unionised, this mean that it negotiates with, or at least consults with, a trade union on matters of interest and concern to its employees. Where an employer and a trade union agree to negotiate, the norm will be that the parties intend this negotiating process to result in a **collective agreement** between the employer and the union. The legal status and consequences of a collective agreement (referred to in Chapter 2) will be explored fully below.

Where an employer agrees to consult with a trade union, it is mutually understood that agreement may not be reached, although both parties will regard an agreement as a desirable outcome. In the course of consultations the function of the trade union is to represent the views of those employees who belong to it and seek to persuade the employer to adopt these views or at least go some way towards accommodating them in formulating its policies and practices. When a trade union has negotiating and/or consultation rights it is engaged in collective representation of its members as it is acting in the interests of its members as a whole within an employing organisation.

Trade unions also have an important role to play in representing an individual member who is having problems at work. As we have seen in earlier chapters, this may be a formal role where the member has invoked a **grievance procedure** or is being subjected to a **disciplinary procedure**, and is exercising the statutory right to be accompanied by a trade union representative at a grievance or disciplinary hearing.

The main statute dealing with trade unions and the world of industrial relations is the Trade Union and Labour Relations (Consolidation) Act (TULRCA) 1992. Section 1 TULRCA defines a trade union as an organisation of workers whose principal purposes include regulating relations with employers or employers' associations. The latter will be a group of separate employers in the same trade, industry or profession who meet with one or more trade unions representing workers in that job sector. For example, university employers engage in national collective bargaining through the University and College Employers' Association with unions representing university staff such as the University and College Union (UCU) and UNISON.

The most effective way in which a trade union can carry out its function of regulating relations between its members and an employer is by securing trade union recognition. This means that an employer has agreed to negotiate with that union with respect to some or all of the contractual terms and conditions of its employees. This process of negotiation is called **collective bargaining** and may result in a collective agreement between the employer and union which alters the terms and conditions of the employees covered by the collective agreement. This may be all employees within the organisation but is more likely to be an agreed **collective bargaining unit** which covers a defined group of employees in the organisation. For example, in a university, members of academic staff are represented by UCU and administrative, technical and other categories of staff are predominantly represented by UNISON. As is typically the case today with employees at managerial level, senior members of a university's staff may be individual members of a union but will not be within the scope of collective bargaining. This means that in practice the university will determine their individual contractual terms and conditions of employment.

Where a trade union is recognised it will negotiate on behalf all the employees who belong to the relevant bargaining unit and this will include those employees who do not belong to the union. However, many employees realise that the more employees who belong to the union the stronger the union will be in its negotiations with the employer. Moreover, employees who choose not to join the union will have no say in the collective bargaining position and strategy the union should adopt in its negotiations with the employer. Similarly, they will not be able to participate in any vote on whether a collective agreement reached between the union and the employer should be ratified by the members so that existing employment contracts will be varied accordingly.

As we saw in the last chapter, recognised and **independent trade unions** have an important role to play in the context of statutory consultations where an employer is proposing **collective redundancies** or a **business transfer**. This chapter will consider other contexts in which employers may be under a legal duty to consult with trade unions or employees' representatives. Whether or not an employer recognises a trade union, its employees have the legal right to join a trade union of their choice and, at the very least outside of working hours, to participate in its activities. These rights are provided by the TULRCA and are in accordance with rights of association guarantee by Article 11 of the European Convention on Human Rights (ECHR).

Trade unions in Britain grew and developed their functions throughout the nineteenth and twentieth centuries, and, as a background to understanding and evaluating the law as it is today, it is valuable to provide a short explanation of how British industrial relations have developed and different theoretical perspectives on the role that trade unions play in British society.

The British system of industrial relations

Case Summary

For much of the nineteenth century trade unions operated in conditions of semi-legality. As a result of a combination of the common law and special statutory provisions the organisation and taking of industrial action constituted criminal offences. Indeed, it was a criminal act for a worker to act in breach of the contact of employment by withdrawing his or her labour. Moreover, the purposes of a trade union were deemed to be in restraint of trade as they were perceived by judges as restricting the freedom of the employer and the worker to reach their own agreement on the basis of which the worker would be employed. As vividly illustrated by the case of *Hornby* v. *Close* (1867) LR 2QB 153, this meant a trade union could not even enforce its rules against its own officials. In this case it was held that was impossible for a union to take legal action against a treasurer who had absconded with its funds as the union operated in restraint of trade and, consequently, its rules were void and unenforceable.

However, full legality did come about in the late nineteenth century with the passing of the Trade Union Act 1871 and the Conspiracy of Protection and Property Act 1875. The combined effects of these Acts were that trade unions were protected from the doctrine of restraint of trade law and the criminal law ceased to be applied to industrial action and picketing providing the latter was peaceful in nature.

The period after 1875 saw the growth of general unions, seeking to organise semi-skilled and unskilled workers. This period, which was one of recession and industrial unrest, also saw the application of the civil law against trade unions through the creation of tortious liabilities which largely continue to apply to this day. The culmination of this process was the *Taff Vale* judgment in 1901, which confirmed that a trade union itself could be directly liable in tort. The effect of this judgment was nullified by the Trade Disputes Act 1906. This Act also provided unions and their officials with statutory immunity for the tortious liabilities that the judges had imposed over the previous decade. The relationship between the law of tort and this system of **statutory immunities** will be fully explained later (see Chapter 9).

Although the organisation of industrial action by trade unions was not in a continuous and systematic way free from legal regulation until after the Second World War, the 1906 Act is generally regarded as providing the basis for a system of industrial relations which was largely free from a legal framework. This system was characterised as one defined by legal abstentionism or voluntarism. The most eminent labour lawyer in Britain in the immediate post-war period was Professor Otto Kahn-Freund, and his seminal analysis of the British system of industrial relations was encapsulated by his concept of **collective *laissez-faire***. Governments influenced by doctrines of *laissez-faire* believe that individual businesses and commercial undertakings should be free from legal constraints in their relations with one another. Kahn-Freund's use of the term 'collective *laissez-faire*' was designed to emphasise that British governments had extended traditional ideas of *laissez-faire* to *collective* relations between employers and trade unions. Therefore, as a matter of policy British governments declined to use the law to intervene in industrial relations.

Whilst it can be argued that the concept of collective *laissez-faire* underestimated the inherent power of the judiciary to intervene in industrial disputes, it cannot be doubted that the concept provided an invaluable basis for contrasting the British system with the highly regulated systems of industrial relations which operated in other western European countries at that time. Today, as will be demonstrated, British industrial relations are also heavily regulated by the law. However, collective *laissez-faire* is not without its legacy. There are two remaining consequences of it. First, it is still presumed that collective agreements between employers and trade unions do not have contractual force and therefore are not legally enforceable. Secondly, although there is now a statutory procedure through which a trade union may be able to secure obligatory recognition by an employer, trade union recognition remains an issue which is largely based on voluntary agreement between an employer and a trade union. In particular, and in contrast to the general position in other EU member states, there is no general legal duty on employers to bargain and consult with trade unions.

It should be appreciated that since the 1870s trade unions have had a special legal status in that they are a particular type of unincorporated association. Under s. 10 TULRCA, whilst trade unions are not legal persons in their own right in the way that companies are, they have quasi-corporate status and can sue and be sued in their own name. Trade unions appoint trustees to hold property on behalf of the union, and any awards of damages granted by a court against a union can be enforced against this property.

Out and about

The majority of readers will never have been members of trade unions and probably have not worked in organisations where trade unions are present. It is therefore valuable, before looking at the relevant law in depth, to gain some idea of what trade unions do on behalf of their members. With this purpose in mind, visit the website of the Trades Union Congress (TUC) – **http://www.tuc.org.uk/**. The TUC is a confederation of trade unions and the overwhelming majority of British unions are affiliated to it.

This site will provide you with information about the TUC itself and its concerns about, and perspectives on, workplace, economic, social and equality issues and rights at work. If you click on 'Unions' at the top of the home page, you will be able to identify all of the unions which are currently affiliated to the TUC. You will see that the largest unions in this country are UNISON, which mainly represents public sector workers, and UNITE, which mainly represents private sector workers. Click on their names to access their websites to look at their activities and policies. If you engage in a career in the educational world then the relevant unions are the NUT, NASUWT and UCU. The main union if you secure work in the civil service is the PCS. Unions which may be of interest to you if you are working in part-time jobs whilst you are studying are USDAW, the shop workers union, and the GMB, which represents workers in the catering and leisure industries.

If you have members of your family and/or friends who are members of trade unions, ask them why they belong to a union and what their experiences of trade union membership are.

Collective labour law and frames of reference

Employment law is one of the more overtly politicised areas of law in our society. This is inevitable given the ways in which employment law connects with and reflects the economic and social policies of any given government. As we have seen, EU law provides an important source of our employment law, and this too has political connotations given that successive British governments, albeit to greater or lesser extents, have shown themselves to be resistant to EU legal intervention in the employment field. The law regulating industrial relations, that is, **collective labour law**, is the most politicised aspect of this already politicised area of our law. Anyone writing or commenting on collective labour law will be affected by their own views on the value of trade unions in our society – indeed, the above account is written from a standpoint which is sympathetic to trade unionism. Industrial relations academics have long recognised that it is impossible, or at least very uncommon, to adopt a neutral approach to discussion of trade unions. Consequently, they have identified the following three different frames of reference within which a system of industrial relations, or employee relations as it is more commonly termed today, and collective labour law can be approached.

1 Unitarism

A unitary perspective on employee relations regards employers and employees as having a common objective, which is maximising the efficiency and productivity of the organisation. The more successful the organisation the greater the benefits to its employees in terms of pay and job security. At an organisational level this approach emphasises the need for strong and effective management. A government which is influenced by unitarist thought, such as Margaret Thatcher's and John Major's governments in the 1980s and the 1990s, will emphasise the need to ensure that market mechanisms function free from external interference. Unitarists will argue that both trade unions and the provision of legal rights at work act as unfair and/or unnecessary constraints upon managerial prerogative and the effective functioning of the market. Similarly, union behaviour and statutory rights impact adversely on the freedom of the individual employee to determine his or her personal relationship with the employer. Therefore, legal regulation of the employment relationship should be restricted to individual contracts of employment freely entered into between employers and their employees.

2 Pluralism

Prior to the election of the Conservative government in 1979, it can be argued that pluralism constituted the dominant school of thought on the part of academics and practitioners, as well as governments both Conservative and Labour, in the post-Second World War era. Pluralists recognise that conflicts between employers and employees are inevitable – particularly at times when employers are seeking to resist pay demands or cut levels of pay, and/or make redundancies and/or increase employee workloads. Pluralists recognise that both trade unions and employment laws have a legitimate role to play in resolving such conflicts in ways that seek to achieve some balance between the competing interests and concerns of employers and employees. Pluralist thinkers will differ on the precise nature and detail of employment rights, and on the extent to which trade unions should benefit from legislative support or be subject to legal controls.

3 Radical/Marxist

This perspective represents an important strand of thought within the trade union movement and is shared, at least to some extent, by politicians such as Tony Benn, and eminent academics such as Lord Wedderburn. This school of thought emphasises that under capitalism there is an inevitable and irreconcilable conflict between employers who own the wealth and resources necessary to produce goods and services and the workers whose labour they rely on to do this. The only way in which this conflict can be ultimately ended is through replacing capitalism with socialism as the economic and social system on which society is based. In the meantime, the function and duty of trade unions is to further the interests of workers and their families by encroaching upon the power of employers and governments to subject workers to their will. Many radicals and Marxists are sceptical about the extent to which the law can be an effective mechanism for the furtherance and defence of workers' interests. Nevertheless, most will take the view that the stronger employment protection laws are, the better the conditions will be for trade unions to maximise their ability to protect workers' interests. In particular, radicals and Marxists will oppose legal restrictions on rights to strike.

It is important to appreciate that the above are only frames of reference – they are not discrete independent categories of thought. The boundaries between unitarists and pluralists in particular will often be blurred. Many unitarists will accept that trade unions are legitimate organisations in a democratic society and that workers should be permitted to join them. They will emphasise that the role of a trade union in modern society is to represent and provide benefits to their members as individuals rather than continue to emphasise collective representation. The Labour governments between 1997 and 2010 can be regarded as combining aspects of pluralism and unitarism as they sought simultaneously to make some improvements to collective and individual employment rights and to promote the (perceived) virtues of the free market. This is also the case with the Coalition government which came to power as a result of the 2010 General Election. It can be argued the Liberal Democrat part of this coalition leans towards pluralism whereas the Conservative majority remain influenced by unitarism.

Whatever perspective is adopted on employee relations and labour law, trade unions are likely to remain a significant feature of our society for some time to come. It is the case that trade union membership fell significantly during the 1980s and that decline has continued to this day. The reasons for this decline were, in part at least, created by changes in the structure of the labour force. The past 30 years have been characterised by permanent mass unemployment and unemployed workers tend not to join trade unions. Most significantly, in the private sector there has been a massive shift away from employment in industries such as coal mining and steel production and manufacturing in general. These always were the sectors of the economy where trade unions were strongest. Most private sector employment today is in the service and leisure industries where even in the 1960s and 1970s trade union organisation was always low.

It is also the case that Margaret Thatcher's and John Major's governments in the 1980s and 1990s were significantly influenced by unitarist philosophies and were hostile to trade unions. These governments enacted significant legal controls on industrial action which have substantially weakened the ability of trade unions to organise effective collective action to further or defend the interests of their members. (This legislation is discussed in the following chapter.) All governments since then, in contrast to the 1960s and 1970s, have to greater or lesser extents displayed some antipathy to the collective role that trade unions play in the workplace and in society in general. It is not surprising that trade unions lose members in such political climates as they lack the necessary power and influence to convince many potential members that their interests are most likely to be secured through union membership. Arguably, this is not a permanent condition, but any pro-union legal reforms are dependent on a political party, which is genuinely sympathetic to trade unions, winning political power. Readers will reach their own conclusion as to whether a revival of trade union power should be regarded as in the overall interests of working people or whether the decline in trade unionism over the past 30 years is to the benefit of society.

As the statistics provided below demonstrate, although unions have declined in size and influence over the past 40 years, they still represent more than six million workers and their activities remain relevant to this section of the workforce. Therefore, the relationship between trade unions and the law remains an important area of study.

Key stats

For the first 25 years after the Second World War trade unions grew significantly in terms of their membership levels and influence in British society. In 1979 there were around 13 million trade union members and trade union density was around half the workforce as a whole. Trade union density means the proportion of the workforce which is in a position to join trade unions and choose to do so. Figure 8.1 demonstrates the rise and fall in trade union membership over the past 100 years or so.

Figure 8.1 Trade union membership levels in UK from 1892 to 2010

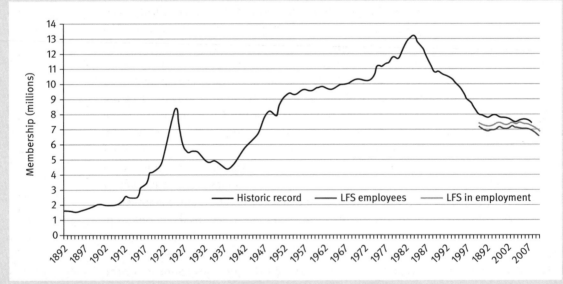

Source: *Labour Force Survey*, Office for National Statistics; Department for Employment (1892–1974); Certification Office (1974–2008/09).

Current statistics show that:

Trade union density for employees in the UK fell by 0.8 percentage points to 26.6% in 2010 compared with 2009. Trade union membership levels for UK employees fell by 2.7% (179,000) to 6.5 million.

Trade union presence in the public sector is still reasonably high. Public sector employees accounted for 62.4% of union members but only 17.6% cent of non-members. Union density was highest in professional occupations at 43.7% whilst sales occupations had the lowest at 12.9%. Contrary to the position historically, women are now generally more likely to be union members than men and this is the consequence of the preponderance of union membership being in the public sector.

In the private sector, between 2000 and 2010, union density grew in the wholesale, retail trade and motor repair sectors but fell in all other sectors with the water supply, electricity and gas supply sectors recording the sharpest fall of over 15 percentage points each. Possibly, this is an ongoing consequence of the privatisation of these industries, which took place in the late 1980s and early 1990s, so that these industries ceased to be part of the public sector.

Source: James Acher, *Trade Union Membership 2010*, National Statistics Publication, Department for Business, Innovation & Skills. The full report can be accessed at **http://www.bis.gov.uk/policies/employment-matters/research/trade-union-stats**

The legal status of collective agreements

As stated above, the main legacy today of the British system of industrial, or employee, relations having developed within a framework of collective *laissez-faire* is that collective agreements negotiated between employers and trade unions do not constitute legally binding contracts. This legal position was confirmed in the case of *Ford* v. *AUEW* [1969] 2 QB 303. In this case, the Engineering Union organised industrial action in breach of procedures contained in a collective agreement between it and the Ford company. The latter sought an injunction to prevent the strike from taking place as the company argued the union was attempting to act in breach of contract. The relevant collective agreement did not contain any statement as to whether or not the collective agreement was intended to be legally enforceable. It was held by the High Court that it was an established principle of the law of contract that it is presumed that collective agreements are not intended by the parties to the agreement to be legally enforceable. It is possible to rebut this presumption, but this is only so where it was clear from the agreement itself, and/or evidence derived from all the surrounding circumstances, that the parties intended it to be legally enforceable, This was not so in this case and therefore, as the union was not seeking to act in breach of contract, the injunction was refused.

Case Summary

This common law presumption against legal enforceability is given statutory force by s. 179(1) TULRCA. This provides that collective agreements concerned with employment matters listed in s. 178(2) TULRCA 1992 are presumed not to be legally enforceable. This presumption can only be rebutted by an express provision contained in a written agreement stipulating that the agreement is intended to be legally enforceable. Section 179(3) clarifies that it is possible to rebut the presumption for part of an agreement only. For this to be so, the parties need to draft their agreement carefully so it is clear which part(s) of the agreement is intended to be legally binding.

Section 178(2) TULRCA defines the types of collective agreement to which the statutory presumption against legal enforceability applies. This will be any agreement covering one or more of the following matters:

(a) terms and conditions of employment, or the physical conditions in which any workers are required to work;

(b) engagement or non-engagement, or termination or suspension of employment or the duties of employment, of one or more workers;

(c) allocation of work or the duties of employment between workers or groups of workers;

(d) matters of discipline;

(e) a worker's membership or non-membership of a trade union;

(f) facilities for officials of trade unions; and

(g) machinery for negotiation or consultation, and other procedures, relating to any of the above matters, including the recognition by employers or employers' associations of the right of a trade union to represent workers in such negotiation or consultation or in the carrying out of such procedures.

It should be understood that this definition of a collective agreement covers all the normal purposes of collective bargaining between an employer and a trade union and therefore reflects established employee relations practice. It will be very rare for a collective agreement to be made which falls outside the scope of s. 178(2). An example of such an agreement would be one which was seeking to promote workplace democracy by providing for worker participation on management boards or on consultation committees in which organisational plans and strategies are discussed. However, the common law presumption against legal enforceability would still apply to an agreement of this sort. The technical difference between the common law and the statutory presumption is that the latter only applies where there is a properly written clause in a collective agreement.

It is worth commenting that the law reflects a preference in Britain, on the part of both employers and trade unions, for a system of non-legally enforceable collective agreements. For some three years, during which the Industrial Relations Act 1971 was in force, the statutory presumption was reversed so that collective agreements were presumed to be legally enforceable. It was commonplace during this period for employers and unions voluntarily to agree that there should be a provision in any collective agreement that they made to the effect that the agreement was not to be legally enforceable.

This is contrary to the position to be found in other EU member states. For example, in Germany and Scandinavia the industrial relations systems are based on collective agreements which cover particular industries, or companies within those industries, which are legally enforceable. An agreement will last for a specified period of time, for example one year, and an employer or a trade union which acts in breach of an agreement can be taken to court. A trade union can only organise industrial action on the expiry of a collective agreement if negotiations for a new agreement break down. In other European countries, such as France and Spain, the legal consequences of collective agreements operate in a different way. A collective agreement will lay down standards which all companies or organisations in that sector of the economy are legally obliged to adhere to even if those organisations are not unionised and were not parties to the relevant collective agreement. European systems of collective bargaining are explained and discussed in the article by Lord Wedderburn, which is cited in the 'Further reading' section of this chapter.

One practical advantage of the British system is that it generates flexibility. If a particular collective agreement appears not to be working as anticipated, the parties can seek to negotiate amendments to it and, if this proves impossible, either or both parties can withdraw from the agreement without fearing legal repercussions. Therefore, collective agreements do not need to be negotiated with the same degree of precision and caution that often characterises the negotiation of a contract. In turn, this facilitates the negotiation of collective agreements at a local, that is, workplace level between managers and elected lay trade union representatives. It is important to emphasise that many collective agreements do have legal status through being incorporated into individual employment contracts in the ways explained below.

People in the law

Set out below are interviews with a lay trade union representative and an HR practitioner to ascertain their perspectives on the value of collective bargaining between employers and trade unions. It is interesting to note that, contrary to more traditional views in the trade union movement, the trade union interviewee favours collective agreements being legally enforceable.

The first interview is with **Mick Tosh**, a port representative of the Rail Maritime and Transport Union (RMT). (In the context of the terminology used in this chapter Mick is not an employed official of the RMT and should be regarded as a workplace or lay representative.)

Please could you identify the advantages to workers of their trade union being recognised by their employer for the purposes of collective bargaining? It gives a level playing field of fairness for all. Pay, conditions and the application of procedures are overseen by an organisation acting in the interest of the members so everyone receives equal treatment. Where there is a recognised union, workers' pay and conditions are better than their co-workers without union recognition. There are also fewer accidents at work in a unionised workforce due to the awareness brought by unions on safety at work.

In contrast with continental Europe, it is the tradition in Britain for collective agreements not to be legally enforce- able as binding contracts. Do you agree with this approach to the nature of collective agreements? Any collective agreements which are reached should be legally binding on all parties. Anything less places workers in a weakened position, which inevitably leads to the possibility of disagreement and confrontation when an employer seeks unilaterally to change or 'interpret' the contract in ways which are detrimental to the employee's rights.

In your view are there any types of collective agreement which you would prefer to be legally enforceable in a court of law? Yes any collectively negotiated amendments to contracts of employment in contexts such as pay, pensions and conditions of employment.

The second interview is with **Peter Brook**, the head of human resources at the University of Portsmouth. This interview exemplifies a pluralist approach to employee relations from a manager's perspective. It is clear that recognising trade unions is a voluntary policy by the university, which it regards as having benefits for it. In contrast to the above interview with Mick Tosh, Peter expresses a clear preference for maintaining the norm of non-legally enforceable collective agreements.

Please could you identify the advantages to an employing organisation of recognising a trade union for the purposes of collective bargaining? It is valuable to have professional negotiators and experienced representatives for the purposes of

collective bargaining. Any change is naturally a shock to an individual so it can help to manage change to have experienced union officials involved. It also adds more credibility to the outcome.

From your experience please could you identify the differences between negotiating with and consulting with a recognised trade union? Generally speaking, it is fair to say that an employer wishes to consult and a trade union wishes to negotiate. An employer has the right to manage their business and to introduce change to their organisations and they will consult about proposed changes. However, when there is an impact on terms and conditions of staff, negotiation will take place.

In contrast with continental Europe, it is the tradition in Britain for collective agreements not to be legally enforceable as binding contracts. Do you agree with this approach to the nature of collective agreements? Yes, I prefer the British approach because it gives more flexibility. Circumstances change all the time but British employment law also provides protection to employees.

In your view are there any types of collective agreement which you would prefer to be legally enforceable in a court of law? No, as I mentioned before, I would see this as a straitjacket. The ability to refer disputes to court will not avoid disputes in the first place. I would prefer to have more flexibility.

Collective agreements and individual employment contracts

Collective agreements can be divided into **substantive agreements** and **procedure agreements**. A substantive agreement will be one which clearly relates to contractual terms and conditions, such as rates of pay and working hours and, typically, will be incorporated into the individual contracts of employment of the employees on whose behalf the union negotiated the agreement.

Procedure agreements are intended to govern the relations between the employer and the relevant trade union, rather than benefit individual employees, and therefore will not

Table 8.1 Legal status of collective agreements

Substantive collective agreements on terms and conditions of employment	Procedure agreements between employers and trade unions
Not legally enforceable between employer and trade union	Not legally enforceable between employer and trade union
Incorporated into an individual employment contract by express terms in that contract and legally enforceable between the employer and the employee	Specific provisions *may* be incorporated into individual contracts of employment and thereby legally enforceable between employers and employees

normally be legally binding as the presumption against legal enforceability will apply. A good example of such an agreement will be a recognition agreement between an employer and a union which sets out the purposes for which the employer agrees to engage in collective bargaining with the union, and the procedures under which collective bargaining will be conducted. Unless a recognition agreement is stated to be legally enforceable, and such a provision would be untypical, then the employer can **derecognise** the union and terminate the agreement at any time. This will be so even if the agreement stipulates a period of notice that the employer must give to the union before any termination of the agreement is to take effect. It is also possible for collective agreements to be of a hybrid nature. An agreement may be largely procedural but may contain substantive clauses which are suitable for incorporation into individual contracts of employment. For example, a recognition agreement may contain provisions setting out the rights of union representatives and members to engage in trade union activities during working hours.

A collective agreement, or specific provisions contained within it, can be incorporated into the individual contracts of employment of relevant employees by express terms in those employment contracts. For the purposes of clarity and certainty, it is useful if the collective agreement itself stipulates whether the agreement as a whole, or particular provisions in it, are intended by the parties to the agreement to be incorporated into individual employment contacts. As discussed below, it is also possible for a court to imply part or all of a collective agreement into employment contracts where the court views the evidence as establishing that this was the intention of both the employer and the trade union parties to the collective agreement. Table 8.1 summarises the legal status and consequences of collective agreements.

Express incorporation

The case of *Marley* v. *Forward Trust* [1986] ICR 891 illustrates the process of express incorporation of a collective agreement into the individual contracts of employees. The case clarifies that there can be incorporation even where the relevant collective agreement was expressed to be binding in honour. The key to express incorporation is that there is a relevant term in the employee's contract. The collective agreement contained a provision giving any employee, who was redeployed due to redundancy, six months in which to assess its suitability. Marley's contract expressly incorporated this agreement. The employers decided to close a regional office and moved Marley to London. Two months later, Marley informed the employer that the position was unsuitable. The

Case Summary

employer treated him as having been moved under a **mobility clause**, and argued that he had resigned from his job. It was held by the Court of Appeal that the terms of the collective agreement had been expressly incorporated into Marley's employment contract and therefore were legally enforceable by him. Consequently, the employer could not rely on the mobility clause and Marley had been dismissed by reason of redundancy.

The best way in which an employer can seek to avoid any doubt as to which collective agreements, or parts of an agreement, are incorporated into the employment contracts of its employees is through listing the relevant agreements in an employee's employment contract at the commencement of his or her employment. It should also be remembered that (as explained in Chapter 2), where an employee has been provided with a written statement of terms in place of a written contract, then collective agreements providing contractual terms should be listed in the statement. The list of collective agreements can and should be kept up to date through informing employees in writing when a collective agreement has been varied or replaced by a new agreement.

Problems of incorporation

In the absence of such a systematic practice, or of an express provision of the sort that was present in *Marley*, there may be problems in establishing whether a collective agreement has been incorporated into individual contracts. Moreover, even in an organisation where the employer has listed collective agreements, which are accepted as incorporated into individual employment contracts, there may still be a dispute as to whether a particular agreement, which has not been so listed, should have been. Employers are not able to deny incorporation simply on the basis that a particular agreement has not been identified as expressly incorporated into its employees' contracts.

Even where there is no express incorporation, incorporation of a collective agreement may still be implied by a court if the circumstances show that this was the intention of the employer. For example, a court may be able to infer from the evidence that an employer has regarded a collective agreement as incorporated into its employees' contracts, and therefore incorporation is implied as a result of the **custom and practice** of that employer. Table 8.2 summarises the general processes whereby collective agreements are expressly or impliedly incorporated into individual contracts of employment.

Table 8.2 Incorporation of collective agreements into employment contracts

Express incorporation	Implied incorporation
Express term in employees' contracts incorporating a collective agreement	Collective agreement must be *suitable* for incorporation
Employment contract or written statement lists collective agreement as incorporated into the contract	Incorporation inferred from evidence such as: • the employer has treated the collective agreement as part of its employment contracts; • the employer's past custom and practice regarding such collective agreements

However, there cannot be implied incorporation of a collective agreement if a court decides that an agreement, or the relevant provision in it, is unsuitable for incorporation. For example, in *Kaur* v. *MG Rover Group* [2005] IRLR 40, Kaur argued that he could not be made compulsorily redundant as this was in breach of two collective agreements made between the company and his trade union. It was held by the Court of Appeal that courts have to look at the content and the character of the relevant parts of the collective agreement to determine whether they were appropriate to constitute terms of the individual contract of employment. The character of the provisions, contained on the collective agreements in this case, was overwhelmingly aspirational. They were not related to the terms and conditions of employees but were part of what were described as 'partnership principles' with the union. At most they constituted a policy that compulsory redundancies should not occur. In so far as they formed part of an agreement with the union, the commitment was solely on a collective basis and was not legally enforceable by Kaur as an individual.

By way of contrast, in *Alexander* v. *Standard Telephone & Cables Ltd* [1991] IRLR 286, a collective agreement between the company and Alexander's trade union stipulated that selection for compulsory redundancy should be on a last in first out (LIFO) basis. Alexander was selected for redundancy in breach of this agreement. It was held that this type of agreement was suitable for incorporation into individual contracts of employment as it was intended to benefit individual employees rather than to govern relations with the union. Although, the collective agreement was not expressly incorporated into the employment contracts of individual employees the court could infer that the employer did intend these particular provisions in the collective agreement to be part of the employment contracts of its employees. Consequently, the provisions could be impliedly incorporated into Alexander's contract.

Incorporation of a collective agreement will not implied if the evidence points away from an employer having treated a collective agreement as incorporated into employees' contracts. In *Griffiths* v. *Bucks CC*]1994] ICR 265, a provision in a collective agreement was suitable for incorporation into individual contracts, but the specific wording of the agreement suggested that this was not the intention of the parties to it. The agreement, which was between a college lecturer's union and the county council, set out as a 'recommendation' that in cases of redundancy an employee should be given at least one year's notice of dismissal. Griffiths was dismissed with his normal contractual notice of three months and he claimed he was entitled to nine months' salary by way of damages for breach of contract. It was held that the agreement did not provide for contractual notice of at least one year, but merely recommended the maximum possible notification of impending redundancy. Therefore, the right to one year's notice had not been incorporated into Griffiths's individual contract and his claim failed. Neither the wording in the agreement nor the employer's previous practice with respect to it suggested the council regarded itself as having agreed to a contractual right to one year's notice.

The recent case of *Malone* v. *British Airways plc* [2011] ICR 125 is controversial as both the collective agreement and the employment contracts of the relevant employees specified that the collective agreement was incorporated into individual employment contracts. The collective agreement concerned workloads and specified the minimum number of cabin crew to be provided on flights. The agreement provided for compensation to crew members if their numbers on a specific flight fell below the required level. The Court of Appeal agreed with UNITE that this provision was suitable for incorporation into individual contracts, but decided that incorporation had not taken place as this could have disastrous commercial consequences for British Airways and therefore could not have been the employer's intention. The provision constituted a collective commitment to the workforce as a whole. It was binding in honour only and did not constitute a contractual obligation owed to individual employees.

This decision can be criticised as it contradicts the ordinary principles of contract law. These principles require courts to enforce the express terms of a contract irrespective of the consequences of doing so on one of the contracting parties. It is not for a court of law to rewrite a contract because it transpires that a contracting party has entered into what turns out to be a bad bargain from that party's perspective. Further analysis and critical discussion of this judgment can be found in the articles by Reynold and Hendy, and Russell, cited in the 'Further reading' section of this chapter.

Case Summary

Where a collective agreement has been incorporated into employment contracts, its terms so incorporated remain legally enforceable by individual employees even if the employer ceases to be a party to the collective agreement. For example, in *Robertson* v. *British Gas* [1983] ICR 351, Robertson's contract of employment stipulated that he was entitled to bonus payments in accordance with a scheme that the employer had negotiated with a trade union. The employer terminated the agreement with the union and argued that after this date Robertson had ceased to be eligible for bonus payments as the scheme no longer existed. It was held that the scheme had been incorporated into Robertson's contract at the time of his appointment and this contract could not be varied by termination of the collective agreement. Therefore, Robertson remained contractually entitled to agreed bonus payments.

Case Summary

The norm is for collective agreements to cover all employees, including those who do not belong to the relevant trade union. Future collective agreements can vary or add to the terms of the contract. However, it may be difficult to incorporate a new collective agreement varying the existing contract of an employee who left the trade union prior to the collective agreement being entered into. In *Singh* v. *British Steel Corp* [1974] IRLR 131, following an unsuccessful pay claim Singh left the trade union and informed the company of this. The company and the union subsequently negotiated a new shift system and grading structure, but Singh refused to work under the new system on the basis that his employment contract could not be varied by a collective agreement with a union that he had left. The union had no authority to negotiate changes to his contract of employment. The court agreed with this argument and held that Singh had not acted in breach of contract by refusing to work the new system. This was, however, a somewhat pyrrhic victory for Singh, as it was held that his dismissal was fair. The company had acted reasonably in dismissing him given that he had refused either to discuss the proposed changes with the company or to invoke the company's grievance procedures.

Conflicts between collective agreements

Collective agreements can be negotiated at a centralised national level covering all employees in a particular trade or profession who are employed by different employers. In recent decades **national collective bargaining** has largely been restricted to the public sector. Today, **local collective bargaining** between a particular employer and a recognised trade union is much more typical as many employers prefer the flexibility of bargaining at company level. Where national bargaining does exist, it is possible that an employer, which is a party to the national agreement, will also enter into a local collective agreement with the trade union which varies the terms of the national agreement. The national agreement may expressly specify that where there is a later local agreement then it is the terms of this local agreement which will govern the contracts of employment of employees employed by that particular employer.

However, where there is no such provision in the national agreement, and the terms of the national agreement and a subsequent local agreement conflict with one another, then it seems it is the former which will normally prevail. In other words, it will still be the provisions of the national agreement which will constitute the contractual terms for the relevant employees.

For example, in *Gascol Conversions Ltd* v. *Mercer* [1974] IRLR 155, Mercer's union made a national agreement with an employers' association, to which Gascol Conversions belonged, providing for a normal 40 hours working week with the expectation that employees would work overtime where necessary at overtime rates. A year later, Gascol Conversions entered into an agreement with union representatives, which was only intended to apply at the local level of the company, to the effect that the normal working week would be for 54 hours. Mercer was subsequently made redundant and he received a redundancy payment calculated on a basic 40-hour week. The Court of Appeal held that it was the national agreement that covered Mercer's contract of employment and which specified the normal hours to be worked in any one week. Therefore, it was correct to calculate Mercer's redundancy payment on the basis of a 40-hour working week. Lord Denning stated that, in his view, national agreements will always prevail over local agreements except where national agreements expressly provide that local agreements are to be given priority as the source of employment terms for the employees covered by the local agreement.

Case Summary

This case is old and was decided at a time when national collective bargaining was much more prevalent than is the case today, where it is largely restricted to the public sector. Nevertheless, the reasoning behind the decision is probably still applicable. Certainly, it is the case that a trade union, which is a party to a national collective agreement, will only be happy with local agreements which are consistent with the provisions of the national agreement or constitute improvements on them. Indeed, it is not uncommon for local trade union negotiators to be required to submit a local agreement for ratification by a higher body within the union before it can be confirmed formally with the employer that local agreement has been reached.

As stated above, national collective bargaining remains significant in the public sector, and a major issue of contention in recent times has been the desire by the Coalition government and public sector employers to make important changes to public sector pension schemes – if possible through collective agreements with public sector unions.

Law in action Proposed changes to public sector pensions

In 2011 and 2012, national collective bargaining involving public sector unions was very much in the news as a result of a dispute between the unions and public sector employers over changes to occupational pension schemes which were required by the government. Overall, this dispute was conducted within a legal framework whereby consultations with the unions were required before the government could make amendments to the various statutory schemes. The one point of agreement between the government, the public sector employers and the unions was that any changes to the statutory schemes could be best secured through negotiation.

However, lack of progress in these negotiations generated a one-day strike by public sector trade unionists on 30 November 2011, with further strikes threatened for 2012. This strike was conducted within the framework of the strike laws (which are discussed in the following chapter). At the time of writing, the dispute had not been resolved. The following is a brief account of the different positions of the unions and the government.

The government's proposals are based on a report it commissioned from Lord Hutton, the former Labour Work and Pensions Secretary. In his report Lord Hutton stated: 'there is no evidence that pay is lower for public sector workers to reflect higher levels of pension provision'. Although 85% of public service employees contribute to a pension, he said that these pensions were far from 'gold-plated', with the average pension in payment currently at a 'modest' £7,800 a year. About half of public service pensioners received less than £5,600 a year. Some private sector schemes are worse than this, but he said that should not affect public sector pensions. In the private sector only 35% of workers sign up for a pension.

According to the government, changes to pensions for public sector workers are essential – as people live longer and the cost of funding public sector pensions is 'unsustainable'. The government wants most public sector workers to:

✦ Pay more into their pensions – workers, on average, would have to pay 3.2 percentage points more in annual pension contributions phased in between 2012 and 2014.

✦ Work for longer – many can access a pension at 60 but the government wants public sector workers, bar the armed forces, police and fire service, to receive their occupational pension at the same time as the state pension in future. The state pension age is due to rise to 66 for both men and women by April 2020.

✦ Accept a pension based on a 'career average' salary, rather than the current final salary arrangement which many of them are currently on.

Unions, however, say the proposals will leave their members paying more and working longer for a lower pension. Moreover, the increases in pension contributions were being proposed at a time when workers are already witnessing a fall in their living standards as a result of a freeze in their pay so that salaries are not keeping pace with inflation.

Source: **http://www.bbc.co.uk/news/uk-13932304** (accessed on 14 January 2012)

Trade union recognition

The collective bargaining process, which is explained above, applies to an employer who has agreed to negotiate with a trade union on one or more of the matters contained in s. 178(2) TULRCA as listed above. Such an agreement constitutes **voluntary recognition** of the trade union concerned. The benefits of trade union recognition to employees who are union members are obvious. Typically, employees as individuals have no bargaining power to negotiate their own terms and conditions of employment. The contract of employment will be drawn up by the employer and offered to the employee on a take it or leave it basis. The union is able to draw on its collective strength and expertise to negotiate terms and conditions for its members which they would probably not be able to secure though individual negotiations with their employers. Indeed, where trade unions are not recognised most employees will never be involved in negotiating any aspect of their employment contracts.

> trade union recognition is not without its advantages for employers

From an employer perspective, this can be seen, and indeed is seen by many employers, as the major disadvantage of recognising a trade union. However, trade union recognition is not without its advantages for employers. Where employers do wish to negotiate on the contracts of employment of their employees it can be more convenient – particularly in larger organisations – to negotiate with a small group of trade union negotiators rather than individually with each and every member of the workforce. This is especially so given that it is the norm for collective agreements to cover all employees in the relevant collective bargaining unit that the union represents, and this will include employees who are not members of the union. Moreover, although this is not a consequence of trade union recognition that trade unions tend to publicise, it is the case that a recognised trade union can assist an employer in maintaining labour discipline. Where a trade union has negotiated a collective agreement, which not all of its members endorse, the union can insist that its members abide by the terms of that agreement. For employers who adopt a pluralist approach to employee relations – of the sort that is explained at the start of this chapter and is exemplified by the above interview with Peter Brook – collective bargaining can be perceived as a way of reassuring members of the workforce that they are employed by an employer who believes in treating employees in a fair-minded manner.

The following statistics demonstrate the current nature and extent of trade union recognition and workplace presence.

Key stats

In 2010, 46.1% of employees reported that trade unions were present in their workplaces, a fall of 2.8 percentage points from 2000. Trade union presence in workplaces was nearly three times higher amongst public sector employees compared with the private sector at 85.7% and 29.6% respectively. The gap between the sectors was even higher for collective agreements coverage at 64.5% for public sector against 16.8% for the private sector. But these figures represent only a slight decline in union presence since 2000 for both private and public sector workplaces of 5.3 and 2.1 percentage points respectively.

It is interesting to note that there is still a premium arising from collective bargaining with respect to levels of pay. The hourly earnings of union members, according to the Labour Force Survey, averaged £14 in 2010, 16.7% more than the earnings of non-members with an average of £12 per hour. The trade union wage premium in 2010 was higher in the public sector at 21.1% compared with 6.7% in the private sector.

Source: James Acher, *Trade Union Membership 2010*, National Statistics Publication, Department for Business, Innovation & Skills. The full report can be accessed at **http://www.bis.gov.uk/policies/employment-matters/research/trade-union-stats**

Voluntary recognition

For recognition to exist, it is necessary that an employer has actually agreed to negotiate with a trade union. The mere fact that an employer meets with trade union representatives is not in itself sufficient to constitute an act of recognition by the employer. This is demonstrated by the Court of Appeal decision in *NUGSAT* v. *Albury Bros Ltd* [1978] IRLR 504. The employer belonged to an employers' association which had entered into various collective agreements with the union setting out conditions of employment which the members of the association agreed to comply with. However, Albury Bros did not have a recognition agreement with the union at company level. It did, however,

Case
Summary

↓

agree to meet with union representatives to discuss certain rates of pay which the union claimed fell below agreed standards. At this meeting the company indicated that it did not intend to change its pay rates. A short while after this meeting a number of employees were dismissed by reason of redundancy. The union claimed that it had been recognised by the company, which had wrongly failed to consult with it prior to making the redundancies. It was held that before an employer can be regarded as having recognised a trade union for the purposes of collective bargaining, clear and unequivocal evidence of an agreement, and/or conduct from which recognition must be inferred, is required. The fact that the company had met with representatives of the union did not constitute sufficient evidence that the company had agreed to recognise the union. Therefore, the company was not subject to a duty to consult with the union prior to making redundancies. This case also clarifies the fact that if a company's employers' association negotiates with a union this does not imply that the company also recognises the union.

Case Summary

The case of *Joshua Wilson & Bros Ltd* v. *USDAW* [1978] IRLR 120 provides an example of how recognition may be inferred from an employer's conduct. In this case, the company complied with a wage increase, which was negotiated with the union at national level for the whole of the industry, after it had been informed of the agreement by a representative of the union. The company had also discussed workloads and disciplinary issues with union representatives, and permitted a union representative to collect union subscriptions on its premises. It was held that taking all of these factors together constituted clear evidence that the company recognised the union. Therefore, it was in breach of its statutory duty when it made collective redundancies without first consulting with the union.

It is, of course, good practice for an employer who wishes voluntarily to recognise a trade union to enter into a written recognition agreement with the union which both confirms that the union is recognised and sets out the issues over which the employer has agreed to bargain collectively with it. However, it is important to understand that an agreement by an employer with a union that the latter may represent *individual* members in meetings with the employer does not constitute recognition, as this is not an agreement permitting the union to negotiate on behalf of the employees as a collective whole.

Case Summary

In *USDAW* v. *Sketchley Ltd* [1981] IRLR 291, following negotiations, the union and the employers signed an agreement in May 1978 entitled 'Recognition for representation agreement . . .'. The agreement provided, *inter alia*, for the appointment of shop stewards and an individual grievance procedure for union members. The agreement expressly stated that it did not confer recognition on the union for negotiation of terms and conditions. It was held that that a distinction had to be drawn between an agreement that permitted a union to represent individual members and an agreement that recognised a union for the purposes of negotiation. It was clear that the agreement in this case conferred upon the union limited rights of representation and expressly excluded rights of negotiation. Therefore, the union was not recognised and there was no obligation on the employer to consult it before making redundancies.

Writing and drafting

The above cases establish that the key factor to recognition of a trade union is that the employer has expressly or impliedly agreed to *negotiate* with the union. In order to avoid doubt and uncertainty, best practice demonstrates that the proper prerequisite for routine collective bargaining is a written recognition agreement between an employer and a trade union. In real life an employer and/or a trade union may seek the advice of a person with legal expertise, although this will not necessarily be a legal practitioner, in drafting collective agreements.

Source: Steve Cole, Photodisc

Therefore imagine that you have been approached by the HR manager of an engineering company which employs 100 staff. It is contemplating recognising the General Workers Union (GWU) for its 80 engineers.

However, it does not want its administrative and managerial staff to be within the scope of collective bargaining. The HR manager has asked you to provide her with a written memorandum containing the 'Heads of agreement' for recognising the GWU. By this she means listing the key issues that the recognition agreement should contain, and stating the main principles on which the agreement will operate.

She has told you that the company is prepared to recognise the GWU for all purposes connected with pay and contractual conditions of employment. However, the company does not want to give the GWU negotiating rights with regard to staffing issues such as recruitment, disciplinary and grievance procedures and dismissals, although it is happy to consult with the union with regard to these matters. The company does not want the recognition agreement, or any part of it, to be legally binding on it either with respect to the GWU or its employees. The company's main motivation for recognising the GWU is to promote a good working environment and avoid conflict with its employees.

Try drafting a 'Heads of agreement' which you think will accord with good employee relations practice but which also reflects the specific policies of the company.

You should spend no more than one hour on this activity.

◆ **Handy tip:** As explained in this chapter, collective agreements are not contracts and therefore are not drafted with the precision of a legal document. Indeed, one of the advantages of collective agreements not being legally enforceable is that this provides the potential for flexible amendment if it proves to be the case that a particular agreement, or a part of it, is not working as anticipated. However, collective agreements are akin to contracts insofar as they are intended to set out the rights and duties of the parties. Ideally, they should comprehensively and unambiguously reflect the intentions of the employer and trade union parties, as this will help avoid industrial disputes in the future. Therefore, in drafting your 'Heads of agreement' you should use your skills as an employment lawyer to identify what issues should be included and the type of language to be used in order to avoid uncertainty and therefore the basis for future conflict.

Independent trade unions

So far in this chapter we have discussed collective bargaining on the implicit assumption that an employer is negotiating with a trade union which has no connection with the employer and is entirely independent of it. However, s. 1 TULRCA defines a trade union as any organisation of workers which includes regulating relations with an employer as one of its purposes. Therefore, it is entirely possible, and indeed is a feature of our employee relations system, that an in-house union or staff association is established by an employer which then negotiates with that union on one or more of the matters contained in s. 178(2) TULRCA. In this situation the employer does recognise a trade union but not one which is independent of it. There are statutory advantages to being a recognised union which has also been certified as an independent trade union, such as the rights to information and consultation in the contexts of proposed collective redundancies and business transfers (explained in the previous chapter), and therefore the process of certification and the meaning of 'independent' must be considered.

The certification officer is a senior civil servant and, as the title suggests, one of the main functions of the certification officer is to ascertain if a trade union, which has applied for a certificate of independence, is genuinely independent of all employers so that the certificate can be granted (see Chapter 1). If the certification officer refuses to grant a certificate, the union can appeal to the EAT with further appeals lying to the Court of Appeal and the Supreme Court. There have been several important cases, discussed below, decided as a result of this process which illuminate the meaning of independent.

Under s. 5 TULRCA for a union to be independent it:

✦ must not be under the domination or control of an employer or of an employers' association; and

✦ must not be not liable to interference by an employer or an employers' association.

Case Summary

The meaning of this provision was considered by the EAT in *Blue Circle Staff Assoc* v. *Certification Officer* [1977] ICR 224. In 1971, the company's salaried staff in conjunction with the company's management formed a staff consultative organisation, a body financed by the employer with the object of promoting better understanding between management and staff. There was no negotiating machinery and the employer was under no obligation to accept recommendations made by the organisation. In 1974, the organisation achieved negotiating rights with the employer. Between 1975 and February 1976, new rules and a new procedure agreement were formulated and the title of 'staff consultative organisation' was changed to 'staff association'. Thereafter the staff association obtained a number of benefits for its members including a revised salary structure and a revised redundancy scheme. The association applied for a certificate of independence which was refused by the certification officer on the basis that the association had not achieved independence from the company. The EAT agreed with the certification officer's assessment of the evidence. It found that: the new rules and procedure agreement had failed to make any significant difference to the negotiating atmosphere; the secretary of the association was an employee of the company; the association's office was on the employers' premises; and the association was not properly financially independent of the company. Overall, the association was still under the employer's domination and therefore had not yet achieved independence from it.

In reaching this decision the EAT identified a checklist of factors to be considered in determining whether a trade union should be considered independent of an employer. This checklist is not a statement of law, as each case must be considered on its own facts, but it nevertheless constitutes helpful guidance. The relevant factors are:

✦ *Finance:* if there is any evidence that a union is getting a direct subsidy from an employer, independence is immediately ruled out.

✦ *Other assistance:* it is necessary to consider what other material support, such as free premises, time off work for officials or office facilities a union is getting from an employer, and whether the union could finance these from its own resources.

✦ *Employer interference*: if a union is very small and weak and gets a good deal of help, on the face of it its independence must be in danger and liable to employer interference.

✦ *History:* the recent history of a union, which was very important in the *Blue Circle* case itself, may be relevant. It was not unusual for a staff association to start as a 'creature of management and grow into something independent'. The Blue Circle staff association had started on this road but still had a way to travel.

✦ *Rules:* the union's rule book should be scrutinised to see if the employer can interfere with or control it, and if there are any restrictions on membership required by the employer. If a union is run by people near the top of a company, this could be detrimental to rank and file members.

✦ *Single company unions:* while they are not debarred from getting certificates, they are more liable to employer interference. Broadly based multi-company unions were more difficult to influence.

✦ *Organisation:* the union's size and recruiting ability should be examined in detail. Particular attention should be paid to whether it is run by competent and experienced officers, the state of its finances, and its branch and committee structure. Again, if the union was run by senior staff in a company, employer interference was a greater risk.

✦ *Attitude:* once the other factors had been assessed, then a 'robust attitude in negotiation' backed up by a good negotiating record could be seen as a sign of genuine independence. It was emphasised by the EAT that a single company union with little resources may still have behaved in a robust or even militant way. In such circumstances, it did not seem common sense to say that a union which has constantly caused trouble for an employer is dependent on that employer. However, the EAT also clarified that a history of militancy is not essential, as a union might have dealt with a good, tactful and sensitive employer who paid well and therefore its members had little to be militant about. In short, a union should not be prevented from securing a certificate of independence because it enjoyed harmonious relations with an employer.

In *Squibb UK Staff Assoc.* v. *Certification Officer* [1979] ICR 235, the words 'liable to interference' were considered by the Court of Appeal. It was held that this phrase means exposed to risk or reasonable possibility, rather than likelihood, of interference by the employer. In this case a number of employees formed a staff association to negotiate with their employers over pay and conditions. The company provided them with facilities including rooms, telephone and stationery. The association applied for certification as an independent trade union. The certification officer refused the application on the

Case Summary

grounds that the association was liable to interference by the company. The Court of Appeal upheld his decision as the extent of the association's financial dependence on the employer meant that it might well be unable to function effectively if the employer withdrew its financial support. The association might not be currently under the employer's domination but its vulnerability to employer interference, as a result of a lack of independent financial resources, meant that it could not be regarded as independent of the company.

Case Summary

The case of *HSD (Hatfield) Employees* v. *Certification Officer* [1978] ICR 21 provides an example of a staff association, which was set up with the cooperation and financial support of a single company, but was able to show that it had ceased to be under the domination of it, and therefore was entitled to a certificate of independence. An unusual aspect of this case was that the association was set up to oppose being nationalised by the government. This suggested that, when its members decided to continue its existence after it had been nationalised, and its activities showed it to be 'fiercely' independent of the new state employer, it had become an independent union. Moreover, this was the case even though the actual members of management remained largely the same people who had run the former company.

One very important advantage to having been certified as an independent trade union is the possible eligibility to secure **statutory recognition** whereby an employer becomes legally obliged to recognise and bargain with that union, even though the employer has refused to recognise that union on a voluntary basis.

The statutory recognition procedure

This procedure is contained in Schedule A1 TULRCA and was introduced by the Employment Relations Act (ERA) 1999. Statutory recognition can only be granted for the purposes of collective bargaining over pay, hours and holidays. If, for example, a trade union is voluntarily recognised by the employer with respect to bargaining over pay then it can invoke the statutory procedure with a view to extending its bargaining rights to hours and holidays.

As part of its desire to maintain a flexible labour market, the Labour government decided that small businesses should be exempted from the statutory procedure. Therefore it applies only to employer organisations employing 21 or more workers. An employer cannot pre-empt the possibility of statutory recognition by constructing an employment relationship whereby it employs workers rather than employees, and/or by conducting its operations under the auspices of separate companies. In calculating the size of an employer both employees and workers are to be included. If an employer is part of a group of associated companies then all the employees and workers in the group should be counted.

> in calculating the size of an employer both employees and workers are to be included

A union acting on its own or in conjunction with one or more other unions may invoke the new procedure where an employer has ignored, or has refused to negotiate on, a valid request for recognition which has been presented to that employer in writing. Application is made to the Central Arbitration Committee (CAC), which (as outlined in Chapter 1), has a similar role to ACAS in that it is an organisation set up by government to facilitate good employee relations. The essential difference between ACAS and the CAC is that the latter is empowered to make binding decisions. The CAC must first establish whether the application is admissible. For this to be so the application must be:

✦ made in writing;

✦ presented by an independent trade union;

✦ supported by at least 10% of the workers that the union wishes to represent with a majority likely to favour recognition.

A practical way in which a trade union can demonstrate it has the support of the workers it wishes to represent is by conducting a straw, that is, informal poll of its members at the workplace in which the majority have voted in favour of recognition. It should be understood that this poll has no legal status other than providing evidence that the relevant workers want their employer to recognise the union.

An employer may voluntarily recognise as many trade unions as it wishes. However, only one trade union can secure recognition through the statutory procedure. Therefore, a request for statutory recognition must be rejected by the CAC if the employer already recognises another trade union or has decided to do so prior to a union invoking the statutory procedure. If the existing recognised union is an independent trade union, no other union can seek to secure statutory recognition.

If the existing recognised union is not independent, workers employed by the organisation can seek to secure statutory derecognition of that union so that it ceases to be recognised by the employer for the purposes of collective bargaining. The statutory derecognition process mirrors the statutory recognition process outlined below. In particular, there is likely to be a secret ballot in which a majority constituting at least 40% of the workers in the relevant bargaining unit votes for the non-independent union to be derecognised. Once the CAC has determined that a non-independent union has been derecognised, an independent union is then able to proceed with a statutory recognition claim. It must be emphasised that it is only the relevant workers who can initiate and undertake the statutory derecognition process. The union that they wish to represent them can have no formal role in this process, though it can provide advice and other logistical forms of support.

Once the CAC has decided that a claim is admissible, it must give the employer and the union the opportunity to agree on the bargaining unit. By this we mean the categories of workers that the employer employs on whose behalf the union will negotiate with respect to pay, hours and holidays. For example, a teachers' union might be regarded as an appropriate union to recognise employees who have an educational role in a school or college, but administrative and technical support staff could well be viewed by the employer as being outside of an appropriate collective bargaining unit for that union to represent. If the parties are unable to reach their own agreement, the CAC will impose a bargaining unit on them. In so determining the collective bargaining unit the CAC must take the following factors into account:

✦ the views of the employer and the union;

✦ the characteristics of the workers and their workplace location;

✦ existing national and local bargaining arrangements;

✦ the value of avoiding small, fragmented, bargaining units.

These factors are designed to ensure that the imposition of statutory recognition will facilitate coherent and workable collective bargaining without disrupting employee relations in other parts of the employer's organisation, or within the industry as a whole. The legislation also stipulates that the paramount consideration that the CAC must take into account is that the bargaining unit it decides upon is compatible with effective management. This is controversial as it appears to prioritise the employer's interests over those of the union and its members. However, the CAC must take into account the views of the union as well as those of the employer on this issue. The CAC is not required to determine which bargaining unit would be the most compatible with effective management providing the unit that is chosen meets the criterion of compatibility.

Case Summary

For example, in *R (Kwik-Fit Ltd)* v. *Central Arbitration Committee* [2002] ICR 1212, the Court of Appeal had to decide whether to uphold the company's application for judicial review of a CAC decision that had upheld the union's proposal on the appropriate collective bargaining unit. The Transport and General Workers Union (TGWU) sought statutory recognition for employees of Kwik-Fit in the Greater London area. The company argued that the most appropriate bargaining unit consisted of employees in the country as a whole as it conducted its management on a centralised national basis. The argument presented to the CAC by the TGWU was based on the fact that the pay and conditions of employees in London varied to some extent with those of the employees in the company as a whole and therefore this bargaining unit was compatible with effective management. The Court of Appeal upheld the decision of the CAC. The bargaining unit may not have been the one that was the *most* compatible with effective management but, nevertheless, as it was so compatible, the CAC had acted properly in determining that this was to be the bargaining unit which was to apply.

Once the collective bargaining unit has been established, the CAC must decide whether a secret ballot should be held to determine the support for recognition by the workers in that unit. Where a majority of the employees in the agreed or determined bargaining unit are members of the trade union, the CAC can grant what can be described as automatic recognition. However, where this is not the case, or the CAC decides that, irrespective of the union's membership levels, it would be in the interests of good industrial relations that a ballot should take place then it will make an order to this effect. A very important factor in this regard is whether there are doubts that all the union's members actually support recognition. It might seem odd that a union member would oppose recognition, but it should be understood that some workers join trade unions in order to secure individual benefits such as advice and representation and do not want their terms and conditions of employment to be negotiated by their union.

Where the CAC orders a ballot to be held, providing it meets the criterion of being a secret ballot, it may be conducted on a postal or workplace basis. The difference between these two forms of secret ballot is that, in the former, ballot papers are sent to the employees' homes and are returned using the ordinary post. In a workplace ballot the papers are issued at work and the employees vote by putting their ballot papers into ballot boxes situated on the employer's premises. It is possible to use a combination of these processes. For example, ballot papers are sent to employees' homes but they vote at work, although employees who are legitimately absent from work will be able to vote by post. Trade unions tend to have a preference for workplace ballots as this facilitates a union encouraging its members to exercise their rights to vote. However, the decision for determining the type of ballot to be conducted rests with the CAC, although this decision is subject to judicial review.

There are various ways in which an employer could frustrate the conducting of a secret ballot or unduly influence its outcome. For example, an employer could refuse to provide the names and addresses of its employees who are not union members. To avoid this happening, an employer is under a statutory duty to co-operate generally with the conducting of a ballot and to give the trade union reasonable access to the workplace to persuade the employees to vote for recognition. If a postal ballot is to be held, the names and home addresses of the workers in the bargaining unit must be disclosed to the CAC.

Both the union and the employer are under a duty to refrain from unfair practices whilst the ballot is being held. In particular, workers must not be offered money to vote in a particular way. There must be no attempt to coerce or intimidate workers, or to threaten them with dismissal or disciplinary action, in order to prevent them from properly exercising their rights to vote.

Handy tip: the Labour government issued a code of practice on rights of access during a recognition ballot, which is still in force. This code can be accessed and downloaded from **http://www.bis.gov.uk/files/file14418.pdf**

If a majority, constituting at least 40% of workers in the bargaining unit, vote in favour of recognition, the CAC must issue a declaration to the effect that the union is recognised for the purposes of collective bargaining on the issues of pay, hours and holidays. Although collective bargaining rights are restricted to these three issues, the union will enjoy all the normal statutory advantages which are conferred on an independent and recognised trade union. These advantages (which were either discussed in the previous chapter or will be discussed later in this chapter) can be summarised as follows:

✦ rights to information and consultation where the union's members may be directly or indirectly affected by the employer's proposal to make 20 or more employees redundant;

✦ rights to information and consultation where the employer is proposing to be a party to a business transfer;

✦ rights to receive certain information from the employer in order to undertake collective bargaining on the matters for which the union is recognised;

✦ employees who are lay representatives of the union, or who are its health and safety representatives or union learning representatives, must be permitted reasonable time off with pay to carry out their trade union duties;

✦ employees must be given reasonable time off, albeit without the right to be paid, to participate in trade union activities.

Statutory recognition normally lasts for three years and will be renewed at the end of this period unless the employer successfully secures statutory derecognition. In most respects the procedure for statutory derecognition is a mirror image of the process for statutory recognition as explained above. Although an employer has the right to seek statutory derecognition once a three-year period has expired, it can be commented that an employer is unlikely to do this unless the composition of the workforce and/or union membership levels have altered significantly during the period of statutory recognition. Figure 8.2, below, sets out the stages of the statutory recognition procedure.

Figure 8.2 The statutory recognition process

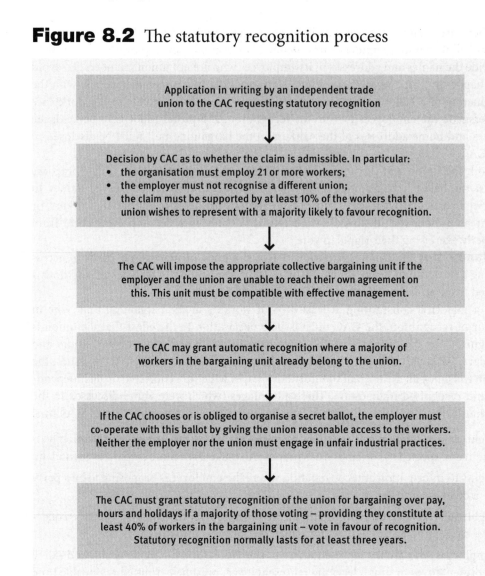

Application in writing by an independent trade union to the CAC requesting statutory recognition

Decision by CAC as to whether the claim is admissible. In particular:
- the organisation must employ 21 or more workers;
- the employer must not recognise a different union;
- the claim must be supported by at least 10% of the workers that the union wishes to represent with a majority likely to favour recognition.

The CAC will impose the appropriate collective bargaining unit if the employer and the union are unable to reach their own agreement on this. This unit must be compatible with effective management.

The CAC may grant automatic recognition where a majority of workers in the bargaining unit already belong to the union.

If the CAC chooses or is obliged to organise a secret ballot, the employer must co-operate with this ballot by giving the union reasonable access to the workers. Neither the employer nor the union must engage in unfair industrial practices.

The CAC must grant statutory recognition of the union for bargaining over pay, hours and holidays if a majority of those voting – providing they constitute at least 40% of workers in the bargaining unit – vote in favour of recognition. Statutory recognition normally lasts for at least three years.

You be the judge

Q: Do think in the following situation that the General Workers Union (GWU) will be able to present a statutory recognition claim?

M Ltd employs 200 production workers. In addition, there are 20 employees who have managerial status. The GWU, which as an affiliate to the TUC is an independent trade union, is seeking to recruit union members at the workplace. Currently, 105 of the production workers have joined the GWU.

Five years ago, M Ltd established the M Company Staff Association. All employees of the company are encouraged to join the staff association, which the company finances. The members elect the officials of the association, and the constitution of the association can be amended at the association's annual general meeting. Officials of the association can represent individual members at meetings and formal hearings with managers up to and including Robert, the managing director. Periodically, Robert meets with officials of the association to discuss pay and conditions of employment. The current employment contracts of the production workers are derived from an agreement between M Ltd and the staff association.

The GWU has written to Robert formally requesting recognition on behalf of the 200 production workers. Robert has replied by stating that he does not believe that there is a need for a formal role for the union within the company, as it already negotiates with the staff association on matters of pay and conditions.

A: As things stand, the GWU's claim could not be accepted by the CAC. Although the GWU meets the general criteria for presenting an admissible statutory recognition claim, in that it is an independent trade union representing the majority of workers in its proposed bargaining unit, its claim could not be accepted by the CAC because the company already voluntarily recognises the staff association.

However, it should be noted that the association is financed by the company and is therefore not an independent trade union. Therefore, it is possible for the production workers to initiate the procedure for the statutory derecognition of the staff association. Were they to do this successfully, the GWU would then be able to present a statutory recognition claim.

The method of collective bargaining

Where statutory recognition is granted, the employer could frustrate the purposes of recognition by refusing to meet with union representatives or engage in meaningful negotiations with them. However, one consequence of statutory recognition is that the parties are required to agree on a 'method of collective bargaining'. Failure to so agree will result in the CAC imposing a method of collective bargaining, that is, a procedure under which collective bargaining is to be conducted. This will generally be based on the model method contained in the Trade Union Recognition (Method of Collective Bargaining) Order 2000, SI 2000/1300. This will require the employer to agree to the establishment of a joint negotiating board (JNB) consisting of at least three representatives from each side. This JNB must meet annually to negotiate on pay, hours and holidays. The model procedure specifies how a union should present its claim and the number of meetings that should take place with the employer's representatives to discuss it.

The CAC may also determine what facilities, such as office space and equipment, the employer should provide the union with to facilitate it in carrying out its collective bargaining functions. Similarly, the CAC can declare what time off rights elected representatives of the union should receive to participate in the annual negotiations, plan a collective bargaining strategy and engage in consultations with the workers they represent. The method of collective bargaining is *presumed* to be legally enforceable, and will have the status of a contract enforceable in the ordinary courts through **specific performance**. It should be clarified that the employer will not be in breach of this procedure if a collective agreement is not entered into, as failure to reach agreement is always a possible outcome where collective bargaining has taken place. The employer will be in breach of the procedure if there is no proper effort by the employer to engage in negotiations in accordance with it.

It should be noted that Part VIII of Schedule A1 contains provisions protecting workers against detriment or dismissal for reasons relating to the invoking of the statutory recognition procedure. These provisions are parallel to those contained in ss. 146, 152 and 153 TULRCA, which are discussed below. Where statutory recognition is granted, the union's officials and members must be permitted the statutory time off rights for trade union purposes that are also explained below.

A union, which has secured statutory recognition, has the same rights to consultation with regard to collective redundancies or a business transfer proposed by an employer, as is the case with a union that has been voluntarily recognised by an employer. Sections 181–183 impose on employers a general duty to disclose information to a union on matters relating to the purposes for which the union engages in collective bargaining with that employer. If the employer refuses to disclose appropriate information, the union may present a complaint to the CAC. This procedure is not often used by trade unions, but is perhaps particularly useful to a union that has secured statutory recognition and the employer remains adverse to meaningful collective bargaining.

Documenting the law

Normally, in this feature we have provided documents which are relevant to proceedings in an employment tribunal or a court of law. As explained above, collective agreements are presumed not to be legally enforceable and, unless they are incorporated into individual contracts of employment, have no legal status. This is normally the legal position with recognition agreements. However, such agreements play a very important role where employers do decide to recognise a trade union for the purposes of collective bargaining, and therefore a model recognition procedure is set out below.

MODEL RECOGNITION AGREEMENT

1 INTRODUCTION

1.1 This Recognition Agreement is between the College and the Union of College Lecturers (UCL) in respect of its teaching staff.

1.2 The College believes that a fully representative union leads to good employee relations and will therefore encourage its academic staff to belong to UCL, although membership is not a condition of employment.

1.3 The College and UCL have a common objective of ensuring the success of the College. Both sides agree that their pursuit of this common objective under this Recognition Agreement shall be by:

✦ **Negotiation – for the purpose of reaching agreements and avoiding disputes;**
✦ **Consultation – for the exchange of views to influence decisions;**
✦ **Communication – for keeping each side fully informed of all relevant matters.**

1.4 The purpose of the Agreement is to set down negotiating, consultative and representational arrangements between the College and the UCL covering all teaching staff other than Heads of Department and the Principal and Deputy Principals of the College.

2 GENERAL PRINCIPLES

2.1 Objectives
The College and the UCL agree:
2.1.1 To promote harmonious employer/employee relations through the development of effective joint negotiating and consultative machinery.
2.1.2 To support collective bargaining as the most effective means of reaching agreement.
2.1.3 To ensure the continuing viability and development of the institution by adopting a flexible approach and pursuing efficient, fair and equitable and cost-effective management and labour practices.

2.1.4 To make genuine and committed efforts to resolve matters of common interest through negotiation and/or consultation.

2.1.5 To engage in the regular review and development of policies, procedures and collective agreements.

2.2 The UCL recognises the College's responsibility to plan, organise and manage its activities according to the objectives set by its Governors.

2.3 The College recognises the UCL's responsibility to represent the interests of its members and to work for good conditions of employment and work.

2.4 The spirit of this Agreement is that collective issues shall wherever possible be settled without recourse to industrial action by either party to it. Both the College and the UCL undertake to arrange discussions within the machinery provided as quickly as possible with the aim of resolving any collective dispute as soon as is reasonably possible.

3 RECOGNITION AND PROCEDURE

3.1 The College recognises the UCL as the exclusive agent for the purposes of collective bargaining on behalf of its teaching staff.

3.2 The College agrees that it will recognise the UCL for all the purposes of collective bargaining as set out in s. 178(2) Trade Union and Labour Relations (Consolidation) Act 1992.

3.3 The College and the UCL confirm that nothing in this agreement, in whole or in part, is intended to be legally enforceable.

3.4 The College and the UCL agree that all collective negotiations and consultations will be conducted through the Joint Negotiating and Consultation Board (JNCB). The maximum number of representatives in the JNCB will normally be six from each party.

3.5 It is recognised that from time to time a full-time official of the UCL may be in attendance in an advisory capacity at meetings of the JNCB. Similarly, the UCL accepts that on occasion it will be appropriate for the College to co-opt members of the management on to the JNCB.

3.6 The JNCB will normally meet on a bi-monthly basis, although additional meetings will take place where both parties agree this is necessary to ensure matters of joint interest are discussed without undue delay and resolved at the earliest stage through constructive dialogue.

3.7 The chair of the JNCB shall alternate annually between the management and trade union sides.

3.8 In the event of the JNCB failing to resolve an issue, the parties may, if mutually agreed to do so, invoke the disputes procedure.

4 VARIATION, DURATION AND TERMINATION OF THIS AGREEMENT

4.1 Variations or changes in this Agreement may only be made with the mutual agreement of both the College and the UCL.

4.2 Either the College or the UCL may terminate this Agreement by giving six months notice in writing to the other party.

4.3 The Agreement shall operate from the date of both parties signing this formal document.

Although the above can be regarded as a model recognition agreement, there is no such thing as a standard agreement as any collective agreement will reflect the specific needs and interests of the parties to it. It should be noted that some recognition agreements will also contain a collective disputes procedure, and/or provisions relating to office facilities to be provided to a trade union on the employer's premises and time-off arrangements for elected trade union representatives and ordinary members. The latter provisions can be regarded as suitable for incorporation into the individual employment contracts of the relevant employees. (An example of a collective disputes procedure will be provided in the following chapter.)

Reflective practice

Revisit the memorandum containing the 'Heads of agreement' for recognition that you have previously drafted. Is there anything you would add to or remove from your memorandum in light of the above? If you have included a disputes procedure and/or provisions relating to trade union facilities and time off rights as items for inclusion in a recognition agreement, this is entirely appropriate as many actual recognition agreements do cover such matters.

Statutory rights to time off

As mentioned above, one of the statutory consequences of recognition, be this secured through a voluntary agreement with an employer or as a result of a trade union successfully invoking the statutory recognition procedure, is that the employer is legally obliged to permit employees to have time off at work for trade union purposes. A distinction must be drawn between employees who are **workplace trade union representatives** and those who are ordinary members of the union. Whilst both categories of employee have the right to reasonable time off, it is only the former who in appropriate circumstances have the right to be paid whilst engaged in trade union duties.

Workplace representatives

The rights provided to workplace representatives are contained in ss. 168 and 169 TULRCA. A workplace representative is an employee who is elected or appointed in accordance with a trade union's own rules to act as an official of an independent and recognised trade union. Traditionally, workplace representatives have been known generically as shop stewards. Mick Tosh from the RMT, who is the trade unionist we interviewed above, is an example of a workplace representative.

Workplace representatives have the statutory right to reasonable time off with pay to undertake trade union duties. This statutory right to time off applies only where the representative is engaged in duties which are both related to or connected with the matters listed in s. 178(2) TULRCA and are in respect of the purposes for which recognition has been granted. Therefore, the extent of time off rights can be limited by the scope of the recognition agreement. For example, where a trade union has secured statutory recognition, time off rights will be restricted to duties related to or connected with annual negotiations with the employer on pay, hours and holidays. Where the trade union has been voluntarily recognised by the employer, the scope of recognition can include any or all of the other issues listed in s. 178(2).

Moreover, even if voluntary recognition is restricted to bargaining over pay and other contractual conditions of employment, it is open to the employer to consent to paid time off rights being extended to any of the other issues contained in s. 178(2). For example, an employer may have agreed to consult with a union on equal opportunities policies relating to the recruitment and promotion of its staff. If the employer agrees to workplace representatives having paid time off rights whilst engaged in such consultations, the statutory right to time off with pay is extended accordingly. An employer is not obliged to extend the scope of paid time off rights, but once it chooses to do this, the statutory duty applies for as long as the relevant agreement with the union remains in force. Under s. 168(1)(c), statutory time off rights also apply to statutory consultations where an employer is proposing collective redundancies or a business transfer.

Out and about

Visit the ACAS website at **http://www.acas.org.uk/CHttpHandler.ashx?id=274.** This will enable you to download the current ACAS Code of Practice on Time Off for Trade Union Duties and Activities, which came into force in January 2010. This code provides useful advice to employers and trade unions in understanding what time off rights involve. The code is not legally binding but contains authoritative guidance as to how the statutory provisions are to be understood and applied. The code provides that reasonable time off may be sought, for example, to:

+ prepare for negotiations with the employer;
+ inform members of the progress of such negotiations;
+ explain the outcomes of negotiations to members;
+ prepare for meetings with the employer about matters for which the trade union has only representational rights.

As you will see, the code recommends that an employer and a recognised trade union enter into their own time off collective agreement. From your reading of the code identify the issues that time off agreements should cover.

Section 168(2) provides for equivalent time off rights to enable workplace representatives to undergo training on courses which have been approved by the TUC or an independent trade union. Appropriate training courses would include those on: the representative's official role; the structure and constitution of the union; developing negotiating and communication skills; how to conduct meetings effectively; and updates on legal changes affecting employee relations at the representative's workplace.

In determining the timing of time off, and the amount that can be taken, the ACAS Code provides that trade unions should be aware of the wide variety of difficulties that employers may encounter where employees are absent from work. It stipulates that the operational requirements of the employer should be taken into account when workplace representatives seek to exercise their rights to time off. Such requirements include:

+ the size of the organisation and the number of workers;
+ the production process;
+ the need to maintain a service to the public;
+ the need for safety and security at all times.

In deciding whether to accept or reject a request for time off an employer can also take into account the amount of time off a representative has already recently been permitted to take.

It is clear from the code that an employer can refuse to permit a representative to take time off where the representative's request can be considered unreasonable because of the genuine operational problems the taking of time off would generate. This is the case even though the representative is seeking to carry out functions or undertake training covered by the provisions of s. 168. This is particularly likely to be the case with training, as this will often be conducted on a day release basis over a period of some weeks or months. Indeed, the code recommends that representatives give an employer at least several weeks' notice that they wish to take time off to attend a training course.

As recommended by the ACAS code, the most effective and certain way for determining time off rights is through collective agreement. As mentioned above, a time off agreement can be part of or appended to a formal recognition agreement. Such an agreement can also identify the facilities that an employer agrees to grant a trade union to enable its representatives and members to engage in trade union activities. There is no statutory obligation on an employer to provide such facilities, but it is common for employer to do so where a trade union has been recognised by voluntary agreement as this is regarded as good industrial relations practice. Such facilities can include an office, and office equipment such as a computer, printer, photocopier and telephone. The employer may also permit employees to use the employer's email system and intranet for trade union purposes.

> the most effective and certain way for determining time off rights is through collective agreement

It should be remembered that (as explained in Chapter 5), under s. 10 ERA 1999, any employee has the right to be accompanied by a trade union representative in formal disciplinary and grievance hearings with employers. This constitutes the only situation where an employer that does not recognise a trade union is subject to a duty to permit trade union representation. Where such a representative is an employee of the employer, the employee must be permitted to take paid time off to carry out this representational function.

Trade union members

Section 170 TULRCA gives similar rights to *unpaid* time off for trade union members to engage in trade activities. The ACAS Code provides that the activities of a trade union member can include:

✦ attending workplace meetings to discuss and vote on the outcome of negotiations with the employer;

✦ meeting with full-time officials of the union to discuss issues relevant to the workforce;

✦ voting in union elections for workplace representatives and the like.

In terms of timing, the code recommends that where workplace meetings are requested, the union should consider holding them, for example, towards the end of a shift or the working week, or before or after a meal break, in order to minimise any disruption to the employer's operations. Again this is the sort of issue that can be most effectively implemented through appropriate provisions in a time off agreement.

Whilst trade union members have the right to reasonable time off to participate in the above types of activities they have no right to be paid whilst they are doing so. However, the ACAS Code recommends that employers consider voluntarily agreeing to pay trade union members when they are engaged in activities that the employer consents to them participating in. This recommendation has no legal status but, again, is in accordance with good employee relations practice. Indeed, it may be in the employer's interests that trade union members can meet at work to vote on the outcomes of negotiations between the employer and their union.

An employee, who may or may not be a workplace representative, may be elected to attend the union's conference or other official internal meetings of the union. Such activities are covered by s. 170 and, although participation in such activities may not be of any direct benefit to an employer, many employers will accept that paying employees whilst they are away from work to attend such meetings is worth the cost given the contribution such a policy will make to maintaining good relations with both the union and the workforce.

The case of *Luce* v. *Bexley LBC* [1990] ICR 591 provides an example of a trade union activity that is beyond the scope of statutory rights. In this case the employer refused Luce, who was a teacher, permission to take time off to attend a lobby of Parliament organised by the TUC to protest against proposed legislation affecting the teaching profession. The EAT upheld the tribunal's decision that the lobby was not a trade union activity within the meaning of the legislation, as the protest was part of a political campaign against government policy, and was not connected either to relations with the employer or the constitutional affairs of the union. It is clear from this decision that not all the official activities of a trade union will constitute trade union activities for the purposes of s. 170.

Case Summary

Where provisions covering payment to employees whilst they are engaged in trade union activities are included in a collective agreement, it is, of course, permissible to provide for the employer's undertaking to pay to be incorporated into individual employment contracts. Where this occurs, the employer has become contractually obliged to honour such undertakings, even though there is no statutory right to payment. Similarly, a collective agreement can stipulate in some detail when workplace representatives are entitled to be paid whilst undertaking their trade union duties. Again such provisions can be incorporated into the employment contracts of the relevant employees. In such circumstances, workplace representatives will have both statutory and contractual rights to payment.

Remedies

With respect to the exercising of *statutory* rights any refusal by an employer to grant reasonable time off or, in the case of a workplace representative to pay the employee whilst he or she is engaged in appropriate trade union duties, may result in the employee presenting a claim to an employment tribunal. Under s. 172(1) TULRCA, tribunals may grant a declaration that the employee's statutory rights have been infringed. This is of practical importance if, for example, an employee has been subject to disciplinary action for taking time off even though the employee's request to do this was (wrongfully) refused by the employer. If the employer has issued the employee with a formal disciplinary warning then the effect of the tribunal's declaration should be that the warning is deleted from the employee's record. Under ss. 172(2) and (3) a tribunal may also award compensation to the employee for any loss suffered, or to cover any payment due to the employee, as a result of exercising statutory time off rights.

The tribunal will reject the employee's claim if he or she was seeking payment for participating in what was in fact a trade union activity rather than a trade union duty. The claim will similarly fail if in the circumstances the employer was acting reasonably in refusing the request for time off. If the employee was engaged in neither a duty nor an activity, the claim must fail.

Union learning representatives and health and safety representatives

Under s. 168A TULRCA, employees who are members of a recognised independent trade union can take reasonable time off *with pay* to undertake the functions of a union learning representative and to receive training relevant to these functions. The role of union learning representative is essentially concerned with enabling a trade union to have an input into the educational and career development of its members at a particular workplace. The functions of a union learning representative include:

✦ analysing the learning or training needs of their colleagues;

✦ providing information and advice about learning or training matters;

✦ arranging learning or training;

✦ promoting the value of learning or training;

✦ consulting the employer about carrying on any such activities.

A recognised trade union has the right to appoint or elect workplace health and safety representatives. Their rights to reasonable paid time off to carry out their functions and receive training are provided by the Safety Representatives Regulations 1977, SI 1977/500. The major functions of health and safety representatives are to carry out regular health and safety inspections at the workplace and to attend and inspect the scene of any accident. The representatives will also sit on health and safety committees established by employers to enable them to inform and consult with employee representatives on health and safety matters.

The time off rights for health and safety representatives operate in a very similar way to time off rights for workplace and learning representatives with one important exception. Generally, employers are obliged to permit union representatives to attend training courses provided by their own trade unions or by the TUC. However, employers may provide their own in-house training to trade union health and safety representatives providing the employer can demonstrate such a course properly and effectively addresses health and safety issues from a trade union perspective. If the employer cannot do this, a representative will have the statutory right to attend a trade union course.

Case Summary

In *White* v. *Pressed Steel Fisher* [1980] IRLR 176 the company refused permission for White, a union safety representative, to attend a union approved health and safety course at a technical college. The company considered that its in-company course provided appropriate training. The company had requested the assistance of the union's education officer in drawing up this course, but the union had refused to comply with this request as it wanted union representatives to attend its own courses. It was held by the EAT that, although there was no necessity for the company's course to be union approved, if the company was unable to show that the trade union aspect of its course was adequately covered, the company would be obliged to permit White to attend the course provided by his union.

In the absence of a recognised trade union, employers must now consult with either elected **employee representatives** or directly with all of their employees as a result of the Health and Safety (Consultation with Employees) Regulations 1996, SI 1996/1513, which implement the Framework Health & Safety Directive, Directive 89/291/EEC. Arguably, this is a less effective method of ensuring that employees are properly involved in discussing workplace health and safety arrangements as trade union representatives can draw on the experience and back-up of their unions. However, the current law does ensure that where there is no recognised trade union the employer must still engage the workforce or representatives of it in health and safety discussions.

You be the judge

Q: In the following situation do you think that Rachel and/or Emily have been denied their statutory rights to take time off for trade union purposes?

The Dickens Academy recognises the NUCL for all the purposes of collective bargaining as listed in s. 178(2) TULRCA. The NUCL is an independent trade union affiliated to the TUC. The academy receives requests from two of its employees, Rachel Pickwick and Emily Cratchett, for time off with pay for trade union duties. Rachel, who has been elected as a workplace representative by NUCL members employed by the academy, wishes to attend a NUCL day school on the working of the Equality Act 2010. This day school is scheduled to take place in the week following Rachel's request during the Academy's examinations period. A repeat day school has been scheduled by the NUCL to take place in one month's time.

Emily, who is a new health and safety representative for the NUCL, wishes to enroll for a TUC health and safety course which is to take place on one day a week over a two-month period. This course is also scheduled to take place in one month's time. Rachel has recently been permitted to take a week's paid leave of absence to attend the annual conference of the NUCL. Emily has never before made a request for time off for work in a trade union capacity. The academy rejects both of these requests.

A: Rachel's request for time off can probably be refused whereas Emily's request should be granted. Although attending the day school should constitute undertaking training for a trade union duty, Rachel's request for time off can probably be refused by the academy. This will be particularly so if her absence will cause operational difficulties to the academy whilst it is conducting its examinations. A relevant factor here is also the time off that Rachel has recently been permitted to take to attend her union's conference. On the other hand, it will be very difficult for the academy to justify rejecting Emily's request unless it can show it is providing her with appropriate in-house training. It is worth noting that were the academy to refuse Rachel time off to attend the repeat day school this would be much more likely to constitute a violation of her statutory rights.

Rights to information and consultation

So far, this chapter has focused on the legal processes and consequences arising out of a situation where an employer recognises a trade union for the purposes of collective bargaining. However (as was explained in the previous chapter), in circumstances where an employer is proposing collective redundancies or a business transfer, but does not recognise a trade union, the employer will still be under an obligation to inform and consult with employees representing the workforce as a whole. These duties of information and consultation are derived from EU Directives. This section of the chapter discusses other duties to inform and consult which are created by EU law and which apply on both transnational and national bases.

European Works Councils

Until 2005, only a relatively small number of UK-based multinationals were legally bound to inform and consult with their UK workforces in permanent collective representative structures, namely European works councils (EWCs). This has been the case since 2000 as a result of the Transnational Information and Consultation of Employees (TICE) Regulations 1999, SI 1999/3323, which implemented the European Works Council (EWC) Directive 94/45/EC in the UK so that it has the same legal force in Britain as is the case in all other EU member states. The Directive covers all European-level undertakings. These are defined as businesses with at least 1,000 employees, operating in more than one member state, and where in at least two states the workforce numbered 100 or more employees. A European-level undertaking is required to initiate negotiations for the establishment of a EWC if it receives a written request to do so from at least 100 employees, or their representatives, in at least two workplaces situated in at least two member states.

The general experience of works councils in EU member states was the inspiration behind the EWC Directive. Consequently, it has been trade unions that in practice have triggered negotiations for the establishment of EWCs, and typically it will be union members and/or officials who negotiate the establishment of the EWC and sit on it as representatives of the workforce. Where an employer fails to agree to the establishment of a EWC the fallback position contained in the Annex to the Directive will come into play. This will be the case where the central management of a European-level undertaking refuses to enter into negotiations within six months of being requested to do so, or if negotiations do not result in agreement within three years of the request. Under this fallback position there must be at least one meeting a year of the EWC. Moreover, there must be further meetings between these annual meetings if the employer wishes to propose changes to the business which are likely to have serious consequences for employees' interests, such as relocation, merger and reduction in size or closure of an undertaking. Under the TICE Regulations this should be as much the situation where a European-level undertaking is based in the UK as it is where the company is based in any other member state.

The Information and Consultation (ICE) Regulations

In April 2005, the Information and Consultation of Employees (ICE) Regulations 2004, SI 2004/3426, which transpose the EC Directive on Information and Consultation in the Workplace, Directive 2002/14/EC, came into force. The general effect of these regulations is that many employers, who only operate at a national level within the UK, may find themselves legally obliged to put in place arrangements to enable them to inform and consult with their workforces or with their representatives. The ICE Regulations only apply to organisations with 50 or more employees. In contrast to the way that organisational size is calculated for statutory recognition (see above), this organisational size is based on employees, not workers, and a part-time employee counts as half a person. Moreover, and again in contrast with the statutory recognition procedure, associated companies cannot be added together to constitute a single undertaking. Therefore, the ICE Regulations will not apply to a network of companies which together employ well over 50 employees but as individual companies employ 49 or fewer employees.

Where an organisation is covered by the regulations, the employer can be compelled to negotiate on or accept the setting up of new information and consultation arrangements. Under regulation 7, this is achieved by the submission of a written request, or a series of written requests made during a six-month period, from 10% of the employees in the undertaking that negotiations take place. It should be noted that this threshold is subject to a minimum of 15 and a maximum of 2,500. In this regard part-time employees resume their biological status as entire persons. However, arithmetically this can work in favour of the employer in increasing the number of employee requests required to meet the 10% threshold. Where there is no dispute concerning the validity of the employee requests the employer has three months to arrange for the election or appointment of negotiating representatives.

Arguably, the 10% threshold is a significant obstacle to the establishment of information and consultation arrangements. This is because employees will often be completely unaware of the existence of the Directive and the ICE Regulations, let alone the detail of the process they must follow to trigger statutory negotiations. Therefore, it is perfectly possible that many employers will never find themselves under any pressure to introduce new information and consultation arrangements, even though they are covered by the ICE Regulations.

> the 10% threshold is a significant obstacle to the establishment of information and consultation arrangements

The statutory fallback provisions

There is no obligation under the ICE Regulations on an employer to agree to the establishment of a permanent representative structure established for information and consultation purposes which is organised along the lines of works councils that operate in other EU member states. It is perfectly permissible for an employer to reach agreement with the workforce that information and consultation will be conducted through direct communication with the workforce as a whole, for example, via email and/or workplace surveys. Alternatively, the workforce may agree that information and consultation will be with representatives appointed by the employer rather than through representatives elected by employees.

However, if the workforce is determined that there will be a permanent structure consisting of elected representatives then ultimately the employer cannot block this. This is because if agreement is not reached between an employer and the negotiating representatives by the end of a six-month negotiating period, then the standard information and consultation provisions contained in Part IV of the regulations will apply. These provisions will also apply if the employer fails to enter into negotiations on the establishment of information and consultation processes within three months of a valid employee request.

The main features of the standard provisions are as follows:

✦ The information and consultation representatives must be elected and it is the employer's responsibility to organise the ballot.

✦ There must be a minimum of two representatives and a maximum of 25, with a norm of one representative per 50 employees or part thereof.

✦ The employer must provide information on 'the recent and probable development of the undertaking's activities and economic situation'.

✦ The employer must inform and consult on the 'situation, structure and probable development of employment within the undertaking and on any anticipatory measures envisaged, in particular, where there is a threat to employment within the undertaking'.

✦ Similarly, the employer must inform and consult on 'decisions likely to lead to substantial changes in work organisation or in contractual relations'.

The duty of an employer to provide information on 'the recent and probable development of the undertaking's activities and economic situation' is explicitly connected to the duties to consult in that the employer must explain the background and rationale for relevant decisions. Examples of the types of information that employers should provide are contained in the guidance notes that accompany the regulations. They include increase or reduction in production or sales, opening and closing of establishments, takeovers and mergers, business reorganisations and the organisation's financial situation.

These duties to consult do not require an employer to conclude an agreement with trade union or other employee representatives and this is, of course, the essential difference between duties to consult and duties to negotiate or bargain. However, where the employer's proposals are 'likely to lead to substantial changes in work organisation or in contractual relations' the employer must initiate consultations with a view to reaching agreement on the decisions that will be made.

This is similarly the case with the purposes of statutory redundancy consultations (see Chapter 7), and there is clearly an overlap here with redundancy consultations. Indeed, it is permissible for the employer to inform information and consultation representatives that statutory redundancy consultations will be carried out under the auspices of TULRCA, that is, with representatives of appropriate recognised trade unions. However, there is an argument that the probability or anticipation of redundancies requires an earlier warning and provision of relevant information than is required under TURLCA. This is therefore a context in which recognised trade unions may find it useful to consider organising their members to trigger the establishment of a works council type structure, which will operate alongside the collective bargaining forum.

It is important to appreciate that the employer may propose changes to contractual terms and conditions in circumstances where there is no risk to jobs and therefore statutory redundancy consultations are not required. However, if the employer is proposing to change working patterns and/or hours, or to introduce new technologies, then under the ICE Regulations the employer will be obliged to inform and consult with elected employee representatives where what in effect is a works council has been set up under the statutory fallback provisions.

Similar points apply to the overlap with statutory consultations over proposed business transfers in that a change in contractual relations includes a change in employer. Under TUPE, an employer is only obliged to consult where it is envisaged that measures affecting employees will occur. Under the ICE Regulations consultation is required simply because a transfer is being proposed.

The fact that the ICE Regulations can cover proposed mergers and takeovers should also at least partly fill the tremendous practical gap in TUPE, in that the latter do not apply where a merger or takeover occurs though a purchase of shares. This is the normal way in which one company acquires another and, prior to the ICE Regulations, there was no obligation to inform and consult with employees and their representatives, even where it was known or anticipated that the merger or takeover would lead to redundancies or to major changes in terms and conditions of employment. However, in this

Table 8.3 Contrasting the statutory duties to inform and consult

Issue for information/ consultation	ICE Regulations	Section 188 TULRCA	TUPE
Redundancies or job losses	As soon as any reduction in the size of the workforce is anticipated	In good time once employer decides redundancy dismissals may be necessary	In good time prior to a relevant transfer if transferor or transferee envisages job losses
Likely changes to work organisation or employment contracts	Consultation required even if no job losses or redundancies will result	No consultation required unless dismissals could occur	In good time prior to a relevant transfer if transferor or transferee envisages such changes
Proposed business transfer	Consultation required if a transfer is being proposed	Not applicable	Date of proposed transfer must be given in good time – consultations required only if transferor or transferee envisages taking any measures
Mergers or takeovers by share purchase	Consultation required if a merger or takeover is being proposed	No consultation required unless redundancy dismissals are proposed	TUPE does not apply

respect it is again unfortunate that the regulations apply to specific undertakings and not to groups of companies. An employer is not obliged to inform and consult where the proposal or decision is that of the parent company, even where that proposal or decision will impact on the undertaking and its employees.

Table 8.3 summarises the different contexts under the ICE Regulations, TULRCA and TUPE when duties to inform and consult with employee representatives will arise.

Enforcement

The CAC is empowered to order employers to take such steps as are necessary to comply with the negotiated agreement or the statutory fallback provisions. Where employers fail to comply, applications can be made to the EAT for a penalty notice which permits the EAT to impose fines of up to £75,000. However, the CAC is not empowered to delay or prevent decisions from being implemented until the appropriate information and consultation procedures have been complied with. Arguably, the most effective mechanism for ensuring that information and consultation processes are meaningful, in that they take place in good time, would be through empowering the CAC to delay the implementation of decisions until full consultation has taken place. As the TUC has stated, the decision taken by the then Labour government not to permit the CAC (or the EAT) to grant what effectively constitutes injunctive relief is a major weakness in the regulations – particularly in the case of organisations that are unlikely to be deterred by a £75,000 fine.

Employees who act as ICE representatives receive similar protection from dismissal or being subjected to any form of discrimination as is enjoyed by trade union representatives of recognised trade unions. Indeed, trade unionists who belong to independent trade unions, even where the union is not recognised, enjoy some protection from dismissal or victimisation by an employer and these general rights of association will now be considered in detail.

Rights of trade union association

The right to belong to a trade union is enshrined in international law as part of the Universal Declaration of Human Rights 1948, and, more particularly, Article 11 of the European Convention on Human Rights. Other relevant international legal instruments include Conventions 87 and 98 of the International Labour Organisation (ILO), which, like the ECHR, have been ratified by British governments. Article 11 of the ECHR is also incorporated into UK law by virtue of the Human Rights Act 1998. The right to belong to a trade union and to participate in its activities are contained in ss. 146 and 152 TULRCA. These sections of TULRCA only apply to members of independent trade unions, but both sections apply to members of non-recognised independent trade unions as well as to members of a union that is recognised by an employer.

Dismissal and detriment

Under s. 152(1) TULRCA a dismissal for membership of an independent trade union or for participation in trade union activities *at an appropriate time* is **automatically unfair**. This means that if an employee claims before an employment tribunal that a dismissal is for such a trade union reason, and the employer is unable to prove that the dismissal was a for reason that is potentially fair under s. 98(2) ERA 1996, then the tribunal must find the dismissal to be unfair (see Chapter 5) – there can be no question of assessing whether or not the employer has acted reasonably. Moreover, no qualifying period of employment is necessary to present a claim under s. 152, although if the employee has less than two years' continuity of employment, the burden of proof is on the employee to show that the dismissal is covered by s. 152. Section 153 renders it similarly automatically unfair to select an employee for redundancy on grounds relating to trade union membership or activities.

The remedies available for a dismissal in breach of ss. 152 and 153 are generally now the same as for ordinary claims for unfair dismissal (as explained in Chapter 5). Orders of **reinstatement** or **re-engagement** may be granted by an employment tribunal. The monetary remedies will be in the forms of **basic** and **compensatory awards**. However, under s. 156, successful claimants will receive a minimum basic award of £5,300. Also, under ss. 161–166 TULRCA, the dismissed employee may be able to obtain interim relief whereby a tribunal makes a Continuation of Contract Order (CCO). Applications for a CCO must be supported in writing by the claimant's union, and may only be granted if tribunal thinks it is likely the claim will be upheld at full hearing. The effect of a CCO is that the employer must continue to employ the claimant, or at least pay his or her salary in full, until the claim is finally decided through tribunal and any appeal proceedings.

The case of *Port of London* v. *Payne* [1994] ICR 555 shows that orders of reinstatement or re-engagement should not be made, even though rights of association are involved, where an employer can show that it is not reasonably practicable to comply with an order. The employees were shop stewards representing dock workers who were made redundant due to restructuring. An industrial tribunal found that the stewards had been selected for redundancy and therefore unfairly dismissed because of their trade union activities and ordered that they be re-engaged. The employers failed to comply with the re-engagement order on the basis that they had no vacancies. At a second remedies hearing the tribunal found that the employers should have sought voluntary redundancies amongst the existing workforce in order to create vacancies and rejected the employer's submission that this would be too onerous, expensive and disruptive. The Court of Appeal decided that the tribunal had erred in finding that the employers had failed to show that it was not practicable for them to comply because there were no available vacancies. The test was of practicability, not possibility, and due consideration should be given to the commercial judgement of management in this regard. What might be considered the unfortunate logic of this decision is that employers are able to rid themselves of turbulent trade unionists providing they are prepared to pay the cost in terms of compensation.

As an alternative to dismissal it may be that an employer has discriminated against an employee for reasons relating to that person's trade unionism. Under s. 146(1) TULRCA, it is unlawful to subject an individual to a **detriment** with the purpose of preventing or deterring that person from joining a trade union or participating in its activities, or penalising that person for doing so. As a result of the Employment Relations Act 2004, workers as well as employees are now protected by s. 146, although it should be noted that only employees are protected by s. 152. This is in accordance with the general policy that only employees are eligible to bring claims of unfair dismissal. As a result of amendments introduced by the Employment Relations Act 2004, the protection provided by s. 146 extends to making use of union services at an appropriate time, and to rejecting an offer made by an employer in contravention of s. 145A or s. 145B which seeks to induce an employee or worker to give up contractual terms derived from collective agreements – this latter issue is discussed further below.

A successful claim under s. 146 will result in the granting of a declaration plus compensation for any financial loss and/or injury to feelings under s. 149. Declarations are of practical importance where, for example, a worker has been disciplined for a trade union reason covered by s. 146, as the declaration will establish that the imposition of any disciplinary penalty, including a formal warning, by an employer was an unlawful act.

It should be noted that equivalent rights and remedies exist with respect to dismissal or detriment for *non*-union membership. In the past this was because trade unions were able to agree with an employer that there would be a **closed shop** whereby joining and remaining as a member of that union would be a condition of employment. However, this is really only of historical interest as closed shops have ceased to be a feature of employee relations in Britain.

Distinguishing between individual and collective discrimination

Claims under ss. 146, 152 and 153 can only be brought if action is taken against the *individual* as opposed to the union. This distinction is illustrated by *Carrington & Others* v. *Therm-a-Stor Ltd* [1983] ICR 208. In this case, the majority of the company's workforce joined a trade union and its secretary requested union recognition. The company was determined to resist trade union recognition and its response was to instruct the foreman to make 20 workers redundant. The evidence showed that in selecting employees for redundancy the foreman did not take into account whether or not the individual employees were union members. It was held that this was action taken by the employer against the union as a collective whole to deter it from making further requests for recognition. As the action was not taken against individual employees by reference to their individual trade union membership or activities, the dismissals were not automatically unfair under s. 153.

We have discussed how redundancy dismissals may be unfair under s. 98(4) ERA (in the previous chapter). It should be noted that had any of these individual employees been eligible to present an ordinary claim of unfair dismissal it can be predicted that such a claim would have succeeded in that the employer had acted unreasonably and therefore contrary to s. 98(4).

The 1990s witnessed a preference on the part of a number of employers to replace collective bargaining over pay with practices for determining the pay of employees on an individual basis. For example, an individual's pay would reflect that employee's productivity or work performance as assessed through a system of employee appraisal. The problem for such employers was that, although there were no legal obstacles to the derecognition of a trade union given that recognition agreements are not normally legally enforceable, the employers were still bound by individual employment contracts which were derived from provisions in collective agreements. The employer response to this was to induce employees to accept replacement of employment contracts derived from collective bargaining with new personal contracts where pay would be determined by the employer. Typically, employers would grant pay bonuses to employees who accepted new personal contracts or, more draconianally, would withhold any further pay increases to employees who refused to give up their existing employment contracts. These sorts of practices raised the question as to whether an employer who penalised workers who insisted on retaining union negotiated employment contracts was acting in a way that was contrary to s. 146.

In *Wilson* v. *Associated Newspapers Ltd* and *Palmer* v. *Associated British Ports* [1995] IRLR 285 the Law Lords accepted that such practices were taken against individuals rather than the union, but decided that the employers were not acting contrary to s. 146 as the employers were not preventing their employees from retaining their individual membership of a trade union. However, in *Wilson & NUJ* v. *UK* [2002] IRLR 568, the European Court of Human Rights declared that the refusal to pay Wilson a salary increase was in violation of his rights to trade union membership as protected by Article 11 ECHR. This decision was reached on the basis that employees should be free to instruct or permit their union to make representations to their employer or to take action to promote their interests. If prevented from doing so, their freedom to belong to a union became illusory. Therefore, s. 146 as it was worded at that time failed to conform to Article 11. UK law did not prohibit employers from offering inducements to employees who renounced the right to union representation, and therefore it wrongly allowed employers to treat employees less favourably if they were not prepared to give up a freedom that was an essential characteristic of union membership.

The Labour government, elected in 1997, amended the 1992 Act to give effect to this ECtHR decision. Consequently, the sorts of practices deployed by the employers in *Wilson* and *Palmer* are unlawful under ss. 145A–145E TULRCA. It should be noted that since the law was changed the trend towards derecognition has disappeared. Moreover, today, a union that was derecognised against the genuine wishes of its members in a workplace would be in a good position to mount a successful statutory recognition claim.

The meaning of 'trade union activities at an appropriate time'

Both ss. 146 and 152 cover what an employee has done as a trade unionist as well belonging to a trade union. This is only the case where the employee can show that he or she was engaged in the activities of an independent trade union at an appropriate time. The distinction between a trade union representative and the ordinary member is again important in this regard. What constitutes a trade union activity on the part of a workplace representative will often not constitute a protected activity for the ordinary member.

For example, in *Chant* v. *Aquaboats Ltd* [1978] ICR 643, the employee, a member of the Union of Construction, Allied Trades and Technicians, complained to the employer that woodworking machinery did not comply with the required safety standards. He persuaded other employees to support his complaint and organised a petition which was signed by a number of employees, a few of whom, had joined the union. The petition was vetted by the local branch of the union before being handed to the employer. It was held by the EAT that 'activities of an independent trade union' did not include an individual's independent activities as a trade unionist. Therefore, the industrial tribunal had correctly found that the organising of the petition was not a trade union activity within the meaning of the legislation and the employee had not been dismissed for an inadmissible reason.

This case also illustrates that where an employee may have been dismissed for acts connected to his or her trade unionism, but the employee cannot bring himself or herself within the scope of s. 152 and does not have the qualifying period of employment to bring an ordinary claim of unfair dismissal, then if that employee is dismissed with notice no form of legal redress will be available to him or her. Had Chant been a workplace or health and safety representative, his claim would almost certainly have succeeded as he would have been engaged in carrying out his official trade union duties.

In order for an employee to be protected by ss. 146 and 152, it is necessary for the employee not only to be engaged in appropriate trade union activities but also to undertake these activities at an appropriate time. Working hours only constitute an appropriate time for trade union activities with the employer's consent. Such consent is much more likely to be given where a union is recognised by an employer. This connects with the statutory obligation, discussed above, on an employer that recognises that union to permit employees who are trade union members to take reasonable time off to carry out trade union duties or activities. Clearly, if an employee is subjected to a detriment or dismissed whilst exercising such statutory rights then this must be a breach of ss. 146 or 152 as well ss. 168 or 170 TULRCA. An employer's right to insist that trade union activities take place outside of working hours is restricted by the obligation to comply with statutory time off rights.

Case Summary

> working hours only constitute an appropriate time for trade union activities with the employer's consent

Trade union activities that are carried out during an employee's own time will clearly be undertaken at an appropriate time as the employer's consent is no longer required.

The case of *Marley Tile Co.* v. *Shaw* [1980] ICR 72 provides a comprehensive example of the operation of ss. 146 and 152 in circumstances where statutory time off rights are not applicable. Shaw was a shop steward of a trade union recognised by the company, but the Court of Appeal found that his dismissal for calling a workplace meeting of his members during working hours was outside the scope of s. 152, as the employer had not consented to this meeting taking place and therefore it was not held at an appropriate time. In fact, it had resulted in the workers stopping work for approximately one hour. In reaching this decision, the court agreed that, as a shop steward in a unionised workplace, Shaw had acted within the scope of his duties in seeking to raise a collective grievance with management and then phoning the union's office to secure advice on how to proceed. Had the meeting been conducted after work or during a lunch break then he would have been protected by the legislation.

The decision also considered the meaning of consent. Shaw stated that he had told members of management that he was going to call the meeting and they had not expressly prohibited him from doing this. He argued that this constituted implied consent. The court held that, although implied consent is a possibility, it could not be found in this case. The context revealed a fractious relationship between Shaw and management so that silence on the latter's part was more indicative of disdain than agreement to his proposed action.

As demonstrated by *Stoke & Roberts* v. *Wheeler-Green Ltd* [1979] IRLR 211, participation in industrial action can never be a trade union activity for the purposes of ss. 146 and 152. The employees, who were shop stewards, were dismissed after they physically blocked access to machines, which they argued were in breach of health and safety requirements. It was held that, although making representations about the machines were within their duties as workplace representatives, they had acted in a way that amounted to them taking industrial action. Therefore, their conduct went beyond what could be considered either as a trade union duty or a trade union activity.

The case of *Robb* v. *Leon Motor Services Ltd* [1978] ICR 506 establishes that seeking to recruit co-workers to a trade union is a trade union activity for ordinary members as well as trade union representatives. However, as was so in this case, the member or representative should not spend an excessive amount of time on recruitment activities during working hours where this involves the employee ceasing to work. Subjecting an employee to a disciplinary penalty in such circumstances is not contrary to s. 146.

As clarified by the EAT in *Zucker* v. *Astrid Jewels Ltd* [1978] ICR 1088, employers cannot ban employees from discussing issues such as trade union membership with co-workers during working hours if this does not conflict with their ability to perform their jobs properly. If conversation or communication between employees whilst carrying out their work is permitted by the employer, the employer cannot prevent the issue of trade union membership from being the topic of conversation, etc. The case also clarifies that official tea breaks and the like, during which employees continue to be paid, should not be considered to be working hours for the purposes of ss. 146 and 152.

Victimisation for previous trade union activities

Sections 146, 152 and 153 may apply to detriments or dismissal arising out of pre-employment activities if these relate to current or proposed trade union activities.

In *Fitzpatrick* v. *British Railways Board* [1991] IRLR 376, the employer dismissed Fitzpatrick when it was discovered that she had a record of political and trade union activism in her employment with previous employers. At the time of her dismissal she did not hold any form of trade union office, and British Rail argued that therefore she was not dismissed for her current or proposed trade union activities. The Court of Appeal held that the evidence showed that the reason for her dismissal was that British Rail was concerned that at some time in the future she would resume her trade union activities and therefore her dismissal was automatically unfair.

This case can be contrasted with the decision in *Birmingham District Council* v. *Beyer* [1977] IRLR 211. In this case Beyer, a well-known trade union activist in the Midlands, applied unsuccessfully for a number of jobs. A notorious practice on the part of some employers in Britain is to draw up and circulate lists of trade union activists, or to pay others to do this on their behalf, with the purpose of excluding persons on the list from employment. Such lists are known colloquially as trade union blacklists. Beyer suspected that he was on such a blacklist and applied for a job using a fake identity, although he did not misrepresent any of his previous work experiences or qualifications. His application for this job was successful but he was dismissed when the council discovered his true identity. It was held that he was dismissed for his misrepresentations and not his trade union activism. Therefore, he was not protected by what is now s. 152 TULRCA.

Since March 2010, the blacklisting of trade unionists has been unlawful as a result of the Employment Relations Act 1999 (Blacklists) Regulations 2010, SI 2010/493. Under these regulations, as implemented by s. 104F ERA 1996, if an employee is dismissed as a result of being on a prohibited list of trade union members, that dismissal will be automatically unfair. The normal remedies for unfair dismissal apply, although a successful claimant will be entitled to a minimum basic award of £5,300. Similarly, if an employee is subjected to a detriment or refused employment as a result of being on such a list, this will be unlawful discrimination. As an alternative to a tribunal claim, individuals can seek an injunction from the High Court to prevent a person from supplying, or acting on, a prohibited list. An injunction can be accompanied by an award of damages which, unlike compensation for unfair dismissal, may include compensation for injury to feelings. Even where a prohibited list is not used, it is generally unlawful to refuse employment to a person because of that person's trade union membership.

Refusal of employment for trade union reasons

Under s. 137(1) TULRCA it is unlawful to refuse a person employment because he or she is, or is not, a member of a union. Under s. 137(2) it is unlawful to refuse employment because a person refuses to leave or join a union, or to make payments in lieu of union subscriptions. Under s. 137(3) refusal of employment will be proved if a job advertisement might 'reasonably be understood' as indicating that a job is only open to union members or to non-union members, or that a person should join or leave a trade union.

In contrast with ss. 146 and 152, it is not expressly unlawful to refuse employment on the basis of an individual's trade union activities. However, in *Harrison* v. *Kent County Council* [1995] ICR 434, the EAT refused to distinguish between union membership and the incidents of it – these were regarded as including a person's previous union activities. In this case, during prior employment with the council, Harrison had been a shop steward and had been involved in a dispute involving strike action. He left the employ of the council but subsequently applied for a new job with it. This job application was rejected by the council on the basis that during Harrison's previous employment with it he had displayed a confrontational and anti-management approach. The employment tribunal found that a major reason for the council's refusal to re-employ Harrison was because of his past union activities but that, since s. 137 only referred to trade union membership and not to trade union activities, the refusal was not unlawful. The EAT decided that the industrial tribunal was wrong to draw a rigid distinction between membership of a trade union and taking part in the activities of a trade union. Where a person was refused employment for a reason related to his union activities it was open to the tribunal to conclude that he had been refused employment because he was a member of the union. Therefore, Harrison may well have been protected by s. 137. It can be noted that, almost certainly, the approach taken by the EAT is required by Article 11 of the ECHR as refusal of employment on the basis of an individual's record as an active trade unionist will be contrary to the right of association.

Remedies

Claims presented to employment tribunals on the basis of s. 137 must be made no later than three months from the date of the conduct to which the complaint relates. In line with the position under discrimination law in general (which is explained in the previous chapter), the claimant can argue that tribunals should draw the **inference of discrimination** where the evidence suggests this has taken place. The burden of proof is then on the employer to show that the decision to refuse employment was not on grounds which are rendered unlawful by s. 137. Under s. 140 TULRCA, if the complaint is upheld a declaration must be granted. The tribunal may also award compensation, which may include compensation for injury to feelings but is subject to the statutory maximum for a compensatory award, which was £72,300 at the time of writing.

As is also the case with general discrimination law, the tribunal may make a recommendation that the employer take action to remove or reduce the adverse effect on the claimant of the discriminatory conduct. An example of such a recommendation will be that the claimant is invited to apply for a post with the employer on the next occasion that a vacancy arises, although the tribunal cannot recommend that the claimant should actually be given the job as this would discriminate against other potential applicants. Failure by the employer, without reasonable justification, to comply with a recommendation may result in the tribunal increasing the award of compensation (subject to the statutory maximum).

Summary

◆ Historically, the British system of industrial relations was characterised by 'voluntarism' or a lack of legal regulation of the relations between employers and trade unions.

◆ Attitudes to industrial relations and collective labour law will be informed by unitarist, pluralist or radical/Marxist perspectives.

◆ In Britain, it is presumed at common law and under s. 179(1) TULRCA that collective agreements between employers and trade unions are not legally enforceable.

◆ Substantive collective agreements or appropriate provisions in procedural agreements may be incorporated into individual employment contracts and will consequently be legally enforceable by employees against their employers.

◆ Employers may voluntarily enter into an agreement with a trade union to recognise it for the purposes of collective bargaining over one or more of the issues listed in s. 178(2) TULRCA.

◆ Such recognition agreements are generally not legally enforceable and can be terminated by the employer at any time with the effect that the union will have become derecognised.

◆ A trade union is independent of an employer if it is not under its domination or control, and it is not vulnerable to employer interference in the way that it operates.

◆ An independent trade union may secure statutory recognition for collective bargaining over pay, hours and holidays which will last for at least three years.

◆ Workplace representatives of a recognised independent trade union have the statutory right to reasonable time off with pay to undertake trade union duties arising out of recognition or for purposes to which the employer has consented.

◆ Workplace representatives of a recognised independent trade union have the statutory right to reasonable time off with pay to undertake training for such trade union duties.

◆ Ordinary members of a recognised independent trade union have the statutory right to reasonable time off without pay to engage in trade union activities such as attending workplace union meetings or voting in union elections.

◆ Under the ICE Regulations, employers may incur duties to inform and consult with trade union or employee representatives over a large range of issues including proposed redundancies, business transfers, mergers, takeovers and changes to terms and conditions of employment.

◆ Under ss. 152 and 153 TULRCA, it is automatically unfair to dismiss an employee, or select an employee for redundancy, because that employee is a member of a trade union or has participated in its activities at an appropriate time.

◆ An appropriate time includes during working hours where the employer's consent has been given or statutory rights to time off apply.

◆ Under s. 146 it is unlawful to subject an employee or a worker to a detriment for membership of an independent trade union, or participation in its activities at an appropriate time or for accessing union services.

◆ Under s. 137, it is unlawful to refuse employment to a person because of that person's trade union membership or previous trade union activities.

Question and answer*

Problem: Wessex Borough Council recognises UNISON, an independent trade union which is affiliated to the TUC, for all the normal purposes of collective bargaining. However, 40 out of its 120 clerical staff are members of the Professional Association of Clerical Officers (PACO), which is a non-TUC affiliated independent trade union. Wessex Borough Council has repeatedly refused to recognise PACO and has a policy of encouraging all its employees to join UNISON. Consequently, UNISON workplace representatives, but not PACO officers, are permitted to use, free of charge, office facilities owned by the council. All employees are permitted to use the council's email system for private matters, providing such use is not excessive.

The council decides to establish a working party, which is entrusted with the task of drafting new disciplinary and grievance procedures. The council invites UNISON representatives to sit on this working party but makes it clear that representation of PACO members will not be permitted. Jill Smith, who is the PACO steward, requests a meeting with Roy Hammond, the Council's personnel officer, to discuss this issue, but Jill's request is refused. In working time, Jill emails PACO's head office for advice. It is suggested to Jill that she should call a workplace meeting of PACO members to discuss what action the association should take. Jill organises this meeting, which takes place in the staff coffee room.

The next day Jill is summoned to Roy Hammond's office and informed that she is to be formally disciplined for engaging in PACO activities in working hours on council property. Jill is also informed that she must remove her three-year old child from the council's crèche, as there are too many children using it and she is the most junior of the relevant employees.

One week after these events, Len Brown is interviewed for a post with the council. Len is well-known in local government circles for being a PACO activist. Len has now received a letter from Wessex County Council informing his that his application has been unsuccessful and that another of the applicants for the post has been appointed. Len has discovered that the successful applicant was less well-qualified and experienced than him.

Advise Jill Smith and Len Brown as to their legal rights and remedies (if any) against Wessex County Council.

You should spend 40 minutes on answering this question.

Essay: 'In Britain, and in contrast to the position in other European countries, the system of collective bargaining operates outside of a legal regulatory framework and collective agreements have no legal status.'

Comment critically on this statement and discuss the implications of collective bargaining for individual contracts of employment.

You should spend 40 minutes on answering this question.

✱ Answer guidance is provided at the end of the chapter.

Further reading

Bowers, J., Duggan, M. and Reade, D. (2011) *The Law of Industrial Action and Trade Union Recognition* **(Oxford University Press: Oxford).**
Chapters 21–23, which are written by Katherine Apps and James Wynne, provide an up-to-date account and analysis of the operation of the statutory recognition procedure.

Davies, P. and Freedland, M. (2007) *Towards a Flexible Labour Market Labour Legislation and Regulation since the 1990s* **(Oxford University Press: Oxford).**
This book provides invaluable critical analysis for any reader who wants to understand the relationship between government policy and collective and individual labour law in the 1990s and at the start of this century. Chapter 2 covers the years of John Major's government and Chapter 3 covers the policies of Tony Blair's New Labour government.

Deakin, S. and Morris, G. (2012) *Labour Law* **(Hart: Oxford).**
This is the seminal text on collective as well as individual labour law. Chapter 1 provides historical and contemporary analysis of the British system of industrial relations and the legal regulation of the employment relationship. Chapters 8 and 9 provide comprehensive coverage and in-depth critical analysis of rights of association and collective bargaining.

Ewing, K. (2005) 'The Functions of Trade Unions', *Industrial Law Journal,* **vol. 34, pp. 1–22.**
This article, written by one of the most eminent labour lawyers in Britain, provides a useful account of what trade unions do both at the workplace and in society as a whole. The article contrasts the functions of trade unions historically with their functions in contemporary society.

Dukes, R. (2008) 'Constitutionalizing Employment Relations: Sinzheimer, Kahn-Freund, and the Role of Labour Law', *Journal of Law and Society,* **vol. 35, pp. 341–63; Ewing, K. (1998) 'The State and Industrial Relations: Collective Laissez-Faire Revisited',** *Historical Studies in Industrial Relations,* **vol. 5, pp. 1–31.**
These two articles are of interest to readers who are interested in discovering more about the historical development of industrial relations in Britain and in discussion of Kahn-Freund's theory of collective *laissez-faire.*

Ewing, K. D. and Truter, G. M. (2005) 'The Information and Consultation of Employees Regulations: Voluntarism's Bitter Legacy', *Modern Law Review,* **vol. 68, pp. 626–41; Hall, M. (2005) 'Assessing the Information and Consultation of Employees Regulations',** *Industrial Law Journal,* **vol. 34, pp. 103–26; Welch, R. and Williams, S. (2005) 'The Information and Consultation Regulations: Much Ado About Nothing?',** *Cambrian Law Review,* **vol. 34, pp. 29–50.**
These articles provide in-depth explanation and analysis of statutory duties to inform and consult with trade union or other employee representatives with emphasis on the ICE Regulations.

Reynold, F. and Hendy, J. (2012) 'Reserving the right to change terms and conditions: how far can the employer go?', *Industrial Law Journal,* **vol. 41, pp. 79–92.**
This article critically discusses recent case law, including *Malone* v. *British Airways,* and examines the extent to which employers may rely on clauses in employment contracts reserving the right to vary the terms and conditions of the employment. It is argued that in cases such as *Malone* variation should only be through the negotiation of a new collective agreement.

Russell, R. (2011) '*Malone and others* v. *British Airways plc***: protection of managerial prerogative?',** *Industrial Law Journal,* **vol. 40, pp. 207–13.**
This case note provides explanation and critical analysis of the decision of the Court of Appeal in *Malone* v. *British Airways* that the relevant part of a collective agreement could not be incorporated into individual employment contracts because of the consequences this would create for the employer.

Wedderburn, Lord (1992) 'Inderogability, Collective Agreements, and Community Law, *Industrial Law Journal*, **vol. 21, pp. 245–64.**

Readers may find this article a little difficult to read but it is well worth the effort. In this article, Lord Wedderburn, who is generally regarded as succeeding Kahn-Freund as the doyen of British labour law, clarifies the legal status of collective agreements in Britain and compares the British system of collective bargaining with the position in a number of other European countries. Lord Wedderburn uses the term 'inderogability' to explain the different ways whereby collective agreements in different countries establish

minimum legal standards to which employers must conform.

Welch, R. (2000) 'Into the Twenty-First Century – the Continuing Indispensability of Collective Bargaining as a Regulator of the Employment Relation', pp. 615–34 in Collins, H., Davies, P. and Rideout, R. (eds) *The Legal Regulation of the Employment Relation* **(Kluwer: London).**

This book chapter assesses the ongoing value to workers of having employment contracts containing term and conditions of employment which are derived from collective agreements. It contrasts the position of such workers with those employed under 'personal' contracts of employment.

Question and answer guidance

Problem:

You should start your answer by explaining that recognition of a trade union is normally the product of voluntary agreement between an employer and a trade union. Therefore, the council is acting lawfully in recognising UNISON but not PACO and restricting facilities to the former. Similarly, it can distinguish between UNISON and PACO with regard to consultation so that only the former has representation on the working party.

Although PACO is not a recognised trade union, it is an independent trade union and therefore Jill is protected by s. 146 TULRCA. As a trade union representative, Jill is engaged in trade union duties in raising a collective grievance with the employer and emailing her union for advice. With regard to the latter act, it is relevant that all employees can use the Council's email system for private purposes – *Zucker* v. *Astrid*. The main problem for Jill is her calling of a union meeting at the workplace. Applying *Marley Tile Co* v. *Shaw* even though this can be regarded as a trade union activity it will not have been carried out at an appropriate time if the meeting takes place in working hours without the employer's consent. Your answer should discuss whether the meeting took place in working hours or, for example, during an official lunch break or after the working day had finished. The council's consent to the holding of the meeting is not required if the meeting took place outside of working hours, but Jill must not be in breach of the council's rules in holding a meeting on its property.

If Jill is protected by s. 146, she will have suffered a detriment in being subjected to disciplinary proceedings. She will be entitled to a declaration to this effect from a tribunal plus an award of compensation to cover injury to feelings. If she can prove a connection to her PACO activities, then withdrawal of her child from the crèche will also be contrary to s. 146 and she will be entitled to compensation to cover the cost of any alternative child-care arrangements.

Len Brown will need to prove that he was refused employment because of his PACO membership and/or previous PACO activities. Appling *Harrison* v. *Kent CC*, this will be contrary to s. 137 TULRCA and he will be entitled to compensation. He will be able to use the fact that the successful applicant was less well-qualified and experienced to argue that the tribunal should draw the inference that he was unlawfully discriminated against.

Essay:

This essay question is asking you to explain the British system of collective bargaining and to clarify the differences between this system and other European systems. In commenting critically on the statement, you should explain the ways in which it is misleading.

Your answer could start by explaining that the statement is correct in so far as it is the norm in Britain that collective agreements are not legally enforceable. If either an employer or a trade union acts in breach of a collective agreement, this is not a breach of contract and the other party cannot take legal action. However, the statement is misleading insofar as collective agreements may be incorporated into individual contracts of employment and are thereby legally enforceable between an employer and its individual employees. In discussing the statement you should clarify that at common law and under s. 179(1) TULRCA there is only a presumption against legal enforceability. This presumption can be rebutted for a whole agreement, or a particular part of it, if the parties agree that their agreement in whole or in part is to be legally enforceable. Your essay could draw on the article in the *Industrial Law Journal* by Lord Wedderburn, which is cited in the further reading above, to provide brief explanation of how collective bargaining operates in other European states.

Your answer should contain a section focusing on the incorporation of collective agreements into individual employment contracts. You should distinguish between substantive and procedure agreements, and clarify that provisions in the latter may be suitable for incorporation even though the agreement as a whole will normally not be legally enforceable. You should discuss cases, such as *Kaur*, *Alexander* and *Griffiths* concerning the difficulties involved in deciding whether a collective agreement has been impliedly incorporated where incorporation is not implemented through express agreement. You should also discuss the decision of the Court of Appeal in *Malone* v. *British Airways* and the academic criticisms that have been made of it, for example, by Russell and by Reynold and Hendy.

Your conclusion could make reference to the fact that employee relations in Britain remain less regulated by the law than is the case with other western European systems. However, the non-legal enforceability of collective agreements does permit a flexibility that is not present in other European systems. Moreover, the experience during the period of the Industrial Relations Act 1971 suggests that both employers and unions in Britain prefer their system of collective bargaining to those which operate elsewhere in Europe.

Visit **www.mylawchamber.co.uk/welch** to access tools to help you develop and test your knowledge of employment law, including interactive 'You be the judge' multiple choice questions, practice exam questions with guidance, annotated weblinks, case summary and key case flashcards, legal newsfeed, legal updates and answer to Lawyers' brief simulation.

mylaw**chamber**
unrivalled support for legal education

Chapter 9
The legal regulation of industrial action

Key points In this chapter we will be looking at:

◆ The economic torts committed by trade unions, their officials or members in organising industrial action

◆ The circumstances in which statutory immunity will apply to protect the organisers of industrial action from liability in tort

◆ Requirements on trade unions to organise secret ballots and adhere to strike notice procedures to avoid losing statutory immunity

◆ Dismissals of individual trade unionists for participation in industrial action

◆ Picketing and the law

Introduction

We examined collective bargaining processes and their legal consequences where employers recognised trade unions (in the previous chapter). The central objective of **collective bargaining** is to provide a mechanism whereby employers and trade unions can make **collective agreements** to resolve conflicts of interests between employers and their work-forces. However, where such agreements cannot be negotiated it is always possible that an industrial dispute will take place, and a trade union will support its members taking industrial action as the only means available to them to exert pressure on an employer to reach agreement with their union. Alternatively, an industrial dispute may occur because an employer refuses **voluntary recognition** of a trade union that a substantial number of its workers belong to.

In most democratic countries in the world, trade unions and their members are granted legal rights to organise and participate in strike action. Indeed, in some countries, including France, Italy and South Africa, rights to strike are part of the rights granted to individual citizens by the constitutions of those countries. This has never been the case in Britain where (as explained in the previous chapter), **collective *laissez-faire***, rather than the provision of a legal framework, was the preferred policy of governments until the 1980s. Until the last quarter of the nineteenth century the taking of industrial action was likely to have attracted criminal liability. Since the 1890s, although the criminal law is seldom of relevance, judges have decided that the organisation of industrial action involves the commission of a number of **economic torts**.

A tort is a civil wrong and the victim of a tort may sue the defendant in damages and seek an **injunction** to prevent the tortious act from commencing or continuing to take place. The imposition of tortious liability on the organisation of industrial action therefore renders it inherently unlawful. In the absence of positive rights to strike, it is only possible for industrial action to be lawful in Britain where Parliament enacts legislation which gives trade unions, their officials and their members protection, or immunity, from the tortious liabilities that organising industrial action inevitably involves.

Statutory immunities from tortious liabilities have existed since the Trade Disputes Act 1906. Depending on the policies of the government in power, the immunities have been relatively wide or relatively narrow. The latter has been the case since 1980, and the current immunities and circumstances in which they will be lost are to be found in Part V of the Trade Union and Labour Relations (Consolidation) Act (TULRCA) 1992. This chapter will explain the torts that are committed through the organisation of industrial action, or through organising and participating in acts of picketing during the course of an industrial dispute.

The way in which the TULRCA operates means that a trade union may often incur legal liability as a result of the actions of its paid officials and/or workplace representatives. Therefore, before examining the law in depth it is useful briefly to explain the typical structure of a trade union in order to understand how legal liability can be incurred. Similarly, it is useful to identify the different forms that industrial action can take.

Trade union structure and forms of industrial action

Different trade unions use different terminology with respect to how their leaders, leading committees and workplace representatives are called. However, the typical structure of any trade union is as follows.

✦ The most senior officer of a trade union will be the president or general secretary who will be elected through a postal ballot by the membership as a whole.

✦ This person is accountable to a national executive committee (NEC) which is also elected through a postal ballot by the membership as a whole.

✦ The general secretary and/or the NEC will appoint national full-time officials, who are employees of the union. Their role is to the assist the general secretary and the NEC in the day-to-day running of the union and in providing services and advice to the union's branches and members.

✦ Many unions will also have regional committees, elected by members in the region, and paid regional officials.

✦ For the ordinary member the most important part of the union is the branch to which he or she belongs. This branch may be based on the workplace or on the town or city in which the workplace is located.

✦ The branch will be run by elected officers and these officers will often be some of the workplace representatives who engage in negotiations and consultation with an employer at workplace level. Typically, they will be assisted by additional representatives. (It is these types of workplace representatives who have rights to paid time-off to carry out their trade union duties which we examined earlier.)

As is to be expected, a trade union will be legally liable for unlawful industrial which is organised by its national leadership. However, as explained fully below, it will also be legally liable, initially at least, for industrial action which is organised by workplace representatives, as such action is *deemed* to be authorised by the union. This is the case even where such representatives have acted beyond the authority conferred on them by their union's constitution. A trade union can avoid legal liability by repudiating the actions of its workplace representatives. If repudiation occurs then, in law, the industrial action has become unofficial.

Forms of industrial action

Industrial action, be it lawful or unlawful, can take different forms, and in order to understand the case law it is useful to explain the different types of industrial action that workers may take.

✦ A strike is a complete withdrawal of labour where members refuse to come into work. Strike action may last indefinitely, but it is more typical today for strike action to take place on specified days or groups of days.

✦ Workers may decide to take **industrial action short of a strike**. Typically, this will take the form of a refusal to carry out particular contractual duties, such as any obligation to work overtime, but otherwise workers will work normally.

✦ Another example of industrial action short of a strike is where workers decide to work strictly to contract by refusing to undertake any work that is not part of their specific or normal contractual duties – this type of action is also known as working to rule. For reasons which are explained later in this chapter, this type of industrial action will often involve employees acting in breach of their contracts of employment but this will not always be the case.

Employers can also take industrial action in the form of a 'lock-out'. This may take the form of workers being formally barred from entering the workplace. Alternatively, employees may be permitted to come into work but are informed that they will not receive their wages or salary unless they agree to end industrial action by working normally. The following statistics provide further insight into the nature of industrial action.

Key stats

Strike statistics cover stoppages of work-in-progress in the UK during a year caused by labour disputes between employers and workers, or between workers and other workers, connected with the terms and conditions of employment. These include 'lock-outs' by employers and 'unlawful' or 'unofficial' strikes. The statistics exclude disputes that do not result in a stoppage of work, for example, work-to-rules and go-slows. Strikes are measured through calculating the working days lost through stoppages of work. These are defined as the number of days not worked by people involved in a dispute at their place of work.

Since the 1980s, at least in part, it is suggested, as a result of mass unemployment and the impact of legal controls on industrial action, the number of working days lost through strikes has steadily declined.

For example 29.5 million working days were lost in 1979, and 27.1 million in 1984. In 2009, the number of working days lost was just 438,000.

Unsurprisingly, given the number of public sector workers who are in trade unions, it is often the case that many more working days are lost during a year in the public sector than was so in the private sector. In 2006 there were 656,000 working days lost in the public sector as against 98,000 days in the private sector.

The figures were higher again in 2011. A significant factor in this increase was the strike action organised by public sector unions in defence of their members' pension rights. In the 12 months to November 2011, there were 1.38 million working days lost from 134 stoppages. In November 2011 alone, there were 988,000 working days lost from eight stoppages. Most of the working days lost in November 2011 were due to the one day strike, on 30 November, which was part of the ongoing (at the time of writing) dispute over public sector pensions. Further details on this dispute are detailed in the 'Law in Action' feature later in this chapter.

Source: Dominic Hale, Office for National Statistics, *Economic and Labour Market Review*, vol. 4(6), June 2010. The figures for 2011 from the Office for National Statistics can be accessed at **http://www.ons.gov.uk/ons/taxonomy/search/index.html?newquery=*&nscl= Labour+Disputes&nscl-orig=Labour+Disputes&content-type=publicationContentTypes&sortDirection=DESCENDING&sortBy=pubdate**

Whether or not industrial action amounts to a full stoppage of work, an employer may decide to dismiss all or some its employees who take that action. Today, there are special unfair dismissal laws that apply in this situation, which this chapter will also examine. However, the law of tort provides the starting point for our examination of the legal regulation of industrial action.

Industrial action and the economic torts

As stated above, where employees take industrial action this normally involves them acting in breach of their employment contracts. Either employees will be totally withdrawing their labour or they will be refusing to carry out specific contractual duties. Except in extremely rare circumstances where an employer consents to employees having time-off to participate in industrial action, employees who take strike action, or industrial action short of a strike, are thereby refusing to obey the reasonable instructions of their employer. This will mean that the employees are committing **repudiatory breaches** of their employment contracts (see Chapter 3).

The relevance of this to the law of tort is that, in *Lumley* v. *Gye* (1853) 2 E&B 216, it was decided that inducing one contracting party to act in breach of contract constitutes a tort against the other contracting party. This case had nothing to do with industrial relations and, in fact, involved a theatre owner persuading an opera singer to break her contract to perform in the plaintiff's theatre. However, since the 1890s, this form of tortious liability has been extended to trade unions which – and to any trade union official, representative or member who – instruct, persuade or encourage employees to take industrial action. Indeed, it is virtually impossible to organise industrial action without inducing another to break his or her contract of employment and thereby committing a tort.

Case Summary

Inducing or procuring a breach of a contract

The essential elements, or component parts, of this tort, were relatively recently confirmed in *TimePlan Education Group Ltd* v. *NUT* [1997] IRLR 457, although, perhaps ironically, the facts of the case illustrate a situation where a tort will not have been committed.

Case Summary

TimePlan was a teacher supply agency, providing local education authorities and school governing bodies with 'supply teachers' to fill temporary vacancies in the UK. Most of TimePlan's teachers came from Australia and New Zealand. The National Union of Teachers (NUT) had for some time been in dispute with TimePlan over the terms and conditions of teachers supplied by the agency, which it claimed fell below the requirements of the School Teachers' Pay and Conditions Act 1991 for teachers employed in state-funded schools. The NUT became aware that the New Zealand Education Institute, (NZEI), a teachers' union in New Zealand, was carrying advertisements for TimePlan in its fortnightly magazine. The NUT wrote to the NZEI outlining the nature of the NUT's dispute with TimePlan and suggesting that the NZEI 'might consider it inappropriate to carry TimePlan advertising in the future'. The NZEI subsequently wrote to TimePlan informing it that the NZEI was obliged to respect the wishes of a sister organisation and that, accordingly, it was suspending the agency's advertisements.

The Court of Appeal held that the tort required all the following elements of the tort to be present:

(a) the union induced or procured the breach of contract by persuading or pressurising a contracting party not to perform the contract;

(b) the union did this with knowledge of the existence of that contract;

(c) the union intended to induce or procure a breach of that contract;

(d) the claimant suffered more than nominal loss as a result of the contract being broken.

In this case, there was no evidence that the NUT knew or could have known that there was an *existing* contract between the NZEI and TimePlan and therefore the union could not have intended to induce the NZEI to act in breach of contract. Its intention was to persuade the NZEI not to engage in *future* business with TimePlan.

The case both confirms the elements of the tort and illustrates how the actual facts of a case will determine whether the tort has been committed. Had the NUT been aware that there was a contract between the NZEI and TimePlan, it would have been liable. It should be understood that it is not necessary for the union or any other organiser of industrial action to know the precise terms of a contract. Moreover, if the union or other organiser knows that a contract may exist, but is recklessly indifferent as to whether or not it does actually exist, then there will be sufficient knowledge for the tort to be committed. In the above case, the NUT was not reckless as the evidence showed its intention was to persuade the NZEI not to make *future* contracts with TimePlan, rather than to break an *existing* contract, whilst the dispute continued.

The element of inducement requires that there is an attempt to encourage, persuade or put pressure on a contracting party to act in breach of contract. Alternatively, in the case of a trade union it may instruct its members to take action that is in breach of their employment contracts. However, where a contracting party is merely given information or advice, which leads to that party deciding to act in breach of contract, the element of inducement will be missing and the tort will not have been committed.

For example, in *Camellia Tanker SA* v. *International Transport Workers Federation (ITWF)* [1976] ICR 274, the union did no more than inform its members that negotiations over pay had broken down. Having received this information the members themselves then decided to take industrial action. It was held that the ITWF had not induced its members to break their employment contracts.

Industrial action short of a strike and employment contracts

Industrial action short of a strike will also normally involve union members in breaking their employment contracts, as they will be refusing to carry out specific duties which are expressly required by the contracts. For example, teachers who boycott all or any of the assessment process will clearly be in breach of their employment contracts even where they are still are prepared to carry out their teaching duties as normal.

However, what if industrial action is regarded by those taking it as working strictly in accordance with the terms of their employment contracts, or it involves a refusal to carry out work which is regarded as voluntary or derived from goodwill? Can it be said that a refusal to perform such work is a breach of contract? On the face of it, it might appear that the answer is no, but it is important to take into account the presence of **judicially implied terms** in contracts of employment, and whether industrial action is in breach of such a term even although an express term in the employment contract has not been broken. We have seen (in Chapter 3) that all employees are under judicially implied duties to act in good faith and to cooperate with their employers. Case law shows how industrial action may involve breach of such duties and thereby involve a union or its officials inducing a breach of contract.

In *Secretary of State for Employment* v. *ASLEF* [1972] ICR 19, ASLEF, the train drivers union, instructed its members to work to rule in a dispute over contractual conditions of employment. This involved the carrying out of a variety of safety checks before a train could leave a railway station. These safety rules were contained in British Rail's rule book but were out of date. The Court of Appeal held that the union had intended its members to act in such ways as would cause serious disruption to train services by wilfully obstructing and impeding the efficiency of their employer's business. The employees were in breach of their contractual duties to work faithfully and to cooperate with the employer's business and ASLEF had thereby committed a tort.

In *BT* v. *Ticehurst* [1992] ICR 383, managers employed by BT participated in industrial action over pay by withdrawing their goodwill. This took the form of them using their discretion over which parts of their job should be prioritised for completion by leaving to last those jobs which were the most important to the employer. It was held that as this was an unprofessional use of their discretion the employees were in breach of the implied duty to cooperate.

As demonstrated by *Cresswell* v. *Inland Revenue* (which is discussed in Chapter 3), employees will also be in breach of this duty if they refuse to work with new technology providing the employer has offered proper training to enable employees to work in new ways.

A refusal to accept overtime working where this is genuinely a voluntary matter may not constitute a breach of employment contract even though the ban on overtime is motivated by an industrial dispute. This was held to be the case by the Privy Council in *Burgess* v. *Stevedoring Services Ltd* [2002] IRLR 810. As a Privy Council decision this is only of persuasive force in Britain, but it is likely to be followed by British courts.

However, it is necessary to take into account that a voluntary duty may have become a contractual duty through **custom and practice**. This was the issue in *Solihull Metropolitan Borough Council* v. *National Union of Teachers (NUT)* [1985] IRLR 211. The NUT instructed its members not to carry out a number of voluntary duties including attending meetings, such as parents' evenings, which took place after school hours. The court held that such duties had been undertaken for so long that they had become part of teachers' normal duties and were incorporated into their contracts of employment. Therefore, in organising this action the NUT was liable in tort for inducing its members to act in breach of their employment contracts.

In *OBG Ltd* v. *Allen*, which is discussed below, the House of Lords suggested that a tort is not committed if there is no intention to induce a breach of contract. Therefore, it is possible that on the facts the NUT might not be liable today, as the NUT genuinely but mistakenly believed the industrial action did not involve its members acting in breach of their employment contracts.

Directly or indirectly committing the tort

In all of the cases so far a union has committed a tort by directly inducing a party to a contract to break that contract. Direct inducement occurs where the union communicates directly with the contracting party and is illustrated diagrammatically in Figure 9.1.

In Figure 9.1 three parties are involved. The trade union (TU) has directly approached its members, who are employed by the employer, to persuade and thereby to induce them to break their contracts of employment with the employer.

It is also possible for the breach of a contract to be procured or brought about indirectly by inducing a third party to act in a way which prevents a contract from being performed. For example, a trade union uses indirect means to procure breach of a commercial contract between the employer with which it has a dispute (the employer in dispute) and another company, which is not involved in the dispute. This will normally be done by persuading employees of a supplier or customer of the employer in dispute not to handle goods or to boycott services to be supplied to or received from the employer in dispute. The supplier or customer is thereby prevented from performing the commercial contract with the employer in dispute. The indirect procurement of the breach of a commercial contract is illustrated diagrammatically by Figure 9.2.

Figure 9.1 Direct inducement to break the contract of employment

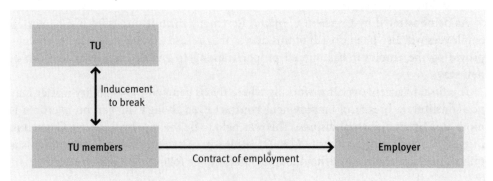

Figure 9.2 Indirectly procuring a breach of a commercial contract

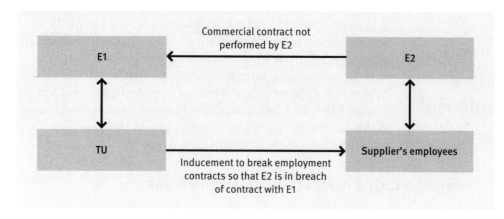

In Figure 9.2 four parties are involved. The trade union (TU) has not directly induced the supplier (E2) to break its commercial contract with the employer in dispute (E1). Rather, it has achieved its purpose of procuring a breach of the commercial contract between E1 and E2 by inducing the employees of the latter to break their employment contracts by refusing to handle the supplies for E1. Consequently, E2 is unable to perform the commercial contract with E1. The trade union intends to procure a breach of the commercial contract between E2 and E1 in order to injure the latter. Therefore, it has committed the same tort as in Figure 9.1 but has done so by indirect means.

It was long believed, as a result of *obiter dicta* of the Court of Appeal in *Torquay Hotel* v. *Cousins* [1969] 1 All ER 522, that where a breach of contract was so procured indirectly, a tort was only committed where this was achieved through the use of **unlawful means**. Such means can be regarded as any form of unlawful activity which is used to achieve the objectives of the perpetrator(s), be those objectives lawful or unlawful. The most clear-cut example of unlawful means is persuading others to act in breach of contract. Therefore, the means that a union uses will be both indirect and unlawful where employees of a customer or supplier to an employer in dispute are induced to act in breach of their employment contracts by refusing to carry out their employer's instructions. This is illustrated by Figure 9.2 above.

However, in a groundbreaking decision in *OBG Ltd* v. *Allan* [2008] 1 AC, the House of Lords reviewed the economic torts as they have developed since the decision in *Torquay Hotel* v. *Cousins*. The *OBG* case brings together three appeals from cases arising in the commercial world, but the facts of these cases shed no light on the issue in the context of industrial disputes. The key relevance of the decision to industrial action is that the Law Lords have ruled that there is just one unified single tort of inducing or procuring a breach of contract. It is not relevant to the establishment of tortious liability whether the breach of contract is achieved by direct or indirect means. Therefore, a trade union is committing the *same* tort irrespective of whether it directly persuades a party to a contract with an employer in dispute to break that contract, or indirectly prevents that party from carrying out the contract by inducing its employees to break their employment contracts.

Causing loss by unlawful means

In *OBG* v. *Allan* the House of Lords also confirmed that the second main economic tort is to cause another to suffer loss by using unlawful means. This loss can be caused either by interfering with a contract to which the claimant is a party or by interfering with that person's trade or business. In other words, interfering with contracts or interfering with business are different practical ways of committing the same tort. As confirmed by the Law Lords, and as elaborated below, the elements of this tort are that there is an intention to cause loss to a person and unlawful means are used to achieve this objective.

> there is an intention to cause loss to a person and unlawful means are used

Interference with a contract by unlawful means

The difference between interfering with a contract, as against inducing or procuring a breach of a contract, is illustrated by the case of *Torquay Hotel* v. *Cousins*. In this case, Esso had entered into a contract to supply oil to Torquay Hotel for the hotel's central heating system. Esso was persuaded by the Transport and General Workers Union (TGWU), which was in dispute with the owner of the hotel, not to perform this contract. Esso could not be sued for breach of contract as it was protected by an exclusion clause. The Court of Appeal held that, nevertheless, there had been direct interference with the performance of the contract and a tort had been committed. It made no difference to the issue of the liability of the union organiser that Esso was not in breach of its contract with the Torquay Hotel.

As a result of the decision in *OBG* v. *Allan*, the *Torquay Hotel* case would be decided differently today as no *actual* breach of contract occurred. There can only be a tort if interference with the commercial contract is brought about by unlawful means. For example, in a case similar to Torquay Hotel, a union instructs drivers employed by an oil company not to deliver supplies to the hotel, or threatens the oil company that it will issue such an instruction if the company does not voluntarily refuse to honour the contract. The inducement of the drivers to act in breach of their employment contracts, or the threat to induce them to do so, provides the necessary unlawful means for tortious interference with a contract to be committed.

The commission of a tort through interfering with the performance of a contract, as opposed to procuring or inducing its breach, by unlawful means is illustrated diagrammatically by Figure 9.3.

In Figure 9.3, as in Figure 9.2, four parties are involved. However, the difference between Figure 9.2 and Figure 9.3 is that in the latter an actual breach of the commercial contract between E2 and E1 has *not* been procured as E2 is protected by the exclusion clause. Nevertheless, TU has interfered with the performance of this contract by persuading the employees of E2 to break their employment contracts. TU has done this with the intention of injuring E1 and, in inducing E2's employees to break their employment contracts, TU has used unlawful means and thereby committed a tort.

Causing loss by interference with business or trade

Causing loss by interference with a person's business or trade is the same tort as causing loss by interfering with a contract but it occurs in a wider context. Interference with business may take place even though the performance of an *existing* contract has not been

Figure 9.3 Interfering with a contract through unlawful means

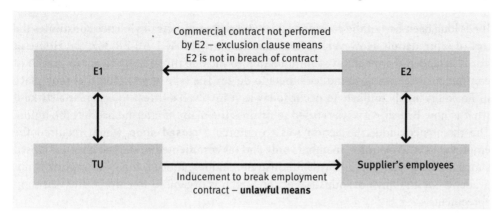

prevented. For example, a union may interfere with an employer's business by persuading other employers and/or consumers not to enter into new contracts with the employer in dispute. Again such interference will only be tortious if unlawful means are used.

In *Middlebrook Mushrooms Ltd* v. *TGWU* [1993] IRLR 232 the company produced mushrooms on their farms. The company wanted to save money by ending overtime arrangements. The company was unable to reach agreement with the TGWU and its employees took industrial action. The company then dismissed all of its employees involved in the industrial action. In response the union organised its members into leafleting shoppers outside supermarkets informing them of the situation and asking them to exercise their freedom of choice by not buying Middlebrook's produce in the store they were entering. The Court of Appeal held that the leafleting was aimed at shoppers and did not result in any breach of a contract. The leafleting was carried out lawfully and, as unlawful means were not present, no tort had been committed even though the leafleting may have affected the business of Middlebrook Mushrooms by some shoppers deciding not to purchase the company's produce. It can be noted that, had union members sought physically to obstruct or prevent shoppers from buying the mushrooms, then any business loss to the company would have been brought about by unlawful means and a tort would have taken place.

For the tort of causing loss by unlawful means to be committed there must be an intention to cause loss to the claimant. Such intent was present in both the *Torquay Hotel* and *Middlebrook Mushrooms* cases as the employer in dispute was the target of the TGWU's actions. The union was interfering with the contracts or business of the employer in dispute to pressurise the employer into acting in a particular way.

The tort will not be committed if a company's business is affected as a consequence of industrial action but this is not the purpose of the action. For example, in *Barretts & Baird Ltd* v. *IPCS* [1987] IRLR 3, the claimant's business was injured as a result of industrial action by civil servants who were in dispute with the government as their employer. This action meant that licenses to export meat were not being granted and the claimant was unable to carry on its trade. It was held that inducing the civil servants to act in breach of their statutory duties to provide licenses may have constituted unlawful means. However, even if this was so, no tort was committed as the loss suffered by the claimant was the consequence, not the purpose, of the industrial action.

Table 9.1 summarises the elements of the main economic torts.

The tort of intimidation

Case Summary

It has long been part of the common law that threatening acts of violence constitutes the tort of intimidation. However, in *Rookes* v. *Barnard* [1964] 1 All ER 367, the House of Lords extended the meaning of intimidation to include threatening to act in breach of contract or threatening to induce others to do so. The type of situation that took place in *Rookes* is highly unlikely to occur today as it involved a threat to organise a strike if what is now British Airways refused to dismiss the plaintiff after he had left the union. The threatened industrial action was to enforce a **closed shop** which required the employer to employ union members only and (as commented in the last chapter) closed shops are no longer part of British industrial relations. Indeed, today, immunity is not available for any form of industrial action which is organised to enforce a closed shop agreement.

It remains the case today that a threat to organise industrial action, despite being a standard negotiating tactic, constitutes the tort of intimidation. However, it was suggested in *OBG* v. *Allan* that threatening to break, or to induce a breach of, a contract should be regarded as an example of causing loss by unlawful means rather than an economic form of intimidation.

Table 9.1 The economic torts

Title of tort	Elements of tort
Directly or indirectly inducing or procuring the breach of an employment or commercial contract	Defendant must have induced a breach of the contract in the knowledge of the existence of the contract and with the intention that the contract be broken
Causing loss by interfering with a contract or a person's business	Defendant must have intended to cause loss to the claimant as against the loss being the consequence of the defendant's actions, and the defendant must have used unlawful means
An example of the above tort is persuading an employer not to enter into a commercial contract with the employer in dispute by threatening to induce the employees of the former to act in breach of their employment contracts	The above elements are present in the example in the first column of the table as the defendant intends to cause loss to the employer in dispute by discouraging others from doing business with that employer. Threatening to induce the employees of a potential supplier or customer of an employer in dispute to break their employment contract provides the requisite unlawful means

You be the judge

Q: Do you think that M, a trade union official, has committed a tort in any of the following situations?

(a) M informs the members that she represents at X Ltd that their request for a wage increase has been rejected by management. On receiving this information the members decide to take immediate strike action.

(b) M informs members at Y Ltd that the company is intending to implement compulsory redundancies and instructs them to implement a ban on voluntary overtime.

(c) M instructs members at Z Ltd not to deliver supplies to A Ltd. The employees of A Ltd are on strike for higher wages and are in the same union as the employees at Z Ltd. There is an exclusion clause in the contract of sale between Z Ltd and A Ltd which protects Z Ltd from any liability for breach of contract.

A: M is not liable in (a), is probably liable in (b) and is definitely liable in (c). In (a), the only tort which M could have committed would be directly inducing her members to act in breach of their employment contracts. However, in line with the decision in *Camellia Tanker*, she has only provided information and the element of inducement is missing. However, note that if M gave this information at a meeting and the information was given in an agitational manner, the element of inducement might be satisfied.

In (b), on the face of it, there is no tort as the members have not acted in breach of contract. However, this is only definitely the case if working overtime is genuinely a voluntary choice for employees. If the long-established practice is for employees to work overtime each and every time they are asked to do so, then a ban on overtime could be considered a breach of the duty to cooperate and/or breach of a term implied by custom and practice. This position is the result of cases such as *BT* v. *Ticehurst* and *Solihull MBC* v. *NUT*. If the employees are in breach of contract then M has clearly induced this breach and consequently has committed a tort.

In (c), in line with the decision in *OBG* v. *Allan*, M has committed the tort of causing loss by unlawful means. Although the commercial contract between A Ltd and Z Ltd has not been broken, M has interfered with its performance with the intention of causing loss to A Ltd. Persuading the employees of Z Ltd to break their employment contracts by refusing to handle goods to be supplied to A is an unlawful way of interfering with the contract between A Ltd and Z Ltd. Therefore, because unlawful means have been used, M has committed a tort.

The statutory immunities

In British law trade unions and their members have not been given rights to organise industrial action. Instead they have been given statutory immunity from liabilities in tort. In recent times the statutory immunities were contained in the Trade Union and Labour Relations Act (TULRA) 1974. The governments of Margaret Thatcher and John Major were influenced by unitarist philosophies which regard collective action by trade unions as unduly harmful to businesses and the economy (as explained in Chapter 8). As part of government policies for reducing trade union power, a number of Acts passed from 1980 onwards incrementally whittled down the scope of the statutory immunities. The changes made by these governments remain the law and the current immunities are to be found in s. 219 Trade Union and Labour Relations (Consolidation) Act (TULRCA) 1992.

Under s. 219(1), an act done by a person in contemplation or furtherance of a trade dispute is not actionable in tort on the grounds only:

(a) that it induces another person to break a contract or interferes or induces another person to interfere with its performance; or

(b) that it consists in his or her threatening that a contract (whether one to which he or she is a party or not) will be broken or its performance interfered with, or that he or she will induce another person to break a contract or interfere with its performance.

Therefore the current immunities expressly cover the torts of:

✦ inducing or procuring breaches of, or interfering with, contracts of employment;

✦ inducing or procuring breaches of, or interfering with, commercial contracts;

✦ intimidation through threatening to do any of the above acts.

However, contrary to the position in the 1970s, the immunities have been amended so, although there is still immunity covering an act constituting interference with a contract, there is no longer any immunity with respect to an act constituting interference with trade or a business. As explained above, as a result of the decision in *OBG* v. *Allan*, such interference is a tort where it is causes loss and is achieved through the use of unlawful means. Therefore, if a union causes loss by interfering with another's contract there may be immunity, but there will not be immunity where a union causes loss by interfering with a person's business or trade, and this so even though the interference takes place in the context of a lawful trade dispute. This may not be logical but it is the result of how the immunities are currently worded. However, it is important to remember that interference with another's business is only tortious if unlawful means are used and this point is at the heart of decision of the House of Lords in *Hadmor Productions* v. *Hamilton* [1982] IRLR 102.

Case Summary

In the case the House of Lords clarified that inducing a breach of contract, etc. cannot constitute unlawful means where the statutory immunity applies. A broadcasting union threatened that its members would break their contracts of employment with Thames Television by refusing to transmit programmes produced by Hadmor, an independent company. The union had committed the tort of intimidation against Thames Television but the evidence established there was a lawful trade dispute with it, as the union feared that some of its employees would be made redundant. Therefore, the threat to induce Thames Television's employees to break their employment contracts was protected by the s. 219 immunity. As there was no *actionable* tort, this meant the threat could not constitute unlawful means. Therefore, even though the union's action was designed to cause loss to Hadmor it could not sue with respect to the interference with its business as no unlawful means had been used.

If the House of Lords had not decided the case in this way it would have led to the peculiar result whereby Thames Television, as the employer in dispute, could not have sued the union for inducing its members to take industrial action, but Hadmor, as a third party whose business was adversely affected by the action, would have been able to sue. Such a conclusion would have led to a restriction on industrial action which even Margaret Thatcher's government had not intended. When this government first amended the immunities in 1980 it was its intention that it should remain fully lawful for a trade union to organise industrial action by inducing its members to break their employment contracts where those members had a genuine trade dispute with their own employer.

However, as has been the case since the immunities were further amended in 1990, statutory immunity does not apply where a trade union organises **secondary industrial**

action. This occurs where a trade union organises industrial action by members who are not dispute with their own employer but who take action in support of other workers. In this situation, inducing or procuring breaches of contracts, or threats to do so, are actionable torts and will constitute unlawful means.

Therefore, as an example, tortious interference with business will be committed if suppliers or customers of an employer in dispute are persuaded by a union not to enter into any new business with the employer in dispute provided this is achieved through the use of unlawful means. This will be the case where a union has induced the employees of customers and suppliers to the employer in dispute to break their employment contracts by refusing to carry out any work connected with the business operations of the latter. The elements of this tort are summarised in Table 9.1 and the issue of secondary industrial action is fully explored below.

What is a lawful trade dispute?

The key to establishing whether the organisation of industrial action is protected by the statutory immunities, in s. 219 TULRCA, is through determining whether the industrial action is '*in contemplation or furtherance of a trade dispute*'. The definition of a trade dispute, as amended in 1982, is now contained in s. 244 TULRCA. Section 244 provides that the following matters can provide the basis of a lawful **trade dispute**:

✦ terms and conditions of employment, or the physical conditions in which any workers are required to work;

✦ engagement or non-engagement, or termination or suspension of employment or the duties of employment, of one or more workers;

✦ allocation of work or the duties of employment as between workers or groups of workers;

✦ matters of discipline;

✦ the membership or non-membership of a trade union on the part of a worker;

✦ facilities for officials of trade unions;

✦ machinery for negotiation or consultation, and other procedures, relating to any of the foregoing matters, including the recognition by employers or employers' associations of the right of a trade union to represent workers in any such negotiation or consultation or in the carrying out of such procedures.

> '*terms and conditions of employment*' include but are not restricted to contractual terms and conditions

It can be noted that these trade dispute matters are identical to the purposes of collective bargaining which are set out in s. 178(2) TULRCA (which we considered in the previous chapter). It should be clarified that 'terms and conditions of employment' include but are not restricted to contractual terms and conditions. Disputes over managerial instructions, which employees are required to comply with, can also provide the basis for a lawful trade dispute.

For example, in *P (A Minor)* v. *NAS/UWT* [2003] ICR 386, P was a pupil at a voluntary aided school in inner London. His teachers found him disruptive, violent and abusive and he was expelled from the school. He was later reinstated but after further incidents of disruption some of the teachers complained to their union, the NASUWT, saying that they should not be required to go on teaching P. The NASUWT balloted the teachers over whether they should refuse to teach P. It was argued on behalf of P that this was not

Case Summary

a dispute over terms and conditions in the teacher's employment contracts but over a rule requiring teachers to comply with all of the headmaster's instructions. The House of Lords decided that, irrespective of whether the instruction to teach P was contractually binding on the teacher, this was a dispute over the conditions under which the teachers were employed. The industrial action was therefore in furtherance of a lawful trade dispute. Indeed, as the Law Lords clarified, it is not uncommon for employees to be in dispute with their employers over what precisely the employer is contractually entitled to instruct them to do.

The meaning of 'in contemplation or furtherance of'

It is not sufficient that a trade union declares an industrial dispute over one or more of the above matters. The union must be able to demonstrate, if it organises action that is tortious, that a dispute is actual or imminent, as otherwise the action will not be in *contemplation* of a trade dispute. For example, in *Bents Brewery* v. *Hogan* [1945] 2 All ER 570, the plaintiff brewery sought a declaration that Hogan, a trade union officer, was not entitled to seek certain information from their employees, which was deemed confidential under their contracts of employment. Hogan had requested this information to enable it to formulate a collective bargaining strategy. It was held that, as a trade dispute with the brewery neither existed nor was imminent, the inducement of its employees to break their contracts of employment was not protected by statutory immunity.

It follows from this case that if collective bargaining breaks down a union can seek confidential information from its members. It may not do so, however, in order to secure information which it believes it will be useful to have in drawing up a claim to be presented to an employer.

The case of *Health Computing Ltd* v. *Meek* [1981] ICR 24 demonstrates that if a union genuinely believes a dispute could imminently occur then industrial action will be regarded as being in contemplation of that dispute. In this case, NALGO (which represented local government officers and is now part of UNISON) opposed the company's plans to develop, market and maintain computer systems and software for use in hospitals and other medical services. NALGO believed that the number of NHS computer employees and opportunities for such employees to do research and development work would be reduced. NALGO therefore instructed its members in the NHS not to cooperate with the company in order to pre-empt the risk of job losses. It was held that this action was in contemplation of a trade dispute as NALGO genuinely believed there was a real risk of future redundancies. It was not necessary for NALGO to wait until there was evidence that redundancies were actually being considered before being able to organise lawful industrial action.

Despite the views of Lord Denning and the Court of Appeal, which resulted in a number of controversial decisions in the late 1970s, it is clear that the words '*in furtherance of*' impose a *subjective* and not an *objective* test. It is enough if a trade union honestly believes that organising the industrial action will further the course of the trade dispute from the perspective of its members. This interpretation was given by the House of Lords in *Express Newspapers Ltd* v. *McShane* [1979] ICR 210. In this case, the Law Lords clarified that it was for a trade union, not the courts, to determine what it considered to be the most effective tactics to be used to enable it to win an industrial dispute. Therefore, it had to be accepted that the NUJ was acting in furtherance of a pay dispute between local journalists and their employers when it called upon national journalists to take supportive action. It should be noted, as is explained further below, that such supportive

Case Summary

Case Summary

Case Summary

or sympathy action is unlawful today, but that is because statutory immunity is lost if workers are organised into taking industrial action in circumstances where they are not in dispute with their own employers.

The meaning of 'wholly or mainly related'

For the statutory immunities to apply, the dispute must be *wholly or mainly related* to one or more of the above employment matters. The meaning of this phrase is demonstrated by the following cases.

In *Mercury Communications* v. *Garner* [1984] ICR 74, the Post Office had a monopoly in telecommunications until 1981, when British Telecom (BT) was established and the Secretary of State was permitted to 'liberalise' that monopoly by licensing rival systems. In February 1982 such a licence was granted to Mercury. To operate their system Mercury needed to be connected to BT's network. Liberalisation was opposed by the union representing Post Office engineering workers as was the government's proposed denationalisation of BT. In March 1982, union members were instructed not to connect Mercury's system. The evidence showed that the union was ideologically opposed to privatisation, but in its literature it had also expressed fears that phone boxes would close – particularly in rural areas – and it feared redundancies would result. It was held by the Court of Appeal that, even if the union's fears over redundancies were genuine, the predominant motive of the union in organising the action was political opposition to government policy. Therefore, although the dispute may have been connected to job losses, it was not wholly or mainly related to this issue and the statutory immunity did not apply. Therefore, an injunction was granted to Mercury to prevent the union from continuing from to organise tortious industrial action.

The *Mercury* case can be contrasted with *Associated Ports* v. *TGWU* [1989] IRLR 291. In this case, the government enacted legislation to abolish the Dock Labour Scheme which had been established by the 1945 Labour government to provide job security to dock workers. Whilst the legislation was going through Parliament, the TGWU, to which the dockers belonged, sought to engage in collective bargaining with the port employers so that a new version of the Dock Labour Scheme would be created through collective agreement. When the employers refused to negotiate the TGWU organised strike action. It was held by the High Court that a lawful trade dispute did exist and the statutory immunity applied. Whilst the TWGU was clearly politically opposed to government policy, the main purpose of the proposed strike related to the employer's refusal to negotiate over terms and conditions of employment.

It is also possible that government policy will adversely impact on the terms and conditions of a trade union's members. In such circumstances the union may organise industrial action providing the reason, or at least the main reason, for doing so is to protect its members' conditions. For example, in *Mayor & Burgesses of the London Borough of Wandsworth* v. *NAS/UWT* [1993] IRLR 344, the NAS organised a boycott of the statutory education assessment tests (SATs), which had been introduced by the government. Although members of the union were critical of the tests on educational grounds, the boycott arose out of a long-standing dispute over teachers' working hours and the chief concern of the union was the excessive and unnecessary workload that the tests would impose on teachers. It was held by the Court of Appeal that the evidence demonstrated that the dispute related *mainly* to terms and conditions of employment of the union's members and was accordingly a lawful trade dispute within the meaning of s. 244 TULRCA.

Case Summary

Case Summary

Case Summary

Identifying whether there is a trade dispute between employees and their own employers

Under s. 244(1) a trade dispute is only lawful if a dispute exists between employees and their own employer. It is not necessary that all the workers who participate in industrial action are personally in dispute with their employer providing they are employed by the employer with whom the dispute lies. This is demonstrated by the case of *BT plc* v. *Communications Workers Union* [2004] IRLR 58. BT sought an injunction to prevent a strike called by the CWU. The strike was called because BT had sought to introduce a productivity scheme, which sought to link pay to employees' productivity. This scheme had been rejected by the CWU's members. BT then proposed to introduce a voluntary scheme rather one which was contained in a collective agreement. This voluntary scheme was also opposed by the union's members though it would only have affected those employees who signed up to it. BT argued there was no trade dispute between it and its employees as a number of employees who were called upon to strike were not in dispute over their own terms and conditions of employment. This argument was rejected by the court as there was no requirement under s. 244(1)(a) TULRCA that only those whose terms and conditions were directly affected could be involved. If the Act prevented employees taking action where there were attempts to change the terms and conditions of only some of them, the union could not represent its members effectively.

A lawful trade dispute can only take place with an existing as against a future employer. In *University College London Hospital NHS Trust* v. *UNISON* [1999] IRLR 31, the University College trust was negotiating with an as yet unidentified private consortium with a view to the latter building and running a new hospital for the trust. Under the arrangement, union members employed by the trust would transfer to the consortium and would become its employees. UNISON sought to persuade the trust to enter into a contractual agreement with the consortium to ensure that the workers who were transferred would be guaranteed equivalent terms and conditions to those who were not transferred. UNISON sought this protection for a period of 30 years. This meant that the protection would be extended to employees who would be employed by the consortium in the future but who had not previously worked for the trust. When the trust refused to enter such an agreement, UNISON balloted for strike action. The Court of Appeal held that this was really a dispute with an, as yet, unidentified future employer rather than a dispute with the trust as the existing employer.

It should be noted that, in *UNISON* v. *UK* [2002] IRLR 497, the ECtHR decided that the failure of the legislation to confer immunity to cover the above type of situation was not a violation of Article 11 ECHR. Whilst this decision explicitly recognised that rights to strike are an aspect of the right of association, the restrictions on these rights in this case were within the margin of appreciation given to a signatory state to protect the general economic interests of society.

Earlier we examined the statutory duty of an employer which recognises a trade union to consult with that union over a proposed **business transfer** (see Chapter 6). This duty clearly applies if it is known that the transferee is proposing to **derecognise** the union and/or terminate collective agreements once the transfer has taken place. It can be argued that there would be a valid trade dispute with the transferor if the latter refuses to co-operate with the union in seeking to secure agreement with the transferee not to implement such plans. If this position is wrong, this means that the union cannot organise lawful industrial action until after the transfer has occurred. By then it may be too late

Case Summary

Case Summary

for effective industrial action to take place. Certainly, this situation can be distinguished from the UNISON case, given that UNISON was seeking a 30-year guarantee and to protect the unidentified future employees of an unidentified future employer.

The following disputes are not disputes between employees and their own employer and therefore cannot be lawful trade disputes:

✦ disputes between workers – for example, demarcation disputes where workers argue over which type of worker should be allocated a particular type of work by the employer;

✦ disputes between different trade unions – for example, where industrial action arises because two trade unions are competing with each other for recognition by the same employer;

✦ disputes over international matters which do not impact on workers' own terms and conditions of employment – for example, industrial action in support of union policy boycotting a political regime in another country.

Secondary action and loss of immunity

Under s. 224(2) TULRCA, with the exception of lawful picketing, there is no immunity where a trade union, or any other person, organises sympathetic or secondary industrial action. This is defined as action which is taken by employees who are not employed by the employer who is a party to a lawful trade dispute. This follows from governmental policy which restricts immunity to disputes between employees and their own employers. During the 1980s, secondary action was permitted in limited circumstances involving customers and suppliers of an employer in dispute but, in 1990, this limited immunity was abolished. The government decided that employers should not have their businesses disrupted through their employees taking industrial action in support of workers in dispute with another employer.

The most common form of secondary action is where a trade union asks union members employed by a supplier or customer of an employer in dispute to take action which enforces a boycott of the employer in dispute. Typically, this will involve the union indirectly procuring a breach of a commercial contract, or interfering with its normal performance, through inducing the employees of a supplier or customer to break their employment contracts. As explained above, this constitutes the use of unlawful means. The effect of s. 224(2) is that immunity is removed from the inducement of the suppliers' or customers' employees to act in breach of contract. Therefore, the union will be liable for inducing or procuring breaches of contracts or for causing loss through the use of unlawful means.

It should be noted that, providing there is a lawful trade dispute, immunity is not lost where a union directly persuades a third party not to carry out its commercial contract with the employer in dispute. However, this is only the case where the persuasion is not accompanied by the use of unlawful means such as threatening to induce the employees of the third party to break their employment contracts.

Section 224(2) also prevents a union from inducing its members in the same union and the same industry as employees in dispute from taking industrial action in support of that dispute. They will not have a dispute with their own employers, and therefore can only take secondary action. This is the case even if the employees of another employer fear that their own employer may copy the actions of the employer in dispute in the future and therefore can be regarded as having a genuine material interest in the outcome of the dispute. For example, the employer in dispute is proposing to cut the pay of and/or impose new contractual conditions on its workforce. Other employers in the industry are less likely to follow suit if industrial action forces the employer in dispute to abandon such proposals.

However, it is permissible for unions representing workers who have genuine separate trade disputes with their own employers to coordinate industrial action so that it is taken simultaneously and/or in planned phased stages to maximise the pressure that that the industrial action generates. The most obvious example of this in recent times was the coordinated strike action in 2011 by public sector trade unionists opposed to their employers implementing government proposals to worsen their pension rights.

Law in action

The reasons for the dispute between public sector workers and their employers over their occupational pensions were documented earlier (see the 'Law in action' feature in Chapter 8). This dispute led to what was effectively a one-day general strike by public sector workers on 30 November 2011. This strike was co-ordinated by the TUC and saw members of unions representing a wide range of public sector workers taking part. They ranged from podiatrists and radiographers to cleaners and construction workers.

The relevant unions were: the Association of Educational Psychologists, Aspect, Association of Teachers and Lecturers, Chartered Society of Physiotherapy, Educational Institute of Scotland, First Division Association, GMB, National Association of Head Teachers, Napo (family court and probation staff), the teachers' union NASUWT, Northern Ireland Public Service Association, National Union of Teachers, Public and Commercial Services Union, Prospect, Society of Chiropodists and Podiatrists, Scottish Secondary Teachers' Association, Society of Radio-

Source: Debbie Rowe, Pearson Education Ltd

graphers, UCAC (one of the Welsh teachers' unions), Union of Construction, Allied Trades and Technicians, University and College Union, Unison and Unite.

At the time of writing, negotiations had still not resulted in any agreement and further industrial action remained a possibility.

Source: http://www.bbc.co.uk/news/uk-13932304 accessed on 14 January 2012.

Case Summary

It is possible for employees to be employed by the same human being, but in circumstances where that person has set up his or her business operations through a network of companies which each employ their own employees. This was the situation in *Dimbleby* v. *NUJ* [1984] ICR 386, where journalists who were members of the NUJ were in dispute over recognition with a specific businessman. This man owned a printing company as well as a company producing a newspaper and both companies operated on the same premises. The recognition dispute was with the newspaper company only. It was held by the Law Lords that union members employed in the printing company, which printed the plaintiff's newspaper, could not be asked to take industrial action as they were not in dispute with the company which actually employed them.

In this type of situation there are no legal grounds for 'piercing the corporate veil' to enable a union to argue that the dispute is with a specific human being as against the different companies that he or she owns. This is the case even though it is one person who makes all the decisions in all of the companies, and from the perspective of the employees they are all employed by the same employer. As explained below, this legal position has also been criticised by the ILO.

It should be noted that, under s. 222, immunity is also lost if it is taken to enforce trade union membership. This was part of the process initiated by governments in the 1980s to end the closed shop as an institution in British industrial relations. Similarly, s. 225 removes immunity from industrial action which is organised to pressurise an employer into employing unionised labour only. More significantly, in terms of the contemporary world of employee relations, immunity is removed by s. 223 from industrial action which is organised as a result of workers being dismissed for taking **unofficial industrial action**. This latter issue is discussed further below.

Handy tip: In answering problem questions concerning liability for industrial action it is advisable to consider issues in the following order:

✦ Has the union or organiser of industrial action committed a tort?

✦ If so, is the union or organiser protected by the trade dispute immunity?

✦ If so, is this immunity lost for any reason – for example, the union has failed to comply with statutory strike procedures (see below) or the industrial action is secondary in nature?

If a tort is not committed, or any tort which is committed attracts statutory immunity, the union and/or organiser of the industrial action will not incur legal liability.

Industrial disputes and the role of ACAS

As mentioned in the introductory chapter, one of ACAS's roles is to assist parties to an industrial dispute in resolving that dispute so that industrial action does not take place or is called off by a trade union. ACAS has no powers to intervene in a dispute. Its involvement must be requested by the parties. However, under ss. 209–212 TULRCA, where its services are requested it can offer **conciliation**, **mediation** and **arbitration**.

Commercial arbitration is particularly important from a legal perspective as it constitutes a mechanism for alternative dispute resolution. This is a system for enabling parties who have a legal dispute to refer that dispute to an expert arbitrator for resolution as an alternative to taking legal action in the ordinary civil courts. Normally an arbitrator's decision is final and there are very limited grounds for challenging that decision in a court of law. It is perfectly possible for the parties to an industrial dispute to refer the dispute to a commercial arbitrator. However, if a dispute is referred to an ACAS arbitrator it is binding in honour only. This position is in line with the general policy for ACAS involvement in disputes, that is, that its role is to secure voluntary settlement.

In order to broaden the circumstances in which ACAS can offer its services to resolve an industrial dispute, the meaning of 'trade dispute' is given a wider meaning by s. 218 TULRCA than that provided by s. 244. For this purpose only the meaning of a trade dispute is based on the law as it was prior to 1982. Therefore ACAS can be involved in disputes which are between workers and workers, as well as employers. A dispute merely needs to be *connected* to a trade dispute matter and includes the situation where secondary action is being proposed or taken by a trade union.

Out and about

Visit the ACAS website on **http://www.acas.org.uk/index.aspx?articleid=2012**.

This will provide you with detailed information and videos about ACAS's role in helping to resolve industrial disputes and, by clicking on the relevant tabs, enable you to ascertain the differences between collective conciliation, collective mediation and collective arbitration in the context of industrial disputes.

Handy tip: On the ACAS website you will find an article entitled 'The role of ACAS in dispute resolution' which you can download and read (see **http://www.acas. gov.uk/index.aspx?articleid=2006**). What does this article tell you about the legal status of arbitration which is conducted under the auspices of ACAS?

Trade union liability

Having identified the circumstances where industrial action will not attract statutory immunity, it is necessary to identify who will incur legal liability. Section 219, as explained above, confers immunity on a trade union or any other person who commits a protected tort in contemplation or furtherance of a trade dispute. Individual organisers of industrial action will typically be paid trade union officials or elected workplace representatives. However, it is perfectly possible that ordinary trade union members, who hold no official or representative position in their union, will also become involved in organising industrial action and will commit torts as a result. This is particularly likely with regard to picketing activity as we shall see below. Section 219 does not differentiate between trade unions and any of these individuals. They all receive statutory immunity in the same way.

However, it is necessary to distinguish between the liability incurred by the union and that incurred by individuals when immunity is not available. Special rules apply to determining when a trade union is liable or can be deemed liable, and to the remedies which can be granted against a trade union. Moreover, as will be discussed in depth below, there is one very important context in which a trade union will lose immunity but its officers and members will not. This is where industrial action is organised in furtherance of a lawful trade dispute but the union fails to comply properly with statutory procedures requiring strike ballots and strike notices.

Determining when a trade union will be liable

The typical way in which trade unions are internally structured was explained above. This structure is important in determining when a union will incur legal liability as a result of the organisation of unlawful industrial action, and when it will be able to avoid liability.

A trade union will be liable in tort where the union has authorised or endorsed the action(s) constituting the tortious act(s). Under s. 20 TULRCA, this will be the case where an act is authorised or endorsed by:

(a) any person empowered by, and who has acted in accordance with, the rules of the union to authorise or endorse such an act; or

(b) the Principal Executive Committee (PEC) or the President or the General Secretary of the union; or

(c) any official of the union, or a committee of a union which is established in accordance with the rules of the union.

Officials may include both paid union officials and elected representatives such as shop stewards. A committee might be a shop stewards committee or a branch committee. The union is bound by the acts of any individuals or committees who, or which, fall within category (c) even where they have acted contrary to the rules of the union, or contrary to the instructions of a higher body or person in the union. For example, a union official or representative has defied the general secretary of a union in organising industrial action. This is because the union is deemed to have authorised the action, but the union will be able to avoid liability through repudiating what the official or committee has done. Repudiation is not possible where the industrial action is authorised or endorsed by the PEC, the president or the general secretary.

Industrial action will not be deemed authorised by the union if it is organised by an unofficial committee of the union set up by rank and file members. However, this will only be the case if no paid official or elected representative is a member of this committee. This is possible but not that likely in the trade union world of today as activists will typically also be trade union representatives.

Where **trade union repudiation** may take place then, under s. 21, it will only be effective where the PEC, president or general secretary repudiates an act 'as soon as reasonably practicable after coming to the knowledge' of any of them. Repudiation must involve:

✦ written notice to the relevant committee or official without delay; and

✦ the union doing 'its best' to give written notice of the fact and date of repudiation without delay to every relevant union member; and

✦ similar written notice to the employer of every such union member.

The effect of repudiation is to render the industrial action unofficial. As will be explained in detail below, workers cannot claim unfair dismissal where the dismissal is for participating in unofficial action. Section 21(3) requires the notice of repudiation to union members to contain a statement informing each member that there is no right to complain of unfair dismissal for participating in unofficial industrial action.

Repudiation will cease to be effective if the PEC, president or general secretary behaves in a manner which is inconsistent with the purported repudiation. For example, the PEC of a union formally repudiates in accordance with s. 21, but then communicates with other trade unions and/or labour movement bodies asking them to 'support their members in struggle'.

Remedies against trade unions

Where a trade union is liable in tort, the employer in dispute and any other business which is a victim of a tort may sue that union. The main remedies which an employer may seek are the normal remedies available to a successful claimant in the law of tort, that is, an award of damages and the granting of an injunction to restrain the defendant from continuing with a tortious act.

Damages

As a matter of law, where a tort is committed by a trade union in the course of authorising or endorsing industrial action, damages may be claimed with reference to the normal forms of loss that are recognised in the law of tort. However, it should be noted that, in practice, employers seldom sue trade unions in order to recover damages. Probably, this is because employers are concerned that claiming damages will adversely impact on employee relations in the future. The main objective of an employer in suing a trade union is not to recover compensation but to secure an injunction, as it is this remedy that will lead to industrial action being called off or brought to an end.

Moreover, the sums of damages that can be awarded against trade unions are subject to statutory caps. This is to recognise that trade unions should not face bankruptcy and therefore lose the ability to represent all of their members as a result of torts committed in the context of industrial conflict.

Under s. 22, the statutory limits vary according to a union's size:

✦ £10,000 if the union has less than 5,000 members;

✦ £50,000 for 5,000 or more but less than 25,000 members;

✦ £125,000 for 25,000 or more but less than 100,000 members;

✦ £250,000 for 100,000 or more members.

It has never been clear and, to date has not been clarified by case law, whether these limits apply to all civil actions arising out of one instance of unlawful action or whether the limit applies to each claimant who is able to being a claim in tort. For example, during the course of a one-day strike, which is later determined to be unlawful, the employer in dispute and a number of other businesses in the industry lose a day's production. It is yet to be decided whether each of these businesses can claim up to the relevant statutory limit, or whether the limit applies to sum total of the claims that are brought. In the latter situation, if the union has, for example, 60,000 member then the maximum damages it would have pay with respect to the strike would be £125,000.

Interim injunctions

An employer may secure an injunction as a result of a full court hearing but, typically, it will be an *interim* injunction that an employer will seek. Such injunctions can be granted very quickly and prevent a trade union from commencing or continuing with the industrial action until and if a full court hearing takes place. At a full hearing a court will either confirm or lift the interim injunction. In recent times interim injunctions have been granted most frequently where employers have argued that unions have failed to comply properly with strike procedures. Such cases are considered in the following section of this chapter.

Interim injunctions may be granted even though it is not certain that industrial action is unlawful. This is obviously problematic for trade unions as it is possible that a future full court hearing may decide that the industrial action has been lawful all along but the union has been prevented from allowing its members to take it because of the interim injunction. On the other hand, if an interim injunction is refused, but a court later decides that the industrial action was unlawful, the employer in dispute and other businesses may suffer substantial financial losses as a result of the unlawful action.

To resolve this dilemma judges apply what is known as the 'balance of convenience' test. In deciding whether to grant or refuse an interim injunction, the judge will determine whether it is the claimant or the union who will suffer the greater inconvenience if it turns out that the decision was wrong, and the only remedy then available at a full hearing will be damages.

Under s. 222(1) TULRCA, judges are required to 'have regard' to the likelihood that at a full hearing the union will be able to show that the industrial action was in contemplation or furtherance of a trade dispute. This has been interpreted as meaning that unions must be able to show that it is 'more likely than not' that the statutory immunity applies. However, the requisite degree of probability of the industrial action being lawful will be higher than this where the consequences of the industrial action for the claimant, other businesses or the public interest can be regarded as particularly serious.

The public interest includes matters such as public safety and the well being of the economy. In *Duport Steels Ltd* v. *Sirs* [1980] ICR 161, the Law Lords lifted an interim injunction which had been wrongly granted by the Court of Appeal to prevent a national strike by steelworkers from taking place. However, the Law Lords implicitly approved the argument that an interim injunction can be granted where industrial action will have a very serious effect on the national economy and there is some element of doubt as to whether statutory immunity is available.

Generally, the courts take the view that if an interim injunction is subsequently lifted the union can commence or resume the industrial action, and therefore the 'balance of convenience' test requires the court to grant an interim injunction. In practice, interim injunctions tend to be refused only where the evidence clearly supports the argument that the industrial action is lawful. It should be noted that appeals can be mounted against the granting or refusal of interim injunctions and, in practice, full court hearings to determine the issue often do not take place. As in *Duport Steels*, an appellate court may lift an interim injunction in circumstances where the lower judge and/or court has misinterpreted the evidence or has made a clear error of law.

Under s. 20(6) TULRCA, in granting an interim injunction, a court can order the union to take such steps as it considers appropriate in order to ensure that:

✦ there is no further inducement of persons to take part or continue with the industrial action; and

✦ no person engages in industrial action after the injunction because he was induced to take part in it prior to the injunction being granted.

The latter power suggests that courts can require a trade union to discipline officials and/ or members who seek to continue with industrial action after the injunction has been granted. It a trade union fails to comply with an injunction and/or any directions given to it under s. 20(6) then it will be in contempt of court. As a result, a trade union can be fined and its assets can be sequestrated, that is, seized if fines are unpaid. Typically, injunctions cover individual leaders and officers of trade unions, as well as the union itself, and individuals can be fined or even imprisoned for civil contempt. In contrast with the 1970s and 1980s, such defiance of a court order by a trade union would be very unusual today. The last major instance of a trade union having its assets sequestrated was with respect to the National Union of Mineworkers during the Miners' Strike of 1984–85.

Case Summary

Writing and drafting

It is clear from what has been covered in this chapter so far that the taking of industrial action can have major adverse consequences for businesses and the general public, as well as causing hardship to workers and their families as a result of loss of income on days when, or during periods in which, industrial action takes place. Industrial action can also have legal repercussions for a trade union in circumstances in which statutory immunity is not available or is lost.

We have already established that the central purpose of collective bargaining is to produce collective agreements between employers and trade unions which prevent industrial disputes from occurring or bring them to an end before they result in industrial action. Reference was made to agreements containing disputes procedures which employers and unions should follow in an attempt to resolve a dispute peacefully, that is, without either side having recourse to industrial action. Typically, such procedures will set out a process for special meetings between union representatives and manage-ment to seek a negotiated settlement to a dispute. Disputes procedures can also pro-vide for reference to ACAS to seek conciliation before industrial action takes place and/ or an employer implements changes to employment contracts or working practices which are contrary to the established position, that is, the status quo.

Imagine that you are a solicitor for a company which is contemplating recognising the General Workers Union (GWU) for the purposes of collective bargaining on behalf of its 500 workers. The company wants to make recognition conditional on the GWU agreeing to a collective dispute procedure which is at least partly legally enforceable.

The company has asked you to draft two procedures – one which is partly legally enforceable and one which is fully legally enforceable – which it can use in its negoti-ations with the GWU.

◆ **Handy tip:** You should bear in mind the 'Out and about' activity above concerning the role that ACAS can play in resolving industrial disputes. In drafting a fully legally enforceable procedure you will need to think about how any dispute can be ultimately resolved – in practice, this is likely to be through a form of arbitration. Do you think it is a good idea for collective dispute procedures to provide for compulsory arbitration?

Strike ballots and procedures

As mentioned above, interim injunctions are often granted against trade unions because a union has failed properly to comply with provisions in the TULRCA concerning strike procedures. Trade unions are required to conduct industrial action ballots, and to provide pre-ballot and pre-strike notices to the employer in dispute. The duty to follow these procedures is on the trade union and, providing there is a lawful trade dispute, only the union loses immunity because strike procedures have not been fully observed. For example, if a trade union official or shop steward organises industrial action after members have voted to take it at a meeting then clearly none of the statutory procedures will have been followed. Nevertheless, that individual will still be protected by statutory immunity if the

> only the union loses immunity because strike procedures have not been fully observed

industrial action is in contemplation or furtherance of a lawful trade dispute. However, as explained above, the union will be liable if it fails to repudiate what the official has done. If an injunction is granted against the union, it will be required to order the official to desist from continuing to organise the industrial action.

The provisions relating to strike procedures are both very detailed and complex. This section of the chapter will provide an overview of what is required of trade unions and will focus on the main issues and major cases.

Handy tip: Readers can obtain the full details of this area of the law by reading the guidance contained in the Department of Employment's Code of Practice on Industrial Action Ballots and Notice to Employers. This can be downloaded in pdf format at **http://www.delni.gov.uk/code_of_practice_industrial_action_ballots_and_notice_to_employers.pdf**

As the following statistics show, strike ballots have become a significant feature of employee relations in this country.

Key stats

Although there has been a significant reduction in work stoppages over recent decades, there have still been a significant number of industrial action ballots. In part, this is because it has become a standard feature of trade union collective bargaining strategies, where it appears that a collective agreement will not be reached, to ballot the relevant members on industrial action to establish in an employer's mind just how strong the support for the trade union's proposals actually is.

For example, in 2006 there were 754,000 days lost through work stoppages. However, there were 1290 ballots for strike action, of which 1,094 were in favour of strike action. In that year there were also 579 ballots for industrial action short of a strike, of which 541 were in favour of the proposed action being taken. It is not uncommon for a strike ballot to demonstrate a majority in favour of strike action without a strike actually being called.

Source: Dominic Hale, Office for National Statistics, *Economic and Labour Market Review*, vol. 4(6), June 2010.

Pre-ballot notices

Under s. 226A TULRCA, a union must, at least seven days before the opening day of an industrial action ballot, notify the employer of the ballot and describe those employees who will be entitled to vote. A copy of the ballot paper must be provided to the employer at least three days prior to the ballot. The notice must:

✦ list the categories of employee who will be balloted;

✦ list their workplaces;

✦ provide figures for the total number of employees concerned;

✦ identify the number of employees for each category and workplace concerned;

✦ explain how the figures provided by the union were arrived at.

Some union members have an arrangement with their employer under which they pay their union subscriptions by a system known as the 'check off'. This means that the employer deducts their subscriptions from their pay and transfers the money directly to the union. Where the check-off system is in place the union can satisfy the requirements of s. 226A simply by giving the employer the information relating to the check-off payments of the relevant categories of employees. The employer will then be able to check its payroll records to identify the employees who will be balloted.

Case Summary

Where some union members pay by check off but others pay their subscriptions directly to the union, the union must supply the above detailed information to the employer as far as the non-check-off members are concerned. In *Metrobus Ltd* v. *Unite the Union* [2009] IRLR 851, the union provided the employer with a pre-ballot notice informing the company that it was balloting 776 of its employees who paid their union subscriptions by check off and 69 other employees so that in total 845 of the company's employees were to be balloted. A majority of the Court of Appeal held that full details of the 69 non-check-off employees should have been provided and therefore the pre-ballot notice was invalid.

Any failure by the union to supply the correct information is fatal in that statutory immunity is automatically lost *vis-à-vis* the employer in dispute – although other employers cannot sue with respect to any failures by the union in this regard. It should be noted that it is not necessary for a union to name the members who will be balloted, although, given the complexity of the statutory provisions, a union may find that this is the easiest way to discharge its obligations and so ensure that statutory immunity is retained.

Many employers regard it as important that trade unions supply accurate information in the pre-ballot notice. One purpose of the notice is to enable the employer in dispute readily to ascertain which of his employees will be entitled to vote in the ballot. This enables the employer to communicate with those employees with a view to persuading them to vote against industrial action. A second purpose of the requirement for a pre-ballot notice is to provide an employer with an advanced warning that industrial action may occur in the imminent future. The employer is able to identify which of its employees may be involved in taking the action, and is therefore able to begin to make plans for countering the effects of industrial action should it subsequently take place.

Case Summary

The case of *BT plc* v. *CWU* [2004] IRLR 58 provides an example of a pre-ballot notice which provided the employer with insufficient information on the employees to be balloted. The CWU informed BT that it was proposing to ballot its 14,001 engineering members employed in BT Retail Customer Services Field Operations. The employer knew that 90% of its employees engaged in this work were union members. However, the CWU had failed to identify the specific number of members at each specific workplace, and therefore the information it supplied was inadequate to meet the statutory requirements.

A logistical problem for a trade union is that the larger the number of members to be balloted and the more complex the operations of the employer are – particularly if they are undertaken over a variety of workplaces – the greater the chances will be that the union will not have up-to-date and accurate records of what its members do and where they are located. In 1990, the then Master of the Rolls, Lord Donaldson described the statutory requirements as 'a minefied in which it is all too easy to stray from the paths of safety and legality' (*Post Office* v. *UCW* [1990] ICR 258). Since 1990, the 'minefield' has, if anything, grown even more hazardous.

Industrial action ballots

Under s. 226, a trade union will lose statutory immunity, even though there is a lawful trade dispute, if the union has failed to conduct a valid ballot of the members it is proposing to call out on industrial action. Under s. 230, a valid ballot must be secret and fully postal. This means that ballot papers must be sent to union members' homes and they vote by returning the ballot papers by pre-paid post. Under s. 226B, the union must appoint an independent scrutineer, who is named on the ballot paper, to oversee the conduct of the ballot and to report to the union as to whether the ballot has been properly conducted and the votes fairly counted. Many trade unions will use the services of the Electoral Reform Society for this purpose.

Law in action

Most readers will be aware of industrial action ballots as they are often drawn to the attention of the public by the media. This is particularly the case with strikes affecting the public in areas such as transport, schools and hospitals. An industrial dispute which generated a lot of media coverage, both in newspapers and on television, and also some important case law was that involving British Airways cabin crew in 2009 and 2010. UNITE, which was the trade union for the cabin crew, decided to ballot its relevant members after BA imposed a pay cut and started to implement redundancies. According to BA, its proposals were necessary to reduce operational costs after it had suffered record business losses.

This ballot had a very high turnout and 92.4% of those who voted supported the strike. Despite this undoubted support for strike action, the High Court decided that under the TULRCA it was obliged to grant an injunction to prevent strikes from taking place in the 2009 Christmas period. Essentially, the High Court agreed with BA that UNITE had blatantly ignored the statutory provisions on strike ballots by allowing members to vote who it knew would have left the company by the time any industrial action took place. Therefore, BA was entitled to act to protect its commercial interests and the interests of its passengers by seeking a court order to prevent unlawful strike action from taking place.

The view of the union was that BA was using complex statutory provisions to discover technical defects in the ballot in circumstances where it was obvious that a large majority of the union's members supported strike action. The members who should not have voted in the ballot made no impact of any meaningful nature on the outcome of the ballot. Even if their votes were taken from the 'yes' vote and added to the 'no' vote, the majority for strike action would still have been very high.

UNITE subsequently held a new ballot. After the ballot, UNITE reported that 78.77% of the 11,691 ballot papers issued were returned. Of those, 80.7% (7,482) supported taking action with 1,789 voting against it. A legal challenge to this ballot was also mounted by BA, but the Court of Appeal ruled that UNITE had properly discharged its legal duty to inform its members of the ballot result. Several strikes then took place with UNITE claiming the strikes to be successful and BA claiming it had been able to get many of its customers to their destinations despite the strike action.

The strike was finally resolved in May 2010 with increases of pay being agreed by BA which were based on the Retail Price Index with a cap of 2.9% for 2011–12 and 3% for 2012–13. In return the cabin crew agreed to changes in working arrangements and UNITE accepted that it would not present any further pay claims until after the pay deal expired in February 2013. An issue that had also caused much bitterness during the strikes was also resolved through BA agreeing that it would restore travel concessions to all of its employees who had participated in the strikes. Previously, BA had threatened that the taking away of these concessions from strikers would be permanent.

Source: 'British Airways cabin crew back strike action', accessed at http://news.bbc.co.uk/1/hi/8527100.stm; Unite briefing note 11 May 2010, accessed at www.unitetheunion.org/ba

Conduct of the ballot

Having identified that a trade union cannot enjoy any statutory immunity if it authorises or endorses industrial action, which has not been sanctioned by a postal ballot, it is necessary to consider the main rules that unions must comply with if a ballot is to be valid.

Under s. 229(4), the ballot paper must contain a statement that participation in a strike or other industrial action may involve the member acting in breach of the contract of employment. Under s. 229(2) it must contain questions which can be answered 'yes' or 'no' (s. 229). In *Post Office* v. *UCW* [1990] ICR 258, the UCW proposed taking strike action or industrial action short of a strike against the Post Office, as its members' employer. It held a ballot but on the ballot paper asked a single question: 'Are you willing to take industrial action up to and including strike action in support of the dispute?' It was held by the Court of Appeal that the ballot was invalid as there should have been separate questions on the ballot paper in respect of each type of action so that members might vote differently if they wished. In this case it was feasible that a majority was voting in favour of industrial action short of a strike but was not in favour of strike action. Had the ballot paper contained separate questions enabling the members to vote for or against strike action, and for or against industrial action short of a strike, the ballot paper would have conformed to the legislation.

Under s. 229(3) TULRCA, the ballot paper must specify who is authorised to call on union members to take industrial action in accordance with the ballot result. This may be a person, persons or committee. Under s. 233, the action must then be called by a specified person if immunity is to be available. The meaning of 'call' was clarified by the Court of Appeal in *Tanks & Drums Ltd* v. *TGWU* (CA) [1992] ICR 1. The ballot papers of the TGWU provided that 'the authority for calling industrial action is vested in the general executive council and through its delegated powers to the general secretary of the union'. Following unsuccessful wage negotiations, the TGWU district organiser contacted the union's regional secretary who in turn contacted the general secretary, who authorised the district secretary to issue the call on the members to take industrial action. The company argued that the call to take industrial action had been made by district organiser when it should have been made by the general secretary. The court refused an injunction. The general secretary had made the decision to call a strike. The district official was merely the means by which the general secretary had communicated this call to his members.

Normally, a union must conduct a ballot on a workplace by workplace basis, and, only where a majority of members at a particular workplace has voted in favour of action, can the members be called upon to take it. However, under s. 228A(1) an aggregated ballot can be held where the members are employed at different workplaces and/or by separate employers, but are employed in the same occupation, or employed under common terms and conditions of employment. This is particularly important in the public sector where **national collecting bargaining** still takes place. Trade unions are able to ballot their national membership in a particular sector irrespective of where they work or who they work for. However, if a ballot is conducted on an aggregated basis then all union members who share the same factor, such as the same terms and conditions of employment, must be balloted. Therefore, it is not possible to exclude from the ballot any workplaces where it is believed by the union that there will be majorities against the action.

Once the union has determined the appropriate balloting constituency, that is, a ballot by workplace or an aggregated ballot then, under s. 227(1), all union members who it is reasonable to believe at the time of the ballot will be induced by the union to take industrial action must be given an equal opportunity to vote. However, failure to ensure that all members receive ballot papers will not always invalidate the ballot.

In *British Railways Board* v. *National Union of Railway Workers (NUR)* [1989] IRLR 349, the NUR balloted its members on industrial action. Over 63,000 ballot papers were issued, and over 51,000 papers were returned with a substantial majority being in favour of strike action. British Railways presented evidence that the NUR had failed to make ballot papers available to about 200 members in the relevant balloting constituency. The Court of Appeal held that the ballot was valid as the union's error was inadvertent and had made no difference to the outcome of the ballot. The NUR had, so far as was reasonably practicable, provided an opportunity of voting to those so entitled. The ballot would have been invalid had there been any intentional failure to provide any member with a ballot paper. Had the inadvertent errors had a material effect on whether or not there was a majority in favour of the strike then, again, the ballot would have been invalid.

Case Summary

Section 232B TULRCA gives statutory force to this judgment by providing that a ballot is not invalidated by accidental errors if they are on a scale which is unlikely to affect the outcome of the ballot. However, an error cannot be regarded as accidental if the union knew or should have known it had balloted members who it was not proposing to call upon to take industrial action.

British Airways plc v. *Unite the Union* [2009] EWHC 3541 is an important recent case on this issue and, as narrated above, also received much media attention. British Airways (BA) applied for an interim injunction to restrain Unite from proceeding with industrial action based on the result of a ballot. Unite called for a 12-day strike over the Christmas period. BA claimed that Unite had wrongly included in its ballot notice, balloting process and notice of industrial action several hundred employees who had volunteered for redundancy and who were due to leave BA's employment by the date of the strike. Cox J agreed with BA that Unite knew that a number of members were taking voluntary redundancies. She held that the union was aware, or ought to have been aware, that the figures provided to BA included those who opted for voluntary redundancy and therefore included members who the union could not have reasonably believed were entitled to vote. It was practicable and reasonable for Unite to enquire as to which members were leaving BA's employment. Unite had never issued instructions to its members about not voting if they were leaving BA's employment by the relevant date, despite having had opportunities to do so. That would have been a practicable and reasonable step. Unite knew that its figures were inaccurate and that the balloting process was flawed. Therefore, the union could not rely on the defence of accidental failure under s. 232B TULRCA. Consequently, it was of no relevance to the court proceedings that there was still a majority of the union's members in favour of the industrial action even if votes of the members who should not have voted were deducted from the yes vote.

Case Summary

In granting an interim injunction, Cox J ruled that the balance of convenience lay in favour of granting the injunction sought by BA. In her view, an award of damages was not an adequate remedy for BA, and a 12-day strike over the Christmas period was fundamentally more damaging to BA and the wider public than a strike taking place at almost any other time of the year. This decision therefore also illustrates how the public interest is a factor to be taken into account in deciding whether an interim injunction should be granted.

It is permissible to call on members who join the union after the industrial action has started to participate in it. Their participation does not invalidate the original ballot. In *London Underground* v. *RMT* [1995] IRLR 636, in furtherance of a lawful trade dispute, the RMT held an industrial action ballot between 4 and 17 August 1995,

Case Summary

obtaining a majority in favour of industrial action. The RMT subsequently gave two notices of its intention to take industrial action pursuant to the ballot on several dates between 25 August and 4 September. In the second notice the RMT included the names of some 672 new members who had joined the union since the date of the ballot. London Underground obtained an injunction to restrain RMT from taking this industrial action on the basis that the action did not have the support of the new members as they had not been balloted. The Court of Appeal lifted the injunction. The court held the Act required only that the industrial action has the support of a ballot, not that industrial action by a particular person has the support of a ballot. There was nothing in the legislation to prevent a union from inducing to take part in the industrial action new members who were not balloted because they were not members of the union at the time that the ballot was held.

Section 231A requires a trade union to inform an employer of the ballot result as soon as is reasonably practicable once the ballot papers have been counted. In *Metrobus* v. *Unite the Union* [2010] ICR 173, there was a delay of two days from the time when Unite could have communicated the ballot result to the employer and when it actually did so. The union argued it had not received the fax containing the ballot result until the day after it was sent, and a Unite official had informed Metrobus as soon as the General Secretary of the union decided that strike action would take place. It was held that it would have been reasonable for Unite to have asked the ballot organisers for the result on the day the ballot closed. It could then immediately have passed that information on to Metrobus. Furthermore, there was no reason in law why the information could not be transmitted to the employer before the union's general secretary had authorised the provision of a pre-strike notice to an employer. This decision perhaps illustrates just how technical this area of the law has become. It is hard to see how such a small delay in communicating the ballot result to the employer could have materially affected the company's ability to formulate a strategy for dealing with the strike.

Section 231 requires a union to give a similar notice to its members regarding the ballot result. This was at the heart of the second case that BA brought against Unite after the union had conducted its second ballot, as narrated above. In *British Airways plc (BA)* v. *Unite the Union* [2010] ICR 1316, Unite appealed against a decision granting BA an interim injunction restraining Unite's members from taking industrial action after a ballot, in February 2010, had again recorded an overwhelming majority in favour of strike action. BA argued that Unite was in breach of s. 231 TULRCA as it had failed to take such steps as were reasonably necessary to ensure that its members voting in the ballot were properly informed of the ballot result. BA contended that it was not sufficient for the purposes of the section for Unite to publish the results on its website, and via union notice boards and news sheets. Emails and text messages should have been sent individually to all of the relevant members containing the requisite information.

The majority of the Court of Appeal upheld Unite's appeal. What was 'reasonably necessary' for the purposes of s. 231 had to be viewed in context. Other provisions of the Act expressed various requirements in more absolute terms, by use of the word 'must', and there was no basis for elevating the provision of information to union members to pre-eminence above the proper conduct of the ballot itself, as the actual result would be unaffected by small-scale failures in the information process. Section 231 did not set out a method of compliance and, in the view of Lord Judge, it would have been absurd if the relevant information could not have been conveyed through modern technology such as websites. There was no requirement for 'active' dissemination of information and no policy reasons why there might be such a requirement. In the circumstances, it would be unreasonable to require Unite to prove that every eligible member had personally been sent his or her own individual information as to the ballot results. Unite had taken the steps necessary to communicate the results to its members, and the methods adopted, via the website, notice boards and news sheets, had been a sensible and practical approach to the statutory duty imposed by s. 231.

Despite the minority view expressed by Lord Neuberger MR that there was no reason why Unite could not have communicated by email or text to all its members the requisite information about the ballot result, this seems a common sense decision. In other contexts, there will be many employers who communicate with their employees in the way that Unite communicated with its members. By focusing on the purpose of the statutory provision, the Court of Appeal's decision is clearly a triumph of substance over form.

Since this second decision in the litigation between British Airways and Unite there have been three more decisions in the context of balloting where, as was so with the above decision, the courts have refrained from interpreting the statutory provisions in a strict fashion.

In *National Union of Rail, Maritime and Transport Workers* v. *Serco Ltd* [2011] ICR 848 the union had sent ballot papers to two members who were not entitled to vote. The employer also argued that the union had failed to carry out an audit of its members to ensure as far as was reasonably practicable that the information provided to the employer in the pre-ballot and pre-strike notices was up to date and accurate. The Court of Appeal lifted an injunction granted by the High Court. The court held that, irrespective of whether the error in giving the two members the opportunity to vote was avoidable, the error was clearly unintentional and thereby accidental within the meaning of s. 232B TULRCA. Moreover, the *de minimis* principle applied to prevent the union from being in breach of duty where it had made an unintentional and trivial mistake involving two out of more than 600 members. In providing the pre-ballot and pre-strike notices the union had done what was reasonably practicable to update its databases, and therefore the information provided to the employer was in accordance with the requirements of the statutory provisions. The fact that its record keeping could have been better did not mean the union had failed to discharge its duties.

In *London Underground Ltd* v. *ASLEF* [2012] IRLR 196, ASLEF, the train drivers union, balloted its London Underground members regarding strike action on Boxing Day in a dispute over payments for working on Boxing Day. London Underground argued that the ballot was invalid as all members employed by the company were balloted not just those who were actually scheduled to work on Boxing Day. Eder J refused to grant an injunction on the basis that there was no evidence that the union intended to restrict strike action to Boxing Day. Indeed ASLEF had issued strike notices for further one-day strikes if the Boxing Day strike failed to secure the union's aims. The judge also stated that members not actually required to work might still want to participate in the action by, for example, joining picket lines. The meaning of taking part in industrial action should not be restricted to those who are to be called upon to withdraw their labour on any particular day.

Eder J also commented on how the decision to grant or refuse an interim injunction should be approached in industrial action cases. In direct contrast to the position adopted by Cox J in the first British Airways case, decided during the previous Christmas period, he stated that the courts should not be concerned with the merits of the dispute, the balance of convenience between the parties or the inconvenience to the public. The sole issue to be considered is the likelihood at full trial of the union successfully pleading that it was protected by statutory immunity. This view is in accordance with that expressed by Lady Justice Smith in the second *British Airways* case, which was that if the union's defence is likely to succeed at trial, a strike must be allowed to go ahead. To decide otherwise would be to deprive the union's members of any effective right to withhold their labour.

The final case in the trilogy is *Balfour Beatty Engineering Services* v. *Unite the Union* [2012] IRLR 452. In this case the employer argued that the union had failed to carry out sufficient checks to ensure its membership lists were accurate and up to date and had therefore failed to do what was reasonably practicable to send ballot papers to all members entitled to vote and only to those members. The High Court refused an injunction on the basis that prior to sending out the ballot papers union officials had taken a variety of steps to check and update the membership database. In interpreting what is meant by 'reasonably practicable' union officials must be given some room to exercise their own judgement as to the steps that should be taken to comply with the balloting requirements. It would be wrong to grant an injunction because a judge might have done something differently. Moreover, the duty on a union is to take reasonably practicable steps as against being required to take *all* steps that are reasonably practicable.

In reaching this decision, Eady J stated that the statutory provisions should be interpreted in a way that was consistent with Article 11 ECHR. He also commented that the union had gone to considerable lengths to ensure the democratic legitimacy of the ballot, and that very sensitive policy issues arose where a balance should be struck between striving for democratic legitimacy and imposing unrealistic burdens on unions and their officers. This approach seems more in accordance with the reasons why ballots and pre-ballot and pre-strike notices are required than was so with the judgments in *Metrobus* and the first *British Airways* case.

The timing of industrial action

Under s. 234, the industrial action must begin no later than four weeks from the date of the ballot, that is, the last day on which votes could have been cast. The case of *Monsanto plc* v. *TGWU* [1986] IRLR 406 examines the interaction between this provision and where industrial action is suspended by a union pending further negotiations with the employer. On 6 May 1986, the TGWU, having held a held a valid ballot, declared that the majority of the balloted workers were in favour of industrial action short of strike action and the action began the next day. On 10 June, the union suspended industrial action while it negotiated with the company. The union's members worked normally until 23 June when the union resumed the industrial action following an unsuccessful meeting between the company and the union about the issues in dispute. The Court of Appeal lifted an injunction as the TGWU had not lost statutory immunity. The court held that neither good industrial relations nor the legislation required that industrial action, suspended during a period of negotiations, could not be resumed without a further ballot.

The above case can be contrasted with *Post Office* v. *UCW* [1990] ICR 258, which is also discussed above. Another issue in this case is the circumstances in which, through lapse of time, a ballot loses validity. The CWU conducted its ballot in August 1988, and organised a series of strikes between September and December 1988. The union then engaged in a publicity campaign, and did not take further industrial action. However, in September 1989 the CWU decided to resume strike action and relied on the 1988 ballot. As explained above, the Court of Appeal found that the 1988 ballot was invalid, but even if the ballot had been valid it could no longer be relied on by the union. The court held that it was implicit in the legislation that industrial action, once begun, must continue without substantial interruption if reliance on the ballot is to continue. It is a question of fact and degree whether in a particular case the protection of the ballot has been exhausted. In the present case, the termination of strike action in December ended the action contemplated by the 1988 ballot. The strike in September 1989 was new and disconnected and required a fresh ballot.

The difference between the Post Office case and *Monsanto* was, that in the latter case, the suspension of the industrial action was for a much shorter period and was clearly to enable the parties to the dispute to ascertain if a negotiated settlement could be achieved.

Under s. 234(1)(b), the four-week period for commencing the industrial action can be extended to eight weeks with the agreement of the employer. This provision is designed to facilitate the postponement of industrial action by giving the union and the employer additional time to negotiate a settlement once it has been established that the workers have voted to take industrial action.

As has been illustrated in several of the cases that we have discussed above, such as the second case brought by BA against UNITE in 2010, an appellate court may decided that an interim injunction was wrongly granted. Under s. 234(2)–(6) a court may extend the period for taking industrial action to 12 weeks from the date of the ballot if legal proceedings had led to the action being called off. It is necessary for the union to apply for a time extension, and such an application cannot be made once eight weeks have elapsed starting with the date of the ballot.

Notices of industrial action

Under s. 234A(1), if a ballot is in favour of industrial action the union must give the employer at least seven days notice before the industrial action may be taken. This seven-day period commences with the day on which the union informs the employer of the ballot result. The union must supply the employer with information identifying the categories of workers who will be called upon to take the industrial action in the same sort of detail that was required in the pre-ballot notice, as explained above. If the union intends to call out workers who were not balloted, such as workers who join the union after the ballot was concluded, the notice should inform the employer of this fact.

If the action is continuous, the notice must specify the date on which the action will start. As explained above, this must normally be no longer than four weeks from the date the ballot concluded. If the action is to be discontinuous, this notice must specify all the dates on which the action is to take place, or a separate notice must be served at least seven days before each day of action occurs.

If the action is suspended, a further seven days notice must be given before the action can recommence unless, in accordance with s. 234A(7B), it is agreed with the employer that if negotiations fail the action will be resumed on or after a specified date.

Who can sue?

It is only an employer who has not received a requisite statutory notice who may seek an injunction. Immunity is not lost *vis-à-vis* other employers or members of the public. However, any victim of a tort may sue the union where a valid ballot has not taken place.

Moreover, under s. 235A, individuals who can show the effect of unlawful industrial action is to prevent or delay the supply of goods or services, or to reduce their quality, may bring an action against the union, if the action has not been repudiated. Note that individuals may also seek injunction against the individual(s) who organise the action if there is no lawful trade dispute, or where the action continues after repudiation by a union. Section 235A applies even where an individual is not able to sue in tort. However, whilst such individuals may secure an injunction against the union or an organiser, they may not claim damages. It can be noted in passing that there is no reported case of any member of the public taking advantage of this statutory provision.

Originally, the main purpose of requiring a union to conduct a secret ballot was to ensure that the union's members genuinely supported the industrial action they were being called upon to take. Under s. 62 TULRCA, any union member who has been or is likely to be induced by the union to take part in the industrial action may seek a court order to restrain the action from taking place on the basis that there has not been a valid ballot. Union members do not need to establish the presence of a tort in order to be granted a court order.

People in the law

Many people, including employment lawyers, will have different views on whether the controls on industrial action which are examined in this chapter should be retained, strengthened or repealed in whole or in part. Set out below are interviews with an experienced trade union workplace representative and the head of a human resources department giving their different perspectives on industrial action and rights to strike. You should appreciate that these interviews represent personal opinions and that the interviewees are not legal experts. However, the views that are provided do represent the typical opinions of trade union activists and human resource practitioners.

The first interview is with **Mick Tosh**, a port representative of the Rail Maritime and Transport Union (RMT).

In your experience what are the most common reasons why a trade union decides to organise industrial action? Unfair and/or unreasonable proposals from the employer towards its employees. Usually these proposals involve changing/reducing pay, conditions or pensions or concern unjust treatment of a colleague.

From a purely personal perspective, do you consider that the taking of indus- trial action is ever justified? Yes, I do not consider that a group of workers ever contemplates industrial action as anything other than a last-straw attempt to get their employer to understand the level of feeling surrounding the issue in a dispute.

The International Labour Organisation has criticised many of the current statutory provisions in UK law regulating the use of industrial action as being in breach of international human rights law. Do you think the law as it stands should be retained or changed? If the latter, should this be to increase or further restrict the circumstances in which industrial action can be lawfully organised or taken? The right to withdraw labour should be enshrined in the law of any decent democracy. The idea that merely being an employer gives you the right to criminalise individuals taking industrial action is not acceptable in a fair minded society. I believe in the use of ballots amongst the workforce to establish the legitimacy of industrial action. This should not be subjected to draconian rules imposed by legislators whose interest is in serving employers and the establishment. Every union member should be given the opportunity to vote and this can best be served by the same methods we use to elect our political representatives.

Do you consider there is any merit to changing UK law so that it operates on the basis of positive rights to strike, as is the case generally in Europe, or do you think the traditional system of statutory immunities should be retained? The immunities only serve to protect the assets of the individual trade union and actually become a burden to the individual union's decision makers when considering whether to call for industrial action. Workers who seek a ballot for action do so because of the injustice they feel is being used against them. They are not interested in the UK's detailed legal measures, they are merely interested in balancing the argument with the remaining option available to them. So yes, I believe it is important to legally enshrine the right to take industrial action rather than worry about whether or not union leadership consider the strike to be official.

The second interview is with **Peter Brook**, head of human resources at the University of Portsmouth.

In your experience what are the most common reasons why a trade union decides to organise industrial action? A trade union does this to bring employers to the negotiating table. The prospect of industrial action is the key muscle that trade unions have to press their demands for improved terms and conditions.

From a purely personal perspective, do you consider that the taking of industrial action is ever justified? Prolonged industrial action can damage the economy and service users. It should only be taken as a last resort after all other steps have been exhausted. It is a safeguard for employees where employers refuse to listen to their staff.

Do you think the law as it stands controlling the right to take industrial action should be retained or changed? If the latter, should this be to increase or further restrict the circumstances in which industrial action can be lawfully organised or taken? The law as it stands is fine. Trade unions should be able to demonstrate majority support for strike action and should not have a problem in following process in order to obtain majority support for their activities. I am uncomfortable with employers who have taken the route of obtaining an injunction first and talking later. I would prefer to see discreet talks rather than legal injunctions.

Do you consider there is any merit to changing UK law so that it operates on the basis of positive rights to strike, as is the case generally in Europe, or do you think the traditional system of statutory immunities should be retained? No, a positive right to strike would need to be balanced against the right of service users to receive uninterrupted service.

Industrial action and dismissal

Having considered the trade dispute immunity, and the statutory requirements imposed on trade unions with respect to strike procedures, it is now necessary to examine the legal position of individual workers and employees who participate in industrial action. Any strike and most other forms of industrial action will amount to a breach of the employment contract by an employee who participates in it. Therefore, at common law, it is always permissible to dismiss an employee where, as typically will be the case, participating in the industrial action constitutes a repudiatory breach of contract. It is always the case that employers may sue their workers for damages to recover the loss suffered through industrial action in breach of contract. However, for practical reasons this is a course of action that employers rarely take.

> the statutory protection given to individual employees against dismissal will only apply to lawful action

It is much more likely that, if employers want to take action against employees who participate in industrial action, this will be in the form of disciplinary action or dismissal. There are no statutory provisions in place with respect to the former, but the ability of employers to dismiss is restricted by legislation. In this context the need for a union to have conducted a valid ballot and to have provided effective pre-ballot and pre-strike notices is of paramount importance. This is because the statutory protection given to individual employees against dismissal will only apply to lawful action which is authorised or endorsed by their trade union. Moreover, if a union has properly repudiated industrial action, it becomes unofficial action. As detailed below, employees who are dismissed for taking unofficial action have no unfair dismissal rights whatsoever.

Protected industrial action

Prior to 1999 it was always permissible for an employer to dismiss employees for participating in industrial action providing the employer dismissed all employees who were taking part in the action at the date of dismissals. These provisions, contained in s. 238 TULRCA, are still important and will be considered below. However, as a result of provisions introduced by the Employment Relations Act 1999, which are contained in s. 238A TULRCA, dismissals for participation in **protected industrial action** will be **automatically unfair**. This will be the case even if all the employees taking the action are dismissed.

Industrial action is protected if it meets the following conditions:

(a) The action must be lawful because the union is protected by the s. 219 immunity by virtue of the action being in contemplation or furtherance of a trade dispute. Moreover, the union must not have lost this immunity for any reason. For example, immunity ceases to apply because the union has failed to comply fully with the strike procedures requiring notices and ballots which are detailed above.

(b) The dismissal relates to participation in industrial action during the protected period. Protection normally ceases to apply once a period of 12 weeks has elapsed since the day on which the employee started to take industrial action. Employees, who are dismissed outside of the protected period, but who had ceased to participate in the action during it, remain protected.

(c) The dismissals occur after the normal 12-week protected period but the protection continues beyond this period because the employer has not taken reasonable procedural steps to resolve the dispute. Section 238A(6) sets out factors to be taken into account by a tribunal in determining whether an employer has taken reasonable steps. It should be noted that the behaviour of the union as well as that of the employer will be relevant. The factors are:

✦ whether the employer or the union has failed to comply with dispute procedures set out in a collective agreement;

✦ whether the employer or the union offered or agreed to resume negotiations after the start of the protected action;

✦ whether the employer or the union has unreasonably refused to refer the dispute to ACAS for conciliation or to make use of mediation services.

Where it is the employer who has, for example, proposed negotiations or a reference to ACAS, a rejection of the proposal by the union will generally result in the action becoming unprotected once the 12-week period has expired.

Only employees are protected by s. 238A but, as the dismissals are automatically unfair, the normal rule applies in that the employees need not have the requisite continuity of employment to present an ordinary claim of unfair dismissal. Moreover, employees have six months, rather than the normal three months, from the date of dismissal to present a claim. The normal remedies for unfair dismissal apply to industrial action dismissals.

Documenting the law

It can be seen from the above that the existence of a collective agreement between an employer and trade union setting out a collective disputes procedure can impact on whether lawful industrial action, which lasts for more than 12 weeks, remains protected so that employees taking the action are protected from dismissal. A model collective disputes procedure is set out below. This agreement stipulates that it is not legally binding between the parties. However, the agreement is not without legal consequence as the status quo clause, contained in section 3 of the agreement, is incorporated into individual employment contracts and is binding on the employer with respect to its employees.

COLLECTIVE DISPUTES PROCEDURE

This procedure has been agreed between the Barchester College of Further Education (BCFE) and the Union of College Lecturers (UCL).

1. **Purpose**
    (i) The purpose of this collective disputes procedure is to provide a framework within which collective disputes can be resolved by discussion between the UCL and the management of BCFE without either side taking recourse to industrial action.
    (ii) The parties to this agreement do not intend it to be legally enforceable.

2. **Scope**
    The scope of the procedure covers matters over which BCFE has agreed to negotiate or consult with the UCL as a result of its recognition agreement with the union. These matters include all the issues listed in s. 178(2) TULRCA 1992.

3. **Status Quo**
   (i) It is agreed that if a dispute, over matters for which the UCL has been recognised, cannot immediately be resolved, then whatever practice or agreement existed prior to the dispute shall continue to operate pending a settlement being reached or this disputes procedure being declared to be exhausted.
   (ii) Where the matters in dispute arise out of the operation of terms and conditions of employment the College agrees that it will make no changes to contracts of employment whilst the dispute procedure is in operation providing the UCL does not seek to ballot on or organise any form of industrial action before the disputes procedure has been exhausted.
   (iii) Clause 3(ii) is incorporated into the individual contracts of employment of lecturers within the scope of the recognition agreement with the UCL.

4. **Procedure**
   Stage One
   The matter shall be raised initially in writing by the chair of the union side in the Joint Negotiation and Consulting Group (JNCG) with the chair of the management side of the Committee declaring that a collective dispute is in existence.

   Stage Two
   A special meeting of the JNCG will take place no later than 10 days from the receipt of this letter with a view to resolving the dispute.

   Stage Three
   If agreement is not reached at Stage Two, then the matter shall be referred to the Principal of the College and a special meeting of the JNCG, with the Principal in attendance, will take place no later than 10 days from the date of referral.

   Stage Four
   If agreement is not reached at Stage 3, then the parties may agree to make a reference to ACAS to request conciliation. If the parties do not agree to make such a reference then this collective disputes procedure will be declared by the parties to have been exhausted.

Reflective practice

Have a look at the dispute procedure that you drafted earlier. Is there anything that you would add to or change in your procedure in light of the above?

Note that the above procedure permits but does not require reference to ACAS. This could be made obligatory, and is a way in which a disputes procedure can be made partly legally enforceable. This would be achieved by including a clause in the first part of the procedure which stipulates that it is intended to be legally enforceable between the parties to the agreement. This would both prevent the employer from acting in breach of the status quo and the union from organising industrial action until after a reference to ACAS had been made. As the procedure stands, there is an incentive for the union not to organise industrial action in breach of procedure as, if it does so, its members lose the protection of the status quo clause in their contracts of employment.

Dispute procedures can be made fully legally enforceable through including no-strike clauses and providing for a dispute to be referred to a commercial arbitrator if the previous stages of the procedure have not resolved the dispute. An employer will be able to seek an injunction if a trade union organises industrial action in breach of the procedure. However, no-strike clauses in employment contracts cannot be enforced by injunctions as a result of s. 236 TULRCA. In other words, a no-strike clause in an employment contract will not enable an employer to secure a court order requiring strikers to return to work.

The decision of a commercial arbitrator will be legally binding on the parties and enforceable by court order. The disadvantage to employers of commercial arbitration is that an award can be imposed on them, which they view as being more expensive than would have been the case had an industrial dispute been allowed to run its course. It is possible for an employer and a trade union to agree that a dispute will be referred to ACAS for arbitration rather than to a commercial arbitrator. ACAS arbitration is not legally enforceable and is binding in honour only.

Unprotected official action

Section 238 TULRCA will apply once lawful industrial action ceases to be protected. The section also applies to unlawful *official* action, that is, action which is not protected by statutory immunity but is authorised or deemed authorised by the union. As explained below, in the latter situation s. 238 ceases to apply if the union has effectively repudiated the action, and the action has consequently become unofficial. The general effect of s. 238 is that an employer must take an all or nothing approach in that if all the employees taking the action are dismissed then tribunals have no jurisdiction to hear unfair dismissal claims. However, if only some of the employees taking the action are dismissed then such selective dismissals will be declared unfair unless the employer can show that it has acted reasonably in accordance with s. 98(4) ERA 1996.

Section 238 applies to exclude a tribunal's jurisdiction to hear unfair dismissal claims providing all the employees participating in the industrial action at the time of the dismissals have been dismissed. The retention of employees who had participated in the industrial action, but who had returned to work prior to the date of the dismissals, will not prevent s. 238 from applying to exclude unfair dismissal claims. Therefore, employers are able to warn employees that they will be dismissed on a specified future date in the hope that this will induce at least some of those involved in the action to resume normal working prior to the specified date.

Similarly, tribunals cannot hear complaints of selective reinstatements or re-engagements if they occur more than three months from the date of the dismissals. In other words, if an employer waits for at least three months from the date of the dismissals it can reinstate some of the employees that it previously dismissed. From a practical perspective, the employer can reinstate employees regarded as good workers whilst employees perceived to be more militant in their attitudes stay dismissed.

As held in *P&O European Ferries (Dover) Ltd* v. *Byrne* [1989] IRLR 254, employers are protected by s. 238 providing all the relevant employees have been dismissed by the end of the tribunal hearing to ascertain whether the tribunal has the jurisdiction to hear the individual unfair dismissal claims. In this case, the employer only discovered at the tribunal that an unidentified employee, who had still been participating in a strike on the date of the dismissals, had not been dismissed. It was decided by the Court of Appeal that it was permissible, even at this late stage, for the employer to require the identity of that employee to be disclosed so that he could then be included in the dismissals with the effect that s. 238 would still apply to exclude the tribunal's jurisdiction.

Case Summary

However, even if all the employees who participated in industrial action are dismissed, s. 238 will not apply where the dismissals are made *after* the industrial action has ended. In *Glenrose (Fish Merchants) Ltd* v. *Chapman*, EAT 245/89, the employees collectively stated that they would refuse to work voluntary overtime on a particular evening in furtherance of a dispute over working hours. The next day the workers turned up for the morning shift at the proper time but were told by the company that they were all dismissed for participating in the overtime ban. The EAT decided that these dismissals were made after the industrial action, not during it, and therefore the tribunal had the jurisdiction to hear individual unfair dismissal claims.

It can be seen in this case that the employees refused to work voluntary overtime and arguably therefore were not acting in breach of their employment contracts. However, it was held by the Court of Appeal in *Power Packing Casemakers Ltd* v. *Faust* [1983] IRLR 117, in a case that also involved employees who were dismissed for collectively refusing to work voluntary overtime, that s. 238 applies to any instance of industrial action including action which may not be in breach of the employment contract. For the purposes of s. 238, industrial action should be regarded as any concerted action by employees, which is taken to exert pressure on their employer. Therefore, had the workers in *Glenrose* been dismissed during the evening shift that they had refused to work then the company would have been protected by s. 238.

It is perfectly possible that during a strike some employees will be absent from work for legitimate reasons such as illness or because they are on holiday. It will be necessary for an employer to dismiss such employees, in order to attract the protection of s. 238, if they can be objectively regarded as participating in the industrial action. For example, an employee whilst on holiday participates in picketing outside of the workplace. That employee is not technically on strike, but will still be participating in it, and should be dismissed along with all the employees who were actually on strike at the date of the dismissals.

As participation in industrial action is to be determined objectively, an employee's motives cannot be taken into account. In *Coates* v. *Modern Methods and Materials Ltd* [1982] IRLR 318, an employee refused to cross a picket line, despite being opposed to a strike, because she was fearful of the consequences of being seen as a strike breaker. It was held that she should be regarded as participating in the strike and therefore had to be included in the dismissals for s. 238 to apply. This would not apply to an employee who attempted to cross a picket line but was physically and unlawfully prevented from doing so. Employers can also permit employees to work from home and employees who do so are clearly not participating in industrial action.

It must be emphasised that even though s. 238 does not apply to exclude a tribunal's jurisdiction, as illustrated by *Sehmi* v. *Gate Gourmet; Sandhu* v. *Gate Gourmet* [2009] IRLR 807, a selective dismissal may be fair if it is reasonable under s. 98(4) ERA 1996. In this case, a large number of employees were involved in unlawful official strike action. The court held that in the circumstances of the case it was appropriate for the employer to consider the strike as creating serious disruption to its operations and to decide to respond quickly and firmly to seek to bring it to an end. Therefore, it was within the range of reasonable responses to dismiss all the employees it believed to be supporting the strike even though not all the strikers were actually dismissed.

Dismissals relating to industrial action

It is possible that a dismissal is connected with industrial action but is not with respect to the dismissed employee's participation in it. For example, a striker is dismissed not for participation in the strike but for an act of violent picketing. This will be a misconduct dismissal covered by s. 98(2) ERA 1996 and, providing proper procedure (as examined in Chapter 5), is followed, the dismissal is likely to be viewed as reasonable and fair under s. 98(4) ERA 1996.

In *Crowther* v. *British Railways* EAT 1118/95, four employees were held to be fairly dismissed for gross misconduct in organising industrial action which was unofficial in the industrial relations sense of the word as it was not genuinely authorised by the union but, at the date of the dismissals, had not yet been repudiated by it. Section 238 does not operate to protect the organisers of industrial action, as against those who participate in it. Nor were the organisers of the action protected by s. 152 TULRCA as the unofficial nature of the action meant that the organisers were not undertaking a trade union duty or activity.

Case Summary

Section 152 does make it automatically unfair to dismiss an employee for undertaking a trade union duty or activity at an appropriate time (see Chapter 8). Therefore, if, as in *Naylor* v. *Orton & Smith Ltd* [1983] ICR 665, a union representative with the approval of the union organises a meeting at which it is decided to organise or call for industrial action, this can be considered a trade union duty providing the meeting takes place outside working hours, or during working hours with the employer's consent. Similarly, attending such a meeting can be considered a trade union activity.

Case Summary

Unofficial industrial action

As is illustrated by the above *Crowther* case unofficial industrial action has two meanings. The industrial relations meaning covers any action where the organiser(s) of the action is acting outside of the union's rules or in defiance of the instructions of a higher body or official within the union. The legal meaning is different to this and is provided by s. 237 TULRCA. For the purposes of this section, action will not be unofficial if the action is deemed to be authorised or endorsed by the participant's trade union, and has not yet been repudiated by it. As detailed above, effective repudiation requires the union to notify relevant union officials and representatives, the workers it believes to be participating in it and their employer of the repudiation.

Moreover, the notice to union members must contain a statement informing them that there is no right to complain of unfair dismissal for participating in unofficial industrial action. Repudiation does not immediately render the action unofficial. It does not become unofficial until after the end of the next working day after the day on which repudiation takes place. If unofficial action is repudiated on a Monday no dismissals should take place until the Wednesday. Saturdays, Sundays and public holidays do not constitute working days for the purposes of s. 237 even if employees normally work on such days. Therefore, if repudiation occurs on a Friday there should be no dismissals until the following Tuesday.

Effectively, employees participating in industrial action have at least one day of grace to return to work before s. 237 applies to render their action unofficial. The effect of s. 237 is that an employee loses any right to complain of unfair dismissal. This means that it is entirely permissible for an employer to dismiss unofficial strikers on a selective basis with the more militant workers being the first to go.

It should also be remembered that unions that fail to repudiate effectively are incurring the risk of liability in tort. The normal consequence of an employer suing in tort would be that an injunction would be granted which would require the union to

Table 9.2 Industrial action dismissals

Type of dismissal	Consequence of dismissal
Dismissal for participation in protected lawful and official industrial action	Dismissal is automatically unfair for participation during the protected period which is normally 12 weeks
Dismissal for participation in official action which takes place outside of the protected period, or which was unlawful and therefore never was protected	Tribunals have no jurisdiction to hear unfair dismissal claims if *all* participants are dismissed. A selective dismissal will be unfair unless it is reasonable under s. 98(4) ERA 1996
Dismissal for participation in industrial action which has become unofficial as a result of trade union repudiation	Dismissed employees have no rights to claim unfair dismissal

take appropriate steps to bring the action to an end, at which point it will become unofficial. As noted above, industrial action which is organised with a view to securing the reinstatement of dismissed unofficial strikers cannot be considered to be in furtherance of a lawful trade dispute as a result of s. 223 TULRCA.

The overall impact of these provisions is that the employer can dismiss at will once industrial action has been rendered unofficial, and the workers so dismissed will have no form of legal redress available to them. Nor can they seek the support of their union without the union incurring the risk of liability in tort. As explained below, the removal of any form of legal protection from unofficial strikers has been declared by the ILO to be a violation of the UK's treaty obligations under ILO Conventions and therefore a breach of international law.

Table 9.2 summarises the different types of industrial action dismissals and their relationship with unfair dismissal law.

Industrial action and wages

Employees who participate in strike action obviously have no right to be paid during the strike. Case law has also established that, with respect to industrial action short of a strike, the employer can choose between withholding payment altogether or making appropriate deductions from wages to cover the work that is not done. This position is the result of the application of the contractual doctrine of partial performance. The employer has the choice between refusing part performance and accepting it and paying for the work that is actually done. Where part performance is refused, the employer is effectively suspending the employees until they agree to work normally. The cases of *Miles* v. *Wakefield District Council* [1987] ICR 368 and *Wiluszynski* v. *London Borough of Tower Hamlets* [1989] ICR 493 illustrate these principles.

Case Summary

In *Miles*, the claimant was employed as a superintendent registrar. His normal week consisted of 37 hours' work, including three hours on Saturday mornings, which was the most popular time for weddings. His trade union instructed him to refuse to conduct weddings on Saturdays as part of industrial action. Miles complied with this instruction but remained willing to work a 37-hour week and to attend on Saturdays to do other work. The council made it clear that it did not accept this and would deduct that part of his salary representing the three hours on Saturday mornings. It was held by the House of Lords that his right to remuneration depended on his being willing to do the work that he was employed to do and if he declined to do such work the employer need not pay him. The deductions from his salary were therefore lawful.

In *Wiluszynski*, the claimant was a member of a union which, as a result of a dispute with the council, called for limited industrial action to be taken in the form of the boycott of giving advice to councillors. Wiluszynski was told that if he took such action he should not come to work at all. If he did attempt to undertake limited work then it would be regarded as voluntary and unauthorised and would not be paid for. Wiluszynski continued to work as instructed by his union and the council refused to pay him for the time worked during the industrial action. It was held by the Court of Appeal that an employee's statement that he will not discharge a material part of his contractual duties is a repudiatory breach of contract. Termination of the contract is not the only remedy available to the employer. If an employee refuses for a period of time to perform a material part of his contractual duties, the employer is entitled to decline to accept the proffered partial performance. Therefore, Wiluszynski was not entitled to receive any of his salary.

In the latter case had Wiluszynski been led by the council to believe that he would have been paid for the work he did, his claim would have succeeded. However, as in *Miles*, the council would have been entitled to make deductions from his salary in respect of the work that he failed to carry out.

Case Summary

You be the judge

Q: Can unfair dismissal be successfully claimed in any of the following situations?

(a) The employees of A Ltd are on official strike for higher wages. Their trade union has fully complied with the statutory requirements for a postal ballot and pre-ballot and pre-strike notices. During week five of the strike A Ltd informs its employees that if they do not return to work on the following Monday they will all be dismissed. On that Monday all the employees remain on strike and all are dismissed.

(b) The employees of A Ltd are on official strike for higher wages. Their trade union has fully complied with the statutory requirements for a postal ballot and pre-ballot and pre-strike notices. During week 14 of the strike A Ltd informs the employees that if they do not return to work on the following Monday they will all be dismissed. On that Monday all the employees remain on strike and all are dismissed.

(c) The employees of A Ltd are persuaded by M, their elected trade union representative, to take immediate strike action in support of a colleague who has been dismissed for his trade union activities. The following day, which is a Wednesday, the union properly repudiates the strike. On the Friday, M, who is also one of the strikers, is dismissed.

A: The dismissals in (a) are automatically unfair, but in (b) and (c) the employees cannot present claims for unfair dismissal.

In (a) the employees have been dismissed whilst they are participating in protected official protected strike action and they will be able to claim that their dismissals are automatically unfair.

In (b) the employees have been dismissed whilst they were participating in unprotected official strike action. As all the relevant employees have been dismissed, an employment tribunal will have no jurisdiction to hear unfair dismissal claims. The action is unprotected because it has lasted for longer than 14 weeks. However, it should be appreciated that if the reason for this is that the employer has refused to return to the negotiating table, despite an offer by the union to suspend the strike pending further negotiations, the strike is likely to still be protected. In this latter situation all the dismissals will be continue to be automatically unfair.

In (c) M has been dismissed for participating in unofficial strike action and M has no right to claim unfair dismissal.

Picketing and the civil law

So far this chapter has focused on the legal position of the organisers of, and participants in, industrial action. Whenever industrial action, particularly strike action, takes place it will often be the case that workers taking the action will picket their place of work, or, indeed, other workplaces in addition to their own. Picketing is not a legal term as such and is akin to other forms of public protest and demonstration. Nevertheless, picketing is normally distinctive in its purposes and form of operation. Picketing is a way of gaining publicity through media coverage of a strike, but its main purpose will be to seek the support of the pickets' colleagues, and the employees of other employers, by asking them not to cross their picket line. To this end, pickets, typically, will position themselves at entrances to workplaces.

Where picketing succeeds in its aim, it will normally involve commission of the economic torts of inducing or procuring a breach of contract, or interfering with the performance of a contract through the use of unlawful means, which were discussed in the first part of this chapter. Picketing, whether it is successful or not, may also involve the commission of public and/or private nuisance and trespass to land. It should be noted that there is never any immunity available with respect to trespass. Therefore, strikers may only picket on their employer's property with the employer's consent.

Private nuisance will be committed where pickets unreasonably interfere with the employer's use or enjoyment of its premises by preventing rights of access to it and impeding the employer's business operations. **Public nuisance** will occur where there is an unreasonable use of the highway – specifically pavements and roads at or near to the employer's premises. If the latter activity causes special damage to the employer, this will provide the employer with a separate cause of action in seeking injunctions to restrain unlawful picketing. Such injunctions can be granted against individual pickets, the person(s) organising the picket and their trade union. The latter may incur **vicarious liability** even where it has not been directly involved in organising the picketing.

This part of the chapter is concerned with the tortious liabilities that organisers of picketing and individual pickets may incur. However, it should be noted in passing that picketing can involve public order issues and pickets may commit criminal offences either at common law such as committing a breach of the peace, or as result of legislation – particularly offences created by the Conspiracy Protection of Property Act 1875, now contained in s. 241 TULRCA, and the Public Order Act 1986. This is particularly so with mass picketing which may involve pickets fighting with the police. However, such picketing has not occurred in a significant way since the miners' strike of 1984–85 and the Wapping printers' strike in 1987.

This chapter is not concerned with the criminal law, although some cases decided by the criminal courts will be discussed, as they involve interpretations of how the immunity from liability in tort in the context of picketing should be understood.

Handy tip: You will find it useful to access and download the government's Code of Practice on Picketing at **http://www.delni.gov.uk/code-of-practice-picketing**. This code is not, in itself, a legal document but it sets out the civil and criminal law, and provides guidance on how lawful picketing should be conducted.

The picketing immunity

Immunity from liability for the economic torts is provided for by s. 220 TULRCA. The immunity is available where all the following conditions apply:

✦ The picketing is in contemplation or furtherance of a trade dispute – this has the same meaning as s. 219, which is discussed fully above.

✦ The purpose of the picketing is peacefully to persuade others to act in a particular way or to communicate information to them – this is the most significant aspect of the immunity and is discussed in further detail below.

✦ The pickets must be at or near their own place of work.

'Own place of work' means the central or single workplace of the employee. If it is impracticable for employees to picket their own place of work then under s. 220(2) employees can picket any of the employer's premises where they actually work or from which their work is administered. This covers, for example, lorry drivers and oil rig workers, who either may have no single workplace or, in the case of the latter, cannot, short of hiring a flotilla of boats, effectively picket it.

The meaning of 'at or near' was considered in *Rayware Ltd* v. *TGWU* [1989] ICR 457. The company's premises were situated within an industrial estate and the entrance to this estate was over half a mile from these premises. In furtherance of a lawful trade dispute, employees of the company set up a picket at the entrance to the estate. This was the nearest they could get to their employer's premises without trespassing on the estate, which was private land. The court agreed with the union that the expression 'at or near' in the Act had to be interpreted in a geographical sense, and also required the using of common sense. The pickets had situated themselves at the nearest point at which a picket could be mounted without committing acts of trespass. Therefore, the picket was lawful.

Case Summary

Under s. 220(3) an ex-employee can picket his former workplace. However, as clarified in *News Group Newspapers Ltd* v. *SOGAT* [1987] ICR 181, this means the actual geographical site at which the employee formerly worked. In this case News International moved its operations from Fleet Street in central London to Wapping in East London. The company's printers took strike action and all of them were dismissed. It was held that the s. 220 immunity did not cover them even peacefully picketing the Wapping plant as they had never worked there. The practical consequence of this decision is that, if an employer transfers its operations after its workers have been dismissed, it is only lawful to picket the now empty premises at which the pickets had actually worked.

Case Summary

Normally, only employees and workers who actually work or worked at a particular workplace are protected by the immunity. Therefore, other individuals who attend a picket line, for example, to demonstrate their support for the industrial action, are not protected by the s. 220 **picketing immunity**, although they may be protected by general rights of assembly. However, s. 220(4) expressly provides that a union official may join a picket line to accompany a member he or she represents, even though that official is not employed at the pickets' place of work. Indeed, the code of practice recommends that trade union officials attend picket lines in order to supervise the behaviour of the pickets and to encourage them to behave in a lawful manner.

The meaning of peaceful persuasion or communication

Pickets will only be behaving lawfully if they do no more than seek peacefully to persuade others not to enter the pickets' workplace and/or peacefully to communicate information to them about the industrial action. It has long been clear that peaceful does not equate with non-violent and that pickets can be acting outside the protection of the picketing even though they are not committing or threatening acts of violence.

Case Summary

In *Tynan* v. *Balmer* [1966] 2 WLR 1181 pickets were frustrated by being ignored by co-workers in cars driving past them and refusing to stop to enable the pickets to talk to them. They therefore mounted a picket involving the pickets constantly walking in a circle on the road. It was held that it did not matter that the picketing was entirely non-violent in nature. The pickets had no right to force motorists to stop and therefore the pickets were guilty of obstructing the highway.

Case Summary

This approach by approved by the Law Lords in *Broome* v. *DPP* [1974] ICR 84. In this case a union official sat in front of a lorry holding a placard summarising what an industrial dispute was about. After approximately nine minutes the official allowed the lorry to enter the premises which were being picketed. Magistrates had held that he was not guilty of obstructing the highway as he was exercising his right peacefully to communicate information to the lorry driver. The House of Lords held that the official was guilty as there is no right to stop a person in order to speak to that person. There is no right to picket. The statutory immunity provides for a freedom to attend a place of work in order to address others who are prepared to stop and listen. In supporting this decision, Lord Reid used the analogy of a hitchhiker, who can stand by, but not in, the road indicating that he or she would like drivers to stop and give a lift. Similarly, pickets can indicate that they would like to speak to persons about to cross the picket line but they cannot obstruct, even by non-violent means, their freedom of movement.

There have been suggestions in some previous cases that if pickets assemble in large numbers then such mass picketing is inherently unlawful as the size of the picket will intimidate others and is designed to impede or deter them from entering their workplace. In *Thomas* v. *NUM*, a case which arose out of the 1984–85 miners' strike and which is discussed below, Scott J stated, at page 906, that in his opinion 'a large number of sullen men lining the entrance to a colliery, offering no violence, saying nothing, but simply standing and glowering would . . . be highly intimidating'.

Moreover, paragraph 51 of the Code of Practice on Picketing states that the number of pickets at a place of entrance or access to a workplace should not exceed six persons. This has led to the view that any group of pickets who total more than six in number are acting unlawfully.

the focus should be on the behaviour and not the number of pickets

However, pickets are exercising their human rights of assembly as guaranteed by Article 11 of the ECHR, and this suggests that there can be no decision in advance to the effect that if pickets total more than a given number they must be acting unlawfully. Rather, the focus should be on the behaviour and not the number of pickets present at a workplace. This view is supported by the decision of the House of Lords in *DPP* v. *Jones* [1999] 2 All ER 457 where 21 people peacefully protested on the road outside of Stonehenge against a refusal by the police to allow them access to 'the Stones' to worship the summer solstice. A majority of the Law Lords decided that the demonstrators were not obstructing the highway, but were exercising a right of lawful peaceful protest on it. In reaching this decision their Lordships made specific reference to the European Convention. As explained above, pickets are essentially protesters or demonstrators, and there is no reason in law to restrict their numbers on the highway in circumstances in which such restrictions would not be applied to other protestors.

Case Summary

The argument that the correct legal approach is to focus on the actual behaviour of pickets is supported by the decision of Fulford J in *Gate Gourmet London Ltd* v. *TGWU* [2005] IRLR 881. In this case unofficial strikers set up a picket line of between six and 20 people at an entrance to the employer's premises. It was held that, although the sheer weight of numbers increased the risk of unlawful activity, this was not inevitable and rights to freedom of expression and assembly as guaranteed by Articles 10 and 11 ECHR also had to be taken into account. He also stated that the fact that the pickets were noisy did not inherently mean they were guilty of intimidating workers who did not support the strike. However, the judge also found that on the facts of the case there had been unlawful acts by the pickets and granted an injunction to the company which limited the number of pickets to six. Therefore Fulford J appeared to have implicitly applied paragraph 51 of the code of practice, but only on the basis of evidence showing that the pickets were behaving in an intimidatory manner. The injunction was not granted merely on the basis of the size of the picket and its noisy nature. In this case, there were also around 200 strikers situated on a hill near to the workplace demonstrating their support for the strike. The judge refused to reduce their numbers until and if evidence was presented to the court establishing that they were behaving unlawfully.

Case Summary

The *Jones* and *Gate Gourmet* cases establish that picketing is not inherently tortious. However, where pickets act in ways which go further than seeking peacefully to persuade or communicate information then they are likely to commit private and public nuisance and, depending on whether they are genuinely issuing threats, the tort of intimidation. Where individual pickets commit torts then they are personally liable as a result. The liability of their union is considered below.

The fact that picketing is not inherently unlawful is of practical importance as pickets will often be unsuccessful in that their activities do not result in workers breaking their contracts by refusing to cross a picket line. In such circumstances, providing pickets do not intimidate or act in ways constituting private or public nuisance they will be doing no more than exercising their rights of peaceful protest. This may cause irritation to the employer whose premises are being picketed, and/or to workers wishing to go into work, but the pickets are not acting unlawfully simply through their presence. This is also important where pickets visit workplaces other than their own, be these premises owned by their employer, other employers in the industry, or perhaps shops at which their employer's products are sold. Providing the pickets do not induce or procure breaches of contracts or interfere with business through the use of unlawful means, it will be of no legal consequence that the s. 220 immunity is not available because the pickets are not at their own place of work.

Picketing and secondary industrial action

Where pickets are lawfully picketing their own place of work their acts may result in secondary industrial action taking place. For example, pickets peacefully persuade a driver employed by a supplier to the employer in dispute not to deliver supplies to the latter. The pickets have committed economic torts through inducing the driver to act in breach of his employment contract, and, in so doing, have procured a breach of the commercial contract between the driver's employer and the employer in dispute. The driver has been induced to take secondary industrial action because he has no trade dispute with his own employer. It should be clarified that the driver in this situation has not incurred any liability in tort. He is in breach of his contract of employment, but that is an issue which is only of concern to the driver and his employer.

However, providing the pickets were situated at their own place of work they and their union will have immunity from liability in these torts. This is because of s. 224(3) TULRCA, which provides that pickets lawfully picketing at their own place of work do not lose immunity if picketing results in secondary action. This is the one exception to the normal position whereby secondary industrial action loses immunity under s. 224.

Liability for picketing

Individual pickets and/or the organiser(s) of picketing can be liable individually under both the civil and criminal law. The trade union's legal liability for the economic torts is determined by ss. 20 and 21 TULRCA, which are explained above. The union will be liable with respect to any acts which are authorised or endorsed, or deemed to be authorised or endorsed, by it. With respect to acts which are deemed to be authorised or endorsed, the union can escape liability if it effectively repudiates them. In the context of picketing this will require issuing instructions to pickets not to continue with particular acts and/or continue to picket at particular locations.

Case Summary

In torts other than the economic torts the liability of a trade union is determined by the doctrine of vicarious liability. This is most important where picketing involves nuisance and/or intimidation. In *Thomas* v. *NUM (S. Wales Area)* [1985] IRLR 136, the National Union of Mineworkers (South Wales Area), organised strike action in South Wales as part of its support for the strike called by the national union. In November 1984 some South Wales union members, including 12 of the 20 plaintiffs, returned to work. Their return was met by picketing and demonstrations in large numbers at the colliery gates. Verbal abuse and threats of violence were made, and the presence of large numbers of police was necessary in order to prevent a breach of the peace. The picketing was organised by the local union lodges. However, it was held that the overall responsibility for the conduct of the strike rested with the South Wales union, and in carrying out arrangements for local picketing individual lodges were acting on behalf of the union. However, although the picketing was in furtherance of a national strike the national union could not incur vicarious liability as the South Wales NUM was an autonomous regional body within the national union.

Case Summary

The case of *News Group Newspapers Ltd* v. *SOGAT* [1987] ICR 181, which arose of the 1987 Wapping dispute, both sheds light on when torts are committed by pickets and their supporters and the vicarious liability of the pickets' trade union. Interim injunctions were granted in favour of the plaintiffs in an action alleging public nuisance, intimidation, harassment and interference with contracts by reason of abusive threatening and violent picketing, marches and demonstrations held in the course of a trade dispute between the plaintiffs and their former employees. Mass demonstrations attempted to prevent traffic passing to and fro from Wapping to delay the distribution of the plaintiff's newspapers. These demonstrations were accompanied by acts of serious violence and public disturbance which the unions contended were not caused by their members. SOGAT, which was the printers union, argued that as the union was not responsible for organising any acts of disorder it could not be vicariously liable for them.

It was held that the conduct of the pickets and demonstrators was an unreasonable use of the highway that caused an obstruction and was therefore unlawful. It was actionable as a public nuisance if the plaintiff could show it had consequently sustained substantial particular damage. The plaintiff could do this because of the need to bus employees into the premises and to provide extra security. With respect to intimidation, the court accepted the argument by SOGAT that idle abuse, swearing and shouting could not in themselves constitute acts which amounted to intimidation. However, the evidence showed that the threats made by the pickets were serious threats to dissuade plaintiff's employees from working at Wapping and taken seriously by those that received them. Therefore, the tort of intimidation had been committed.

SOGAT was not liable simply because it organised a march or picketing during which tortious acts were committed by third parties, even though such acts could have been foreseen. However, there was sufficient evidence to show that SOGAT had continued to organise the picketing and demonstrations over a period of time in the knowledge that numerous acts of nuisance and intimidation had occurred and would continue to do so. The union could and should have exercised substantial control over its members to require them to act lawfully. Even if this was not the case, SOGAT could have avoided the commission of further torts by ceasing to organise the activities in question.

This case establishes that a trade union cannot wash its hands of unlawful acts by its members. Effectively, a union must instruct its members not continue to commit unlawful acts. In particular, a union must genuinely cease to have any formal involvement in activities which had led to the torts being committed.

Rights to strike and international law

As detailed throughout this chapter, since the beginning of the 1980s governments have imposed or retained significant restrictions on trade unions authorising or supporting their members taking industrial action. The picketing immunity has been restricted to the specific workplace of workers on strike. The content of a lawful trade dispute has been narrowed, sympathetic or secondary industrial action is unlawful and the procedures that a union must follow to ensure it does not lose the trade dispute immunity are detailed and complex.

Those who support these legal controls will regard them as justified because they believe that what they regard as excessive trade union power is damaging to the British economy and damaging to business. They will argue that companies based in other countries in the world would not set up operations in Britain if there was a real risk of systematic industrial unrest. Therefore, reducing the circumstances in which industrial action can lawfully take place contributes to business growth and reducing unemployment. This is in contrast with the 1960s and 1970s where industrial conflict generated both unemployment and inflation.

Those who oppose the legal controls regard them as reducing the ability of trade unions to organise collective action to further or defend the interests of their members.

They will argue that, as trade unions have the desire to represent the interests of all working people and their families, the majority of people in our society are disadvantaged by legal controls that have resulted in a weakened trade union movement. This has gone hand in hand with deregulation of the labour market, increased job insecurity and a growth in casual and part-time patterns of working. In short, weakening the trade unions has undermined the securing of workplace justice and dignity.

Readers will have their own views as to which of these positions they agree with or veer towards. However, it is legitimate for employment lawyers to argue that British governments should ensure that British law is in accordance with international legal standards. This is not the case with the current statutory provisions regulating the organisation and taking of industrial action.

As documented by Keith Ewing in his book which is cited in the 'Further reading' section at the end of this chapter, the International Labour Organisation (ILO), which is part of the United Nations, published several reports more than 20 years ago which condemn many of the current controls on industrial action as being excessive and in violation of Britain's obligations under international law as a result of its ratification of ILO Conventions. These include Convention 87, which the ILO has made explicitly clear upholds the right to strike as one of the 'essential means available to workers and their organisations to promote and protect their economic and social interests'. The ILO has criticised the following aspects of British law in particular:

✦ reducing the scope of a lawful trade dispute to *exclude* disputes which have a political dimension in so far as industrial action is organised in opposition to government policies which impact on workers' industrial and social interests;

✦ the absolute prohibition of any form of sympathetic industrial action as workers should be able to take sympathy action where the action they are supporting is in itself lawful;

✦ the ability of employers to render industrial action as unlawful secondary action by taking refuge behind one or more subsidiary companies when in reality there is just one employer as was the situation in *Dimbleby* v. *NUJ*, which is discussed above;

✦ the removal of *any* form of unfair dismissal protection from workers engaged in unofficial industrial action.

The ILO has also criticised the complexity of the legislation. Therefore, although the ILO has stated that it is in accordance with the Convention for the law to provide for balloting and other pre-strike procedures, these should not operate in a complex manner so as to interfere unreasonably with rights to strike. Given the decisions in the *Metrobus* and the first *British Airways* case discussed above, it is questionable whether the detail of the legislation is compatible with Convention 87. Alternatively, it could be argued that the procedures are in accordance with the Convention providing the approach taken in the second *British Airways* case and subsequent cases such as *RMT* v. *Serco* is consistently applied.

The ILO has called on British governments to amend the current statutory provisions so that the requirements of international law are met. For example, replacing the phrase '*wholly or mainly related to*' in s. 219 TULRCA with the phrase '*connected to*', which was the position before 1980, would lead to a different decision in the case of *Mercury Communications* v. *Garner*, which is discussed above. The industrial dispute in this case was *mainly* about the government's decision to privatise BT but it was also *connected* to the fear that privatisation would result in redundancies.

The ILO's calls have largely fallen on deaf ears – not only during the years of Margaret Thatcher's and John Major's Conservative governments but also during the 13 years of New Labour government. All of these governments have maintained the position that, the requirements of international law notwithstanding, the restrictions on industrial action are in the interests of British business and the British economy.

The one change made by Tony Blair's government was the introduction of the 12-week period during which lawful industrial action is protected and any dismissals are automatically unfair. It is not certain whether this change in the law, important though it is, has satisfied the criticisms of the ILO to the effect that British law does not give adequate protection to strikers against dismissal.

Rights versus immunities

The ILO has stated that a system of immunities rather than a system of positive rights is not in itself contrary to the ILO Convention. However, the ILO has noted that the system is very complicated, and it is problematic that the flexibility of the common law is such that existing immunities can be circumvented through the development of new tortious liabilities. An example of this process was the development by the House of Lords in *Rookes* v. *Barnard*, see above, of the tort of intimidation to cover threats to strike as well as threats to inflict violence.

Nevertheless, it is perfectly possible to support pro-union reforms and be in favour of the retention of the system of immunities. This was the view of Lord Wedderburn, who was the leading British labour lawyer of his time and who, very sadly, died in early 2012. Wedderburn argued that the system of immunities constitutes the provision of rights in a negative form and that any system of rights – positive or negative – is susceptible to judicial restriction and the creation of new liabilities. Wedderburn's view was that the emphasis should not be on the form in which rights are provided, but on the establishment of autonomous labour courts which would be staffed by lawyers experienced in employment law rather than by the traditional judiciary.

Other labour lawyers, including one of the authors of this text (Roger Welch), have argued that there are advantages to any pro-union reform being in the form of positive rights replacing statutory immunities. In particular, this would prevent judges, politicians and the media from characterising what are intended to be rights to strike as privileges to break the law. The question can be posed in this way. Is it better to provide rights and then decide what restrictions, if any, it is reasonable and just to impose on them? Or is it better to retain a system where industrial action is inherently defined as law-breaking and then identify the circumstances where this law-breaking should be protected from the imposition of normal legal liabilities?

It should be clarified that moving from a system of immunities to a system of rights would not prevent governments from deciding what restrictions should be imposed on rights to strike to provide a reasonable balance between the interests of employers and the interests of trade unions and their members. However, irrespective of whether future British governments retain the system of immunities or adopt a system of positive rights, it should be the case that any restrictions on industrial action are in line with the requirements of the ILO and therefore compatible with international law.

Summary

 Taking industrial action generally involves employees in acting in breach of express or implied terms in their contracts of employment.

A trade union or person which or who organises industrial action will typically commit the tort of inducing or procuring breaches of employment contracts and/or commercial contracts.

Organisers of industrial action may also commit a tort by interfering with contracts or business where this causes loss and unlawful means have been used.

Trade unions and persons have immunity under s. 219 TULRCA for inducing or procuring breaches of contracts or for interfering with their performance, or threatening to do so, providing industrial action is in contemplation or furtherance of a lawful trade dispute.

A trade dispute is only lawful if it is wholly or mainly related to a dispute between workers and their own employer over one or more of the matters set out by s. 244 TULRCA.

Other than in the context of lawful picketing, the organisation of secondary industrial action which is taken by workers who do not have a trade dispute with their own employer cannot attract statutory immunity.

 The trade dispute immunity available to a trade union is lost if the union fails to secure support for industrial action through a valid postal ballot, and/or fails to provide valid pre-ballot and pre-strike notice to the employer in dispute.

 Employees who take official and protected industrial action will be automatically unfairly dismissed for taking industrial action during the protected period which will normally be for 12 weeks from date the action first started.

Where industrial action is official but unprotected, employment tribunals have no jurisdiction to hear unfair dismissal claims if *all* the workers taking the action at the date of the dismissals have been dismissed.

 Selective dismissals of employees taking official unprotected industrial action will be unfair if the employer has failed to act reasonably in deciding to make the dismissals.

Industrial action which is deemed to be authorised or endorsed by a trade union will become unofficial if the union effectively repudiates it.

Employees who are dismissed for participating in unofficial industrial action have no rights to claim unfair dismissal.

Picketing in contemplation or furtherance of a lawful trade dispute is lawful under s. 220 TULRCA providing workers are picketing their own place of work, and are doing no more than seeking peacefully to persuade others not to work or peacefully to communicate information to them.

Where a trade union has no immunity or loses immunity for authorising or organising industrial action, the most common remedy that employers seek is an interim injunction to restrain the industrial action from taking place or continuing.

Question and answer*

Problem: Camberwick Co. Ltd is a manufacturer of toys and has one factory in Camberwick and a second factory in Trumpton. An associated company, Toyland Co Ltd, owns a number of retail outlets in the South to distribute these toys. Dougal is the major shareholder and managing director of both of these companies. Both companies recognise the General Workers Union (GWU) for the purposes of collective bargaining. All production workers at Camberwick and Trumpton are members of the GWU.

Camberwick Co. Ltd announces that over the next two months it will be transferring part of its work from the factory in Camberwick to its factory in Trumpton. As a result of this transfer, it is proposing to halve the workforce of 500 at Camberwick. The company intends to distribute redundancies notices in three months' time after full consultations with the GWU. The production workers at Camberwick are balloted on strike action to oppose the company's plans. The ballot produces an 80% majority in favour of the strike action. Two weeks after the conclusion of the ballot Richard Franks, the general secretary of the GWU, instructs the members at Camberwick to strike and picket the factory with effect from the following day. During the first week of the strike the following events occur:

(a) On the Monday, 50 of the strikers picket the four entrances to the Camberwick factory. Twenty GWU members, who had voted against the strike, turn up for work but decide not to cross the picket line.

(b) On the Tuesday, a lorry driver, employed by Toyland Co Ltd to collect toys for delivery to Toyland's shops, is dissuaded by two pickets from entering the factory.

(c) On the Wednesday, Ivor Jones, the senior shop steward at Camberwick, sends a delegation of pickets to the Trumpton factory to urge GWU members to refuse, with immediate effect, to accept any work transferred from the Camberwick factory.

(d) On the Thursday, strikers picket supermarkets and toyshops in Camberwick with a view to persuading shoppers not to buy Camberwick products.

Consider the legal rights and liabilities that arise out of this situation. You should assume that the GWU has complied with all the appropriate statutory procedures concerning balloting and the provision of notices to Camberwick Co. Ltd. prior to calling the strike.

You should spend 40 minutes on answering this question.

Essay: 'British law regulating the organisation of and participation in industrial action strikes an appropriate balance between the rights of workers to withdraw their labour and the interests of businesses and the public in maintaining a healthy economy.'

Critically discuss this statement.

In an examination you would spend 40 minutes on answering this question. However, this question is also suitable for setting as an in-course assessment, in which case, having done your research, you should spend around three hours in writing it.

✱ Answer guidance is provided at the end of the chapter.

Further reading

IDS (2010) *Industrial Action, Employment Law Handbook* **(London: Income Data Services).**

Chapters 2 to 5 of this book provide a comprehensive explanation of the torts committed through organising industrial action, where statutory immunity is available and when it is lost.

Bowers, J., Duggan, M. and Reade, D. (2011) *The Law of Industrial Action and Trade Union Recognition* **(Oxford: OUP).**

Chapters 3 to 5 provide a similar comprehensive explanation of the torts and the immunities, although this text is written in a more technical style.

Deakin, S. and Morris, G. (2012) *Labour Law* **(Hart: Oxford).**

Chapter 11 both comprehensively explains the law regulating industrial action and provides critical and contextual analysis of it.

Deakin, S. and Randall, J. (2009) 'Rethinking the Economic Torts', *Modern Law Review,* **vol. 72(4), pp. 519–53; Simpson, B. (2007) 'Economic tort liability in labour disputes: the potential impact of the House of Lords' decision in OBG v. Allan',** *Industrial Law Journal,* **vol. 36(4), pp. 468–79.**

Both of these articles analyse the economic torts in the aftermath of the decision of the House of Lords in *OBG* v. *Allan.* As these writers demonstrate, although the law had been clarified with respect to inducing and procuring breaches of contracts, other areas of the economic torts remain unclear – such as the scope of unlawful means and the lawfulness of industrial action which brings about breaches of statutory duty.

Dukes, R. (2010) 'The Right to Strike under UK Law: Not Much More than a Slogan', *Industrial Law Journal,* **vol. 39(1), pp. 82–91; Ewing, K. D. (2011) 'Fighting Back Resisting "Union-Busting" and "Strike-Breaking" in the BA Dispute' (Liverpool: Institute of Employment Rights); Prassl, J. (2011) 'Industrial Action at British Airways:**
a Case Study', *Contemporary Issues in Law,* **vol. 11(2), pp. 117–38.**

The complex procedures on strike ballots and notices have generated some recent important decisions. The article by Dukes contains critical analysis of the decision in *Metrobus.* The paper by Ewing and the article by Prassl contain critical and contextual analysis of the *British Airways* cases.

Ewing, K. D. (1994) *Britain and the ILO* **(London: Institute of Employment Rights).**

This short book explains the origins of the ILO and analyses the criticisms of British legislation by it. The book also contains copies of the ILO reports on British law.

Ewing K. D. (ed.) (2006) *The Right to Strike: From the Trade Disputes Act 1906 to a Trade Union Freedom Bill 2006* **(Liverpool: IER).**

This book contains a number of essays by labour lawyers and industrial relations academics which analyse pivotal cases such as *Quinn* v. *Leathem,* the *Taff Vale* decision and *Rookes* v. *Barnard.* The concluding chapter recommends changes to the British legislation which, if enacted, would bring British law more into line with the ILO Conventions.

Hanson, C. (1991) *Taming the Trade Unions: a Guide to the Thatcher Government's Employment Reforms 1980–90* **(Basingstoke: Macmillan).**

There is little academic literature which is sympathetic to the legal controls on industrial action, which British governments have put in place or retained since 1980. This text is an exception to this. Otherwise, the best sources for ascertaining government thinking are official documents. In particular, *Trade Union Immunities* Cmnd. Paper 8218, 1981; *Democracy in Trade Unions* Cmnd. Paper 8778, 1983; and *Fairness at Work* Cm. Paper 3968, 1998. The first two documents should be available in your law library but the last paper can be accessed online at http://webarchive.nationalarchives.gov.uk/+/http://www.berr.gov.uk/files/file24436.pdf

Wedderburn, Lord (1987) 'From Here to Autonomy', *Industrial Law Journal,* **vol. 16(1), pp. 1–29; Welch, R. (1995) 'Judges and the Law in British Industrial Relations: Towards A European Right to Strike' (1995)** *Social & Legal Studies,* **vol. 4(3), pp. 175–96.**

The ILO has suggested that the British system of immunities can operate to restrict rights to strike by making the law unduly complex. These two articles discuss, from a pro-union perspective, the pros and cons of replacing the system of immunities with a system of positive rights.

Wallington, P. (1985) 'Policing the Miners' Strike', *Industrial Law Journal,* **vol. 14(1), pp. 145–59.**

Picketing which has resulted in public disorder has not been a significant feature of industrial disputes since the 1980s. However, as the *Gate Gourmet* case in 2005 illustrates, such issues arising out of picketing can still occur and are likely to do so in the future. This article, written at the time of the miners' strike, analyses and discusses the civil and criminal law regulating picketing.

Question and answer guidance

Problem: In problem questions on industrial action there is a tendency to go immediately into the legislation rather than to start by identifying the tort or torts that have been committed. As suggested above, the best approach is to discuss tortious liability, then the availability of the trade dispute immunity, and then whether immunity has been lost.

In your answer to this problem there is no need to dwell on ballots and strike procedures as you are told the union has complied with the statutory requirements. However, you should explain that the GWU in calling the strike has induced its members at Camberwick to break their contracts of employment. Your answer should explain why this is by setting out the elements of the tort. As the dispute is over threatened job losses, there is a lawful trade dispute within the meaning of s. 244 and the strike is in contemplation or furtherance of this dispute. You could cite the *Meek* case to clarify that the strike is in contemplation of job losses even though they have not yet been formally proposed. You could also state the strike is commencing within four weeks from the date of the ballot, and it is assumed that the ballot paper specified the general secretary as the authorised person to call the strike.

In (a) the pickets have induced colleagues to break their employment contracts by not entering work, and the emphasis of your answer should be on the availability of the s. 220 immunity. In particular, have the pickets impeded entrance to the workplace in any way? If they have then they will also have committed private and/or public nuisance as they will have done more than peacefully sought to persuade their colleagues not to cross the picket line. However, it is possible that the picket is lawful, despite the numbers involved and the s. 220 immunity applies.

In (b) given there are only two pickets it can be assumed they have acted peacefully. However, they have committed torts by inducing the driver to break his employment contract and by procuring a breach of the commercial contract between Camberwick and Toyland. Explain this is secondary industrial action as Toyland is a separate company despite it being owned by the same person – *Dimbleby* v. *NUJ*. However, providing the pickets have acted lawfully they are protected by s. 224(3).

In (c) the pickets can have no immunity from any torts committed as they are not at their own place of work. However, they may not have committed any torts unless, of course, they do successfully induce the Trumpton workers to break their employment contracts.

Similarly, in (d) no immunity exists but the *Middlebrook Mushroom* case can be applied to argue that, although there may interference with business, this will not have been achieved by unlawful means if the strikers do no more than hand out leaflets. In (d) it is likely that no tort has been committed.

Your answer can conclude by explaining that injunctions can be obtained against individual pickets who act unlawfully and the organiser(s) of any unlawful picketing. This includes the union unless it repudiates unlawful picketing and instructs its members to act lawfully.

Essay:
This essay requires you to discuss critically the legislation regulating industrial action. Before discussing the law it is important that your answer demonstrates knowledge and understanding of it. You should focus on the key issues, which are the economic torts, the operation of the s. 219 trade dispute immunity, the rules requiring postal ballots and pre-ballot and pre-strike notices, and the dismissal of strikers.

In discussing the law you should draw on a variety of standpoints ranging from those of governments to the reports of the ILO and the opinions of academic writers, as contained in a number of the articles and papers in the above 'Further reading', such as the work by Dukes, Ewing and Hanson. Whilst, it is not appropriate to reference the interviews given in this chapter in your essay, you can still reflect on them as a source of ideas and arguments.

It is important in your conclusion that you explicitly address the statement contained in the essay question by giving your own reasoned views. Readers' views will vary and will range from: agreement with the statement that the law should stay as it is, or even that further controls on industrial action are desirable; proposals to make some changes to the law to remove some of the existing restrictions on industrial action; proposals to restore the wide immunities or rights to strike that existed in the 1970s.

Visit **www.mylawchamber.co.uk/welch** to access tools to help you develop and test your knowledge of employment law, including interactive 'You be the judge' multiple choice questions, practice exam questions with guidance, annotated weblinks, case summary and key case flashcards, legal newsfeed, legal updates and answer to Lawyers' brief simulation.

Chapter 10
Lawyer's brief

Introduction

The previous chapters of this book have been concerned with explaining and discussing the substantive law regulating employment relationships. This final chapter gives you the opportunity to put into practice many of the skills and knowledge that you have learned throughout the rest of the book. What you will see in this chapter is a series of documents presented in much the same way as you would see them in a file of a working solicitor. In addition to these documents, the chapter contains a number of tasks which have been designed to test your understanding of employment law and how the law relating to wrongful dismissal and unfair dismissal is applied in practice. You will play the part of a solicitor in a law firm who has been instructed by a senior partner to advise and represent a client who has contacted your firm for legal advice after being dismissed from his employment.

The brief

You are Christopher or Christine Ford, employed as a solicitor in the legal firm of Claridge Wittingham, which is situated in the county town of Wessex in southern England. You have been instructed by Guy Claridge to advise and represent John Slocombe, a senior human resource manager, who has been summarily dismissed for gross misconduct, in the form of fighting, by his employer, Wessex County Council. John believes that the Council did not have good reasons for dismissing him and failed to follow proper procedures prior to his dismissal. He also believes his dismissal was a breach of his employment contract as he was dismissed without notice. He is seeking legal advice on how to present and argue employment tribunal claims for wrongful and unfair dismissal. John anticipates that the Council will contest the claim and is prepared to reach a settlement, negotiated under the auspices of ACAS, if this is sufficiently advantageous to him. He has supplied the firm with his letter of dismissal, his **written statement of terms** and a personal witness statement. The firm has also obtained statements from the other key witnesses. These documents are set out below.

Drafting a form ET1

As explained in Chapter 1, a claimant must complete and submit form ET1 to an employment tribunal office in order to present a tribunal claim. This claim must be presented to the tribunal no later than three months from the **effective date of termination** of the claimant's contract (ETD). For the purposes of this activity, you should assume the claim is presented in time irrespective of the actual date on which you drafted the form.

Writing and drafting

Based on the evidence contained in documents 1–6 below, you should draft a form ET1 on behalf of John so that he can present claims of wrongful dismissal and unfair dismissal to an employment tribunal.

You can access a blank form ET1 and the official guidance for completing it from **http://www.justice.gov.uk/global/forms/hmcts/tribunals/employment/index.htm**

◆ **Handy tip:** Remember, in real life you would submit a form by clicking on the red button towards the top of the form. You should *not* click on this button as otherwise your fictional form could end up in a tribunal office.

As suggested in the 'Reflective practice' feature in Chapter 1 on page 17, you can also access the following URL – **http://etclaims.co.uk/tag/et1/** – to obtain practical advice on drafting an ET1.

Whilst this is not essential for the purposes of undertaking the activities set out in this chapter, should you wish to read further on tribunal procedure and practice then the best source is *IDS Handbook on Tribunal Practice and Procedure*, 2006, London: Income Data Services. Pages 72 to 80 of Chapter 2 cover completing a Form ET1. Pages 284 to 314 of Chapter 9 detail the rules relating to ACAS conciliated settlements. Pages 375 to 378 of Chapter 11 provide advice on making closing statements to a tribunal.

Document 1

John's letter of dismissal

Martha Longhurst
Head of the Human Resource Department
Wessex County Council
Alfred Square
Alfchester
Hants
AF1 0DR

John Slocombe
'Beachcroft'
The Limehouse
Upper Breeding
Wessex
AF3 1PQ

15 March 201*

Dear Mr Slocombe

It is with regret that I have to inform you that the Chief Executive of the Council has decided to uphold the decision to dismiss you summarily for the gross misconduct you committed in fighting in public with a junior colleague, Susan James, on 29 January. Consequently, you should regard the date of this letter as your last day of employment by the Council.

The Council has paid into your bank account your accrued five days' holiday pay. This is based on your annual net pay of £37,200 and constitutes a sum of £509.59.

You should be advised that in accordance with the statutory pension scheme your annual pension at the date of the termination of your contract amounts to £7,244. This sum is one eightieth of your annual gross salary multiplied by your ten years and 196 days employment with us. Your lump sum, which is three times your annual pension, amounts to £21,732. You will be entitled to access these sums in full once you reach pensionable age. Depending on the outcome of possible changes to the scheme this will be either the age of 60, 65, or 66.

Yours sincerely
Martha Longhurst, Head of Human Resources

Document 2

John's written statement of terms

WESSEX COUNTY COUNCIL
WRITTEN STATEMENT OF TERMS

1 **The Employer:** Wessex County Council

2 **The Employee:** John Horace Slocombe

3 **Date of Commencement**
Your employment with the Council commenced on 1 September 200*. None of your previous periods of employment constitute continuity of employment with Wessex County Council.

4 **Place of work**
Your main place of work is County Hall, Alfred Square, Alfchester, Hampshire, AF1 0DR. You will be required from time to time to visit any building in the County where Council employees are employed.

5 **Job title and responsibilities**
You are employed by the Council as a Senior Human Resource Manager. You will work as directed by your line manager, the Head of the Human Resources Department. Your main duties include dealing with personnel, disciplinary, grievance and welfare issues with respect to individual Council employees and negotiating and consulting with the trade unions recognised by the Council and representatives of the Wessex Staff Association.

6 **Remuneration**
Your current salary is £55,000 per annum. This salary is subject to periodic review by the Chief Executive of the Council and may be increased on the recommendation of your line manager.

7 **Hours of work**
You are employed for 40 hours a week on Mondays to Fridays between 8.30 and 17.30. You may be required to work outside of these hours where this is necessitated by the demands of the job. Where this proves necessary you will be entitled to time off in lieu to be taken on days agreed with your line manager.

8 **Holidays**
8.1 The Council's holiday year runs 1 January to 31 December. In addition to statutory Bank Holidays you are entitled to 30 working days paid holiday. Unused holiday entitlement may not be carried forward into the next holiday year, except by agreement with your line manager.
8.2 The timing of your holidays is subject to the agreement of your line manager. You may request that up to three weeks of your normal holiday period be taken in one continuous period, and such a request will not be unreasonably refused.
8.3 In the holiday year in which your employment commences or terminates, your holiday entitlement will accrue on a pro-rata basis for each complete month of service; on the termination of your employment holiday pay will be worked out on a similar basis.

9 **Sickness**
Up to any consecutive period of six months, you are contractually entitled to time off with full pay if you are absent from work due to illness or injury.

10 **Staff appraisal**
In relation to the performance of your duties you will be required to participate in an appraisal scheme approved by the Chief Executive of the Council and included in the staff handbook.

11 **Pension**

You are entitled to participate in the statutory Local Government Employees pension scheme** subject to its terms and conditions from time to time in force. The scheme is contracted out of the State Earnings Related Pension Scheme. The maximum number of years of service that can be counted towards your pension is 40 years. Your pension will be calculated on the basis of multiplying one eightieth of your final salary by your pensionable years of employment. You will also be entitled to a one-off lump sum payment which will be three times the sum of your annual pension. Should you choose not to join the statutory scheme you must join the State pension scheme or take out a personal pension.

12 **Grievance and disciplinary procedures**

These procedures, which are based on and fully compliant with the ACAS Code of Practice, are set out in the staff handbook. In cases of alleged serious misconduct the Council reserves the right to suspend an employee on full pay whilst the matter is being investigated, and pending any consequent formal disciplinary proceedings that it is decided to take.

13 **Termination of employment**

Your appointment shall be terminable, except in the case of gross misconduct, by your giving the Council two months' notice in writing or by the Council giving you two months' notice in writing.

14 **Variation**

Trade unions are not recognised for employees in your job grade and therefore your terms and conditions of employment are not subject to variation by collective agreement. Subject to the approval of the Chief Executive of the Council, any variation to your contract will be by agreement between you and your line manager.

Signed: Martha Longhurst
Head of the Human Resources Department, for and on behalf of Wessex County Council.

Date: 15 August 200*

ACCEPTANCE

I accept the terms and conditions of my employment as set out above.

Signed: John Horace Slocombe
Date: 22 August 200*

**Readers should be advised that the pension scheme in the above written statement is fictional and should not be understood as based on the actual occupational scheme that applies to local government employees.

Consider this

What information can you obtain from the above documents that will assist you in specifying in the ET1 the monetary remedies that John should receive if either or both his claims succeed?

 Handy tip: Remember that John will be able to recover **damages** for **wrongful dismissal** and a **basic award** and a **compensatory award** for **unfair dismissal**.

Document 3

John Slocombe's witness statement

My full name is John Horace Slocombe, and at the date of my dismissal I was aged 50 years and three months, and I had been employed by the Council for just over ten and a half years as a human resource manager. As you can see from the letter sent to me by Martha Longhurst, I was summarily dismissed on 15 March for professional gross misconduct.

I want to sue the Council for everything I can get. They have treated me shoddily. I have worked for them for over ten years without a stain on my record and this is how they treat me. Summary dismissal! My professional reputation is totally ruined and, since my dismissal, I have been unable to secure any form of paid employment.

This all came about when I caught Susan drinking one Friday lunchtime. It was on her birthday I remember. So that was 29 January. She was so drunk that she was unsteady on her feet and her breath smelt strongly. I happened to notice Susan as I was walking through the reception area of the Council, and I approached her with a view to asking her if she had been drinking. I did not get the chance to speak when she started swearing at me. She accused me of picking on her and then she tried to slap my face. The only way I could defend myself was by raising my arm to ward off her blow but, unfortunately, because she was so drunk, she lost her balance and fell to the ground. I have to admit to being angry and I may have sworn at her.

The next day I was summoned to the office of Martha Longhurst, the Head of Department. She told me she had received a complaint against me from Susan and had interviewed her accordingly. She also told me that she had interviewed two of the reception staff who had observed what had happened and also my colleague Imelda Bewes, who happened to be present too. Imelda and I go back a long way. We have played badminton together for years. She told me that Susan had complained about me to her before Christmas and that Susan had alleged I had been harassing and bullying her. That's a lot of rubbish. Everyone knows that I treat all staff fairly. It's true that when Susan first started working here I did ask her out for a meal but she declined and that was the end of it. I never thought any more about it. It was some time after that that I formed the view that Susan was too big for her boots. She thought she was too well qualified for the job with her degree, but in fact she was quite lazy and inefficient. I did her a favour by informally warning her in my office that she could well be in danger of not passing her probationary year.

Sod's law dictated that there was a reporter from the local rag when this all occurred. I don't know why she decided to make a story out of it which was published that night under the headline 'Drunken brawl in council offices'. In my interview with Martha I did explain to her that despite my view of Susan I did at all times treat her appropriately, and, on the day in question, I was taken completely by surprise and was only trying to defend myself. OK I did call her a drunken bitch but that is absolutely the only thing I did which was wrong. Hardly gross misconduct in my professional view. Nevertheless Martha then informed me that she would be initiating disciplinary proceedings and the end result has been my being sacked as you know from my letter of dismissal. I have learnt that Susan did get the sack too but she received salary in lieu of notice.

After my initial interview with Martha I was suspended upon full pay. I was not happy about this but my contract does provide for suspension. Two days later I received a letter at home informing me that I was to attend a formal disciplinary hearing and reminding me of my right to be accompanied by a trade union representative or friend. On 19 February, I duly attended the formal disciplinary hearing accompanied by my trade union representative. To our surprise, Martha chaired the hearing. This is contrary to the Council's own disciplinary procedure, which stipulates that, other than in exceptional circumstances, a neutral manager should chair a disciplinary hearing. Martha was hardly neutral given that, as our Head of Department, she had investigated Susan's complaint against me. We formally protested about Martha chairing the hearing, but when it became clear that Martha was determined to proceed I had no option other than to give my evidence.

Imelda, and the two receptionists in the foyer of the Council also gave evidence. No other colleagues from the HR Department were called as witnesses. Susan had been asked to attend but she failed to turn up. However, I am aware that Martha has a transcript of her interview with Susan at which she complained about me. At the end of the hearing I reiterated that I was innocent of all but minor misconduct and asked that my impeccable work record be taken into account. The next day I was informed by letter that I was to be dismissed summarily but reminding me that I had the right of appeal to the Chief Executive. The letter also set out the procedure I should follow in exercising my right of appeal. This appeal took place a fortnight later. At the appeal hearing the eye witnesses all again gave evidence as did Martha. This time they didn't even try to get Susan to attend. I was again accompanied by my trade union representative, and again gave my evidence and pleaded my work record, but to no avail. The end result was the letter of dismissal which you have in your possession.

Although I have made several job applications, since my dismissal I have not been able to secure any employment as a HR practitioner, in either the public or private sectors, at any grade. Indeed, I have not even been able to get a job in my local pub, because they tell me that as a professional person I am over qualified and not suitable for that type of employment.

Document 4

Martha Longhurts's witness statement

My full name is Martha Petrunia Longhurst and I am the Head of Human Resources at Wessex County Council. I was promoted from within this department to this position three years ago. I like to think that I know my staff well.

This unfortunate matter started with Susan James coming into my office in tears on 29 January. She accused John Slocombe, one of the human resource managers in our department, of assaulting her, swearing at her and knocking her to the ground. I thought it appropriate to interview her then and there once she had calmed down. She did smell of alcohol but I calmed her with a strong sweet tea. During this interview she told me that John had struck her and sworn at her. She also alleged that he had persistently picked on her and that this was all because she had turned him down during her first week of employment when he had asked her out for a meal and/or to the cinema – she couldn't quite remember which. She also stated that she felt very uncomfortable on one occasion when John had got her alone in his office and threatened her with the fact that she was going to fail her probationary year.

I decided that I needed to investigate these accusations more fully so the next day I interviewed two reception staff, who were eye witnesses to the altercation between John and Susan, and another of my managers, Imelda, who was also present in the reception area at the time. Prior to these interviews I had also seen a copy of the local newspaper that was published the previous evening. It transpired that one of their journalists was also present at the time and had published a story that was highly embarrassing to the Council under the headline 'Drunken brawl in Council offices'. I then interviewed John who denied fighting and said that he was doing no more than acting in self defence when confronted with a drunken and aggressive colleague. He did admit to calling her a drunken bitch. I decided that there were sufficient grounds to suspend him on full pay as provided for in his contract of employment pending disciplinary proceedings.

I also decided to recommend to the Council that it should dismiss Susan James with pay in lieu of notice. It does seem that she was not regarded highly by her colleagues, and the easiest thing to do was to terminate her employment before she had worked long enough to secure unfair dismissal rights. Consequently, Susan was dismissed on the basis of my recommendation.

Two days after his suspension, John received a letter at his home informing him that he was to attend a formal disciplinary hearing and reminding him of his right to be accompanied by a trade union representative or friend. On 19 February, he duly attended the formal disciplinary hearing accompanied by his trade union representative. I chaired the hearing, as I believed it was necessary to act promptly in dealing with this matter, and none of my other managerial colleagues were available on that day to chair the hearing. John gave evidence as did Imelda, and the 2 receptionists who were eyewitnesses to the fight between John and Susan. All three of these witnesses were in agreement as to what occurred, and their view of the facts is contained in Imelda Bewes's witness statement. I did not regard it as necessary to ask any other colleagues from the HR Department to give evidence. Susan had been asked to attend but she failed to turn up. However, I do have in my possession a transcript of my interview with her on 29 January at which she complained about John.

At the end of the hearing John reiterated that he was innocent of all but minor misconduct and asked that his impeccable work record be taken into account. Despite these pleas of mitigation, I was of the view that in all the circumstances John was guilty of professional gross misconduct and that it was appropriate to dismiss him summarily. The next day John was informed by letter that, subject to his right of appeal, he was to be dismissed summarily. This letter set out the procedure to be followed for exercising the right of appeal to the Chief Executive. This appeal took place a fortnight later. At the appeal hearing the eye witnesses all again gave evidence as did I. However, this time it was decided there was no point in trying to get Susan to attend. John was again accompanied by his trade union representative and again gave evidence and pleaded his work record, but the Chief Executive confirmed the decision to dismiss John.

Consider this

John and Martha's evidence can be regarded as providing different perspectives on the same set of facts and both believe their evidence to be accurate. How can you use their evidence to John's best advantage in completing the ET1? To what extent do these statements provide mutually reinforcing evidence of what actually occurred?

Document 5

Witness statement for Susan James

This evidence is based on an interview she had with Martha Longhurst immediately after the incident with John.

My full name is Susan Janette James. My date of birth is 29 January 1980, and I have a degree in Human Resource Management from the University of Wessex. I started work with Wessex County Council last September. I was employed in the HR department as a clerical assistant. If John had not got it in for me I would have had promotion by now.

I always had a problem with Mr Slocombe, John. He was my line manager in the HR department. The problem is that he fancies me and always has. In my first week at the Council he asked me to go to the cinema with him. As if I would – it was very embarrassing. I told him he was far too old for me. And ever since then he was always picking on me. He gave me the worst jobs he could think of – the really boring ones which anyone with half a brain could do. In my last week at the Council he had me cataloguing pension files and then I had to update database entries. I ask you! I'm qualified to set up and use professional databases. I gave a presentation on them at Uni in my final year. I got a first for that piece of work.

Anyway he did always give me the boring jobs, you ask anyone. He didn't seem to know, or at least care, that I'm a graduate. Just before Christmas he had me moving files. I'm probably the smallest in the department but did he ask Peter or Bill, the only other two blokes in HR? And I always have to type up the minutes and get everyone to ensure their desk is clear at night so no confidential information is left on view. If I had wanted to be a secretary would I have gone to Uni?

Well the incident happened on my birthday. I had been out to lunch with my best friends Sharon and Liz. We went to The Foxglove Inn. It does very good food and its overlooking the cathedral. On my way back, I wasn't late it was just before 2 o'clock, I was approached by John – in fact, he nearly walked straight into me, great oaf. I know I'm not very tall but he needs to look where he's going. I did shout at him. But I thought he hadn't seen me. I was wearing my new shoes with quite high heels and I thought he was going to knock me over and ruin them. Well he just stared at me and accused me of being drunk. And I lost it. It was his fault and he didn't even apologise. I gave him a bit of my mind. I realise now that I shouldn't have been quite so loud when we were surrounded by members of the public. And I expect the alcohol had loosened my tongue. Not that I was drunk. No I had had only a couple of cocktails. Liz has insisted on buying me the one called the 'Birthday Bounce' and so I had to let Sharon buy me one too didn't I? I think I may have used a swear word or two but it got his attention at least.

Well I told him that he needed to look where he was going and to give other people a bit of consideration and that led to me saying that he ought to give me a bit of consideration and not keep giving me all the shitty jobs like minutes and filing. Just because I wouldn't go out with him!

And then he hit me! He knocked me over. I was quite frightened at that stage. He can be quite intimidating being so tall. He must weigh 16 stone! And he started swearing at me. He called me a drunken bitch. It was lucky I didn't break anything. I was very shaken up. I was so embarrassed being spoken to like that in front of everyone. I was really humiliated and he is a senior manager. He ought to know better.

No, this isn't the only incident with John. He had frightened me once before. I had only been at the Council for a couple of months when he called me into his office. I was frightened then. I didn't know what he was going to say to me. I knew he didn't like me. No he had never asked me out again. He never made any suggestive comments or tried to touch me. Thank goodness, fat old git! Anyway he shut the door and told me I was lazy. I couldn't believe it. He told me to pull my socks up or I would fail my probation and lose my job. He wouldn't listen to my side of the story. He just opened the door again and told me to get on with my filing.

I was so upset that I went to see Imelda Bewes, the other senior HR manager, and said that I thought John was bullying me, taking advantage of his seniority to make my life misery and all because I wouldn't go out with him. Imelda suggested that I read the grievance procedure and think about making a formal complaint against him. I thought thanks a lot for nothing. If I make a complaint he'll just make my life worse than ever.

Did I try to hit him? No, for goodness sake! I'm not that stupid. I'm five foot three and he's over six foot. I couldn't even reach. I was just waving my arms about to make my points clear. I was quite cross that he hadn't seen me coming. As a result of all this I have lost my job. Totally unfair, but there is nothing I can do about it, as I can't claim unfair dismissal and I have received all the notice and holiday pay I was entitled to.

Consider this

Whilst you should assume that Susan believes all that she says this is obviously a very emotional and not very reliable piece of evidence. Consider what the statement suggests to you about Susan's character and how this can be used to John's advantage.

Document 6

Witness statement from Imelda Bewes

My name is Imelda Louise Bewes and I can confirm that on 29 January I was an eyewitness to an incident that took place between two colleagues – John Slocombe and Susan James. This incident took place in the Council's reception area and two other members of the reception staff were also eyewitnesses. The three of us all agree that the following took place.

Susan, who appeared to be the worse for wear through drink as she was staggering slightly, was approached by John. Susan shouted at John and essentially told him to look where he was going. John asked her if she had been drinking. Susan's response was to accuse John of always picking on her and then tried to slap his face. John raised his arm to ward off the attempted slap and to push her away from him and she fell to the ground. Susan was obviously shaken by this but otherwise was clearly not physically hurt. As he pushed her John also swore at her saying 'Get off me you drunken bitch'. It is fair to say John was taken by surprise, but, in my view, given that he is an experienced HR manager, John did not handle the situation well. This was made worse given, as luck would have it, that there was a reporter from the local paper present who wrote a story for the local evening newspaper, which blew up the whole incident out of all proportion, under the headline 'Drunken brawl in Council offices'. Obviously, this did reflect rather badly on the Council.

At the start of last December, Susan James did have an informal conversation with me during which she accused John of picking on her because she had turned him down for a date. She also said that earlier that day, John had called her into his office out of the blue, had accused her of being lazy and had had threatened her with failing her probationary year. I simply advised her to initiate the formal grievance procedure if she believed she was being bullied. I am a friend of John's, though I can assure you that this account is totally objective. I mentioned Susan's conversation with me to John and he assured me that he was not hostile to Susan because she had turned down his offer of a date. However, he did not regard her as a good worker and had, indeed, informally warned her in private in his office that she was in danger of failing her probationary year.

I have made discreet inquiries with other colleagues in the HR Department and they do share John's view that Susan can be uncooperative – in fact the general view is that she seems to think she is too good for the job. They told me they have noticed that John is untypically brusque with Susan, but otherwise treats her in the same way as he treats them. They also confirmed that they think John is a fair manager and have always got on well with him. On the other hand, they thought Susan was a 'bit snooty' as she seemed to think that because she had a degree she should have had a more responsible role. They also said Susan had boasted that John 'fancied her but that she was not going to go out with a fat middle-aged old git'.

In short, all other colleagues think John is a fair manager and, like me, do not see him as someone who is going to single out a junior colleague in a bullying way. I do admit that in hindsight I should have mentioned the problems between John and Susan to Martha, the Head of the HR Department, but at the time I just assumed the problem would blow over.

Consider this

Imelda is the nearest you have to a neutral and therefore objective witness. Moreover, her evidence as to what happened on the day of the incident is reinforced by two other eyewitnesses. Imelda's evidence is very important as it is likely to provide the basis on which a tribunal will make its decision on the facts. Therefore, think carefully about how the information supplied by Imelda can be used in the ET1 to support John's claims.

Negotiating an ACAS settlement

In Chapter 1 it was explained that, after the tribunal office receives forms ET1 and ET3, the documents are sent to ACAS. The purpose of this is to enable ACAS to help individual employers and employees reach an **ACAS conciliated settlement** as an alternative to proceeding with a tribunal claim. If a claim is voluntarily settled under the auspices of a conciliation officer employed by ACAS then the claim is withdrawn from the tribunal and the settlement is legally binding.

Writing and drafting

This second activity is designed to give you experience of formulating a negotiating strategy on behalf of your client. You should assume that an ACAS conciliation Officer has contacted John and Wessex County Council and both parties have indicated that they are interested in seeing if a conciliated settlement can be reached. Based on John's instructions, which are contained below in Document 7, write a negotiating strategy that sets out the approach that you propose to follow were a face to face negotiation to take place with a lawyer from the firm representing Wessex County Council.

Consider this

In formulating your strategy you should take into account that you are aware from the ET3 that the Council presented to the tribunal that the Council's view of its decision to dismiss John is as follows.

Wessex County Council is convinced that it acted fairly in deciding to dismiss John for gross misconduct as his behaviour towards Susan was entirely inappropriate for a senior human resource manager, and he brought the Council into disrepute by participating in a fight in full view of the public. Moreover, this fight damaged the Council's reputation as a result of it being reported in a local newspaper. The Council believes that, given that John was able to exercise a right of appeal, it followed a reasonable procedure prior to reaching its decision to dismiss John. The Council also believes that John's behaviour constituted a **repudiatory breach** of contract justifying his **summary dismissal**.

In drafting your negotiating strategy you should anticipate that the Council will be absolutely resistant to reinstating John but might be prepared to offer a sum by way of compensation in return for all the details of John's claim and any settlement being kept confidential. You are aware that an employer such as a County Council will have an interest in avoiding a tribunal hearing because of the inconvenience, time and cost to it and the possible further adverse publicity a tribunal hearing could entail. Therefore, the more that you can persuade it that John will win his tribunal claim, the more likely it is that the Council will agree to a financial settlement on terms favourable to John.

Document 7

Instructions from John

I am inclined to pursue claims for both unfair and wrongful dismissal to the employment tribunal. It strongly remains my view that the Council should not have found me guilty of gross misconduct and that it should have understood that Susan was the real cause of the problem. It was clearly unfair that Martha chaired the initial disciplinary hearing as she had previously taken the decision to suspend me. However, if it is possible to secure a reasonable deal with the Council through negotiation then I am prepared to reach a settlement in this way.

Ideally, I would like reinstatement as I believe that my dismissal has ruined my career as a human resource manager in terms of obtaining a post in another organisation. Since my dismissal I have applied for several jobs in the HR field and all of my applications have been rejected without me even being short listed for an interview. Therefore, I am prepared to drop the tribunal claim if the Council agrees to my reinstatement with payment in full of arrears in salary, restoration of my lost pension benefits and continuity of employment. As I have never had a problem with any colleague including Martha Longhurst, I will be able to do my job effectively given that Susan has been dismissed. My prior impeccable work record is evidence that I am a good HR manager.

Should the Council refuse to reinstate me, and, as my legal representatives, you are of the view that I am unlikely to obtain this remedy from the tribunal, I am prepared to accept a settlement based on compensation. I want a basic award, based on my actual gross pay, rather than the statutory limit, and a compensatory award above the statutory limit to reflect loss of earnings and pension rights for the rest of my working life up to at least the age of 60. I also believe compensation should reflect the damage to my professional reputation and the injury to my feelings caused by the Council's decision to dismiss me. I need a good reference to give me some chance of securing another post as a human resource manager in the future.

I give you, as my legal representatives, the discretion to accept a lower sum of compensation than this providing you are of the view that the offered sum is greater or at least equal to what I would receive from a tribunal.

It is possible that during the negotiation you form the view that I will probably lose at a tribunal. Should this prove to be the case, the minimum I will accept is salary for loss of notice and a good reference. If the Council is not prepared to agree even to this, then I will cut my losses and proceed with a tribunal hearing.

◆ **Handy tip:** It will be useful to bear in mind the following guidance in drafting a negotiating strategy.

✦ Negotiation is about give and take. If you are not prepared to concede anything, there is no point to entering into a negotiation. Both sides must expect to make concessions. Therefore, your strategy should involve identifying what points are concedable or negotiable and what are not. In real life this would, of course, be done in consultation with your client. Before you commence the negotiation, you should also have an idea of how strong your legal position and arguments are in comparison to the likely position and arguments of the opposing firm.

✦ The first task is to draw up a list of issues which are ranked in terms of importance to your client, as can be determined from the client instructions, and in accordance with how strong they are from a legal perspective. As far as possible, you might also wish to calculate how much each issues is worth in monetary terms, although you cannot put a price on an apology or a good reference. In determining the strength of your legal position in respect of any given issue, you need to draw on the approach to legal problems which you are familiar with as part of your law programme. What is the relevant law? Are there any inconsistencies or ambiguities in the previously decided case law? Has there been an EAT or a decision of Court of Appeal or House of Lords/Supreme Court which favours one party's position? How should the law best be applied to the facts to develop arguments in favour of a particular party?

✦ If a negotiation takes place, it is a good tactic to attempt to take the initiative and provide your opponents with an agenda listing the issues. However, if you do this, you must be careful not to give away unintentionally the strengths and weaknesses of your position. In putting forward your case it is always best to start with your strongest argument.

✦ Identify your client's fallback position and anticipate at what stage in the negotiation it would be appropriate to reveal this position. Clearly, the initial objective is to achieve the optimum outcome in accordance with your client's instruction, and it is important in the initial stage of the negotiation that you do not prematurely disclose your client's fallback position. Nevertheless, a lawyer conducting a negotiation should not unduly prolong the negotiation by continuing to seek to secure the optimum outcome after it has become clear the opposing client's firm is not going to concede this. Unnecessarily dragging things out tends to create irritation and result in a negative atmosphere, which is not conducive to reaching an agreement. In practice, any negotiator knows that the other side will have a fallback position, and, normally, the real objective of the opening phase of a negotiation is to seek to tease out what this fallback position is. Sticking to your guns is only really appropriate where you are confident that all the cards are stacked in your favour, that is, if a tribunal hearing does take place you are convinced that your client will win.

Consider this

In preparing your negotiating strategy you will need to identify the amount of compensation John could receive from an employment tribunal. For this purpose you can work on the basis of the following data.

✦ If John not been dismissed, he would have would have worked for another 10 years, and would have retired from the Council at the age of 60, giving him a total of 20 years' employment with the Council.

✦ Any amounts of compensation, which are awarded, will be on the basis of John's current **gross pay** of £55,000 and/or **net pay** of £37,200.

✦ With respect to his pension, this means that had John been dismissed with two months' notice his annual pension entitlement from the age of 60 would have been £7,362 and his one-off lump sum would have been £22,088.

✦ Had he continued working with the Council to the age of 60, his pension entitlement would have been £13,750 and his lump sum payment would have been £41,250.

✦ It is anticipated that after John's retirement at the age of 60 his life of expectancy would have been 20 years.

Also it should be remembered that tribunals cannot award **damages** in excess of £25,000 for breach of contract. Moreover, the **basic award** for unfair dismissal is calculated on the basis of a **statutory week's pay**. Both the basic award and the **compensatory award** are subject statutory caps. As you know, a basic and a compensatory award can be reduced by a tribunal on grounds of employee contributory misconduct. You will need to take this into account in identifying the minimum sum of compensation you will be prepared to recommend to John that he accepts.

Drafting a closing statement to a tribunal

In undertaking this activity you should assume that your attempt to negotiate a settlement on behalf of John failed as John was not prepared to accept the offer made by the Council. Consequently, he engaged you to represent him at the tribunal hearing to determine his claims of wrongful and unfair dismissal.

Writing and drafting

Once a tribunal has heard all of the evidence, the parties have the right to present closing statements to the tribunal before it gives its decision. Therefore, you should draft a closing statement to be put to the tribunal on behalf of John. In drafting your statement you should operate on the basis that the parties and the tribunal have accepted that the dismissal is potentially fair under s. 98(2) ERA as the Council genuinely believed John to be guilty of misconduct.

The statement should be in the form of a speech to the tribunal consisting of legal argument on behalf of John based on the evidence contained in all the witness statements to be found in Documents 3–6 above. Although some of this evidence conflicts, the tribunal has accepted that each witness genuinely believes that they have stated the truth. Your closing statement should consist of applying the law to the facts in a way that benefits John's case.

Consider this

In writing your statement you should bear in mind the following points:

✦ You should not misrepresent or distort the evidence in any way but you should emphasise those aspects of the evidence that most benefit your client's case.

✦ You should apply the law to this evidence in a way that constitutes persuasive legal argument in favour of your client.

✦ Where, as here, your client is making more than one claim, keep the legal issues separate and do not conflate your legal arguments in a way that confuses the different nature of the claims.

✦ As there are two claims, take into account that some of the evidence may be relevant to one of these claims but not to the other.

✦ Tribunals do not like to be bombarded with case authorities, but your submission should cite cases where you believe that doing so will strengthen your client's case.

✦ Relevant statutory sources should also be briefly cited.

✦ You should only go into the facts of a previous case if you regard this as necessary either because it is a precedent that strongly supports your argument, or it is a case that favours the other side and you are arguing why and how it should be distinguished from your case.

◆ Whilst you are using the law in a way that supports your client's claim, it is important to remember that you should identify arguments that the other side are likely to use in order to produce counter arguments to the tribunal.

Handy tip: In drafting your statement you should write as you would speak in addressing an employment tribunal. Indeed, what you are really doing is writing out your speech in advance. Most practitioners would do this in real life so they could commit the speech to memory but also have it in front of them in the tribunal to refer to it quickly if need be. As you are writing as you would speak, you can use the first person, for example, I am arguing and the like. Alternatively, if you prefer, you can use the third person, as you will be used to doing in assessed work on your course. In other words, you can write it is argued, it is submitted, it is contended and so on.

In undertaking this activity you are drawing on problem-solving skills that you are familiar with using in tackling problem questions on your course and which are exemplified by the problem questions at the end of each of the previous chapters. The key difference in writing arguments to be presented to a tribunal is that you are not approaching the problem as a disinterested third party. In problem questions you identify legal arguments in favour of both parties and weigh up the different circumstances in which each party is likely to win. In making a submission to a tribunal, whilst you still need to anticipate and respond to the legal argument that the other side is likely to use, you are presenting arguments to seek to persuade the tribunal to find in favour of your client. Therefore, in drafting your closing statement you are not writing in the neutral way that you normally write answers to problem questions.

Writing and drafting

If John's claims of wrongful and/or unfair dismissal succeeds then there will be a separate remedies hearing. You will continue to represent John at this hearing and you should write arguments on his behalf with respect to the remedies the tribunal should award. On your advice, John is no longer seeking reinstatement. Therefore, you are only concerned with the issue of financial compensation and using arguments to maximise the amount of money John will receive.

Handy tip: You can ascertain the current financial limits for basic and compensatory by googling compensation limits for unfair dismissal plus the current year. At the time of writing, this information could be accessed at: **http://www.xperthr.co.uk/article/111519/award-limits-and-amounts-payable-under-employment-legislation-from-1-february-2012.aspx**

The calculator for redundancy payments and therefore basic awards can be accessed at: **http://www.direct.gov.uk/redundancy.dsb**

Consider this

In a remedies hearing, the tribunal will hear evidence as to whether the claimant has sought to obtain new employment, for how much longer the claimant would have worked for the employer had he not been dismissed and what his final salary would have been at the date on which the employment would have normally terminated. This is particularly difficult to predict in the current economic climate when public sector pay rates have been frozen, rates of inflation are unpredictable and the rules for public sector pensions are in a state of flux.

To keep matters manageable, you should work on the basis that the tribunal has decided to accept the following evidential points. First, the tribunal has accepted that John has made genuine attempts to secure new employment in the human resource management profession and that he is unlikely to secure such a post in the future. Secondly, it has decided that had John not been dismissed he would have worked for another 10 years, and would have retired from the Council at the age of 60, giving him a total of 20 years' employment with the Council. The tribunal has decided to calculate any amounts of compensation on the basis of, as appropriate, his current gross salary of £55,000 and net salary of £37,200.

With respect to his pension, this means that had John been dismissed with two months' notice his annual pension entitlement from the age of 60 would have been £7,362 and his one-off lump sum would have been £22,088.

Had he continued working with the Council to the age of 60, his pension entitlement would have been £13,750 and his lump sum payment would have been £41,250. The tribunal has decided that after his retirement at the age of 60 his life of expectancy would have been 20 years.

Reflective practice

Once you have carried out the activities set out in this chapter, you can access an outline answer by visiting **www.mylawchamber.co.uk/welch**

This answer will summarise arguments for and against John winning his claims and provide a breakdown of the amounts of compensation John might receive if either or both of his claims were successful. You can reflect on this outline answer and compare it with your closing statement.

Glossary

Glossary terms are highlighted in the text in **bold**.

ACAS Code on Disciplinary and Grievance Procedures The ACAS Code lays down the disciplinary procedures that employers should follow prior to reaching a decision to impose any formal disciplinary penalty on an employee or any decision to dismiss. In particular, employers should convene formal hearings prior to reaching any decisions of a disciplinary nature and where possible should provide for rights of appeal. As held by the House of Lords in *Polkey*, if the ACAS Code is not followed, an employee is likely to succeed in a claim for unfair dismissal unless it can reasonably regarded by the employer as futile or useless to follow the relevant part of the code. The code also sets out the grievance procedures an employee should follow if he or she wishes to complain about how he or she is being treated at work. Where the code is not adhered to, any damages for wrongful dismissal or the compensatory award for unfair dismissal will be increased or reduced by up to 25% depending on whether it was the employer's or employee's fault that the code was not properly followed.

ACAS conciliated settlements Where a claim has been presented to an employment tribunal, the parties may agree to negotiate a conciliated settlement with the assistance of an ACAS conciliation officer. If a conciliated settlement is reached, the claim is withdrawn and the settlement is legally enforceable.

Additional award A tribunal may award reinstatement or re-engagement to an employee who has successfully claimed unfair dismissal. Where the employer refuses to allow the employee to return to work, the tribunal will make an additional award as well as granting the employee a basic award and a compensatory award. An additional award will consist of 26–52 statutory weeks' pay.

Affirmation Where one contracting party commits a repudiatory breach of contract, the other party may treat the contract as at an end or choose to continue with it. This is known as affirmation. In the employment context it is most important where, for example, an employee continues with the employment contract where the employer has acted in breach of mutual trust and confidence. Such affirmation means the employee can no longer terminate the contract and claim constructive dismissal.

Arbitration Where an employer is in dispute with an employee or a trade union, the dispute can be referred for resolution to an independent arbitrator. Normally, the arbitrator's decision is final and cannot be challenged in a court. Commercial arbitration is legally binding but arbitration conducted by ACAS is binding in honour only.

Associative discrimination This is where an employee is discriminated against because he or she associates with a person with a protected characteristic. For example, a woman is refused promotion because the employer fears she will need time off from work to care for her disabled husband.

Automatically unfair dismissals An employee must normally have two years' continuous employment to bring a claim of unfair dismissal. However, some dismissals are automatically unfair and apply from the commencement of the employment contract. If a dismissal was for an automatically unfair reason, a claim of unfair dismissal must succeed. For example, under s. 99 ERA 1996 a dismissal by reason of pregnancy is an automatically unfair dismissal.

Basic award Employees who successfully claim unfair dismissal will be given a basic award. As is the case with a statutory redundancy payment, the award is calculated on the basis of an employee's gross week's pay, age and completed years of employment. Only the last 20 years of employment can be taken into account and a week's pay is subject to a statutory cap. Deductions can be made to the basic award on grounds of the employee's contributory misconduct.

Bilka-Kaufhaus principles This test comes from a ruling of the European Court of Justice where it was stated that to justify indirect discrimination an employer must (a) establish a genuine objective commercial or organisational need for the policy that constitutes the discrimination and (b) the advantage so gained by the employer must satisfy the requirement of proportionality, that is, it must not be outweighed by the discrimination suffered by the claimant. Moreover, it must not be possible for the employer to secure its interests by other non-discriminatory means.

Burden of proof An individual who wish to pursue a claim before an employment tribunal must prove the claim in the normal way for civil cases by showing that the facts on which the claim is based were, on the *balance of probabilities*, what actually occurred. In an unfair dismissal claim this burden of proof is on the employer to establish the real reason for the dismissal. In claims presented under the Equality Act a tribunal may draw the inference of discrimination to assist a claimant in proving discrimination.

Business efficacy As with any other type of contract, a court can decide to imply a term into a contract of employment where this can be regarded as giving business efficacy to the contract. This means that a term is being implied into a contract to ensure the contract works in a proper businesslike manner and in accordance with what the parties themselves must have intended.

Business transfer Where an employer is selling all or part of its operations to another employer, the transfer will generally be subject to the TUPE Regulations unless the transfer is in the form of a company buying the majority shareholding in the selling company. Under the TUPE Regulations the employees of the transferor are transferred to the transferee on their existing terms and conditions of employment. Any dismissals will be automatically unfair unless they are for an economic, technical or organisational (ETO) reason.

Closed shop agreement This was a particular type of collective agreement under which an employer agreed only to employ members of the trade union. An employee would be dismissed if he or she refused to join the union or ceased to be a member of it. Such agreements are no longer enforceable and have fallen into disuse.

Collective agreement A collective agreement is made between an employer and a trade union as a result **of collective bargaining**. Such agreements are not normally legally enforceable and thus breach of a collective agreement will not enable a trade union to sue an employer (or vice versa) for breach of contract. However, the contents of substantive collective agreements are normally incorporated into the employment contracts of relevant individual employees so that breach of a collective agreement may enable an individual employee to sue the employer (or vice versa) for breach of contract. Most of the contents of a procedure agreement are not suitable for incorporation and have no legal force.

Collective bargaining This is the process by which employers seek to negotiate on a range of issues including terms and conditions of employment, the implementation of redundancies, disciplinary procedures and health and safety. Collective bargaining produces collective agreements. Whilst collective agreements are presumed not to be legally enforceable between the employer and the union, appropriate substantive agreements, for example, on pay and other terms of employment, will normally be incorporated into the individual contracts of the employees in the collective bargaining unit. Such terms are then enforceable as between the employer and an individual employee.

Collective bargaining unit This term is used to describe those workers within the scope of a recognition agreement who a trade union will represent for collective bargaining purposes. If a union is seeking statutory recognition and the parties cannot agree the collective bargaining unit, the CAC must determine the appropriate unit. In so doing the CAC must pay particular regard to the unit being compatible with effective management.

Collective labour law Much employment law is concerned with the regulation of the individual relationship between an employer and an employee. Collective labour law regulates the relationship between employers and trade unions. However, it is also concerned with individual rights such as the right of an employee or a worker to join a trade union and participate in its activities.

Collective *laissez-faire* This is the term coined by Kahn-Freund to distinguish between the British and other European systems of industrial relations. Employers and trade unions were able to establish their own relations outside of a state imposed legal framework. Relations between employers and unions and between employers and their employees have both become substantially regulated by law since the early 1970s. However, one ongoing consequence of collective *laissez-faire* is that collective agreements between employers and trade unions are presumed not to be legally enforceable.

Collective redundancies This is any proposal by an employer to make 20 or more redundancy dismissals. An employer is then obliged to inform and consult with a recognised trade union or, if there is no union, with employee representatives.

Compensatory award This is the main monetary award granted to an employee who successfully claims unfair dismissal. Unlike damages for wrongful dismissal the compensatory award can cover loss of earnings for any period of unemployment after the claimant's period of notice or fixed-term contract would have expired. The compensatory award is subject to a statutory cap and can be reduced on grounds of an employee's contributory misconduct. The award may also be subject to a Polkey reduction.

Compromise agreement This is an alternative to an ACAS conciliated settlement. For a compromise agreement to be legally binding, it must be in writing and the claimant must have been independently advised by a lawyer or other qualified person such as a trade union officer.

Conciliation Claims presented to employment tribunals are referred to ACAS to give the parties the opportunity to resolve their dispute through an ACAS conciliated settlement. ACAS has an important role in collective disputes between employers and trade unions by offering its services to facilitate the parties returning to the negotiating table to resolve their dispute through agreement.

Confidential information The duty of fidelity is one of the judicially implied terms in contracts of employment. Employees are in breach of this duty if they disclose information that an employer has designated as confidential to a competitor or misuse such information for their own benefit. It was held in *Faccenda Chicken* v. *Fowler* that injunctions are only available to prevent an employee from misusing information that is no more than confidential whilst he or she is still an employee. However, employers can still prevent employees from disclosing or misusing trade secrets after their employment has ended.

Continuous employment Many statutory employment protection rights are conditional on employees having a specified period of continuous employment. In the case of claims of unfair dismissal and for a statutory redundancy payment this period is for two years. Continuity of employment is maintained even in weeks where the employee does not work providing the employment contract continues in existence. A break in this contract breaks continuity. However, continuity will not be broken if the employee is without a contract for up to 26 weeks through illness or injury, and the contract is renewed when the employee is fit to return to work. A short period of lay-off may also not break continuity where a tribunal can regard this as a temporary cessation of the employment contract.

Constructive dismissal This is where an employee is deemed to be dismissed even though it is the employee who terminated the contract. The leading case on the definition of constructive dismissal is *Western Excavating* v. *Sharp*. If an employer commits a repudiatory breach of contract, for example, by destroying mutual trust and confidence, an employee may resign and claim damages for constructive wrongful dismissal and/or present a claim of unfair dismissal. If the employee chooses affirmation, he loses the right to claim constructive dismissal.

Control test Traditionally, this states that for a worker to be an employee he must be told what to and how to do it. This test has long been inadequate as professional workers are not normally told how to do their job by the employer. Under the multiple test adopted in the *Ready Mixed* case, control is one of a number of factors to take into account in determining whether a person doing work for another is an employee. This will not be so if a person is engaged in business on his or her own account as that person will then be an independent contractor. As held by the House of Lords in *Carmichael* v. *National Power*, control is part of the irreducible minimum a worker must satisfy to be considered an employee. Control can be exercised in a number of ways, such as instructing an employee when and where to work, stipulating the procedures that must be followed for an employee to exercise his or her holiday entitlement, imposing dress codes and subjecting employees to disciplinary procedures.

Custom and practice Occasionally, a term can be implied into a contract of employment by reference to the employer's previous established practice. The custom must be certain, general and reasonable. Where a collective agreement has not been expressly incorporated into an individual's contract of employment, a court may decide that it should impliedly incorporate the collective agreement because it can be inferred from the employer's established practice that it regards the collective agreement as being part of the employment contracts of its individual employees.

Damages The purpose of damages is to compensate the injured party for the damage, that is, the financial loss, which the breach of contract has caused him to suffer. As confirmed by the House of Lords in *Unisys Ltd* v. *Johnson*, the wrongful dismissal of an employee will not enable an employee to claim damages for loss of reputation or any other loss arising out of the manner of the dismissal. Typically, a sum of damages is restricted to net pay for the contractual notice period or the remainder of a fixed-term contract.

Derecognition A decision by an employer to terminate collective bargaining arrangements with a trade union. Derecognition may be partial in that an employer may only be seeking to remove certain employees from the scope of collective bargaining. As a recognition agreement is a collective agreement, there is normally no legal barrier to derecognition as the agreement will not be legally enforceable. However, if a union has secured statutory recognition, it may not be derecognised unilaterally by an employer. The statutory derecognition procedure will have to be followed.

Detriment Any act or omission by an employer which is short of a dismissal but disadvantages an individual in circumstances which constitute unlawful discrimination. Examples include demotion and withdrawal of benefits granted to other employees.

Direct discrimination An employer will have committed an act of direct discrimination if it treats an employee with one protected characteristic less favourably than employees not sharing that characteristic. For example, an employer treats employees of one sex differently to employees of the opposite sex. Other than in the context of age, unlike indirect discrimination, an employer is not able to justify direct discrimination. However, it is a defence if it can be shown that possessing a particular protected characteristic is a genuine occupational requirement for a job. Direct age discrimination can only be justified where an employer's policy, for example, to impose a compulsory retirement age, is underpinned by public interest aims such as promoting inter-generational fairness or preserving an employee's personal dignity.

Directive EU employment law is typically made in the form of Directives. A Directive does not become law within a member state until it has been implemented at national level. In the UK this will be by legislation or statutory instrument. However, a Directive which is sufficiently clear and certain will take **vertical direct effect** against state bodies including public sector employers.

Directly applicable This term refers to those forms of EU law which automatically become law within member states so that, unlike Directives, they do not require prior national implementation. Article 157 TFEU providing for the right of equal pay for work of equal value is a major example of directly applicable EU law. Any employee or worker can enforce Article 157 against the employer, and if there is a conflict between national legislation and Article 157 then tribunals and courts must apply the latter to decide a case.

Disciplinary procedures An employer should draft and adhere to formal procedures in order to discipline employees. Such disciplinary procedures should be followed each and every time that an employer is considering imposing a disciplinary penalty on an employee such as a formal warning. Disciplinary procedures should conform to the ACAS Code. Where an employer's procedures do not do this, or in a given situation the disciplinary procedures are not properly followed, a dismissal is likely to be procedurally unfair as a result of the decision of the House of Lords in *Polkey*.

Duty of cooperation As well as being subject to a duty of obedience, an employee is under a judicially implied duty to cooperate with the employer by working beyond the strict terms of a contract where failure to do so can be regarded as wilfully impeding the employer's business operations. For example, as long as an employer provides reasonable training, an employee must adapt to change by coming to terms with new technology as the most effective way of performing his or her job. Breach of the duty to cooperate can constitute a form of industrial action short of a strike.

Duty of fidelity Under this judicially implied duty employees should not copy trade secrets or lists of customers etc for their own use of use by a competitor. 'Moonlighting', which is where an employee undertakes a second job in his own time, may also constitute a breach of this duty where an employee has access to trade secrets but wishes to 'moonlight' for a competitor. Injunctions may be available to prevent an ex-employee misusing such information even though he or she has left the relevant employment. Some employers find it more effective to use garden leave terms or post-employment restraints but such terms will not be enforceable if they are unreasonable and therefore a restraint of trade.

Duty of obedience As a result of a judicially implied term, employees must obey all lawful and reasonable instructions of an employer. Breach of this duty may entitle an employer to dismiss the employee summarily. However, this will only be so if the employee has committed a repudiatory breach of contract through gross misconduct. If the disobedience is not sufficiently serious, the employee may claim damages for wrongful dismissal. Moreover, where an employee has been dismissed for disobedience, a claim of unfair dismissal will also succeed if the dismissal is beyond the range of reasonable responses and/or procedurally unfair because the ACAS Code was not followed by the employer.

Economic dismissals These are dismissals which are not connected to the behaviour of the employee but occur as a result of the business needs of the employer. Such dismissals include redundancy dismissals, dismissals connected with a business transfer and dismissals resulting from a unilateral variation of contract terms by an employer.

Economic, technical or organisational (ETO) reason A dismissal connected with a business transfer covered by the TUPE Regulations is automatically unfair unless it is for an ETO reason. For example, the reason for the dismissal is to keep a business viable or to maintain its profitability. Such a dismissal will be fair providing it is within the range of reasonable responses.

Economic torts The main economic tort is committed by inducing or procuring the breach of an employment or a commercial contract. A trade union commits this tort where it calls a strike. A tort may attract statutory immunity but not where secondary industrial action has taken place (other than in the context of lawful picketing). As held by the House of Lords in *OBG Ltd* v. *Allan*, causing loss by unlawful means is also a tort where a trade union targets an employer with the intention of injuring that employer's business. Statutory immunity is not always available for this tort.

Effective date of termination (EDT) This is the date on which an employee's employment contract comes to end. This will be the date on which an employee's notice or fixed-term contract expires. Alternatively, it will be date an employee is dismissed if the dismissal is without notice, or the date an employee leaves the employment if the employee resigns. Typically, employees have three months from the EDT to present a claim to an employment tribunal.

Employee representatives A number of statutory duties to inform and consult, for example, over proposed collective redundancies or business transfers, are owed to recognised trade unions. As a result of EU law, if there is no recognised trade union, employers owe these duties to employee representatives who are elected or appointed by the workforce.

Employee status As endorsed by the House of Lords in *Carmichael* v. *National Power*, there is an irreducible minimum for a person doing work for another to have a contract of employment and therefore possess employee status. This irreducible minimum consists of control, mutuality of obligations and the duty to provide personal performance. Only employees enjoy certain statutory rights such as the right to claim unfair dismissal and the right to claim a statutory redundancy payment. On the other hand, discrimination law operates throughout the field of employment and therefore protects workers and independent contractors as well as employees.

Employers' negligence Any employer owes a duty of reasonable care to its employees both under tort law and as a result of a judicially implied term in employment contracts. An employer will not have been negligent if it has taken reasonable care as the employer will then not be in breach of the duty of care. The employer's personal duty of care should be contrasted with vicarious liability. An employer is vicariously liable for any tort committed by an employee whilst the employee was acting within the course of employment.

Equal value If an employee is unable to bring a like work claim, she may be able to identify a male comparator doing an entirely different job involving, for example, different responsibilities, and who is on a higher rate of pay. She may then be able to argue her job is of an equal value to the employer as his, and therefore she should receive the same rate of pay. Equal value claims may be defeated at a preliminary hearing stage if a tribunal regards the claim as hopeless, or the employer has already conducted a valid job evaluation study (JES) under which the claimant's job has been given a lower value to that done by the male comparator. If the claim proceeds, the tribunal will normally commission an independent expert to conduct a JES. If the jobs are determined to be of equal value, the claimant will succeed unless the employer successfully pleads the material factor defence.

European Court of Human Rights The European Court of Human Rights (ECtHR) was established by the European Convention on Human Rights to determine whether nation states which have ratified the Convention have acted in breach of its provisions. It can hear inter-state cases and, in contrast to the European Court of Justice, can hear claims brought by individuals. Under the Human Rights Act (HRA) 1998 UK courts should follow its decisions in preference to national precedent. Under s. 3 HRA, where possible, UK statutes should be interpreted in a way that is consistent with decisions of the ECtHR. However, the decisions of the ECtHR do not render conflicting UK statutory provisions invalid as the HRA does not contradict the doctrine of parliamentary sovereignty. EU law remains the one exception to the doctrine of parliamentary sovereignty.

European Court of Justice (ECJ) The European Court of Justice (ECJ) was established by the Treaty of Rome in 1957 as the court for the EEC. Today, its composition and powers are to be found in the TFEU. Its main forms of jurisdiction are hearing cases brought by the European Commission against member states and giving preliminary rulings which interpret EU Law. In contrast to the European Court of Human Rights individuals have no right of access to the ECJ. As a result of the supremacy of EU law, national courts should follow decisions and rulings of the ECJ in preference to national judicial precedent.

Fixed-term contract This type of employment contract stipulates the date on which it will expire. Under the Fixed-Term Employees Regulations, employees employed on fixed-term contract should normally be treated equally with employees on permanent contracts. If employees are employed on successive fixed-term contracts for four years, their contracts normally become permanent.

Garden leave An employer places an employee on garden leave if the employee is required to work out an unusually long period of notice prior to resigning but is not permitted to work during this period. It was established in *Provident Financial Group* v. *Hayward* that imposing garden leave is in breach of the judicially implied term to provide work. However, it is permitted to incorporate an express term in the contract providing for garden leave. Such a term will not be enforceable if it constitutes a restraint of trade.

Genuine occupational requirement (GOR) Whilst it is not possible to justify direct discrimination (with the very important exception of age where both direct discrimination and indirect discrimination may be justified), an employer may be able show that there is a genuine occupational requirement that an employee be of a particular race, sex etc. The GOR defence can only be pleaded successfully where an employer can show that the requirement is a proportionate means of achieving a legitimate aim.

Grievance procedures The ACAS Code provides for grievance procedures that employers should adopt and employees should invoke before, for example, resigning to bring claims of constructive dismissal. Where the grievance procedures are not adhered to and the claim succeeds, a tribunal may increase or reduce the compensatory award for unfair dismissal or damages for wrongful dismissal by up to 25% depending on whether it was the employer's or the claimant's fault that the procedures were not properly followed.

Gross misconduct An employee is guilty of gross misconduct if he or she commits misconduct amounting to a repudiatory breach of contract. Where this is the case, a summary dismissal will be lawful. A misconduct dismissal will be fair if the employer has acted within the range of reasonable responses in regarding an employee's misconduct as gross providing, in line with the HL decision in *Polkey*, an employer has adhered to procedures in the ACAS Code before reaching a decision to dismiss.

Gross pay The wage or salary an employee receives before the employer has deducted income tax and national insurance contributions. A statutory week's pay is based on gross pay.

Independent contractors These are self-employed persons who run their own businesses to carry out work for others. Independent contractors are not covered by employment protection rights but are protected by discrimination law contained in the Equality Act 2010. An employing organisation cannot be vicariously liable for the acts of an independent contractor.

Independent trade union To be independent, as defined by s. 5 TULRCA 1992, a trade union must be neither controlled nor dominated by an employer. A union which is financed by an employer is vulnerable to employer interference and is not independent. An independent trade union which has entered into a recognition agreement with an employer, or which has secured statutory recognition, will acquire a number of rights including the right to be informed and consulted over collective redundancies or a proposed business transfer.

Indirect discrimination If an employer applies a provision, criterion or practice (PCP) that has a disproportionate and detrimental effect on members of a group sharing a particular protected characteristic, the PCP will be unlawful unless it can be objectively justified in accordance with the Bilka-Kaufhaus principles. Justification will only succeed where the PCP is a proportionate means of securing the employer's commercial or organisational interests.

Indirect effect EU Directives and the rights guaranteed by the European Convention on Human Rights, as incorporated unto UK law by the Human Rights Act 1998, cannot be directly enforced by most employees against their employers unless an employer constitutes a state employer or public authority. However, EU Directives and Convention rights take indirect effect as, where possible, British courts must interpret national law in a way that it is consistent with a Directive or the Convention.

Industrial action short of a strike Not all industrial action involves workers totally withdrawing their labour by taking strike action. Industrial action short of a strike occurs where union members state that they will not undertake particular contractual duties but will otherwise work normally. An overtime ban is an example of such action and this may constitute a breach of an express term in an employee's contract or breach of the duty to cooperate.

Inference of discrimination In discrimination claims the claimant must satisfy the normal burden of proof. However, tribunals may draw the inference of discrimination from facts that suggest discrimination. For example, on paper the claimant was the strongest candidate for the post applied for. Discrimination could be regarded as proved if an employer is unable to satisfy the tribunal that there were non-discriminatory reasons for appointing another candidate.

Injunctions An injunction is an equitable remedy which is available at the discretion of the court. It will not be granted unless an award of damages is an inadequate remedy. Injunctions are available to encourage but not compel performance of personal contracts – contrast *Warner Bros* v. *Nelson* and *Page One Records* v. *Britton*. Injunctions may also be granted to enforce garden leave. Employees may secure injunctions to prevent dismissals taking place until disciplinary procedures in their contracts have been properly followed. However, the granting of such injunctions is rare and the courts prefer to grant damages to cover the period the employee would have been employed had the procedures been carried out. Injunctions are most frequently granted to enforce the implied duty of fidelity, or express terms providing for garden leave or post-employment restraints in circumstances where the employer has a legitimate trade interest to protect such as a trade secret. A term will not be enforced if it constitutes an invalid restraint of trade. Employers may also seek injunctions – particularly interim injunctions – to prevent trade unions from organising or continuing with industrial action which does not attract statutory immunity.

Judicially implied terms A number of terms are judicially implied into contracts of employment. The effect of such terms is to impose duties on both employer and employees. With respect to the former, the most important obligation is maintain mutual trust and confidence. Judicially implied duties on employees include obedience, cooperation and fidelity.

Judicial review Individuals who are post holders and have their terms and employment regulated by statute rather than contract may be able to apply for judicial review, if, for example, a dismissal is in breach of principles of natural justice such as denial of the right to be heard. The *Sharon Shoesmith* case provides a recent example of judicial review being successfully pursued.

Lay-off If an employee is laid-off, he or she is not provided with any work whatsoever. Alternatively, an employee may be put on short-term working where he or she is employed for less than half the working week. An employee who is laid-off or kept on short-term working without pay for four or more consecutive weeks may resign and claim a statutory redundancy payment. Alternatively, where the consecutive period is no more than three weeks, an employee has this right where the lay-off or short-term working is for a total of six weeks in any period of 13 weeks. If an employment contract is terminated by a lay-off, but the employee is subsequently rehired, the period of lay-off will break the employee's continuous employment unless it constitutes a temporary cessation.

Local collective bargaining Although national collective bargaining still takes place, it is much more common today for an individual employer in a particular work sector to engage in its own local collective bargaining with a recognised trade union representing its employees.

Like work An employee will be able to bring a like work claim for equal pay if she can show the male comparator is doing the same job as her or that the two jobs are broadly similar and any differences are of no practical importance. The claim will succeed unless the employer is able to plead the material factor defence. If a woman is employed on a different job to the male comparator, she may be able to bring an equal value claim.

Material factor Where a woman succeeds in a like work claim or an equal value claim, the employer may be able to plead that the pay differential between her and the male comparator is due to a material factor other than sex. Examples of material factors include better qualifications and/or greater experience. Where the material factor involves indirect sex discrimination, such as market forces or higher pay rates for full-time employees, the employer must be able to justify the material factor in accordance with the Bilka-Kaufhaus principles.

Mediation As with conciliation, the purpose of mediation is to assist parties to reach their own agreement to resolve a dispute. The difference is largely one of timing in that mediation refers to resolution of a dispute at an early stage. Conciliation, for example in the form of an ACAS conciliated settlement, occurs after an employee has presented a claim to an employment tribunal or a trade union has embarked on balloting or organising industrial action.

Mitigation of loss Where an employee has been wrongfully dismissed, an award of damages will be reduced by the extent to which the employee has failed to avoid or reduce the loss resulting from the dismissal by, for example, accepting a suitable job offer. Similarly, a compensatory award for unfair dismissal may be reduced on this basis.

Mobility clause A term in an employment contract which an employer can invoke to require an employer to move to a different workplace. An employee will be in breach of the duty of obedience if the employee refuses to move in accordance with the clause unless the manner in which the clause is invoked by the employer breaches mutual trust and confidence – *United Bank* v. *Akhtar*. An employee may be subjected to a redundancy dismissal, even though there is a mobility clause in the contract, where the employee is being instructed to move from his or her established place of work. However, refusing to move may constitute unreasonable refusal of an offer of suitable alternative employment, in which case the employee will lose the right to a statutory redundancy payment.

Mutuality of obligations This is present where an employer is contractually obliged to offer work and the employee is contractually obliged to perform that work. As held in *Carmichael* v. *National Power*, a mutuality of obligations is part of the irreducible minimum for possessing employee status. Thus casual workers will often not be employees and will not have statutory rights under ERA 1996. However, in *Nethermere Ltd* v. *Taverna* it was held that the regularity of the relationship between the company and homeworkers established a mutuality of obligations through umbrella contracts, as in practice the company always provided work which was performed by the homeworkers as required.

Mutual trust and confidence This fundamental judicially implied term in the contract of employment requires employers to treat employees with respect and not to act in any way which will constitute a destruction of trust and confidence. The term imposes obligations on employees with respect to the duties of cooperation and fidelity. Breach of the term by the employer will enable an employee to resign and claim constructive dismissal.

National collective bargaining It is possible for all employers in a particular work sector to negotiate with one or more trade unions on a centralised national basis. If a national collective agreement is reached, the agreement may become part of the employment contracts of all employees employed in that sector. A good example of national collective bargaining is provided by university employers who negotiate with a number of trade unions representing academic and other university staff.

Net pay The wage or salary an employee receives after the employer has deducted income tax and national insurance contributions from the employee's gross pay.

Offers of suitable alternative employment If an employer has implemented a redundancy dismissal, it may make an offer of alternative employment to the redundant employee. This may be an offer of a different job at the same place of work or the same job or a different job at a different location. The offer will be one of suitable alternative employment if the new job is objectively identical or similar to the previous job. If the offer is suitable, the employee will lose the entitlement to a statutory redundancy payment if the offer is unreasonably refused. A refusal will be reasonable if it is the result of genuine family commitments (for example, relocation would disrupt the career of a spouse or partner).

Perceptive discrimination This occurs where an employee is discriminated against because he or she is wrongly perceived to possess a protected characteristic. For example, a heterosexual employee is bullied by colleagues because he is perceived to be gay.

Picketing immunity The picketing immunity is provided by s. 220 TULRCA. For the statutory immunity to apply the pickets must (a) be picketing at their own place of work and (b) be doing no more than peacefully communicating information and/or peacefully persuading others not to cross the picket line. If pickets persuade another person to act in breach of contract, they will commit an economic tort. Lawful picketing provides the one example where there can be statutory immunity from torts committed through organising secondary industrial action. For example, a van driver employed by another company is persuaded by the pickets not to enter their workplace. Picketing which involves obstruction, even if non-violent, will be outside the immunity and thus unlawful – see *Broome* v. *DPP*. Such picketing will involve the commission of a private and/or public nuisance.

Polkey In *Polkey* v. *Dayton Services* the House of Lords decided that a dismissal will normally be *procedurally* unfair where an employer has failed to follow the ACAS Code. A dismissal can only be fair where the employer can show that a reasonable employer could take the view that following the code in the particular circumstances was futile or useless. In particular, an employer cannot argue that a dismissal is fair because the failure to follow the code made no difference to the employer's decision to dismiss.

Polkey reductions Although an employer cannot argue that a dismissal is fair because the failure to follow the code made no difference to the employer's decision to dismiss, a tribunal can decide to grant a nil compensatory award on this basis. Therefore, although the tribunal must find the dismissal to be fair, the claimant will not receive any compensation.

Positive discrimination This is where an employer discriminates in favour of a person with a protected characteristic. For example, an employer decides that only a woman will be appointed to a new post because women are underrepresented in the workforce. Such discrimination is unlawful, although employers are permitted to take positive action to encourage members of an underrepresented group to apply for a job. Positive discrimination may be *required* in the context of disability discrimination where the employer is under a duty to make a reasonable adjustment.

Post-employment restraint An express term in an employment contract prohibiting an employee from working for a competing employer after the contract has ended. Such a term is *prima facie* in restraint of trade and invalid. However, the restraint will be enforced where its purpose is to protect the legitimate business objectives of the employer, such as preventing a competitor from obtaining a trade secret, and its duration and area of geographical operation are no longer and wider than necessary to protect the employer's interests.

Preliminary rulings Such rulings are given by the European Court of Justice (ECJ) under Article 267 of the TFEU. Their purpose is to ensure that national courts across member states interpret EU law, including Directives, in a consistent and uniform manner. Only national courts (not the parties to a case) can request a preliminary ruling. The national court will ask the ECJ to give an interpretation on the relevant point(s) of EU law. The ECJ's ruling provides this interpretation which is sent back to the relevant national court. The national court then applies the ruling to decide the case. Many such rulings have been given by the ECJ in the context of discrimination and equal pay law.

Private nuisance This tort is committed by unreasonably interfering with another's use of or enjoyment of his land. Pickets who act beyond the picketing immunity frequently commit this tort against the occupier of the premises being picketed.

Procedure agreement A collective agreement between an employer and a trade union setting out the procedures under which collective bargaining between the parties will be conducted. Procedure agreements are presumed not to be legally enforceable.

Proportionality/proportionate means Under the Bilka-Kaufhaus principles an employer may be able to justify indirect discrimination on the basis that a PCP is necessary to meet its objective commercial or organisational interests. However, justification will fail on grounds of proportionality where the interests can be secured by non-discriminatory means or the advantages to the employer are outweighed by the discrimination. The genuine occupational requirement defence will also fail if it is not a proportionate way to achieve the employer's legitimate objectives.

Protected characteristic The Equality Act 2010 renders it unlawful for an employer to engage in direct discrimination or indirect discrimination against an employee who possesses a protected characteristic. These characteristics are age, disability, gender reassignment, marriage and civil partnership, pregnancy and maternity, race, religion or belief, sex and sexual orientation.

Protected industrial action Industrial action is protected if the action is official and lawful. A dismissal for participation in protected industrial action is an automatically unfair dismissal. Industrial action normally ceases to be protected once it has lasted for longer than 12 weeks unless the continuation of the industrial action is the fault of the employer. Where industrial action is official but unprotected, tribunals have no jurisdiction to hear unfair dismissal claims if all the employees participating in the action have been dismissed. Selective dismissals for participating in official unprotected action will normally be beyond the range of reasonable responses and therefore unfair.

Provision, criterion or practice (PCP) A PCP may be in the form of an employer's policy which constitutes indirect discrimination against an employee with a protected characteristic. For example, an employer refuses to allow a mother with a very young child to work part-time as it has a policy of only employing full-time employees. This indirectly discriminates against women and will be unlawful unless it can be justified in accordance with the Bilka-Kaufhaus principles.

Public authority Under s. 6 HRA, Convention rights can only be directly enforced by employees who are employed by a core public authority. Such employers include the armed forces, civil service, police, local government and probably the NHS. Employees of other public sector employers and all private sector employers cannot directly enforce Convention rights against their employer. However, under EU law Directives may take vertical direct effect between employees and state employers; and this is very wide in scope as it covers all public sector employers and also private employers such as water companies who are substantially regulated by statute – see *Griffin* v. *Southern Water Co.*

Public nuisance This tort is committed where pickets stand on the public highway, that is the pavement and/or the road, and obstruct entry to a workplace. This tort enables any person who suffers special damage to sue. Typically, this will be the occupier of the premises being picketed. Public nuisance also constitutes the crime of obstruction of the highway.

Range of reasonable responses test In a claim of unfair dismissal this is the test that a tribunal must adopt in determining whether a dismissal is unfair under s. 98(4) ERA 1996. As confirmed by the Court of Appeal in *Post Office* v. *Foley*, a tribunal may not substitute its own decision for that of a reasonable employer. It is not enough that the tribunal regards the dismissal as harsh. The decision to dismiss will only be unreasonable and thus unfair if it was one that no reasonable employer would have reached.

Reasonable adjustment An employer can only justify unfavourable treatment of a disabled employee where there is no reasonable adjustment an employer can make to the workplace, or to equipment or to patterns of working which enables the employee to work despite the disability. Making a reasonable adjustment may require an employee to engage in positive discrimination in favour of a disabled employee by, for example, as in *Archibald* v. *Fyfe*, redeploying him or her in a new post without requiring that employee to undergo a normal process of competitive interview.

Recognised trade union A trade union is recognised by an employer if the employer has voluntarily entered into a recognition agreement with that union and has agreed to negotiate with it over some or all of the purposes of collective bargaining such as pay and hours of work. Alternatively, a trade union may have successfully secured statutory recognition. An independent trade union which is recognised has statutory rights to disclosure of information and to statutory consultations with respect to health and safety, collective redundancies and proposed business transfers. Its elected workplace representatives have rights to reasonable time off with pay to carry out their duties as determined by the scope of recognition.

Recognition agreement A collective agreement entered into by an employer under which that employer voluntarily recognises a trade union for some or all of the purposes of collective bargaining as defined in s. 178 TULRCA 1992. Such agreements are not normally legally enforceable and therefore there is no legal bar to derecognition. However, this is not the case if a trade union has secured statutory recognition.

Recommendations This tribunal remedy is available to a claimant who succeeds in a discrimination claim under the Equality Act or with respect to refusal of employment for trade union membership or activities. Employers do not have to comply with a tribunal recommendation stipulating the steps to be taken to end or alleviate the discrimination, but a failure to comply may result in additional compensation being granted to the claimant.

Redundancy dismissal An employee is dismissed by reason of redundancy if the workplace is closed or the employer requires fewer employees to do particular job (work of a particular kind). Unless a redundancy dismissal is also an unfair dismissal, the employee's only entitlement is to a statutory redundancy payment. A redundancy dismissal will be unfair if, for example, an employer uses arbitrary or discriminatory selection methods.

Reinstatement This remedy may be granted by an employment tribunal to an employee who has succeeded in a claim of unfair dismissal. If the employer complies with the order, the employee will return to his or her job and will receive arrears in pay, etc. If the employer refuses to comply, the employee will receive an additional award of between 26 to 52 statutory weeks' pay. He or she will also receive a basic award and a compensatory award.

Re-engagement This is an alternative remedy to reinstatement. The difference between reinstatement and re-engagement is that in case of the latter the tribunal is instructing an employer to give the employee an alternative job or the same job but at a different workplace.

Repudiatory breach This is where a party commits a breach of contract which goes to the root of the contract. The injured party may choose between repudiation and affirmation. If the injured party chooses the former, the contract is at an end. An employer may summarily dismiss an employee who has committed gross misconduct constituting a repudiatory breach. Such a dismissal will be wrongful where any misconduct is not sufficiently serious to go to the root of the contract. If the employer commits a repudiatory breach, the employee may resign and claim constructive dismissal.

Restraint of trade Terms in employment contracts which seek to prevent an employee from working for others (or for him or herself) after the contract has ended (post-employment restraints) are *prima facie* a restraint of trade and thus void and unenforceable. However, such clauses can be enforced if the employer has legitimate interests to protect, such as trade secrets, and the clause is otherwise reasonable with respect to its duration and geographical scope. Where a restraint is valid, the employer will normally secure an injunction to prevent an ex-employee from acting in breach of it. An express term in a contract providing for garden leave will constitute an invalid restraint of trade unless it is reasonable. At common law the purposes of a trade union are regarded as being a restraint of trade. However, the TULRCA confers statutory protection on trade unions from the consequences of this.

Secondary industrial action This takes place in any situation where a worker who has been induced to take industrial action has no dispute with his/her own employer. Statutory immunity is withdrawn from liability for economic torts committed in the course of secondary industrial action except where this takes place in the context of lawful picketing – s. 224 TULRCA.

Specific performance In ordinary contract law there are circumstances in which a court can compel performance of a contract through granting a decree of specific performance. This remedy generally has no role to play in employment law as it is contrary to public policy to compel an employer to employ an employee or an employee to work for an employer. For example, courts cannot compel workers engaged in strike action to return to work. Specific performance is available as a remedy in the context of statutory recognition where an employer has failed to comply with a procedure imposed by the CAC for collective bargaining with the recognised union.

Statutory immunity This refers to the situation where Parliament through legislation has conferred protection from liabilities in tort, incurred in the course of industrial action, to trade unions and/or individuals. Such immunity from the economic torts is conferred by s. 219 TULRCA and, in the case of lawful picketing, by s. 220. For immunity to be available, the tort must be committed in contemplation or furtherance of a trade dispute. Moreover, even where this is the case a trade union (but not an individual) will lose immunity if there is no valid postal ballot or the union has failed to provide the necessary pre-ballot and pre-strike statutory notices to the employer in dispute.

Statutory recognition Under Schedule AI TULRCA, a trade union can pursue a statutory procedure to seek a declaration from the CAC which imposes recognition on an employer with respect to workers in a collective bargaining unit for the purposes of negotiating pay, hours and holidays. If an employer and a union cannot agree a method of collective bargaining the CAC may impose the model procedures contained in the Method of Collective Bargaining Order 2000. Such a decision by the CAC is enforceable by specific performance.

Statutory redundancy payment A statutory redundancy payment must be made to an employee who is subject to a redundancy dismissal where the employee has at least two years' continuous employment. The payment is calculated on the basis of an employee's gross week's pay, age and completed years of employment. Only the last 20 years of employment can be taken into account and a week's pay is subject to a statutory cap. The basic award for unfair dismissal is calculated in exactly the same way.

Statutory week's pay A statutory week's pay provides the basis for calculating a number of remedies that employment tribunals may grant for breach of an employee's employment rights. These remedies include the additional award and basic award for unfair dismissal and a statutory redundancy payment. A week's pay is calculated on the basis of an employee's gross pay and is normally subject to a statutory cap.

Substantive agreements A collective agreement between an employer and a trade union covering the terms and conditions of employees in a collective bargaining unit. Although such agreements are presumed not to be legally enforceable, they may be incorporated into individual employment contracts and legally enforceable between the employer and the individual employee.

Summary dismissal This is where an employee is dismissed without notice or prior to the expiry of a fixed-term contract. Such a dismissal is wrongful if the employee is not guilty of gross misconduct constituting a repudiatory breach of contract. Such a dismissal will be unfair if the dismissal is outside the range of reasonable responses.

Trade dispute The content of a lawful trade dispute can be found in s. 244 TULRCA. This includes disputes over pay, hours and other terms and conditions of employment. It also includes disputes over issues such as redundancies, disciplinary dismissals, health and safety and collective bargaining arrangements. If a dispute between employees and their own employer relates wholly or mainly to such matters, a union or person organising the industrial action will have statutory immunity from the economic torts under s. 219 TULRCA.

Trade union repudiation A trade union can repudiate industrial action organised by its officials or workplace representatives. Where repudiation is effective, the trade union can no longer be sued where the industrial action is unlawful. After repudiation, industrial action becomes unofficial and employees dismissed for taking unofficial industrial action have no rights to claim unfair dismissal.

Umbrella contracts This term comes from cases involving homeworkers such as the *Nethermere* v. *Taverna* case. If over a significant period of time an employer provides a person with work which that person agrees to carry out, this creates an umbrella contract generating mutuality of obligations and therefore that person will have employee status.

Unfair dismissal Employees with two years' continuous employment are eligible to claim unfair dismissal. A dismissal must be for a potentially fair reason such, as incapability, misconduct or redundancy. A dismissal is unfair if an employer has acted beyond the range of reasonable responses in deciding to dismiss. Alternatively, the dismissal may be procedurally unfair in line with the House of Lords' decision in *Polkey* because the employer has failed to follow the ACAS Code. In contrast to wrongful dismissal, a dismissal may be unfair even though the employer is not in breach of contract. The remedies for unfair dismissal include reinstatement, re-engagement, the basic award and the compensatory award.

Unilateral variation of contract terms An employer unilaterally varies the terms and conditions of its employees if it imposes contractual changes on them without their agreement. An employer which acts in this way is acting in breach of contract. However, if an individual employee refuses to accept changes to his or her contract where other employees have done so then any subsequent dismissal – actual or constructive – may be fair if the employer has acted within the range of reasonable responses in deciding that changes to employment contracts are

necessary to save the business or to make it more efficient or competitive.

Unlawful means Any unlawful act committed by a trade union which, typically, will be committed through the organisation of industrial action. The most common types of unlawful means involve inducing or procuring breaches of contracts or threatening to do so. Unlawful means will have been used if a trade union persuades a supplier not to enter into a commercial contract with an employer with whom its members are in dispute by threatening to induce the supplying company's employees to act in breach of their employment contracts if a commercial contract is made. The union will consequently be liable in tort for causing loss by unlawful means.

Unofficial industrial action Industrial action which continues after trade union repudiation of it becomes unofficial. Workers who are dismissed for participating in unofficial industrial action have no rights to claim unfair dismissal.

Vicarious liability Under the common law doctrine of vicarious liability an employer will be legally liable for any torts committed by an employee providing the latter is acting within the scope of his employment. An employer may incur statutory vicarious liability in the context of the harassment of an employee by his or her colleagues. However, an employer will avoid statutory vicarious liability where it has taken reasonable steps to prevent acts of harassment from taking place or continuing. Trade unions are vicariously liable for unlawful behaviour in the form of nuisance and intimidation committed by their officials and/or members in the course of picketing.

Vertical direct effect EU Directives do not become part of UK law until they are given legal effect by a statute or statutory instrument. However, if a Directive is sufficiently certain, clear and precise, it can be enforced from the date the Directive comes into effect by employees of state employers. This includes all public sector employers and private companies which are significantly regulated by statute such as privatised water companies.

Voluntary redundancy Where an employer is intending to make redundancy dismissals, he may select employees for redundancy by inviting employees to volunteer for dismissal. Typically, this will be in return for enhanced redundancy payments in place of statutory redundancy payments.

Voluntary recognition An employer may voluntarily decide to enter into a recognition agreement with a trade union for the purposes of collective bargaining. It can be contrasted with statutory recognition where the CAC has imposed an order on an employer requiring it to recognise a trade union for bargaining over pay, hours and holiday.

Voluntary severance As an alternative to redundancy dismissals, employers may invite employees to apply to leave their employment in return for an agreed financial package. Such employees are not dismissed as termination of their employment contracts is by mutual agreement with the employer.

Workers These are individuals who are not independent contractors or who do not possess employee status but who undertake work for an employer. Examples of such workers include agency workers and casual workers. Workers enjoy fewer statutory rights than is the case with employees. However, for example, they are protected by the National Minimum Wage Act 1998 and the Working Time Regulations 1998. They are also protected from discrimination by the Equality Act 2010.

Workplace trade union representatives These are employees who are elected by trade union members in an employing organisation to represent the workforce and individual members over workplace issues. These lay representatives are entitled to reasonable paid time-off to carry out their duties if they are representatives of a recognised trade union.

Written statement of terms Under s. 1 ERA 1996, an employee who has not been given a full written contract of employment has the statutory right to a written statement which sets out the main terms and conditions under which the employee is employed. The information that must be supplied to an employee includes full details on how the rate of remuneration is calculated, the hours the employee is required to work, holiday entitlement and the place(s) the employee is required to attend for work.

Wrongful dismissal An employee will be wrongfully dismissed if he is dismissed summarily, that is, without due notice or during the currency of a fixed-term contract. Such a dismissal will not be wrongful if the employee has committed a repudiatory breach of contract. An award of damages is the normal remedy available for wrongful dismissal. Damages may only cover the loss caused by the employer's breach of contract. For example, net pay during the notice period that the employee was contractually entitled to be given. It is important to remember that wrongful dismissal is part of the common law, that is, ordinary contract law, in contrast with unfair dismissal which is based on statute law.

Index